THE CULTURAL STUDY OF MUSIC

A CRITICAL INTRODUCTION

SECOND EDITION

EDITED BY
MARTIN CLAYTON
TREVOR HERBERT
RICHARD MIDDLETON

Routledge
Taylor & Francis Group

NEW YORK AND LONDON

Senior Editor: Constance Ditzel
Senior Editorial Assistant: Mike Andrews
Production Editor: Sarah Stone
Marketing Manager: Joon Won Moon
Text Design: Keystroke
Copy Editor: John Banks
Proofreader: Ruth Jeavons
Cover Design: Jayne Varney

Second edition published 2012
by Routledge
711 Third Avenue, New York, NY 10017

Simultaneously published in the UK
by Routledge
2 Park Square, Milton Park, Abingdon, Oxon OX14 4RN

Routledge is an imprint of the Taylor & Francis Group, an informa business

© 2012 Taylor & Francis

First edition published by Routledge 2003

Library of Congress Cataloging-in-Publication Data
The cultural study of music : a critical introduction / edited by Martin Clayton,
Trevor Herbert, Richard Middleton. – 2nd ed.
p. cm.
Includes bibliographical references and index.
1. Music–Social aspects. 2. Musicology. I. Clayton, Martin. II. Herbert, Trevor. III. Middleton,
Richard.
ML3798.C85 2011
306.4'842–dc23
2011024301

ISBN: 978-0-415-88190-6 (hbk)
ISBN: 978-0-415-88191-3 (pbk)
ISBN: 978-0-203-14945-4 (ebk)

Typeset in Minion and Scala Sans
by Keystroke, Station Road, Codsall, Wolverhampton
Printed and bound in the United States of America on acid-free paper
by Sheridan Books, Inc.

Contents

PREFACE TO THE SECOND EDITION

The first edition of *The Cultural Study of Music* was published in 2003 and it is gratifying that we have been given the opportunity to produce a new edition, which is significantly extended and revised. It was clear soon after the 2003 publication was released that the book was receiving a very positive reception in what publishers sometimes describe as "several market segments." By this they mean (we think) that people were finding the book interesting and helpful in different ways and perhaps for different purposes. We have always felt that the book's original success was due to two key features. We had been fortunate enough to attract a group of extremely distinguished writers from both sides of the Atlantic who had responded to the brief we gave them with chapters that were thought-provoking and original. Also, we had, perhaps to a greater extent than we may have fully grasped as we assembled our ideas in 2001/2, identified an important place and need for a book of the type it turned out to be: one that covers cultural approaches to the study of music by focusing on themes from several of the perspectives from which music and the activities associated with it can be investigated and critiqued.

We stuck steadfastly to a few self-imposed rules when assembling the first edition and as they have served us so well we have not deserted them. For example, while we have been clear about the themes that we wanted to be addressed in the book, we have not made dogmatic interventions into the content of individual chapters or the way they should be written. To put this somewhat differently, authors have been given freedom to develop and set out their ideas in the way they individually see fit, beyond of course the normal and common sense processes that editors need to follow to assure coherence and avoid unnecessary overlap. Also, we have not encouraged an overly didactic or "user friendly" approach just for the sake of it, because, while the idea of user-friendliness can be applied confidently to some software applications and electric toasters, it provides challenges to writers on cultural phenomena among whom it is a somewhat suspect concept anyway: how, after all, can several different discursive styles applied to different types of problem be distilled into a mode of delivery that anticipates universal comprehension?

This point is worth making because one of the comments that emerged from reviews of the first edition (each of which we valued greatly), touched on this issue. The comment concerned the variety of styles that authors employed and our apparent reluctance to marshal them into a common tone and temperament. One suggestion which rather undermined the very basis of the perceived problem was that a quick fix could be applied in the form of a "how to do it" chapter ("it" presumably meaning cultural criticism), stationed stoically, as a sort of optional portal, at the start of the book. We decided against this idea because it misses one of the fundamental points that the book as a whole is intended to convey: that there is no single way of "doing it," but there are lots of different ways of thinking about music so that its purpose and power can be understood with greater confidence, richness, and clarity.

THE NEW EDITION

So how is this new edition different from the first and how is its purpose and utility to be understood by the many different people who might want to use it? The detail of how the two editions differ is explained in the Introduction, but the main changes can be summarized briefly here. A good deal has changed in music studies since 2003, not least in the areas and debates that are explored in the book. At the same time, the underlying issues are no less pertinent than they were a decade ago, and in many cases present themselves in still-familiar forms. For this new edition, we invited all contributors to the first edition to participate again. We are grateful to all of them for agreeing to do so, and for the revisions and updating that have been made. In many cases, the revisions are substantial: two contributors to the original edition wrote completely new essays. Everyone took the opportunity to consider how they might take account of new interventions into their areas of interest; the further reading lists and bibliography have been revised; and an entirely new, comprehensive index has been compiled.

In addition we have added new chapters, nine in all, some of which fill gaps in the original edition while others reveal new areas of interest that have emerged in the ensuing years, often through the endeavors of the very authors who are now included in what was already a distinguished list. Themes important in music studies that can be explored from a cultural perspective and that are new to this edition include technology, religion, race, and, politics, and the coverage of "identity," especially gender and sexual identities, is extended.

READERSHIP

On the question of the utility of the book we can only say that it is a resource that can be used in different ways to serve different needs and purposes. We know, for example, that a large part of the readership is in colleges and universities where the book is used in music departments to extend students' thinking about music and in other departments where it has been found that cultural studies more generally are exemplified rather well by considering various styles of music through the types of approach taken by our contributors. Students and those who teach them—and those who fit into neither category—are likely to benefit from reading the Introduction for the context it provides before reading those chapters dealing with the topics that interest them. The present edition uses a new structure that groups smaller numbers of chapters into a greater number of thematic segments. We hope that this approach provides helpful routes through which the contributions can be encountered and studied.

What we now have then is a considerably extended (by more than a third) and enhanced volume which brings together work from a yet larger field of expertise.

We as editors are especially proud of *The Cultural Study of Music* and owe a debt of gratitude to each of the authors who have contributed to this new edition. We must also acknowledge the considerable assistance we have received in preparing this new edition by our editor, Constance Ditzel (who first proposed the idea) and her assistant, Denny Tek; by our ever efficient secretary and administrator, Lisa Lewzey of the Open University; and by our intrepid indexer, Annette Musker. Our grateful thanks to all.

Martin Clayton
Trevor Herbert
Richard Middleton
June 2011

Notes on Contributors

Kofi Agawu is Professor of Music at Princeton University and Adjunct Professor at the University of Ghana, Legon. He is the author of *Playing with signs: A semiotic interpretation of classic music* (Princeton University Press, 1991), *African rhythm: A Northern Ewe perspective* (Cambridge University Press, 1995), *Representing African music: Postcolonial notes, queries, positions* (Routledge, 2003), and *Music as discourse: Semiotic adventures in Romantic music* (Oxford University Press, 2009). He was elected Corresponding Fellow of the British Academy in 2010.

Ian Biddle is Senior Lecturer in Music at Newcastle University. A cultural theorist and musicologist, he works on a variety of topics in music- and sound-related areas. His work ranges from the cultural history of music and masculinity; theorizing music's intervention in communities and subjectivities; sound, soundscapes, and urban experience; and the politics of noise. He has interests in memory studies, sound studies, Italian workerist and autonomist theory, psychoanalysis, and theoretical approaches to "affective" states. He is co-founder and co-ordinating editor (with Richard Middleton) of the journal *Radical Musicology*.

Philip V. Bohlman is the Mary Werkman Distinguished Service Professor of the Humanities and of Music at the University of Chicago and Honorarprofessor at the Hochschule für Musik und Theater Hannover. He is active also as a performer, serving as the Artistic Director of the "New Budapest Orpheum Society," a Jewish cabaret that has recorded three CDs, most recently *Jewish Cabaret in Exile* (Cedille Records,

2009). Among his recent publications are *Jewish music and modernity* (Oxford University Press, 2008), *Focus: Music, nationalism, and the making of the new Europe* (Routledge, 2011), and *Balkan epic: Song, history, modernity* (Scarecrow, 2011), coedited with Nada Petković. For his research he has received the Edward Dent Medal from the Royal Music Association, the Berlin Prize from the American Academy in Berlin, the Donald Tovey Prize from Oxford University, and the Derek Allen Prize from the British Academy. His current research includes field studies of religion and the arts in India, music in European Muslim communities, and the Eurovision Song Contest.

Georgina Born is Professor of Music and Anthropology at the University of Oxford, and Honorary Professor of Anthropology at University College London. She researches contemporary music, media, and cultural production. Her books include *Rationalizing culture: IRCAM, Boulez, and the institutionalization of the musical avant-garde* (1995), *Western music and its others: Difference, representation, and appropriation in music* (edited with David Hesmondhalgh, 2000) and *Uncertain vision: Birt, Dyke and the reinvention of the BBC* (2005). From 2010 to 2015 she is directing the international research program "Music, Digitization, Mediation: Towards Interdisciplinary Music Studies." An edited collection—*Music, sound, and the transformation of public and private space*—is forthcoming.

David Brackett teaches in the Schulich School of Music of McGill University where he is Chair of the Musicology Program. His publications include *Interpreting popular music* (Cambridge University Press, 1995; reprint, University of California Press, 2000), and *The pop, rock, and soul reader: Histories and debates* (Oxford University Press), now in its second edition. His current work focuses on the interconnections between musical categories and group identification.

David Clarke is Professor of Music at the University of Newcastle upon Tyne, U.K. He is a music theorist who has written on the aesthetics of musical modernism and postmodernism, on music and language, and on questions of music and cultural pluralism. He is author of *The music and thought of Michael Tippett: Modern times and metaphysics* (Cambridge University Press, 2001), and co-editor (with Eric Clarke) of *Music and consciousness: Philosophical, psychological, and cultural perspectives* (Oxford University Press, 2011). He is currently working on articles on Indian classical music.

Eric F. Clarke is Heather Professor of Music at Oxford, and Professorial Fellow of Wadham College. He has published widely on various issues in the psychology of music, musical meaning, and the analysis of pop music, including *Empirical musicology* (2004, co-edited with Nicholas Cook), *Ways of listening* (2005), *Music and mind in everyday life* (2010, co-authored with Nicola Dibben and Stephanie Pitts), and *Music and consciousness* (2011, co-edited with David Clarke). He is an Associate Director of the AHRC Centre for Musical Performance as Creative Practice (2009–14) and was elected a Fellow of the British Academy in 2010.

Martin Clayton is Professor of Ethnomusicology at Durham University. His books include *Time in Indian music: Rhythm, metre and form in North Indian rag performance* (2000), *Music, time and place: Essays in comparative musicology* (2007), *Music and orientalism in the British Empire, 1780s to 1940s: Portrayal of the East* (2007) and *Music, words and voice: A reader* (2007).

Nicholas Cook took up the 1684 Professorship of Music at the University of Cambridge in 2009, having previously directed the AHRC Research Centre for the History and Analysis of Recorded Music at Royal Holloway, University of London. His most recent book, *The Schenker project: Culture, race, and music theory in fin-de-siècle Vienna*, won the SMT's 2010 Wallace Berry Award, and he is now completing *Changing the music object: Analysing performance*. He is a Fellow of the British Academy and of Academia Europaea.

Ian Cross was initially a guitarist, and since 1986 has taught in the Faculty of Music at the University of Cambridge, where he is Director of the Centre for Music & Science and also a Fellow of Wolfson College. His research is interdisciplinary, guided by the aim of developing an integrated understanding of music as grounded in both biology and culture; he has published widely in the fields of music cognition, music theory, ethnomusicology, archeological acoustics, psychoacoustics and, most recently, music and language evolution.

Kevin Dawe is Professor of Ethnomusicology at the University of Leeds. His publications include the single-authored books, *The new guitarscape* (Ashgate, 2010) and *Music and musicians in Crete* (Scarecrow, 2007), the edited collection *Island musics* (Berg, 2004), and the co-edited collections *Guitar cultures* (Berg, 2001) with Andy Bennett and *The Mediterranean in music* (Scarecrow, 2005) with David Cooper. He is currently conducting research into the fretless guitar scene in Turkey, as well as preparing a book on green issues in relation to the guitar-making industry.

Nicola Dibben is a Senior Lecturer in the Department of Music at the University of Sheffield and co-ordinating editor of the journal *Popular Music* (Cambridge University Press). She is author of *Björk* (Equinox Press, 2009), a co-author of *Music and mind in everyday life* (Oxford University Press, 2010), and has published over 25 book chapters and journal articles on music, mind, and culture.

Jeffers Engelhardt is Assistant Professor of the Anthropology of Music at Amherst College. He is currently finishing a book on music and Orthodox Christianity in Estonia. His fieldwork in Estonia and Kenya deals with music and religion, secularity, postsocialism, cultural rights, development, and new media. He has published widely in journals and edited volumes.

Ruth Finnegan FBA is Emeritus Professor/Visiting Research Professor, Faculty of Social Sciences, The Open University, and Honorary Fellow, Somerville College Oxford. Her books include *Oral literature in Africa* (1970), *Oral poetry* (1977, 1992), *Literacy and orality* (1988), *The hidden musicians: Music-making in an English town* (1989, 2nd ed. 2007), *Oral traditions and the verbal arts* (1992), *Tales of the city* (1998), *Communicating: The multiple modes of human interconnection* (2002), *The oral and beyond: Doing things with words in Africa* (2007), and *Why do we quote? The culture and history of quotation* (2011).

Simon Frith is Tovey Professor of Music at the University of Edinburgh. He is currently working on a three-volume history of live music in Britain since the 1950s. His most recent book is *The art of record production*, edited with Simon Zagorski-Thomas for Ashgate. He is chair of the Judges of the Mercury Music Prize.

Lucy Green is Professor of Music Education at the London University Institute of Education, U.K. Her research interests are in the sociology of music education, specializing in issues of meaning, ideology, gender, popular music, informal learning, and new pedagogies. She is the author of four books and numerous articles and book chapters; has given keynotes in countries across the world; and serves on the editorial boards of eleven journals. She led the research and development project "Informal Learning in the Music Classroom" within the British venture "Musical Futures," which is now being implemented in Australia, the U.S.A., Canada, Brazil, and other countries. Her current research is taking this work forward into instrumental tuition.

Antoine Hennion is Professor at MINES ParisTech and the former Director of the Centre for the Sociology of Innovation (CSI). He has written extensively on the sociology of music, media and cultural industries (radio, design, advertising). He is now studying amateurs, and diverse forms of attachment and detachment, from taste and sports to aging, or disability. His book *La Passion musicale* (1993, reprinted, 2007) will be published in English in 2012. Other recent books: *La grandeur de Bach* (2000, with J.-M. Fauquet), *Figures de l'amateur* (2000, with S. Maisonneuve and É. Gomart), *Le vin et l'environnement* (2011, with G. Teil).

Trevor Herbert was a professional trombone player before joining the staff of the Open University where he is now Professor of Music. He has written extensively on all aspects of the repertoires, performance practices, and cultural history associated with brass instruments. He is co-editor of *The Cambridge companion to brass instruments* (Cambridge University Press, 1996), editor of *The British brass band: A musical and social history* (Oxford University Press, 2000) and his monograph *The trombone* was published by Yale in 2006. He has also written on the cultural history of Wales and is co-editor of the seven volume *Welsh history and its sources* series.

David Hesmondhalgh is Head of the Institute of Communications Studies at the University of Leeds. He is author of *The cultural industries* (two editions, 2002 and 2007, another due in 2012) and *Creative labour: Media work in three cultural industries* (2011), co-written with Sarah Baker. He is also editor or co-editor of five volumes, including *The media and social theory* (with Jason Toynbee, 2008) and *Western music and its others: Difference, appropriation and representation in music* (with Georgina Born, 2000). The issues discussed in his chapter will be explored in greater depth in a book he is writing for Blackwell, provisionally entitled *The politics of music*.

Bennett Hogg is a composer, improviser, and cultural theorist who teaches at Newcastle University. Much of his creative work has been in the field of electroacoustic composition, and he is also involved in a series of environmental sound art projects. His academic research is focused on ideas of embodiment and technology in music from the perspectives of phenomenology and consciousness studies, the intellectual and creative legacies of surrealism and other "modernisms," and psychoanalytical perspectives on voice and vocality. He is currently co-editing an issue of *The Contemporary Music Review* on "resistant materials" with long-time academic collaborator Sally Jane Norman, director of the Attenborough Centre for the Creative Arts at Sussex University. He is committed to Small's idea of "musicking"—music as verb rather than noun—and to Varela's "enactive consciousness," taking the view that music and consciousness are things we *do*, not things we have.

Lawrence Kramer is Distinguished Professor of English and Music at Fordham University. He is the author of ten books on the cultural study of music, beginning with *Music as cultural practice* (1990) and most recently including *Interpreting music* (2010). He is the editor of the journal *19th-Century Music* and a composer whose works have been performed internationally.

Adam Krims is Professor of Music Analysis at the University of Nottingham, holding the only professorship in that area in the United Kingdom. He is author of the award-winning books *Rap music and the poetics of identity* (2000) and *Music and urban geography* (2007), as well as numerous essays and articles on contemporary music and music culture, urban change, and political economy. His most recent work focuses on Historically-Informed Performance (HIP) and its integration with the cities on which it relies for much of its basic workings, as well as the ways in which cities come to be musically "creative."

Dave Laing is a visiting research fellow at the Institute of Popular Music, University of Liverpool and a freelance researcher, editor, and author. He is associate editor of the journal *Popular Music History*. His books include *The sound of our time* (1970), *One chord wonders* (1985) and *Buddy Holly* (2010). He was co-editor of *The Faber/Da Capo companion to 20th century popular music* (1990) and of the *Continuum encyclopaedia of popular music of the world* (2002–5).

Fred Everett Maus teaches in the Music Department of the University of Virginia. He has published on narrative and drama in classical instrumental music; aesthetics and analysis, including issues of musical unity, musical time, and embodiment; music, gender, and sexuality; popular music studies (Pet Shop Boys, R.E.M.); and curricular and pedagogical issues.

Richard Middleton is Emeritus Professor of Music at Newcastle University in England, and a Fellow of the British Academy. Born in Yorkshire, he now lives in Galloway in southwest Scotland (which once, long ago, was part of Northumbria), and enjoys inhabiting multiple territories whose borders, historical, political, and cultural, do not always align. *Musical belongings* (2009), a collection of his essays on popular music originally published between 1979 and 2009, casts light on an intellectual journey towards a musicology of political commitment that can at the same time accommodate an entirely welcome sense of cultural instability.

Other books on popular music include *Pop music and the blues* (1972), *Studying popular music* (1990), *Voicing the popular* (2006), and the edited volume, *Reading pop* (2000). Professor Middleton was a founding editor of the journal *Popular Music*.

John Mowitt is Professor in the department of Cultural Studies and Comparative Literature at the University of Minnesota. He is the author of numerous texts on the topics of culture, theory, and politics, most recently his book, *Re-takes: Postcoloniality and foreign film languages*, (2005) and the co-edited volume, *The dreams of interpretation: A century down the royal road* (2007), both from the University of Minnesota Press. He recently collaborated with the composer Jarrod Fowler to transpose his book *Percussion: drumming, beating, striking* (Duke University Press, 2002) from a printed to a sonic text. His current project, *Radio: Essays in bad reception*, is forthcoming from the University of California Press. He is also a senior co-editor of the journal *Cultural Critique*, a leading Anglophone academic publication in the field of cultural studies and critical theory.

Ronald Radano is Professor of Musicology and Ethnomusicology at the University of Wisconsin-Madison. He has written extensively on U.S. black music and on the study of music and race. He is co-editor of two book series, Chicago Studies in Ethnomusicology and Duke University Press's Refiguring American Music.

John Shepherd is Associate Provost (Academic Quality Assurance), Dean of the Faculty of Graduate and Postdoctoral Affairs, and Chancellor's Professor of Music and Sociology at Carleton University, Ottawa, Canada. His publications include *Music as social text* (Cambridge: Polity Press, 1991), and *Music and cultural theory* (with Peter Wicke) (Cambridge: Polity Press, 1997). With David Horn, he is a principal editor of the *Continuum encyclopedia of popular music of the world*. Dr. Shepherd was in 2000 elected a Fellow of the Royal Society of Canada in recognition of his role as "a leading architect of a post-War critical musicology".

Mark Slobin is the Richard K. Winslow Professor of Music at Wesleyan University and the author or editor of many books on Afghanistan and Central Asia, eastern European Jewish music, and ethnomusicology theory, the most recent being *Folk music: A very short introduction* (2010).

Martin Stokes is a University Lecturer in the Faculty of Music at Oxford, and a Fellow of St. John's College. He has published widely on issues of history and theory in ethnomusicology, and on the music of the Middle East. His most recent book is *The republic of love: Cultural intimacy in Turkish popular music.*

Will Straw is Professor of Communications in the Department of Art History and Communications at McGill University and the Director of the McGill Institute for the Study of Canada. From 1997 to 2004, he was Director of the Graduate Program in Communications. Dr. Straw is the author of *Cyanide and sin: Visualizing crime in 1950s America* and of over 100 articles on film, popular culture, and urban culture. His current music-related research focuses on the material culture of music in relation to recording formats.

Jeff Todd Titon is Professor of Music at Brown University. His books include *Powerhouse for God* (1988), *Early downhome blues* (2nd ed., 1995), and *Worlds of music* (5th ed., 2008). From 1990 to 1995 he served as editor of *Ethnomusicology*, the Journal of the Society for Ethnomusicology. Currently he is developing an ecological approach to music and sustainability. Blog: http://sustainablemusic.blogspot.com/.

Gary Tomlinson is Professor of Music and Humanities at Yale University and a recipient of numerous awards, including MacArthur and Guggenheim fellowships. His work has ranged from early modern Italy through the history of opera, from anthropological method to cultural critique and post-structuralist theory, and from Aztec and Inca song to Miles Davis. His books include *Music in Renaissance magic* (1993), *Metaphysical song: An essay on opera* (1999), *The singing of the New World: Indigenous voice in the era of European contact* (2007), and *Music and historical critique* (2007). His current research concerns the evolutionary emergence of music.

Jason Toynbee is Senior Lecturer in the Department of Sociology at The Open University. His research is in copyright and creativity, and ethnicity and the postcolonial condition. He often takes case studies from popular music, as with his books *Making popular music: Musicians, institutions and creativity* (Arnold, 2000) and *Bob Marley: Herald of a postcolonial world?* (Polity, 2007). He is also the author of journal articles and book chapters on these themes as well a co-editor of *The popular music studies reader* (Routledge, 2006), *Analysing media texts* (Open University Press, 2006), *The media and social theory* (Routledge, 2008), and *Migrating music* (Routledge, 2011).

Rob C. Wegman is a historical musicologist specializing in music from the twelfth to the sixteenth centuries. He is the author of *Born for the muses:*

The life and masses of Jacob Obrecht (1993) and *The crisis of music in early modern Europe, 1470–1530* (2005), and has published numerous essays on music and culture in late-medieval and early modern Europe. He teaches at Princeton University.

INTRODUCTION
Music Studies and the Idea of Culture

RICHARD MIDDLETON

Culture: the word is one of the most complex in the English language, as Raymond Williams (1983, 87) points out, but this has proved little handicap to its spread; it's *everywhere*. We cultivate culture (*sic*), celebrate it, argue and struggle over it; we territorialize it (for example, in "cultural quarters"), preserve it (as "heritage"), institutionalize and administer it (through UNESCO, for instance); we even *live* it, as "popular" or "everyday" culture, or just as "customs" or "way of life." The idea of culture doesn't always get a good press, however. When Hermann Göring heard the word, so legend has it, he reached for his revolver.[1] But negative indictments, whether in the name of a simplistic naturalism or a vulgar-Nietzschean posthumanism, aren't culture's only enemy. Indeed, as a result of its ubiquity, it is often over-positivized—instrumentalized to death, so to speak. Buffeted, traduced, and prostituted—by political nobodies, state functionaries, advertising hucksters, muddled "post-industrial" planners, media narcissists, reactionary bigots, racists, and misogynists fighting "culture wars" across the planet— "culture" might seem to be a word begging to be put out of its misery. It wouldn't work. So integral is "culture" to the formations of modern society that it would rise again—or else some cognate term would appear to stand in its place. The battleground it occupies is irreducible. The idea of culture is still, as perhaps it always has been, *fraught*.

To say this is at the same time to cut against a different conventional wisdom. Williams also liked to affirm that culture is ordinary (rather than confined to elites, shrines, and special occasions), but this insight has been given a banal twist. In the 1980s and 1990s, the "cultural turn" in music studies was presented as a radical shift and widely received as such. Now, it is commonly suggested, its lessons have been absorbed. Cultural musicology is mainstream. Job done. At least one reviewer of the first edition of this book found it difficult to understand what all the culturalist fuss was about:

> The premise of this book must seem a little odd to those outside the field of musicology. Its title speaks of the "cultural study" of music as if "culture" were a novel standpoint from which music could be regarded, and the blurb . . . asks . . . "What is the relation between music and culture?" . . . The puzzled layman's attitude to all this would I think express itself as follows: isn't music a *part* of culture? Isn't specifying "the relation between music and culture" like trying to specify the relation between shoes and fashion, or soufflés and French cuisine? . . . "Culture" and the "cultural study of music" are not really a new paradigm for the discipline . . . but a peg on which to hang an interestingly mixed bag of topics, approaches and concerns.
>
> (Pritchard 2007, 145–146)

This seems to over-simplify the idea of culture in several ways, giving the impression, first, that "music" fits unproblematically into "culture", as part to whole (admittedly this is an improvement on the older idea that "culture" is just "context"); second, that the idea of "culture" is, equally unproblematically, a universal (rather than itself culturally situated, hence requiring exegesis); and third, that this idea is unchanging, that "culture" is just *there* (rather than requiring to be historically located). The coexistence of such views—which seem quite widespread—with the sense of conflict I sketched at the outset suggests that closure of the debate is, to put it no higher, a touch premature. If the cultural approach in music studies has become routine, or if it represents little more than a return, after the neo-positivist hegemony of mid-twentieth-century musicology, to an earlier norm—which the reviewer cited above comes close to arguing—then it seems strange that the resettlement of the field and its subdisciplines, commonly associated with the period from the 1990s on, has not been more straightforward and is patently incomplete (Born 2010a). It's true that the library shelves now groan with book series in culturalist subdisciplines such as ethnomusicology and popular music studies; that new approaches associated with them and with "critical" or "new" musicology are now welcome in the elite journals; that they have been monumentalized in the proliferating Ashgate book series, *Contemporary Thinkers in Critical Musicology*. True as well that, as has often been observed, these approaches sometimes come with an imperializing swagger, betraying an unbecoming and misleading triumphalism.

But the fact that resentment at this "success" has not gone away, and that this element of discomfort is paralleled on the "other side" by an anxiety that the political thrust driving the new approaches has fallen short (Bohlman 1993; Cusick 2008; Middleton 2009, Introduction), points towards a less sanguine mood. I will come back to the idea that the crisis in music studies widely diagnosed a decade or two ago may not in fact be over, simply observing for now that routine and unease are strange bedfellows. Or are they? The drift of much post-Nietzschean thought suggests the answer is: No—an answer we might link, via Heideggerian as much as Freudian traditions, with the concept of *Unheimlichkeit*, the uncanny (to use the less than ideal English equivalent), the foreign or strange that is at the same time strangely familiar. And here, in the problematic of *home* (homeland and homeless, homes made and homes lost, belonging and exclusion, ours and theirs, property, common or addressed), and the messages that circulate around it (sometimes successful, sometimes—address unknown?—less so), we may find the nub of the issue.

Where, then, do we stand today with the idea of culture?

Always historicize, as Fredric Jameson likes to instruct us. The idea for the first edition of this book arose in the mid-1990s in a quite specific moment. Members of the newly formed Musics and Cultures Research Group at The Open University in Britain found that, although their work as individuals stemmed from a variety of disciplinary positions, they shared a sense that, to quote the book proposal:

> A tendency towards increasing concern with "culture" has been manifested in music scholarship for some time, and in a variety of ways. It would be too much to say that the various trajectories are converging, let alone that all will crystallize into a single field of "cultural musicology." Nonetheless, different approaches are interacting, and with increasing intensity, such that it is clear that a new paradigm may well be on the horizon. All the disciplines involved in the study of music will continue to be changed by this process, and some form of reconfiguration seems inevitable.

Already in 2003, as the first edition appeared, the degree of programmatic confidence signaled, however hesitantly, in that statement looked premature. In the period since, new proposals and interventions have continued to appear, accompanied however by further waves of accommodation, compromise, and resistance. The horizon against which any new paradigm might coalesce seems little nearer. This alone would justify continued engagement with the questions that initially exercised us, especially when so many other essays in intradisciplinary reassessment concentrate on one perspective alone (gender, the canon, history, musical analysis, or whatever the case may be).

To look across the full range of disciplinary perspectives is important. Indeed, the parallelism displayed in the early histories of the different strands of "musics and cultures" research, together with their varied dialogues, seems to be integral to its problematic. To bring together into the historical picture the cultural turn in ethnomusicology associated above all with Alan Merriam's *The Anthropology of Music* (1964) and carried forward subsequently by Blacking, Keil, Feld, and many others; the maturing (from Howard Becker to Hennion, Frith, and DeNora) of a cultural sociology exercised with music; the emergence of Anglophone cultural studies in the 1970s, its work on music partly overlapping with the equally new area of popular music studies (Frith, Hebdige, Middleton, Tagg); and the development of the "new" or "critical musicology," its birth conventionally dated from Joseph Kerman's *Musicology* (1985), and most influentially represented in the work of such scholars as McClary, Tomlinson, Leppert, and Kramer, is to outline a concurrence of narratives, roughly through the final three decades of the twentieth century, following distinctive but often mutually affecting routes, which taken as a whole mark a historical node in thinking about music of indisputable significance. This story, of course, is a story of the Western, particularly the Anglophone, academy. But then, notwithstanding the fruits of a multitude of ethnographic fieldwork projects, that academy has been conspicuously poor at learning from other intellectual traditions, or recognizing the full scope of its own impact on them—surely one reason for the political unease circulating within radical quarters of musicology which I have already noted.

It is hard to delineate with precision all that these various trajectories have in common, beyond a position against pure musical autonomy: "Music is more than *notes*" represents the bottom line, an idea whose seeming banality today perhaps might be taken to signal its triumph. But this idea would hardly have come as a surprise to Baroque theorists of *Affektenlehre*, or medieval thinkers about music and theology, or even Plato (not to mention classical Indian or Chinese music theorists). What was new in the late twentieth century, however, was precisely the concept of *culture*, in a specific sense associated with the post-Enlightenment world. I will return to the ramifications of this concept; for now, it is enough to note the political thrust of its usages in late modernity, which, within music studies, has generated a whole range of characteristic impulses: attacks on "the canon," on "great composer history," and on "transcendental" aesthetics; critiques of "positivistic" historiographies and analytical methods; deconstructions of patriarchal, ethnocentric, and other "ideological" interpretations; valorization of popular music cultures; the relativizing of differences between musical systems; and so on. On this level, the new approaches all stand for the proposition that *culture matters*, and that therefore any attempts to study music without situating it culturally are illegitimate (and probably self-interested).

But on this level, as already observed, some will ask what all the fuss is about. Surely this at least is one battle that *has* been won. Does anyone still believe that musicology is the study of the scores of the great masters and nothing more? In this sense, aren't we all, to a greater or lesser extent, culturalists now? To locate the debate on this terrain is to succumb to the parochialism of much of the old musicology itself. A tendency to treat the category of "culture" as transparent and universal, and therefore its accommodation as purely pragmatic, needs to be brought up against its historicity: as Francis Mulhern (2000, xiii) has pointed out, "culture" is a *topic*, and, as one of the most successful topics of late-modern discourse, has assumed the status of a commonplace—one of "those places in discourse in which an entire group meets and recognises itself" (Bourdieu 1993b, 168). It is this dimension of the commonsensical that explains how culture can so often still be taken for granted; to advance the debate, eventually perhaps to reconfigure the field, demands as a minimum the recognition that an introduction to the cultural study of music should be *critical* (which means, also, *self*-critical); and a useful starting point is the awareness that the concepts of both "culture" and "critique," in their recognizable modern meanings, emerged concurrently in the moment of the European Enlightenment.

Previously, the discourse of culture had metaphorically linked the cultivation of mind and of ground: the culturing of inner and outer nature, through education on the one hand and by farmers on the other, formed a coherent conceptual field. But, while many ramifications of this metaphor have survived, in the late eighteenth century—in England and especially in Germany—the idea of "culture" took on a more politicized edge: it assumed the role of critique (*Kulturkritik*, as the Germans put it), posed against the contemporary concept (typically French) of *civilization*. "Culture" now stood for inward, spiritual qualities, a wholeness of life, as against the apparently external, mechanical, alienating characteristics of Enlightenment democracy, in the emergent phase of industrial capitalism. This new culture concept soon split into divergent tendencies. The humanistic proposition of a universal measure of value ("the best which has been thought and said in the world . . . the study of perfection," in Matthew Arnold's words of 1869 [1963, 6, 11]) was one, and it possessed a distinct moral dimension: right thinking led to right living. But this perspective could be narrowed to a focus on culture as art—the best art, naturally, the art of an elite—or, in a later variant, to the sphere of meaning as such, the symbolic order. A third tendency—the *völkisch* turn—began with Herder's equation of cultures (plural rather than singular) with distinctive ways of life, each embodying a national soul; in this approach, a people "has a culture," and its value is incommensurate with any other. It is easy to recognize the influence of this view on the development of the discipline of cultural anthropology and on early ethnomusicology, but it also fed into many strands of cultural studies.

These three tendencies have competed, interacted, and mutated. That story has been told many times, classically by Raymond Williams (1961, 1965, 1981), and in more recent books by (among others) Adam Kuper (1999), Terry Eagleton (2000), and Francis Mulhern (2000). It doesn't need repeating here. It is worth drawing attention, though, to a few of the most important features; these take the form of continuities on the one hand, and contradictions on the other.

The continuities arise precisely from the culture concept's historicity. Culture may, in one sense, be a universal attribute of humankind, but we cannot escape the specific provenance of culture theory and its historical development. In the tradition this development represents, culture always has a political force (even when it is posed as antipolitical); indeed, it often threatens to absorb or displace the sphere of politics as more conventionally understood. In part this is because culture functions as an other: it "is always defined in opposition to something else" (Kuper 1999, 14)—economics, society, psychology, biology—and its representations have their roots elsewhere: in a golden past, in a utopian future, in the captivating unfamiliarity of "primitive" societies, of the "folk," the "people," the anthropologically *different*. It is defined, too, in opposition to Nature: Culture is what is learned, what is cultivated; it is just what is not in the genes, and culture theories have figured in a long-standing critical relationship not only with raciologies of various sorts but also with more reputable disciplines of evolutionist anthropology, social Darwinism and, today, evolutionary psychology. At the same time, culture can seem "natural"; and indeed, the organic metaphor—good culture as wholeness and health—has a strong presence in much of the theory. Terry Eagleton has worked hard to close this gap: "If culture really does go all the way down, then it seems to play just the same role as nature, and feels just as natural to us"; but this coherence is deceptive: "what is peculiar about a symbol-making creature is that it is of its nature to transcend itself. . . . It is not that culture is our nature, but that it is *of* our nature, which makes our life difficult. . . . Culture is the 'supplement' which plugs a gap at the heart of our nature, and our material needs are then reinflected in its terms. . . . Human nature is naturally unnatural, overflowing the measure simply by virtue of what it is" (Eagleton 2000, 94, 97, 99, 101). The gap, then, is inescapable—indeed "natural." But its representations, in such formulations as these, are historically specific—part of the history of the theory; and the tension between nature and culture is part of a broader crisis of knowledge. If the culture idea—from Vico through Marx, Nietzsche, and Freud to Sartre, Williams, and Habermas—is a secular theory of a species making itself, then it carries along with it an inevitable strand of reflexivity which ensures that it will always fall short of what it claims. Eagleton again: "What is it that connects culture as utopian critique, culture as way of life and culture as artistic creation?" (20). The answer is that all are responses to "the failure of culture as actual civilisation—as the grand narrative of human self-development" (23); "culture in this sense arises when civilisation begins to seem self-contradictory. . . . Our very notion of culture thus rests on a peculiarly modern alienation of the social from the economic, meaning from material life. . . . It [culture] is itself the illness to which it proposes a cure" (31).

To even glance at the continuities within culture theories is thus to find the contradictions also flooding out. There is a strong strand right across the theories emphasizing culture as the sphere of meaning, of collective symbolic discourse, webs of significance, processes of signification; culture in this view is the dimension in which humans interpret their activities, institutions, and beliefs to themselves. Yet an equally strong tradition emphasizes that, far from being just a commentary, culture is *everything*. Thus, Raymond Williams, who talked often of culture in terms that focused on signifying practices, "meaning-bearing activity in all its forms" (Mulhern 2000, xiii), nevertheless offered as his considered formula for a theory of culture "a theory of relations between elements in a whole way of life" (Williams 1961, 12). In a reciprocal tension, cultural anthropology, while never forgetting Tylor's classic definition—"the complex whole" (1871, 1)—has also, particularly since the 1950s, followed Talcott Parsons's narrower perspective in claiming the study of collective consciousness as the specific province for the discipline, alongside and by contrast with the different arenas policed by sociology, economics, and psychology; and indeed the "hermeneutic turn" evident in the work of many of Parsons's successors in American anthropology—from Geertz to Clifford—further extends the idea of culture as a "text," and sidelines these other arenas almost completely. There are many variants of this tension. It can be written in terms of a distinction between culture as *practice* (e.g., Bourdieu 1977) and culture as the sphere of *subjectivity*, of identity formation (e.g., Bhabha 1994; Morley and Chen 1996). Or it can be figured through the picture of culture as a specific sector or subsystem in a complex set of relationships with other systems—this is Parsons's view, but an even more influential theory is of course that associated with Marx—in contrast with the idea that culture is more of a register, a level of thought and discourse applicable to all social spheres: this is the thrust of the later Williams's cultural materialism, neatly encapsulated by Stuart Hall—"Culture is not *a* practice. . . . It is threaded through *all* social practices, and is the sum of their interrelationship" (Hall 1980, 59).

Other significant contradictions within the nexus of culture theories often relate to, but sometimes cut across, this one. Is culture a human universal, and if so, is it ethically or aesthetically normative or merely a capacity that is ontologically given? Alternatively, can culture be thought of only relative to history, place, and context, and if so, are cultures radically noncomparable? If the latter is the case, judgment across boundaries—which, in today's fragmented, fluid societies, can be quite localized—would seem to be ruled out, let alone general projects of human emancipation. But if culture is taken to be a putative substantive universal, it is hard to avoid the elitism of Arnold, T. S. Eliot, and other proponents of traditional *Kulturkritik*. Should culture be seen, then, as making any sort of claim to special or specialist value or ambition, or is it, to come back to Williams's telling word, radically *ordinary*, the property of everyman (and woman)? A final question (final for now) might be this: If culture is learned, and if, especially, it is seen as providing in today's world the mechanisms for ever-mutable self-identifications, does this mean that it is entirely "performative"? Or is there, still, any sense in which culture can be regarded as authentic (or not)—as "true (or not) to . . . (something)"? Part of the price paid for the seeming triumph of the culture idea is the difficulty this leaves in specifying that "something."

With these questions, the political dimension of the culture idea emerges clearly. Mulhern has, intriguingly, connected the apparently different traditions of European (initially German) *Kulturkritik* and Anglophone cultural studies, the leftist, relativistic populism of the second acting, it would seem, as a radical critique of the elitist universalism of the first. What links them, he argues, is their displacement or absorption of "real" politics: they offer an alternative locus of authority, which acts as "a 'magical solution' to the poverty of politics in bourgeois society" (2000, 168), providing "a symbolic metapolitical resolution of the contradictions of capitalist modernity" (169). From distinct viewpoints, both Eagleton (2000) and Kuper (1999) also note the overweening status of culture in contemporary understanding and explanation, attacking the tendency to reduce issues to a purely cultural level, and often an especially localist, relativistic cultural level at that. All three writers call for a greater modesty on the part of culture theorists, a recognition that culture is not all there is. For Kuper, "unless we separate out the various processes that are lumped together under the heading of culture, and then look beyond the field of culture to other processes, we will not get far in understanding any of it" (1999, 247).

Such issues seemed particularly pressing in the early years of this century, as the first edition of this book was prepared; they are no less so now.

"Identity politics" have inscribed cultural claims and sufferings as primary weapons of struggle, in ways that can as easily have reactionary as progressive outcomes. The culture wars, inside and outside the academy, especially in the United States, have positioned elitists against populists. But, as Eagleton points out (2000, chapter 3), they function as a proxy for broader conflicts: between concepts of culture as civility, as identity, and as commerce; and on the global level, between a singular culture standing, in mystificatory fashion, for a hegemonic new world order and a host of threatened little worlds and neglected or threatening outlooks and problems. After September 11, 2001, Samuel Huntington's prophecy that henceforth "the great divisions among humankind and the dominating source of conflict will be cultural" (quoted, Kuper 1999, 3) took on a particularly terrifying quality as the reduction of political, economic, and social difference (not to say injustice) to culture *tout court* assumed official status. To resist such facile culturalism is a *political* imperative; lives depend on it. One might assume that Huntington's idea has been so discredited, not least by the fallout from the "war on terror," as to no longer require refutation. This would be a mistake. Its basic thrust is still there in, for example, Niall Ferguson's recent book (2011), *Civilisation: The West and the Rest* (the underlying framework can be conjugated: I am civilized, you belong to a culture, he is a barbarian, a formula that Ferguson cites, but without comment); to make no mention of current attempts, by politicians across Europe and the U.S.A., to distract attention from the economic crisis by attacking "the rest" (Mexicans in Arizona, Roma in France and Italy, Muslims everywhere, "multiculturalism" as policy in Germany and Britain). In this perspective, "culture" is elided with (what is coded as) "family" or "home" and presented, often with apparent innocence, as what Mulhern calls "customary difference"; "Culture today," he points out, "consists above all else in customs we do not share with the others" (Mulhern 2009, 4). The "multicultural fix" (ibid., 5–6), the liberal variant of this position, represents gains that demand defence, but at the same time if we cannot push past this, beyond cultural stereotypes, into what is or could be commonality and shared perceptions of injustice, we shall be stranded at the level of "tolerance" and little more.

Even if, heeding the call for modesty, we acknowledge the limited power of music scholars to change the world, it remains important to note the degree of congruence between Mulhern and the other writers I have cited (Eagleton, Kuper), a congruence which suggests that an important turn in conceptions of the culture idea may be in progress. If we take a fresh look at the cultural inscription of music—where necessary "disaggregating" spheres, to use Kuper's word, and reconfiguring relationships—we may both improve our understanding of culture and clear some room for politics, both "real" and "cultural" politics. We may also, who knows, happen upon a new paradigm for the cultural study of music.

The contents of this book could in one sense certainly be seen as congruent with a policy of disaggregation. The editors proposed no particular concept of culture and no line was laid down. Our strongest suggestion to authors was that they write stimulating essays, placing the stress at least as much on where music studies might (or ought to) be heading as on summaries of work done on their topic to date. The choice of topics emerged out of our own understandings of where the key issues are currently located. This was true of the first edition—all of those essays reappear here, although most of them are revised to a greater or lesser extent—and it is true of the chapters added to this second edition. Of course, the new topics we have selected will indicate our sense of the areas that have taken on a new or increased prominence during recent years. And, while the contents of the new chapters considered as a whole should not be taken as an attempt to summarize overall shifts in the field, some newly prominent emphases emerge in striking ways. One such emphasis is the *materiality* of musical practice, explored in relation to technologies and locations of music, cultural apparatuses within which it circulates, and the embodiment of practitioners and listeners. Another arises from a sense that the social embedding of music should be considered in broader terms than has often been the case in the past, to take in such parameters as race, religion, and emotional well-being. A third trend brings in an increased recognition of (or return to) the importance of political economy, including Marxist models—although it is fair to add that, at the same time, there is a contrasting emphasis that pushes even further than in past work against all totalizing analytical frameworks.

The existence of such trends in scholarship means that, although our initial planning was, as already indicated, based on topics rather than any overarching plan, it is not so surprising that, when we surveyed the content of the essays as a whole, many shared themes, focuses, and links became apparent. This indeed was even more the case with the second edition than the first and led to a structure organized around different perspectives on what might be thought of as the musical event: when, where, and how does this take place, who is involved, whose interests are served? The perspectives concern both methodology (how is this topic best studied?) and ideology (how should the disciplinary field be divided up?). *Part 1: When?* raises questions of historiography as these are affected by changing understandings of the development of human culture. *Part 2: Where?* explores locations of music, conceptualizing these in terms not only of geography but also culture and genre, and the interactions of all these in dialogues of interpretation. *Part 3: How?* is concerned with the routes, technologies, and institutions through which music comes into being. *Part 4: Whose?* investigates the social forces involved in these processes and the resulting social formations within which ownership of music is claimed. Finally *Part 5: Who?* is concerned with the subjects who respond to, make sense of, are constructed by, music.

If, overall, this sequence is understood as suggesting a trajectory from wide-angle to more closely focused perspectives, this should not be taken as an attempt to prescribe a particular reading strategy. Part of the condition of writing or editing any book is that, happily enough, one has no control over the ways in which it will be read and discussed. There is certainly no presumption that the book will generally be read cover-to-cover: In fact, for many purposes readers will find it useful to read, successively, two or more chapters dealing with closely related topics. The arguments will sometimes be mutually reinforcing and sometimes contradictory—they do not serve some overbearing model of the cultural study of music so much as reveal a patchwork of distinct, but also overlapping and complementary, conceptions of how such study might work. Links, overlaps, and dialogues crisscross the entire book and many chapters could have found a home in a different section from the one in which they have been placed. In preparing this volume, nonetheless, we had it in mind to facilitate certain kinds of usage. Thus, it should be not only suitable for use in university teaching at master's or final-year undergraduate level, but also accessible to readers outside the academic establishment (hence, for instance, the almost complete absence of notes and the inclusion of a list of further reading at the end of each chapter); and it should be accessible not only to musicians but also to anyone interested in the ways in which cultural approaches have been, and can be, applied to music (no author relies on music notation in developing his or her argument).

Perhaps any edited book—and even more, any co-edited book—situates itself inevitably in a certain field of turbulence of the sort sketched in the preceding section, in which coherence and diversity pull in different directions. Authorial names at the head of individual chapters (including this Introduction) signal the responsibilities of individual agency but also mask the inadequacies of such markers. The collegial roles of the three editors in the planning and production of this book (despite their diverse intellectual standpoints), not to mention the part played by every single contributor, should be taken as symptoms of what, in any enterprise of this sort, can only be, indeed, an exercise in social authorship of the happiest kind. But the pressures associated with such authorship are doubly appropriate here given the subject matter of the book and the state of play in the disciplinary field. The content of the book taken as a whole—mediated inescapably by the structure we have imposed upon it, but at the same time erupting through this structure in a range of tantalizing figurations—reveals not only processes of disaggregation but also a certain mood of reaggregation, or at least a reconfiguring, a search for connections. (Of course, different structures would have shaped the story differently.) At the very least, the fear of many recent writers—Eagleton, Mulhern, Kuper—that culturalism rampant and reductive, in its most relativistic but also imperialist mode, might signal a triumph of the culture concept that was altogether reactionary, is not borne out. Is this because music studies, typically, are behind the game? Or, unusually, ahead? Or is it the effect of the bewitching idiosyncrasy of music itself, its specificity so hard to ignore, its dependency on economic, social, technological, and political processes equally irreducible?

In an important intervention, James Currie (2009) disaggregates with a vengeance. First, though, he mounts an incisive critique of what he initially terms "contextualism" in the radical musicological movements of the past two decades, later specifying this more precisely in terms of the abandonment of totalizing narrative in favor of an emphasis on cultural localism and a politics of difference. These movements, despite the gains they have undoubtedly brought, find themselves in crisis, a crisis in large part attributable to a sense of political impotence in the face of what, at a higher level of social and economic analysis, presents itself clearly as a *totality*, namely the now-universal frame of global neo-liberal capitalism. Drawing on the arguments of Alain Badiou and Slavoj Žižek, Currie shows that the political ambitions accompanying the cultural inscription of music, when confronted with the intimidating, all-pervasive power of this frame, have inevitably fallen short. At this point, one might expect Currie to follow the example of Badiou and Žižek, and attempt to push past the impasse in search of some new synthesis or some sort of metapolitics of culture. Instead he takes a sidestep. At the present juncture, he suggests, we would do better to leave musicology to get on with its political soul-searching and turn (or return) to music itself, to the possibility that what is most important in the cultural status of music is precisely what is musical about it; to (re)turn, then, to what is "music after all." This argument about the "otherness" of music is addressed through perspectives drawn from phenomenology (Heidegger), from the Hegelian dialectical concept of negation, and from Adorno's utopianism; and then, in a second move, is applied to musicology as well:

> While musicology is off negotiating its own political problematic, what music in the meantime does while it is doing nothing is to instigate in the subjects who are exposed to it the very shift that musicology itself needs to undergo. Music negates (us). So could musicology perhaps achieve more politically by doing less, hanging out mindlessly with the unemployed, with music after all?
>
> (Currie 2009, 182)

The argument is telling (though Currie, it might be objected, tends to ignore works by radically minded scholars which *do* engage with "totality" in some sense: Tomlinson's (1999) philosophical history of opera, Erlmann's (1999) study of music and today's global imaginary, Bohlman's (2004) exploration of the politics of European musico-cultural identity, my own rather Žižekian account of "the popular" (2006), to name but four). Many chapters in the present book speak to the specificity of music, to the idea that what is special about music as a cultural practice is just what other discourses cannot capture, and it is surely worth hanging on to the notion that this realm may be the key to what music brings to culture, and thence to potential political practice. Equally, however, there are arguments why the otherness of music, its "ungraspability" (as compared, say, to material objects), is dependent on, and inextricably bound up with, the mediations through which it actually comes into existence—and these would include the ways we talk, and write, about it. Making all due allowance for the particularity of music, how far have we moved here beyond Oscar Wilde's "All art is quite useless" (which, he probably meant to imply, is precisely its use)? Or Susan Sontag's (1966) call for an erotics of art "beyond interpretation"? Or the "jargon of authenticity" subjected long ago (including its Heideggerian core) to Adorno's withering critique ([1973] 2003)?[2] What is placed before us is the familiar tale of music's *autonomy*. But "autonomy" *is* cultural, is a state of culture. The musical *Ding an sich* lies not *beyond* culture but *behind* it on an endless Möbius strip. Music's eloquent "silence," its resistance to the probes of the cultural sciences, makes sense only in the context of that "worldliness" which is its other side: penetrated incessantly by our prattle about it, it cannot stop meaning, however much we would like it to. Its negations—to follow Currie's lead into quasi-theological language—have the ambiguous valency of the *apophatic*. They are, like photographic negatives, *uncanny*.

What Currie is after, one suspects, is a glimpse of what Lacanians call the Real. But it's worth pointing out that, for Lacan, the Real is not located in some archaic, subterranean layer underneath the Symbolic (underneath discourse, culture, politics, we might say), a territory we can penetrate only if we abandon culture and leap blindly into these mysterious depths; rather, it comes into being *with* the Symbolic, it is just what the Symbolic cannot handle, running "behind" it, repressed but at the same time providing vital subversive energy. From this point of view, music *qua* Real, as Currie (I think) envisages it—like Lacanian thought itself—can readily be situated in a well-established post-Romantic schema (which in turn has still older roots in theological antinomies of reason and revelation). In Currie's formulation, music performs a metonymic substitution, taking up in effect the political role of culture, that is, of Romantic *Kulturkritik*, in a manner that is perfectly traditional but is now positioned against the claims of culture itself; it acts as an ethically preferable, "spiritual" Other to the machineries (including the musicological machines) of secular system, discourse, and way of life. It is indeed important to distinguish the different domains, to disaggregate; but their relation is a condition of this separation and underpins it; this is what boundaries do. The antinomies of the regime of culture are not easily escaped. It is not that "negations" aren't necessary nor potentially productive, it is that they are always already spoken for (indeed spoken) within the system which they purport to escape.

Adorno puts it beautifully: "In the universally mediated world everything experienced in primary terms is culturally preformed. Whoever wants the other has to start with the immanence of culture, in order to break out through it" (Adorno [1973] 2003, 81). It is not hard to agree, then, with both the sentiment and the tone of James Clifford's rumination: "Culture is a deeply compromised idea I cannot yet do without" (quoted, Kuper 1999, 212). Some Marxists have suggested that the primacy of economics in Marxism might be specific to the historical stage of capitalism (hence Marx's theory really represented a cultural self-diagnosis). It would be rash, especially at the present moment, to assume that this phase has been superseded. Drawing an analogy from this formula, however, we might do well to regard the concept of culture (and especially its rise to apparent hegemony, a move itself not without effects on late-twentieth-century Marxist theory) as a staging post. Full of important leads, still indispensable to thinking, but always overambitious, never fully identical to its objects, the idea of culture would then appear as a moment that we need to push past, while retaining what is valuable in its patrimony, most particularly the insistent question it makes manifest: if, in a fractured world, culture, as idea and instance, inevitably falls short—short of its own promise and desire—what follows? What sort of ground, what sort of *home*—might present itself? Here negation could earn its keep, prompting a rediscovery of "lost causes" (Žižek 2009b), turnings not taken and doors unopened, that might help point us towards a future beyond the present limits of culture.

NOTES

1 The actual source appears to be a play premiered in 1933 in Berlin. But the general idea—action trumps thought, "culture" is for Jews, homosexuals, and other misfits—is of course an *idée fixe* in Nazi ideology, and Göring probably said something of the sort.

2 To be fair, Currie ends up in a position that is more Adornian (via Richard Leppert) than Heideggerian (via Carolyn Abbate). Nevertheless, it's entertaining to speculate what Adorno would have made of the fact that he is lined up here on the same side of the argument as the leading representative of the philosophical tendency for which the Frankfurt School had especial scorn.

PART 1

WHEN?
Musical Histories

CHAPTER 1

MUSIC AND BIOCULTURAL EVOLUTION

IAN CROSS

INTRODUCTION

How should we understand music? The ways in which we can answer this question are conditioned by the status that we are willing to grant to music. If music is a universal human behavior, part of "human nature," then it should be possible to understand music by identifying and applying general principles of the type found within formal and scientific theories. And music has been claimed as "a universal behavior" by Alan Merriam (1964, 227), though Blacking (1995, 224) is more circumspect in stating that "every known human society has what trained musicologists would recognize as 'music.'"

But this view is difficult to square with much ethnomusicological, and most recent musicological, scholarship, which would replace music with musics, holding that musics are musics only in their cultural contexts. Musics make sense as musics only if we can resonate with the histories, values, conventions, institutions, and technologies that enfold them; musics can be approached only through culturally situated acts of interpretation. Such interpretive acts, as Bohlman (1999) makes clear, unveil a multiplicity of musical ontologies, some or most of which may be mutually irreconcilable: hence a multiplicity of "musics."

In the first view, there is a singular phenomenon called music, which has material manifestations and some knowable relationship to human biology, mind, and behavior. In the second view, music exists as musics, diverse, multiple, and unknowable within a single unitary framework. But in this second view music seems to have lost much of its materiality, and while the materialities of "musics" may be heterogeneous and heteronomous, they are irrefutably grounded in human behaviors.

From a materialist perspective, underlying human behaviors are minds, and underlying minds are embodied human brains. Underlying embodied human brains are human biologies, and underlying human biologies are the processes of evolution. Musics as culturally situated, minded human behaviors—musics as material phenomena—thus stand in some to-be-determined relationship to human evolution. Of course it might be the case that the cultural dynamics of music owe little or nothing to the evolutionary processes that underlie our biologies. But this position is tenable only if our biological being can be cleanly dissociated from our cultural lives, and given that our cultural lives are mainly evidenced in material behaviors and their traces, a clean dissociation between culture and biology—or between music and evolution—is unfeasible. To state this is *not* to argue that musics are reducible to—are knowable wholly in terms of—an understanding of evolution, merely that the relation between musics and evolution needs to be explored and specified.

Current theories of evolution are concerned with the ways in which the operation of processes of random variation, natural selection, and differential reproduction within a population leads to changes in the state and makeup of that population. Random variation leads to the emergence of entities with different attributes or capacities; natural selection, operating through ecological pressures, leads to the preferential survival of those types of entities whose capacities are best adapted to immediately prevailing sets of circumstances; and those entities that are best adapted have a better chance of reproducing and passing on their genes than do less-well-adapted entities. It is important to note that the entities referred to above might be genes themselves, organisms, or individual or group behaviors (see, e.g., Boyd and Richerson 2010). An evolutionary approach will tend to focus on the attributes that allow a gene, a behavior, an organism, or a specific intra- or intergroup dynamic to be functional in the processes of evolution, that is, to be adaptive in contributing to the differential success in survival and reproduction of the entities that make up the population.

Hence an evolutionary perspective seems to offer an integrated framework that has explanatory power with respect to individuals' biological components and behaviors, as well as with respect to groups of individuals (and the existence of groups of individuals is a necessary though not sufficient premise for the existence of culture). So evolutionary thinking may provide a means of exploring relationships between human biology, behavior, and culture. There are, however, very good reasons why anthropologists and psychologists have been wary of applying an evolutionary perspective to human behaviors and culture. The genetic determinism and racist stereotyping that the evolutionary thinking of the first half of the twentieth century appeared to sanction led to some of the worst barbarities in recorded history.

But contemporary evolutionary thinking offers comfort neither to genetic determinists nor to racists. Evolution is currently seen as impacting on human mind and behavior not by shaping or determining complex behaviors directly, but by providing general constraints on how minds interact, and develop so as to be able and motivated to interact, with their physical and social environments. And modern genetics has shown that two gorillas five miles apart in a central African rain forest are likely to differ more in their genetic makeup than are a Basque inhabitant of San Sebastian and an Aboriginal Australian from the Northern Territories. Despite recent evidence for a limited amount of gene flow between archaic humans and modern humans (Reich et al. 2010; Green et al. 2010), we are one single species—Homo sapiens—recently emerged from Africa. However, our biological homogeneity stands in extreme contrast to our cultural diversity; for a species whose members are, biologically speaking, all much the same, we have developed a superabundance of different ways of living—an enormous plurality of cultures.

Bearing this prodigious cultural diversity in mind, are there reasons to expect that musics, as culturally situated human behaviors, have anything other than a contingent relationship to evolutionary processes? In the first place, a hint of a more than contingent relationship can be found in music's ancient provenance as a human behavior. The earliest unambiguously musical artifacts identified to date are bone and mammoth-tusk ivory pipes dated to around 40,000 BP found at Hohle Fels in southern Germany, uncovered in contexts that associate them with modern Homo sapiens (Conard et al. 2009). The pipes predate almost all known visual art, and in any case a capacity for musicality (most likely vocal) would predate the construction of a sophisticated musical artifact such as a pipe, probably by a considerable period. Archaeology thus suggests that human musicality is ancient; the fact that music appears about as early as possible in the traces of Homo sapiens in Europe, together with the fact that musicality is an attribute both of the peoples of the pre-Hispanic Americas and of the Aboriginal peoples of precolonial Australia, provides good grounds for believing that music accompanied modern humans out of Africa.

And not only is music ancient, but musicality may be universal for all members of the human species; it has been claimed that "musical ability [is] a general characteristic of the human species rather than a rare talent" (Blacking 1995, 236). Of course, there are societies within which the term music does not seem to offer a good fit to any discretely identifiable set of cultural practices. But this does not seem to connote an absence of activities that might be interpretable as "musical." This lack of fit might arise because such "musical" behaviors are so embedded in broader categories of cultural practice as to be inextricable from them (as is the case in many African societies); or it may arise because "music" is a proscribed activity (as under the Taliban regime in Afghanistan). Even in this latter case, behaviors interpretable as "musical" may be manifested in contexts such as *tarana* (devotional song), though unacknowledged as music by the participants (Baily 2004).

Music is thus humanly ancient and ubiquitous, making it a good candidate to be considered as an evolutionarily adaptive behavior. But both music's ancient provenance and its universality are more suggestive than conclusive. It may be that musics are contingently human. Perhaps they are human behaviors that are not adaptive (in the evolutionary sense), which have arisen simply because humans have evolved other capacities that music can parasitically exploit, or they might be behaviors that have specifiable and determinate functions but that have neither played a role in, nor been impacted upon by, processes of human evolution.

MUSIC AS A GENERIC HUMAN CAPACITY

In order to evaluate the relationship between music and the processes of evolution we have to start by ascertaining whether or not music is a generic capacity of the human species; is there a sense in which we can claim that all humans are musical? A positive answer to this question will require that we are able to identify phenomena across all human societies—and across all typical members of those societies—that we can categorize as "music"; only then will we be in a position to determine whether or not this generic "music" has any specifiable function that has the potential to be considered as adaptive.

As we have seen, ethnomusicologists generally agree that all known societies have music, or perhaps more accurately, musics. However, the question of what precisely counts as "music" poses a significant problem; the diversity of cultural practices that ethnomusicologists have characterised as "music" seems to present no essential diagnostic features that would allow "music" to be identified unambiguously. Nevertheless, a pragmatic solution to the problem can be found in the ethnomusicologist Klaus Wachsmann's (1971, 384) suggestion that what ethnomusicologists and others tend to identify as "music" in cultures other than their own are simply the phenomena that sufficiently "*resemble* the phenomena which I am in the habit of calling music in my home ground."

While this may not seem to get us very far, we can at least start by suggesting that "musics" in cultures other than our own will tend to share some objective properties with the music with which we are familiar, typically employing complex patterns of sound that may be articulated in any or all of the dimensions of pitch, rhythm, timbre and intensity, typically by the voice. Most musics tend to "sound like" music, their sonic surfaces and structural organizations tending to exhibit similar features. These shared features can be understood as rooted in generic constraints on human perceptual, cognitive and motoric capacities (see Stevens and Byron 2009). A less evident shared property relates to the tendency of musics to exhibit temporally cyclical event-structures organized around an underlying, regular pulse. This not only allows the foci of listeners' attention to be modulated according to the music's underlying pulse (Jones and Boltz 1989) in presentational contexts, but also enables performers engaged in musical interactions (both formally trained specialists and enculturated individuals) to coordinate their musical behaviors in time—to *entrain* with each other (Clayton, Sager, and Will 2005). Aside from commonalities of structure, engagement with music across cultures tends to be associated with changes in the affective states of participants; universally, engagement with music tends to elicit emotion (see Fritz et al. 2009; Juslin and Sloboda 2010) and music is conceived of as emotionally expressive (see, e.g., Feld 1984).

Music also tends to be experienced as powerfully meaningful, but the meanings that are experienced embody the paradox of being somehow immediate and "natural" (e.g., Feld 1981, 28), yet at the same time indeterminate or ambiguous (e.g., Qureshi 1987)—what I have described elsewhere (Cross 1999) as "floating intentionality." As Alan Merriam (1964, 32–33) noted, across cultures—and even from a perspective rooted in one particular society—music is more than just sound; it is also manifested as concept and as behavior. The concepts that underpin music may take quite different forms in different cultures, as might the practices that embody or that give rise to those concepts; hence, although the acoustical manifestations of music in two different cultures may appear quite similar to a Western listener, their conceptual and behavioral contexts may render them quite distinct as musics. For example, not only may music may be conceived of or enacted for entertainment or for its aesthetic value, it may be embedded in, and be instrumental in respect of, other domains of social action. It may be presentational, or it may appear as a participatory, communicative medium entailing active contributions from all culture members (e.g., Turino 2008) that involve both sound and movement; it may be an integral component of coping with social change (Cross and Woodruff 2009) or may be central to the maintenance of aspects of the social order (Marett 2005).

Despite the immense range of contexts in which musics manifest themselves in different societies, and the wide range of cultural functions that they appear to fulfill, music is part of the cultural repertoire of every known society, and there is a general presumption that all culture-members will be able to respond to it and engage with it. Blacking's claim that "musical ability [is] a general characteristic of the human species" can be glossed by suggesting that each culture typically expects its members to be able to engage with music in culturally appropriate ways, irrespective of whether the primary mode of engagement with music in a particular society is presentational, differentiating between those who perform and those whose capacity to engage with music is limited to listening and appreciation, or participatory, imputing to each culture-member the capacity actively to contribute to collective musical behavior. In general, while the participatory mode is prevalent in pre-industrial or traditional societies (see Turino 1999), in contemporary Western societies the presentational mode predominates, privileging acts of listening; however, the participatory mode, involving collaborative music-making by nonspecialists, remains widespread in present-day urban societies, as shown in the work of Finnegan (1989) and others.

PROSPECTIVELY ADAPTIVE ATTRIBUTES OF MUSIC

Across cultures, then, music appears to have several clearly identifiable attributes; it is complexly structured, affectively significant, attentionally entraining, and immediately—yet indeterminately—meaningful. If we restrict our view of music to the "folk-theoretic" (Walton 2007) terms in which it is typically conceptualized within Western societies—as an autonomous aural commodity that has hedonic (and perhaps aesthetic) value—then our identification of these generic attributes of music may be interesting but seem to offer little in the way of help in understanding the nature of any relationships between music and evolutionary theory. From this perspective music seems to have complexity but to lack purpose, incongruous features that have led evolutionary theorists such as Steven Pinker to dismiss music as a trivial pursuit—a "technology," in his terms. For Pinker (1994), its complexity is parasitic on our capacity for language, while our use of it to move our emotions is on a par with our use of recreational drugs to simulate the pleasure engendered by the release of endorphins. He suggests that our faculty for music simply exploits capacities such as language, auditory scene analysis, motor control, etc., that can be postulated to have become universal components of the human behavioral repertoire through evolutionary processes because of their incontestable adaptive value. Pinker's view still holds sway in much of the scientific literature that has addressed music and evolution (see, e.g., Balter 2004). However, as should be evident, such a view is tenable only if almost all the world's musics other than those of the last one hundred and fifty years of technologized Western societies are excluded from consideration, and if we completely disregard the fact that music is experienced as meaningful.

If we think of music as primarily interactive and communicative, as fused with other domains of human thought and behavior rather than constituting an autonomous domain in its own right, then its complexity, its immediacy and indeterminacy of meaning, together with its tendency to occur in contexts of entrainment, endow it with considerable powers. Its cyclic periodic structures afford individuals interacting through music the experience that their behaviors are coordinated with other participants, endowing musical interaction with the impression that each participant is somehow sharing each other's time and laying the ground for the emergence of a sense of mutual affiliation. Its floating intentionality allows each participant to hold to their own interpretations of the meaning of the collective musical act without ever having to make those interpretations explicit for each other. At the same time, music's immediacy of meaning—its *apparent* honesty—legitimates the sense that what each participant feels and understands is also felt and understood by the others.

In these respects, music appears quite different from language as a communicative medium. For most linguists and psycholinguists, the key feature of language is its capacity to represent and communicate complex propositions about states of affairs in the world. As Pinker and Jackendoff (2005, 219) put it, "language is a mapping between sounds and meanings"; the principal task of language is to enable information that can have semantic specificity—that can unambiguously denote things such as objects, agents, attitudes, or events—to be exchanged between speakers and listeners. Music, considered as a communicative system, cannot do this; it cannot be employed to communicate complex yet unambiguous propositions about states of affairs in the world, indeed, it cannot even communicate simple propositions. But at least some of the time language, or more properly, speech, does *not* convey complex semantic information.

For example, on meeting someone in passing with whom one is casually acquainted, one might say "How are you?", expecting a formulaic "Fine, thanks—and you?" response, the interaction reaching an anticipated close with one's own response of "Oh, fine." This linguistic interaction is not concerned with exchanging information but with establishing or reestablishing a social relationship—it is phatic (Coupland and Coupland 1992). In such phatic contexts, where language is being used *relationally* rather than *transactionally*, it is fulfilling a function that seems more like that which I have postulated for music; it is acting, albeit transiently, as an affiliative and nonconflictual means of interaction. However, that function could be suppressed in the instance outlined above were one's initial enquiry to be interpreted as a genuine desire to elicit information rather than as a ritualized act of social facilitation. Language's capacity to be interpreted as unambiguously referential underwrites a potential for conflict between participants' interpretations of a shared discursive act. Music, in the view presented here, constitutes a more efficacious medium for sustained non-conflictual, affiliative social interaction precisely because of music's lack of capacity to be interpreted as unequivocally conveying a specific meaning. Nevertheless, there appears to be a significant overlap between the capacities of music and speech, and it can be suggested that "music" and "language" constitute culture-specific categories of communicative interaction that are distinguishable by being at opposite poles of the capacity for unambiguous reference (Cross 2005).

That music has potency in the social domain is a consistent theme of the ethnomusicological literature, summed up in Bruno Nettl's proposal that one of the fundamental functions of music is "to support the integrity of individual social groups" (Nettl 2005, 253). The ideas outlined here put a particular gloss on Nettl's proposal, suggesting that music's socially facilitative effects depend on the attributes identified above as common across cultures and implying that music, as a communicative medium, is likely to have a significant role in minimizing within-group conflict or, to put it another way, in collaboratively establishing a degree of social equilibrium. Indeed, as McLeod (1974, 113) notes, across a wide range of societies music is particularly associated with "the public presentation of social uncertainty," and elsewhere (Cross 2009) I have proposed that music, as a generic human capacity, can best be interpreted as a communicative medium that is optimal for the management of situations of social uncertainty.

MUSIC AND EVOLUTION

This proposal provides a baseline for understanding music as having a generic role across human societies, and may also offer a way of understanding how musicality—the capacity for music—comes to be instated in the human genome. Music is self-evidently functional in the social domain, facilitating social interaction and sustaining the integrity of social relationships. Such relationships are intensely important for humans; we are an intensely social species, and we are extremely flexible in the ways in which we manifest that sociality in comparison with other species, including most of our close evolutionary precursors (Foley and Gamble 2009). Indeed, humans exhibit a range of cultural variability (and of flexibility in accommodating to new cultural environments) that is of a different order from all other species. Boyd and Richerson (2009) propose that the course of human evolution is marked by an increasing capacity for social interaction driven by adaptive enhancement of the ability to learn from others, leading to the emergence of intra-group (cultural) and inter-group (inter-cultural) selection pressures that drove the evolution of cooperative, prosocial behaviors.

Tomasello et al. (2005) have suggested that it is the possession of a *capacity for culture* that is a generic feature of modern humans, marking us as fundamentally different from other species. The capacity for culture is manifested in our ability to "share intentionality" with others; we are able to interact with others in ways that indicate that we can infer and share their feelings, attentional foci, intentions, and goals. We are able to do this because we have highly developed (and largely pre-conscious) powers of attributing "mindedness" to others, on the basis of their (largely pre-conscious) behaviors (Frith 2008); gaze direction, facial and brachiomanual (hand and arm) gestures, degree of spatial and temporal alignment of others' actions with our own, all provide cues that we can use in making inferences about the feelings, mental states, and attitudes of those with whom we are interacting. This "mind-reading" ability, generally termed "Theory of Mind" (Leslie 1987), is evident from infancy, though its developmental trajectory through childhood to maturity is complex and susceptible to a degree of cultural influence (Liu et al. 2008).

Music plays on and exploits these cues (particularly temporal alignment of action and sound) in providing a framework for affiliative—prosocial— interaction. We can suggest that "something like music" is likely to have played a role in enabling our ancestors to get on with each other: to form, maintain and re-form stable yet flexible groups or cultures. In effect, in an evolutionary scenario in which the capacity to create and maintain social relationships is as important for survival as are any overt attributes of the individual (such as strength, speed, perceptual acuity, etc.), music's powers of stimulating and consolidating the appearance of social accord would have had considerable adaptive value in the overall repertoire of human behaviors. Over the course of human evolution music could have served as a means of managing intra- and inter-group interactions, helping to nurture the human facility for complex sociality that underpins the capacity for culture. As I have suggested elsewhere (Cross 2003), it may have emerged as a mode of communicative interaction as a mechanism for regulating, and coopting into the adult repertoire of thought and behavior, juvenile exploratory patterns of thought and behavior, under the selection pressure of the increasing altriciality (extension in duration of the juvenile phase relative to total lifespan) that is evident across our ancestor species in the hominin lineage (Bogin 1999).

As I have suggested above, music and language overlap considerably in the functions that they can fulfill as communicative media (and, indeed, in the structures and forms that they use to effect their ends); the distinction drawn between "music" and "language" in present-day Western cultures may reflect historic and contemporary cultural practices rather than any clean or intrinsic distinction between the two domains. Hence I would propose that rather than music preceding language in human evolution (as Mithen 2005 argues, following Darwin's suggestion of 1871: see Darwin 2004), or indeed language preceding music (after Spencer 1858), music and language are best conceived of as having co-evolved as components of a generalized human communicative toolkit. It is possible that they manifested themselves in ways that might be dimly discernible from the perspective of the present day with *Homo heidelbergensis* (the immediate predecessors of both ourselves, *Homo sapiens*, and our sibling species, *Homo neanderthalensis*) some half a million years ago; but it seems more likely that only with the emergence of *Homo sapiens* some 200,000 years ago did music and language assume forms with which we contemporary humans could fully resonate. According to this interpretation, more archaic humans (such as *Homo ergaster*) are likely to have had to make do with communicative capacities that fully integrated phatic and (limited) referential functionality.

In the end we can speculate almost endlessly about whether music has been evolutionarily adaptive, nonadaptive, an exaptation (an accidental but evolutionarily beneficial consequence of the evolution of other capacities), or merely a technology (as Pinker proposes). The evidence will always be likely to remain susceptible to multiple and contested interpretations, as is clear from the theories summarized in Cross (2007). However, it seems to me that the evidence most strongly supports the view that music *could* have been unequivocally adaptive; it is certainly socially efficacious in present-day societies, and given music's universality and ubiquity across all societies including traditional cultures there is every reason to suppose that social efficacy is an ancient characteristic. In the light of music's early appearance in our archeological record, all this lends weight to the idea that the capacity for music is an adaptive characteristic of the human species.

Nevertheless, the fact that we can account for certain generic aspects of music within an evolutionary frame does not provide an account of music *per se*, nor does it provide a warrant for science in general, or evolutionary theory in particular, to claim intellectual hegemony over the exploration of music. What has been outlined here is a generic account of music that reflects commonalities across cultures and that is concordant with an evolutionary understanding of the human faculty of musicality; but it cannot capture or reflect any single or particular cultural manifestation of music, and all music is inescapably culturally situated. For that, we must turn to ideas, methods, and disciplines represented elsewhere in this volume. That said, a generic account of music as a human capacity may provide those concerned with music in contemporary society with some moral, or even political, capital. If it is the case that the ideas outlined in this chapter have some validity—if it is the case that there is no other mechanism or vehicle that can perform for humans what music can perform *as a communicative medium*—then at the least we have a basis for claiming that to remain human we require the right to be able to be musical.

FURTHER READING

Blacking, John. 1995. *Music, culture and experience.* London: University of Chicago Press.

Conard, Nicholas J., Maria Malina, et al. 2009. New flutes document the earliest musical tradition in Southwestern Germany. *Nature* 460, 7256: 737–740.

Cross, Ian. 2007. Music and cognitive evolution. Pp. 649–667 in *Handbook of evolutionary psychology.* Edited by Robin I. M. Dunbar and Louise Barrett. Oxford: Oxford University Press.

Cross, Ian. 2009. The evolutionary nature of musical meaning. *Musicae Scientiae.* Special Issue: Music and Evolution: 147–167.

Darwin, Charles. [1871] 2004. *The descent of man and selection in relation to sex.* 2nd ed. 2 vols. London: Penguin Books.

Fritz, Thomas, Sebastian Jentschke, et al. 2009. Universal recognition of three basic emotions in music. *Current Biology* 19(7): 573–576.

Jones, Mari Riess, and Marilyn Boltz. 1989. Dynamic attending and responses to time. *Psychological Review* 96(3): 459–491.

Mithen, Steven. 2005. *The singing Neanderthals: The origins of music, language, mind and body.* London: Weidenfeld and Nicolson.

Nettl, Bruno. 2005. *The study of ethnomusicology: Thirty-one issues and concepts.* 2nd ed. Urbana and Chicago: University of Illinois Press.

Stevens, Catherine, and Tim Byron. 2009. Universals in music processing. Pp. 14–23 in *Oxford handbook of music psychology.* Edited by Susan Hallam, Ian Cross, and Michael Thaut. Oxford: Oxford University Press.

Tomasello, Michael, M. Carpenter, et al. 2005. Understanding and sharing intentions: The origins of cultural cognition. *Behavioral and Brain Sciences* 28(5): 675–691.

CHAPTER 2

MUSIC AND CULTURE
Historiographies of Disjuncture, Ethnographies of Displacement

PHILIP V. BOHLMAN

JANUARY 2011

Displacement, deportation, forced migration, immigration reform. Ten years after I wrote the essay for the first edition of the present volume, the words echoing the historiographies of disjuncture have become disturbingly ominous. They are words tied to actions, to the politics of the decade that followed the turn of a century and a millennium. They are dissonant with the tones of hopefulness that tentatively sounded in the first version of the essay. I locate the present version in a historical moment as if arrested by the immediacy called forth by the deluge of events ushering in new historiographies of disjuncture as 2010 gave way to 2011. In the spring of 2010, the American state of Arizona passed a law permitting police to demand that Mexicans in the state produce immigration papers or face immediate deportation. In the summer of 2010 the government of France, led by President Nicolas Sarkozy, passed legislation that would deport Roma "back" to Eastern Europe, upon which their homes and settlements in France would be destroyed. In Germany the politically powerful economist Thilo Sarrazin mustered statistics intending to prove that Muslims were responsible for the cultural decline of Germany (Sarrazin 2010). In the ethnographic moment in which I write, political disjuncture sweeps across Tunisia and Egypt, already destabilizing the historically destabilized Middle East. At the beginning of 2011, new anxiety arises in Europe, fearful of a wave of North African refugees crossing its borders, leading some European governments to call for emergency restrictions on the very borders opened across Europe by the 2007 Schengen Process.

I turn to the questions of empire, racism, nationalism, and displacement raised again by these events throughout this chapter, but in the present introduction I state a single question baldly: What do they have to do with music? At a level too simple to overlook we recognize that the cultural groups involved have long enjoyed a popular presence in music, while at the same time that presence in culture is marginalized. Latin and Roma music, the nationalist repertories of *ma'luf* in Tunisia and the spectacularly popular Umm Kulthum in Egypt: the musically popular coexists with the culturally unpopular to sustain the *longue durée* of disjuncture. We have been there before, and here we are again. And that is the most disturbing thought of all as I return to this chapter after a decade in which the circulation of music's global diversity is increasingly celebrated while cultural diversity faces unrelenting denigration. Writing in 2011, I turn to disjuncture again, forced to reconcile myself to the knowledge that its historiographical force lessened not in the least during the past decade.

JANUARY 2001 AND BEYOND

Historically, it has never been easy to talk about music and culture together, much less define them in ways that draw them together. Definitions of music that we might extract from widely used dictionaries neither include the word *culture* nor refer to any intrinsic or extrinsic property of the "arranging of sounds in time" or "a musical composition" (*American Heritage Dictionary*) that has anything to do with culture. Definitions of culture, too, rarely refer to music in any explicit way. Music and culture, broadly or narrowly defined, are not convenient discursive fits. When we do try to fit them together—and at base, this is what the authors contributing to *The Cultural Study of Music* are committed to doing—not everyone is happy. We have all had music teachers who have insisted that "music is music," and that it "doesn't need to be about culture." We have all known social scientists who have kept music at arm's length from culture because it is so many "notes on a page," a technical language spoken by specialists and not the generalists who want culture to be an umbrella for all human activity.

In the first edition of this book I took the difficulty with which we formulate definitions of music and culture that fit together as my point of departure; in the present edition that difficulty has returned, this time also as a point of arrival. I am not concerned here with finding definitional compromises or forging discursive methods that will repair the bad fit. I do not propose that we look for the widespread presence of music in culture, nor do I take an ameliorative position urging us to recognize traces of culture everywhere in music. The bad fit, instead, results from what I call *disjuncture* once again in this chapter. That disjuncture has been with us for a very long period of history, and it shows no signs of disappearing, even as the second edition of the present book appears.

In this chapter, I take as a given that disjuncture itself is one of the historically most critical reasons to study music and culture. Employing an approach that combines historiography and ethnography, this chapter strikes out in a direction that may be different from others in the book. First, I should suggest that, historically, there is far greater acceptance that music and culture are related, if not inextricably so, than many commonly assume. Second, the question that concerns me as a critic with the ethnographic present is why so many theories and aesthetics of music resist that acceptance. Above all, why does the historiography of Western art music, which includes historical musicology, music theory, ethnomusicology, and popular-music studies, cling to the counterintuitive assumption that music and culture are separate? Third, I wish to suggest that one reason there is resistance to accepting the relatedness of music and culture results from the paradoxical unwillingness to admit to the full range of cultural work that music makes possible. Finally, I turn to the revision of this chapter after ten years with an enhanced sense for the indispensability of political and moral imperative, and with a conviction that the cultural study of music is inseparable from the history of the present and the ethnographic encounter with our own world.

HISTORIOGRAPHICAL MOMENT 1—EMPIRE AND COLONIAL ENCOUNTER

The historiography of music and culture begins with the moment of encounter. The awareness of difference intensifies encounter, and that awareness engenders wonder and awe, which, however, lie precariously close to fear and violence. Music marks the moment of encounter, for it stands out as the form of communication that is at once most familiar and most incomprehensible. Even more than language, music is the key to understanding and to the power that will turn initial encounter into prolonged dominance. To music, then, accrues the potential to articulate colonial power and chart empire, and that potential was never lost on those most eager to colonize and missionize the worlds of the others they encountered (see, e.g., Pagden 1993).

Encounter transformed music into a resource that fired the engines of modernity, first in the Early Modern era that followed on the heels of the Age of Discovery, and then the modernity that accompanied the Enlightenment. Music and, by extension, music history underwent an ontological transformation of revolutionary proportions when they accompanied conquest and missionizing. Music represented culture in two ways: as a form of expression common to humanity, and as one of the most extreme manifestations of difference. On the one hand, the essence of a universal culture was borne by music; that is, the commonness that the colonizer and the colonized shared. On the other hand, the fact that music might embody profound differences accounted for the ways it was totally incompatible with the culture of the colonizer. Missionaries and colonial officials were quick to recognize such contradictions, which were exaggerated by the incongruities that marked moments of encounter.

Among the first missionaries to write an early-modern travel account was the Calvinist Jean de Léry, whose descriptions of Tupinamba song, dance, and ritual from a 1557 to 1558 sojourn near the Bay of Rio de Janeiro were reproduced by European writers such as Montaigne in his celebrated essay, "Des Cannibales" (cf. de Léry 1578; Montaigne [1580] 1952), and Johann Gottfried Herder in the first collections of musical works to bear the name *folk song* (Herder 1778–1779). The musical and the cultural differ from each other in such accounts, sometimes radically so. For de Léry and Montaigne the possibility that music could accompany seemingly horrific cultural acts, especially cannibalism, made it most unfamiliar, while songs seemingly consonant with European repertories nonetheless accounted for familiarity (Greenblatt 1991, 14–19). Jesuit missionaries, charged with the obligation to convert, frequently found music to be their most effective weapon, transcribing and recomposing music from the cultures they encountered into a new global language that would allow them to "sing salvation" (Aracena 1999). New practices of inscription and transcription, therefore, were crucial to the acts of possession that transformed colonial encounter into forms of domination.

The nature of encounter is highly contested in the debates about the relation between music and culture in modern musical scholarship. Anthropologists urging a move away from comparative musicology in the 1950s elevated encounter to a position of primacy. Until music was encountered in its cultural contexts, so the slogan went, there could be no comparison. Effectively, such anthropological claims on encounter undercut the privileged position that music had enjoyed in comparative musicology. With the expansion of postcolonial studies beginning in the 1980s criticism turned more sharply toward the moment of encounter. Culture, once the privileged site of social sciences, was no longer a safe haven for study. Everything about encounter was questioned, stripping culture of its former privilege, even in the eyes of many anthropologists. Concomitantly, forms of representation, the arts, and performance—and, of course, music—rose in significance, as if they had been immune to the exercise of power all along. Although there was a greater willingness to include music, at least tangentially, in cultural studies, the disjuncture between culture and music in many ways widened. From a historiographical standpoint the vital question is not that such contradictory issues of music and culture accrue to encounter, but why musical scholarship and the cultural study of music persist in their failure to close the gap that encounter continues to expose.

HISTORIOGRAPHICAL MOMENT 2—RACISM

The most remarkable thing about the use of music to formulate a sweeping vocabulary of racism in German-language musical scholarship during the first half of the twentieth century is that racist musicology took shape so unremarkably at the very core of musical and cultural study. As a link shared by music and culture, race was simply a given. So unremarkable was the presence of racism in German-language musicology from the 1920s through World War II and the Holocaust that it was only in the 1990s that scholars began to unravel the full extent to which modern musicology failed to extricate itself from an earlier musicology that was itself a racist response to modernism. In particular, Pamela Potter's study of Nazi musicology uncovered the step-by-step acquiescence of German musicologists to the steady racialization of German thought in both the public and scientific spheres (Potter 1998).

The question of racism in the scientific study of music is far more deeply and historically located in the disjuncture between music and culture than we wish to admit. The musicological language of racism forged by Nazi scholars became convincing for a number of different reasons, but I concentrate here on only one: The racial traits of music were immanent in nature. Racism grows from the impulse to witness music in nature, one of the original uses of "culture" in the interpretation of music. Nature in two forms, human biology and the human transformation of natural landscapes, could explain not only cultural difference but also cultural dominance. Basic intervallic structure in music and the scales that formed around it, for example, were based in the measurements of skull shape, which in turn formed global patterns based on racial groups (e.g., Metzler 1938). The differentiation of musical structure according to biological structure required collaboration across several disciplines, with historical and comparative musicologists at one end of a disciplinary continuum and physical anthropologists and folklorists at the other. It was furthermore significant for the use of nature to justify racial differences in music that these differences were not limited to Central Europe or even to Europe, but rather stretched across the entire globe (see, e.g., a 1938 map of racial differences, translated into English, that appears in Bohlman 2000, 658).

Maps of racial traits in music were not simply representations of racist fantasies, for they were used to justify cultural work of the most extreme kind, above all the German military expansion. One of the central projects of German folk song scholarship during the Weimar, Nazi, and Cold War periods, for example, was the publication of a series of anthologies—a total of forty-seven appeared in print—that charted "German folksong landscapes" (*deutsche Volksliedlandschaften*) across Europe, musically claiming the continent as German through repertories that would show how German folk song grew from the soil of Poland and Ukraine or was fundamental to the Christianity of Alsace-Lorraine (see Bohlman 2002 for a study of individual volumes). German folk song, thus, was imbued with the meaning of *Blut und Boden* ("blood and soil"), nature in its most German essence.

The musicological accountability that began to emerge at the end of the twentieth century notwithstanding, there was a disturbing lack of willingness to confront the involvement of musical scholars such as Hans Heinrich Eggebrecht as a soldier who had served with German army troops charged with murdering Jews during the Holocaust, but who falsified his war records after World War II to ease his path to a career as one of the major musical scholars of the postwar generation and the author of major works of music history, such as *Musik im Abendland* (Eggebrecht 1991), with its racialization of Western music and its history. The failure to connect Eggebrecht, the soldier, to Eggebrecht, the musicologist, rests once again on claims that music and culture are themselves disconnected.

Stereotypes of race exacerbate the disjuncture between music and culture. So common are such stereotypes that it is only when they are most brutally misused that they attract our attention. The several subdisciplines of musical scholarship have all relied to greater or lesser degrees on stereotypes of race to explain local distinctiveness and to construct global theory. The boundary between terminology that is racial and language that is racist, as Stephen Blum (1991) has demonstrated in his thorough examination of European discourse about African music, is at best blurred and often entirely indistinguishable. Even as ethnomusicologists at the beginning of the twenty-first century increasingly questioned the reliance on racialized and racist stereotypes in the study of the music of Africa and the African diaspora, there remained resistance to abandoning biological and natural explanations for music's distinctiveness (e.g., Blacking 1995).

The contradiction that ethnomusicologists were unable to resolve in their examination of differences that so critically characterized the gap between music and culture resulted from the inability to separate the racial from the racist in music. The "racial" was regarded positively, as an explanation for difference. The "racist" was regarded negatively, as a perversion of difference. To eliminate one or the other would also eliminate difference in music itself, which by the end of the twentieth century had been elevated to the common ground shared by all the subdisciplines of musical scholarship (e.g., Solie 1993; Radano and Bohlman 2000; Brown 2007).

HISTORIOGRAPHICAL MOMENT 3—NATIONALISM

More than any other form of identity, nationalism closes the gap between music and culture. In so doing, it heightens the disjuncture created by conflicting musical processes for constructing the nation. The nation that emerges from the intersecting domain shared by music and culture is remarkable for both its vastness and the detail of its landscapes, and it is for this reason that nationalists so eagerly reach toward music, and that so much power accrues to music when it is enlisted for nationalist ends. At the end of the first decade of the twenty-first century, there still is no music that is as often celebrated and maligned as that which represents the cultural identities to which we ascribe the label *nationalist* (see Bohlman 2011).

In the post-Enlightenment era of nationalism, music acquired the potential to articulate nationalism by representing place. The nation grew as an amalgamation of places, for example, from the welter of dialects that nineteenth-century nationalists identified in folk song. There was an expansion of folk song repertories in concentric patterns as local songs constituted regional repertories, which in turn stretched across a national repertory. Following the rhetorical model of Herder, who affixed national labels to folk musics in relatively democratic fashion, proclaiming the possibility that national "peoples" (*Völker*) without politically independent nations gave "voice" to the nation through songs (Herder 1778–1779), nineteenth-century nationalists constructed enormous canons of folk song from the collective endeavors of folklorists, linguists, ethnologists, philologists, and musicologists. The landscapes of the nation and its songs were isomorphic.

The problem of musical nationalism emerged when that relation between music and culture was disturbed; when, for example, the landscape of national song was imagined to extend beyond a nation's borders. European nationalists were especially adept at discovering national songs beyond their borders and mustering those songs to imperialist ends. German "speech islands" (*Sprachinseln*)—linguistically bounded regions, especially in eastern and southeastern Europe, where German was spoken by a minority population—were one of the primary justifications for German expansionism in the late nineteenth century. Hungarian nationalists, among them Béla Bartók, were no less willing to point to the presence of regions where Hungarian songs were still sung, especially in Romania, Serbia, and Slovakia, and to encourage the mobilization of national forces, including national armies, to unite the periphery to the center, thus reinforcing the national musical repertory (e.g., Trumpener 1996).

The nationalist expansion of the nineteenth century culminated in the implosion of the European nation in the twentieth, particularly in the global tragedies of the two world wars. Among those symbols of the nation demonstrating the greatest resilience to the implosion was national music. Within years after the realignment of national borders following World War I, national song projects took shape, more often than not challenging the very validity of the new national borders. As former colonial and imperial holdings beyond Europe began to construct national myths and to transform these into national histories, national music quickly became invested with the power to serve as international political capital, mapping the rest of the world according to European musical geographies (e.g., Chakrabarty 2000; cf. the essays in Stokes 1994).

At the beginning of the twentieth century, many predicted that the potential of music to do the cultural work of nationalism would diminish as music's historical trajectory pulled it toward increasing complexity and aesthetic autonomy. At the end of the twentieth century, there were predictions that music would lose the functions of nationalism because its movement across national borders would erase those borders. The predictions that framed the past century, however, have not come to pass. Quite the contrary, during a century in which the destructive force of nationalism was almost unimaginably extreme, new nationalist ontologies accrued to music. National music was liberated from the soil, that is, from the bounded landscape and geography of the nation. The emerging technologies of the period between the world wars, particularly the growing availability of radio and recordings, invested music with the possibility of creating what Brian Currid calls a "national acoustics," whereby a national public experiences the nation through regularly listening to its musical broadcasts (Currid 2006). National publics experience the nation in even more complex ways than the populations that gather at specific moments to perform the nation in the phenomenon Benedict Anderson calls "unisonality" (Anderson [1983; 1991] 2006).

In the first decade of the twenty-first century, nationalism has re-emerged in many of the same places from which it seemed to recede at the end of the twentieth century, notably along the ethnic and religious seams of former empires, particularly in the zones of war in the Middle East and South Asia, and along the east–west and north–south axes in Europe. As my own ethnographic work took me with growing frequency into Eastern Europe and India, I witnessed a virtually unchecked proliferation of musical culture brokers who seized on music's ideological power in the national conflicts in the Balkans or in the perpetuation of religious sectarianism in India

(Bohlman 2009). Medieval epic songs about Serbia, Kosovo, and the Ottoman Empire had passed through the nineteenth-century filters of Romantic nationalism to afford multiple variants for every region of the former Yugoslavia before spinning out postmodern texts for hip-hop artists across southeastern Europe (see Bohlman and Petković 2011). The revival of religious and popular musics was everywhere, in the service of the nation at its sacred roots (e.g., Poland) or seeking to establish its place in Europe through the convergence of music and culture in the Eurovision Song Contest (e.g., Ukraine and Serbia; see Bohlman 2007). The musical diversity in Eastern Europe in 2011 is one of many signs that nationalism dominates the present even more than the past.

HISTORIOGRAPHICAL MOMENT 4—ETHNOGRAPHIES OF DISPLACEMENT

It was with eschatology—the end of things—that I sought to use the fourth of my historiographical sections in the 2003 version of this chapter. I searched for a turn, even a telos, at which music and culture crowded in upon each other in a common domain of disjuncture. The twentieth century, I argued, had witnessed unprecedented levels of human destruction and death, and music, too, was present in unprecedented ways at moments of massive violence and death. Music, too, was a participant in the cultural work of persecution and genocide. As the end of the twentieth century and the beginning of a new millennium approached, eschatological meaning itself intensified, and with it music was implicated in the imminent end of history. The eschatological power of music results from both its cultural and musical sides. The former is evident in the overt use of music to mark moments of death; for example, in the concentration camps of the Holocaust. The latter resides in the temporal phenomena that shape the ontologies of music, in other words, the power of music to calibrate and shape—as well as negate—time. Historiographically, I had miscalculated, or at least failed to remember the extent to which the present cannot evade history.

It is with historiographical ethnography, therefore, that I draw closer toward the conclusion of this chapter, but not of history itself. I return, then, to the resurgence of displacement with which I established the basic vocabulary of the present at the outset of the chapter. It is with three acts of displacement that we return to the ethnographic present. Each act has a history that is ongoing—for which there is no end in sight—thus, each expands its global reach and international significance as the ethnographic present continues. Such is the very presence of displacement as a chronic context for the interaction of music and culture.

In spring 2010, the state legislature of the American state of Arizona passed House Bill 2281, a law that permitted and in some cases demanded that Arizona police require any individual to show documentation of the right to reside in the United States. Individuals without proper documentation, that is immigrant papers, green cards, or legal citizenship, should be immediately deported. The target of HB2281 was clear, no less than its intent: Migrants from Mexico should not be allowed to live in the state of Arizona.

In August 2010, the government of France began to remove Roma from their settlements in France and deport them to Eastern Europe, after giving them €300. The only Roma officially targeted by the action, aggressively backed by President Nicolas Sarkozy, were those believed to be displaced Roma, especially those who had migrated across the open borders of Europe from Romania and Bulgaria since the implementation of the Schengen Process of 2007. The question of deporting migrants dominated the summit of EU leaders on 17 September 2010, and France was joined by other EU countries in claiming its right to deport migrants as it saw fit.

In late August 2010, after weeks of pre-publication hype, Thilo Sarrazin, a German economist who had served in the highest commissions to rebuild the economy of a reunified Germany, as Finance Senator for Berlin, and from 2009 as a member of the board of directors of the German central bank (Deutsche Bundesbank), published a book that called for stemming the cultural decline of Germany by restricting the presence of Muslims, especially Turkish migrants, who displayed a statistical unwillingness to adopt the culture of Germany, with its history of educational excellence, economic superiority, and industrial efficiency, which had sustained the nation since the Enlightenment (Sarrazin 2010). Sarrazin made extensive use of economic statistics to justify his claims, and he mixed these with the pseudo-scientific evidence of genetic traits evident in Germany's elite class of intellectuals, even referring to the genetic superiority of some Europeans. Coupling his statistics with epigraphs from Goethe at the beginning of many chapters, Sarrazin deepened the historical debate about whether the Germany of Goethe and Schiller, Bach and Beethoven, could ever be home to non-Germans.

Ironically, the three cases of displacement unequivocally accept the interrelatedness of culture and identity, and by extension a musical identity that lies somewhere else, that is, in the place to which Mexicans, Roma, and Turkish workers might be displaced. The stakes for establishing place with music become ever higher as the struggle to locate it in common culture becomes ever more costly (cf. the essays in Clausen et al. 2009).

MUSIC'S EMBEDDEDNESS IN CULTURE

It is hardly new to make a case that music and culture relate to each other, even that one is inseparable from the other. When Guido Adler inscribed the tablets for a modern science of *Musikwissenschaft* in 1885, culture was there, all over the place, and it accompanied the many subdisciplinary branches that constituted Adler's vision for a comprehensive study of music (Adler 1885). Later comprehensive models for the study of music continued the methodological practice of connecting music and culture (see, e.g., C. Seeger 1977). While most ethnomusicologists concerned themselves with the appropriate prepositional connective between the two—music *in* culture, music *as* culture—historical musicologists and music theorists, at least the progressive ones who looked beyond canonic art-music repertories, wrestled with ways of interpreting text in relation to context.

It would seem that the battle was won long ago. And yet, the debates that fill the pages of this volume, in its second edition even more than in its first, remind us that the matter is no closer to being settled than it ever was. The "musicological juncture" for which Charles Seeger famously called continues to elude us, and the nagging question that stimulates the polemics argued by the authors whose essays fill this volume is, Why? If the fact that there is a relation between music and culture is not at issue, what, then, is?

At issue, of course, is why that relation is skewed, why there is imbalance, which in turn destabilizes the ways in which we understand the presence of music in culture and vice versa. Metaphysically, musicological juncture—or any other kind of juncture in the study of music—may well be inherently impossible, for music and culture occupy two fundamentally different phenomenological domains. Rather than juncture, it is disjuncture that makes for a very specific kind of embeddedness. That embeddedness results not from an attraction based on similarity but instead from an affiliation predicated on difference. And this in turn produces the anxiety of disjuncture.

Culture allows for the domestication and possession of music, but it also allows for forms of domination. Music is well fitted to do cultural work, but the more we engage it in cultural work, the more its ontology as an aesthetic object is sullied. This is how it has always been. Any music historiography that would ignore that, by seeking to establish neat interrelations between music and culture, would necessarily also ignore the power that emerges when music interacts with culture in ways we do not want. Wish as we might that the relation between music and culture had changed in some clearly positive way between the editions of this volume, the stark reality remains that music may be so embedded in and tangled with culture that it cannot rise above culture. Accordingly, we must remain vigilant in our search for historiographies of disjuncture that might well reveal that music's relation to culture is not what we have thought it was, and that music itself is not what we imagine it to be.

FURTHER READING

Agnew, Vanessa. 2008. *Enlightenment Orpheus: The power of music in other worlds.* New York: Oxford University Press.

Bohlman, Philip V. 2002. *World music: A very short introduction.* Oxford: Oxford University Press.

Brown, Julie, ed. 2007. *Western music and race.* Cambridge, U.K.: Cambridge University Press.

Clausen, Bernd, Ursula Hemetek, Eva Sæther, and the European Music Council, eds. 2009. *Music in motion: Diversity and dialogue in Europe.* Bielefeld, Germany: Transcript Verlag.

Irving, D. R. M. 2010. *Colonial counterpoint: Music in early modern Manila.* New York: Oxford University Press.

Jankowsky, Richard C. 2010. *Stambeli: Music, trance, and alterity in Tunisia.* Chicago: University of Chicago Press.

Levi, Erik, and Florian Scheding, eds. 2010. *Music and displacement: Diasporas, mobilities, and dislocations in Europe and beyond.* Lanham, MD: Scarecrow Press.

Magrini, Tullia, ed. 2003. *Music and gender: Perspectives from the Mediterranean.* Chicago: University of Chicago Press.

Radano, Ronald, and Philip V. Bohlman, eds. 2000. *Music and the racial imagination.* Chicago: University of Chicago Press.

Ramsey, Guthrie P., Jr. 2003. *Race music: Black cultures from bebop to hip-hop.* Berkeley: University of California Press.

Tomlinson, Gary. 2007. *The singing of the New World: Indigenous voice in the era of European contact.* Cambridge, U.K.: Cambridge University Press.

CHAPTER 3

HISTORICAL MUSICOLOGY
Is It Still Possible?

ROB C. WEGMAN

In recent years, historical musicology has come close to critiquing itself out of business. Scholars have argued ever more vigorously that the pursuit of music history is driven—and its results contaminated—by the values, creative impulses, dreams, illusions, and neuroses of our time. Historical inquiry, they concur, is fundamentally *creative*, expressive of who we are. Nor could it be otherwise. Without the firm interpretive hand of the music historian, the massive flood of unsorted, undigested, unprocessed material that we euphemistically call "historical evidence" would remain devoid of any apparent sense or meaning. That material is the clay, the raw material, that we are irresistibly driven to cut, shape, and mold in our image. We pick and choose, select and combine, whatever evidence we need to fill out the patterns we wish to perceive. That is why history is so rewarding. It is the creative act of imposing order on chaos.

Of course we do need the illusion that the shape, the pattern, and the order are more than just the products of our imagination—that they have a basis in historical reality. This illusion has traditionally been provided by the ideals of objectivity and authenticity. Yet these ideals have been questioned as well, and with good reason. A historical fact, by itself, may be objective and incontrovertible. But the choice to single it out, from among innumerable other facts, is unavoidably arbitrary, revealing of our interests. Still, it is that choice, and the interpretation that guides it, that endows a fact with its historical significance. Without interpretation, we are not engaged in history, but in collecting and storing raw data. Positivists might insist that it is possible for interpretations to be objectively valid if they are inductively derived from empirical evidence, somewhat like natural laws or universal principles. Yet the endeavor to prove that induction can yield objective and incontrovertible knowledge defeated epistemologists long ago.

More problematically, perhaps, what is the touchstone of objectivity and authenticity? "Objective" or "authentic" in terms of what? "Historical reality," one might be tempted to answer. Yet historical reality cannot by definition be objective, or at least not objectively knowable. It is a metaphysical entity. It cannot be empirically known by us (otherwise it would not be historical), only postulated—that is, once again, created. This is not to deny that people in the past must have had a sense of their reality. Yet that sense would have been *subjective* even then: it might well have varied enormously depending on whom you asked. If there is such a singular, objective, and transcendent thing as "historical reality," then surely it can be knowable only to God.

Even after the modernist ideals of objectivity and authenticity are abandoned, however, there typically remains a powerful yearning for a past that has a reality of its own, an autonomous existence, transcending the distorting fictions inherent in our modern perspective. This yearning has recently given rise to a new proposal: the idea of a dialogue with the past. Starting, once again, from the premise that history ought to be more than the product of our creative imagination, advocates of this approach insist that the past can be—and indeed should be—an equal partner in a cross-historical dialogue. This so-called ethnographic approach, advocated especially by "new musicologists," has come under criticism as well (Taruskin 1997, xx–xxx). The chief objection is that it succeeds merely in replacing one illusion with another. We can disown the products of our imagination by attempting to show that they correspond to historical truth, and we can disown them by postulating "others" whose "authentic" voice we then hope to hear somehow within our own ventriloquizing. But what's the difference? If the Other is not the product of our historical imagination, then what can it be, except yet another metaphysical postulate?

Whither historical musicology? Is it still possible? That is the critical question. It concerns every historical musicologist, and it affects all our work. In this chapter I outline an introduction to the debate, clarifying its terms, and, in a polemic conclusion, offering some of my own thoughts.

The problem outlined above is of course anything but new. What we are reliving in the current debate over historical musicology, arguably, is the same "crisis of historicism" that erupted in German scholarship in the 1920s. That crisis affected musicology no less than it did other disciplines. Its impact can be witnessed, for example, in Heinrich Besseler's well-known textbook on the history of early music *Die Musik des Mittelalters und der Renaissance*, published in 1931. Besseler opened his book with a separate chapter devoted to the "core problem" of historicism, a problem whose causes he explained as follows (Besseler 1931, 3; my translation):

> In the nineteenth century, early music, as a living tradition, retained an active presence only in isolated vestiges. As a phenomenon in its totality it had to be rediscovered, yet this discovery was guided by the needs and longings of the present. What modernity failed to offer was sought and found in history. It was inevitable that its image [of the past] would conform to its own wishful dreams, that selection and interpretation, evaluation and cognizance, were determined by the ideas of an age which yearned for the past in order to use it for its own fulfilment. No consideration of history may pass over the task of elucidating the motives behind such discoveries, and of raising awareness of the manifold reinterpretations which the legacy of earlier eras undergoes as it passes from one generation to another.

These words were written more than seventy years ago, yet they seem to have lost none of their relevance today. What is perhaps most noteworthy about them, given musicology's traditional aspirations to scientific status, is their emphasis on the *psychological* nature of the problem. The issue was not merely one of methodology. According to Besseler, the rediscovery of early music had been driven by unconscious needs and longings, wishful dreams, and a yearning for fulfillment. At the root of all this, he suggested, was a sense of disillusion with modernity, which had failed to offer what it was hoped the encounter with history would provide.

If this was indeed the core problem, then it should not surprise us that its recognition provoked a crisis. The ideals that had captivated nineteenth-century scholars turned out to be contaminated by the very problems from which the past had seemed to offer an escape. The needs, longings, dreams, and yearnings had finally been exposed for what they were: symptoms of modernity. Even the encounter with history, in short, had ended in disillusion. If musicologists were to draw any lessons from this, Besseler concluded, they should continue to expose those symptoms in all historical inquiry, by engaging in rigorous self-scrutiny and self-criticism.

This injunction is of course still being repeated in current debates over historical musicology. Gary Tomlinson, for instance, has argued that "in broad terms, a postmodern musicology will be characterized most distinctively by its insistent questioning of its own methods and practices" (Tomlinson 1993, 21). If we are to implement genuine renewal in the discipline, he suggested, "we might begin to interrogate our love for the music we study" (p. 24). As these words indicate, the terms of the debate may not have changed all that much since the early twentieth century. Our passion for the music of the past may be as ardent as were the needs, longings, dreams, and yearnings of nineteenth-century musicology. Yet for Tomlinson, no less than for Besseler, they may also be self-serving and self-centered. That is why they need to be interrogated.

It can never hurt to repeat that injunction, perhaps not even after seventy years. At the same time, one wonders if persistent self-interrogation is likely to tell us much that we didn't already know. In essence, after all, the problem we are confronting here is that of the *subjectivity* of human knowledge, the fact that it always bears the imprint of the feelings, thoughts, and concerns of those who produce it. This problem is of course paradigmatic of the Western intellectual tradition, and surely there is no need to remind ourselves of it at every turn. We are fallible human beings, and everything we do will always have its problems: so what else is new? On the other hand, the particular psychological mechanism that Besseler identified—history as the projected fulfillment of modern longings—does seem to invite closer analysis. This mechanism has been studied by a number of writers, and it is commonly understood as exhibiting *narcissistic* impulses (Davies 1989). I suspect that this was Besseler's understanding as well, even if he didn't say it in so many words. For the archetypal myth of Narcissus matches his analysis very closely, and in fact matches the current debate over historical musicology equally well.

Like Narcissus, or so critics remind us, we have gazed into a fountain, and have become enamored of the image reflected in its surface. The fountain, one might say, is the totality of the available historical evidence, and the image it returns is the product of our historical vision. We have wanted that image to be real, objective, autonomous, authentic, other. Like Narcissus, however, we have been frustrated in our attempts to capture the image—that is, to demonstrate its objective reality. Sooner or later we were bound to make a painful discovery. "Oh, I am he!" Narcissus cried, "now I know for sure the image is my own; it's for myself I burn with love; I fan the flames I feel" (Ovid 1986, 64–65). That was the moment of truth. Historical evidence, by itself, may be as real and tangible as the water in the fountain. Yet the past, as we read it into that evidence, has no objective reality, no independent existence, no autonomy, no otherness. Rather, it is always and necessarily the reflection of the viewing subject, the product of our historical imagination. That is why the Narcissus myth is of enduring relevance: it epitomizes the Western discovery of subjectivity (Kristeva 1987).

Let us pause briefly to review the key issues in this analogy. First of all, what have we lost with the discovery? What we have lost is "the past," as a realm that has an autonomous existence independent from our historical vision—just as Narcissus lost the object of his love when he discovered it to be his own reflection. Second, what do we think we have gained? Like Narcissus, we may have gained self-knowledge. The past "as it really was" may be a delusion, yet at least we can try to understand how we have fashioned it in our image. That, as noted before, is what Besseler urged historians to do, and that is what we are still being urged to do today. Finally, why was the discovery a painful one? Because historical musicology, like Narcissus, had invested its deepest needs, longings, dreams, and yearnings in the image it perceived. Its love for the past was staked precisely on the objective reality of that image. Yet this love affair ended in the 1920s, and the aspirations of historical musicology have remained unfulfilled ever since.

The syndrome is a recognizable one: what causes the pain is, in effect, a narcissistic injury. We have loved the past, in all its apparent authenticity and objectivity, but we have been duped. We have made fools of ourselves. There is no past that could have asked us to love it, and like Narcissus, we feel shame and embarrassment at having imagined one. For Narcissus, the initial response was one of despair. Grieving over the lost image that had fueled his love, he cried out: "What now? Woo or be wooed? Why woo at all?" (Ovid 1986, 466). The response in our time is not dissimilar. What now, we wonder? Why pursue historical musicology at all? Is it still possible? Why aspire to authenticity in performance, to objectivity in historical knowledge? Why converse with imagined others, as if they actually had the power to speak to us? It has all been exposed as a fruitless pathological delusion.

Another response, however, is indignation. The past that we knew and loved has let us down, and so it must be repudiated as the delusion it was. Such repudiation has become a popular pastime in present-day scholarship. When scholars dismiss every image that was ever constructed of the past, preferably by previous generations of musicologists, they are not merely expressing a difference of historical interpretation. There is more at stake. We cannot forgive traditional musicology for having indulged and gratified its infatuation with the past, for this is a pleasure that we must deny ourselves. We are only too aware of, after all, how deeply satisfying it can be to identify with the past, to imagine it to be real, to love it with a passion. As we all know, there is an irresistible attraction to exercising the historical imagination: its very subjectivity confirms how much it is a part of who we are.

To indict and interrogate that subjectivity may be conscientious, but it does involve us in inner conflict. We settle that conflict at a high price. When an archival scholar is thrilled about the discovery of a new document, and when a critic dismisses such work as positivistic fact-gathering, it is the latter who is the poorer, not the former. For the archival scholar is capable of perceiving historical meaning and significance in the document, whereas the critic cannot acknowledge it as more than a "mere" fact. The latter may be right, of course. The fountain is just a body of still water. And where we perceived an image of a living past, there is in fact just a mountain of inert evidence. It will always be tempting to be carried away by the historical imagination, yet we must remind ourselves that this faculty is, in the end, subjective. For that very reason, however, it is painful, exceedingly painful, not to be able to allow it free rein, to deny ourselves the sheer exhilaration of exercising it without inhibition.

The chief reward for this self-restraint, this self-abnegation, is the knowledge that we are at least more conscientious than others have been. That knowledge may do little to ease our pain, yet it does bring a further reward. For we have also earned ourselves the right to cast judgment on those who have been less conscientious than we. It is here that we can give free rein at least to our indignation, and allow ourselves the *ersatz* exhilaration of exercising it without inhibition. Targets are easy to find. For there are many things for which we cannot forgive traditional musicology—Western hegemony, positivism, objectivism, modernism, metaphysics, essentialism, reification, whatnot. It is not that those paradigms are merely unsatisfactory or inadequate. That, after all, would be true of every paradigm we might adopt in their place. The problem is that they have offered us a past that we must forsake. The more we have loved that past, or envy others for their love of it, the more we resent the paradigms for having accommodated that love.

Yet our anger is directed at musicology as well, and this anger is of a particularly bitter and unforgiving kind. To the extent that we have only ourselves to blame, the narcissistic injury calls for punishment. "Then in his grief he tore his robe," as Ovid wrote of Narcissus (Ovid 1986, 3: 480–481), "and beat his pale cold fists upon his naked breast." We, too, must engage in merciless self-criticism, perpetually reminding ourselves of our failings, and finding even a perverse pleasure in exposing them. "The narcissistic self," as historian Martin L. Davies noted, "evinces a depressive, destructive aggressivity, repudiating the unworthy Other [that is, our image of the past] with an intensity matched only by its own internal self-castigation [that is, our self-criticism]" (Davies 1989, 266).

These, needless to say, are not the signs of healthy critical debate. They are symptoms, rather, of a profound and despairing sense of melancholia. In recent years, historical musicology has developed a moral conscience, a superego, of unprecedented righteousness and severity. Under the guise of critical reflection, it keeps reminding the discipline of its unworthiness. Everything you do, it says, everything you have ever done, has been self-serving, self-centered, and self-indulgent. Or, to put it in more familiar terms, everything has been hegemonic, positivist, objectivist, modernist, essentialist, totalizing. We indulge and placate that superego not just by accepting its accusations but also by seeking to satisfy its demands. We cannot simply throw ourselves into an encounter with the past, or so the reasoning goes, for we have no idea how base our hidden motives may be, and how badly we may need to expiate them. That is why, over the last decade or so, musicologists have become engaged in a desperate search for legitimation—a predicament summed up by the question, is it still possible? This search has typically led away from historical inquiry as such into the realm of critical theory. By now, we are close to reaching the stage where we cannot make any step, no matter how small, without theorizing it first. Without such legitimation, we feel, historical musicology may not be possible at all.

This search for legitimation is doomed to failure, however. As I said before, the problem comes down, at bottom, to the subjectivity of human knowledge. If this problem is paradigmatic of the Western intellectual tradition, then of course we cannot theorize ourselves out of it, no matter how hard we might try. Why then do we persist? Chiefly, I suspect, because we feel *incriminated* by our subjectivity. And we cannot see any legitimation for the pursuit of history if everything we do is bound to incriminate us further. We are fallible human beings, true, but we ought not to be. That is why we have lost the confidence to look into the fountain. Every image we see reminds us of our subjectivity, and confirms our unworthiness to engage in historical inquiry. If only we could prove ourselves worthy again, if only we could discover some legitimation for what we do, that confidence might be restored.

And yet: worthy of whom, worthy of what? Surely our subjectivity cannot make us unworthy of ourselves. For to be subjective is to indulge oneself—and self-indulgence typically fosters a sense of self-worth. That is why the pursuit of history is so rewarding, and yet so problematic. We distrust our subjectivity precisely because it has made us too self-indulgent, too pleased with ourselves. If this makes us unworthy, then surely we must be unworthy of the Other—that is, the past, which we readily confess to having stifled under our mastery pose, our "hegemonizing" gestures. That is what our moral conscience tells us. Go theorize, it says, and then look again: you will see that there really is an objective past where you used to see your own image, that there really are others where you used to hear your own voice. Your work so far has been unworthy of that past, unworthy of those others. But you can redeem yourself, and renew the discipline, if you can manage to see them now, in all their reality, through the corrective lens of critical theory.

This, needless to add, is merely another lapse into narcissism. And yet, it is this perpetual relapse, alternated by the perpetual rediscovery of our subjectivity, that keeps the debate going round in circles. For every image that is exposed as subjective, a new one is theorized as real. If we are to follow

Gary Tomlinson, for example, "the primary stimulus for musicology, instead of our love for this or that music, might more luminously be our love of, concern for, belief in, alienating distance from—choose your words—the others who have made this or that music in the process of making their world" (Tomlinson 1993, 24). That is to say, if narcissistic identification with music is self-serving, narcissistic identification with others might be selfless. One would like to believe Tomlinson, but the premise does strain credulity. No amount of theorizing can endow historical others with an objective existence. They are dead and gone, and can only be revived in the historical imagination. Surely one cannot blame that imagination for being unworthy of the others it calls into being. Yet for Tomlinson, its inherent subjectivity is detrimental to the *real* others who (he imagines) exist beyond its ken. If only we could prove worthy of those others, by escaping from the prison of our subjectivity, historical musicology might be redeemed at last. This aspiration does indeed seem to motivate his call for disciplinary renewal. Several critics have drawn attention to the "aversion to old-fashioned subjectivity," "distrust of subjectivity," indeed "antisubjectivity" that appears to underwrite his harsh indictments of traditional musicology, and his desire to break away from it (Kramer 1993, 32, 33; Taruskin 1997, xxv). As Charles Rosen concluded, "he ends up by asking, in short, for a value-free history, although he knows that this ideal of objectivity is impossible" (Rosen 1994b, 62).

Can we break away from this vicious circle? If we want to, I suspect, we probably can. As far as narcissism is concerned, the solution seems deceptively simple. Throughout Western history, at least until the modern period, it has been taken as self-evident that the past has no objective reality or existence (Ligota 1982, 3–6; cf. also Schott 1968, 192–193). "When a true narrative of the past is related," as St. Augustine observed in his *Confessions* (XI.xviii.23), "the memory produces not the actual events, which have passed away, but words conceived from images of them" (St. Augustine 1991, 233–243). For St. Augustine this was not a painful discovery at all; on the contrary, it was a matter of common sense. After all, "who can measure the past which does not now exist, or the future which does not yet exist, unless perhaps someone dares to assert that he can measure what has no existence?" (XI. xvi. 21). To the extent that the past has any reality, it dwells only in the memory of those who narrate history. There is no Other to fall in love with, only a self that may choose to dwell in "the fields and vast palaces of memory" (X. viii. 12).

Still, I doubt that narcissism is necessarily the problem here. Nor, for that matter, are Western hegemony, positivism, objectivism, modernism, metaphysics, essentialism, reification, and all the rest. The real issue probably lies elsewhere. Let me put it quite bluntly: if we cannot accept that we are fallible human beings, that everything we do will always have its problems, then historical musicology will indeed be possible no longer. To put it even more bluntly: There is a certain arrogance in depreciating a worthwhile endeavor, in this case historical musicology, merely because we cannot attain perfection in it. Narcissism may be a human weakness, but instead of excoriating it for that reason, we might learn to live with it. True, narcissistic history may potentially trap us in delusion. Yet the fiction of a "real" past has undeniable heuristic value, and may well bring out the best in us—our historical imagination, for instance, or our subjectivity, or excitement, or yes, our love.

What, exactly, have we become afraid of? We know that there is no real past, that there are no real others of whom we could be unworthy. The only world that is real is the one we live in today. History adds a rich dimension to that world. If we are in danger of being unworthy of anything or anyone, it is probably our readers—*real* others, whom we may perplex with our scholarly angst, annoy with our narcissistic self-torment, and exasperate with our defensive theorizing. It is only the paralyzing fear to take human risks that might render historical musicology impossible. Or rather, perhaps, it is the fear that we may not be forgiven for our failings. Yet we cannot ask anyone's forgiveness if we are unable to forgive ourselves, and the scholars who worked before us. That, I suspect, may be the hardest thing of all: to find it in our hearts to understand and accept those failings—before we blame them on the discipline, and critique it out of business altogether.

FURTHER READING

Besseler, Heinrich. 1931. *Die Musik des Mittelalters und der Renaissance*. Potsdam, Germany: Akademische Verlagsgesellschaft Athenaion.

Davies, Martin L. 1989. History as narcissism. *Journal of European Studies* 19: 265–291.

Kramer, Lawrence. 1993. Music criticism and the postmodern turn: In contrary motion with Gary Tomlinson. *Current Musicology* 53: 25–35.

Kristeva, Julia. 1987. Narcissus: The new insanity. Pp. 103–121 in *Tales of Love*. Translated by Leon S. Roudiez. New York: Columbia University Press.

Ligota, Chistopher R. 1982. "This story is not true": Fact and fiction in antiquity. *Journal of the Warburg and Courtauld Institutes* 45: 1–13.

Ovid. 1986. *Metamorphoses*. Translated by A. D. Melville. Oxford: Oxford University Press.

Rosen, Charles. 1994. Music à la Mode. *New York Review of Books*, June 23, 55–62.

Schott, Rüdiger. 1968. Das Geschichtsbewusstsein schriftloser Völker. *Archiv für Begriffsgeschichte* 12: 166–205.

St. Augustine. 1991. *Confessions*. Translated by Henry Chadwick. Oxford: Oxford University Press.

Taruskin, Richard. 1997. *Defining Russia musically: Historical and hermeneutical essays*. Princeton: Princeton University Press.

Tomlinson, Gary. 1993. Musical pasts and postmodern musicologies: A response to Lawrence Kramer. *Current Musicology* 53: 18–24.

CHAPTER 4

SOCIAL HISTORY AND MUSIC HISTORY

TREVOR HERBERT

"The past is dead and gone. History is what historians make of it." This aphorism neatly summarizes the key issue. Unlike historians, some musicians and sectors of the listening public believe that the past can be reclaimed. They expect its past repertoires and practices to be regularly enacted. In fact, the word *past* in this context can be something of a misnomer. The repertoires of our own time are the repertoires of all time, to the extent that we know of them and choose to call on them. This is a condition that music shares with other creative disciplines. But to music historians it has a special edge because of the concerns of both the academy and the box office.

There are other disjunctions between the idea of history as seen by professional historians and the way history is used by musicians. Historians, particularly those for whom social and cultural history have been subsidiary to political and constitutional history, have typically used music as the fodder of footnotes, merely illustrating background social and cultural patterns. But can social history—particularly in its newer cultural forms, and employing wider discourses than are offered simply by economic and demographic parameters—offer alternative perspectives to music history, and, if it can, will it matter? The critical reflection within both disciplines in the closing decades of the twentieth century, forced as it was by wider theoretical debates, makes such questions especially compelling. My purpose here is to give an overview of some traditions of history and music history, and—in the light of newer, more radical approaches to historical discourse—to examine convergences and divergences between the two disciplines. The main question I want to pose is whether there are new avenues for genuine social histories of Western art music.

HISTORY AND SOCIAL HISTORY

There are long-standing debates about how historians do what they claim to do. They center on the philosophical, methodological, and even ethical assumptions that underpin the business of being a historian. The polemic most often utilized in Britain for illustrating this is the one that emerged in the 1960s between E. H. Carr and other English historians, especially Sir Geoffrey Elton. Carr's contention was that histories are as much about the time of their making as they are about the past. He held that the barrier that stands between historians and their subjects is that of their own cultural and ideological baggage. He counseled skepticism about the historian's "fetishism for facts." Like Croce, he held that all history is "contemporary history" (Carr 1961, 21) because it inevitably interprets the past in light of prevailing conditions. This does not mean he believed that histories could not be written or that the historian's task was futile. He answered his own question, "What is history?" with the retort that it is "a continuous process of interaction between the historian and his facts, an unending dialogue between the present and the past."

Elton (1967), on the other hand, held faith with the notion that the accumulation of authentic facts and the application of skilled synthesis through sophisticated historical method provided a perfectly reliable basis for the assemblage of an objective history. In effect, he believed that it was possible, through the careful scrutiny and objective synthesis of primary sources, to write histories that—if they were done properly—could be definitive. Elton, like many of his generation and persuasion, saw grand narratives of political and constitutional history as both the basis upon which, and the framework within which, any history should be constructed. It is easy to see why the Carr/Elton dichotomy became the primary exercise most commonly encountered in British universities by brand-new history students who had left home harboring the innocent and optimistic belief that the past was there before them, just waiting to be revealed.

Social history developed uneasily and relatively recently as a subdiscipline of history. On April 7, 1966, the *Times Literary Supplement* famously devoted most of its pages to an evaluation of history, the British history profession, and historical writings. Several of Britain's leading figures set out their stalls. Prominent on the front page was a piece by Geoffrey Thomas in which he reported that the long-established *English Historical Review* had already been eclipsed by the social-history-oriented *Past and Present*, whose subscribers held conferences at which such sociological topics as "work and leisure," "social mobility," and "popular religion" were featured.

The impact of social history on the discipline of history represented a sea change for those steeped in the "Great Men" tradition. The French *Annales* school was an important force for change. Its participants sought to understand society as "a total, integrated organism." Strong advocacy for social history as a distinct species of history also came from those who developed a broadly Marxist focus. Many embraced a wider range of evidence than political historians would have countenanced. They identified culture as "the driving force of historical change" and denied "simple correlations between economic forces and cultural constructs" (Desan 1989, 50–51). They also espoused methodologies that would routinely pay equal, or more than equal, regard to society as a whole, as opposed to just its dominant figures. The most important presence in this respect was probably E. P. Thompson, whose massive and influential *The Making of the English Working Class* (1963) offered both a new type of narrative and a working illustration of his "history from below" thesis—a systematic reversal of the practice of tracing the past by following the downward flow from the highest point of hegemony. His mission, as he famously put it, was to "rescue" the people "from the enormous condescension of posterity."

It became tempting to associate social history with themes that are primarily positioned to the political left, but this is misleading. Equally misleading was the claim by its detractors that it is a "soft history" or that it merely functions as a symptom of political change. When the *Journal of Social History* was launched in 1976, its editors self-confidently announced that "Social history must be iconoclastic, corrosive of received explanations; creative in producing new concepts and deriving new methods; and aggressive, encouraging incursions into all fields of historical analysis." Those editors may not have anticipated how soon their words would be put to the test. The theoretical upheavals that emerged in light of debates prompted by cultural studies stimulated waves of self-examination that questioned the fundamentals of the historian's craft.

Music History

For the greatest part of the twentieth century music history was conditioned by concerns that emerged as defining features of musicology in the nineteenth century. Central was the perceived need to identify, verify, classify, and catalog the sources for the body of works that make up and to a large extent define Western art music. Additionally, and especially since the late 1960s, music historians sought to gain an understanding of historical performance practices. These lines of inquiry (and their attendant ideologies) gained focus and emphasis through key forums in the musical establishment, especially learned societies, which were oriented around quite particular discourses, the points of reference of which were well-formed value systems, and around the musical academy, which developed similarly focused curricula.

The preoccupation with the assemblage of data about a canonical repertoire and information about how it was performed implied an essentially linear approach to music history, in which the main points of reference—periodizations, canonical composers, the emergence of genres, styles, and so on—appeared obvious and unquestionable. Inherent too was the implication that the past (as reflected in its histories) was a progression, in which each historical "moment" developed out of, or in reaction to, that which preceded it. A further nuance that might be drawn from this (if certain historical models were followed) was that such narratives told of a continuous path of positive progression from which societies and their cultures benefited incrementally. The task of the music historian was to add more detail to the musical "grand narrative," to fill in some gaps, or to tell the story with a different accent and different points of emphasis—but the basic story was almost always, more or less, the same.

The other underlying assumption of many music histories up to the closing decades of the twentieth century was that music is essentially autonomous: that social and other cultural factors have a contextual, rather than a more intimate or even causal, relationship with musical creativity or practice. Richard Leppert and Susan McClary recognized this when surveying the musicological map in 1987:

> Briefly stated, the disciplines of music theory and musicology are grounded on the assumption of musical autonomy. They cautiously keep separate considerations of biography, patronage, place and dates from those of musical syntax and structure. Both disciplines likewise claim objectivity, the illusion of which is possible only when questions considered valid can, in fact, be answered without qualification.
>
> (Leppert and McClary 1987, viii)

The parallels between trends in the disciplines of history and music history are easy to spot. By the late 1960s both had become susceptible to central positivist narratives in which a certain type of knowledge and inquiry was privileged; both sought to garner historical "facts" and use them as the basis for "objective" histories; and both became infatuated with orthodox methodologies. Eventually both also came to be challenged from within and without. By the opening years of the twenty-first century new thematic approaches to musicology had taken root and these in turn had almost invariably attracted some of their proponents to take on historical perspectives that implicitly offered an alternative to traditional trends in historical musicology. Some such approaches have rich socio-historical detail because their topics demand such an approach. The obvious example is jazz because its musical difference, as most writers on the subject have exemplified, cannot really be explained without reference to the social and economic circumstances of its origin and development. The persistent question however is whether social history approaches are applicable only to those segments of the musical past in which the vernacular is clearly and indisputably visible.

Music History, Social History, Postmodernist History

Henry Raynor's substantial *Social History of Music* (1972) opens with the declaration that it attempts "to fill some part of the gap between the normal and necessary history of music which deals with the development of musical styles and the general history of the world in which composers carried out their function" (p. vii). Whatever are the merits of Raynor's book, there are no prizes for guessing what "the normal and necessary history of music" means, who the "composers" are, or that to him the term *general history of the world* is a largely unproblematic concept. But others were pioneering alternative ways of interrogating musical processes from social, economic, and cultural perspectives. Among the more obviously important contributions are those of Cyril Ehrlich (1985, 1990), John Rosselli (1984, 1991), Lawrence Levine (1988), William Weber (1992), Thomas Brothers (2006) and Tim Blanning (2008). Each of the aforementioned (just one of whom is primarily a musicologist) has demonstrated that musical practices are usually dependent on social, economic, and cultural interactions traversing a wider terrain than is immediately occupied by the music makers. This paradigm will hardly surprise ethnomusicologists and anthropologists, but music historians have often questioned the legitimacy of discursive approaches that are not demonstrably focused on musical texts.

A further albatross that music historians have shared with historians is born of the preoccupation with historical "facts" and the spooky notion that, in the right hands, their original meaning is resistant to the layers of interpretive, cultural, and ideological mediations to which they are susceptible. In the positivist tradition, it often seems, legitimate histories are those that are not merely objective but *neutral*: devoid of imaginative engagement with their subjects. This is hard to countenance, given that all histories are exercises in conjecture based on the chance survival (sometimes following careless disposal) of documents and artifacts. The patchwork of musical topics that has received close scrutiny is also partly random: a consequence of fashion, taste, ideology, and accident. Then there is the mode of historical rhetoric, the figures of speech and tones of which are utterly of the present. A denial of imaginative engagement between the music historian and historical material implies a denial of what is already embryonic in much musicological writing.

It would, of course, be grotesquely inaccurate to ascribe to all music histories the characterization that I have given here. Such perspectives have long been questioned by historians and musicologists (e.g., R. G. Collingwood, Hayden White, Arthur Mendel, Richard Taruskin, Joseph Kerman). To these names can be added many more who have focused on popular music. Furthermore, as musicology has changed to embrace a wider spectrum of thematic approaches it has also acquired new, sometime hybrid methodologies and modes of inquiry. But even amidst such change the prevailing orthodoxy of Western art music history continues to incline to the elite and to many of its more enduring traditions. That topics relating to the canonical repertoire are central to most research is hardly reprehensible; more questionable are the self-limiting methods that are employed, and the neglect of the "lost peoples" of music history who are left to languish in a historical void—constituencies whose obscurity is made more certain by the effects of globalization. For example, there has been relatively little curiosity about the lives and culture of rank-and-file musicians, of the attitudes of popular audiences, or of the interaction between amateurs and professionals.

Social histories of music should as a matter of course expose the interactions between the widest spheres of society and musical practices. One can identify a range of revitalizing elements introduced into the discipline of history from cultural studies that could invite a closer engagement between music history and social history. These often take their most challenging form under the influence of what became known as postmodernism. Postmodernism emphasizes a range of social determinants (such as gender and ethnicity) that challenge the Marxist focus on class, and accommodates incidents, events, and characters that fall outside the modernist emphasis on reason and progress. Above all, it resists prioritization of one aspect of history over another, rather than accepting a central privileged narrative as the point of reference for events and movements that fall outside it.

The postmodernist emphasis on themes and practices that fall outside the more traditional parameters of historical methodology is especially evident in microhistory, an approach that emerged in Italian historical thinking in the early 1980s (e.g., Ginzburg 1980; Muir and Ruggiero 1991). Microhistories take the opposite tack to the large-scale, "grand narrative" approach that deals with major themes running over several centuries: "they build on the obscure and unknown rather than on the great and the famous. . . . [They] take very small incidents in everyday life and retell them as stories, analysing them as metaphorical and symbolic clues to larger things" (Evans 1997, 245). Thus they often disclose something of the relationship between the popular and the elite so as to inform a wider historical picture.

Can and should such approaches inform music history? The obvious difference between music history and history in its most general sense is the one that I indicated at the start of this chapter: music histories always carry some responsibility to cast light on repertoires and their creation, performance, and reception. Can music be autonomous and yet need a social history to enliven our understanding of it? Does Western art music history suffer from a lack of narrative depth—especially in terms of the social strata that its investigations touch upon—even in the parameters that it has defined for itself? An alternative view is that this matters little anyway: "the work's the thing" and socio-historical approaches have no value unless they cast light on the material content of music or the manner of its performance. A comparison can be found in approaches to biography: "The essential truth is simple. Flaubert was born. Flaubert wrote his novel. Flaubert died. It is his work which is unique, that matters, not the ordinary experience he shared with so many others" (Faulks 2011, 5). It is an attractive idea but this sort of restriction seems to be a denial of even the basic function of "history" as a harbinger of those elements that contribute to our collective memory, let alone the many practicalities that social history explains about cultural artifacts.

AN ILLUSTRATION: THE CASE OF THE VALVE—MUSIC HISTORY OR SOCIAL HISTORY?

In 1814, Heinrich Stölzel, an otherwise obscure horn player working in the orchestra of the Prince von Pless in Prussia, invented what is believed to be the first widely adopted valve brass instrument. Soon, other makers adopted this or similar inventions and applied them to treble instruments such as trumpets. These instruments provided the raw prototype for the valve trumpets that are used today. Before Stölzel's invention, and leaving aside some of the transitional models (such as the *Klappentrompete*) that were contemporary with it, "natural trumpets" with crooks were essentially identical to those that had probably been in use since at least the sixteenth century. The implications of this invention were important: Valve instruments are much easier to play than "natural" instruments, the players of which had rare skills that were taught privately, mainly within family dynasties.

Any good music history book will tell you that valves were invented in the second decade of the nineteenth century. Few mention that hardly anyone used them for the best part of the next quarter century. There were two related reasons for this. First, few people needed them: there was little standard repertoire that actually required them, and players of instruments of older designs saw no need to desert their sophisticated techniques in order to learn the use of a new contraption. Second, the market for these instruments was entirely among professional players—a small group of men, probably no more than a handful in each of the larger European and American towns that supported professional musicians. These men lived distant from, and were probably unknown to, each other. Indeed, even though Stölzel's invention was listed in the *Allgemeine musikalische Zeitung* in 1815, one wonders how widely valve instruments were known and understood by players across Europe, let alone across the Atlantic.

At this point, social and economic factors combined to initiate one of the most momentous changes to the idiom of a family of instruments in the history of Western music. The earlier designs were given considerable refinement by (among others) the Belgian inventor Adolphe Sax, who moved to Paris in the 1840s. There, in 1844, he had a chance encounter with an itinerant group of British brass-playing entertainers called the Distin family—an encounter that turned out to be cataclysmic. Following the meeting the Distins adopted the British sales agency for Sax's valve instruments. British makers, following the Distins' lead, recognized that a new market existed in the sprawling industrial conurbations of Victorian Britain. They seized on the possibility that groups of working men could be encouraged to form bands. Realizing that the main barrier to their ambition lay in the economic circumstances of their potential clients, they opportunistically seized on issues of social cohesion that worried the dominant classes. They extolled communal music making to community leaders (such as factory owners) as a "rational recreation": a recreation that would be morally—even spiritually—constructive, and would promote civic responsibility. They then put into potential purchasers' heads the idea that if the said community leader's name could be used to guarantee a loan, the instruments could be delivered promptly and paid for on a deferred payment basis.

The strategy worked like a charm. Thousands of bands were formed, and industrialists across the country happily underwrote the debts. Railroad companies also saw a chance to make a profit by sponsoring band contests for which trains were needed to carry bandsmen and their hundreds of supporters. Such congregations of brass players had never previously assembled. They provided unprecedented opportunities for the standardization of a new brass-playing idiom. The repertoire they played was drawn from third-hand arrangements of Italian operatic overtures and the like. Some of it survives, and it reveals that many of these players were consummate virtuosos.

But how did they play? What were the sonic values that they had in mind when they were learning? Who did they imitate other than each other? They had no relationship with the continuum of the art-music brass-playing tradition. It is virtually certain that what we have here is an *ab initio* encounter of a vernacular population with the sophisticated tools of art music.

Miscellaneous fragments of documentary evidence, together with the handwritten (sometimes crudely annotated) music, give important insights into these questions. The repertoires can be reconstructed. Evidence about how contest adjudicators evaluated performances, personal exchanges between players, and similar documents allow us to get close to establishing a series of snapshots of the lives and musical preoccupations of these bandsmen. This type of investigation informs a wider music history. The brass band phenomenon occurred throughout the world in one guise or another. The American manifestation is especially interesting, because a version of it is so germane to embryonic forms of jazz.

This narrative is a case study of the interaction between an important musical development and the historical process within which it unfolded. It is not perhaps on a sufficiently minute and mundane scale to pass as microhistory. But should it be read as music history or as social history? Perhaps it is both, but it deals with a topic with which the traditional positivist music history, by default, has never sullied its hands. Undoubtedly part of the reason for this is that few brass players have found their way into the academy (compared, say, to keyboard players). The reason that some might offer for regarding this example as merely contextual is that it does not touch on any repertoire that can stand up to the value judgments or assumptions that are normally present in music histories. But does that matter?

Of course such approaches bring their own set of problems. Some have cast doubt on cultural history "defined only in terms of topics of inquiry" (Hunt 1989, 9). But histories in which evidence about small units of the past are investigated to analyze the relationships between musical and socioeconomic processes, and to inform wider structures of music history, offer potential. Such histories might focus on the experience of individuals and groups in order to understand the larger social mass. One group ripe for such treatment is the professional rank and file of instrumental players, a sector of Western music history that has generally been left in obscurity.

By necessity, this type of endeavor requires the sustenance of traditional empirical historical methods to provide reliable data about people, societies, institutions, and their economic and cultural condition. History that is based merely on ideas and that is contemptuous of the need for a relentless pursuit and sensitive scrutiny of sources is not really history at all—it is historical fiction. Microhistorians demonstrate meticulous concern about questions of selectivity and significance, and also "respect the strictest positivist standards" of source evaluation (Muir and Ruggiero, 1991, xii), but they use the information in new and highly imaginative ways. However, such approaches to the social history of music should also imply a setting aside of the goal of cool objectivity in favor of open advocacy—a refreshing tendency often found in gender and gay studies in music. Empiricist data are not self-revealing. They require and demand clear mediation and forthright advocacy. What is needed now are social histories of music that are both intimate and red in tooth and claw. E. P. Thompson always wore his subjectivity on his sleeve. His work engaged with the type of grand narrative that I now suggest is inappropriate for social histories of music, but his style and manner are difficult to quarrel with. In 1966 he commented on a passage in the preface to Volume 6 of the *Cambridge Economic History of Europe*, in which the editors signaled that a distant future volume would "perhaps . . . deal with the social changes involved with the modern world." "In that 'perhaps,'" Thompson observed, "we have the poor bloody infantry of the industrial revolution, without whose labour and skill it would have remained an untested hypothesis." It is a pity that Thompson wrote nothing about music.

FURTHER READING

Arnold, John H. 2000. *History: A very short introduction.* Oxford: Oxford University Press.

Blanning, Tim. 2008. *The triumph of music: Composers, musicians and their audiences, 1700 to the present.* London: Penguin.

Carr, Edward H. 1961. *What is history?* New York: St. Martin's Press.

Ehrlich, Cyril. 1985. *The music profession in Britain since the eighteenth century.* Oxford: Clarendon Press.

Elton, Geoffrey R. 1967. *The practice of history.* London: Methuen.

Evans, Richard J. 1997. *In defence of history.* London: Granta Books.

Hunt, Lynn A., ed. 1989. *The new cultural history.* Berkeley: University of California Press.

Jenkins, Keith. 1995. *On "What is history?": From Carr and Elton to Rorty and White.* New York: Routledge.

Leppert, Richard, and Susan McClary. 1987. *Music and society: The politics of composition, performance and reception.* Cambridge, U.K.: Cambridge University Press.

Levine, Lawrence W. 1988. *Highbrow/lowbrow: The emergence of cultural hierarchy in America.* Cambridge, MA: Harvard University Press.

Muir, Edward, and Guido Ruggiero, eds. 1991. *Microhistory and the lost peoples of Europe.* Translated by E. Branch. Baltimore: Johns Hopkins University Press.

Rosselli, John. 1991. *Music and musicians in nineteenth-century Italy.* Portland, OR: Amadeus Press.

CHAPTER 5

MUSICOLOGY, ANTHROPOLOGY, HISTORY[1]

GARY TOMLINSON

In their present-day forms, ethnography and historiography are twins, born of the same parentage at the same moment in the eighteenth-century dawn of Western modernity. They have most often seemed, however, to be nonidentical, even antithetical twins, each trait of the one answering to a corresponding but converse trait in the other. This complementary relation has been remarked on and analyzed almost since the eighteenth century itself. One summary, offered by Michel de Certeau in the wake of Lévi-Straussian structuralism, puts it this way: Where ethnography has taken as its object *orality*, historiography scrutinizes *written* traces; where the one has wanted to describe an atemporal *space* of culture, the other follows change through *time*; the one starts from a gesture of radical estrangement and *alterity*, the other from an assumption of transparent *identity*; the first analyzes collective phenomena of a cultural *unconscious*, the second the *consciousness* of historical self-knowledge (de Certeau 1988, 209–210).

These contrasts have certainly been blurred, revised, and rearranged over the two centuries of development of anthropology and history as modern disciplines. In much recent work we witness anthropology gauging informants' consciousness of change through time and weighing written documents from an otherwise irretrievable past (e.g., Sahlins 1985; Comaroff and Comaroff 1992), or, conversely, history setting itself to recover an unwritten legacy and discover the distant otherness of its once-familiarized actors (Ginzburg 1985; Burke 1987; de Certeau 1988). Such moves must broach a basic doubt whether any substantive differences separate the two disciplines—any differences, that is, other than those sanctioned by time-worn ideologies or ethnographers' fond hopes for the survival of lived experience in their written accounts.

Nevertheless, the disciplinary differences of history and anthropology have never been effaced altogether. These distinct endeavors continue to elaborate, if tacitly or, often these days, in a climate of explicit self-critique, an ideology that limns a historical, alphabetic, conscious Western self and opposes to it a static, unlettered, un-self-conscious other.

The relation, over more than two centuries, of musicology to this set of disciplinary distinctions and their equivocation is a complex one. This is true not merely because music scholarship assays a performative mode akin to the anthropologist's orality, or because it moves in the medium of writing naturalized in historiography but uneasily wedded, as a means at odds with its sources, to ethnography. On a deeper level it is true because music itself was, at the moment of musicology's appearance, being refashioned in a manner that set it in opposition to the voices behind ethnography. It was assuming a place in European ideology that would eventually exalt it, ally it more tightly with the written than ever before, and distance it from related non-European activities that an earlier, more ecumenical designation had embraced.

*Music*ology—the very name incorporates a word that came, across the European eighteenth century, to betoken a "fine" art at the center of new aesthetic concerns and that designated, by the mid nineteenth century, the *finest* art, the art to whose transcendental, spiritual capacities all others looked with envy. Across the century from 1750 to 1850, music lodged itself at the heart of a discourse that pried Europe and its histories apart from non-European lives and cultures. Perched finally at the apex of the new aesthetics, it functioned as a kind of limit-case of European uniqueness in world history and an affirmation of the gap, within the cultural formation of modernity, between history and anthropology. Music, in this sense, silenced many non-European activities that it might instead have amplified.

There is another side, however, to musicology's connection with the twins ethnography and historiography. If, on the one hand, the new aesthetics of music and the musicology to which it gave rise widened the distance between history and anthropology, on the other hand, an older ideology of singing worked to emphasize their affinities and draw them together. The common conception of musicology as a discipline invented after the full emergence of Romantic views of music—invented even in the late nineteenth century, with a *fons et origo* in Guido Adler's famous manifesto of 1885 (Adler 1885; Mugglestone 1981)—works to conceal this earlier formation. It not only forgets the large literature on music history produced in the eighteenth century but also ignores a fact of subtler, deeper import: the presence of singing at the heart of eighteenth-century accounts of the history of European society, of Europe's relation to other societies, and indeed of the origins of all societies.

The central position of song in writings offering generalized theories of the origins of language and society tended to unite rather than distinguish European and non-European musical experiences. This position, solidified across the 1700s in the writings of Vico, Condillac, Rousseau, Herder, and others, situated singing at the nexus of the emergent disciplines of ethnography and historiography. It could even offer song as the nexus itself—as a vanishing point, so to speak, of distinctions of European from other societies. Musicology, then, is not solely the nineteenth- and twentieth-century grandchild of an anthropology and a historiography long since sundered. An earlier musicological impulse (or *cantological*, as I have called it elsewhere, half seriously, to distinguish it from later developments) preceded the full emergence of modern historiography and ethnography, formed, even, a part of their parentage, and resisted, at the moment of their birth, their too-clear separation.

Song, not music, was the fundamental category here. In a period when a full-blown modern conception of music had not yet taken hold, song could still pose itself as an expressive mode shared by Europe with the rest of the world. This is the general role it played in the protoethnographic accounts of European travelers, explorers, and missionaries through the sixteenth and seventeenth centuries. Here the singing of non-Europeans was not differentiated in any categorical way from European song, but rather was assimilated into it, gauged against it, at times celebrated in comparison with it, and set with it at different points along the same spectrum of sense-transcending expressive functions (usually extending from the divine to the demonic).

Later, in writings such as Rousseau's *Essay on the Origins of Language* and Vico's *New Science*, an element of historicity, in some measure novel, entered into European views. Now non-European singing was conceived not as equivalent (in whatever manner) to contemporary European practices but as a survival in far-off places of practices Europe had long since outgrown. This perceiving of historical distance in geographical and cultural difference hinted at later distinctions of historiography and ethnography while still resisting them in the commonality of song itself. Non-European singing was still *commensurable* with European singing, though it was *displaced* from it along a historical axis.

Song, in this dispensation, presented authors such as Vico and Rousseau with the conundrum of Derrida's supplement (Tomlinson 2007, chap. 1). At once envisaged as the earliest, most immediate, and most passionate of utterances—the form in which language first emerged—and as a modulated and disciplined art of the present day, song was endowed with expressive features both primitive and modern, brutally direct and delicately metaphorical, barbarously non-European and of consummate (European) refinement. The conundrum points forward to later developments in European ideology while at the same time affirming for us the proximity, at this moment, of historical and anthropological perspectives. Around 1750, song offered a category, at once conceptual and perceptual, in which anthropology and historiography began to assume their modern outlines while resisting the oppositions that would later separate them.

The *music* that came to counter such *song* in the decades before 1800 was not conceived as a European version of worldwide activities but instead as a European métier opposed to practices elsewhere, however much it might superficially resemble them. It was sanctioned within views novel in the late eighteenth century: new conceptions of the nonmimetic expressive capacities of music and of music's transcendence of the sensible world (Dahlhaus 1989a), a novel discreteness and fixity of the musical work itself (Goehr 1992), even a revising of the human subject that perceived all these things (Tomlinson 1999). It was represented above all by the burgeoning genres, institutions, and traditions of instrumental music. If around 1700 song had offered a conceptual umbrella under which the world's musical activities, non-European and European, might gather (if uneasily), now instrumental music—music without words, *nonsong*—posed a new, exclusionary category redolent of European spiritual superiority. Such a category could not help but carry deep implications for both anthropology and historiography.

An early marking of this new category is Kant's positioning of instrumental music in his analysis of beauty in his *Critique of Judgment* (Kant [1790] 2000 pt. 1, bk. 1, section 16: "The Judgment of Taste, by Which an Object is Declared to Be Beautiful Under the Condition of a Definite Concept, Is Not Pure"). The free or unattached, hence pure, beauty Kant finds in such music—in "music fantasies (i.e., pieces without any topic [*Thema*]) and in fact all music without words"—is foreign to most other human products, such as the human body itself, buildings, even horses (seemingly conceived only, by Kant, as livestock). The beauty of these human products depends on the concepts of the ends or purposes envisaged for them; it therefore emerges from a human moral and rational order. The beauty of instrumental music, instead, manifests a kind of errancy, an independence from such humanist moral orders that likens it to the meaningless beauty of flowers, exotic birds, and seashells.

The converse of Kant's example is implicit but clear: Song, music with words, must manifest a dependent beauty. Kant considers song only *in absentia*, so to speak, by specifying that free beauty is restricted to instrumental music; but this restriction poses a deep-seated differentiation of the two. In this distinction (though he certainly would not have relished the consequence), Kant prepared the ground for the ennoblement of instrumental music throughout the nineteenth century that would take forms as different as the complexities of Wagner's relation to Beethoven or Hanslick's ([1885] 1974) resolute separation of music from speech and musical from other beauty. In its own time the effect of Kant's differentiation was to mark off, within a solidifying and narrowing conception of aesthetics considered as the philosophy of beauty, one precinct for singing, a different one for playing.

The rationale behind Kant's two types of musical beauty is, however, anything but transparent. If the beauty of buildings and horses must be conceived as connected to their purposeful human ends, under what view of humanity and music both does instrumental music escape this service? How could Kant have convinced himself, finally, that *any* music could instance a beauty dissociated from all human ends? The puzzle suggests the pressure of ideological constructs on Kant's thinking, and it is not resolved by the shifting, in the decades after him, of the capacities of certain instrumental music from the category of "free beauty" to that of the "sublime."

Kant's assignment of categorically differing modes of beauty to nonsong and song punctuated a period when instrumental practices in elite Europe—the ascendancy of symphony, concerto, and sonata, the challenging of the supremacy of opera by public concerts featuring instrumental virtuosity, and so on—called forth a sense of European musical accomplishment and uniqueness that needed to be squared with the global ubiquity of singing. In the years after Kant, indeed, the achievements of recent European instrumental music could be viewed as the culmination of a progressive world history. In 1800 Herder, writing in *Kalligone*, his response to Kant's *Critique*, described "the slow progress of music's history" toward the moment, in his own Europe, when it "developed into a self-sufficient art, *sui-generis*, dispensing with words" (Le Huray and Day 1981, 257; Goehr 1992, 155). It was a very short step, soon taken, from the Kantian distinction of instrumental and vocal musics to the assertion of Europe as the privileged endpoint of music history.

If in this way Kant's remark on instrumental music points toward a Eurocentric separation of music history from music anthropology, Johann Nikolaus Forkel's *Allgemeine Geschichte der Musik* ([1788] 1967), from the same years, spins out a full-fledged narrative of their divorce. The novel force of Forkel's account lies neither in its frankly progressive tone, common enough in his predecessors, nor even in its less commonplace linkage of the advancement of music to the evolution of language. Instead the crucial, innovative move by which Forkel pries music history apart from music anthropology is his insistence that music progresses in tandem not only with language but also with *writing*.

Forkel asserts first that music and language develop in parallel ways from their earliest origins to their "highest perfection" (Forkel [1788] 1967; Allanbrook 1998, 280). But "Language and writing always proceeded at an equal pace in their development; therefore music and notation can be presumed to have done the same." Peoples who use imperfect music notations can, then, attain only "imperfect, extremely unordered" musics (p. 288). A perfect music depends on a perfected music writing. In language writing, Forkel reasons (echoing many eighteenth-century predecessors), the approach to perfection moves from pictographic through ideographic to alphabetic stages. Alphabetic writing emerges only after a people's attainment of a level of intellectual sophistication in which writing can be abstracted from the things it represents; ideographs show a less-developed mode of abstraction, pictographs no abstraction at all. Since music writing is the inscribing of airy, invisible bodies, it requires, like alphabetism, a high degree of abstraction. Therefore, Forkel sweepingly concludes, "No people could arrive at any method at all for translating its melodies into signs before the invention of alphabetical writing" (p. 287).

Forkel's specific inferences concerning the history of music notation are complex. After the invention of the alphabet this history reverses, in a way, the evolution of language writing, moving from an incipient alphabetic mode toward something akin to pictography. But we need not follow these particulars to be staggered by the blunt force of Forkel's syllogism: *Musical perfection is dependent on notational perfection; notational perfection follows alphabetism; therefore musical perfection follows alphabetism.* Forkel subsumes the evolution of musics worldwide under a history pointing toward the circum-Mediterranean achievement of the alphabet. In doing so he creates for music both a *course* of history and a *space* of anthropology, separating the two in their specific domains: the first traversed by alphabetic societies and their precursors, the second inhabited by analphabetic peoples. Societies with the alphabet can move closer to a perfect musical art; those without must move elsewhere or not move at all. "How long a people can tolerate [the] first crude state of music cannot be precisely determined," Forkel writes. "We still find it today, however, among many Asiatic, African, and American peoples, whom we also know to have made no progress for millennia in other branches of culture" (p. 285).

In the service of a music history and anthropology thus clearly distinguished, Forkel has deployed oppositions closely related to those described by de Certeau (1988) in separating general historiography and ethnography. European music history will evolve from writing, while music anthropology encounters a space of orality. Europe's writing will enable a progressive evolution contrasting with the cultural stasis of others ("We still find it today . . ."). The alphabetic writing that enables musical perfection, finally, will arise from a mode of consciousness—the capability for abstraction—not attained by others. By 1788, the date of the introductory volume of Forkel's work, the history of European musical development could be plotted as a story of the progress of writing, the anthropology of non-European musics as the trackless space of writing's absence.

The exemplary instances of Forkel and Kant may seem at first glance to touch on each other only tangentially. The one offers a differentiation of beauty in song from beauty in instrumental music that militated toward a Eurocentric music history, the other an emphasis on alphabetism that could separate music history from music anthropology. The two cases are, however, connected at a deep level. Each is predicated on a mode of abstraction: for Forkel, the capacity that leads to alphabetic writing and then to music notation and musical perfection; for Kant a humanly created instance of beauty somehow loosed from all human ends. (These changes are connected also to the archeological shifts discerned about 1800 by Foucault [1970, chaps. 7–8], in which previously hidden functions came into view as new conditions of knowledge. Foucault's labor, newly perceived as the determinant of knowledge of exchange and value, and his biological functions, cutting from beneath across the expanse of eighteenth-century taxonomy, are comparable to Forkel's capacity for abstraction and Kant's ethico-functional distinction of categories of beauty.)

Each of these abstractions, moreover, represents a separation of the musical materials involved from their human creative matrices—a manner, that is, of *decontextualization*. The beauty of instrumental music is, for Kant, like that of tulips and parrots. In drawing this similarity he detached (mysteriously) instrumental music from the human means and ends of its production, dissemination, and consumption. Forkel's move away from context is less self-evident than this but no less basic to his thought. For him alphabetism represents an attainment of human consciousness whereby a system of writing looses itself from the conditions of visual perception, a detachment signally absent from pictography; in general alphabetism amounts to a mark of the separation in advanced peoples of concepts from sense stimuli. Music writing follows as a related (if obverse) detaching of sense from intellect. The attainment of a sophisticated music notation yields something like a pictographic representation of invisible, disembodied aural perceptions. In notation invisible sounds take on visible form, marking the soul's conceptual ability to discern, finally, the subtlest differences among them (Allanbrook 1998, 282). This increased conceptual power of the soul, not some change in sense perception, enables the perfection of music. The whole advancement of music is idealist, relying on the conceptual abstraction manifested in music notation. The progress of *situated* musical practice follows from the possibility music writing offers of its *detachment* from its situation.

It is not hard to recognize in Forkel's and Kant's modes of decontextu-alization ingredients of the novel conception of musical autonomy that would take strong root in nineteenth-century Europe. From thinking related both directly and indirectly to Kant's detached musical beauty sprang, as I have already suggested, the ideology of absolute music: the view that special capabilities and privileges adhere to music without text or program, "that instrumental music purely and clearly expresses the true nature of music by its very lack of concept, object, and purpose" (Dahlhaus 1989a, 7). The sepa-ration itself of such music from its context, in the views of its proponents, marked its transcending of history and the material world.

Viewed against the backdrop of the cantological intuitions of a slightly earlier European moment, this conception of musical autonomy appears as a powerful philosophical assertion by elite Europe of its own unique achievement and status. In historical terms—the terms already set forth by Herder in 1800, as we have seen—it presents the European instrumental traditions of its time as the telos of all musical progress. In doing this it simultaneously posits for territories beyond Europe a set of anthropological limitations. These locales are, now more than before, spaces of primitive (that is, static or ahistorical) or regressive (historically failed) musical prac-tices. In coming to seem a marker of European distinction, *instrumentalism* is now set off in complex ideological opposition to non-European *vocalism.* The singing that Rousseau could still offer as a trait shared across all humanity is now instead an index of human difference. (Later, near the end of the era of European colonialism, this view of instrumental music found its reflection in European or European-influenced conceptualizations of other elite musics. Bruno Nettl has argued that European instrumentalism had a profound impact on the emergence, around 1900, of the instrumental *radif* basic to the theory and pedagogy of modern Persian classical music [Nettl 1987, 133–137]. Indian classical traditions have also felt the impact of modern Western instrumentalism since the late nineteenth century.)

The example of Forkel, for its part, shows us how this European coop-tation of musical (hence artistic, creative, imaginative) history is allied from the start with conceptions of writing. From the early nineteenth century on, conceptions of absolute music ran together with views related to Forkel's of the determining importance of notation in music history. The result was another crystallizing of ideological forms and new practices reflecting them.

The idea of instrumental music as an autonomous, nonmimetic expres-sive means, together with the emergent formation of the modern conception of the discrete musical work, invested new and substantial powers in the written form of the work. The notated music came to be viewed less as a preliminary script for performance than as the locus of the truest revelation of the composer's intent, the unique and full inscription of the composer's expressive spirit which was elsewhere—in any one performance—only partially revealed. Music writing itself seemed an inscriptive means endowed with nonsemantic and mysterious significance. It was now conceivable, to a degree that it had not been before, that the work as embodied in music writing, divorced from its contexts of production, performance, and reception, could become the avatar of the transcendent spaces absolute music could attain and inhabit. The notated work took on almost magical characteristics, projecting spirit outward in legible form and traversing the distance between musical exegete and composer. The search for the secrets of this written work could in large degree ignore and thus conceal the social interactions of performers and audience at the scene itself of musicking. The language here gestures intentionally toward Marx, for by 1900 the musical score shows many of the hallmarks of the fetishized commodity of late capitalism.

The ability for abstraction that Forkel had seen as a prerequisite for music writing and hence musical advancement has here posed itself in the European mind as a new, quintessentially musical ability: the ability to comprehend an unperformed work from its writing alone. The idealism behind this proposition is a direct outgrowth of the idealism attendant on notions of absolute music all told; but this variant of the general idealism relies on the fixed inscription of the work. The music writing that Forkel had held up as a *sine qua non* of an advanced musical tradition has exerted its full prerogatives. (A related development appears about this time in conceptions of drama: Coleridge, Hazlitt, and others advance the idea that Shakespeare's plays are more fully—more ideally—experienced in reading than in witnessing performances. See Heller 1990.)

The two primary activities that mark the emergence of modern musicology in the late nineteenth century grew up in the shadow of this idealization of music writing. First, the huge projects of establishing "critical" editions for Bach, Handel, and other composers, which arose in these years and continued at an accelerating pace across the early twentieth century, mark the new faith in the work fixed in music writing, in the possibility of representing it as a stable, authoritative text, and in the belief that this text can bring us closer to the singular expressive intent that motivated the composer.

The search for the expressive secrets of the score, meanwhile, blossomed from descriptive beginnings, in writings such as those of E. T. A. Hoffmann, into modern music analysis ([1810] 1989). Analysis, in this light, can be seen to be the interpretive praxis that arose from the decontextualization of instrumental music at the moment of the apotheosis of music writing as manifestation of transcendent spirit. Moreover, as an outgrowth of

Eurocentric conceptions of music, analysis was linked to Europe's positing of its own musical (and other) uniqueness in world history. In a profound circularity it was positioned so as to confirm a Hegelian culmination of world musical history in the very absolute music that helped define it (for the position of Beethoven in this formation, see Burnham 1995, 101–2). Enacting this pseudo-confirmation, analysis offered criteria constructed on a foundation of European views, including an ideology of writing, as a universal gauge of musical worth.

We can sense here the colonial dilemma, as we might call it, that conditioned from the start the kind of musicology that attends mostly to discrete works fixed in music writing. Such musicology starts from a historically local and recent mode of musical self-awareness and idealization and projects it outward from Europe toward the rest of the world. This impulse is probably inevitable and, if carefully scrutinized, is not necessarily a bad thing. But the scrutiny is essential. It points up the place of musicology in a Eurocentric self-knowledge that characterizes in varying degrees all the modern humanities. (Literature, in this regard, is a category in many ways similar to music; see Eagleton 1983, chap. 1.) It locates music in the modern university's pedagogical effort of humanistic *Bildung*, itself in some measure circular. The posing of such self-knowledge becomes problematic when it is not accompanied by more or less strenuous attempts to gain *other*-knowledge—when, to paraphrase Paul Ricoeur's famous aphorism, knowledge of the self is thought to be meaningful without detour through knowledge of relatively distant others.

We can appreciate also, in these discursive formations, the difficulty ethnomusicology would face as it emerged, in the mid twentieth century, from a Eurocentric musicology to offer itself as the alternative to self-knowledge. Preordained as the study of de Certeau's oral, ahistorical, unwritten cultures in a disciplinary matrix that was from the first defined by European powers of writing, it was unable simply to ignore the formations that shaped its sibling discipline. It reacted against them, instead, from a position still partially within them. Ethnomusicology's deep, even constitutive ambivalence, at once fascinated and wary, in the face of music analysis, the score, and the inscription of unwritten traditions and practices shows this as clearly as any other feature. Modern ethnomusicology and musicology, like modern historiography and ethnography before them, arose as antithetical twins; but they arose as a single, dualistic reflex of the emergence of music from song.

The disciplinary genealogy sketched here encourages some general observations about the relations of music studies to anthropology and history. First, it shows the opposition of modern musicology and ethnomusicology for what it originally was: a disciplinary artifact arising from a new stage, attained not much before 1800, in the evolution of European conceptions of self and others. In this light, modern musicology itself, and not only ethnomusicology, appears as a discipline erected on propositions of cultural difference, European versus non-European. In founding itself on such propositions, it was from the start ethnographic through and through—though the conditions of its local culture led it to found itself in such a way as to conceal its sources. (Again Marx's commodity comes to mind.) Meanwhile ethnomusicology arose, defensively, as a reaction to musicology's concealment of the truth that it was always already a particular instance of ethnomusicology.

Second, an anamnesis is needed to foster alternatives to the conceptual categories that created and still sustain these disciplinary constructs. This might assume a number of different forms: a commemoration of the fact that European musical thought preceded Europe's modern distinction of anthropology from history; a recognition of the ways this earlier musical thought gathered together human activities that would be categorically separated by the impact of later discourses; and an injunction, implicit in this recognition, not to ignore the *longue durée* of European music history, as happens increasingly in our music departments and curricula. The anamnesis might take the form of a realization that the powers of voice have come to pose themselves in our musical culture as a potent and in some measure suspect "other" of instrumentalism. It might take the form, finally, of a meditation on the shape of a future musicology that would show that song, universal corollary of the human propensity to language, is not so much a musical thing as music is *songish* (to borrow from Dryden a useful word).

All this suggests that a re-elaborated musicology needs to embrace the fact of its position within a more general ethnomusicology. This is not to privilege one musical subdiscipline over another, but to widen the purview of both. It would not involve a repudiation of musicology's canons—of its canon of works, with common-practice instrumental pieces at its heart, or of its methodological canons, revolving around close scrutiny of these works; such canon-making seems to be another inevitable impulse of the humanistic *Bildung* discussed above. It would, however, relocate these canons in a broader disciplinary and historical panorama and, in the same motion, ensure that their deployment was accompanied by an ideological critique of the sort sketched above.

The usefulness of such a critique lies finally in its clearing the way for meaningful comparison of varieties of musicking across large stretches of human history and culture—ultimately, across the whole stretch of human history and culture available to us. I mean here to espouse a sweeping *neocomparativism* that could explore ever broader questions about the place of music in human experience, aspiration, and achievement. Such questions, usually foreclosed by the localism of conventional music studies, are easily propounded: What is the significance of the ubiquitous relation between speech and song, activities at once proximate and distinct in all cultures? Why are song and religion or song and drama constantly linked? How does the body in musical motion meet the material world through prosthetic technologies of instrument making, and how are these related to other technologies? What are the peculiar powers of repetitive musical structures, and how are they differently deployed in different situations? How do the institutions characteristic of human society allow political power to accrue to musical acts? How are musical traditions altered by music writing, and how are we to understand the urge to this inscription? And so forth.

Questions such as these open onto vistas of dizzying breadth. They widen, for example, the issue of musical formalism far beyond its parochial limitations in nineteenth- and twentieth-century Europe-derived aesthetics, thereby bringing to light its transhuman dimensions and connecting it with recent cognitive and evolutionary studies and computational modelling of music processing. Such questions also put in new perspective music's relation to the larger world of human communication, thereby gesturing still farther afield, toward deep histories of biosemiosis that carry extra-human (and even post-human) implications. Raising the topic of music's broadest semiotic reach and history, meanwhile, displaces those conceptions of musical meaning hovering close to theories of symbolism—another nineteenth-century product—with an information-based approach that answers to our growing understanding of the valences of human affect and connects music directly to the broad fluxes of information that govern the biome. All these topics, then, bring music into focus as one of a few complex human behaviors with the potential to reveal deep currents of human commonality as well as recurring patterns of human engagement with ecological affordance. The second of these in particular could indicate new avenues for the study of musicking as embodied knowledge, narrowing the divide between interpretation and praxis at a moment when scholars have begun to emphasize what one has termed the "practice turn" in our disciplines (see Born 2010a; also Abbate 2004; Currie 2009).

Such a reconceived musicology would not efface the delineation of human difference that music studies, in their localism, have long pursued. The human ability to proliferate such cultural variety is, after all, itself a profound bond linking us all, one now well understood as the most spectacular evolved trait distinguishing our species from every other one on the planet today (see Sperber 1999, cxv). The neocomparativism here envisaged would take off from the particularism that has marked most musical ethnography and, certainly, most Eurocentric music history and criticism. It would not obviate situated, detailed studies of musical matters but rather transform them by making the means of their situating and the definition of their detail objects of its own scrutiny. It should go without saying, also, that this approach would differ from earlier comparativisms in its critical dismemberment of the hegemonic, Europe-first strategies on which they rested.

Perhaps it also does not need emphasizing that such a neocomparativism would efface the lingering, fragile, but often defended divide between ethnographic and historical approaches. It would bring historical depth to ethnomusicological areas not usually conceived in this way and, at the same time, foster a cross-cultural perspective on European musics too often walled off from the rest of the world. In doing so, in other words, it would enact in music studies the exchange I noted at the outset of this chapter, confounding the differences that European ideologies have for two hundred years presumed between historical and anthropological approaches.

In the end, at a moment when musicology is emerging from a period of strenuous attempts to clarify the differences among its various subdisciplines, the affinities of all our efforts instead need to be emphasized. The challenge facing music scholarship today is to feel its way toward intuitions about musicking that preceded and have always surrounded the opposition of history and ethnography. As it does so, it will map a unified field on which localism and globalism, formalism and expressivism, embodied praxis and hermeneutics, and finally difference and sameness all told appear as mutually constituting pairs.

NOTES

1   This chapter is a revised version of one published under the same title in *Il Saggiatore musicale* (8.1, 2001, pp. 21–37).

FURTHER READING

Burnham, Scott. 1995. *Beethoven hero.* Princeton: Princeton University Press.

Chakrabarty, Dipesh. 2000. *Provincializing Europe: Postcolonial thought and historical difference.* Princeton: Princeton University Press.

Clifford, James. 1983. On ethnographic authority. *Representations* 2: 118–46.

De Certeau, Michel. 1988. *The writing of history.* Translated by Tom Conley. New York: Columbia University Press.

Derrida, Jacques. 1976. *Of grammatology.* Translated by Gayatri Chakravorty Spivak. Baltimore: Johns Hopkins University Press.

Fabian, Johannes. 1983. *Time and the other: How anthropology makes its object.* New York: Columbia University Press.

Goehr, Lydia. 1992. *The imaginary museum of musical works.* Oxford: Clarendon Press.

Richerson, Peter J., and Robert Boyd. 2005. *Not by genes alone: How culture transformed human evolution.* Chicago: University of Chicago Press.

Smail, Daniel Lord. 2008. *On deep history and the brain.* Berkeley: University of California Press.

Tomlinson, Gary. 1999. Vico's songs: Detours at the origins of (ethno)musicology. *The Musical Quarterly* 83: 344–377.

—— 2007. Monumental musicology. *Journal of the Royal Musical Association* 132: 349–374.

PART **2**

WHERE?
Locations of Music

CHAPTER 6

TEXTUAL ANALYSIS OR THICK DESCRIPTION?

JEFF TODD TITON

In the last decades of his long and productive life, the ethnomusicologist David McAllester used to tell a story about the founding of the Society for Ethnomusicology. On a cold November afternoon in 1952, three of the four founders, McAllester, Alan Merriam, and Willard Rhodes, were driving to New Haven to see Charles Seeger and involve him in their plans. They had just "hatched their plot" to start something new, a society for scholars engaged in the study of the music of the world's peoples. Sitting in the back seat and bursting with enthusiasm, McAllester sang a Navajo song, not quietly. After a few moments of this in the close confines of their car, Merriam, from the driver's seat, turned his head around and said, "Must you sing, McAllester?" (McAllester 1989; 2006)

McAllester always ended the story there, but we can assume that this Boston-bred intellectual who later realized his dream of becoming a Native American when he was adopted into the family of his principal consultant, the Navajo Frank Mitchell, understood that he was interfering with Merriam's thoughts, and ceased. For McAllester, the story was in his singing and Merriam's response, for it revealed that ethnomusicology would from the start need to accommodate both scientific and humanistic approaches to its subject, the study of people making music all over the world. McAllester wanted to be remembered as one of the pioneering humanists.

The title of this chapter was assigned to me, by the book's editors; and in its either/or formulation it suggests a distinction between scientific analysis and humanistic interpretation. This is a difference that some ethnomusicologists have tended to maximize, as McAllester did, and that others have worked to minimize, viewing analysis and interpretation as complementary procedures. In this chapter I touch on scientific and humanistic approaches to the cultural study of music, concentrating on Geertz's humanistic "thick description," which has been enormously influential in the cultural study of music among North American ethnomusicologists. I conclude with a look at recent developments in applied ethnomusicology; that is, in putting the cultural study of music to practical use.

Ethnomusicology's forebears, the comparative musicologists Stumpf, Hornbostel, Sachs, Herzog and others, as well as those such as Bartók and Brăiloiu who regarded traditional music as folklore, were proud that theirs was a scientific project. Indeed, the fundamental premise of their work, we would say now, was that music was best understood as a "text" to be analyzed, using the term "text" in its broad sense as any object of study (Titon 1995b). These late-nineteenth- and early-twentieth-century forebears asked grand questions: how did music originate, and how did it grow and spread among the world's peoples? How could musical affinities among varied human groups reveal the paths of migrations and diffusions? What did the variety of musical instruments found throughout the world signify, and how could they be classified and compared? It seemed obvious that the appropriate musical text was analogous with a musical score, a rendering of a performance in written Western musical notation. But notation was not used in most of the world's music. For that reason, the comparative musicologists had to construct, or transcribe, musical texts from performance, a practice that was greatly aided after the late nineteenth century by the phonograph recording, which permitted rehearings of the same performance, and which enabled one scientist to review the musical text constructed by another with a copy of the recording at the ear.

Having isolated these musical texts, the comparative musicologists conducted scientific analysis upon them: examination of constituent parts and their interactions to form the whole. The discovery of intervallic, scalar, contour, rhythmic and harmonic patterns made it possible to acknowledge differences and group similar musical performances together, which facilitated description and classification of these larger bodies of music that were characteristic of certain geographical areas and that belonged to particular cultural groups. Thus classified, they were meant to be compared cross-culturally to arrive at generalizations about music and culture that would yield answers to their grand questions. What we mean by the modern term science developed in Europe in the nineteenth century from what had until then been called natural philosophy (the analytical and experimental side of the study of nature) and natural history (its descriptive, classificatory, and comparative side). In their fascination with scales and intervals, their transcriptions, analyses, and comparative work, Stumpf, Hornbostel, Bartók and the others were operating as natural philosophers, while in their descriptive, classificatory and historical work (for example, in the Sachs–Hornbostel classification of musical instruments) they were operating as natural historians. However, for various reasons they failed to achieve the successes they had envisioned, and by the 1960s and 1970s comparative musicology appeared to exhaust itself in Alan Lomax's cantometrics project (Lomax and Berkowitz 1972).

Science, however, had not disappeared from ethnomusicology; scientific breakthroughs such as atomic bombs, the polio vaccine, and explorations in outer space had given science increased prestige, and, in this climate, ethnomusicologists continued to think of themselves as doing science. During its first two decades, prominent members of the Society for Ethnomusicology engaged in a soul-searching quest for identity. In the Society's journal, *Ethnomusicology*, one scholar after another put forth a different definition of ethnomusicology, but none seriously questioned whether it ought to be a science. Discussion ensued over whether it was a discipline with a single, characteristic methodology; or if it was an interdisciplinary field that could accommodate different goals and methods for the cultural study of music. Merriam, the loudest advocate for science, consistently and frequently expressed the view that ethnomusicology ought to model itself on the social science of cultural anthropology; as he famously wrote, ethnomusicology was "sciencing about music" (1964, 25). In the last decades of the twentieth century, Marcia Herndon, Norma McLeod, Steven Feld, John Shepherd, Anthony Seeger and others moved ethnomusicology in the direction of an ethnoscience of music wherein the notion of "text" expanded to become a performance event, a social text that proceeded by behavioral rules (Herndon and McLeod, 1979; Feld 1982; Seeger 1987). Today, the study of musical expression as rule-governed behavior still animates scientific approaches to music. Feeling liberated from the racist stigma of cultural evolutionism, a new generation of scientists speculates once more about music as an adaptational tool in human evolution (see Wallin, Merker, and Brown 2000). And neuroscientists and cognitive ethnomusicologists are asking intriguing questions about music, the body, and the brain (see Hallam, Cross, and Thaut 2009; and the "Call and Response" section of *Ethnomusicology* 53(3) [2009]).

In this way, contemporary scientific approaches yield insights into the cultural study of music as human behavior governed by biological constraints and cultural rules; but, for the past thirty years or so, many North American ethnomusicologists have been asking different questions, ones that bear on the relation of music to region, race, class, gender, politics, ethnicity, belief, identity, money, power, and the production of knowledge. These questions concern music as lived experience, as commodity, as social practice, and as cultural symbol. Of course, these questions arise from the powerful critique of science that took hold in the last quarter of the twentieth century in the ideologically driven fields of critical theory, deconstruction, feminism, post-structuralism, and postcolonialism, among others. This intellectual climate encourages a humanities approach to the cultural study of music, one that foregrounds ideology and prefers interpretation to analysis. No scholar had more impact on ethnomusicological representations of people making music during the last thirty-five years than the cultural anthropologist Clifford Geertz (1926–2006), whose methodology involving "thick description" of cultural "texts" moved fieldwork-based disciplines away from scientific method and toward the interpretive practices of the humanities.

Geertz's intellectual project was to reconfigure cultural anthropology through redefining its key concept, culture, as an assemblage of texts (in the broad sense) whose meanings were to be interpreted (Titon 1995b). Rejecting scientific approaches involving cultural analysis, Geertz states, refines, and illustrates the idea that culture is not like an organism whose structures and functions are to be analyzed; nor like a game with tacitly understood rules governing behavior; nor like a drama, with stages, actors, and performances; but, rather, culture is a system of symbols embedded in social action. Drawing on the French philosopher Paul Ricoeur's idea that action can be "read" and interpreted, Geertz declares that this symbol system, residing in social action, is in fact a great text; that "the culture of a people is an ensemble of texts, themselves ensembles, which the anthropologist strains to *read* over the shoulders of those to whom they properly belong" (1973, 452; my italics). Geertz asserts, further, that cultural anthropologists are not only readers but also, fundamentally, writers; that is, they "inscribe social discourse" and turn a passing event into an "account which exists in its inscriptions and can be reconsulted" (1973, 19). Reading, interpreting, and writing as a model may not seem remarkable at first, but it was a cry for a humanities-based approach to the work of cultural anthropology, and was very much opposed to the then-dominant rule-governed, analytical model based on the sciences—the very same ethno-science model that certain of Merriam's students and intellectual heirs were employing in the cultural study of music.

Geertz's theory of "thick description" follows from these assertions. Thick description is best understood as a method by which to apprehend and interpret cultural texts. Borrowing this term from the English philosopher Gilbert Ryle, Geertz explains how often a subtle and complex understanding is required to grasp the meaning of even the simplest act: in Ryle's thought experiment, the act is the blink of an eye (Geertz 1973, 6). Is this an involuntary twitch, asks Ryle, or is it a wink? And if a wink, is it a conspiratory signal, or is it perhaps a faked wink meant to deceive a third party? Ryle thus distinguishes between "thin description" (the blink described as a contraction of an eyelid) and "thick description" (the wink understood as "practicing a burlesque of a friend faking a wink to deceive an innocent into thinking a conspiracy is in motion"). To put this into Geertz's terminology, thick description renders a more satisfactory "reading" (interpretation) of the "text" (the wink).

For Geertz, then, thick description is what anthropologists ought to do: unpack the meanings of the symbols that reside in texts and comprise a culture. This involves understanding the layers, the "multiplicity of complex conceptual structures" that the anthropologist "must contrive somehow first to grasp and then to render" in writing (1973, 6–7, 10). No easy task, even in one's own society, let alone among complete strangers. Although Geertz published a number of ethnographic works, his essay on the Balinese cockfight, which appeared at about the same time as his groundbreaking theoretical articles, is usually taken as his case in point, his best exercise in thick description. The essay is a *tour de force*, a dazzlingly persuasive, densely detailed, dandily written account of how cockfights in Bali symbolize much in Balinese culture and character. The essay contains profuse descriptions and interpretations of the cocks, the fighting, the wagering, how wagering symbolizes social relations, and the way Balinese beliefs and character can be read in the varieties of behavior exhibited around the cockfight; it is impossible to summarize. I only restate my admiration for it below and comment on a few aspects of it as I begin to tug at the loose ends of Geertz's enterprise—not in an attempt to unravel it all, although I do unravel it some; but rather to show how it might be redone in a more persuasive way, one which leads toward collaborative ethnographic enterprises and applied ethnomusicology in the cultural study of music.

One of the striking early things in Geertz's cockfight essay is his story of how he and his wife gained community acceptance by "getting caught, or almost caught, in a vice raid." Geertz and his wife were observing a cockfight; the police raided it; everyone ran away; Geertz and wife (alas, she is never named; she always appears as "my wife") joined a fleeing Balinese man and wound up in his courtyard. The Balinese man's "wife, who had apparently been through this sort of thing before," set a table, the two couples sat down and composed themselves, and they presented a united front when the police arrived shortly afterwards. The next day "the village was a completely different world for us," Geertz wrote, and they were "suddenly the center of all attention, the object of a great outpouring of warmth, interest, and most especially, amusement. . . . In Bali, to be teased is to be accepted. It was the turning point as far as our relationship to the community was concerned, and we were quite literally 'in.'" The incident made it possible for Geertz to achieve "that mysterious necessity of anthropological fieldwork, rapport. . . . It led to a sudden and unusually complete acceptance into a society extremely difficult for outsiders to penetrate. It gave me the kind of immediate, inside-view grasp of an aspect of 'peasant mentality' that anthropologists not fortunate enough to flee headlong with their subjects from armed authorities normally do not get" (1973, 416).

This charming and clever narrative functions to establish Geertz's ethnographic authority as someone who is "in," who is "accepted," who has established "rapport" with, and therefore has good access to, the people and culture under study. Yet, a little later, in his essay "From the Native's Point of View," Geertz dissociated himself from those social scientists who, following George Herbert Mead, advocated rapport as a means toward empathetic understanding. For Geertz, "understanding the form and pressure of . . . natives' inner lives is more like grasping a proverb, catching an allusion, seeing a joke—or, as I have suggested, reading a poem—than it is like achieving communion" ([1974] 1977, 492). From that point in his essay, he is enmeshed in thick description of the cockfight. By the end of the piece we learn that the cockfight is a "paradigmatic human event" in which "the Balinese forms and discovers his temperament and his society's temper at the same time" (1973, 450–451). He is so thorough, so smart, so graceful, and so reassuring that the reader is lulled, and does not worry that Geertz's is the only authoritative voice speaking from within the inscribed account. Geertz very seldom quotes his Balinese informants, and when he does it usually appears in a footnote, well below the level of the discourse inscribed as thick description. That is, although we are given to understand that Geertz has conversed with the Balinese about cockfights, the kind of interpretation he is after is presumably not something that Balinese would be able to articulate. Upon reflection, one wonders what the Balinese think of Geertz's take on the cockfight. We never know, and he implies that it does not matter.

For many ethnomusicologists in the twenty-first century, it does matter. Suppose that a Balinese wrote an account of North American culture based on the "paradigmatic human event" of the professional football game. As a ritual, Sunday afternoon football in the United States surely rivals the Balinese cockfight in rich cultural symbolism. Ritual violence and mock war drama; hierarchy and racism (the Balinese might remark on the preponderance of black athletes at every position except quarterback and head coach); gambling and organized crime; spectating and various kinds of vicarious behavior and misbehavior in the stands; sports talk shows—all this and more would be grist for the symbol mill, as football becomes a quasi-religious ritual akin to the Balinese cockfight in which, to paraphrase Geertz, "the American forms and discovers his temperament and his society's temper at the same time."

Well, some Americans. Males, principally, and not all American males either. But note that this interpretation is not something that a Balinese has supplied; as a participant in the culture, my culture, I have articulated it on the basis of a few seconds' thought. A Balinese ethnographer would come up with something different. Of interest, then, would be to show the Balinese and his or her American informants in dialogue over the interpretation of football. Interpretive accounts and inscriptions thus become multivoiced, and meaning in them often turns out to be incomplete as well as contested. This is the collaborative direction in which ethnomusicological ethnography has moved "thick description" in the past quarter century (see Lassiter 2000).

In reconfiguring thick description to include dialogue and to show the process of interpretation proceeding through fieldwork into reflection and inscription, a more engaged relationship is obtained between the ethnomusicological ethnographer and those people whose music is under study. Words like rapport and informant and interview do not always suffice to describe it; they give way to words like friend, field partner, and conversation. Indeed, researchers enter into gift relationships that require reciprocal obligations. In his ethnographic book on music in Bulgaria, Timothy Rice writes of his long-time friendship with Kostadin, a bagpiper and his principal "informant," who became, among other things, Rice's bagpipe teacher. The relationship made Rice understand that just as he expected certain things of Kostadin, so Kostadin had invested a good deal of expectation in Rice's study of the bagpipe (Rice 1994). In becoming bimusical (i.e., in becoming competent in a second music) Rice understood that Kostadin was his teacher in more ways than one (Titon 1995a). In his ethnographic work on "sound and sentiment" among the Kaluli in Papua New Guinea, Steven Feld discusses the reception of his book among the people he wrote about. Just as the Balinese cockfight is paradigmatic for Geertz, among the Kaluli the myth of the boy who turns into a Muni bird is paradigmatic for Feld. Yet Feld reports that his Kaluli friend asked why he had chosen that particular myth and not another that in his view had an equal, if not better, claim (Feld 1990). It would be as if an American had questioned the Balinese ethnographer's choice of football, suggesting that something different, but equally important, could be learned about American culture by examining the behavior of couples on a "date," the activities surrounding a rock concert or the purchase of a house, or a day in the life of a Wall Street broker; and then as if the resulting discussion were included in the ethnography, further thickening the description to the point of contestation.

Empathy in ethnomusicology's "new fieldwork" (Barz and Cooley [1997] 2008) not only thickens the description through dialogue, it also introduces the subjectivities of emotion and reflexivity. European intellectuals, in my experience, are skeptical of empathy as a scholarly method; but as developed in North American ethnomusicology, or in the practice of medicine for that matter, empathy does not mean standing in other peoples' shoes (feeling their pain) as much as it means engagement. Better than the distanced procedure of symbolic analysis, empathy, or the experience of those moments of "subject shift" when one is thrown outside of oneself (Titon 1995a), offers insight into what Geertz described as "the structure of feelings" in a society. Empathy has led, also, to a resurgence of applied ethnomusicology; that is, to ethnomusicology in the public interest: ethnomusicologists advocating on behalf of musical communities as well as, or instead of, extracting musical life from them and then producing ethnomusicological knowledge primarily for the academic world (*Ethnomusicology* 36(3) [1992]). I shall have more to say about this toward the end of this chapter.

In these new ethnomusicological writings the thickening description names the people and shows them in dialogue, thus becoming multivocal (Levin and Suzukei 2006 is a fine illustration). Interpretation of action read as a text requires that the ethnographer inscribe the observed action into a narrative description-interpretation. So, for example, Geertz evokes, describes, and narrates the cockfight; the result is a highly processed account from the ethnographer's viewpoint. Missing, as I have said, from Geertz's text are the voices of the handlers, the wagerers, the spectators, and what it is, exactly, that they say—that is, the texts, in the conventional sense, generated in the performance of the cockfight. These, if given in Geertz's ethnography, would be on display, as it were, as grist for the mill of everyone's interpretive efforts, whether Geertz's or the reader's.

Geertz has been criticized for being too much a literary critic, reading culture; but as I see it, his problem in the cockfight essay is that he is not enough of one. That is, a literary critic always places the text of the poem, play, or novel in front of the reader so that the process of interpretation can be followed with the exact words of the original text in mind. Geertz's text is both highly processed and predigested; the original text has long since disappeared. Geertz would surely respond that, in observing human activity, there is no such thing as apprehending an original text; that every text is always already an interpretation. This, however, is one of the difficulties with reading action as a text. The fact is that certain actions do generate texts (words) in the conventional sense, and the endless conversations in the field generate them as well. As a writer Geertz operates more as a Jamesian novelist than a literary critic, a comparison that I think would have pleased him.

Geertz has pointed out that, even when the ethnographer includes many voices in a written account, the ethnographer retains control over those voices, writing as a kind of ethnographic ventriloquist. To be sure, just as an ethnographic filmmaker selects those scenes, filmed from "real life," to be ordered into the final sense-making film cut, so, unless we have multiple authorship (Guilbault et al. 1993; also Titon, Cornett, and Wallhausser 1997 and 2003, and Levin and Suzukei 2006), the ethnographic writer selects, from among the many statements by the many voices, what will be included in the ethnographic account. But when the multiply voiced texts are on display, they offer the reader far more interpretive possibilities than are present when the interpretation comes through the inflection of a single voice. To illustrate I will immodestly do something that Geertz often did; that is, turn to one's own research and writing.

The preface to *Powerhouse for God* (1988) is an exercise in multivoiced, thick description, a narrative of a luncheon conversation in which my friend John Sherfey, the principal figure in this ethnographic monograph on music, language, and life in a Baptist church in rural Virginia, presents himself to a visitor from the Library of Congress, by telling a story from his own experience to illustrate, indirectly, the kind of person he is. I evoked the scene, describing it as best as I remembered it; I printed the text of the dialogue between Sherfey and the man from Washington; I interpreted the dialogue in light of my particular concerns once it was finished. Is this "ethnographic ventriloquism" (Geertz 1988, 145)? It cannot be, for the text of the dialogue is given complete (although my description of people's gestures had to be reconstructed from memory) and verbatim, because I had tape-recorded it. (I was, at that time, in that fieldwork stage of documenting everything.) My understanding of the dialogue in its context and in the context of my research is meant to introduce the reader both to John Sherfey and to the subject of the book; but the reader is free to interpret it otherwise, for the reader always has the text of the conversation at hand, not a highly processed or predigested description of the conversation. Including conventional (what Geertz would call "raw") texts for analysis not only thickens the description but allows for the possibility of multiple interpretations.

As my generation of North American ethnomusicologists came of age in the socially conscious 1960s, we increasingly viewed fieldwork not only as a means of obtaining cultural information but as an opportunity to give something back to those people whose music we were studying. As we became acquainted with them, we began to understand their musical goals and to see how we might collaborate with them to help them reach those goals. Researching the history of their music could be helpful not only in terms of the increase of knowledge circulating among scholars but also to the musical communities that were the sites of our fieldwork. If they had musical careers, it was possible to help them gain publicity, to promote them at various musical venues, to help them make recordings, to arrange for granting agencies to become aware of their talents. If they thought of themselves primarily as family and community musicians, it was possible to encourage them, honor them within their communities, and help them maintain the conditions under which their music was able to flourish.

Such individual acts of reciprocity and collective acts of collaboration began to formalize themselves in a reconception of the cultural study of music as an applied endeavor, not merely as an attempt to gather knowledge for the academic world of scholarly knowledge, but for use among the peoples and musical communities one was studying. Ethnomusicologists had begun to see themselves not only as engaged in the cultural study of music but also as culture workers strategizing and administering policy on behalf of the traditional arts. In the United States, for example, the 1960s folk revivals became a breeding ground for a new class of applied folklorists and ethnomusicologists, and in the 1970s they established three federal government institutions in Washington, DC, that formalized the conservation of traditional expressive culture: the Folk Arts Division of the National Endowment for the Arts; the Office of Folklife Studies at the Smithsonian Institution; and the American Folklife Center at the Library of Congress. In the 1980s the Arts Councils in most states of the U.S. hired folklorists and ethnomusicologists to encourage the traditional arts among their constituents. In the 1990s the National Endowment for the Arts was led by the ethnomusicologist William Ivey, while the National Endowment for the Humanities was led by the folklorist William Ferris whose scholarly research was centered in blues music. These were more than titular victories; they symbolized how far the cultural study of music had entered government policy.

In the new century, top–down national and international cultural policies initiated by UNESCO and other institutions, concerning such things as music and intangible cultural heritage, tourism and the creative economy, cultural rights, the digital commons and intellectual property law, have increased opportunities for applied work in the cultural study of music. At the same time, participatory action research and bottom–up collaborations among ethnomusicologists and members of musical communities continue to offer a complementary model. Applied ethnomusicology puts ethnomusicological research to use; contemporary examples include medical ethnomusicology, music and conflict resolution, and cultural policymaking. An enlightened cultural policy with regard to music, based on principles of social justice and human and cultural rights, results in good stewardship of the dynamic musical heritage of all the world's peoples, and brings human beings closer together. The cultural study of music today involves scientific analysis, interpretive scholarship, and the practical application of insights gained from both.

FURTHER READING

Barz, Gregory F., and Timothy J. Cooley. [1997] 2008. *Shadows in the field: New perspectives for fieldwork in ethnomusicology.* 2nd ed. New York: Oxford University Press.

Ethnomusicology, 1992. Volume 36(3). Special issue on *Music and the Public Interest.*

Ethnomusicology, 2009. Volume 53(3). "Call and Response," pp. 478–518.

Feld, Steven. 1990. *Sound and sentiment: Birds, weeping, poetics, and song in Kaluli expression.* 2nd ed. Philadelphia: University of Pennsylvania Press.

Geertz, Clifford. [1972] 1973. Deep play: Notes on the Balinese cockfight. Pp. 412–453 in Geertz, *The interpretation of cultures.* New York: Basic Books.

Geertz, Clifford. 1973. Thick description: Toward an interpretive theory of culture. Pp. 3–30 in Geertz, *The interpretation of cultures.* New York: Basic Books.

Geertz, Clifford. 1988. *Works and lives.* Stanford, CA: Stanford University Press.

Hallam, Susan, Ian Cross, and Michael Thaut, eds. 2009. *The Oxford handbook of music psychology.* New York: Oxford University Press.

Kisliuk, Michelle Robin. 1998. *Seize the dance!: BaAka musical life and the ethnography of performance.* New York: Oxford University Press.

Lassiter, Luke. 2000. *The Chicago guide to collaborative ethnography.* Chicago: University of Chicago Press.

Titon, Jeff Todd. 2008-present. Research blog on music and sustainability. Access at http://www.sustainablemusic.blogspot.com.

CHAPTER 7

COMPARING MUSIC, COMPARING MUSICOLOGY

MARTIN CLAYTON

My aim in this chapter is to offer some observations on the past, present, and future of comparison in musicology. These comments concern the necessity of comparison, but also the profound difficulties it presents: Understanding both the importance and problems of comparison is an important part of any cultural study of music. In order to introduce and to illustrate these observations, I make reference to a couple of quite different examples, both of which include an autobiographical element. The first of these concerns a particular performance event and my experience of and reaction to it. The second example refers to my own research on the temporal organization in North Indian classical music, which I published in the book *Time in Indian Music* (2000). The rationale for introducing such different examples is precisely in order to ask to what extent they may be compared: in fact my concern is not only how *music* can be compared, but also how far *modes of describing music* can be compared. I move from the description and comparison of my own examples to a more general discussion of comparison in musicology, and in particular the legacy of the academic field known between about 1880 and 1950 as "comparative musicology." I begin my argument with a musical performance as experienced, and a discussion of the relationship between such experiences and musical discourse.

LONDON, DECEMBER 16, 2001

The event I alluded to above was the Icelandic pop singer Björk's performance at the Royal Opera House in London, England, in December 2001. I do not present a review of the concert here, still less do I burden you with an account of the emotional roller-coaster that my co-celebrants and I enjoyed over the course of the evening. On the contrary, I would argue that much of what I consider important in the event could not be adequately expressed in words. Suffice it to say, as we stumbled out into the chilly London night my companions and I were all but speechless. We tried, with little success, to share our reactions to the evening's performance, until—abandoning the attempt—we digressed into a comparison of "all-time top five live performances," as if transformed into characters from Nick Hornby's novel *High Fidelity* ([1995] 2000). Fascinated by our inability to even attempt a verbal account of the evening's experience, the next day I checked Björk's website (www.bjork.com/unity) for the reviews which I knew our fellow concertgoers would soon be posting. Somehow, although the challenge of transforming the experience into words had defeated me, it seemed important that someone should at least *try*, and perhaps delay the dissipation of our memories.

At the heart of any musicological work, comparative or otherwise, lies the relationship between our experiences, and the discourse we generate around those experiences (and through which we explain and interpret them). Musicology cannot enter the domain of unmediated experience, since the academic discipline is by its very nature discursive. This is an essential condition of the musicological enterprise, a condition that becomes problematic only when we confuse that discourse with a true or sufficient account of music, rather than recognizing it as an adjunct to experience.

In 1885 Guido Adler began a famous and influential article defining the scope and aims of musicology by suggesting that the experiences of singing, playing, and listening were not in themselves sufficient for the operation of "tonal art," which required self-conscious reflection. As he put it, from the top:

> Musicology originated simultaneously with the art of organising tones. As long as natural song breaks forth from the throat freely and without reflection; as long as the tonal products well up, unclear and unorganised, so long also there can be no question of a tonal art. Only in that moment when a tone is compared and measured according to its pitch . . . only then can one speak of a musical knowledge as well as an art of working with tonal material.
>
> (Mugglestone 1981, 5)

While I would express the relationship between music and discourse somewhat differently, I think Adler's observation on the importance of this relationship remains valuable. For a century or more after Adler's article, most musicologists fell shy of discussing the epistemological basis of music-theoretical discourse. Yet, as the music theorist and composer Benjamin Boretz has suggested, such questions are actually crucial to our endeavors. For Boretz theoretical description was not so much a necessary condition of music as a description erroneously taken for the experience, which in the process became simplified and impoverished (1992). I argue (with acknowledgment to both Adler and Boretz) that musicology needs to resist this error, something I characterize as the collapse of experience into discourse.

Musicology, while it cannot *contain* unmediated experience, can at least enact a sense of its own complex relationship with the material fact of people experiencing music. I call this relationship "complex" because musicological discourse does not only comment on practice and experience; it is not merely parasitical. It also influences that very practice and experience, insofar as musicians and listeners are aware of it. Verbal and graphical discourse can describe, interpret, or otherwise account for musical experience; at the same time, the music we make or choose to listen to is inevitably influenced by this paramusical activity; thus, each feeds off the other.

Time in Indian Music as Comparative Musicology

In the early 1990s I was preparing a doctoral thesis on rhythm in North Indian classical music. Through a combination of tuition, practice, informal ethnography, and reading, I felt that I was well on the way to acquiring an understanding of the matter at hand—the system of temporal organization operating in this repertory—and would in due course distill something I might usefully share with others. When I did so my readership would be made up of people expecting me to tell them something comprehensible about Indian music: in particular, how does it work, and how does it relate to Indian culture in general? (Perhaps also, how does it differ from Western music?)

In order to meet this challenge I needed a language; a body of terminology, and of the concepts and ideas to which those terms refer. There was no shortage there, since I had two sets of terms and concepts: one Indian, which I imagined would be useful in explaining how the music works, and the other English, which I assumed my readers would understand.[1] Naturally then, my task seemed to comprise the translation of Indian musicological discourse into English.

So far so good? Well, not exactly. I had understood my task as the translation of a set of repertory-specific and culture-bound concepts (tala, laya, laykari, and so on) into a general, ahistorical, and culturally neutral set of concepts (rhythm, meter, anacrusis, etc.). But as I also knew, these concepts are anything but culturally neutral, general terms: they have their own history, tied up with a long tradition of Western musical thought. What I was doing, in fact, was implicitly comparing Indian rhythmic organization to Western rhythmic organization. But I didn't want to write a comparative study, but rather to write about Indian music on its own terms, so for a while I neglected to resolve this contradiction.

Ultimately I took on the comparative challenge somewhat more explicitly, acknowledging at the same time the problematic nature of the English concepts and terms when applied cross-culturally. Bitten by the comparativist bug, I also tried some comparison within the tradition, examining the relationships not only between different genres, but also between what musicians' discourse was telling me and what I could observe empirically in the music. I became convinced of the need in ethnomusicological analysis to examine both musical sound and discourse, and to interpret the relationships between the two.

Ethnomusicological orthodoxy at the time, to which I subscribed no less than any of my contemporaries, held (as Bruno Nettl put it) that one must "study each music in terms of the theoretical system that its own culture provides for it" (1973, 151). I came to believe that this model was too simplistic, and that any theoretical system must itself be considered critically, *alongside* the music with which it is associated. In the case of North Indian classical music, the relationship between the two proved to be rather complex: I have no doubt that the same would be true elsewhere, and is equally true of the relationship between European music theory (of whatever period) and the music it describes. It can hardly be otherwise.

So much for studying Indian music on its own terms. First, those terms can only belong to the discursive field that surrounds music. Second, musical discourse does not have its own terms: on the contrary, the terms of musical discourse are precisely those that metaphorically link sound to other domains of experience. This is a significant problem with discussing the connections between music and culture: the language we use to construct music is language that already embodies metaphorical links to other domains of culture and experience—the high and low, large and small, balanced and symmetrical, all of the materiality and structure we impute to music (Lakoff and Johnson 1980).

The implication of this line of argument is that notions of musical text, structure, and system are exposed as problematic. Each (text, structure, system) inheres in discourse: but what ontological status do they have as part of a musical experience? Does sonata form exist in music as experienced, or only in music as discussed? Does raga exist as a system in our preverbal musical percepts and memories, or only in our internalizations of paramusical discourse? Such questions have rarely been considered in mainstream musicology, although they are touched on in psychological studies of topics such as categorization and schema formation—in other words, studies attempting to clarify what kind of cognitive structures or processes are implicated in an individual's experience of music (e.g., Krumhansl 1990; Leman 1995; Zbikowski 2002). Given the present state of the field, these questions do not dispose themselves to easy answers.

Attention to the distinctions and relationships among sound, experience, and discourse (such as I am proposing above) does not simplify the business of musicology. This attention does, however, help us to face some problems we have generally avoided. It also opens an important space for empirical work: What features of the sound energy can be specified in a way that permits meaningful comparison? More productive than a retreat from comparison (or indeed a headlong rush toward it) would be an acknowledgment of comparison's inevitability, and a concerted attempt to deal with the epistemological and ontological questions that inevitably arise (what kind of things are we comparing, and how do we know?).

COMPARING MUSIC, COMPARING DISCOURSE

What, if anything, does this have to do with my experience of Björk's performance at the Royal Opera House? I speculated above that the impulse to discuss and interpret this experience might be linked to an urge to fix my memory of that moment—my angst at the slow evaporation of an emotionally charged state. The reason I found this discussion and interpretation so difficult is, I suspect, connected to that very experiential intensity: verbalizing intense musical experiences is as difficult, and perhaps as futile, as verbalizing other moments of emotional intensity. And the reason I resisted—I could, after all, have said *something*—is perhaps that given the choice, allowing the moment to fade slowly is easier to bear than reducing it quickly to something known, controlled, and impotent. Another factor is revealed by my reaction to those website reviews—*Ah yes, it wasn't just me then*. In this way discourse can reassure us that intense personal reactions are to a degree shared within the community of listeners, which in turn acts as a kind of validation of that experience.

However reluctant I may be, Björk's performances and recordings are nonetheless surrounded by webs of discourse: some generated by the artist herself (in her book, in published interviews, in her lyrics); some by critics and reviewers; a great deal by fans. A sample of the latter can be observed in the form of fans' concert reviews, in which one can discern some common themes. A great deal of this informal public exchange concerns practicalities (what did she sing, what did she wear, what was the sound quality like, and so forth), while some is explicitly comparative ("Was this better than Union

Chapel??" (SC); "one of the best [concerts] I have ever experienced in my life" [JD]).[2] But the issues that seem to emerge as most important are the emotional intensity of the performance, and the sense of relationship members of the audience feel with the singer. A few examples:

> "Björk wanted to give us the full experience and succeeded beyond expectations" (SC).

> "This evening's concert was extremely powerful and emotive, I felt Björk wanted us to experience something quite different . . ." (SC).

> "I was very lucky to see Björk in concert on Sunday night. I'm having great difficulty finding words that can describe how brilliant the whole evening was" (JD).

> "Last night was definitely a religious experience" (PP).

Can this kind of discourse be compared to the theorizing about tala in Indian classical music? I suggest that it can: not that these discourses function in exactly the same way or have precisely the same effects, but that both exist in a dialectical relationship with particular musical repertories and performances. In both cases, familiarity with the discourse affects the way one experiences subsequent performances. In both cases, discourse begets discourse, metaphorically creating a field within which consensus may be reached over the meaning and importance of the musical experience.

An obvious difference between the two cases is that fans' reviews of Björk's concerts do not generally address musical theory *per se*. Such an approach is possible, and one imagines that it is realized in some contexts— perhaps by the musicians when rehearsing and recording the music, or by a minority of fans in other situations. But the dominant mode of discourse among fans is one in which the primacy of the occasion and the quality of the experience are affirmed and not transgressed. Experience and discourse cannot collapse into each other in this case.

In the case of music-theoretical discourse, such as I commented on and contributed to in *Time in Indian Music*, this collapse is all too likely. Since all music theory is discursive, it is always to some degree alienated from the experiences it describes. Much musicological writing tacitly assumes the existence of musical works, repertories, forms, styles, and systems: entities that can be described by a musicological discourse that nonetheless appears to remain outside those musical facts. Since I am arguing that these "facts" are all actually discursive artifacts, it follows that the work of musicology is not to describe musical facts but to be implicated in a wider discursive field. This implication has a purpose, and part of that purpose is the control or delimitation of musical practice and its interpretation. The illusion is that musical works and forms exist, but are only imperfectly described—in fact they exist only as imperfect descriptions, while the more immediate business of musical experience is denied serious attention.

In the one example then, fans' exchanges preserve the centrality of the experience, and refuse to collapse everything into discourse. This has the effect of strengthening the sense of community shared by listeners (and, perhaps, further estranges those who don't "get it"), but does little in terms of the production of academic knowledge: it tells us very little about why we felt as we did. In the second example, the theoretical discourse has vastly more to say about the music "itself." On the other hand (as Boretz suggests) the production of this discursive knowledge threatens to substitute itself for our musical experience, in such a way that we listen only for that which signifies the structures described by theory, and to deafen us to all other features of a given performance.

COMPARATIVE MUSICOLOGY COMPARED

How, finally, do the issues I raised above relate to the legacy of "comparative musicology"? This discipline, now remembered as ethnomusicology's forerunner, was in fact listed by Adler as one of the subdivisions of his science (his field was divided into historical and systematic approaches; comparative musicology came under the latter). It is clear from Adler's work, however, that comparison—alongside ethnography—was reserved for "other" music, that it had little to do with the serious business of "tonal art." The succeeding generation, in the form of scholars such as Carl Stumpf (1911) and Erich Moritz von Hornbostel ([1905] 1975), confirmed the place of comparative musicology on the academic map, although the comparative method was mainly implicit in their development of general analytical principles (principles that were not, of course, applied to Western art music). Where Western art music and other repertories were considered together was in compendia such as Hubert Parry's *Evolution of the Art of Music* (1896). In such works it was abundantly clear that, while all musics might be part of the same evolutionary scheme, they by no means enjoyed equal status.

We must thank Hornbostel for setting out his vision of comparative musicology with great clarity. In an article of 1905 entitled "The Problems of Comparative Musicology," he explained his debt to anatomy and linguistics and their shared reliance on an evolutionary model.

> Systematization and theory depend on comparison. In this sense all learning is comparative, and comparison is a general and not a special method. Yet one generally speaks of *comparative anatomy, comparative linguistics,*

etc. This surely infers the application of a particular approach. Medical anatomy is almost exclusively concerned with the structure of the human body; zoology . . . treats the anatomy of the individual animal species separately. . . . Now comparative anatomy presents cross-sections, so-to-speak, of the entire complex: it traces the individual organs through the entire realm of living beings and thus recognizes, for instance, vertebrae in the cephallic bones of man and a sort of eye in the outer epidermis of a leaf. The knowledge thus acquired yields new principles of classification and at the same time stimulates new and specialized investigations.

The development of linguistics followed a similar course. Initially, philology examined the individual languages separately, until comparative linguistics began to tie connecting threads. Here again the concept of evolution presented itself: it pointed to new paths and led to new groupings.
(Hornbostel [1905] 1975, 250)

Whatever Hornbostel thought he was comparing in music, they were clearly *entities*, made up of *parts* that fitted together logically and according to common structural principles. The individual entities were, moreover, exemplars of species—the logic of his own comparison with other disciplines is that comparative musicology would look for deep similarities and differences among *types* (repertories, music cultures?), and would not be concerned with the detail of individual *instances* (performances?). Another implication of this approach is that the boundaries between musical repertories would be seen as relatively stable, and hybridization a slow and difficult process, while individual music cultures were related to each other more or less closely, like languages or animal species.

It is notable that early comparative musicology offered few attempts at large-scale comparison (Carl Stumpf's *Die Anfänge der Musik* being the most obvious exception). Grand surveys and sweeping generalizations were on the whole more the preserve of music historians such as Parry. If the hope was to rewrite such evolutionary history on a more scientific basis, the aim was hardly realized before the political traumas of the 1930s shattered the academic status quo. Comparative musicology re-emerged in North America after World War II with what proved to be a brief flowering. The most ambitious and commented-upon postwar comparative project was Alan Lomax's Cantometrics (Lomax 1968), a brave attempt to correlate features of singing styles with aspects of social organization. However, if anyone in this period can be regarded as Hornbostel's intellectual heir, it must surely be his student Mieczyslaw Kolinski, who developed a series of ingenious empirical (or quasi-empirical) methods of comparative analysis, described in a series of articles published from the 1950s to the 1970s (for a bibliography see Beckwith 1982). By this time, however, the intellectual climate was changing, and as a result Kolinski's work was largely ignored, and most of the potential his methods offered was wasted.

The comparative musicology project had effectively collapsed, and part of the reason for this was the place Adler and his followers had allotted it in the greater scheme of things. Evolutionism meant that, however marginal comparative musicology may have been in Adler's scheme, it nonetheless formed an inseparable part of musicology as a whole. Back in the late nineteenth century, musicology and comparative musicology had been united in their goal of describing a comprehensive history of world music. Once social evolutionism collapsed, Western music scholarship didn't feel the need for comparative musicology, and could retreat into the insular stance from which it is still slowly emerging, while comparative musicology's marginality intensified. On the other hand, if the ideology that had given comparison its urgency was now dead, why should comparative musicologists worry any more about comparison?

Comparative musicology was gradually superseded by ethnomusicology, with its anthropological methodologies and mistrust of grand comparative schemes. Where early comparative musicologists sought to compare different musical structures on a common basis, later ethnomusicologists tried to replace this with another view, structuralist in a different sense, in which the structural principles of music related to those found in other cultural domains. As I argued above, there were two major problems with this: (1) that comparison is inescapable, and a retreat from comparison results only in irrational implicit comparisons; and (2) that structure in music is itself contingent, and needs to be recognized as a discursive artifact. From the point of view of the epistemological basis of comparison in musicology, neither nineteenth-century comparative musicology nor late-twentieth-century ethnomusicology satisfies: it can hardly be denied that a new paradigm is needed.

I have argued that comparison is inevitable in musicology. I have also argued, however, that comparison is problematic as long as we confuse experience with discourse, and as long as we do not recognize the contingency of musical "structure." What we *might* look for is a kind of metatheory that is able to take into account the contingency of the very idea of the musical structure. The underlying intention of this metatheory would be to address the relationship among *sound,* as an integral aspect of human interaction; the *experience* of producing, perceiving, and responding to that sound; and the processes by which people imagine that sound to possess structure or to convey meaning.

I have discussed and illustrated comparison on a number of different levels, in order to demonstrate the point of its inescapability: to either retreat from or rush toward comparison would be equally futile. What can we learn from comparing Indian musical practice with Western music theory? One concert with others? The way fans talk about a Björk concert with the ways musicologists analyze a classical symphony? These examples are not far removed from the everyday business of musicology, although they perhaps make the basis of comparison more explicit than is normal, or take comparison into areas not previously explored. My point is not that we need more comparison, but that we could be more conscious of what we compare, and on what basis.

It would also be a long overdue step to acknowledge that Adler was wrong to restrict comparative musicology to the study of "others," and wrong to place comparative musicology as a subdivision of musicology rather than vice versa. Establishing a rational basis for comparison in academic musical discourse may one day prove to be the critical step in the rapprochement between subdisciplines, and the development of a post-Adlerian consensus on the organization of our field.

NOTES

1   The use of the adjective *Indian* here for musical terminology is shorthand for "in various Indian languages, such as Sanskrit, Hindi, and Urdu."
2   I am very grateful to the authors of these comments, Simon Cheung, John Dalgano, and Pierre du Plessis, for permission to quote them; also to Lina/lunargirl at bjork.com for her help in contacting these reviewers.

FURTHER READING

björk.com/unity. Website: www.bjork.com
Boretz, Benjamin. 1992. Experiences with no names. *Perspectives of New Music* 30: 272–283.
Cavicchi, Daniel 1998. *Tramps like us. Music and meaning among Springsteen fans.* New York: Oxford University Press.
Clayton, Martin. 2000. *Time in Indian music. Rhythm, metre and form in North Indian rāg performance.* Oxford: Clarendon Press.
Falck, Robert, and Timothy Rice. 1982. *Cross-cultural perspectives on music. Essays in memory of Mieczyslaw Kolinski from his students, colleagues, and friends.* Toronto: University of Toronto Press.
Hornbostel, Erich Moritz von. [1905] 1975. *Hornbostel opera omnia.* Edited by Klaus Wachsmann, Dieter Christensen, and Hans-Peter Reinecke. The Hague: Martinus Nijhoff.
Hornby, Nick. [1995] 2000. *High fidelity.* London: Penguin Books.
Lakoff, George, and Mark Johnson. 1980. *Metaphors we live by.* Chicago: University of Chicago Press.
Mugglestone, Erica. 1981. Guido Adler's "The scope, method and aim of musicology" (1885): An English translation with an historico-analytical commentary. *Yearbook for Traditional Music* 13: 1–21.
Nettl, Bruno. [1973] 1992. Comparison and comparative method in ethnomusicology. Pp. 148–161 in *Ethnomusicology: History, definitions, and scope: A core collection of scholarly articles.* Edited by Kay K. Shelemay. New York: Garland.
Nettl, Bruno, and Philip Bohlman. 1991. *Comparative musicology and anthropology of music. Essays on the history of ethnomusicology.* Chicago: University of Chicago Press.
Smith, F. Joseph. 1979. *The experiencing of musical sound. Prelude to a phenomenology of music.* New York: Gordon and Breach.

CHAPTER 8

THE DESTINY OF "DIASPORA" IN ETHNOMUSICOLOGY

MARK SLOBIN

In this update of the chapter I wrote for the first edition of the present volume, I begin with a look back at how the term "diaspora" emerged and evolved, generally and in ethnomusicology, then move to a survey of its current usage and prospects for the cultural study of music. Starting in the 1970s, diaspora spilled over its traditional boundaries as designator of the far-flung fate of a small number of groups—principally the Jews—outside their homeland. The 1956 *Shorter Oxford English Dictionary* has a two-word definition, derived from biblical sources: "The Dispersion." By 1991, the *Random House Webster's College Dictionary* follows the Jews with "any group that has been dispersed outside its traditional homeland." Diaspora's meaning has expanded as part of our ever greater interest in issues of deterritorialization, displacement, dislocation. With typical Anglo-Saxon verbal flexibility, it is used as a noun ("in diaspora") or adjective ("a diaspora mentality"), and when a suffix is attached, there is no uniformity, some liking "diasporan" while others (like myself) prefer "diasporic."

The creation of a learned journal, *Diaspora*, in 1991 was a sign of recognition of the word's move into prominence. In his oft-quoted opening, the journal's founder and permanent editor says succinctly: "We use 'diaspora' provisionally to indicate our belief that the term that once described Jewish, Greek, and Armenian dispersion now shares meanings with a larger semantic domain that includes words like immigrant, expatriate, refugee, guestworker, exile community, overseas community, ethnic community" (Tololyan 1991, 4).

As suits the world we live in, diaspora studies resemble a tangled thicket of terminology more than a pruned, topiary trope. From the earliest citations of the problem, such as Tololyan's, through today, writers have acknowledged that diaspora is heavily contextual. The term has expanded so widely and penetrated so deeply into diverse discourses that we now get summary-and-survey articles to guide readers and to query its survival value in the shifting tides of "transnational studies," the phrase that is the subtitle for the journal *Diaspora* itself. By 2003, the editors of a reader titled *Theorizing Diaspora* exclaim that "the explosion in various fields . . . in work about diaspora makes it difficult to ascertain how and why the term is being deployed in critical scholarship" (Braziel and Mannur 2003, 3). By 2005, Rogers Brubaker (2005, 1) slyly suggests "a 'diaspora' diaspora—a dispersion of the meanings of the term in semantic, conceptual and disciplinary space."

Ethnomusicology had made little use of the word "diaspora" until well into the 1990s. As the academic atmosphere drifted toward a new discourse centered on individual and small-group identity, diaspora wafted into view, particularly with the appearance of James Clifford's influential article of 1994. "Diaspora" began to lead a double life. At its simplest, it merely marks the existence of an identified population that feels that it is away from its homeland, however imagined, however distant in time and space. The subtler meanings of "diaspora" acknowledge that this involves more than just demographics. Some sort of consciousness of a separation, a gap, a disjuncture must be present for the term to move beyond a formalization of census data. Once analysis moves into this territory, the terrain gets very swampy indeed. Whose consciousness? Governments, NGOs, advertisers, packagers, self-proclaimed community leaders, refugees, immigrants, third-generation heritage-seekers—and the list goes on. A phrase like Appadurai's (1996, 10) "diasporic public spheres" can cover too many different types of situations, from Hollywood movies to street protests, to be very useful. Gilroy's approach is more helpful when he distinguishes between a "spatial focus on the diaspora idea" and issues of "diaspora temporality and historicity, memory and narrativity" (Gilroy 1993, 191). Gilroy needs the distinction because there are so many black cultures and countercultures to contend with in trying to grapple with a broad concept like his "black Atlantic." More prosaically, Barnor Hesse (2000, 20) simply distinguishes between "cartographic" diaspora—the demographic fact of a displaced population—and "dispositional" diaspora, which denotes "communities that invest in imagining themselves as part of a diaspora."

What's an ethnomusicologist to do? Having previously made little use of the term "diaspora," ethnomusicology has had to absorb, modify, and partially abandon it in the compressed time-frame typical of current academic thought. When I began in the 1960s, we talked about immigrants, minorities, or ethnic groups, and worked hard at figuring out "acculturation," by now a vanished term. Finally, by the 1980s, we began to take "refugees" seriously as a special category (Reyes 1986, Baily 1984). Given the newly fluid formulation of the term, what could music contribute to both widening and deepening the discussion? By 1994, I edited a set of essays for *Diaspora* on "Music in Diaspora" (by Gage Averill, Su Zheng, Maria Teresa Velez, Anders Hammarlund, and John Baily; *Diaspora* 3(3), 4(1)). The aim was to showcase the importance of music to nonmusic diaspora scholars. My framing remarks say that "music offers a richness of methodological possibilities and points of view, opening new windows on diasporic neighborhoods," and ends by hoping that "readers of *Diaspora* can gain some sense of the value of using the filter of music to sort out some of the thorny issues of diasporic studies" (Slobin 1994, 243, 251). By 2002, Keila Diehl's multilayered study of Tibetan music in Dharamsala, India, is subtitled "music in the life of a Tibetan refugee community," but is carefully grounded with a quotation from Clifford about "diaspora" (Diehl 2002, 56).

Like all such adapted terms, "diaspora" has been at once valuable, commonplace, and misplaced in our discourse. It most certainly refuses to be standardized in its reach or its resonance. Our recent writings have matched the interdisciplinary sophistication of the term's use and have more than fulfilled my hopes that ethnomusicology could make a substantial contribution to diaspora discourse. In what follows, I tack between the recent musical and general literature to suggest just a few of the many themes arising from the current improvisations on the term.

First, let me sketch out the extremes. At one end stands the simple acceptance of the word as a given, as in the 2010 anthology that asks the question: "How can we spread 'the African diaspora' across the waffled surface of the disciplines?" (Olaniyan and Sweet 2010) Responding to this task in the music essay for the volume, Melvin L. Butler sets as his goal "to convey a sense of how ethnomusicologists have conceptualized the African Diaspora." Neither he nor the editors ever define the term around which the book is organized. The other end of the spectrum finds authors downgrading, if not outright erasing, that pesky word "diaspora." *Music and Displacement* (Levi and Scheding 2010) moves the term down to the subtitle, along with "mobilities" and "dislocations," and rarely cites it. The series editors' foreword sets up this strategy: "Migrants and minorities, refugees and exiles, *Gastarbeiter* and peoples in diaspora, all of them were victims of displacement" (Bohlman and Stokes 2010, vii). Here, diaspora seems only a limited and undefined case of a larger discourse about music and dislocation. The volume editors immediately push diaspora to the background as a way of foregrounding their replacement term: "While questions of place, migration, and diaspora may attract greater interest today among musicologists, displacement studies remains in its infancy in the sphere of music" (Scheding and Levi 2010, 1–2). So in this anthology, diaspora's application is largely relegated to specific cases—Jewish, Albanian, Irish—rather than figuring as a core concept of analysis. Even in highly specific cases that look like a diasporic music study, such as Frances Aparicio's book on salsa, the word may be firmly backgrounded, only very occasionally appearing in a sentence describing salsa as "a metaphor for race, class, and gender conflicts within the diverse Puerto Rican communities (the island and the diasporas), as well as across Latin America, the United States, and the international scene" (Aparicio 1998, 66). Here Aparicio sets multiple Puerto Rican diasporas into motion, nesting them within giant overlapping geocultural spheres stretching off into an "international scene," which seems too broad to define further. Aparicio takes little comfort in "diaspora" as a productive core term.

Between these strong strategies for dealing with diaspora lies a whole set of stimulating and often subtle case studies. They proceed not by seeing diaspora as a static entity or as political posturing, two approaches that Brubaker critiques, but rather by agreeing with him that "it may be more fruitful, and certainly more precise, to speak of diasporic stances, projects, claims, idioms, practices, and so on," all of which allow music to step forward and take its rightful role in diasporic studies. One more caveat before getting down to cases. Diaspora studies often asserts—sometimes loudly—that there's something new going on here or, in Braziel and Mannur's (2003, 3) formulation, that "diaspora offers critical spaces for thinking about the discordant movements of modernity." But when does modernity start and end? Aren't "discordant movements" always with us? Forced resettlement, migration, and other necessary conditions for declaring diaspora mark the human condition. What is, perhaps, new is the level of self-consciousness, interconnectedness, and political awareness with which populations, "homelands," nation-states, and transnational structures interact, made much easier by recent technological shifts and the chance for everyday multi-sitedness. Another novelty is the extent to which researchers themselves reveal their own feelings about diaspora, as resettled citizens and thinkers. Su Zheng, whose *Claiming Diaspora* (2010) offers a comprehensive and far-reaching analysis of how a stratified, multi-stranded immigrant group defines itself musically, declares her dual challenge: on the one hand to interpret "the diasporic sensibilities and feelings expressed through musical sound and words" among Chinese Americans, and on the other "to assert my own voice in current cultural and identity debates." She goes so far as to say "this tension is underscored in the book's structure and content" (Zheng 2010, 22).

Zheng finds three ways that "diaspora" can help to organize her overview of Chinese American music.

> In this book, I consider diaspora as a descriptive term to illustrate Chinese Americans' past and present social and cultural experiences and their structures of feelings, memories, and imaginations through rich ethnographic treatment; as an analytical category to probe the deeper meanings and implications of diasporic conditions of Chinese American expressive cultural forms and practices; as a mode of awareness for critiquing and problematizing the pervasive, often Western-centered notion of the bipolar order of the totalizing global system and fragmented local responses, and at the same time, as a vehicle for oppositional politics against the oppressive and hegemonic national narratives and cultural formations.
>
> (Ibid., 11)

This threefold move is important for Zheng to reveal the internal complexity of the group she is both studying and representing. She suggests a triangulation among the observer/group member, the other diasporic insiders, and the outside power structure, all three sharing the same analytical space. Her sense of the "descriptive" goes far beyond its usual neutrality to include insiders' states of mind. "Analytical category" might be reserved for the observer's assessment. "Mode of awareness" leaves open the question of just who is making the critique of the established order, the diasporic subjects or the analyst, as does the strong insistence on "oppositional politics," and on the idea that politics complements the oppressive narratives of the power structure.

The payoff for present purposes is that when it comes to "diaspora," Zheng explains, Chinese Americans express great ambivalence, approaching or retreating from the term, across generation, location, class, political leaning, marketing, and other variables. Whether people want to be diasporic, and if so, when, why, and how, has become much more of an issue. To cite her book title, do people want to "claim" diaspora? These days, diaspora analysis is more about agency than ascription. Every micro-study that flows into the literature has to start with a panorama, move to a long shot, and progressively zoom in to account for local affiliation and taste.

This is Gregory Dietrich's sequence as he describes "dancing the diaspora" for Indian-American youth in Chicago. There, Desis stake out a local space within the international diasporic Indian popular music scene. Going beyond a general Indian-American consciousness, they assert a "local *Indo-Chicagoan* identity" (Dietrich 2004, 104). Looking even further inward, Dietrich finds that the dancing Desis form a very mixed population of regional, ethnic, and religious backgrounds, so the practice acts as glue for a very fragmented picture. How does this work? Like the adhesive in some bonding agents, you need two components for hardening. Hindi film music offers a first-layer adhesive, since it works as a unifier among and across Indian diasporas worldwide, enjoying an aesthetic complex that is "simultaneously traditional and cosmopolitan (ibid., 106). The second ingredient is African-American hip-hop style, which provides a "coolness" through the sound and social structure of house music. It offers the added bonus of bridging, if not bonding, two stereotyped, oppressed American minority groups. Zooming in still closer to observe musical style, Dietrich says that in the local Indian sampling the "Indian" melody track is primary, while the African American-derived beat is "considered secondary and subordinate to the tune" (ibid., 110). Diasporic definition is in the details.

This last point moves Dietrich's writing into the zone of *inter-diasporic research*, perhaps best represented by work on New York's intersection of Latino and African American musicians, from the 1930s on (Glasser 1995, Guridy 2010). As Jason Stanyek (2004, 102) puts it, "African diasporic musical practice has been a particularly fertile ground not only for the development of hybrid forms but also for the enactment of intercultural collaborations." The combination of "hybrid," "intercultural," and "diasporic" in a single sentence creates a conceptual knot that is not easy to disentangle. "Not only" seems to imply that hybrid musical forms evolve as part of agency from within a "group," however defined, and should be taken for granted, whereas "intercultural" action moves creativity into in-between spaces, the original location of "hybridity" in, say, the work of Homi Bhabha. Diaspora, somewhat assumed here, acts as a kind of ground bass for this multipart improvisation. The circulation of these terms still seems uncertain, but what remains clear is that inter-diasporic action, whether collaborative, reactive, or even hostile, remains seriously under-represented in ethnomusicology.

Often, *supercultural supervision* sets the conditions or mediates the relationship between groups, as in the current "21st-century paradox that Korean food, still considered exotic by many Americans, has begun to gain widespread acceptance when wrapped in a Mexican flatbread. . . . [T]he tortilla and the toppings are a way to tell our customers that this food is O.K., that this food is American," says Mr. Ban, an entrepreneur who understands the terms of diasporic encounter (Edge 2010). Musically, the American film has long played this kind of role in imagining or erasing overlaps among diasporic populations under the watchful eye of mainstream musical representation (Slobin 2008). Or, as in the case of a Nike commercial (scored by a former Wesleyan student versed in world music), the superculture can erase group identity while celebrating competition. Here's the scenario: an African-American and Asian-American man sprint down a New York street, fighting for a taxi, to a flamenco soundtrack. Sneakers are trans-diasporic. But often enough, the mainstream cannot handle intercultural patterns, or the internal dynamics of complex communities, as Deborah Pacini Hernandez (2010, 13) points out: "Latinos' layered identities and musical practices have always rattled an industry loathe to deal with the ambiguity of hybridity."

Intra-diasporic music making really could use more attention, even among ethnomusicologists. This might require both a close-up and a panoramic lens. The latter leads to looking for linkages between scattered communities that share a short- or long-term lineage. Contacts wax and wane over time among groups nominally tied by descent or identification who may or may not stay in touch with each other on a circuit of sensibility. Multi-sited musical diaspora studies have begun to increase, from Kay Shelemay's transcontinental Syrian Jews (1998) to Tina Ramnarine's cross-Carnival study (2007). Moving to close-up focus on a tightly knit community may turn up just as much diversity. Elizabeth McAlister has zeroed in on current Haitian diasporic practices, evoking clashing structures of feeling and belief systems. She argues that looking at, or listening to, a resettled population as a fairly unified whole scants the set of choices that subgroups make to locate themselves conceptually, not geographically. Some Haitians draw on an African imaginary to think diasporically, some on Caribbean "roots," and a third group biblically: "Many Caribbean Christians conceive of their 'spiritual lineage,' their past and their future, in ways that mirror a 'classic' diasporic consciousness" (McAlister 2011, 2). So the original, Jewish, reference for the term keeps its power among Christians who are "nostalgic" for ancient Jerusalem and "envision an immanent 'return' in the future" in the New Jerusalem. This allows groups "to produce sonic indexes that create deep associations and a sense of belonging," and may even facilitate the spread of evangelicalism. Based in religious studies while doing ethnomusicology, McAlister sees music as "a sonic compass pointing out cosmic directionalities," offering a "spatial valence" and what Paul C. Johnson calls a "diasporic horizon" (cited in ibid., 5). She readily draws on Brubaker's idea that "to be diasporic" is part of "an idiom, a stance, or claim" (ibid.) rather than just part of a statistical, demographic, geographic, or historical situation.

Some Haitians reference a Kongo background for their Rara practices, whether the celebration is in Haiti or Brooklyn, a situation of doubled diaspora. By cutting back the parts of their music that belong to Voudou practice, Haitians abroad open up multiple possibilities of orientation towards Africa and the Caribbean. Christians, however, who form perhaps one-third of the Haitian diaspora, range much more eclectically, drawing on Christian music that may be available from Francophone Africa, Europe,

Canada, and the Antilles. The resulting mix is "a hybrid of Haitian, French, and American influences" (ibid., 14). This does not mean they give up their strong grounding in Haitianness, since they stay within compatriot Christian congregations and use the Creole language. So McAlister thinks they live "simultaneously in two imagined diasporas—one of which might be described as ethnic and one religious," where music offers the multiplicity that sonic sources provide so generously. McAlister's sense of a split diaspora, with each segment seeing different "ethnic horizons," plays differently when more than one diaspora share a single national space, as described by Jocelyne Guilbault for Trinidad and Tobago (Guilbault 2005). "Discrepant diasporas" in that island region, along with the internal split between Afro-Trinidadian and Indo-Trinidadian communities, may provoke a narrowing, rather than a widening, in the service of a "national" music that moves away from the big picture of multiplicity.

Spreading the storyline out over time only opens up more extended vistas of diasporic development. A 2010 special issue of *Journal of American Music* devoted to the Irish takes analysis from the 1850s to the 2000s. Among immigrants who become "ethnic groups," in Western societies, what was once the "host country" (if not always hospitable) becomes a kind of "homeland" of the music as it evolves in emigration. This story is too well known to need retelling here, but two pivotal issues stand out: the importance of key activists who collect and distribute the music within the community, and that of commercial recording companies which rather arbitrarily archive and spread certain players and styles, who then become incredibly influential. The collecting work first of Boston's William Bradbury Ryan (1880s) and of his emulator in Chicago, Francis O'Neill, showed how tenacious early-generation emigrants can be in sustaining what the Irish call *duchlas*, a word which has "a multiplicity of interrelated meanings, from place, heritage, and homeland, to patrimony and inheritance" (Collins 2010, 492). What we see today as "heritage" efforts by later-generation communities have strong roots in diasporic consciousness, even if sentiment ebbs and flows over the decades.

Recording spanned that gap by offering people tangible, audible proof of cultural continuity, even for the folks "back home" in the country of origin. The 1920s New York Irish discs, particularly of Michael Coleman, sparked a surge of new interest in old tunes in Ireland at a critical historical juncture there, influencing regional and national style in all parameters, from ornamentation to instrumentation. An accidental evolution ends up looking overdetermined. Other resonance patterns from studio sounds might argue for a more indeterminate set of effects. Ted McGraw (2010) describes how the McNulty Family, Irish-American vaudeville headliners from the 1930s to the 1950s, developed a diasporic style that ended up shaping the music of

Newfoundland, through a single arrangement they happened to make of a local poet's lyrics. The McNulty sound dominated Newfoundland's musical profile for the next couple of decades, according to McGraw. So musically, a diaspora can help to create a homeland for others.

The influence of *diasporic musical return* comes either through recordings or in person. Chris Waterman's study (1990) of how Nigerian returnees from the Western hemisphere surprisingly reconfigured "African" popular music points to the unpredictability of musical flow-cycles. Despite Waterman's pioneering work, research on returnees, as a special branch of music studies, has yet to take hold as a topic, even as the general subject is finding its place in diaspora studies. On Takeyuki Tsuda's account, ethnic return migration is no simple matter, since the reverse immigrants might well create a new ethnic minority rather than integrating into the "homeland" they think they are coming back to. If they feel rejected in the land of origin, they end up being more attached to the country they came from. Homeland might not be "home," even musically: "We find Japanese Brazilians dancing samba (often for the first time) in their ethnic homeland of Japan and German *Aussiedeler* singing Russian songs in Germany" (Tsuda 2009, 335).

Music can return to putative homelands even without whole communities shifting. A particularly complex pattern of recirculation marks the Jewish-based system called "klezmer." Its core repertoire emerged from diasporic Eastern European Jewish life, flourished in another diaspora in the United States from the 1880s through the 1930s, was largely exterminated in Europe by Nazism and Stalinism, made a big comeback in North America, starting in the mid-1970s, and returned to Europe as an American import in the 1990s. It became a "heritage" music for new Jewish immigrants coming from Eastern Europe to Germany, in yet another diaspora. Complicating the picture is the fact that "klezmer" as we know it today had not flourished in Germany before 1945. Meanwhile, in Israel, a diaspora that became a homeland, "klezmer" as a concept was not a familiar construct. It has only recently appeared there, as an Americanism. In such a situation, diaspora carries little analytical weight as a term of choice except when redefined imaginatively. For a musician like Michael Alpert, a Jewish-American from Los Angeles playing Eastern European melodies in Berlin, "homeland" is multiply meaningful. The music itself becomes a kind of homeland to the musician's compounded sense of diaspora. In liner notes to Brave Old World's album *Beyond the Pale*, Alpert says: "In 1993, Germany is one of the very few countries where you can make a living playing Jewish music. But for whom . . .?" "So play me a sweet Diaspora song, with a longing that's pure," is a line from the song "Berlin 1990" that made it to Germany's hit charts.

Sonic diaspora, rather than the motion of displaced people or traveling musicians, introduces further levels of complexity. If homeland-diaspora music circulation flows largely through media, a greater range of practice and attitudes can arise. Emerging work on African hip-hop (Charry 2011) pushes the issue into new territory. No single interpretation of rap as diasporic or "African" looks stable across the stretch of the continent, since the situation varies locally, generationally, aesthetically and politically. Young people's intensive involvement with American-based music is highly cosmopolitan, but at the same time insular, since African hip-hop has not yet achieved serious visibility in the U.S. or elsewhere. Diasporic domination also marks the Tamil hip-hop scene, in which Malaysian Tamil artists have become the source of the style, distributed both through media channels and through invited touring (Aaron Paige, personal communication). Any given situation of diasporic music flow can be simultaneously embodied and schizophonic.

Beyond recordings, concert circuits, and ethnic returnees, musical instruments flow in a *material-culture diaspora.* The *mbira,* the gamelan, the digeridu, the *djembe,* and other extremely popular objects diffuse from homelands around the globe. While diasporic musicians might direct this instrument traffic as mediators or gatekeepers, the very objects themselves take unexpected twists and turns, as they end up in the hands of outsiders. Some of my graduate students have worked on this theme, with different findings. Looking at the *mbira*-based African scene in the U.S., Nina Rubin found flashpoints between the ideas of diasporic Zimbabweans and those of the "Americans" who flock to workshops. The inexorable rise of the *djembe* and other drumming-circle tools came with similar negotiations among visiting or long-term resident Africans and non-African enthusiasts, as described, for example, in the memoirs of the foundational figure Babatunde Olatunji (2005). The didgeridu, in Peter Hadley's comprehensive dissertation study, lies at the far end of the spectrum, as its evolution abroad has rarely been pushed or shaped by the Aboriginal Australian population from whom it originates—there just isn't a diasporic community of aboriginal players or marketers. Nearby on this continuum lie the many gamelans of the United Kingdom, chronicled by Maria Mendonça (2002), which thrive in settings from prisons to schools to physical rehab sites, all without a diasporic Indonesian presence. Can we speak of the diaspora of an instrument? "Dispersal" or "dispersion," from exactly the same origins, might fill the bill, though each term has its own strengths and weaknesses.

In short, although we are dealing with musical processes as old as humankind, there's no way around the emergence of new and sometimes unprecedented patterns of flow of musical materials, and I haven't even touched on the *Internet as diasporic agent* (e.g. Lundberg 2003). In this short chapter, I have not been able to offer maximal geographic coverage. Many world diasporas receive little ethnomusicological attention as yet, and there remain gray zones in definitions of, say, refugee music, or who counts as an immigrant. The International Folk Music Council's Study Group on Music and Minorities keeps its name, suitably sweeping a wide variety of situations, some diasporic, others not, under its colorful carpet. And local usages vary considerably. For example, my contacts say that in Austria "diaspora" remains a common and helpful term for ethnomusicologists, whereas in Sweden it has never had much purchase.

To what extent "diaspora" will continue to satisfy the need for a cover-all term remains an open question. There are precedents for the slippage of once-steady terms, as Stuart Hall (2000, 209) noted for "multiculturalism," also implicating "diaspora": Wrapping up an entire volume devoted to the term, Hall can't help allowing that "like other related terms—for example, 'race,' ethnicity, identity, diaspora—multiculturalism is now so discursively entangled that it can only be used 'under erasure.'" Perhaps everything is sliding away from these sorts of terms towards a recognition of new forms of "transnational citizenship," as Nicholas van Hear (1998) suggests. Robin Cohen (also 1998) disagrees, saying that, yes, we need "new conceptual maps and fresh case studies," and that "the old idea of 'diaspora' may provide this framework." On whatever terms, ethnomusicologists have contributed many of the freshest studies and most stimulating guides to this unsettled discourse.

FURTHER READING

Baily, John, and Michael Collyer. 2006. Introduction and special issue, Music and migration. *Journal of Ethnic and Migration Studies* 32(2).

Diehl, Keila. 2002. *Echoes from Dharamsala: Music in the life of a Tibetan refugee community.* Berkeley and Los Angeles: University of California Press.

Guilbault, Jocelyne. 2005. Audible entanglements: Nation and diasporas in Trinidad's calypso music scene. *Small Axe* 9(1): 40–63.

Levi, E., and F. Scheding, eds. 2010. *Music and displacement: Diasporas, mobilities, and dislocations in Europe and beyond.* Lanham, MD: Scarecrow Press.

Pacini Hernandez, Deborah. 2010. *Oye como va: Hybridity and identity in Latino popular music.* Philadelphia: Temple University Press.

Ramnarine, Tina. 2007. *Beautiful cosmos: Performance and belonging in the Caribbean diaspora.* London: Pluto Press.

Shelemay, Kay Kaufman. 2006 [published 2011]. Ethiopian musical invention in diaspora: A tale of three musicians. *Diaspora* 15 (2/3): 303–320.

Slobin, Mark. 1994. Music in diaspora: The view from Euro-America. *Diaspora* 3(3): 234–252.

Slobin, Mark. 2001. *Fiddler on the move: Exploring the klezmer world.* New York: Oxford University Press.

Turino, Thomas, and James Lea. 2004. *Identity and the arts in diaspora communities.* Warren, MI: Harmonie Park Press.

Zheng, Su. 2009. *Claiming diaspora: Music, transnationalism, and cultural politics in Asian/Chinese America.* New York: Oxford University Press.

CHAPTER 9

GLOBALIZATION AND THE POLITICS OF WORLD MUSIC

MARTIN STOKES

The expression "World Music" acquired currency in Europe and North America after a meeting in 1987 of concert promoters, journalists, musicians, and independent record company owners in The Empress of Russia, a pub in Islington, London. "We created a handle for something that was already there, but needed to be identified," Ben Mandelson, one of those present, observed recently (Cottrell 2010, 62). By the early 1990s, it was a major media phenomenon, embraced by the mainstream recording indutry, and attracting journalistic celebration and academic critique in equal measure. The "needs" in question were primarily those of marketing and distribution. But the label was also intended to bind together, again in Ben Mandelson's words, "a bunch of people who were already friends, already working on things that they loved and supported" (Cottrell 2010, 63).

Was something identifiable already there? Or was that something summoned into existence by the term? It is by no means easy to say. Philip Sweeney, a prominent music journalist, was one of the first to offer a definition of the field for consumers in need of guidance:

> Broadly speaking, I have focused on music which is popular in the sense that it is not art or classical music, is in regular use by ordinary people to dance to, is listened to via radio or cassette, is perhaps performed, and is not artificially preserved folklore . . . I have also attempted to remove the great body of music belonging to Anglo-American dominated pop and

> rock mainstream, and the music of those local artists worldwide who
> simply recreate this style, and to describe what is left.
>
> (Sweeney 1991, ix–x)

Philip Sweeney's confident definitions were very much of their moment. If one were to survey the global mediascape, Anglo-American pop and rock, "art" and "classical" music, and "artificially preserved folklore" could all be stripped away. The music of the world's "ordinary people" would then be plain to see. The benefits were enticing: the discovery of new musical pleasures, a global democratization of musical taste. Sweeney's optimism echoed that of the globalization theorists of the time. Barriers to the circulation of people, things, and ideas were being removed. A millennial mood was in the air. History itself, some claimed, had come to an end. Politics was now a matter of managing "flows" between nation-states; the trickle-down of wealth and creativity unleashed in this way would sort out questions of distribution and social justice *within* the nation-state.

In retrospect it is not hard to link the transformations of the late 1980s, today labeled "globalization," and the disasters of the first decade of the twenty-first century: major wars in the Middle East, genocidal ethnic conflict in Africa, epidemic financial crises in the industrial heartlands. But these had scarcely been anticipated. And there was much to distract the intelligentsia at that moment. Globalization provoked radical rethinking in academic fields in which the nation-state and the dominance of Europe had previously been unquestioned: literature, history, sociology, politics. A critique of globalization eventually developed, however, and, along with it, a critique of world music. Three elements of this critique concern me in what follows: cultural imperialism, hybridity, and authenticity.

Firstly, cultural imperialism. Sweeney's anxiety about the domination of "Anglo-American pop" was shared by many at the time under the general rubric of the "cultural imperialism hypothesis." Before the Web and file sharing fundamentally altered the picture in the Western world, a handful of major recording companies did indeed dominate the musical landscape: Time-Warner, Thorn-EMI, Bertelsmann, Sony, PolyGram and Matsushita ("the majors"). In the mid-1990s, the International Federation for Phonographic Industries estimated that the majors controlled approximately 80–90 per cent of the sales of (legally) recorded music worldwide. Their products—then, Madonna, Michael Jackson, George Michael and others—were globally ubiquitous. There were few parts of the world that had not, even then, produced their own versions of rock, country music, rap, and hip-hop. On the face of it, the "cultural imperialism hypothesis," which suggested that wealthy, Western-based, multinational corporations control global markets and global musical tastes, had much to recommend it.

But there are problems with this way of looking at things. It assumes a simple causal linkage between technologies of sound reproduction, musical styles ("the Anglo-American mainstream"), and a variety of political and aesthetic effects ("homogeneous" music, "passive" consumers, the quasi-colonial "domination" of media corporations). These linkages are, surely, complex and many-stranded; they need to be observed and figured out, rather than assumed, in a given situation. Rock, for example, thrived in situations, for instance in Eastern Europe during the Cold War, where recordings were extremely hard to come by. This is a situation that can hardly be characterized in terms of passive consumption. And it can rarely be characterized purely in terms of the circulation of a particular form of mediation, the sound recording. Musical style in the modern world travels along other vectors: with people via aural/oral transmission, with instruments and technologies, and with social institutions that connect people globally—sport, religion, political organizations, and so forth.

Far from imposing a cultural hegemony, as the cultural imperialism hypothesis suggests, the majors were often obliged to respond to the lead of smaller, independent companies. In Europe, following the punk rock explosion in the 1970s, the independents became highly responsive to new confluences of youth, black and migrant culture in European and American cities. World music styles such as *rai*, a North African migrant music, were shaped and nurtured by independent recording companies, like the French label Barcley. PolyGram bought Barcley in 1978, and reaped the benefits when a *rai* album, Khaled's *Didi* of 1992, became an unexpected hit and sold in significant numbers across Europe. Khaled's success had a major impact on *rai* production in North Africa, accelerating transformations already under way. A genre formerly dominated by women (like Cheikha Remitti) gradually became a male-dominated genre. Sounds earlier engineered and marketed with a North African audience in mind were fused with a variety of transatlantic black styles, and oriented to a broad European and American audience. But PolyGram would not have enjoyed this success without Barcley's cultivation of various subcultural and migrant markets in France. *Rai* does not make much sense in terms of, at least, the conventional outlines of the cultural imperialism hypothesis. One might, equally, describe *rai* as a kind of countercultural imperialism, as "globalization from below."

The cultural imperialism hypothesis also assumes a rather simple line separating "Anglo-American dominated pop and rock" from the rest. Historically speaking, things are far more complicated. "Anglo-American dominated pop and rock" has always incorporated a variety of African and Latin elements, meaning that its musical effects, when "returned" to Africa and the Latin American world, have been complex and varied. "Afropop," a term referring to practices deriving from popular genres like *chimurenga* in

Zimbabwe, *m'blax* in Senegal, *mbaqanga* in South Africa, *jújù* and *highlife* in Nigeria, *makossa* and *bikutsi* in Cameroon, owes its distinctive patterns and textures to the meeting of various Afro-Cuban musics, well known because of their popularity amongst French colonial elites in West and Central Africa, with the traditional interlocking instrumental practices of the region. François ("Franco") Luambo Makiadi's Zairean *rumba*, forged in the 1950s, was widely imitated across the continent in subsequent decades as a result of political identification with both Cuba (for its revolution) and Zaire (for its glamour and modernity). "Mainstream Anglo-American" pop and rock has circulated in Africa, then, on ground that had already been transformed by encounters connecting Africa and New World musical practice, encounters stretching back over significant periods of time.

Secondly, hybridity. Let us turn, once again, to Philip Sweeney. In an article in *The Independent* on July 9, 1992 ("The Word Made Flesh"), Sweeney suggested we might understand World music

> as a sort of new mutated "First World" genre, a conscious fusion of traditional "Third World" forms with elements of Anglo-American rock and jazz. "I play world music," Salif Keita told me last year, "not African music." The new crossover/fusion area of music-making is currently booming, typified by the Brussels-based Belgian-Zairean female quintet Zap Mama, whose *a cappella* arrangements mixing European, Central African pygmy, Zulu and Arab melodies, among other things, have made them one of the hottest attractions at this summer's European festivals.

World music is defined here in terms of fusion, crossover, and the cosmopolitanism of musicians like Salif Keita. One must subject these terms, which simultaneously suggest and conceal struggles, accommodations, and distinctions, to scrutiny. Keita had followed a number of West African musicians to Paris, notably Manu Dibango, today remembered by many as the inventor of "Afrobeat." In a poignant memoir, Dibango describes the difficulties of life as an African musician in Paris in the 1950s, and, later, America. Dibango struggled with conflicting expectations and demands on his identity. In France he was expected to behave, musically, as a conduit for jazz, i.e. black American culture. In America, he was expected to behave, musically, as an African; back in Cameroon, it was his European and American experience that mattered. "I am a divided man," he notes plaintively at the outset of his autobiography (1994, 2), but he eventually came to regard with an amused detachment the way Americans and Europeans interpreted his Africanness. Keita's confident self-identification as a "world musician" strikes a different and more confident tone. But it is also, one feels, shadowed by the doubts and anxieties Dibango describes in his memoir, and the very real struggles faced by countless African migrants in

Europe and America's cities today. Cosmopolitans fashion their own world. Migrants have to fit into worlds made by other people, as anthropologist Anna Tsing once observed (Tsing 2002). "Crossover/fusion" involves power relations that must always be carefully considered.

Zap Mama, the well-known "Brussels-based Belgian-Zairean female quintet" led by Marie Daulne, provides Sweeney with his second example of "crossover/fusion." Daulne was born in Zaire, of a Belgian father and Zairean mother, and grew up in Belgium. Following Zap Mama's initial success, she returned to Congo to learn traditional central African vocal techniques. After extensive travels, and a stay in New York, she returned to Belgium. Her story is reminiscent of Manu Dibango's, though her struggles with her identity led in different directions. Manu Dibango seems ultimately to have come to understand his Africanness as a position, or stance, in a complex field of musical representations. Daulne, on the other hand, seems to have been animated by a more active fantasy of Africanness in music, one significantly shaped by ethnographic recordings. The track "Babenzélé," for example, on *Adventures in Afropea* of 1993, closely mimics the densely layered interlocking of voices, whistles, and hand clapping on Simha Arom's 1966 ethnographic recording, made among the Babenzélé, in the Central African Republic. Arom's Central African recordings sparked other musical fantasies of the African rain forest, many of which, as Steven Feld has suggested, respond as much to one another as to the Arom "original"—a process he describes as "schizophonic mimesis" (Feld 2000).

For all of its studied fidelity to the Arom recording, the Zap Mama version contains a variety of subtly added elements. The women's voices, for example, provide a sparse harmonic underpinning, in the form of an oscillation of tonic and dominant seventh chords throughout. Such combinations of the musical values of European a cappella singing and African vocal technique prompt Sweeney to characterize their music as "hybrid." The term assumes the irreducible *difference* of the hybridized elements. This can be an unhelpful way of conceptualizing relationships between stylistic elements. As we have already noted with regard to African and Western pop, the connections are often more salient than the differences. "Anglo-American pop" comprises densely compacted African, Latin, and Old World European folk elements. "African" musical practices are of similarly diverse origins, comprising, amongst other things, European elements that go back to the earliest days of slavery, colonialism, and missionary activity. Every element of a hybridized style is itself a hybrid, a bricolage of previous encounters, assimilations, and blendings.

Such formulations of hybridity also suggest anxiety about identity in a world increasingly shaped by movement and migration. This anxiety surfaces with particular force in the cities of the industrialized world, particularly those that have started to label themselves, with a certain degree of self-congratulation, as "global cities." Migrancy has supplied many of the industrial world's cities with a cheap and increasingly ethnicized supply of labor. The interaction of migrant groups has produced vigorous new forms of literature, cinema, music, and cuisine. "Hyphenated identities"—Franco-Maghrebi, "Newyorican," Irish-American, British-Asian and so forth—are no longer seen by most people as signs of a problem, an inability to be fully one thing or another. Quite the reverse: they signify kinds of empowerment, repertoires of cosmopolitanism. And "migrant chic" enables city managers to celebrate diversity and cultural dynamism, and thus market their city in an increasingly competitive global environment.

But this celebratory picture is hard to sustain. Globalization has involved the fragmentation of an increasingly casualized urban workforce, and desperate competition for niches within it. The growth of the service sector at the expense of heavy industry has entailed conflicts between white and migrant working classes, between men and women. Even as migrancy is celebrated as a sign of globalized, postmodern cultural vitality, new tensions are coming into play. These spill over into protest, rioting, violence, a politics of the street that cannot easily be subsumed by bureaucratic multicultur-alism: the Rushdie affair of 1989, the Solingen arson attacks in 1993, the Parisian *banlieue* riots of 2005. Multilingual migrant rap and hip-hop scenes across northwestern Europe suggest complex new social fault lines and fractures along lines of race, gender, and sexuality. To describe them as "hybrid" is to obscure their politics.

Thirdly, authenticity. Authenticity and hybridity may seem opposed, but they are conceptually linked. Hybridity, understood as a mixing of styles, entails the prior existence of "unmixed" styles, the basic elements of the mix. The idea of African-American music, for instance, involves certain assumptions about its "Africanness," about identifiably authentic "African" elements in genres as diverse as jazz, blues, and hip-hop. Indeed, a great deal of the talk that has surrounded world music keeps a deeply fantasized notion of an authentic "Africa" very firmly in place. Rock doyen and impresario Peter Gabriel, for example, described his attraction to African music in Philip Sweeney's volume in the following terms:

> It was the choir I was drawn to initially—by Ladysmith Black Mambazo and others with their close kinship to Gospel and their blend of spirituality and sensuality at the same time . . . the spirituality of South African music appealed especially. . . . One of the most striking things about West African percussion is the fluidity of the rhythms. This is partly due to the actual equipment used. The little drumsticks that Senegalese drummers like Doudou N'Diaye use are often freshly cut from the tree, so they're much more flexible than western drumsticks. They're also much shorter.

The result is a more liquid tone, somewhere between a hand and a western drumstick in sound.

(Sweeney 1991, 2)

For Gabriel, Africa is an antidote to the modern West, with its categorical and rigid distinctions between spirituality and sensuality, the body and technology, nature and culture. A musical practice that escapes, or has never known, these binary oppositions can also—by extension—be valued for its "fluidity," "flexibility," and "liquidity." (The resonance of these terms with characterizations of capital and labor in the context of globalization is important to note.) The West offers an alternative: a drumstick or a hand. Africa provides the space in between. Such ways of understanding African music have a long history. They took shape in the circulation of black popular musical styles between America, Europe, and South Africa in the last decades of the nineteenth century. They are also entangled with the broader history of European orientalism. "Others," whether "African" or "Oriental," tend to be characterized in terms that point to the uniqueness of Europe's modernity (including the things it is deemed, in a complex compensatory maneuver, to lack). African music has then habitually been understood in terms of what it is *not*, and such understandings have evolved in a complex field of representations over a considerable period of time. The more elusive the "Africanness" of African music has proved, the more energetically it seems to have been pursued and fetishized.

World music discourse in the late 1980s and early 1990s has, then, been characterized as the everyday popular music of people obscured (because colonized) by the Anglo-American mainstream, as a music of migrancy and hybridity, and as the bearer of a kind of authenticity, an antidote to Western modernity. I have noted, in passing, some of the problems with these characterizations, drawing on the work of a variety of scholars in popular music studies and ethnomusicology. Such criticisms accumulated, I would argue, in response to a growing anxiety with the broader political and technological transformations associated with the term "globalization" in the late 1980s and early 1990s, an anxiety that subsequently took the form of a serious and critical investigation of world music aesthetics, and the various environments (studios, festivals, radio stations) in which world music was produced.

Does world music really deserve this kind of criticism? Were its consequences really so dire? The world music phenomenon may have perpetuated a naive and romanticized understanding of parts of the world the West needs to understand more critically. It may have empowered certain members of certain communities, and silenced others. It may, in some contexts, have demonstrably deepened cultural dependence upon Western markets and the tastes of Western consumers. Multiculturalism may often have reduced rich musical traditions to mute tokens of otherness, to be noticed administratively or exploited commercially, but not engaged in meaningful, or lasting, dialogue. These are some of the problems associated with the world music phenomenon, and it is no bad thing to draw attention to them.

But the diversity of intellectual, creative and commercial purposes articulated by the world music phenomenon must also be recognized. Connections have been made, ideas exchanged, pleasures gained, and everyday music making in local contexts changed in fundamental ways. Cultural creativity on the margins of our own societies, previously invisible and inaudible, has been recognized outside of those margins; we have started to *hear* our social environment more inclusively. The media interest in world music in the 1980s created an atmosphere of normalcy, of everydayness regarding unfamiliar music from around the world, on which ethnomusicology has thrived. And this may yet—despite the inevitable backlash against multiculturalism—succeed in making the cultural study of music, still heavily focused on the West, the cultural study of *all* music.

Like globalization, the topic of world music—so intricately entangled with it—has polarized critical opinions. A broader historical perspective suggests that this is no new thing. One might, in conclusion, reflect briefly on the ways in which contemporary discussions of world music echo those of a much earlier period. In an early period of diplomatic and commercial overtures to the Ottoman court, early in the seventeenth century, French scholars encountered what was, for them, a radically different kind of music. Charles Perrault joined others, later in that century, in wondering about the connections between what they were hearing and the music of the ancient (biblical and Greek) world that they knew from scholarship. His own musing, on a wide range of "parallels" between the ancient and modern world, took the form of an imagined debate between three characters: the Abbot, representing the church, the President, representing academia, and the Chevalier, representing nobility. Perrault published the various volumes of his *Parallèle des Anciens et des Modernes* (*Parallel between Ancients and Moderns*) between1688 and 1692. One of the later volumes discusses music along with astronomy, geography, navigation, war, philosophy, and medicine.

In this particular conversation, the Abbot takes the lead. He starts with a provocative observation: we think we know music, but actually know very little about music as the term is understood by most of the world. "The music of the Ancients is still today the music of all the earth," he notes, "except for one part of Europe . . .", i.e., our own. The Abbot has heard stories about this "ancient" music, encountered at events and soirées in the French embassy in Constantinople. And they had got him wondering. When the French played their favorite opera overtures, "the Turks could not stand it, considering the mixture of parts, to which they were not accustomed (i.e. polyphony), to be a chaotic racket." Musical values, he thinks, might be relative, and not absolute. His companions are momentarily dumbstruck. The Abbot continues. Like the Ancients, the Orientals have only cultivated monophony. As a result, he says, they have developed a level of sensitivity to tuning and temperament that we have lost.

Finally the President manages to splutter a response. The Germans, he observes, have invented keyboards in which the "irregularities" of the current keyboard tunings could be remedied by the addition of extra keys, to distinguish a D sharp from an E flat, and so forth. Surely our lack of sensitivity in this regard, a necessary casualty of musical progress, can be remedied by German technology? But the Abbot presses on. Oriental musicians must be regarded, in certain respects, not only as more sensitive, but, he suggests, as more skillful than ours. When our violinists played their favorite tunes, the "Persian" musician at court could play them back instantly. ("Persians," from various parts of today's Central Asia, represented the dominant musical stratum in the Ottoman court in this period.) Challenged in return, the French violinist could manage "no more than four notes" of the tune the Persian musician played.

The Abbot, Voltaire-like, playfully provokes his companions with suggestions that, from a certain perspective at least, it might be we who lack civilization, not they. He acknowledges, in passing, the areas in which Western musicians enjoy superiority—in technology, in music literacy, in multipart polyphony. But he does so with an equivocation that seems calculated to provoke his colleagues. Every defense mounted in favor of the West by the President elicits a fresh line of argument from the Abbot about the things "they" can do that "we" cannot. In the end, the Chevalier attempts to steer the conversation onto less contentious ground. Hadn't Petis de la Croix, sent to study this music by the King, succeeded in learning this music tolerably well? Surely this indicates that these differences can be overcome? The Abbot is suddenly struck by another flight of fancy. Having learned the music, "it would be nice to mix some bits of it into the Fêtes and Divertissements that His Majesty gave at his Court; to do a scene, for example, where the singers, dressed as Turks and playing the same instruments that are played in Constantinople, would sing the same songs and dance the same dances as are sung and danced before the Grand Seigneur, and another scene where the musicians would sing the same songs that are sung before the Sophi of Persia or the Grand Moghul." The idea intrigues the President, who muses that it would be like being "transported in a single moment to all the different parts of the world."

Many aspects of the contemporary politics of world music seem to be prefigured in this seventeenth-century exchange. Difference, in Perrault's

Parallèle, is ultimately imagined in the service of royal power, i.e., the global status quo. But until then, the conversation is playful and unsettled. No real conclusions seem to be drawn. Aesthetic values may be relative, and the problems with our own musical practices may now be more clearly grasped. But the practical consequences of these insights for Perrault's protagonists, and, arguably, for us today, are far from clear. Will technology-driven initiatives provide answers, or create more problems? Does exchange bring people closer, or keep them in their place? Can knowledge be shared equitably, or will it inevitably generate competition and rivalry? Our questions, today, are expressed in terms of democracy, mutuality, and sustainability, concerns that play out in discussions of world music as in broader discussions of globalization. They took shape at the beginning of the European Enlightenment, and show no signs of losing their force today.

FURTHER READING

Cottrell, Stephen. 2010. An interview with Ben Mandelson. *Ethnomusicology Forum* 19(1): 57–68.

Dibango, Manu. 1994. *Three kilos of coffee: An autobiography*. Chicago: University of Chicago Press.

Erlmann, Veit. 1999. *Music, modernity, and the global imagination: South Africa and the West*. Oxford: Oxford University Press.

Feld, Steven. 2000. The poetics and politics of Pygmy Pop. Pp 280–304 in *Western music and its others: Difference, representation and appropriation in music*. Edited by Georgina Born and David Hesmondhalgh. Berkeley: University of California Press.

Frith, Simon. 2000. The discourse of world music. Pp. 305–322 in *Western music and its others: Difference, representation and appropriation in music*. Edited by Georgina Born and David Hesmondhalgh. Berkeley: University of California Press.

Gross, Jane, David McMurray, and Ted Swedenburg. 2003. Arab noise and Ramadan nights: Rai, rap and Franco-Magrebi Identities. Pp. 198–230 in *The anthropology of globalization: A reader*. Edited by Jonathan Inda and Renato Rosaldo. Oxford: Blackwell.

Shain, Richard. 2009. The Re(public) of salsa: Afro-Cuban music in fin-de-siècle Dakar. *Africa* 79(2), 186–206.

Slobin, Mark. 1993. *Subcultural Sounds: Micromusics of the West*. Hanover, NH: Wesleyan University Press.

Sweeney, Philip. 1991. *Virgin directory of world music*. London: Virgin.

Taylor, Timothy. 1997. *Global pop: World music, world markets*. London: Routledge.

Tsing, Anna. 2002. Conclusion: The global situation. Pp. 453–482 in *The anthropology of globalization: A reader*. Edited by Jonathan Inda and Renato Rosaldo. Oxford: Blackwell.

Turino, Thomas. 2000. *Nationalists, cosmopolitans, and popular music in Zimbabwe*. Chicago: Chicago University Press.

CHAPTER 10

CONTESTING DIFFERENCE
A Critique of Africanist Ethnomusicology

KOFI AGAWU

Difference may well be *the* sign of our times. In the United States, for example, feminist theories seeking to negotiate the problematic of gender, to come to terms with various forms of essentialism, or to counter real-world discrimination, have placed difference firmly on the critical agenda. Gay and lesbian studies, too, are centrally concerned with alternative episte-mologies, and with resisting coarse constructions of difference that may prove to be socio-politically disadvantageous to their communities. And perhaps most notably, race as a category permeates a good deal of human-istic discourse, providing innumerable opportunities for a wide range of reflection upon difference. There are, as is to be expected, many points of divergence, but if we had to isolate one overriding concern, it might well be the attempt, in Gayatri Spivak's words, to undermine "the story of the straight, white, Judeo-Christian, heterosexual man of property as the ethical universal" (Spivak with Rooney 1989, 146). Discussion of difference among music scholars is already under way, inspired in part by a number of inter-disciplinary conversations, and in part by a widely shared feeling that only a few of music's many contexts have been given adequate scholarly attention (e.g., Solie 1993; Brett, Wood, and Thomas 1994; Born and Hesmondhalgh 2000; Radano and Bohlman 2000). It is perhaps a little surprising that such discussion is not more prominent in Africanist ethnomusicology, a field that regularly traffics in difference. Although Martin Stokes characterizes the 1990s as a period in which the larger discipline of ethnomusicology "was absorbed by the question of difference, particularly in relation to matters of ethnicity, nation, race, gender and sexuality" (Stokes 2001, 388), signs of this absorption and subsequent reflection are not prominent in the subfield of Africanist ethnomusicology. Indeed, Christopher Waterman proffered an opposing view in 1991, claiming that "the portrayal of similarity and difference" is a subject "infrequently discussed" in Africanist ethnomusicology (Waterman 1991, 179). Waterman was well aware that ethnomusicology had always drawn *implicitly* on notions of difference, distance, and alterity. Explicit, open, and critical discussion of such notions was, however, strangely muted.

The purpose of this chapter is to develop a critique of notions of difference manifest in writings on African music. I proceed in three stages. First, I quote and comment upon a handful of thematizations of difference in Africanist ethnomusicology. Then I ask whether difference is "real." Finally, I take an explicitly political stance in urging a resistance to difference.

THEMATIZING DIFFERENCE

Difference is regularly invoked by ethnomusicologists. Erich von Hornbostel, for example, opened his seminal 1928 article on "African Negro Music" with the question "What is African music like as compared to our own?" His brief answer was, "African and (modern) European music are constructed on *entirely different principles*" (my emphasis). Why Hornbostel chose to emphasize differences over similarities, instead of granting similarities alongside differences, probably had less to do with the comparative method as such than with an inherited tradition of European representations of others. Perhaps Hegel's ghost was hovering over Hornbostel's pages, reminding the comparative musicologist of words written a century earlier: "[The African character] is difficult to comprehend, because it is so totally different from our own culture, and so remote and alien in relation to our own mode of consciousness" (Hegel [1822–28] [1975], cited in Eze 1997, 126; see Eze 1997 for other Enlightenment texts on race and Taiwo n.d. for a discussion of Hegel's view of Africa).

Interesting is the way in which Hornbostel, in the course of the article, concedes many points of similarity between the two musics. In fact, his phrase "entirely different principles" could easily be replaced by "similar principles" or, more daringly, by "the same general principles" without altering the (in)coherence of his argument. There is a danger of undercomplicating the challenge of comparison, however, for in the absence of explicit criteria for distinguishing between similarities and differences, a rigorous analysis cannot be undertaken. My interest here is not in proving the truth or falsity of Hornbostel's remark but in observing that his initially declared "difference" is a summary of his knowledge, not some fictional, unenlightened starting point to be proved untenable by a process of discovery. As such, it contradicts the other summary of his knowledge, the analytically achieved sameness that emerges from the article *per se*. This contradiction is fascinating: by constructing phenomena, objects, or people as "different," one stakes a claim to power over them.

A. M. Jones, too, opens his *Studies in African Music* of 1959 with a loud bang on the difference cymbal:

> Anyone who goes to Africa is bound to hear the music of the country and is equally certain to notice that it is not the same as our Western music. True, the people sing, in solo or chorus, as we do, and their instruments though lacking the precision of Western technology, will still recognizably belong to the familiar families of wind, string, or percussion. Yet the music produced is obviously not the same sort of music as that to which we in the West are accustomed. . . . The plain fact is that African music is a strange and novel object when encountered by a Western musician.
>
> (Jones 1959, 1)

Jones acknowledged similarities and differences but, like Hornbostel, *chose* to give the edge to "strange[ness] and novel[ty]." Difference for him constituted premise as well as conclusion. As premise, difference served to enliven the process of discovery insofar as it allowed the Englishman to read African musical procedures as originating from an unfamiliar conceptual base. As conclusion, difference facilitated a symbolic affirmation of a prior, indeed naturalized view of African music as phenomenologically distinct from that of the West. Such acts of framing are not inevitable; they represent choices made within a broader economy of representational practices and impulses.

Hugh Tracey was equally forthright when, as Honorary Secretary of the African Music Society, he addressed the International Folk Music Council on July 14, 1953, on "The State of Folk Music in Bantu Africa":

> We Europeans are at a great disadvantage in talking about African music. Unlike most other members of this conference we do not represent or discuss our own music but that of *a people radically unlike ourselves* among whom we live. It is only because we have found that the African is pathetically incapable of defending his own culture and indeed is largely indifferent to its fate that we, who subscribe wholeheartedly to the ideals of our International Council, are attempting to tide over the period during which irreparable damage can be done and until Africans themselves will be capable of appearing at our conferences as well-informed representatives of their own peoples.
>
> (Tracey 1954, 8; my emphasis)

The ringing characterization of Africans as "a people radically unlike ourselves" speaks to a persistent strategy of "differencing" that reaches back to the European Enlightenment. It is a habit that remains as alive today as it was in the 1950s, though it may take less blatant forms. Although Tracey understood that one consequence of the rise of global capital was the subjugation of African voices, although he construed the European's role in Africa as historically temporary, and although he felt confident that Africans would eventually possess the wherewithal to represent themselves, his own project and that of other Africanist ethnomusicologists did not pursue the task of transferring power to "Africans themselves" with any urgency. Nor was such a strategy finally implementable, for maintaining an imbalance of power is logically necessary for ethnomusicological practice. Balancing the distribution of power would remove one of ethnomusicology's crucial enabling mechanisms.

Hornbostel, Jones, and Tracey belong to an earlier generation, and so it may be thought that such acts of "differencing" are now a matter of the past. Yet, in more recent writing, Hegelian ideas of difference continue to be promulgated, sometimes in a direct and aggressively essentialist mode. Peter Cooke, for example, in a 1999 article subtitled "Listening to Instrumental Music in Africa South of the Sahara," sets out to prove that Africans "may well listen in a different way from the way Europeans do" (Cooke 1999, 73). Similarly, John Chernoff finds a peculiar link between the senses of hearing and smelling in Ghana: "'Hearing' music, like 'hearing' a language or 'hearing' the truth or 'hearing' the scent of a soup, refers to perception as a form of recognition" (Chernoff 1997, 23).

The impulse to cast African realities into *a priori* categories of difference is so strong that both authors are led to make generalizations and inferences on the basis of questionable evidence. Thus Cooke makes much of the words attributed to an illiterate but highly skilled musician (Kakraba-Lobi), while Chernoff invests in a literal translation of the verb "to hear" by an individual with limited fluency in English. Both authors in effect strategically under-complicate European practice in order to demonstrate Africa's ostensible uniqueness. Doing so, however, deprives Africa of full participation in our global critical conversation. While Africans deserve full recognition for whatever is unique about their critical and cultural practices, they do not need fake or facile attributions.

IS DIFFERENCE REAL?

At first sight, difference is a real, commonsensical phenomenon. Faced with a range of objects, I may distinguish them by number, size, color, texture, or function. The system of language enables me to invoke basic, meaning-producing oppositions. Thus, notes played on an instrument may be high or low, short or long, soft or loud, dark or bright. Chords may be consonant or dissonant, mellow or harsh, open- or close-spaced. These and thousands of such distinctions are employed routinely in (musicians') daily discourses. They are for the most part self-evident at a first level of articulation.

Meaning is difference. This fundamental insight has been worked over many times, with discussions extending into semiotic, linguistic, psychoanalytical, and other areas. Without difference, the ethnomusicologists would say after Saussure, there can be no meaning. So while a specific construction of meaning can accentuate one or another political or ideological motivation, the will to communicate and the practical need to build from difference are shared by all producers of texts about music. The enterprise of ethnomusicology is, in this sense, not different from any other branch of learning.

A little reflection on the complex processes of meaning formation, however, undermines our confidence that differences are self-evident or natural. They are, in fact, propped up by other textual constructions and motivated in ways that are not (necessarily) immediately apparent. What, for example, does the term *black* mean when applied to a group of people in the United States? To some, it is a perfectly adequate descriptive category for one's racial makeup. "Race" in this understanding is distributed into two essential categories, "white" and "black" ("yellow" is underused since it does not carry the force of the two polar opposites, while various hybrids are generally consigned to the categories "black" or "nonwhite," never "white"). But since very few people are literally "black" or "white"—"brown" and "pink" might be more accurate substitutes for the metaphorically challenged, those enamored of iconic signs—we need to translate signs from one realm of experience into another. But what about "black" as a social construction? Here, and depending on context, one might consciously (or, more often, subconsciously, and hence dangerously) tap into a series of historical or social texts that construe blackness in terms of slavery, sports, entertainment, preferential policies, urban violence, and so on. So, while at one level the terms *black* and *white* seem self-evident as descriptive categories, they are, in fact burdened with meaning (Gates 1986 provides an excellent introduction to issues of race and interpretation).

Differences, then, are not simply there for the perceiving subject. We do not perceive in a vacuum. Categories of perception are made, not given. Every act of perception carries implicit baggage from a history of habits of constructing the world. It should not seem strange at all—to choose a final set of examples—that not all of us notice hair types as markers of distinction among people. Similarly, in societies where intergenerational intercourse is marked, aging does not carry a stigma, and reference to an ethnographer as "an old man" is not an insult. Nor should one be upset at being described as "fatso" in communities in which plumpness is a sign of well-being. (Those who are thin are those who have not had enough to eat.)

To return to music: there is nothing self-evident about the categories used to distinguish African musics from Western music: functional as opposed to contemplative; communal rather than individualistic; spontaneous rather than calculated; rhythmically complex rather than simple; melodically unsophisticated rather than ornate; improvised rather than precomposed; and based in oral rather than written practices. These binarisms range from the possible to the irrational. Each subtends an asymmetrical relation in which one term is marked, the other unmarked. As ideology, these enduring characterizations speak to meaning as difference constructed by particular individuals for particular purposes.

RESISTING DIFFERENCE

There are two possible responses to the conditions described in the first part of this chapter: deny that there is anything problematic about the acts of differencing; or, accept the problem and abandon the Africanist ethno-musicological project altogether. The former recommends continuing with business as usual, while the latter advocates the end of all transactions. Might there be a less radical solution? In what alternative terms might we cast a principled pursuit of difference?

In a discussion of multiculturalism, Charles Taylor sought ways of inter-preting degrees of difference and distance between cultures (Taylor 1994). Here is his Gadamer-inspired recommendation, one that has the added benefit for us of a musical analogy:

> [F]or a sufficiently different culture, the very understanding of what it is to be of worth will be strange and unfamiliar to us. To approach, say, a raga with the presumptions of value implicit in the well-tempered clavier would be forever to miss the point. What has to happen is what Gadamer has called a "fusion of horizons". We learn to move in a broader horizon, within which what we have formerly taken for granted as the background to valuation can be situated as one possibility alongside the different back-ground of formerly unfamiliar culture. The "fusion of horizons" operates through our developing new vocabularies of comparison, by means of which we can articulate these contrasts.
>
> (Taylor 1994, 67)

A very reasonable proposition, this, indeed one that, far from being new, has been endorsed by social anthropologists committed to participant observation. It is also well known to ethnomusicologists whose ethnographies consciously incorporate "the native's point of view." Taylor's strategy for cross-cultural understanding promises to overcome certain ethical dilemmas raised by our dealing with Others. It provides a way of acknowledging, contextualizing, and eventually containing difference.

But isn't Taylor's program (and the numerous others that resonate with it) essentially a "Western" or "European" program? How does one decide, to start with, that a given culture is "sufficiently different"? If differences are constructed, then doesn't the judgment that one culture is "sufficiently different" from another presuppose a prior set of analytical acts? Isn't there a danger of monopolizing the ability to name something as different, a danger of granting that ability to those in the metropolis and denying it to those in the South? And whose are the resulting "broader horizons"—ours or theirs? Are they not essentially an expansion of Western horizons? Is it possible to achieve a genuine fusion of horizons between cultures located in radically different economic spheres? Is cross-cultural understanding ultimately possible?

These questions prompt us to consider an alternative strategy. Taylor notwithstanding, we might approach a raga with "the presumptions of value" implicit in Bach's *Well-Tempered Clavier* in order to pursue to the limits our initial impression—for it is no more than that—that the two musics are "sufficiently different." If we probe the contexts of both musics with equal commitment and sensitivity, and if we accept the theory that the impulses that lie behind certain expressive gestures are translatable (Henrotte 1985), we may well find that operating at different levels of perception are differences as well as residual similarities. We should be able to bring the "presumptions of value" implicit in a raga to bear upon an investigation of the *Well-Tempered Clavier*, thus allowing flow in both directions. For although Taylor, writing from "our" point of view, naturally assumes that we have the first option of checking out the other's horizon, it ought to be possible to imagine a reversal of this scheme. In short, it ought to be possible for others to "other" us if they so desire.

Taylor's efforts here suggest an attempt to relativize and ultimately decenter the West in order to draw other world cultures into a discussion space arranged along more egalitarian lines. ("Arranged by whom?" we should remember to ask, in order not to forget that the construction of egalitarianism itself represents an exercise of power.) Such a reorientation may produce a convergence at the background level of ostensibly different cultural systems. Backgrounds or deep structures bear uncanny resemblances to one another, so what Taylor calls our "background of valuation" may turn out to be a version of the Asian's, Australian's, or African's. But as we approach this "fusion of horizons" from the discrete polarity separating "our horizon" from "their horizon," we need to ask where this third space is located, and (since space is usually owned) to whom it belongs. Taylor implies that the new space is ultimately an extension of the West's; it is *our* "vocabularies of comparison" that will be enriched in the process. So while bringing more of the Other into view, Taylor's program does not—indeed cannot—eliminate the foundational terms of *Self* or Other, terms locked in a violent hierarchy in which Self as subject reproduces and completes itself as object or other. So, once again, a version of "Eurocentric cross-culturalism" is what is likely to emerge from an attempt to fuse horizons (Spivak with Rooney 1989, 133; see also Bhabha 1994, 85–92).

Embracing Sameness?

If differencing has produced such distorted, ideologically one-sided, and politically disadvantageous representation, and if a reasonable proposition to fuse horizons fails to overcome its core difficulty, why not eliminate it altogether and substitute a carefully defined sameness? The proposition that we dispense with difference might sound reactionary at first, scandalous perhaps, or merely silly. To attempt to eliminate that which is not ultimately eliminable is to attempt a critique in the spirit of a deconstruction (Spivak with Rooney 1989). It is to gnaw at limits and to resist the naturalized oppositions upon which knowledge of African music has been based without escaping the regime of oppositions. It is to insist on the provisional nature of our musical ethnographies, to persist in reordering concepts positioned at the center or in the margin. Only through such a persistent critique can we hope to refine theories born of a will to difference; only through critique can we stem the tide that reduces the hugely complex edifice of African musical practices to a series of "characteristics."

There is no method for attending to sameness, only a presence of mind, an attitude, a way of seeing the world. For fieldworkers who presume sameness rather than difference, the challenge of constructing an ethnographic report would be construed as the challenge of developing a theory of translation that aims to show how the materiality of culture constrains musical practice in specific ways. The idea would be to unearth the impulses that motivate acts of performance, and to seek to interpret them in terms of broader, perhaps even generic, cultural impulses. Such a project would ultimately look beyond the immediate material level, not by denying that Africans blow on elephant horns, cover drums with animal skin, or make flutes out of bamboo, but by emphasizing the contingency of their material and conceptual investments. Objects function as means to an end, and it is the complex of actions elicited by such objects that betrays the translatable impulses behind performance. Focusing on such impulses promotes a cross-cultural vision without denying the accidental specifics of local (African) practices.

Contesting difference through an embrace of sameness might also prompt a fresh critique of essentialism. Such a critique should facilitate a better understanding of the peculiar juxtapositions of cultural practices that define modern Africa. It would explain how a Sierra Leonean, Nigerian, or Ghanaian can be equally moved by a hymn, a traditional dance, a local proverb, a quotation from Shakespeare, a piece of reggae, the Wedding March, and the latest Highlife music. Eliminating the will to difference facilitates a better appreciation of the precarious grounds on which contemporary African reality stands, grounds shaped by religious, political, and ethical impositions that are sedimented at various levels of depth. Sameness prepares an understanding of (modern) African culture as a form of improvised theater, a makeshift culture whose actors respond to social pressures on an ad hoc, ongoing basis. It is not a culture of frozen artifacts imbued with spiritual essences.

A premise of sameness might also reorient our studies of theoretical (including aesthetic) discourses by causing us to regard with suspicion some of what is reported to have been said by informants in their own languages. Languages evolve according to need, and needs are defined across a spectrum of human activities. Accidents occur just as frequently as intended actions. So the condition of any African language today is best considered in light of its genealogy and refracted histories, including real and hypothetical occurrences. The fact, for example, that there are no terms corresponding directly with *music* or *rhythm* in many African languages—a fact, incidentally, that has caused difference-seeking ethnotheorists to rejoice—is significant only in a restricted sense. Its significance is retrospective, not prospective. For what matters is not what is known but *what is knowable*. This future-oriented appraisal paves the way for empowerment by placing the accent not on what an objectifying Western discourse deems significant but on the potential of African languages to support a self-sufficient and sophisticated practice of critical reflection.

The transformative, contingent, if-only, frankly political approach advocated here has certain practical consequences. One of them concerns the production of ethnography. Awareness of the precarious nature of material investments should lead to an abandonment of ethnography and an embrace of fiction. It should lead to a rejection of all first-level, ostensibly objective descriptions, and a substitution of second- or third-level suppositions, some of them openly speculative, none of them realist. If realism is capable of producing only partial, misleading, or distorted truths, then why not follow an approach that rejects realism's pretensions without denying its own imperfections? Why not tap the imaginative realm for possibilities?

The idea of sameness makes some people nervous. We surely do not want to all look alike, play the same instruments, listen to the same music, deploy the same critical language. Sameness carries the threat of hegemonic homogenization analogous to the cultural effects of the movement of global capital. What I am arguing for, however, is not sameness but the hypostatized presumption of sameness, which in turn precedes action and representation. We no longer worry about the exact traces left by our acts of representation because the ethical bases of our motivations are beyond question. Restoring a notional sameness to the work of ethnomusicology will go a long way toward achieving something that has hitherto remained only a theoretical possibility, namely, an ethical study of African music.

FURTHER READING

Agawu, Kofi. 1995. The invention of "African rhythm." *Journal of the American Musicological Society* 48(3): 380–395.

Appiah, Kwame Anthony. 1992. *In my father's house: Africa in the philosophy of culture*. New York: Oxford University Press.

Ekpo, Dennis. 1995. Towards a post-Africanism: Contemporary African thought and post-modernism. *Textual Practice* 9(1): 121–135.

Minow, Martha. 1990. *Making all the difference: Inclusion, exclusion, and American law*. Ithaca: Cornell University Press.

Mudimbe, V. Y. 1988. *The invention of Africa: Gnosis, philosophy, and the order of knowledge*. Bloomington: Indiana University Press.

Nzewi, Meki. 1997. *African music: Theoretical content and creative continuum: The culture exponent's definitions*. Olderhausen, Germany: Institut für Didaktik populärer Musik.

Radano, Ronald, and Philip Bohlman, eds. 2000. *Music and the racial imagination*. Chicago: University of Chicago Press.

Scherzinger, Martin. 2001. Negotiating the music-theory/African-music nexus: A political critique of ethnomusicological anti-formalism and a strategic analysis of the harmonic patterning of the Shona Mbira song *Nyamaropa*. *Perspectives of New Music* 39(1): 5–118.

Solie, Ruth. 1993. Introduction: On difference. Pp. 1–20 in *Musicology and difference: Gender and sexuality in music scholarship*. Berkeley: University of California Press.

Spivak, Gayatri. 1999. *A critique of postcolonial reason: Toward a history of the vanishing present*. Cambridge, MA: Harvard University Press.

CHAPTER 11

WHAT A DIFFERENCE A NAME MAKES
Two Instances of African-American Popular Music[1]

DAVID BRACKETT

In 1959, after a ten-year reign as the "Queen of the Harlem Blues" or "Queen of the Juke Boxes" (depending on which source one reads), Dinah Washington, an African-American rhythm and blues star known for her gospel-tinged, blues–jazz vocal style, recorded "What a Diff'rence a Day Made." This recording, which became Washington's biggest pop hit, bathed her voice in the amniotic fluid of sumptuous strings and oohing choruses redolent of that part of "mainstream" (read: white) popular music that had not yet succumbed to rock 'n' roll—but even this treatment could not quench her unrivaled ability to make the most cosmopolitan ballad funky. It was not until 1993, however, by which time her 1959 hit had little in common with contemporary R&B, that Washington achieved the ultimate in crossover recognition when the U.S. Postmaster General issued a postage stamp bearing her visage.

What a difference 34 years had made: The name of African-American popular music now gestured toward a different bundle of musical styles and cultural discourses, while the arrangement of popular music categories continued to produce a vision of difference in which that name remained marginal to the mainstream. Complete, nonmarginalized acceptance could occur, or so it would seem, only according to a time frame resembling that of the acceptance of subjects for postage stamps: that all such subjects must have died at least ten years prior to acquiring an exchange value of 29 cents (the value of a first-class stamp in 1993; Dinah Washington died in 1963).

In the preceding paragraphs, I used the terms *rhythm and blues, mainstream popular music,* and *crossover:* conventional labels used by those who make, consume, and profit from popular music in the United States. The very conventionality of such terms may obscure their demographic associations, the functions they have served, and the images of society they both model and produce. When the demographic associations of one of these terms, *rhythm and blues,* become explicit and are then folded into the more general category of "African-American music," questions occasionally arise as to the connections between musical style, biology, and historical origins. Debates circle around either the assertion of an essential connection between race and style based on the phantasmatic power of such ideas in subjects' everyday lives, or the refutation of such connections due to the difficulty of producing a scientifically delimited list of traits, leading in some cases to a concomitant assertion that African-American music is constructed through discourses about race, power, and identity.

I attempt to chart an alternative path between these positions, a path not dissimilar to Paul Gilroy's "anti-anti-essentialism" (Gilroy 1993, 99–103; see also hooks 1992; Brackett 1995, 108–119). I do this by examining one particular practice that both constructs and emerges from the concept of African-American music: the process of categorizing styles sustained in the relationship among musicians, audiences, and the mass media/music industry apparatus. This process is part of the "phantasmatic power" of identification (Ivy 1995) alluded to in the preceding paragraph. The term *phantasmatic* does not indicate that identities are fictions, but rather refers to the role of temporal deferral or displacement that characterizes the process of identification in relation to a sense of racial, gender, national (etc.) origins.

However, even the tertiary division of essentialism/anti-essentialism/anti-anti-essentialism does not adequately convey a sense of the complexity of musical identification. Georgina Born has developed a four-pronged model ranging from identifications that are relatively homologous to those that are relatively imaginary (in Born and Hesmondhalgh 2000, 31–47). While a psychoanalytic theory of musical identification might argue that all identifications are imaginary to some extent, or, following Lacan, that the Imaginary refers to a specific register of subject formation, and while such an observation touches on how identification with cultural Others may fulfill psychic needs, the usage here suggests that some types of identification with forms of mass culture are relatively homologous. That is to say, that these forms rest on an identification with an extant social/demographic category; these contrast with those which may or may not prefigure a grouping, but which do not refer to a pre-existing identification. Such a distinction is crucial to understanding the functioning of musical categories in popular music even if the "extant" categories are themselves in a constant state of flux, and are modified once they are pressed into service; this distinction also helps explain how, for example, people who are not African Americans can participate in African-American music as producers and consumers.

To examine how this sense of difference between musical categories emerges as "real," I look at two moments in recent U.S. history: the years around 1947, and those around 1996. Examining how styles are categorized illuminates how a sense of "black music" emanates from its relationship to other categories of music coexisting within a given period, and thus demonstrates how structures of difference permeate the circulation of both musical sounds and verbal discourse about music (Middleton 1990, 241). While the experience of popular music as connoting particular demographic groups may be widespread and gain tacit acceptance in a particular place at a particular historical moment, it need not derive from a belief solely in either transhistorical essences or in arbitrary rhetorical effects. Somewhat paradoxically, the linkage between musical style and demographics, while experienced and acted upon as "real," may also be revealed as arbitrary when similar categories of popular music are compared from contrasting historical periods.

The context for the particular connotations of musical categories under discussion in this chapter centers on social and historical relations in the United States: My remarks may be suggestive for other geopolitical contexts to the extent that the particular connotations studied here have been successfully exported. Associations among musical categories, style elements, and audiences have existed in the United States since the 1920s, when the recording industry organized the popular music field around the divisions of "popular," "race," and "old-time" (often referred to as "hillbilly") musics, each supposedly referring to a distinct musical style with its own audience. These categories developed in tandem with popularity charts that reflect the intersection of three forces: the public's fascination with the measurement of its preferences, its tacit acceptance of categories, and the music industry's use of these categories. While various charts had tracked the success of "mainstream" popular music since 1890, the economic importance of race and old-time music had grown by the 1940s to the point that popularity in those fields began to be represented in separate charts (see Figure 11.1). While historically the content of the term *mainstream* is malleable and stylistically heterogeneous, its durability lies in its continuing ability to provide a "center" for other, "alternative," or "marginal" genres (Toynbee 2002; Brackett 2002, 2005). At this point in the 1940s the assumed mainstream pop audience was Northern, urban, middle- or upper-class, and white. The charts for the "marginal" musics also assumed an audience—African

American for "race"; rural, Southern white for "hillbilly." Note particularly the instability (displayed in Figure 11.1) of the nomenclature used to describe "black music" relative to country or pop. Although rhythm and blues or R&B is the default name for popular music associated with African Americans, neither of the other categories is so explicitly tied to race.

To understand how a distinct black popular music circulates in relation to the mainstream, one must look closely at the *specific* interconnections among institutional policies, discourses of categorization, and elements of musical style within a narrow period of time. Such a proposal runs counter to the suggestions of some scholars who emphasize the difficulty in connecting musical sound to genre labels (for example, see Frith 1998: 86). While it is certainly all too easy to make transhistorical generalizations that collapse under a welter of exceptions, the key to the formulation proposed here is the emphasis on a narrow historical frame and on the analysis of discursive regularities. The years around 1947 prove instructive: while the music industry was in the process of slowly recognizing the importance of black popular music, it effectively excluded the representation of black music from the mainstream. Or, perhaps I should say that the mainstream at that moment included only one form of black music, and one of its more

1939–1949	1949–1969	1969–1982	1982–1990	1990–1997	Contemporary Radio Format ca. 1996	Video Channel, ca. 1996
Popular	Popular/ Hot 100	Hot 100	Hot 100	Hot 100	Top 40/ Contemporary Hit Radio	MTV Top 20 Video Countdown
Harlem Hit Parade (1942–44)/ American Folk (1945)/ Race (1946)	Rhythm and Blues	Soul	Black	Rhythm and Blues	Urban Contemporary (UC)/ Quiet Storm/ R&B/Rap	MTV Jams/ BET
Hillbilly (1939)/ American Folk (1945–49)	Country and Western/ Country (1960)	Country	Country	Country	Country	CMT
Other categories					Adult Contemporary	VH-1
					AOR (Album Oriented Rock	

FIGURE 11.1 Popularity chart and radio format nomenclature, 1939–97 (as found in *Billboard* magazine)

curious manifestations at that. A standout among these curiosities was Count Basie's smash hit from 1947, "Open the Door, Richard": Hitting number one on the Honor Roll of Hits on March 1, 1947, "Open the Door" stakes its claim as Basie's most successful recording, and one of relatively few recordings by African-American artists to appear on the (mainstream) pop charts during the period in question. Basie's success is particularly marked in that the Honor Roll of Hits ranked the top ten songs by synthesizing the radio play, record sales, and jukebox play charts from the "popular" category; reaching the top of this chart thus represented a greater achievement than topping any of the individual charts.

However, if we are to avoid charges of essentialism, the name of an African American on the label of "Open the Door, Richard" is not enough to qualify it as an example of black popular music. In fact, the presence of Basie's recording on the Honor Roll might militate against understanding "Open the Door" as "race music" owing to its very appearance on a mainstream chart. It takes but a glance across the page of the March 1, 1947, issue of *Billboard* to reassure us that "Open the Door, Richard" is indeed well represented in the race charts, with different versions of the song (including Basie's) occupying five of the seven slots. As some five versions of the song appear on the mainstream top 30 "jukebox" chart, "Open the Door" would seem to be an archetypal example of a crossover song: a song that appears on more than one chart, thus by implication appealing to more than one segment of the *Billboard*-partitioned audience, and thereby one that relies on both homological and imaginary acts of identification.

Determining what difference, if any, existed between songs represented on the race charts and those on the mainstream charts requires closer scrutiny of the constitution of the categories at this time. *Billboard's* definition, that "Records listed are race-type disks most played in the nation's juke boxes, according to the Billboard's weekly survey among juke box operators", is of little help, for the identity of those "race-type disks" remains a mystery. Analyzing the race chart tells us that at the crudest level there does appear to be a simple relationship of racial identity, as almost all the recordings on the chart are secular recordings made by African Americans. The majority of crossovers from the race chart to the mainstream chart during this period, however, do tend to be novelty tunes such as "Open the Door, Richard."

The sound of "Open the Door," along with the fact that it was Count Basie's most successful foray into the mainstream charts, may come as a bit of a surprise to those who know Count Basie as the innovative pianist and leader of one of the most successful black swing bands. In terms of musical style, the song certainly departs from what jazz fans would associate with Basie: his trademark tinkling piano is present but subordinated to novelty effects such as the repeated snare drum "knocks," the vamp that marks time during the narrative, the chorus sung in unison, and the spoken narrative itself, which describes the misfortunes of one of Basie's band members (Harry "Sweets" Edison) when he is locked out of his apartment by his roommate, a fellow band member by the name of Richard. The lyrics and performance style reveal that this novelty number presents a type of vaudeville humor with a long history in minstrelsy. The associations with novelty and minstrelsy occur also in many of the most successful recordings of the man widely regarded as the first crossover artist, Louis Jordan. Jordan's jukebox hits such as "Choo Choo Ch'Boogie" and "Ain't Nobody Here But Us Chickens," however much they might have been signifyin' trickster tales, double-coded to provide empowering messages to African Americans, at least partly invoked minstrelsy codes to white audiences (Lott 1993), and reveal much about what imaginary modes of identification were necessary at that time for crossover success.

Jordan is often cited as the first crossover artist, but closely examining music industry publications during this time, though not literally contradicting this commonplace, reveals a layer of complication. While the race charts recorded only jukebox activity, there were many separate charts for mainstream popular music representing record sales and radio play in addition to jukebox revenue. A handful of recordings by African-American artists did register on the mainstream record sales and jukebox charts, but they almost never showed up on charts representing radio play, and they never appeared on the chart surveying network radio play (network radio shows were nationally syndicated and had the broadest audiences). It is open to question, therefore, how widely Jordan's recordings were actually played on the radio, the medium least bound by physical or geographical limitations.

A cautionary word is in order here: the preceding discussion does not endorse the idea of *Billboard*'s charts as transparent windows through which the popularity of recordings may be viewed in an absolute sense; rather, the charts are particular representations of popularity that circulated and thereby affected public notions of what was popular. However, to dismiss the information contained in popularity charts is to believe in the possibility of an unmediated means of conveying popularity. If we can relinquish the vision of a perfect re-creation of a historical moment, then a space is opened where analyzing the charts as a symbolic mediation of that period becomes plausible. The charts at this time may then be understood as *representing* the idea that crossover artists such as Louis Jordan were selling records and being played on jukeboxes but not being heard widely on the radio, unlike the vast majority of mainstream popular hits. These ideas then circulated among the readership of these publications, where they were presumably accepted as real to the extent that they resonated with other widely accepted discourses about race and music. This scenario suggests that these recordings became popular without the aid of network radio, and were not likely to have been heard by white audiences who did not happen to purchase the record or find themselves in a venue where a jukebox was playing "Choo Choo Ch'Boogie."

The most telling deviation from the mainstream that one finds among the race records chart—as well as, one assumes, on the jukeboxes and the few radio shows devoted to black popular music at the time—is a *variety* of styles that did not cross over to the mainstream (in addition to the novelty songs that did). If the categories of race music and mainstream popular music are depicted as two overlapping circles (see Figure 11.2), then the crossover novelty songs exist within the portion of the circles that overlaps, while the noncrossover songs reside in the nonoverlapping part of the circle. Here, in the part of the race music circle that does not overlap, resides the critical difference that separates black popular music from mainstream popular music at this time.

Hence, listening to the most popular race recordings of the time that did not cross over—songs such as Cecil Gant's "I Wonder," Wynonie Harris's "Good Rockin' Tonight," or Amos Milburn's "Chicken-Shack Boogie"—may indicate the musical practices that differentiated race music from the mainstream. These noncrossover songs feature up-tempo boogie-woogie

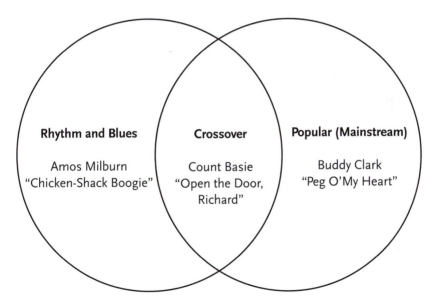

FIGURE 11.2 The circular logic of race and mainstream popularity charts, c. 1946–47

rhythms, slow blues grooves, guitars and saxophones with distorted or "dirty" timbres, strongly emphasized back beats, and extensive improvisation; they include lyrics filled with current African-American slang and playful double-entendres that extol the virtues of partying, enunciated with diction that may not have been easily intelligible to white listeners of the time. In the style that was coming to be called rhythm and blues or "jump blues," listeners could hear echoes of the small-band jazz that had emanated from Count Basie's Kansas City Six or Kansas City Seven groups, recordings that Basie made around ten years earlier when his songs were not heard on popular radio stations, back when there was little thought of asking for a door to be opened. In 1946–47, on jukeboxes in black neighborhoods, and on the few isolated radio shows scattered throughout the country that played race music for an hour or two, listeners could hear new permutations of the country blues, the classic blues, or piano-based boogie-woogie, now filled out with ensembles of bass, drums, guitar, saxophones, and trumpets, and fronted by blues shouters, gospel wailers, and jazz insinuators—musical elements, personas, and styles that were rare or nonexistent in the mainstream popular music of the time.

During the same years, a new phenomenon began to gather momentum. The possibility arose that, under certain amorphous circumstances, an African-American performer could sing mainstream pop ballads in a style that differed little from the crooning that had come to dominate popular music following World War II. Most closely associated with Bing Crosby in the years before 1946, after the war this relaxed singing style had spread to ascending male stars such as Perry Como, Dick Haymes, and Buddy Clark, as well as to female balladeers like Dinah Shore and Margaret Whiting. Nat "King" Cole, still recording under the aegis of the "King Cole Trio" at this point, was the exception that proved the rule. In recordings such as "You Call It Madness (But I Call It Love)" and "(I Love You) For Sentimental Reasons," Cole crooned effortlessly with flawless "standard" American diction in front of his subdued, yet jazzy and tasteful, trio of piano, guitar, and bass to spatially separate (but sonically equal) lovers, regardless of their race. Benefiting from the confluence of the crooner wave with the last vestiges of acceptance for jazz-influenced music associated with the swing bands, a year later Cole parlayed this success into orchestra-backed recordings such as "Nature Boy" (in 1948). Cole's success flew in the face of music industry wisdom of the time; he, as well as other African-American vocalists such as Billy Eckstine, encountered resistance in their efforts to record pop ballads, frequently being limited to recording only the blues that record company personnel deemed appropriate and commercially viable (DeVeaux 1997, 340–363).

To look at the concept of "African-American music" in action fifty years later is to observe both the persistent meaningfulness of the term and its radical instability. Two examples from 1996 illustrate how the concept continued to mark difference, thereby participating in the process of producing meaning in the popular music field while at the same time continuing to float free from essential connections to biology or from historically invariant style traits. By the mid-1990s the relationship between style and marketing category had become simultaneously simplified and more complex. Many of the same factors involved in crossover still existed, but were adapted to the new medium of music television, with different channels targeting specific demographic groups, or with different programs on a single channel employing niche marketing. Beginning in the early 1980s, music television channels and music video shows interacted with a greatly expanded number of style categories for popular music, some of which had strong correlations with radio formats, others of which responded to the vibrations of dance clubs (see Figure 11.1). The properties of the new medium heightened awareness of the social connotations of pop music categories, granting crossover a visual immediacy that it had previously lacked. Music television reveals the physical characteristics of recording artists and putative cultural contexts in a way that radio cannot (unless we include that material signifier of the body conveyed through sound waves alone: *Le grain de la voix*, residue of the real), and these, together with the types of advertisements played during shows, supplement informal ethnography in analyzing the relationship of audience demographics to particular shows.

Music videos also provide a graphic reminder of who we, the audience, are to imagine ourselves to be, as videos represent a diegetic audience corresponding to the demographic of the target audience. For example, many rap videos are staged to show the participants partying and having a good time in what appears to be the artist's community, surrounded by his or her group of friends (see Rose 1994, 8–15). In the video for the Southern dance-rap hit from the summer of 1996, "C'mon n' Ride It (the Train)," we find a group of African Americans located somewhere between outer space and a frenzied bumping and grinding dance party, while the performers, the Quad City DJs, are represented as shamanic personages summoning the image of African-American hypersexuality from the mass-cultural unconscious. This video followed a classic crossover pattern, appearing first on MTV's video "ghetto," the MTV Jams Countdown (a show paralleling the R&B chart—see Figure 11.1) in June, and eventually making it to the multiracial, all-beautiful teen family of the MTV Top 20 Video Countdown (a show paralleling the mainstream, Hot 100 chart) in August. "C'mon n' Ride It" never did show up on the VH-1 countdown, which caters to a bourgeois, aged 25 to 54, largely white audience, and parallels the Adult

Contemporary chart, which arose with a new radio format in the 1980s (Barnes 1988). The song has tight links to other contemporary R&B hits with its incessantly repeated short riff; its largely synthesized, electronic, instrumental sound; and its alternation of sung chorus with rapped verse.

Another almost exactly contemporaneous video unsettles any potentially essential linkages. "Give Me One Reason" is recorded/performed by Tracy Chapman, who, although she is African American, has, since her emergence in 1987, been associated with the modern singer-songwriter pop genre, a genre with connotations of a predominantly white audience. Her song quickly hit number 1 in June of 1996 on the VH-1 countdown, slowly climbed up MTV's Top 20 countdown, making it as high as number 8, and never appeared in the MTV Jams countdown. The representation of the audience in "Give Me One Reason" differs markedly from that in "C'mon n' Ride It," with images of racially mixed couples dancing to an integrated, sexually androgynous band. Musically, the differences are quite profound as well; Chapman's song is a blues, which is a form associated historically with African Americans, but one that has been more often used by white musicians over the last forty or so years. The instrumentation is that of the urban blues bands from an earlier time, and the song features a guitar solo, another performance gesture enacted most often in public since 1965 by white males, and one enacted in the video, in yet another act of musico-semiological reversal, by an androgynous woman.

In fact, this "earlier time" of the urban blues band is the period over sixty years ago discussed previously in this chapter, and in many ways "Give Me One Reason" has more in common with "race music" of the 1940s than with contemporary R&B. Is Tracy Chapman the Nat King Cole of the 1990s? Well, no: as the Quad City DJs demonstrated, a recording that is strongly coded as "black" could cross over in the mid-1990s to MTV's mainstream countdown if not to VH-1's. Conversely, while Cole had a large, African-American audience, it is most likely that Chapman's core audience lies in the (mostly white) Adult Contemporary category (Figure 11.3 provides a graphic representation of the different crossover trajectories of "Give Me One Reason" and "C'mon n' Ride It").

Regardless of how many rap recordings show up on the mainstream Hot 100 chart or how many white rappers or black singer-songwriters receive mass exposure, the concept of crossover remains viable because popular music categories continue to create meaningful distinctions between demographically marked styles or genres of music (in a tempting homology, we could observe that regardless of how "integrated" U.S. society may be at any given moment, census workers must still check off a racial designation on their forms). In other words, and to refer to a paradigm presented earlier, crossover represents a move from a predominantly homological

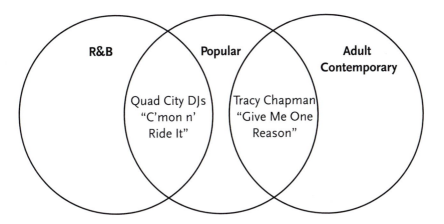

FIGURE 11.3 The circular logic of R&B, popular, and adult contemporary charts, c. 1996

identification of a recording marked as marginal, to a mode of identification blending homological and imaginary identifications. Crossover thus relies on pre-existing categories, which provide sites to move away from and towards, and it therefore seems to reinforce these categories; yet the process whereby recordings move from one category to another also undermines assumptions about connections between categories and audiences, and points to the complexity and instability of individual identities.

While I have stressed here the radical discontinuity of several examples of black popular music separated by fifty years, my approach need not exclude historical continuities or gradual transformations. For example, Samuel A. Floyd, Jr. (1991, 1995) has described the musical elements that developed within the ring shout, elements that have subsequently constituted a group of musical "tropes" that black music repeatedly draws from. In both the periods described in this chapter, at least part of the sense of difference between black popular music and mainstream popular music derives from the way in which these elements are employed. Perhaps Amos Milburn's "Chicken-Shack Boogie" is linked to "C'mon n' Ride It" by Floyd's call-response trope; or by other theories, such as Olly Wilson's (1974) "conceptual approach," Amiri Baraka's (1967) "changing same," or Ralph Ellison's (1964: 131) "concord of sensibilities," all of which seek to explain the practical expression of that sense of constantly reinforced racialized subjectivity that goes by the name of African-American difference. Stressing ideological continuity over musical consistency, Ronald Radano has emphasized the mutual imbrication of musical blackness with musical whiteness, the shifting conceptions of each produced as part of an obsession with racial difference in the U.S. (Radano 2003). This sense of difference, reiterated in synchronic reformulations of the popular music field, marks a phantasmatic zone in the generalized (un)consciousness of the U.S. consumer who uses it to decode (in the words of Tower of Power) "What Is Hip" and to find CDs in the local megastore.

"Race Music," "The Harlem Hit Parade," "Rhythm and Blues," "Soul Music," "Black Music," "R&B," "Urban Contemporary": to repeat a point made earlier, of all the categories used by the popular music industry, the category associated with African Americans has been the most explicitly tied to race and the most unstable. One can speculate that this instability of naming is tied to changing mainstream notions in the United States about what might constitute acceptable modes of representation for African Americans. This speculative analysis could be pressed further still, to the idea that the naming of categories in popular music mediates (and simultaneously participates in producing) U.S. society's vision of itself and the position of African Americans in that society. This catharsis for socio-historical cognitive dissonance influences the range of the possible: that is, who can hear what at any given time and who will reap the economic rewards. The process of crossover indicates that the category of African-American popular music exists as a colony for the mainstream, producing goods that may then circulate as part of a tarnished golden triangle (the same is true of country music). Recordings by black artists are thus held to a different standard by having to "prove themselves first" with success on the black chart, unless they already have a track record of crossover success (see Brackett 1994).

The arrangement of categories in the popular music field continues to make a difference: to imagine the field without difference is to imagine popular music without meaning. And to imagine the erasure of race from the play of this difference is to imagine a stage of society in the United States that has not yet come into existence.

NOTE

1   Work for this project was supported by a grant from the National Endowment for the Humanities.

FURTHER READING

Baraka, Amiri. 1967. *Black music.* New York: William Morrow.
Barnes, Ken. 1988. Top 40 radio: A fragment of the popular imagination. Pp. 8–50 in *Facing the music.* Edited by Simon Frith. New York: Pantheon.
Brackett, David. 1994. The practice and politics of crossover in American popular music, 1963–65. *Musical Quarterly* 78(4): 774–797.
Brackett, David. 2002. (In search of) musical meaning: Genres, categories, and crossover. Pp. 65–83 in *Popular music studies.* Edited by David Hesmondhalgh and Keith Negus. London: Arnold.

DeVeaux, Scott. 1997. *The birth of bebop: A social and musical history.* Berkeley: University of California Press.

Floyd, Samuel A., Jr. 1991. Ring shout! Literary studies, historical studies, and black music inquiry. *Black Music Research Journal* 11(2): 265–288.

Floyd, Samuel A., Jr. 1995. *The power of black music: Interpreting its history from Africa to the United States.* New York: Oxford University Press.

Gilroy, Paul. 1993. *The black Atlantic: Modernity and double consciousness.* Cambridge, MA: Harvard University Press.

hooks, bell. 1992. *Black looks: Race and representation.* Boston, MA: South End Press.

Ivy, Marilyn. 1995. *Discourses of the vanishing: Modernity, phantasm, Japan.* Chicago: University of Chicago Press.

Rose, Tricia. 1994. *Black noise: Rap music and black culture in contemporary America.* Hanover, NH: University Press of New England.

Toynbee, Jason. 2002. Mainstreaming: Hegemony, market and the aesthetics of the centre in popular music. Pp. 149–163 in *Popular music studies.* Edited by David Hesmondhalgh and Keith Negus. London: Arnold.

CHAPTER 12

MUSIC, SPACE, AND PLACE
The Geography of Music

ADAM KRIMS

While commentators have been correct to suggest that music studies' engagement with geography is a recent and innovative thing, in a sense we have routinely relied on geographic concepts as long as musicology, at least, has existed. Thus the presumed proliferation of "national" styles in the nineteenth century, long a part of mainstream histories of "art" music, presented its own roughly hewn geography of Europe; and while many scholars (e.g., Taruskin 2008, 25–29) have correctly complained that such conceptions create a *de facto* center and various peripheries, such maps have long supported the ways in which scholars have discussed musical compositions. Inside and outside academia, music performance traditions are frequently tagged to national traditions, presumably handed down through the pedagogy of key teachers; though I have argued elsewhere that such concepts—"Russian" piano style, "Czech" string playing, and so on—may more usefully be re-scaled to the urban level (Krims 2010), in either case, the correspondence of musical sound to physical space underlies the label conceptually. Musicologists, especially, deploy geographic terms and concepts in order to delimit hubs of activity, though not always entirely accurately: thus, Anthony Newcomb's authoritative *The Madrigal at Ferrara: 1579–1597* (1980) delineates its scope at the urban scale, whereas the agglomeration of activity described within the book is largely confined to the court of Este, and, quite arguably, the interaction of the music produced there with that of other courts outside Ferrara was more significant than its interaction with the city as a whole. Of course, musicology of this and earlier periods understandably tends to focus on courts and the church (though Pacheco [2009] correctly underlines the erasure of the bulk of urban music that such foci tend to elide). Such slips of geographic focus result, perhaps, from our taking geographic terms and ideas for granted, borrowing them as needed without a sense of their weight, a sense of the decades, or centuries, of intellectual background and still-lively debates that lie behind many of them—and their potentially profound importance for the kinds of things that we discuss as music scholars. While taking geography for granted, we have sometimes lost any sense of its true power.

There is one more respect in which music scholars (especially ethno-musicologists, but also musicologists, and, to some extent, music theorists) have engaged geographic concepts, in this case somewhat more critically and consciously: we have sometimes factored both place and landscape into our studies of music. "Landscape" and "place" are not entirely separable objects, of course, and in the theoretically strongest studies, both emerge as interactions among locality, cultural interpretations of that locality, and the music being discussed. They are not only "constructed" but also, more important, profoundly *historical*, emerging from tensions and struggles that are constantly changing and inflected; at the intersections of time, space, and cultural struggle, landscapes are also, of course, constructed musically. Thus, Daniel Grimley's (2006) study of Grieg's music and landscape shows the tension between the regressive aspects of his landscape conception (such as the Nynorsk dialect of Arne Garborg's verse novella *Haugtussa*) and the progressive harmonic language that allies his music with pan-European expansions of chromatic possibility.

More commonly, however, "place" becomes something like the geographic equivalent of "identity," referring to a discursively constructed notion (or, for those more enamored of agonistic models, sets of "contested" notions) defining a locality in some way. Of course, related themes such as the creation of new subject positions may also come into play, once identity is at issue. Some scholars (e.g., Mitchell 2009), even go to the lengths of equating place with identity, and underlining the purely discursive nature of its rubric (e.g., in the "psychogeography" of his title); and perhaps also thus underlining the limiting nature of such investigations. It need not be rehearsed here how early Birmingham school studies in whose tradition Mitchell and others' work emphasized discursive constructions as a supplement (Gramsci-style) to (but also, of course, constructive of) political economy, and then eventually allowed that political economy to stand as a rather static background against which all of the "action" takes place in artistic (and other) discourse. Mitchell's investigation, certainly interesting in itself, rehearses that fetishized focus with an admirable clarity. Ironically enough, Gramsci's concern was to explain how it is that working classes do not necessarily develop revolutionary consciousness, and thus to offer a model capable of integrating "base" and "superstructure" (concepts whose conventionalized hierarchical relationship constitutes by far the most widespread tradition of Marxism—although it may not have been Marx's own [Sayer1987, 83–112]); he did this by arguing for a need to coordinate analysis of conditions in the two. In the practice of those in the "cultural studies" tradition claiming his name, however, that "base" may become a two-dimensional, essentially background, material for understanding the crucially important "superstructure" which always seems to end up as the focus of investigation.

Mitchell's explicit embrace of the culturalist ideology behind many notions of "place" can usefully be contrasted with the majority (most prominently among ethnomusicologists, but increasingly among musicologists, popular-music scholars, and even some music theorists) that engage "place" in the less self-conscious manner that simply assumes the requisite social premises. Thus Sunardi (2010), to take just one recent example, focuses on local discourses, music, dance, and gesture in eastern Java, and how local performers distinguish their art from that of central Java; even the often weakly refracted notion of "dominant" and "subversive" localities that "place studies" also share with cultural-studies works on "identity" need not (and does not) appear in Sunardi's study, which nonetheless presents useful and engaging information on local perceptions of art. In the most extreme cases of theoretical abnegation, "place" can come to have almost no meaning at all, other than referenced locality (e.g., Van Glahn 1996), thinning material geographic content to near-nothing; happily, though, that is a worst-case scenario. More normally, "place" takes its position in musical studies as a light and trim framework onto which essentially empirical work is trussed, flexible enough to sustain just about any particulars and light enough so as not to obscure the concretes which inevitably take the foreground. And of course, such empirical investigations are often of immeasurable value, even if the framework of "place", in them, adds little heft in itself.

If cultural geography is a factor in musicological work on representation, then the material forces of social space remain little addressed in such work (except indirectly, through the potential material consequences of representation). This more difficult but potentially powerful task falls to the work that at least somewhat engages economic geography, which necessarily implicates itself in the broader social structure, even directly into the beating heart of capital itself (a giddy possibility that always threatens the sublime, if, indeed, any pleasure at all). The connection of the changing built environment to music always comes indirectly, often from the *habitus* of the environments that we occupy and the degree and kinds of attention that they demand, or from new uses of music that merge with practices of interior design (Sterne 1997; Krims 2007); the change in musical practices is not determined by the built environment (and its economically intertwined shaping), but rather is conditioned by it, and tracing such connections can lead the music scholar into obscure and unfamiliar territory, the aesthetic byways, snuggled to the breast of capital, that turn out to be the very mainstream of musical culture (as I argued may have happened with Anonymous 4, whose vocal timbres merged with a more generalized tendency, in parts of the classical recording industry, to position music as design for bourgeois urban interiors [Krims 2007, 127–161]).

Of course, the worlds of discourse and built environment affect each other, meld into each other at certain points, and overall interact in ways that are complex and saturated with genuine geographic interest. And certainly, studying one need not preclude studying the other; on the contrary, one of the signal lessons that came out from debates about cultural-industry clusters and urban geography is just how crucially discourse about "creative" cities has shaped urban policy and thus, of course, the built environment of cities all over the world (see, e.g., Evans 2009). So, of course, the boundaries between the built environment and "place" can be permeable and are by no means always stable or predictable.

So why talk about "space" and the built environment, economic geography and so many aspects of urban change that seem, at an uncritical first glance, so remote from the worlds of music? Perhaps it is exactly because of that apparent remove, because of the possibility that it is precisely these far-reaching changes in cities themselves which we tend to miss as conditioners of musical practice. The surprising thing, after all, would be if, for example, all the sweeping changes in urban areas of the developed world in the past forty or so years were to have absolutely no effect on the aesthetic worlds that are produced within them; and those who are interested in critical geography—geography that asks questions—should not be satisfied only to uncover the important but often rather conspicuous connections of geographic discourse (i.e., "place") to musical life. We who live in the capitalist world live in spaces, in built environments, whose contours are constantly developing at the pace of capital itself (and of course, most intensely in precisely those "global cities" [Sassen 1991] that lie at the heart of world commerce); and such changes have a number of concrete effects whose shaping of musical production and consumption can be far-ranging. For one thing, most bluntly but also quite comprehensively, changes in the kind and manner of industrial production bring new populations into close contact in the urban theatre (Peterson 2010); these populations vary not only in ethnic origin, but also in educational level and background, life experience, professional training and activity, sexual orientation, and all manner of aesthetic predilections and tastes (Hutton 2010; Wynne and

O'Connor 1998). The experience of the city here changes, as the kinds of stores, bars, restaurants, theaters and cinemas, bookstores, clubs, and other urban amenities mutate to serve the incoming populations, presenting new object worlds and configurations in space in which to experience them. In those areas that feature creative quarters (increasingly prominent in urban planning and development since the beginning of the "post-industrial" era), there congregate (often with residences) workers especially involved in the "creative" and/or "knowledge-based economy" (Currid 2007), for whom aesthetic taste and judgment form a particularly high priority and the aesthetic experience of the city looms especially large. The generalized aestheticizing of the contemporary city (Ley 2003) is a much broader phenomenon than this, applying every bit as much to upscale offices and residences as to cultural quarters, and thus further underlining the intimate role that aesthetics and the arts play in urban production and character (and vice versa). And, both as the principal locus of the relevant professions and also the location providing the greatest concentration of relevant amenities, the large city becomes the site *par excellence* of that breakdown of barriers between work and leisure, between production and consumption, often cited as characteristic both of "post-industrial" cultural production and of "post-Fordist" urban industry (Breedveld 1996). Negus (1992), among others, had already documented how this was central to the lives of decision-makers in the music industry, how their musical judgments were formed as much during nights out with friends as during official visits to performances of prospective artists. Such adventures in urban space, and mutations in the way that people live through it, turn out to be momentous in their consequences for musical production and consumption. (The surprising thing would be if it were not.) We may, of course, ask ourselves (or the people whom we study) how they value locality, observing how they symbolically tag their cities as being a certain way, listening to their music for representations of "place"—but all of these things, as valuable as they may be in themselves, do not explain to us the musical consequences of (or, if one prefers, music's role in) these profound, and profoundly aesthetic (and aestheticized) changes in urban life. On top of this argument focused on the working practices of urban musical producers, one may add, albeit more speculatively, the more aestheticized spaces of (especially developed) cities themselves (Ley 2003; Harvey 1990; Zukin 1982); moving through such aesthetically saturated spaces as a *habitus*, and especially hearing music's deployment as design in such spaces (Sterne 1997; Krims 2007), urban musical workers, including engineers and producers, A&R executives and promoters, develop new senses of musical space, and of the relationship between music and the spaces in which it is deployed and consumed (Bull 2007). Research on these developments can only be called nascent but holds, in my view, the greatest potential for revealing the changes of music in the social fabric. And while these examples are contemporary, by no means is that relevance confined solely to (post-)industrialized times; much, if not most, of the tradition of "Western Art Music" was composed in, and for, cities with determinate structure and thus highly framed social relations and aesthetic possibilities.

One can, of course, far more directly and easily observe people's attachment to their (or other) localities, their ideas about the layout of the world and its music, their subject positions, and the ways that music helps to build their notions of the world and its spaces; and the vast majority of music studies that have dealt with music and geography have thus turned to that rubric of *place*. Hardly an ethnomusicological study of a locality (e.g., Averill 1997; Stokes 1997) does not deal with this in some way, often (as Averill) agonistically; and while the basic concept may in itself be simple, the way in which it unfolds in the messy and multi-textured world of music's route through social life can be endlessly complex and fascinating to follow. At its best, a study of music and place measures the way in which artists' and audiences' engagement produces friction with the constraints in their social situation; and while an easy temptation to a cultural-studies-style celebration of that friction lies just down that lane, the most engaging commentators of music-and-place hold that friction in suspension, leaving it as a blunt and appropriately mixed force of social conflict (again, as Averill does). Such a suspension also best captures the true permeability, the free interaction, of space and place, of built environment, social habits (which are, after all, constitutive of both space *and* place), music, and human ideation. The humanistic interest of the best investigations of place can be a (for many, much-needed) corrective to the more ambiguous (though also more ambitious) study of space, especially the latter's presumed danger of sliding into a grim determinism. Even the sunnier, cultural studies-inspired investigations of place (e.g., Lipsitz 1994) can offer such a balm—and, of course, capture a truth, no matter how partial. There is no reason not to benefit from such work and the humanistically motivated scholars who offer them, in ample supply.

The under-studied status of musical *space*, on the other hand, probably stems not only from the need for mediation discussed above, but also from the lack of a tradition of *political economy* in music studies. While cultural studies has been slowly, but quite surely and eventually on an impressive scale, seeping into the theoretical tool bag of many music scholars, political economy (perhaps owing to its grounding in the social sciences, rather than in the humanities) continues to lag. A good, critical version of materialist music geography (i.e., one that studies the built environment and its relation to music) requires the support of something like political economy, in order that the researcher may both take seriously the lessons of postmodern critique (e.g., the mediating force of discourse) and still not reduce the reality of social life to ideation. Were critical realism to have established itself in music studies as it has in many of the social sciences (Jessop 2005), some basis for a serious political economy could be established; but, as things stand, the soft idealism of cultural studies (often disowned, of course) seems to reign, at least implicitly, in musical approaches. This may explain why the one attempt to assemble some essays dealing with political economy was dashed before it started (Qureshi 2002), in the end including only a handful of attempts actually to engage that tradition alongside many more examples of the cultural studies approaches that were, by then, already very much mainstream procedure. Those of us who have been publishing work on political economy must wonder, however, whether a real engagement with music and space can survive without a living tradition of political economy, or at least something like it. After all, while the relationship between music and people's subjectivity (i.e., place) can be simple enough to establish, with discourse as the mediating term, establishing an analogous relationship between the built environment and spatial practices, on the one hand, and music, on the other, requires very different forms of mediation. There one is dealing with relationships that usually cannot be established in ethnographic interviews or inferred from music lyrics, journalism, and album design. Or rather, these last discursive sources of mediation will not disclose much more than the blunt fact of changes in representation; it can always be a wholesale change confined to that representational level. Tagging those changes, in turn, to anything more broadly based in the production of life within a community (or whatever scale one picks) calls for a theoretical structure that renders holistic music and production.[1] Perhaps political economy is not the sole framework in which such an analysis may take place, but, at a minimum, the project requires something that ties music and non-discursive social organization together. If one prefers to think of *habitus* as a way of doing the trick, it may well; speaking of a *habitus* of music and space might enable one to relate the use of "classical" music for relaxation to a more generalized ethereality in music performance, for instance (Krims 2001). After all, if one has practiced music as a way to aestheticize, say, a domestic interior, then one can easily see the enactment of that with music recordings more generally, without requiring the more demanding theoretical apparatus that relates both phenomena to production most generally. A political-economy approach to such a development may prove more satisfyingly complete to some, while others may find such an impulse reductive, determinist, and so on. "Chaq'un(e) sa theorie!", to some extent. But it is worth noting, here, that even the considerably lighter *habitus* framework is needed precisely because it mediates nondiscursively between music and practices of production (in this case, the production of interior space). If a healthy, vibrant scholarly culture of studying music-and-space is to survive, then some such mediating, nondiscursive term will be needed.

And indeed, there are signs that scholars, especially in the past few years, have been meeting this challenge. Bas van Heur (2010) has been studying the changes in built environment, industrial organization, social relations, and music that have been taking place in cities both large and small. Scholars within musicology, music theory, and ethnomusicology looking to engage with such contributions, on a more properly "musicological" level, need only begin with his helpful elaborations of the development and distribution of music genres (Nye 2009), a map that is simultaneously social, musical, and a formation of a unique contemporary moment of capital.

Why the fetishizing of cities, if indeed this is a fetish? The United Nations Population Fund predicted, in 2007, that by the following year more than half the world's population would be living in cities (UNFPA 2007). That blunt statistic alone should suggest the importance of the ways in which cities go to shaping the ebbs and flows of social life; but, of course, even long before most of us lived in some city or other, the centrality of cities to musical creation had been the case at least since the advent of the industrial era (and in many cases, before then, as merely the example of Vienna handily demonstrates). Of course, rural and small-town musical activities existed as well, and continue to exist, and there is no reason to turn a blind eye to them; the origins of blues in the Mississippi delta, and not only the "folk" musics but also the "art"-music production outside the major urban centers, certainly merit their own consideration. But even the Delta blues did not radiate its ultimate fate simply through the juke joints of the South; it was through Memphis and New York City, that the music found its reach, and, in the times since then, networks of (since then) vertically disintegrated centers of music production have come to dominate the music industry (Scott 2000). Cities do not dominate music production, however, simply through the concentration of major recording companies. They also dominate music production as target professional (and residential) preferences for aspiring musicians; as hosts to densely interconnected networks of workers in allied industries such as film, Web design, television, and advertising; as target work and living locations for educated young, childless workers seeking the amenities and variety of the metropolis; and, perhaps most elusively but also most centrally, as formation points of taste, originators, and important disseminators, of trends (Currid 2007).

Understanding those environments that help to produce and disseminate those trends would seem to be crucial to any scholar with a serious interest in topics like the history of musical style and traditions of music performance (which surely are largely cultivated in major cities [Krims 2010]). In the industrial era, with royal courts largely out of the picture and the influence of the Church on musical life largely sidelined, cities become very much the center of musical developments; and yet, where are the studies of the cities historically crucial to mainstream musical history (Vienna, Paris, Berlin, Naples, Rome, and so on) that take most seriously their status and structures *as cities*? There are such studies, of course (such as David Harvey's excellent study of nineteenth-century Paris [Harvey 2003]), but they generally do not foreground the music that these cities contributed to producing and disseminating. That task falls to us music scholars.

NOTE

1 Here, "production" can mean, but need not mean, something economic. Life is produced and reproduced in any number of ways; the production of space is one of them, and the key here is to connect that to the kinds of music produced, circulated, and consumed.

FURTHER READING

Cohen, Sara. 2007. *Decline, renewal and the city in popular music culture: Beyond the Beatles.* Aldershot, U.K.: Ashgate.

Grimley, Daniel. 2006. *Grieg: Music, landscape, and Norwegian identity.* Woodbridge, U.K.: Boydell and Brewer.

Krims, Adam. 2007. *Music and urban geography.* New York: Routledge.

Leyshon, Andrew, David Matless, and George Revill, eds. 1998. *The place of music.* New York: Guilford.

Lipsitz, George. 1997. *Dangerous crossroads: Popular music, postmodernism, and the focus of place.* London: Verso.

Stokes, Martin, ed. 1997. *Ethnicity, identity, and music: The musical construction of place.* Oxford: Berg.

Van Heur, Bas. 2010. *Creative networks and the city: Towards a cultural political economy of aesthetic production.* Bielefeld, Germany: Transcript Verlag.

Whiteley, Sheila, Andy Bennett, and Stan Hawkins, eds. 2005. *Music, space and place: Popular music and cultural identity.* Aldershot, U.K.: Ashgate.

CHAPTER 13

MUSIC AND EVERYDAY LIFE

SIMON FRITH

In the British House of Commons on March 15, 2000, Robert Key, the Conservative MP for Salisbury, begged to move "That leave be given to bring in a Bill to prohibit the broadcasting of recorded music in certain public places" (Hansard [Parliamentary Debates]. Sixth Series, 1999–2000, vol. 346, pp. 326–327).

Key was speaking on behalf of Pipedown, the Campaign for Freedom from Piped Music, but suggested that there would be widespread public support for the measure. He cited a 1997 *Sunday Times* survey that found piped music to be number three in the list of things most hated about modern life. He noted that, following a survey of its users, Gatwick Airport had stopped playing canned music. He drew on medical findings. "All uninvited noise raises the blood pressure and depresses the immune system." He added information from the Chartered Institute of Environmental Health. "The commonest type of offending noise is not pneumatic drills, cars or aircraft but music."

The bill was greeted enthusiastically in the media, perhaps because everyone knew it wouldn't get anywhere. But as a solution to the problem of public music, Key's bill was actually quite modest. He didn't seek to ban piped music from places where people choose to go (stores, hotels, sports clubs). His measure was meant to regulate involuntary listening. It covered hospitals and surgeries, local authority swimming pools, bus and railroad stations and journeys, and the streets. He didn't propose, as he might have, that in the future no one should listen to music except in premises licensed for that purpose.

It is not as if private places are free of musical pollution. How many people now travel by car in silence? Who now doesn't shave or bathe to music, cook or iron to music, read or write to music? Thanks to the radio and recording technologies, music is now the soundtrack of everyday life, and no law is going to change that. And our ears are as likely to be assaulted these days by classical music as by pop. It's not just that music is everywhere but that all music is everywhere. Works composed for specific secular or religious occasions (marches, masses), in specific places (Thailand, Texas), can turn up as if at random on TV commercials and restaurant tape loops. There's no longer any necessary connection between the occasion for making music and the occasion of listening to it. Hence the peculiarity of our present situation: If music was once that organization of sounds that could be distinguished from noise, it has become the epitome of noise itself, more offensive, if Robert Key is to be believed, than the sound of jackhammers.

One theme of twentieth-century composition was to make music out of noise, to reclaim the everyday for art, as it were, to write works *for* jackhammers. Noise-as-music has as many instances as music-as-noise: Cage and Stockhausen wrote works including "live" radio (*Imaginary Landscape No 4* and *Kurzwellen* [*Short Waves*]). Avant-garde composers took up Pierre Schaeffer's and Pierre Henry's idea of *musique concrète* in a variety of genres. Eric Satie, following a different strategy, proposed *musique d'ameublement*, furniture music, which would be unnoticed in the everyday hubbub, an idea followed up much later by Brian Eno in his *Music for Airports*. And, of course, many rock musicians—in heavy metal bands and their offshoots, in the postpunk industrial and noise scenes—have made electronic amplification and the distorting effects of high volume and feedback a central part of their aesthetic.

But what concerns me here is another of John Cage's contributions, his question: What now is silence?

Two points are striking here. First, silence is so rare that it has become, in itself, increasingly valuable. We live now not just with the permanent sense of traffic roar, the routine interruption of sirens and car alarms and mobile phones, but also with the ongoing electric hum of the refrigerator, the central heating, the neon lights, the digital clock. Silence has become the indicator of an unusual intensity of feeling—emotional intensity in the Hollywood film; public solemnity in the two-minute silence on Veterans' Day; the one-minute silence before kickoff in which to honor someone's death. It was, presumably, this that prompted the Independent Television Commission in Britain to censure Independent Television News (ITN) for broadcasting a "sick and tasteless" sequence of news in which "the collapse of the World Trade Center in New York was set to music." The music (from

Charles Gounod's *Judex*) may have been, as ITN claimed, suitable, with "a sombre, funereal tone," but the very attempt to show these images in time to music "was inappropriate and breached the programme code." And silence, as something valuable, to be bought, means not complete silence, but the absence of human or electronic or artificial sounds. Nature—the country retreat, the unspoiled beach or bush or jungle, the mountain wilderness—is the most precious holiday resource.

Because we seem to value silence, to covet it, it is perhaps surprising that silence is also now something to be feared—on radio, in seminars, on the telephone. Here silence becomes something to be *filled*, and music becomes not that which isn't noise, but that which isn't no noise (i.e., silence). Popular music, something once used to drown out other sounds—on the streets, in the music hall and variety theater, in the pub and parlor singsong—is now used to ensure that there is never no sound at all. If the BBC were to reintroduce Lord Reith's rule that programs should be followed by silence, to allow listeners to reflect on what they had heard, I have no doubt that the switchboard would be jammed with complaints: Has something gone *wrong*?

In the House of Commons, Robert Key suggested that there is an important difference between choosing to listen to music in public places and having to listen to it, and, given people's apparent need to fill their lives with music, the implication is that the problem is *what* we have to hear: other people's music, not our own. And certainly the routine use of the term *muzak* to dismiss a certain sort of light instrumental arrangement suggests that what's involved here is a matter of taste. But this may be misleading. People are equally upset by what seems to be the *inappropriate* use of music they do like: Mozart as we wait for a plane to take off; Credence Clearwater or the Clash on a commercial; Miles Davis in a bank. I don't know of any systematic research into what most offends people about the use of music in public places but an unscientific survey of friends and newspaper columnists suggests that what is played matters less than its circumstances.

On the one hand, people seem less offended by live music: children singing in a playground, a brass band or choir in the park, an Andean troupe or reggae guitarist in the shopping mall. A busker singing "Wonderwall" or "Hey! Mr Tambourine Man" badly is less offensive than the original record. The issue here is not aesthetics but sociability. Live music is music as a social event, an aspect of a social situation—play, display, celebration, begging. It is an organic, a living aspect of public life (hence the term *live music*), whatever its technical or aesthetic qualities. Canned music, piped music (terms almost always used with negative connotations of the mechanical), has been removed from its social origins. Like some alien force it moves relentlessly forward regardless of any human responses to it.

On the other hand, anecdotal polling suggests that there are experiences of public music that are particularly offensive whatever the music involved. Music while a telephone is on hold; iPod leak on trains and buses; the bass boom from a car at traffic lights; the endless loop of Christmas songs in December; the sound of other people's parties. The offense here is against one's sense of one's own space—it is being invaded; but it reflects too, I think, resentment, resentment at being so obviously excluded by other people. Music, that is to say, has become a defensive as well as an offensive weapon (just as it has become a way of negotiating shared space, as in the club or on the dance floor).

The question of how and why music got implicated in our sense of personal space is fascinating and has been little explored. It is not just a matter of music in public places; music is equally important in organizing domestic space. From a sociological perspective, that is, we can better understand the domestic relations of intimacy and distance, power and affection, by mapping patterns of musical use than we can explain musical tastes by reference to social variables. How is family space regulated musically? Family members (teenagers most notoriously) mark off their own space with their music—volume as a barrier. But what happens in communal spaces—the kitchen, the car? Who decides what plays? What music is ruled out *tout court* and why?

I doubt if there's anyone nowadays who couldn't map the history of family relationships along musical lines. It's a moot point whether changes in domestic ideology meant new markets for new kinds of domestic electrical goods, or whether it was the new musical possibilities that changed families, but I have no doubt that a sociology of contemporary courtship, romance, sex, and friendship could start with the role of music in these relationships: the exploration of each other's tastes, the shifting degrees of tolerance and intolerance for other people's records, the importance of the musical gift, the attempts to change other people's music habits, to resist changing one's own. I'll come back to this. First I want to digress into some brief remarks about the role in all this of music radio.

I believe that radio was the most significant twentieth-century mass medium. It was radio that transformed the use of domestic space, blurring the boundary between the public and the private, idealizing the family hearth as the site of ease and entertainment, establishing the rhythm of everydayness: the BBC *Children's Hour, Breakfast Time, Friday Night Is Music Night!* It was radio that shaped the new voice of public intimacy, that created Britain as a mediated collectivity, that gave ordinary people a public platform (creating the concept of "ordinary people" in the first place). It was radio that made sport a national symbol, that created the very idea of "light entertainment." Where radio led, television simply followed. And it was radio (rather than film) that established the possibility of music as an ever-playing soundtrack to our lives.

If television in all its varieties were to be abolished, it would make little difference to a classical music world that is, though, almost entirely dependent on radio not just for broadcasts but also for the support of orchestras and concerts, for commissions and record sales. And while the pop world would have to adapt its ways if television no longer played a part in star making, radio is still the most important source of popular musical discourse, defining genres and genre communities, shaping music history and nostalgia, determining what we mean by "popular" music in the first place.

It was radio that created the musical map that we now use to distinguish high and low music, youth and older people's music, the specialist musical interest, and the mainstream. Radio is important not least as a means of access to music otherwise inaccessible, whether in the BBC's systematic policy of musical education or in the furtive teenage use of Radio Luxembourg, the American Forces network, and pirate radio stations as windows on another world.

But here I want to use radio to address another issue: the question of musical choice. In the early days of the music industry, it was assumed that the phonograph and the radio were competing for domestic attention, and it is often suggested that the U.S. record industry survived the Depression years of the 1930s only because of the success of the jukebox (an interesting example of a technological device for imposing private musical choices on a public). It seemed a matter of common sense that, if someone owned a record they could play at will, they wouldn't turn on the radio to hear it. Or, alternatively, if they knew the radio would be routinely playing the latest hits, why would they spend money on getting the records for themselves?

In practice, though, this is not how radio choice works. From the 1950s' rise of top 40 radio in the United States to the 1990s British success of Classic FM, it has become accepted industry wisdom that people are more likely to stay tuned to a radio station the more likely it is to play music that is familiar to them, records that they already own or have just bought. It is much harder to maintain listening figures for programs or stations that routinely play the odd or unfamiliar. And radio remains, of course, the essential tool for selling music of all sorts: The more a track is played, the more likely it is that listeners will buy it.

What seems to be involved in radio listening, then, is a constant movement between predictability and surprise. On "our" station we expect to hear our kind of music, without ever being quite sure what will come next. It's as if we're happy to let someone else have the burden of choice. And radio is also a way of suggesting a broader taste community. Our personal musical likes and dislikes are publicly confirmed, and deejays and presenters have a particularly important role in treating music as a form of social communication. The only kind of radio that acquires the condition of muzak is that deejayless ambient format in which no voice is heard (unless it is selling something).

Radio has also been important in developing the skill of switching attention, moving back and forth between hearing music and listening to it, treating it as background or foreground. It's a skill that is taken for granted by film scorers, and one that we exercise everyday without thought as we walk down the street or sit in the pub. Public music irritates, one could say, when what should be in the background forces itself on us as foreground, but the question that interests me, and to which I will return, is why it is, when we are now so skilled at screening out music that doesn't much interest us, that some songs or voices or melodies or beats just reach out and grab our attention anyway.

For Adorno "all contemporary music life is dominated by the commodity character" and it is the resulting "fetish character in music" that explains "the regression in listening" (Adorno [1938] 1991). Or, as we would say these days, music is a matter of brand and lifestyle. Take this report from the music industry trade paper *Music Week*:

> There was further good news for Classic FM last week when its TV-advertised Time to Relax entered the compilation chart at number nine. "Getting listeners to buy into the Classic brand is at the heart of what we do," says [Roger] Lewis [Classic FM program controller]. "As well as the albums we have the magazine, a credit card and even a dating agency. We are seeing a classical music phenomenon in the UK, as suddenly it's cool to be classical."
>
> (*Music Week*, November 3, 2001)

But underlying such brash commercialism are two broader transformations in how music now works in society, the transformations to which Adorno is in part referring when he uses the term *commodity character*. On the one hand, we primarily think of music in terms of its *use*; on the other hand, usefulness means *individual* use.

It is the use of music as a commercial tool to which we mostly object these days: its use to manipulate us in the market. There can be few people who are unaware of how music is used by advertisers and retailers. But it is equally important to note that people nowadays routinely use music to manipulate their moods and organize their activities *for themselves*.

The pioneering researchers of music and everyday life in Britain, sociologist Tia DeNora and psychologist John A. Sloboda, both emphasize the extent to which people now regard music as a personal tool, something to be used, in DeNora's terms, for "emotional self-regulation" (DeNora 2000). As a "technology of self," music has become crucial to the ways in which people organize memory, identity, their autonomy. Both writers suggest that the driving force of people's everyday use is the need to be in control, and that today this means integrating emotional and aesthetic control: creating the setting for the appropriate display of feeling (whether to oneself or to others). Sloboda's research also shows that people are more likely to use music to accompany chores than pleasures, tasks done as duties rather than enjoyed for their own sake (Sloboda and O'Neill 2001). Joggers routinely wear an iPod; walkers do not. Once the dinner party conversation comes to life no one bothers to put on a new CD.

In many societies, as ethnomusicologists have told us, the functions of music could be described in almost exclusively social terms: Music was used in games and for dancing; to organize work and war; in ceremonies and rituals; to mark the moments of birth, marriage, and death; to celebrate harvest and coronation; and to articulate religious beliefs and traditional practices. People might have enjoyed music individually, but its purpose was not to make them feel good. Compare assumptions now about the use of music. In a survey of 210 works on "the power of music" (commissioned by The Performing Right Society), Susan Hallam notes how contemporary research is focused on the use of music for therapy and medical treatment, for enhancing children's learning abilities, and for influencing individual behavior. Among her "key points" are these:

> Music can promote relaxation, alleviate anxiety and pain, promote appropriate behaviour in vulnerable groups and enhance the quality of life of those who are beyond medical help.
> People can use music in their lives to manipulate their moods, alleviate the boredom of tedious tasks, and create environments appropriate for particular social events.
> The easy availability of music in everyday life is encouraging individuals to use music to optimise their sense of well being.
>
> (Hallam 2001, 1)

And she concludes her survey of research by suggesting that

> [t]here is also need for more systematic investigation of the ways that music can impact on groups of people in social settings. To date, research has tended to focus on commercial and work environments. The way that music may affect behaviour in public places has been neglected. Such research, for instance, might explore whether particular types of music might stimulate orderly exits from large public functions, reduce the incidence of disorder in particular settings, increase tolerance when people have to queue for relatively long periods of time or engender feelings of well being and safety in public places.
>
> (Hallam 2001, 19)

There are, in fact, already reports of music being used for such social engineering—classical music played in railroad stations to make them unsuitable as youth hangouts, for example—and what I want to note about this is less dismay that music should have become a technology of discipline rather than delight, than that it marks a significant shift in our understanding of *how* music is powerful. While the Taliban outlawed music with the traditional anxiety that it is a source of collective disorder, a challenge to religious authority, in modern societies discipline is internalized. What's at stake is not what people want to do but usually (until released by music) don't, but what they don't want to do in the first place. Music remains "a powerful medium of social order," but its power is exercised less through group psychology, the orchestration of crowds, than through individual psychology, the articulation of self.

Tia DeNora concludes her book on *Music in Everyday Life* by suggesting that

> [f]urther explorations of music as it is used and deployed in daily life in relation to agency's configuration will only serve to highlight what Adorno, and the Greek philosophers, regarded as a fundamental matter in relation to the polis, the citizen and the configuration of consciousness; namely, that music is much more than a decorative art; that it is a powerful medium of social order. Conceived in this way, and documented through empirical research, music's presence is clearly political, in every sense that the political can be conceived.
>
> (DeNora 2000, 163)

I want to conclude by reiterating DeNora's suggestion that music is much more than a decorative art. In *The Sociology of Rock*, published in 1978, I began with the observation that while recorded music was usually included in a list of the contemporary mass media in textbooks, it was rarely otherwise examined. More than thirty years on and the situation hasn't really changed. The cinema, television, newspapers, magazines, and advertising are still regarded in the academy as more socially and politically significant than records. And so it needs stressing that what people listen to is more important for their sense of themselves than what they watch or read. Patterns of music use provide a better map of social life than viewing or reading habits. Music just *matters* more than any other medium, and this brings me back to my starting point and the ways in which music is now heard as offensive. It is because music is now used to mark private territory that it can also "invade" it; it is because music has become so deeply implicated in people's personas that it can be misused; and it is because music is now so widely employed as an emotional tool that its misuse is genuinely upsetting.

But there are two further points I want to make. First, DeNora and Sloboda tend to refer musical meaning to its emotional function for individuals, but music remains equally important as a means of communication and as a form of sociability. Most academic research on everyday music focuses, as I have focused here, on music listening. But what is equally remarkable is the sheer amount of *music making* in which people are engaged, and my point here is not just that people do, in large numbers, join choirs, form rock and pop groups, play around with record decks, and set up home studios, but also that these musical activities are central to their understanding of who they are. Music making provides, as Ruth Finnegan argues, critical pathways through life (Finnegan 1989). And music making is less about managing one's own emotional life than about enjoying being together in groups, real and imagined. Future research in music and the everyday needs to integrate the study of music making with the study of musical use. To my mind, ongoing investigation of people's tastes and the current research focus on issues of identity are much less interesting projects than an ethnography that would try to map in detail people's *timetable of engagement*, the reasons why particular music gets particular attention at particular moments, and how these moments are, in turn, imbricated in people's social networks.

Second, and to register finally my unease at treating music in simple functional terms, we need to balance accounts of how people use music to manage their emotions with accounts of how music still has the unexpected power to disrupt us emotionally. The ancient myths of musical power—the stories of the Sirens, Orpheus, the Pied Piper—have a continued force not primarily because of advertisers' ceaseless attempts to lead us astray but because of the much more mysterious power of music *in itself*. How is it that a voice suddenly reaches us, out of the background, whether we are paying attention or not? Whatever the strength of those commercial and technological forces that turn the transcendent into the trite, I don't think we have lost the sense that music, the musical experience, is *special*, that it is a way of one person reaching another without deceit. There's still no better way than through music to be surprised by life.

FURTHER READING

Bennett, Tony, M. Emmison, and John Frow. 1999. *Accounting for tastes: Australian everyday cultures.* Cambridge, U.K.: Cambridge University Press.

Booth, Wayne. 1999. *For the love of it: Amateuring and its rivals.* Chicago: University of Chicago Press.

Hargreaves, D. J., and A. C. North, 1997. *The social psychology of music.* Oxford: Oxford University Press.

Hennion, Antoine, Sophie Maisonneuve, and Emilie Gomart. 2000. *Figures de l'amateur: Formes, objets, pratiques de l'amour de la musique aujourd'hui.* Paris: La Documentation Française.

Lanza, Joseph. 1994. *Elevator music: A surreal history of muzak, easy-listening and other moodsong.* London: Quartet.

Scannell, Paddy. 1996. *Radio, television and modern life.* Oxford: Blackwell.

PART 3

How?
Processes, Practices, and Institutions of Music

CHAPTER 14

MUSIC, CULTURE, AND CREATIVITY

JASON TOYNBEE

Although creativity might seem an obvious topic for the cultural study of music, until recently little attention has been paid to it, certainly within the field of cultural studies. Perhaps the main factor has been a populist current that runs through the field as a whole (McGuigan 1992). Its logic goes like this. Authorship and creativity are associated with high art; high art is elitist; therefore creativity is not an appropriate subject for cultural studies, concerned as it is with the culture of the people. Several intellectual tributaries have then strengthened this position. Structuralism, particularly important in the 1970s, focused on relations between elements in the text while ignoring the stage of production. Post-structuralism went even further. For example, in his highly influential essay "The Death of the Author," Roland Barthes (1977) lampooned the "author-god" and argued that the meaning of literature is realized at the moment of reception rather than creation. Finally, the ethnographic tradition in cultural studies, where culture equates to way of life, has focused almost entirely on the consumption of artifacts. Interestingly, the concept of creativity does persist here, but as "symbolic creativity," a phenomenon that animates everyday activities, like listening and dancing to music (Willis 1990). From this perspective, then, creativity is widely distributed through the cultural practices of ordinary people (Gauntlett 2007)

My response to all these tendencies in cultural studies that want to do away with creativity, or dissolve it into the everyday, is a banal plea for moderation: don't go so far. For while listening and dancing *are* surely creative, music (like any other symbolic system) is in an obvious sense fashioned by those who design and perform it. Production comes first, in other words, and, depending on the division of labor that exists in any particular case, it is the composer, instrumentalist, singer, and engineer who shape the phenomenal form of the musical text.

Actually, there has been a resurgence of academic interest in understanding the nature of creative labor recently (see Hesmondhalgh and Baker 2011), as well as in the way such work might constitute a form of practice that depends on "virtues" intrinsic to it (Banks 2007). Such research has been important in showing not only the micro-organisation of creativity in cultural production but also its normative dimension, namely how creative work matters ethically. By and large, though, this new strand has not tried to explain creative action in terms of outcomes, or how music makers come to create the artifacts they do—their compositions, recordings, performances, and so on. Nor has there been much consideration of aesthetic value, a key issue because, as Keith Negus and Michael Pickering (2004) suggest, to consider creativity necessarily involves some form of evaluation. We need to establish which songs and symphonies are genuinely creative as opposed to merely competent.

And that is where consumption comes back in, not so much as a cultural practice in its own right as with the cultural studies work on audiences and the everyday, but more in terms of the social production of value and the accreditation of creativity. If we take as wide a range of musical creators as Chopin, Louis Armstrong, and Lady Gaga, their creativity is manifested precisely through post hoc evaluation, a process of diffusion and reception that is cultural in the widest possible sense. The issue cannot then be reduced to one of choosing either production or reception as the moment in which cultural value is realized. Rather, *both* count in any analysis of creativity. To state this not only challenges the skepticism about creative work found in cultural studies, it also constitutes a reproach to Romanticism, the strongest account we have of creativity as a factor of production.

Romantic discourse asserts that music comes from within and is a direct product of the psyche of the creator. A passage from a letter by Tchaikovsky shows this quite nicely:

> Generally speaking, the germ of a future composition comes suddenly and unexpectedly. If the soil is ready—that is to say, if the disposition for work is there—it takes root with extraordinary force and rapidity, shoots up through the earth, puts forth branches, leaves and, finally, blossoms. . . . It would be vain to try to put into words that immeasurable sense of bliss which comes over me directly [when] a new idea awakens in me and begins to assume a definite form. I forget everything and behave like a madman. Everything within me starts pulsing and quivering; hardly have I begun the sketch ere one thought follows another.
>
> (Tchaikovsky [1878] 1970, 57)

Three main points, utterly typical of Romantic discourse, can be pulled out of this passage, I think. First, the creative process is solipsistic. Both *germ* and *soil* are located within Tchaikovsky's own psyche and have no connection to other music making, past or present. Second, creation is involuntary, and involves possession by a creative demon that is not subject to conscious control. Third, composition takes place in stages, from inchoate "new idea" to "definite form." This is a transformational approach to creation whose origins, as George Steiner points out, can be traced to the Christian doctrine of transubstantiation (Steiner 2001, 46–48). Such an understanding of creativity has become hugely influential, and not just in the realm of art music. Both jazz and rock fans have adopted the heroic mode and, along with it, a tendency to lionize artist-creators (Frith 1998). It is clear too that the musicians themselves tend to understand their work in Romantic terms— as the outpouring of a tortured, solitary soul (e.g., Wenner 1972 for John Lennon; Mingus 1995). However, I want to argue that there are fundamental problems with such a conception.

Above all, it treats creation as a mystical process, and creators as a select band of individual geniuses. In doing so, Romanticism ignores the profoundly social nature of authorship in all forms of culture, including music. Writers from quite different traditions help to open up this alternative approach to creativity. So, the sociologist Howard Becker (1982) makes the point that new art works emerge only through the interaction of artists, co-workers, and audiences. When interaction is intensely repeated, it may solidify in conventions that organize both the way the artist works and how the audience responds. However, the artist is not necessarily aware of such conventions. Rather, in making a creative choice he or she works intuitively. Becker calls this the "editorial moment," that is, when the artist identifies creative options and then selects from them according to informal criteria that represent, in the case of music, an ideal listener's point of audition. For Becker, then, creation involves small amounts of individual agency and large amounts of regular, if complex, social interaction. Even the most intense and solitary moments of creative passion depend on careful monitoring of choices from a (virtual) position outside the creator's own subjectivity, and in the thick of the culture in which he or she works. As Becker puts it, "art worlds rather than artists make art" (pp. 198–199).

The Soviet literary critic Mikhail Bakhtin (1981) then complements this approach. Like Becker, he is concerned with interaction, but more in relation to the ingredients of art—in his case speech as it feeds into the novel. The defining attribute of the novelistic form, Bakhtin suggests, is dialogue, and this consists not only of the idiomatic utterances of characters but also of a huge range of "speech genres" quoted by characters or embedded in the discourse of the narrator. In an important sense, then, the novel is a fabric woven from voices that already exist, and that therefore have socially ascribed connotations and even structural significance. To use Bakhtin's terms, the dynamism of the novel derives from the "interanimation" of these voices, a process that "refracts" authorial intention rather than directly expressing it.

There is a problem with applying Bakhtin's theory of dialogism to music, namely its basis in a radically dissimilar system of communication—language. In everyday life in the industrialized world people do still produce music; for example, in amateur productions, karaoke, or casual whistling. But this is on a much smaller scale than the speaking they do. As a result, musical genres, whether classical or pop, are considerably less demotic than language genres. Furthermore, it is hard to find any musical equivalent of the utterance, a univocal syntagma with one dominating parameter in the shape of semantic content. Music, of course, is always multiparametric, generally polyphonic, and has little or no denotative meaning. A further significant divergence between language and music lies in the fact that dialogue is defined precisely by the diachronic segmentation of differently voiced utterances. Antiphony in music has a similar function, but its importance varies enormously by genre. Rarely is it of defining significance.

If these are necessary caveats, I still want to argue that the general principle of dialogism, particularly the notion that cultural production consists of the interanimation of social materials, is so cogent that it must lie at the center of any theory of creativity. How might it be applied to music then? Quite simply, music needs to be understood as an ensemble of coded voices. On the one hand, these may be sounds that come from a recognizable place and time: the sliding tones of the early Billie Holiday, say, or a baroque harpsichord in busy chime. In this respect coded voices are comparable to Bakhtin's utterances, being pieces of musical fabric with an identifiable source and therefore also a particular social milieu. On the other hand the emphasis may be more on what Umberto Eco calls, in his theory of semiotics, "system code," namely "elements oppositionally structured and governed by combinatorial rules that can generate both finite and infinite strings or chains of these elements" (1976, 38). Here it is relatively abstract rules and forms that are most at stake. Examples include the movement structure of the concerto or the metrical organization of the British electronic dance genre called grime.

Now, as Eco stresses, while fabric and code may be distinguished analytically, in practice "[s]ignification encompasses the whole of cultural life" (p. 46). Or, in the terms used here, the coded voice can always be located on a continuum running between the formal and the phenomenal. Thus Billie Holiday's voice—the particular thing we hear—is also always a generative, rule-governed system, while the structure of the baroque concerto can never be completely separated from the sound of a baroque concerto performed. Clearly, this approach runs counter to the strict separation of form and sounded work generally found in musical analysis. And it is opposed also to the closely related idea–expression dichotomy in copyright law. This attempts to demarcate the uncopyrightable idea at stake in a piece of music or other symbolic artifact, which may circulate freely, from its specific expression in the work itself. The latter is the property of its creator and protected by copyright. My point would be that such binaries are much better conceived in terms of tendencies, which are co-present to varying degrees in what I have been calling the *coded voice*. This certainly makes it a broad category. Yet that very breadth enables a powerful, large-scale theory of the process of musical creation to be constructed.

At a general level, then, the author's work can be understood as the identification of coded voices and their arrangement in meaningful dialogue. Most of these arrangements will be already given. Whether we consider genres and movements in classical music (the sonata, the string quartet, impressionism, and so on) or in pop (rap, new country, sixteen-bar verse-chorus structures, etc.), the collocation of coded voices is highly conventional. In effect, competence as a social author consists of being able to identify and deploy appropriate voices so as to meet a minimum threshold of stylistic accomplishment. However, this does not necessarily amount to creativity. Earlier on I emphasized the importance of listener recognition in evaluation. We might say now that what is being recognized in the case of a "creative" work is a particular relation to the stylistic norm. This may involve transcendence of the norm, or even, in the case of avant-garde aesthetics, its transgression. But just as often, the work will strive to implement or express the norm completely. This is a centripetal tendency where what is at stake is crystallization of style.

Whatever form such relationships with stylistic norms may take, though, the question remains: how do they come into being? Or, to put this in a different way, why are some music makers particularly creative? We can usefully call on another sociologist of culture here. Pierre Bourdieu (1993b) argues that two structuring factors tend to shape the making of art. First there is the "field of production," marked by a system of positions. The contemporary musical field is clearly enormous. It is a great landscape of scenes and schools, each one made up of a cluster of music makers working with a particular set of stylistic norms. But the key point is that any particular position, with certain quantities and kinds of status attached to it, attracts particular music makers.

Second, from the other direction as it were, aspiring musical creators are disposed to aim for a particular position in the field according to "habitus," the way of going on in the world that every actor "carries" with her. It is largely acquired during the early years, and is determined by a complex of social factors such as class, education, and gender. Critically, the push of musician habitus and the pull of the field tend to converge, and it is through the highly charged *near* alignment of these forces that a "space of possibles" (Bourdieu 1993b, 176–177, 182–185) then opens up. What Bourdieu calls possibles are nothing less than creative choices in the terms I am using here. They are made much more frequently when the field starts to shift, or when new kinds of authors begin to push forward. In these circumstances the space of possibles expands, and creative possibilities further out along the "radius of creativity" become audible (Toynbee 2000, 35–42).

Let me try to depict this graphically. Imagine a circular space of possible creative choices delimited by a certain radius. At the center is what I call the "social author." A cluster of densely distributed dots around her represent those regularly selected choices required for the competent production of a text in a given genre. Moving out along the radius, an increasingly thin distribution of dots indicates not only the increasing difficulty of making choices beyond the datum of genre, but also a larger and larger space of possibilities. It is less predictable what will be done out here. Eventually, inscribed by the end of the radius is a fuzzy perimeter or virtual horizon of possibility beyond which the author cannot identify any coded voices at all.

Three points need to be made about the thinly dispersed choices toward the outside of the radius. First, they still represent the selection of *coded* voices. So, in the case of transgressive creative acts, which yield unlikely sounds and structures, there must be recognition of their meaningfulness on the part of the audience. To this end cues are offered or countercodes implied. Equally, where crystallization is at stake, detailed attention to the main strands of the style reveals subcodes that can then be explored and developed. In either case the new is produced through a process of linking back to the "body of conventions" (Becker 1982, 30) that governs the more obvious choices around the center. Such a process encapsulates a defining paradox about creativity: difference needs to be recognized. The second point is that the literally eccentric choices in the model depend on combination. Arthur Koestler (1975, 35–38) argues that "bisociation" is central to creativity. He means by this the putting together of previously unconnected components that then produce a surprising synthesis. Bisociation is very much what is at stake further out along the radius as choices become more and more thinly distributed. Third, highly creative choices are often made when a social author arrives at a position in the field that is *not* strongly indicated by habitus. In other words, the "wrong" kind of background and disposition can produce the conditions for a particularly creative combination of voices. Hector Berlioz with his less than fully adequate formal training in composition is a case in point. From another angle, so is John

Cale—Welsh, working class, and overtrained for the New York rock scene of the mid-1960s.

These mechanisms of recognition, combination, and "misalignment" of habitus and field are all real causal factors which generate creative acts. Still, creativity cannot be reduced to them. For creativity, like all social processes, is *emergent*, that is to say it cannot be fully explained by its generative structures. On the one hand these provide the conditions of possibility of creative practice. On the other, such practices have a certain autonomy which derives precisely from combination, association, and the coming into being of the practices at a higher ontological level than the generative structures from which they emerge (see Bhaskar 1998, 97–99 for discussion of emergence more generally).

Up to now I have been making rather broad claims about creativity, and suggesting that they apply to all types of musical production. This is an important step in the argument. Too frequently Western art music and its Others are counterposed as radically distinct when in fact common problems of structure and meaning are encountered everywhere in musical analysis (McClary and Walser 1990). Yet there *are* important differences across the musical field and between popular and classical music in particular. In considering creativity we cannot avoid them.

To begin with there is the issue of distribution of creative roles. In Western classical music, composition and performance are generally separated. Composers may play or conduct their own works of course. Nonetheless, the apparatus of sheet music and concert hall reinforces the creative supremacy of the composer in her or his absence and the corresponding subservience of performers (Small 1987). In contrast, pop's division of labor varies to a considerable degree. There is, however—particularly since the 1960s—a strong tendency toward the sharing of creative functions. In a sense this represents the re-traditionalization of music, a "return" to the kind of people's music making found throughout the world in premodern societies. The strongest example of this is the small rock band with its own "writers" as in the archetypal group, The Beatles (MacDonald 1995). Conversely, in the Motown "factory" system responsibility for molding the sound of a recording is split among writers, arrangers, singers, players, and producers (George 1985). What both examples have in common, though, is a high degree of flat, art-world interaction between creative actors. This divergence between pop and classical music is then associated with another difference. Classical music consists of a canon of emphatically first-rate work composed by great *auteurs*. On the other hand, pop has a historically varying system of genres and stars, but also one-off hits and sublime oddities. Another way of putting this is to say that the field of classical music is relatively unified and stable, while the popular field is fragmented and volatile.

Finally, there are differences to do with form. Andrew Chester has argued that popular music may be defined by the "intensional development" of materials. He means by this inflection and variation within a basic form—the 12-bar blues, say. This is a method of creativity that involves "inward" movement toward complexity along many dimensions. And it depends too on articulation of parameters (intonation or the sound of the human voice, for example) that are assumed to be fixed in classical music. Conversely, classical music is characterized by extensional development. Here "[t]he complex is created by combination of the simple, which remains discrete and unchanged in the complex unity" (Chester [1970] 1990, 315). Nicholas Cook makes a similar point. Composers in the tonal tradition, he suggests, work by elaborating simple motifs so as to produce a progressively more complex structure (Cook 1990, 187–216).

It seems to me that the distinction between intension and extension is extremely illuminating for the study of creativity. What is more, it complements Franco Fabbri's semiotic approach to musical codes and generic change. Fabbri's musical code is very like the system code delineated by Eco—it is a set of combinatorial rules. Crucially, though, Fabbri sets up two historical types: "rich" and "poor" (1982, 61–62). Rich codes are associated with the durable rules of classical music. They are capable of generating complex musical texts. Clearly, rich codes also have the capacity to generate *long* texts where not only are motivic atoms recombined over the length of a piece, but large-scale harmonic development may also take place. By contrast, the poor codes of pop yield *short* texts (the mythical perfect pop record plays for 2 minutes 30 seconds), which deteriorate quickly as musical communities become "analytically competent," and find successive texts more and more predictable. It might be said, then, that the intensionality of the poor code consists of a movement down into the synchronic microcoding of texture and meter, or what might be described as a process of 'intensification' (for an elaboration of this in the case of Jamaican popular music see Toynbee 2007, 92–94).

How does such a way of conceiving the structure of classical music and pop impact on the analysis of creativity? In the first place we need to recognize that textual organization is fully social in both cases. Becker's point about conventions being highly regularized forms of interaction applies here. Code is simply repeated social action: a "doing it this way." But then, almost immediately, we encounter a significant difference between the two broad types. On the one hand the social authors of popular music tend to be code shapers. As we have seen, the poverty of pop codes means that sooner or later redundancy sets in, and this is quickly followed by bending or even breaking of rules. Moreover, because the field is relatively open there is no formal induction or exclusion through academic training. As a result the habitus of aspiring music makers varies strongly. Sometimes they may not achieve competence in a code before they enter the field. Sometimes it may not be clear exactly what competence consists of.

Thus, from a sociological perspective as much as a textual one, popular music is volatile and has a tendency to mutate. To put it another way, the most creative episodes in popular music making always involve code shaping and generic change.

In classical music, on the other hand, codes have been relatively stable. Edward Said describes functional tonality from Mozart to Mahler as "a police regime of the signifier." This was a language that suppressed radical transformation (1992, 56). It also involved a system of authorship whereby composers worked *through* a set of rules. Code might be adapted by the handful of great composers (in the conventional wisdom greatness consisted of "making one's own" the language of tonality), but it could never be fundamentally altered. Arguably, the advent of serialism did represent something more radical. Yet as Schoenberg himself proposed, serialism was actually "an organisation granting logic, coherence and unity." It would therefore enable one "to compose as before" (quoted in Griffiths 1978, 91). In the terms we have been using above, serialism represented a renewal of extensive composition through the application of a new rich code. Twentieth-century inflections of the tonal system (neoclassicism, for example) then constitute a less radical version of the same move. It is only with the various kinds of avant-gardism, minimalism, *musique concrète*, and electronica that code-shaping itself becomes an important principle of the creative process. And even here the field demands academic credentials of a very particular and historically invariant kind from its novitiates. Composers must not only be competent in the use of consecrated codes, they must also be grammarians, able to state how breaking and making rules "works."

In this chapter I have been arguing that creativity in music needs to be reconceived as a cultural process rather than a heroic act. New music—in other words significantly different music—is made by social authors who work in networks, collaborating (and sometimes fighting) with co-workers, critics, industry, and audiences. Social authorship also implies a social semiotics in that creation is a matter of selecting from a pool of coded voices that are shared within a given musical community. If these are general characteristics, a relative openness of the field to authors from a variety of cultures, and hence with diverse forms of competence, has tended to differentiate pop from classical music. In addition pop's short texts and poor codes have demanded that its authors be code *shapers*, constantly making new combinations of voice.

Creativity is thus manifestly a cultural process. But how then to account for the persistence of a romantic myth of the individual creator in the post-Romantic age—from, say, Elliott Carter to Missy Elliott? It would perhaps be easiest to explain this in political-economic terms. The industry strives to reduce uncertainty of demand by marketing a few big stars (Miège 1989). And in popular music it has been convenient to graft stardom onto the authorship cult of small group or performer-writer that has predominated in the rock era. As for art music, the system of commissioning and state subsidy represents nothing but the bureaucratization of the individual creator in the modern age. Still, the romantic cult of creativity is not just imposed. Listeners actively embrace it, partly for reasons of efficiency. To admire a limited number of great artists makes learning and sharing knowledge about music more economic (M. Adler 1985). And music makers of course want romanticism too. Perhaps the key factor here is the endemic likelihood of failure. In such a situation, to imagine oneself a lone creator with a special gift provides both a pretext for autonomy—"I am instructed by my muse"—and an excuse for failure—"society cannot understand what I do." Finally, for the handful of stars who benefit from intellectual property, the cult of individual genius justifies their copyright income.

In effect, then, romantic discourse about creativity ties together industry, artist, and audience. Or to put it another way, capitalist ideology built on insecurity and the profit motive suppresses the social nature of the creative process (Stratton 1982). Yet such ideological work can never be complete. For the myth of the heroic creator is always already premised on a utopian imperative: if music transcends everyday life (though arguably it *organizes* the quotidian too: see Frith, Chapter 13 above), then so must its producers in their abundant creative capabilities and extraordinary personalities. Ultimately this represents a goal for everyone. We should all be creators together, and in this way transform the limited social practice of music making into something universal and collective. Looked at this way, the contradiction between romantic ideology and the reality of social author-ship is simply one more symptom of the contradictions within the capitalist system as a whole.

FURTHER READING

Bourdieu, Pierre. 1996. *The rules of art: Genesis and structure of the literary field.* Cambridge, U.K.: Polity Press.

Csikszentmihalyi, Mihaly. 1999. Implications of a systems perspective for the study of creativity. Pp. 313–335 in *Handbook of creativity.* Edited by Robert J. Sternberg. Cambridge, U.K.: Cambridge University Press.

Elder Vass, D. 2007. Reconciling Archer and Bourdieu in an emergentist theory of action, *Sociological Theory* 25(4): 325–346.

Gardner, Howard. 1993. *Creating minds: An anatomy of creativity.* New York: Basic Books.

Keil, Charles. 1994. Participatory discrepancies and the power of music. Pp. 96–108 in *Music grooves: Essays and dialogues*. Edited by Charles Keil and Steven Feld. Chicago: University of Chicago Press.

Moore, Allan. 2001. *Rock: The primary text. Developing a musicology of rock*. 2nd ed. Aldershot, U.K: Ashgate.

Sawyer, R. 2006. Group creativity: musical performance and collaboration, *Psychology of Music* 34(2): 148–165.

CHAPTER 15

MUSICAL AUTONOMY REVISITED

DAVID CLARKE

> Attempts to annul what is contradictory in the development of art, by playing off a "moralizing" against an "autonomous" art, miss the point because they overlook what is liberating in autonomous and what is regressive in moralizing art.
>
> Peter Bürger

EXPOSITION

The concept of musical autonomy has been having a hard time of it lately. Be it from quarters sociological, new-historicist, or feminist (the list goes on, but this gives the gist), the word is out that to construe music purely as an art for its own sake is to perpetuate a discredited ideology. Charges against the autonomy concept are several. It is bourgeois and hegemonic: it wants to present its socially and historically specific paradigm as universal and as the measure against which all other musics are evaluated (so distorting our reception of popular, vernacular, and non-Western musics). It is reifying and atrophying: its promotion of music as meaningful purely in its own terms, allegedly floating free from historical and social contingencies, underwrites a canon of putatively timeless masterworks—the fossilized museum culture of classical music. It is patriarchal and sexist: until recently this canon has deflected both feminist critique and female participation because, on the one hand, its music, putatively formed only out of its own stuff, denies the influence of anything so worldly as gender (McClary 1991, 55), while, on the other hand, in the record of actual social practice, the principal genres of autonomous music—symphony, sonata, string quartet—and their associated aesthetic of greatness have been the prerogative of male composers (Scott 1994). Carrying the burden of so many sins, then, it is only to be expected that autonomous music has found it necessary to commit suicide (Chua 1999, 221–223, 266–275), only to find itself "as dead as Elvis," surviving like the inert cinders of a formerly living practice (Kramer 1995, 227–242).

Look around you, though, and these critical generalities get muddied in the complex particulars of empirical life. Consider, for example, how for a season in parts of Britain free instrumental lessons in schools and a flourishing culture of local youth orchestras held out the possibility of breaking the middle-class monopoly on access to the practice of classical music (and its associated autonomist aesthetic). Consider too the game of cultural negotiation required of a schoolkid learning, say, the violin under this initiative, who has to juxtapose a classical musical practice—with its connotations of effeminacy—alongside a youth culture infused by conspicuous mass musical consumption. From this perspective, what is hegemonic and what is emancipatory, what is atrophied and what is vital, may look a little different. Readers will have probably suspected an autobiographical element at work here; but the intention is not to be anecdotal. Rather I want to suggest that the social and cultural mediations acquired by autonomous classical music in the grand sweep of history may be open to redefinition and revaluation, and that this possibility may be prompted by, among other things, personal and local histories that don't entirely square with the characterizations of autonomy in recent critical accounts.

In advancing the possibility of other critical positions, however, I don't wish to institutionalize a simplistic for-or-against model of argument or allegiance. It seems to me to be as futile to deny that autonomous musical practices are ideologically problematic as it is to claim that they no longer have valuable cultural work to do. I am more inclined to argue for bringing these contradictions to a fuller consciousness and considering how they can be worked through within our contemporary cultural situation. This is a position broadly analogous with Fredric Jameson's refusal to come down squarely on one side or the other of the modernism–postmodernism debate, citing instead the idea of a "historical and dialectic analysis" which "cannot afford the impoverished luxury of . . . absolute moralizing judgements: the dialectic is 'beyond good and evil' in the sense of some easy taking of sides" (1988, 381). Part of that dialectical consciousness certainly involves heeding Lydia Goehr's call for a revaluation of the autonomous artwork's alleged "universal and absolute validity" (1992, 273)—in other words putting the autonomy aesthetic in its place, as one musical species among many. But I want to argue for a more dynamic, frictional view of musical autonomy within this pluralist situation: as a modern concept that may still have important critical currency within a postmodern cultural landscape. In this sense, then, Jameson's framework is indeed relevant (and I mention it again below), as is his call for a historically informed understanding of the situation.

DEVELOPMENT

The historiography of autonomous music—music emancipated from ritual or ceremonial function; music whose meaning is not dependent on an accompanying text or imagery—is itself a site of polemic, not least regarding dating (cf. Strohm 2000; Goehr 2000). These differences notwithstanding, I pursue below one of the dominant narratives of autonomous music, which locates its emergence around 1800. This situates aesthetic autonomy within the wider conditions of *modernity* in which—following the Enlightenment's cultivation of Reason—rationality, morality, and sensuality separate into radically independent modalities of knowledge (Bernstein 1992, 5–6). There is space here only to sketch some of the key points of this history, but more detailed accounts may be found in writings referenced in the process.

What also needs stressing—something implicit in this account so far—is the potential for slippage between the idea of autonomy and other concepts that while not synonymous nevertheless overlap semantically. Start talking about such autonomous forms as the symphony and sonata, for example, and the concept of a musical *work* (as opposed to the n-dozenth piece exemplifying a genre) lurks not far behind; and this notion in turn is something peculiar to, though not a sole defining criterion of, *Western classical music* (Horn 2000). On a broader canvas still, the idea of autonomy is difficult to unhitch from the idea of the aesthetic as such—that strong concept of art (Art with a capital A) that differentiates it from merely socially functional practices. And then there is the concept of *absolute music* (and its associated notion of *formalism*), often treated as interchangeable with the idea of autonomous instrumental music, but in fact, like all the other terms mentioned, arising within its own historically and culturally specific discourse. In one way or another all these terms contribute to a constellation around the musical autonomy idea. Indeed it is arguably their convergence in the period following the Enlightenment that defines what I term the *strong* autonomy concept. (And I later consider whether new configurations of the idea could be related to a dispersal and redistribution of these elements.)

The roots of the concept lie in changing constructions of musical meaning, specifically the meaning of *instrumental music*, at the turn of the eighteenth and nineteenth centuries. Already among the Enlightenment *philosophes* we can detect a move away from previous understandings of instrumental music as *mimetic*—as emulating sounds in nature, or imitative of the human voice itself, or an analogue for rhetorical oratory—toward a view that such music may be its own justification. For example, the ency-clopedist Marmontel writes: "If through a veil of sound [instrumental] music allows the listener to see and feel what he pleases depending on his individual state of mind at the concert then it has served its purpose" (quoted in Ford 1991, 42). For Kant such a "play of sensations" ([1790] 1952, 184) put music at the top of the merely *agreeable* arts but at the bottom of the more highly rated *fine* arts (p. 195). However, other theorists writing around the turn of the nineteenth century developed a concept of fine art that, more than just accommodating instrumental music under its banner, would eventually make it its definitive paradigm.

This predominantly Germanophone line of thought belongs to the moment of early romanticism or idealism—related but not identical philosophical–aesthetic movements (cf. Goehr 1992, 148–75; Bonds 1997, 389ff.). Key writers include Wackenroder, Tieck, Novalis, Schelling, and E. T. A. Hoffmann. But there were numerous others, among them Christian Gottfried Körner, who in an essay published in 1795 posited a new level to which a composer might elevate music: "he should *idealize* his material. . . . he should . . . present the infinite as an intuition [*Anschauung*], which outside of art is permitted merely as thought [*zu denken*]" (quoted in Bonds 1997, 402 n. 46; my translation). Similar sentiments are found in Hoffmann's famous 1810 review of Beethoven's Fifth Symphony: "Music reveals to man an unknown realm, a world quite separate from the outer sensual world surrounding him, a world in which he leaves behind all feelings circumscribed by intellect in order to embrace the inexpressible" (Hoffmann [1810] 1989, 236).

Taken together, Körner's and Hoffmann's statements suggest a contract between composer and listener—and their mutual empowerment. The lofty responsibilities ascribed to the former by Körner (entirely consistent with romantic notions of genius) are reciprocated in the equally committed attentiveness assumed of the latter in Hoffmann's comments. What Rose Subotnik has identified (and critiqued) as the "structural listening" (Subotnik 1991, 277–283) assumed of art music today is already evident in idealized notions of listening promoted by the early Romantics—for exam-ple, by Wackenroder in 1792 as "the most attentive observations of the notes and their progression" (cited in Bonds 1997, 394). But, notwithstanding Bonds's claim that "it was not a change in the contemporary repertory that was transporting listeners to a higher realm, but rather a change in the perceived nature of aesthetic cognition," it seems unlikely that listeners were propelled toward the absolute merely by their own perceptual projections: something was also happening to the work of music itself.

Indeed it was becoming just that—a work: not merely a transient event in sound, but some *thing* with the potential to endure, a textlike object for "reverent contemplation [*Andacht*]" (Herder's phrase of 1800: see Bonds 1997, 410). This is evident in the changing appearance and status of the symphony—the most exemplary and public genre of "independent music" at this time (Dahlhaus 1989a, 10–14). From its beginnings in Enlightenment concert life as a rococo genre amounting to little more than a curtain-raiser—literally an overture—the symphony had become, by the end of the eighteenth century, something composed on a larger, more complex scale (see Zaslaw 1989, 517–525). The last symphonies of Mozart composed in 1788 would provide as good an illustration as any of what Friedrich Schlegel may have had in mind when a decade later he rhetorically posed the question: "Must not pure instrumental music itself create a text of its own? And does not its theme get developed, confirmed, varied, and contrasted like the object of meditation in a philosophical sequence of ideas?" (quoted in Dahlhaus 1989a, 107). Music can attain the status of a philosophical discourse, Schlegel implies, through an affinity with philosophy's own discursive medium, language. A striking paradox: music becomes most essentially itself ("pure . . . music") through its mimesis of something other than itself;[1] it extends toward the infinite by intending into itself.

A further paradox ensues. Music's very self-referentiality, its articulation of the linguistically unsignifiable, elicits a whole new style of highly poeticized writing about music from critics of the time. As Bonds points out, this paradox need not be perplexing if the tendency to rhapsodize poetically is seen as a free subjective response to the experience of musical immanence, and not as an attempt to translate into language what a piece "really" means (Bonds 1997, 413ff.). It was only later in the century with Eduard Hanslick's polemical conception of *absolute music* (a term used pejoratively by his adversary Wagner, but which Hanslick adopted and sought to transvalue in his own riposte) that the suppression of such subjective poetic responses began to be institutionalized. Hanslick's rigorously objective, formalist conception of music—of which "it is impossible to form any but a musical conception, [and which] can be comprehended and enjoyed only for and in itself" ([1885] 1974, 70)—could be seen to be close to that assumed in many music-analytical methodologies of the nineteenth, twentieth, and twenty-first centuries. Yet while Hanslick's understanding of absolute music had paradoxically stamped out any reference to the absolute, this was achieved only by cutting certain poetic, extramusical references from the first (1854) edition of his treatise *The Beautiful in Music* (Dahlhaus 1989a, 28–29; Bonds 1997, 414–417) so that subsequent editions established a greater critical distance from exponents of program music such as Liszt, and from Wagner's total artwork, which sought a synthesis of musical and literary content.

RETRANSITION

From the time that Kant ascribed to it the character of "purposiveness without a purpose," the independent realm of the aesthetic can be seen as possessing an implicit political dimension. Music's very longing for an "other" world transcending the here and now in fact bears critical witness to the historical and cultural conditions it disdains to acknowledge. Stephen Rumph (1995) interprets Hoffmann's music criticism in just such a light: while Hoffmann claims that for musicians "our kingdom is not of this world," the poetic imagery he deploys in his review of Beethoven's Fifth and other writings alludes to the very real political conditions of a Prussia under Napoleonic occupation (see also Chua 1999, 8–11). Similarly, Goehr explores the notion of a "double-sided autonomy" in which the formalist properties of music were attractive to romantic composers of various persuasions precisely because, having "no meaning to speak of," music could be used to envision an alternative cultural and political order—while escaping the scrutiny of the censor (Goehr 1993, 186–188). And for bourgeois consumers in a modernizing society characterized by increasing scientific rationalization, growing industrialization, and an associated market economy, autonomous art offered a world of imaginative experience that was Other to the means–end orientation and commodity production of the empirical social world (Paddison 1996, 38). Moreover, as romantic hopes for social transformation faded after the failed revolutions of 1848, the realm of the aesthetic increasingly came to represent a retreat from life (arguably still a kind of political gesture). This moment coincided with Hanslick's formalist agenda, and was followed by the Wagnerphile French symbolists' search for a hermetic poetry that would emulate music's apparent disconnection from the everyday world of things.

We now approach the moment of aesthetic modernism at the turn of the twentieth century, when, decades before the critiques of scholars, the domain of the aesthetic acquired a critical self-consciousness of its own ideology while asserting its continuing social necessity. The result was a situation in which, as Adorno puts it, "art revolts against its essential concepts while at the same time being inconceivable without them" (1984, 465). The prismatic distortion of form in Stravinsky and the distension of tonal connections beyond breaking point in Schoenberg's quest for emancipated dissonance are both manifestations of the immanent critique of the very devices musical art used to construct an autonomous domain for itself. Repudiating historically established codes of communication, autonomous music now denies its bourgeois consumers illusory solace from reality. Further, in the multiple serial works of the 1950s, such as Pierre Boulez's *Structures 1a*, autonomous music reaches an absolute of objective musical formalism in which total structural integrity is achieved at the price of maximum indifference to sensuous appearance and subjective enjoyment. This extreme is iconic of high modernism's resistance to the world of commodities: contemporaneously with the rise of rock 'n' roll, such music now radically asserts, "under the guise of a self-referential, formal autonomy, . . . its absolute difference from popular musics" (Born and Hesmondhalgh 2000, 16). On the one hand, then, there is a high modernist practice that retains its purity as an autonomous art by moving to an aesthetic vanishing point where only a minority care to venture; on the other hand, there is a mass cultural practice assimilated to its role as part of a market economy and embracing its mundaneness, its worldliness. This polarized cultural condition—what Andreas Huyssen (1986) has termed *The Great Divide*—forms the context against which any revaluation of the autonomy concept must be considered.

RECAPITULATION/DEVELOPMENT II

We are too knowing these days not to recognize the paradox of "independent music" as a historically situated cultural category. What is necessary, I argue, is fully to embrace the dialectics of the situation. I don't think we need regard the sentiment behind Scott Burnham's statement that "[o]ne might . . . claim that we *need* to understand music as music, as an autonomous language, if we want to grant it the power to speak of other things" (2001, 215; emphasis in original) as conciliatory liberalism. Rather, this might support the dialectical notion of an autonomous *moment* of musical signification within the larger interplay of social and cultural codes that bring that signification to its full articulation. Goehr's depiction of musical autonomy as *double-edged* (as an inwardly oriented resistance to outer political circumstances) might be worked up to its full tension; indeed something cognate is implicit in Lucy Green's dialectic of inherent and delineated musical meaning. For Green, music is inherently meaningful on one level by dint of its temporal organization of sounds. Nevertheless those sounds do not point "only to themselves": on another level they also "point outwards from music and towards its role as a social product"; they delineate their situation within "a web of meanings in the social world" (1988, 27–28). Importantly, Green argues that it is only the existence of an inherent dimension to music that enables it to find new delineations among different social constituencies (2005, 90–91). Further, she makes the point that this dialectic is not specific to any particular kind of music; it operates just as strongly, say, for popular music as for classical music. Likewise, Adam Krims, in arguing forcibly for rap music's consideration as a cultural formation (and indeed for music theory as a subdivision of cultural studies), also argues for its identity-constituting processes as being played out in the sonic particularity of the songs themselves: "One must, at some point, work through [rap's] musical poetics . . ., not to aestheticize it or abstract it away from social life, but *precisely to factor in that the people one is studying are taking the music seriously, as music*—and that their cultural engagement is mediated by that 'musical' level" (2000, 40).

Hand-in-hand with the autonomy concept's double-edgedness, then, comes the possibility of its *dispersal*. If we are open to thinking of autonomy as dialectically enmeshed in music's social and cultural formations, so, conversely, we might also speculate whether elements of its constellation might also be recognizable within other genres of music, including those usually documented more explicitly for their socio-cultural significance. This could be figured as a loosening or unbonding of various elements of the strong autonomy concept (the cognate features outlined earlier—work concept, high-art aesthetic, and so on). For example, under this dispersed paradigm we might endorse the possibility of an autonomous moment in Indian classical music—which demands an attentive listenership, and reflects a strong focus on its own musical processes, but which, crucially, carries no concept of a musical work;[2] or in rock music—which places emphasis on composition (though not in isolation from performer and performance), and whose aesthetic values include "seriousness," subjective authenticity, and autonomy, but which clearly (except for progressive rock) does not seek "high art" status as such (Keightley 2001, 127–139). Another case might be certain subgenres of late-twentieth-century dance music concerned largely with "purely musical" sounds, such as Detroit techno or garage. Most obviously a celebration of collective hedonism, a resource for identification as, variably, black, white, young, or gay (or some combination, mediation, or blurring of these categories), this musical genre also contains ample possibility for celebrating creativity through its formations and trans-formations of sounds in time, its play of sounds across actual and virtual spaces (perhaps a quite literal example of "sounding forms in motion"—as Hanslick aphoristically characterized absolute music).

Lest this last seem an anachronistic (or, worse, imperialistic) projection of a nineteenth-century concept onto modern-day practices, possible links between these two conjunctures are suggested by historical accounts of the cultural mediation of music and technology. David Toop (1994) refers to the "labyrinthine entwinements of culture" that connect present-day electronic evocations of "possible worlds" to scores such as Satie's *Parade* of 1917, with its evocation of machine noises, and to the player piano technology and other "musical automata" of the earlier twentieth century. Such connections would find corroboration in research by Anna Sofie Christiansen (2001) into the aesthetic discourses that mediated the reception of mechanical music in Weimar Germany.[3] Christiansen describes how, in writings of the

1920s, mechanical instruments such as player pianos were seen to hold the potential to attain a more absolute, objectivized relationship between composition and performance by cutting out the expressive mediation of the performer to attain a kind of transcendent piano playing "in itself" (the Kantian *an sich*) or an idealized form of expression, an absolute immediacy between the geometric patterns of the piano roll and "the sounding forms in motion" that resulted (an allusion to Hanslick in a review by Alfred Einstein of a mechanical concert). This unexpected convergence of twentieth-century technology and nineteenth-century idealism offers a suggestive gloss on Toop's speculations regarding the potential of present-day electronica to recover some remnant of spirituality within a world of "mechanisation and commerce." Yet music's power to stand free of the ever more technologically determined world that mediates it depends on a delicate game of alliance and resistance; Arved Ashby (2010) reflects these negotiations in his account of the ongoing vicissitudes of absolute music in the era of recorded sound—in which the concept has found new ways to be (and new ways to be problematized), and in which, following the advent of MP3 and iPod technologies, it has entered a new historical phase of its ambivalent relationship with the commodity.

Recontextualizing the idea of absolute music, then, does not necessarily make it any less contentious. Simon Reynolds for one is entertainingly disparaging of the kind of dance subgenres found on the Warp label for which Toop writes. Such "'electronic listening music' or 'new complexity techno': the particularly use-less, uselessly peculiar sonic *objets d'art* constructed by the likes of Autechre and Christian Vogel" is pilloried as nothing more than "small boys playing with tekno toys, lost in their own little world of chromatics and texture and contour" (Reynolds 1998, 90–91). Reynolds's spleen is vented at the complicity of dance genres in promoting a contradictory aesthetics in which radical political potential is simultaneously melded with and undermined by a depoliticized escapism: this is "music of resistance and acquiescence, utopian idealism and nihilistic hedonism" (p. 92). While clearly a different figuration of an idealist escape from the empirical world from that described by the likes of Hoffmann (with underpinnings now perhaps more pharmacological than philosophical), the situation is not dissimilar—and prompts similar critique, albeit now from the standpoint of a postmodern rather than post-Enlightenment culture. What is equally important, however, is to see this debate now being played out on the other side of "the great divide" between classical and popular culture.

Reynolds's comments seem to tell of a frustration at the blunting of the double-edged potential of dance music. On a broader canvas this might be symptomatic of a postmodern condition, in which individuals' engagement with culture involves a degree of acquiescence toward its basis in a market-driven economy dominated by the commodity—an acquiescence that in its most radical postmodern guise might take the form of outright celebration (emblematically, learning from Las Vegas [Venturi et al. 1977]). If, as Fredric Jameson suggests, "we are *within* the culture of postmodernism to the point where its facile repudiation is as impossible as an equally facile celebration of it is complacent and corrupt" (1988, 381), this is nevertheless not to preclude fostering a consciousness of resistance from within. And it is here that cultural forms of all kinds have a role to play—a role to which the epithet "modernist" might still be appropriate, and a role in which a critically aware autonomist practice might still have something to contribute. On the one hand this might mean the ongoing "classical" modernism of a Harrison Birtwistle or Brian Ferneyhough—a modernism that, while getting long in the tooth, retains a necessary critical bite, and whose autonomist aesthetic remains key to its mandate to "challenge the limits of mainstream political and cultural discourse" (Scherzinger 2004, 94). On the other hand, and pursuing the notion of an autonomy dispersed across "the great divide," we might also look for resistance within popular musical genres (Bloomfield 1993) in which a reflexive, creative use of sonic materials cuts into our normative social consciousness, and provides a phenomenal space in which we might for a moment experience the world differently, without simply becoming amnesiac about its problematics.

The music of postdance composer David Kosten, produced under the alias Faultline, offers a glimpse of such a possibility (and a constructive response to Reynolds's critique). Belonging less to the genre of crossover music, the Faultline album *Closer Colder* (1999) is compelling more for the way it invites oppositional categories and then deconstructs them—dualisms such as classical/popular, modernist/postmodernist, physical/mental, and autonomous/referential. The groove of the CD's opening track, "Awake," is made from spluttering, distorted splinters of sounds that invoke a harsh, desolate postindustrial landscape, over which is mixed the periodic entries of effulgent singing cellos—the humane embrace of the maternal and personal. In similarly non- (or only partially) synthetic fashion, the urges to dance, to listen, and to reflect are co-present but not coterminous. We are simultaneously drawn inward, to the artifice of the music's own poetic strategies, and oriented outward to the social world referenced by its samples (including, on the final track, "Partyline Honey," a telephone sex chatline); intrinsic and extrinsic musical meanings are rendered utterly permeable to each other.

CODA

My intention with these few pointers is emphatically not to argue for so-called "intelligent dance music" as a monolithic paradigm for some would-be idea of "new autonomy." But there are alternatives between making a fetish of the autonomy idea and wanting to bury it; it is imaginable that (borrowing Peter Bürger's phraseology) what is truthful about autonomous art, its "apartness . . . from the praxis of life," need not lead to untruth, "the hypostatization of the fact," the occlusion of the social and historical determination of that apartness (Bürger 1984, 46). Hence I invoke dance and postdance genres here as possible examples on the way to envisioning a more mutable, pliable construction of autonomy, adapted to our relativized, postmodern frame, oblivious neither to other determinants of musical experience—words, dancing, images, bodies, technology, and so on—nor to the social medium in which it operates. In societies whose history has rendered them less than fully congenial places for all their members, the autonomous moment available to music—embodying the notion of something valuable in and for itself—might still offer a moment of subjective resistance against social domination or means–end-oriented rationality.[4] It may still serve as a reminder that, to paraphrase Adorno (Jarvis 1998, 216), "that which is" need not be "*all* that there is."

NOTES

1 In Clarke (1996a) I explore in greater detail how music might acquire an autonomous dimension when its own structural processes achieve certain homologies with linguistic structures.

2 Martin Clayton's equivocation as to whether "cultural ideology, patterns and norms may be reflected in [in this case Indian] music" is not unconnected with this argument (Clayton 2000, 5–7, 10–11).

3 I am grateful to Matthew Sansom for drawing my attention to Toop's sleevenote and the Warp album that it accompanies; and to Anna Sofie Christiansen for kindly making her unpublished paper available to me.

4 A closely related sentiment (or ideology?) distinguishes Julian Johnson's apologia for classical music (2002) from the orientations of subsequent treatments of the same topic by Joshua Fineberg (2006) and Lawrence Kramer (2007). Johnson's disinclination to concede a comparably emancipatory potential to popular music—a position congruent with his resolutely Adornian theoretical line—has provoked a predictably mixed critical reception, which nonetheless ought not to eclipse much that is salutary in his account.

FURTHER READING

Biddle, Ian D. 1995. Autonomy, ontology and the ideal: Music theory and philosophical aesthetics in early nineteenth-century German thought. Ph.D. thesis, University of Newcastle upon Tyne.

Clarke, David. Forthcoming. Between hermeneutics and formalism: The Lento from Tippett's Concerto for Orchestra (Or: music analysis after Lawrence Kramer). *Music Analysis*, 29(3).

Dahlhaus, Carl. 1982. *Esthetics of music*. Translated by William W. Austin. Cambridge, U.K.: Cambridge University Press.

Dahlhaus, Carl. 1989. The metaphysic of instrumental music. Pp. 88–96 in *Nineteenth-century music*. Translated by J. Bradford Robinson. Berkeley: University of California Press.

Kivy, Peter. 1990. *Music alone: Philosophical reflections on the purely musical experience*. Ithaca, NY: Cornell University Press.

Neubauer, John. 1988. *The emancipation of music from language*. New Haven, CT: Yale University Press.

Scruton, Roger. 2001. Absolute music. Pp. 36–37 in *The new Grove dictionary of music and musicians*. 2nd ed. Edited by Stanley Sadie. London: Macmillan.

Stravinsky, Igor. 1942. *Poetics of music: In the form of six lessons*. Cambridge, MA: Harvard University Press.

Treitler, Leo. 1989. Mozart and the idea of absolute music. Pp. 176–214 in *Music and the historical imagination*. Cambridge, MA, and London: Harvard University Press.

Wolff, Janet. 1987. The ideology of autonomous art. Pp. 1–12 in *Music and society: The politics of composition, performance and reception*. Edited by Richard Leppert and Susan McClary. Cambridge, U.K.: Cambridge University Press.

CHAPTER 16

MUSIC AS PERFORMANCE

NICHOLAS COOK

The case for the prosecution is easily made. You can blame it on Stravinsky, who claimed that music should be executed and not interpreted, or on Schoenberg, who wrote that the performer was "totally unnecessary except as his interpretations make the music understandable to an audience unfortunate enough not to be able to read it in print" (Newlin 1980, 164). Or you can blame it on the recording industry, which has created a performance style designed for infinite iterability, resulting over the course of the twentieth century in a "general change of emphasis . . . from the characterization of musical events to the reproduction of a text" (Philip 1992, 230), or on musicology's origins as a nineteenth-century discipline modeled on philology, and therefore treating music as a written text. Any way you choose, the charge is the same: Because they think of performance as in essence the reproduction of a text, musicologists don't understand music as a performing art. In fact this orientation is built into our very language for music: You can "just play," but it's odd to speak of "just performing," because the basic grammar of performance is that you perform *something*, you give a performance "of" something. In other words, language—and especially musicological language—leads us to construct the process of performance as supplementary to the product that occasions it, and it is this that leads us to talk quite naturally about music "and" its performance, just as film theorists speak of the film "and" the music, as if performance were not as much part of music as music is of film. (As it happens, this chapter was originally commissioned under the title "Music and Performance.")

The 1990s saw a sustained critique of the idea of the reified musical work, triggered largely by Lydia Goehr's *The Imaginary Museum of Musical Works*

(1992). This critique is the necessary starting point for developing a concept of performance that is not just performance "of," or—as I have expressed it in my title—thinking of music *as* (not *and*) performance. Richard Taruskin (1995) and Christopher Small (1998), to name just two, suggested some ways in which this might proceed, but in this chapter I want to draw on aspects of interdisciplinary performance studies and ethnomusicology that I see as particularly relevant to an understanding of music as performance. The shift from a text-based to a performance-based understanding of music parallels the breaking away of theater studies from literary studies that led to Shakespeare's texts being seen not as literary "works" but rather as the traces of theatrical productions: Philip Gossett has transferred this approach to opera in his editions of Verdi and Rossini. And the conjunction of theater studies and anthropology (supposedly the result of a chance conversation between Richard Schechner and Victor Turner) gave rise to what is normally called simply "performance studies", in Schechner's (2004, 8) words a "broad spectrum approach" to performance that sees all "performative behavior, not just the performing arts, as a subject for serious scholarly study." Seen in such terms, the rituals and paraphernalia of medieval courts might be seen as performances of kingship, or punk culture as the performance of an oppositional identity.

Fundamental to this expanded concept of performance is the idea that it generates meaning, rather than simply reproducing a meaning that resides elsewhere. This insight drew on the philosopher of language J. L. Austin's (1962) concept of the performative, according to which promises, curses, and bets do not represent actions or states of affairs, but are in themselves actions (what Austin called "speech acts"). Judith Butler (1988, 527) gave Austin's concept an edgier dimension when she applied it to the construction of gender, claiming that gender "is real only to the extent that it is performed." Traditionally gender had been understood as the behavioural expression of the biological distinction between male and female: Butler (1988, 528) turned this concept upside down, arguing that gendered behaviors "effectively constitute the identity they are said to express or reveal." In the same way, placing emphasis on performance as a site for the generation of meaning turns the traditional relationship between work and performance upside down, as illustrated by the dance and theater theorist Nick Kaye's characterization of performance as "a primary postmodern mode": as he sees it, the performance-oriented practices of artists like Foreman, Cunningham, or Cage subvert the "discrete or bounded 'work of art'" definitive of modernism, or dissolve it into "the contingencies and instabilities of the 'event' . . . penetrated by unstable and unpredictable exchanges and processes" (Kaye 1994, 22, 32, 117). Given the extent to which the reified musical work is built into the very language of musicology, the same kind of tension is probably inherent in any attempt to write about music as performance. But then nobody without a taste for the impossible should become a musicologist.

Keir Elam (quoted in Aston and Savona 1991, 104) has written, with reference to theatrical performance, of the "relationship of mutual and shifting constraints between two kinds of text, neither of which is prior and neither of which is precisely 'immanent' within the other, since each text is radically transformed by its relations with the other." Though his characterization of performance as "text" reflects an earlier phase of theatrical semiotics (the quotation dates from 1977), Elam's formulation vividly captures the interaction that is constitutive of music as performance. The contemporary performance studies paradigm stresses the extent to which signification is constructed through the act of performance, and generally through acts of negotiation both between performers, and between them and audiences. In other words, performative meaning is understood as subsisting in process, and hence by definition is irreducible to product; as Charles Bernstein (1998, 21) expresses it with reference to poetry reading, "Sound . . . can never be completely recuperated as ideas, as content, as narrative, as extralexical meaning."

To understand music as performance, then, means to see it as an irreducibly social phenomenon, even when only a single individual is involved. (There is a comparison with religious ritual, which involves the enaction of socially agreed-on forms of expression even when conducted in private.) According to Ingrid Monson (1996, 186), "the formal features of musical texts are just one aspect—a subset, so to speak—of a broader sense of the musical, which also includes the contextual and the cultural. Rather than being conceived as foundational or separable from context, structure is taken to have as one of its central functions the construction of social context." Seen this way, however, the term *text*, with its connotations of New Critical autonomy and structuralism, is perhaps less helpful than the more distinctively theatrical term *script*. Whereas to think of a Mozart quartet as a "text" is to construe it as a half-sonic, half-ideal object reproduced in performance, to think of it as a "script" is to see it as choreographing a series of real-time, social interactions between players: a series of mutual acts of listening and communal gestures that enact a particular vision of human society, the communication of which to the audience is one of the special characteristics of chamber music.

Thinking of music as "script" rather than "text" implies a reorientation of the relationship between notation and performance. The traditional model of musical transmission, borrowed from philology, is the stemma: a kind of family tree in which successive interpretations move vertically away from the composer's original vision. The text, then, is the embodiment of this vision, and the traditional aim of source criticism is to ensure as close an alignment as possible between the two, just as the traditional aim of historically informed performance is to translate the vision into sound. But the performance studies paradigm in effect turns this model by 90 degrees: as Richard Schechner (1998, 28) expresses it, it emphasizes "explorations of horizontal relationships among related forms rather than a searching vertically for unprovable origins." In other words, it seeks to understand performances primarily in relation to other performances (Schechner's "related forms") rather than to the notated text; a given performance of Beethoven's Ninth Symphony, for example, will acquire its meaning from its relationship to the horizon of expectations established by other performances.

The reorientation does not stop there. Busoni famously refused to admit any ontological distinction among scores, performances, and arrangements, because he saw all of them as equally transcriptions of an abstract, platonic idea. Current performance theory reaches the same conclusion from the opposite premise: there is no ontological distinction among the different modes of a work's existence, its different instantiations, because there is no original. Charles Bernstein (1998, 10) invokes Alfred Lord's study of the Homerian epic in order to oppose the reduction of poem to text: "I believe," wrote Lord, "that once we know the facts of oral composition we must cease to find an original of any traditional song. From an oral point of view each performance is original." And Stan Godlovitch (1998, 96) sees the related practice of storytelling as the best model for musical performance, not only because it emphasizes presentation, skill, and communication, but also because "this view of the relationship between works and performances puts the former in their proper musical place primarily as vehicles and opportunities for the latter in the larger business of making music." Instead of a single work located "vertically" in relation to its performances, then, we have an unlimited number of instantiations, all on the same "horizontal" plane.

Or have we moved too fast and too far? Is it really credible to claim that we have no "original" in the case of, say, the Ninth Symphony when we have Beethoven's text? I have two answers to this. The first is that Beethoven's text exists only as an interpretive construct; there is a variety of largely contradictory sources (the autograph, copyists' scores, early printed editions, and so on), and it might be argued that urtext editions of Beethoven's symphonies do not so much replace earlier texts as add new ones. (To put it another way, new editorial work constantly constructs new "originals.") The second answer is that while these historically privileged texts have a particular significance and authority within the field encompassed by the Ninth Symphony, they do not exhaust the work's identity: in a passage that I have quoted so often that I might as well quote it once more, Lawrence Rosenwald

(1993, 62) characterizes the identity of the Ninth Symphony as "something existing in the relation between its notation and the field of its performances." This precisely captures what I am trying to convey: that Beethoven's text (whatever that means) has an obviously privileged role and yet relates horizontally, as Schechner would put it, to the symphony's other instantiations, resulting in just the kind of intertextual field to which Elam referred. In other words, the work does not exist "above" the field of its instantiations, but rather encompasses it—which, of course, is why the Ninth Symphony is still evolving. There is a sense, then, in which to refer (like Godlovitch) to work "and" performance is just as wrongheaded as speaking of music "and" performance.

But somehow there is a remainder. It is only when you have started thinking of music as performance that the peculiarly time-resisting properties of works in the Western "art" tradition come fully into relief. The real-time process of performance routinely leaves not a few, fragmentary memories (like a holiday, say) but rather the sense that we have experienced a *piece* of music, an imaginary object that somehow continues to exist long after the sounds have died away. "The belief that quartets and symphonies of Mozart and Beethoven rise above history can never be completely erased," Charles Rosen (1994a, 89) affirms, because "the autonomy was written into them." Rosen's confident tone belies the fragility of this snatching of eternity, so to speak, from the jaws of evanescence: the fantastical idea that there might be such a thing as music, rather than simply acts of making and receiving it, is arguably the basic premise of the Western "art" tradition.

But what kind of musicological practice might this translate into? An obvious way of studying music as performance is to study those traces or representations of past performances that make up the recorded heritage, thereby unlocking a century-long archive of acoustical texts comparable in extent and significance to the notated texts around which musicology originally came into being. Some musicologists, such as José Bowen and Eric Grunin, have used computers to make comparisons of performance timing across large numbers of recordings of "the same work"; this approach directly reflects the idea of music as a horizontal field of instantiations, and allows for a range of stylistic measures and the extrapolation of statistical trends, but does not easily provide the kind of insight into the specific qualities of specific interpretations that score-based analysis characteristically offers. (It suffers, in short, from the traditional problems of style analysis.) The alternative, as illustrated by the work of Joel Lester, is to seek to relate performance interpretation to the available analytical readings of a particular composition, in effect working from analysis to recording; here the danger is of replicating what the theater theorist Susan Melrose (1994,

215) terms the "page to stage" approach, and so reinforcing the very presupposition (that music is in essence a text reproduced in performance) that studying music as performance was supposed to interrogate. Work in this area has continued apace since this chapter was first written, for instance from the researchers associated with the AHRC Research Centre for the History and Analysis of Recorded Music (London, 2004–9), much of it in effect attempting to find a middle way between these two alternatives. It is too early, however, to speak of established and generally accepted methods or even goals.

Another route to understanding music as performance might be to focus on the functioning of the performing body, both in itself and in relation to other dimensions of the performance event: there has been an explosion of work in the area of performance gesture, though interpretations of this term have varied so widely as to render it almost meaningless. But again the conceptual framework is crucial. Melrose (1994, 210) observes that structuralist approaches to theatrical performance attributed significance to the body only to the extent that they constructed it as "text" (and the same might be said of the performance timing approaches I have just described). The contemporary performance studies paradigm, by contrast, seeks to understand the body in the same way as it understands sound, as a site of resistance to text, for as Charles Bernstein (1998, 21) puts it, "Sound is language's flesh, its opacity, as meaning marks its material embeddedness in the world of things." And in both cases performance is understood to be in "fundamental opposition to the desire for depth," as Kaye (1994, 69) puts it. His choice of words is particularly suggestive in a musical context, given the extent to which analytical discussions of performance have represented it as a more or less transparent revelation of underlying structure (an obvious example is the Schenkerian concept of performing from the middleground). Set that aside, and a variety of terms might come into play to articulate more opaque relationships between work and performance: quotation, commentary, critique, parody, irony, or travesty, for example.

But a further conceptual ingredient is crucial. Melrose (1994, 225) quotes Ariane Mnouchkine's observation that "the goal of text analysis is to attempt to explain everything. Whereas the role of the actor . . . is not at all to explicate the text." It is just this distinction that theoretical approaches to musical performance generally seek to deny. After all, you cannot perform from the middleground unless you have an authoritative knowledge of the text, and William Rothstein reveals the assumption that this must be the foundation of articulate performance when he says (by way of the exception that proves the rule) that it is sometimes better to conceal than to project structure: on such occasions, he says, "the performer adopts *temporarily* the viewpoint of one or two characters in the drama, so to speak, rather than assuming omniscience at every moment" (Rothstein 1995, 238; my italics). By comparison a postmodern approach, as advocated by Kevin Korsyn (1999, 65), would question the possibility of what he calls "a central point of intelligibility, a privileged position for the spectator"—or, in this case, the performer. As might be expected, Korsyn invokes Bakhtin's concept of dialogic in order to make his point, drawing a comparison between music and Bakhtin's concept of novelistic discourse as "an artistically organized system for bringing different languages in contact with one another, a system having as its goal the illumination of one language by means of another" (p. 61). This image of different languages being brought into contact with one another—an image strikingly reminiscent of the Elam quotation—provides a fertile framework for the analysis of musical performance, and indeed it is hard to think of an area in which the Bakhtinian concepts of heteroglossia and double-voiced discourse might be applied in a more literal manner.

This is not an original observation. Richard Middleton (2000) has appropriated Bakhtin's concepts for the analysis of popular music, linking them to Henry Louis Gates Jr.'s (1988) concept of "Signifyin(g)"; Monson (1996, 98–106) has made the same linkage in connection with the tissue of intertextual reference that is jazz improvisation, also throwing W. E. B. Du Bois's concept of African-American "double-consciousness" into the mix. Such approaches not only add depth to such concepts as parody, irony, and the rest, but also put the emphasis firmly on the quality of creativity, of performative difference, which Gates invokes when he defines Signifyin(g) as "[r]epetition with a signal difference" (discussed in Monson 1996, 103); this semiotically charged figuring of iteration as commentary, ventriloquism, or even impersonation lies at the core of, for instance, Hendrix's Monterey covers of *Like a Rolling Stone* or *Sgt. Pepper's Lonely Hearts Club Band*. That approaches such as these, developed for the articulation of characteristic features of African-American culture, should be well adapted for the analysis of jazz and popular music is not surprising. I would go further, however, and suggest that just as the spread of African-American musical practices has gone far toward establishing a global common practice, so the concepts of Signifyin(g) and double-consciousness can help to articulate the creativity that has always been present in the performance culture of Western "art" music, but has long been repressed by the text-dominated discourses of musicology. Or to put it another way, thinking of "art" musical performances as reproducing texts may be less useful than thinking of them as culturally privileged forms of intertextual reference.

The issue of omniscience, of the availability or otherwise of a central point of intelligibility, also has a direct effect upon the relationship between the performance analyst and the phenomena under investigation, and it is the component of the contemporary performance studies synthesis that I have not yet directly discussed that makes this clearest: ethnomusicology. Through its functionalist orientation (i.e., its insistence on understanding any practice within the totality of its cultural context), ethnomusicology from the start distanced itself from the model of detached observation and taxonomic analysis that characterized its predecessor discipline, comparative musicology. Instead, it emphasized the necessity of fieldwork, understood as prolonged and intimate association with, within the target culture, during which musical practices would be observed in context, where possible through participant observation, and an understanding of native conceptualization accordingly acquired. Nevertheless the aim remained one of, if not omniscience, then at least an authoritative and objective understanding of cultural practice.

More recent approaches to fieldwork, however, question the availability of such a central point of intelligibility in just the same way that Korsyn does; it is for this reason that Michelle Kisliuk (1997, 33) describes the claim of ethnomusicological and other ethnography "to interpret reality for its 'informants'" as a "pretense." The result is that, in Jeff Todd Titon's words (1997, 87), "Fieldwork is no longer viewed principally as observing and collecting (although it surely involves that) but as experiencing and understanding music," and he continues: "The new fieldwork leads us to ask what it is like for a person (ourselves included) to make and to know music as lived experience." In a word, it stresses personal participation in the performative generation of meaning that is music, and as most conspicuously represented by such books as Kisliuk's *Seize the Dance!* (1998) or Louise Meintjes's *Sound of Africa!* (2003), it gives rise to a literary practice that is as close to travel writing or even autobiography as to the traditional literature of ethnomusicology, and that is also acutely conscious of its performative nature as writing. As Titon (1997, 96) puts it, citing Geertz, the performative approach "forces us to face the fact that we are primarily authors, not reporters."

Applied to more traditional musicological contexts, an ethnographic approach questions conventional constructions of relevance. For the drama theorist Baz Kershaw (1992, 22), it is "a fundamental tenet of performance theory . . . that no item in the environment of performance can be discounted as irrelevant to its impact," and Bernstein (1998, 14) provides an all-too-graphic illustration of what this might mean when he characterizes "gasps, stutters, hiccups, burps, coughs, slurs, microrepetitions, oscillations in volume, 'incorrect' pronunciations, and so on" as "semantic features of the performed poem . . . and not as extraneous interruption." The point Bernstein is making is that "one of the primary techniques of poetry performance is the disruption of rationalizable patterns of sound through the intervallic irruption of acoustic elements not recuperable by monological analysis" (p. 13), and one might say that in music the performance "of" paradigm—the equivalent of Bernstein's "monological analysis"—filters out such dimensions of performance as are not directly referable to the work being performed. An ethnographic approach, by contrast, seeks to understand the performance of a particular piece in the context of the total performance event, encompassing issues of program planning, stage presentation, dress, articulation with written texts, and so forth. To date, this approach is more familiar in the context of popular music than of the "art" tradition, and the work of Les Back offers a representative example that parallels both Kisliuk's selfconsciously performative writing and, in its invocation of Deleuze and Guattari's cultural "rhizomes," Schechner's concept of the horizontal: Back shows by such means how the performances of the Birmingham (U.K.) based musician Apache Indian function as an arena for complex negotiations of cultural identity reflecting, as he puts it, "a diasporic triple consciousness that is simultaneously the child of Africa, Asia, and Europe" (1996, 75).

For the musicologist such work may be simultaneously stimulating, because of the virtuosity with which cultural meaning is read in the multifarious dimensions of the performance event, and frustrating, because of its lack of engagement with the specifics of music. How might we put the music back into performance analysis? One model is provided by Monson's analyses of jazz improvisation, in which extended transcriptions are aligned with prose commentary, and counterpointed by quotations from and discussions of performers' discourse. Again, the kind of communicative interaction between performers that Chris Smith (1998) has analyzed in relation to Miles Davis is equally evident within the dynamics of—to repeat my previous example—a string quartet playing Mozart: Here there is an opportunity to combine ethnographic and traditional music-theoretical approaches, and perhaps also the computer-based approaches I mentioned, in an analysis of the relationship between notated "script" and social interaction. And if this kind of work is harder with the Western "art" repertory than with jazz improvisation, because of the danger of relapsing into the performance "of" paradigm, then a useful half-way house is offered by analysis of the longitudinal process by which "art" music interpretations come into being, that is, of practice and rehearsal; as illustrated for example by the work of Elaine King, Jane Ginsborg, or Roger Chaffin and his co-workers, this is a topic now attracting interest from music theorists, psychologists, and sociologists.

But analyzing music as performance does not necessarily mean analyzing specific performances or recordings at all. John Potter (1998, 182) offers an analysis of a passage from Antoine Brumel's *Missa Victimae Paschali* that focuses on the intimate negotiations and conjunctions between the performers, and the manner in which these inflect the performance: "Throughout, the voices are setting up patterns of tension and relaxation, acutely conscious of each other, both seeking to accommodate each others' desires and to satisfy themselves." At the end of the first bar, a particular dissonance "is only a passing moment but it creates a moment of acute pleasure that they may wish to prolong," thereby subverting the tempo (p. 180); the third voice (with successive eighth notes on the first beat of the following bar) has to re-establish the tempo, but by the end of the bar, with the suspension, it is the superius who controls the negotiations of tempo between the performers. "I have not chosen an actual performance," Potter writes, "since the potential degree of realization of the points I wish to make will vary from performance to performance" (p. 178). But the points themselves are scripted in Brumel's music; that is, they can be recovered from the score provided the analyst has the requisite knowledge of performance practice (Potter is a professional singer whose experience ranges from medieval music to *Tommy*)—and provided that the dissonances in question are understood not just as textual features, as attributes of the musical object, but as prompts to the enaction of social relationships in the real time of performance.

And the analysis of social interaction between performers offered by writers like Potter and Monson prompts a final thought on the potential of performance analysis for a culturally oriented musicology. The underlying objective of such a musicology, to understand music as both reflection and generator of social meaning, is most ambitiously expressed in Adorno's claim that music "presents social problems through its own material and according to its own formal laws—problems which music contains within itself in the innermost cells of its technique" (Adorno 1978, quoted and discussed in Martin 1995, 100). Music, in other words, becomes a resource for understanding society. Adorno's own analyses of music have proved a constant source of frustration, however, while even his apologist Rose Subotnik (1976, 271) has described his concept of the interface between music and society as "indirect, complex, unconscious, undocumented, and mysterious." But the problem disappears if, instead of seeing musical works as texts within which social structures are encoded, we see them as scripts in response to which social relationships are enacted: The object of analysis is now present and self-evident in the interactions between performers, and in the acoustic traces that they leave. To call music a performing art, then, is not just to say that we perform it; it is to say that through it we perform social meaning.

FURTHER READING

Auslander, Philip. 1999. *Liveness: Performance in a mediatized culture.* London: Routledge.

Cook, Nicholas et al., eds. 2009. *The Cambridge companion to recorded music.* Cambridge, U.K.: Cambridge University Press.

Davis, Tracy, ed. 2008. *The Cambridge companion to performance studies.* Cambridge, U.K.: Cambridge University Press.

Godlovitch, Stan. 1998. *Musical performance: A philosophical study.* London: Routledge.

Monson, Ingrid. 1996. *Saying something: Jazz improvisation and interaction.* Chicago: University of Chicago Press.

Philip, Robert. 1992. *Early recordings and musical style: Changing tastes in instrumental performance, 1900–1950.* Cambridge, U.K.: Cambridge University Press.

Philip, Robert. 2004. *Performing music in the age of recording.* New Haven, CT: Yale University Press

Potter, John. 1998. *Vocal authority: Singing style and ideology.* Cambridge, U.K.: Cambridge University Press.

Rink, John, ed. 1995. *The practice of performance: Studies in musical interpretation.* Cambridge, U.K.: Cambridge University Press.

Rink, John, ed. 2002. *Musical performance: A guide to understanding.* Cambridge, U.K.: Cambridge University Press

Schechner, Richard. 2006. *Performance studies: An introduction.* 2nd edn. New York: Routledge.

Taruskin, Richard. 1995. *Text and act: Essays on music and performance.* New York: Oxford University Press.

CHAPTER 17

THE CULTURAL STUDY OF MUSICAL INSTRUMENTS

KEVIN DAWE

A musical instrument is much more than the sum of its parts. It can be measured and weighed, its acoustic properties investigated, the ecology of its wood documented, its metals sourced, the site of its sound activation identified, and its sound spectrum plotted. However, made to be played, whether one person's noise or another person's music, when musical instruments sound out they are invariably made to make meaning (changing soundscapes, affecting emotions, moving bodies, demarcating identities, mobilising ideas, demonstrating beliefs, motioning values) which, in turn, makes them potent social and cultural phenomena. As sites of meaning construction, musical instruments are embodiments of culturally based belief and value systems, an artistic and scientific legacy, a part of the political economy attuned by, or the outcome of, a range of associated ideas, concepts and practical skills: they are one way in which cultural and social identity (a sense of self in relation to others, making sense of one's place in the order of things) is constructed and maintained. For example, I note the prominence and rootedness of the ʿūd in the soundscape of Arab music cultures and its significance for the development of a musical cosmology, mythology, and performance practice system over several centuries (see Jenkins and Olsen 1976; Shiloah 1995; Touma 2003; Marcus 2007).

The fact is that a musical instrument is much more than *the thing itself.* Musical instruments are generally not regarded as "things" at all, at least not for long, but acquire meaningful status as part of individual-collective musical worlds, wherein they develop a "social life" (Appadurai 1986) akin to that of "social beings" (after Gell 1998 and 2006), becoming empowered (DeVale 1989; Doubleday 2008), providing a solid basis for cultural memory (Fisher et al. 2006) and participation in social life (Turino 2008). Whether Wedgewood, Model T Ford, Hoover, Moog or Rickenbacker, the objects of material culture (see Forty 1986; Miller 2005; Woodward 2007) go on to acquire a degree of power and agency in the contexts of their use, as symbols of transformation if you will (Jung 1977), extending the influence (and intentionality) of their creators and patrons outward and onward through the passage of time and the stages of human life. The fact that musical instruments by design and definition are produced to create humanly organized sound provides them with an empowering multi-sensorial dimensionality that eludes many other objects of material culture.

Musical instruments continue to develop, emerge out of, mutate, or resonate as a part of a continual convergence of a wide range of meaningful developments in music, culture, design, and technology (Arthur 2009). Here I use the term "technology" in the widest sense possible to subsume old and new, acoustic and electric, and analogue and digital sound-producing devices. I also include among "musical instruments" the human body, drumming upon the surface of water (and thus hands and water), bark whistles, bone flutes, harpsichords, electric guitars, synthesisers, a DJ's mixing desks, and a recording studio. Whether one includes the syrinx of both birds and ancient Greeks—both still appreciated *musically* in human cultures—is beyond the scope of this chapter. The focus here is upon the contests and negotiations that attend musical instruments as social and cultural phenomenon in more recent times, and the various models we might use to understand and define them.

The evidence is clear that musical instruments, as played today, might fruitfully be incorporated into various sound-culture models or, rather, models of the soundscape that prioritize the *cultural* value and agency of "things" or the sound-producing objects we call musical instruments (or "music instruments" or the "instruments of music", descriptors which subtly contract or expand the meaning attached to "musical instruments" here). Drawing on the historical impact and value of musical instruments (and their study) but focusing on the present day, one might include among such models: "music-cultures" (Titon and Slobin 1996), "sonic cultures" (Greene and Porcello 2005), and "technoculture" (communications, culture and technology) (Penley and Ross 1991; Lysloff and Gay 2003), among numerous other locations or convergences of culture (see Bhabha 1994, Jenkins 2006, respectively), which incorporate, overlap, and interpenetrate with the life of musical instruments. Musical instruments exist as a part of an intricate web of sound-producing and sound-carrying/relaying/filtering/

processing devices that can be heard—directly or indirectly—around the world (whether the instrument itself or some other form of representation of it, for instance, on a mobile phone or the Internet). Surely, any attempt to answer the question "What is a musical instrument?" must now look to the multifarious and far-reaching relationship between music, culture, and technology, a complex, intense, and interacting network that, in the realm of human experience, provides a challenge to the senses as an extension of both the human body and mind. I am not suggesting we lose the term "musical instrument" altogether, even if many cultures around the world would not be familiar with such a term. However, the *boundaries* that have traditionally separated or demarcated musical instruments from other objects and technologies, as well as academic disciplines, must surely be questioned.

Musical instruments have the potential to spread out across the various domains of human culture and society, creating "instrumentscapes" (Dawe 2010) at both a local and, increasingly, an international level. This is, of course, in line with models of the components of the global cultural-political economy, with its "scapes" and "flows" within which musical instruments, and all human beings, are now firmly caught up (Hall 1991; Appadurai 1992; Palan 1996). Here, ethnicity, media, finance, technology, and ideology bear upon the shaping of instrumentscapes, honing facets of their objectification. At the local level, there may even be attempts to encourage or silence musical instruments (and their makers and performers); for example, encouraged as part of youth orchestras in Venezuela ("National system of youth orchestras in Venezuela": http://www.pri.org/theworld/?q= node/296) or discouraged in the case of the making and playing of the *'ūd* in Iraq ("Demise of the oud makes for sad music": http://articles.sfgate.com/ 2010-04-04/news/20834564_1_oud-iraq-baghdad-slum).

In attempting to draw attention to new and emerging frames of reference for the study of musical instruments, this chapter focuses on the following themes: (1) the study of musical instruments as part of the study of material culture and the technology of globalization: *Whose global order?;* (2) the social power and agency of objects in specific localities/contexts: *Localizing the instrument;* (3) representational/discursive systems (the approaches, ideologies, and agendas that shape musical instruments, from facets of their performance to their study): *Entangled objects.*

Whose Global Order?

Debate about the field of "organology" (the study of musical instruments) suggests that there is indeed some effort to combine centuries of scientific work (including classifying and measuring) with new perspectives offered by the cultural study of music (involving ethnography and material culture studies, for instance). Perhaps not surprisingly, the difficulties involved in this process (i.e., the bringing together of both scientific and cultural perspectives) have been encountered to a great extent in organologists' efforts to design classification schemes capable of incorporating all the musical instruments of the world. No wonder then that, as Sue Carole DeVale notes, many have assumed that the field "attends only or primarily to the classification of instruments" (DeVale 1990, 1–2).

One can only applaud the panopticism of some scholars in their efforts to treat musical instruments within the framework of classification systems. At least they have given serious attention to musical instruments outside of the Western world in constructing systems "into which facts can be integrated in order to show their relationships and affinities" (Montagu and Burton 1971, 49). After all, how else does one set about achieving order out of the chaos of such a diverse set of objects? As an ethnomusicologist I would suggest nonetheless that schemes constructed and used by the people who built and played the instruments should be used wherever possible (Zemp 1978; Dawe 2001).

Obviously, objects need some kind of sorting and interpretation, if they are to be displayed to effect in a museum exhibition, form a "collection," and be accessible and retrievable for research and display purposes. After all, this is where most of us encounter historical musical instruments or musical instruments from around the world. There is no doubt that the schemes developed since the late nineteenth century have been useful in providing the means whereby even nonspecialist workers are able to assemble, organize, and maintain museum collections of musical instruments and their catalogues. The schemes apply a basic Eurocentric logic to collections of musical instruments from different parts of the world. After all, instruments from around the world use similar sound-activating devices (for example, strings, membranes) and resonators (for example, the "bodies" or boxes of guitars and other lutes, the tubes of flutes). These and other recurring features provide some scientifically based criteria with which to sort instruments into groups or types.

The most widely acknowledged classification system (and the one upon which others are based) is that of Hornbostel and Sachs ([1914] 1961). Based on a system devised by Mahillon, it uses four main taxa: idiophones, aerophones, chordophones, and membranophones. The criteria used to define groups and types are continuously tested and refined (creating microgroupings) through an ongoing investigation of material and acoustic properties, methods of construction, sound qualities, techniques required to produce sounds, and tuning systems, while applying scientific techniques of preservation, conservation, restoration, measurement, and classification.

The system is quite broad in scope but, nevertheless, produces a cognitive scheme that is but one model of reality (a monoculture). Usually, a downward classification is employed, moving from a highly abstract level downward to a more specific level; for example, idiophones, idiophones struck, struck directly, struck upon, and so on. The highest classes are broken down into their subclasses until the individuals that are their members are reached. Yet Margaret Kartomi notes that downward classification is based on any arbitrary viewpoint that disregards historical factors (Kartomi 1990).

Such schemes establish an ordering system that shows up particular aspects of design that the musical instruments in a collection have in common, and enable them to be placed in an access and retrieval system, facilitating an overview of the science of musical instruments and their construction techniques and materials analysis from around the world. Increasingly, an attempt to bring to life the musical instrument collections of the world is made, providing a broadly-ranging educational experience and resource. (See, for instance, The Musical Instrument Museum in Phoenix, Arizona website at themim.org or The Virtual Instrument Museum http://learningobjects.wesleyan.edu/vim/.)

LOCALIZING THE INSTRUMENT

The making of musical instruments (like the playing of them) requires a range of psychobiological, socio-psychological, and socio-cultural skills (whether the maker is Antonio Stradivari, Paul Reed Smith, or one of thousands of other makers, dead or alive). Indeed, musical instruments can provide unique insights into the body–machine interface in their development, construction, and the ways in which they are played. They can reveal much about the use and value of the body in musical performance, the senses at work upon but also stimulated by the musical instrument. The musical instrument (and the materials and tools of its construction) is a kind of "sensescape" to which we respond, sensing (touching, feeling) the instrument (after Howes 2005, cf. Classen 2005, and see Dawe 2010 for a deeper discussion of these issues in relation to the guitar). At another level, as socially constructed and meaningful, the morphology of musical instruments reveals through their shape, decoration, and iconography features of the body politic, as embodiments of the values, politics, and aesthetics of the community of musicians that they serve. They are at once physical and metaphorical, social constructions and material objects. In fact, as sound producers they are "socially constructed to convey meaning" (Feld 1983, 78) and remain "saturated with meaning" (after Derrida 1978). These approaches can be compatible. John Baily's research on the long-necked lutes of Afghanistan reveals as much about human motor patterning in musical performance as about the relation between changes in the construction of musical instruments and music made to be meaningful in a multicultural nation-state (Baily 1976).

The Australian didjeridu, as manufactured and played by Aboriginal people (they call themselves "Yolngu," and in northeast Arnhem Land the instrument is called *yidaki* [Neuenfeldt 1997, vii]), is very much a part of a unique cultural heritage. The instrument is used in ceremonies and ritual practices that are thoroughly shaped by Aboriginal experience, thoughts, skills, needs, and desires, and it has great importance as an emblem and marker of ethnic and cultural identity. In anthropological terms, this is the emic perspective, which aims for "the understanding of cultural representations from the point of view of a native of the culture" (Barfield 1997, 148). It is debatable whether musical instruments can ever have similar cultural resonance, let alone the same meaning, for those who do not have the same experience as, in this example, the Aboriginal people and without detailed information about their religion, beliefs, ritual practices, social structure, and musical system.

I want to further illustrate the need for detailed in-the-field study with reference to Alan Merriam's brilliant analysis of drum making in an African village in the late 1960s. Although Merriam presents what many consider to be an outmoded or simple form of functionalist analysis, his study must surely be seen as one of the first and finest examples of musical scholarship to show how completely musical instruments are entangled in a web of culture. He brings the complexity of the processes involved in musical instrument making to life in his study of the Bala (Basongye) drum, in an article that epitomizes his approach to the "anthropology of music" (Merriam 1964). He writes:

> [A] substantial number of bits and pieces of culture patterns were revealed, and these included, among others: taboos; children's games; patterns of badinage and boasting; real and ideal behaviour; technological information such as types of woods, the sources of colors, and tool-use patterns; linguistic information, including terms for parts of the drum, tools, woods . . . ideas of Europeans; concepts of design; institutional friendships; learning by imitation . . . and tricks and jokes. Almost every one of these items requires further research, but all of them were spin-offs from the central procedure being studied.
>
> (Merriam 1969, 99)

Despite some of the issues his approach raises, Merriam's analysis of the role of drum making within Bala society provides a rich and complex model of the ways in which the drum making fits into and even shapes a particular cultural context with "the systematic description of a single contemporary culture . . . through ethnographic fieldwork" (Barfield 1997, 157). Another excellent example of musical instrument ethnography at work is Regula Qureshi's wide-ranging and fascinating discussion of the ways in which the North Indian *sarangi* (an upright, bowed lute) relates to and intersects with many facets of the cultural contexts in which it is found. Qureshi notes:

> [T]he complex and intensely affective meanings which were being shared in wide-ranging conversations around the musical, physical, and meta-phorical site of the sarangi. I faced a rich palette of responses to that single instrument and its sound: moral depravity as well as emotion, devotion, feudal domination and servitude, with women who sing for men, and men who play for women. This led me to explore how people experience the sarangi, how players, listeners and patrons negotiate the contradictory, multiply referenced meanings of its music and how the power of music serves the interests of power.
>
> (Qureshi 1997, 5–6)

Qureshi's ethnography of what it was like to learn the sarangi as a participant observer provides us with a rich insight into how gender, power, and emotion are socially and culturally achieved, affected, and built around a musical instrument. I have endeavored to work with this form of analysis in my own study of the *lyra*, a three-stringed, upright, bowed lute found on the island of Crete (see Dawe 2007). The pear-shaped, fiddlelike features of the lyra suggest both "Western" and "Eastern" influences—it could be Turkish or Venetian, some say Minoan. Indeed, the notion that the lyra has its origins in antiquity suits local constructions of island identity well. Even today there is an extensive folklore that grounds the instrument in a world of pastoralists and mountain villages, up where the air is pure and where Zeus was born.

The lyra-laouto ensemble (the *laouto* is a four-course, plucked, long-necked lute) is a powerful manifestation of the body politic, not only reflecting the values and beliefs of many individuals and communities (urban, village, neighborhood, and family) but also helping to shape them. "The tradition," namely "lyra music," has been significantly updated, reinvented even, in an attempt to make it relevant to contemporary Cretan society—a feat achieved largely through the establishment and the apparatus of a local recording industry. However, the lyra is still regarded as quintessentially Cretan, a man's instrument, its "body," "neck," "eyes," "heart," and "soul" having special symbolic resonance and technical significance. The stylos or "pillar," a device that takes the weight of the bridge and acts as a carrier for the transmission of vibrations between the bridge and the back of the instrument, is said to be the site where the psyche or "soul" of the lyra resides. Indeed, if this pillar is missing, the instrument loses volume and tone—its sound will die, and so too, it is said, will the lyra.

The sound of the lyra moves between sweet and bittersweet tones, expressing a range of emotions experienced by sensitive but strong men in the face of what life can throw at them (see Dawe 2007 for a discussion of the interplay among music, poetry, and manhood ideals in Crete). Local musical aesthetics largely revolve around and interpenetrate the instrument itself, as it continues to reinforce long-held ideals that can be seen to make up a poetics of manhood and to form the basis of notions of professional musical performance practice in modern Crete. I argue that the Cretan music ensemble, with the lyra as its focal point, belongs to, and subscribes to, what Chris Shilling calls, elsewhere, a "body project" (Shilling 2005). To play lyra and laouto, musicians (99.9 percent male) have to subscribe to a grueling regime imposed by "tradition," by teachers, by other authorities, and by those with "the knowledge." They have to learn a wide range of musical techniques within a complex repertory, acquire the necessary mental and physical dexterity, stay awake at celebrations lasting up to fifteen hours, and manage an audience of a thousand inebriated guests; in short, a host of skills that require the disciplining of the body and the sharpening of the mind. According to Shilling, "in the affluent West there is a tendency for the body to be seen as an entity which is in the process of becoming; a project which should be worked at and accomplished as part of an individual's self-identity" (2005, 5). I am convinced that a culturally-specific Cretan body project can be similarly identified, which demands that individuals be consciously and actively concerned about the management, maintenance, and appearance of their bodies (whether at celebrations or on CD covers). The Cretan body project is managed in Cretan terms, embodiment is culturally constructed, and the connection to the body (in performance, visual culture, and folklore) bears upon the lyra, especially, as a masculine instrument. The lyra is not only emblematic of cultural difference in Crete, setting it apart from the outside world, it is also engendered, empowered, as a finely tuned physical and metaphorical site of performance where the body politic is constantly negotiated and reinforced.

Throughout the island, many examples from the iconography of records, posters, and the promotional materials of tourism, as well as displays in music shops and folk-life museums, draw attention to musical instruments and their potential as powerful icons of ethnicity. Indeed, images and displays provide a visual counterpoint to talk about music. They also reveal something about the nature and interaction of the forces that create, sustain, and move musical instruments around. For example, instrument displays in music shops convey much about the types of music popular in the area. In Crete, the fact that lyres are on display with Greek bouzoukis, Turkish *bağlama* (long-necked lutes), and electric guitars speaks volumes about the aspirations of the local musical community, about old and new trends in the local music scene, and about locally held values and beliefs. Musical instrument shops and workshops are therefore microcosms of the greater musical world at large, and have an important and often understated role in the construction of local musical culture.

ENTANGLED OBJECTS

In trying to build upon the work of scholars like Merriam and Qureshi, but also Sue Carole DeVale (1989) and Margaret Kartomi (1990), I and other researchers interested in musical instruments as cultural objects have used the tools of the field researcher and the ethnographer (Dournon 1981), because, as Clifford and Marcus state with force, "ethnography decodes and recodes, telling the grounds of collective order and diversity, inclusion and exclusion" (Clifford and Marcus 1986, 2–3). We should view musical instruments not just as part of some imposed scientific ordering system but as part of the semantic fields that make up cosmologies and worldviews (created and carried in the same minds that envision locally built musical instruments). How could we set about building information about "didjeridu culture" or the socio-economics of Bala drum making or the musical culture of the Indian sarangi or the Cretan lyra into the classification schemes offered by scholars in the West? How can we hope to capture, contrast, and compare a small part of a musical and artistic world in isolation—the musical instrument as mere object—without reference to its sound, affect, meaning, and social and economic status? It seems the world of musical instruments is much more complex and entangled than was first thought.

Throughout the twentieth century, scholars such as Izikowitz, Dräger, Hood, and Ramey tried to develop classification schemes that incorporated clusters of morphological, technomorphic, sociological, and anthropomorphic information as well as noting the performance practice characteristics and the facets determining the sound that an instrument produces (Kartomi 1990). And in an article published in 1986, Dale Olsen even suggested that a classification scheme like the one devised by Hornbostel and Sachs should include a separate category called "corpophones" for "instruments" such as the singing voice that comprise parts of the human body. But can these schemes tell us in detail about a particular musical culture and the role of a musical instrument within it?

The nonfit of imposed cross-cultural classification systems of musical instruments that make assumptions on a global scale from one viewpoint (with sometimes quite small samples) is problematic. Ultimately, emergent culture-specific systems are tied to systems of meaning beyond the scientific worldview. However useful these systems are, mistranslation, misrepresentation, and incompleteness are clearly possible using systems that quite clearly place "old instruments in new contexts" (after Neuenfeldt 1998) and in a new relationship with other musical instruments. Musical instruments are, not unexpectedly, made and played in new contexts as musical practices and industries develop but, as James Clifford notes:

> Every appropriation of culture, whether by insiders or outsiders, implies a specific temporal position and form of historical narration. Gathering, owning, classifying, and valuing are certainly not restricted to the West; but elsewhere these activities need not be associated with accumulation (rather than redistribution) or with preservation (rather than natural or historical decay). The Western practice of culture collecting has its own genealogy, enmeshed in distinct European notions of temporality and order.
>
> (Clifford 1988, 232)

Increasingly, musical instruments from around the world are pulled into new social and cultural arenas that are "enmeshed in distinct European notions of temporality and order"—classification is but one arena in which they have become enmeshed. A series of "partial truths" (Clifford and Marcus 1986) may be continuously reflected in as many different ways as there are models of musical instruments in the glass cabinets of museums, the grooves of world-beat records, and the photographic memorabilia of tourism, advertising, and the media (despite the best efforts of museum curators).

Building on analyses of the exchange of material goods in both colonial and postcolonial periods throughout the Pacific region, Nicholas Thomas notes that in that context "objects are not what they were made to be but what they have become" (Thomas 1991, 4). In general, we consume objects and give them meaning, and in doing so, reproduce them, so to speak, in our own image—we colonize them. Thomas goes on to say that a view such as this contradicts "a pervasive identification in museum research and material culture studies which stabilises the identity of a thing in its fixed and founded material form" (1991, 4). Whether museum exhibit or "world music" production, the focus is not on studying what musical instruments once might have been but on "what they have become" as "old instruments in new contexts" (after Neuenfeldt 1998). Thomas notes that "creative re-contextualisation and indeed re-authorship may thus follow from the taking, purchase or theft" of material goods. He goes on to say that "since exhibitions or museums of history are no less prominent now than in the epoch of the world's fairs, that is a sort of entanglement that most of us cannot step aside from" (Thomas 1991, 5). It is conceivable that musical instruments become so entangled with museum culture and colonization by the "host" that their meaning and exchange value are useful, and function only in relation to, the concepts that make up museum culture. Again, according to James Clifford, this "entanglement" is a means of colonizing, owning, and accumulating the objects of "outsiders," where "collecting has long been a strategy for the deployment of a possessive self, culture, and authenticity" (Clifford 1988, 218; see also Clifford 1992; Vergo 1991). These are surely some of the more pithy issues that organologists will need to engage with while attempting to collect and piece together what Margaret Kartomi has called "the broad picture." Clifford and Marcus's comment that ethnography "poses questions at the boundaries of civilisations, cultures, classes, races, and genders" (Clifford and Marcus 1986) seems particularly apt here. After all, these boundaries are just the places where we need to ask more and more questions about the humanly organized and culturally based phenomenon that is the musical instrument.

FURTHER READING

Appadurai, Arjun, ed. 1986. *The social life of things: Commodities in cultural perspective*. Cambridge, U.K.: Cambridge University Press.

Berliner, Paul. [1978] 1993. *The soul of mbira: Music and traditions of the Shona people of Zimbabwe*. Chicago: University of Chicago Press.

Birley, Margaret, Heidrun Eicher, and Arnold Myers. 2000. *Voices for the silenced: Guidelines for interpreting musical instruments in museum collections*. Electronic publication (this update, September 7, 2011). http://www.music.ed. ac.uk/euchmi/cimcim/iwte.html.

Bourdieu, Pierre. 1993. *The field of cultural production*. Cambridge, U.K.: Polity Press.

Diamond, Beverley, M. Sam Cronk, and Franziska von Rosen. 1995. *Visions of sound: Musical instruments of first nations communities in northeastern America*. Chicago: University of Chicago Press.

Foucault, Michel. 1970. *The order of things*. London: Tavistock.

Journal of Material Culture. Vol. 1, no. 1. 1996. Thousand Oaks, CA: Sage (mcu.sagepub.com/).

Leppert, Richard. 1988. *Music and image: Domesticity, ideology and socio-cultural formation in eighteenth-century England*. Cambridge, U.K.: Cambridge University Press.

Leppert, Richard. 1993 *The sight of sound: Music, representation, and the history of the body*. Berkeley: University of California Press.

Taylor, Timothy. 2002. *Strange sounds: Music, technology and culture*. New York: Routledge.

Théberge, Paul. 1998. *Any sound you can imagine: Making music/consuming technology*. Hanover, NH: University Press of New England.

Waksman, Steve. 1999. *Instruments of desire: The electric guitar and the shaping of musical experience*. Cambridge, MA: Harvard University Press.

CHAPTER 18

Music Education, Cultural Capital, and Social Group Identity

Lucy Green

A society without music has never been discovered. But although music making is a universal feature of human society, it is by no means universally undertaken by every individual within a society. The more highly specialized is the division of labor generally, the more likely it is that music will also become a specialized sphere of action: listened to and enjoyed by many, but practiced by only a few. In Europe five hundred years ago, not only the church and court but also the ordinary home, the street, the field, and the tavern all represented places where music was actively created by almost everyone, and in many non-Western societies music making has always been a normal part of everyday life. Nowadays, while technological developments have increased the availability of music for the listener, only a relatively small percentage of the adult population is engaged in active music making.

Over the last hundred and fifty years, there has been a gradual expansion in the sophistication, availability, and state funding of formal music education in schools, colleges and universities in many parts of the world. The decline of music making has occurred in tandem with the expansion of music education. Whether this complementary process is a matter of mere irony, whether music education has developed as a response to falling participation levels in music making, or whether it has been a contributory factor in causing that fall is not possible to demonstrate, at least not in a single chapter. But what is open to examination here is the role of music education in the production and reproduction of certain ideological assumptions and material conditions, which together contribute to overall patterns of musical life in the wider society. I focus on two linked areas: ideologies, particularly those relating to processes of canonization and the split between classical and popular musics; and social groups, specifically those defined by class, gender, and ethnicity. The discussion considers changes in ideologies of musical value and competence, and their part in the production and reproduction of social groups through formal music education in schools over the last forty years of the twentieth century. Many of the examples and illustrations relate specifically to Britain, while I also refer to research in a variety of other countries, and raise issues affecting formal music education globally.

The concept of ideology refers to ideas, values, and assumptions that are neither "true" nor "false," but that, rather, render the world intelligible and legitimate. Even though different ideologies can come into direct conflict, such as in war and revolution, ideologies normally help to maintain social values and relations, either in the forms in which these values and relations already exist or in the least destabilizing ways possible. Thus ideologies tend to benefit those social groups that are already in relatively beneficent positions. Until recently, musical ideologies have suggested that classical music lays claim to the greatest value, by possessing transcendent qualities such as universality, complexity, originality, or autonomy. Such qualities not only operate as markers for ascertaining musical value in itself but also provide various means of distinguishing classical music from other musics. The case of popular music provides a clear example of this, insofar as it is understood, by contrast to classical music, as ephemeral, trivial, derivative, or commercial. But what makes the assumption of the superiority of classical music ideological is not that it is necessarily "wrong." Rather, it tends to perpetuate the values of particular, interested social groups at the expense of others while at the same time appearing to be "objective" or disinterested (Green 1988, 1999).

Schooling helps to perpetuate existing ideologies, assimilate ideological challenges, and produce new ideologies in line with changing economic and social conditions. Formal education imbues children with self-images, expectations, and achievement orientations that correspond in various ways to their existing social situations, guiding them toward adult values and roles that, although often involving overt resistance along the way, are ultimately adaptable to the current economic and social climate, and at the same time largely similar to those that derive from their parents. This process does not take the form of overt discrimination, since a vital ideological aspect of education, whether in a capitalist democracy, a communist state or many other types of society, is precisely to offer equal opportunities to all children. However, whereas real equality of opportunity presupposes equality in values and incentives at the starting post, those children who come to school already sharing the values and incentives propagated and rewarded by the school stand more chance of succeeding. As Bourdieu famously put it, the school "demands of everyone alike that they already have what it does not provide" (1973, 80).

Music education participates in the construction and perpetuation of ideologies about musical value. For the first seventy years or so of the twentieth century, music in schools, including schools in many non-Western countries, was overwhelmingly concerned with Western classical music and settings of folk songs by prestigious composers. For while formal music education of various kinds occurs in many parts of the world, where schooling is concerned Western models have been most influential, especially in countries that were colonized or where missionaries had set up formal schooling programs, often involving hymn singing. Thus, for different reasons and to differing degrees, countries as far apart as Singapore, Ghana, Cyprus, Japan, Brazil, and Hong Kong as well as many others have employed Western models of music education in schools, with mainly Western classical music as the content.

During the 1970s, a small number of music educators, mainly in Britain, Scandinavia, Australia, and to a lesser extent North America, began to argue that popular music should be included in the school curriculum (Swanwick 1968; Vulliamy 1977a, b; Tagg 1998; Cutietta 1991; Volk 1998). However, reception of such ideas was often lukewarm, and, even when the ideas were accepted, this did not necessarily indicate any fundamental changes in musical ideologies. This was partly because many educators assumed that, if popular music was valuable, then it must share the qualities of classical music. So, for example, popular music was argued to have "universal" appeal; much popular music was said to be "complex" or "original"; or a distinction was drawn between different kinds of popular music, some of which was assumed to be "autonomous" (such as progressive rock), as distinct from other types that were assumed to be "commercial" (such as chart pop) (Green 1988, 1999).

Despite some commentators assuming that classical and popular music shared such qualities, when it came to classroom practice teachers often approached the two musics rather differently from each other. Research in Britain (Swanwick 1968; Vulliamy 1977b; Green 1988) suggested that the treatment of classical music generally focused upon singing and "musical appreciation," based on the assumption of the music's transcendent value. For older children and those taking specialist instrumental lessons, teaching also tackled the intramusical forms and processes: in other words the notes and how they fit together, or how they are to be executed in performance. By contrast, when teachers began to include popular music in the classroom, the aim was not so much to instill appreciation of the music's transcendent value as to encourage an appreciation of its relative value, or in other words its inferiority; to appeal to pupils' existing taste as a stepping-stone toward improving upon it; or to keep pupils entertained (especially those who were liable to be "disruptive"). Furthermore, rather than intramusical processes (the "notes"), teachers tended to concentrate on extramusical associations related to the social circumstances of the music's production and reception, such as the social functions or effects of the music, the dress of the performers, or the lyrics (Green 1988).

Therefore not only explicit but also implicit messages about the value of classical and popular music were conveyed, as a result of the emphasis of study upon a particular *aspect* of music. For if teachers present music only or largely in terms of its intramusical contents, the suggestion is that the significant aspects of the music are not tied to any specific social situation and are therefore autonomous and universal, that they involve complexity, and that they make possible the development of originality. Contrastingly, if teachers draw attention only or mainly to extramusical associations, this suggests that the "music itself" is a servant of its social context, which bolsters the appearance that it cannot be universal or autonomous, resulting in a lack of attention to the music's level of complexity, and this in turn affirms the unlikelihood of its ever affording any means for creative originality.

The treatment of classical and popular music in British schools was thus ideological, both in a parallel and in a contradictory manner. On the one hand, when teachers, curricula, syllabuses, or books *theoretically supported* the value of popular music, they tended to do so by appealing to the very same qualities of universality, complexity, originality, or autonomy upon which the value of classical music rested. But this approach was not necessarily pertinent to understanding or evaluating popular music, as has since been demonstrated by musicologists (e.g., Middleton 1990; Walser 1993; Moore 1993; Brackett 1995). On the other hand, when popular music was *actually used* in the classroom, teachers approached it as if it lacked those very characteristics of universality, complexity, originality, and autonomy purportedly possessed by classical music, and the ultimate superiority of classical music was thus affirmed and legitimated by default. Through such processes, not only in schools but also from the nursery to the university, music education has been a central mechanism in the establishment and maintenance of the classical canon. This canon has developed not as a result of the perpetuation of an arbitrary set of musical values by teachers and lecturers, but as a result of possessing various intra- and extramusical qualities that have marked it for "greatness" according to expert consensus arrived at through music criticism, analysis, and historiography, all of which have been closely tied to processes of educational success and legitimacy.

Just as ideology is reproduced through education, so too are social groups. Here I consider some of the changing processes through which music education and some of its associated ideologies have contributed to the reproduction of three kinds of groups: social class, gender, and ethnicity. This reproduction occurs both at the broad societal level in terms of cultural and economic relations between social groups, and at the level of the individual in terms of personal identity.

Children from all social classes in many countries are generally far more interested in various types of popular music than in classical music, and many children, especially from working-class backgrounds, come from families that do not consider classical music to be especially valuable. Despite or perhaps partly because of this, for the greater part of the twentieth century, as discussed above, Western classical music was accepted as the most valuable and relevant curriculum content for all children in many parts of the world. The ideology of this music's superiority corresponded with the perspectives of a minority of upper- and middle-class children, whereas it deviated from the musical tastes of other children from these classes, and of many working-class children. These latter children came to school already lacking what the school "demanded" in order to achieve music-educational success. Furthermore, since knowledge and skills in Western classical music are often supported by private instrumental lessons, children from families that could not afford to pay the fees missed out on the lessons. Therefore, both for cultural reasons concerning musical value, and for economic reasons concerning access to musical tuition, working-class children were less likely to select music courses, and, even when they did select them, they tended to be disadvantaged. They therefore achieved less educational success in music than middle-class children. Through such means, ideologies about musical value participate in the construction of patterns of music-educational success and failure, or success and drop-out rates, and in so doing serve to perpetuate existing cultural and economic relations between social classes.

During the 1980s and 1990s, increasing numbers of educators across the globe joined the challenge to the implicit and explicit assumption of Western classical music's canonization and superiority within schooling. This rise in protest was caused partly by broader social movements outside education, including developments in technology, globalization, and localization; the continuing effects of decolonization; changes in demography; and in gender, social class, and race relations. The expansion of the music industry made a huge variety of global musical styles available to listeners almost anywhere. At the same time the threat of musical monopolization by the American-dominated popular music industry caused some governments and pressure groups to raise the cultural and educational status of indigenous, local, and national classical, traditional, and popular musics. The relationships of people from differing social groups to music underwent rapid changes: certain styles of music were no longer exclusively associated with certain social classes; women in some parts of the world became less restricted in their musical roles than previously; and particular musics no longer "belonged" primarily to particular ethnic groups.

Today, the music curriculum in many countries reflects these developments, in that it includes a mixture of folk, traditional, popular, jazz, and classical musics from all around the world (Volk 1998; Campbell 1991). Not only curriculum content but also the values and attitudes of many teachers have undergone an apparent transformation. For example, whereas research conducted in England in 1982 suggested that schoolteachers regarded classical music as unquestionably the most important, valid, and in many cases the only legitimate music for inclusion in the curriculum, by 1998 a parallel sample of teachers indicated that the most important area of the curriculum was popular music, with classical and "world music" in almost equal second position (Green 2001, 2002).

However, the mere entrance of a wider variety of musical styles into an education system does not automatically halt the construction and perpetuation of ideologies of musical value. Rather, value hierarchies and canonization processes can continue to operate, only across different styles. Two issues related to popular music can illustrate this. One refers to curriculum content. Precisely by virtue of its entrance into education and the concomitant production of a scholarly literature, popular music develops canons within itself, often based on assumptions that it lays claim to universal, complex, original, or autonomous properties. In this way, it conjoins rather than dismantles the same evaluative axes upon which classical canons are built. The other issue refers to teaching strategies. Alongside formal music education, informal methods of acquiring musical skills and knowledge have always flourished, leading to the production of most of the world's popular, folk, traditional, classical, and jazz musics throughout history. The majority of musicians in these realms have largely acquired their skills and knowledge through informal means, outside, and even in contradistinction to, institutionalized education; and have employed quite different learning methods to those of Western formal music pedagogy (e.g., Green 2001, 2008). Yet in spite of the presence of popular musics in the curriculum, the assumptions of this formal pedagogy have continued to inform most music education literature and teaching materials, at least until very recently. It is one thing to bring a variety of musics into the classroom, but, if the learning practices of the relevant musicians are ignored, a peculiar, classroom version of the music is likely to emerge, stripped of the very methods by which the music has always been created, and therefore bearing little resemblance to its existence in the world outside. So, although covering a wider array of musics, new canons emerge within education, and are positioned in contradistinction to "other" musics that remain beyond the school.

Currently, widespread and potentially radical changes are occurring within formal music education, which are affecting the reproduction of both the ideological aspects of musical value and the sociological aspects of musical opportunity. For, rather than remaining as mere curriculum *content*, popular musics are now being brought into education in ways which affect teaching (and thereby, learning) *strategies*. This has occurred as increasing numbers of teachers in many countries of the world have begun to incorporate adapted versions of informal music learning practices into the formal environment. (For a range of cross-cultural discussions of this, see e.g. Green 2008; Lebler 2007; or three special issues of journals: the *British Journal of Music Education*, Vol. 27(1), March 2010; *Action, Criticism and Theory in Music Education*, Vol. 8(2), October 2009; *Visions of Research in Music Education*, Vol. 12, 2008). These informally based teaching and learning strategies involve, for example, a higher amount of student choice in what music is learnt; more emphasis on aural learning methods including the copying of recordings; and more self-directed learning and group work. Concerning the reproduction of social class, there are some signs that such changes are leading to increased motivation, and wider, more diverse opportunities for children and young people from different class and cultural backgrounds to take part and succeed in music, from the school to the higher educational sphere. However, contestation over musical value is unlikely ever to disappear, and only time will tell whether such changes in the educational sphere are to have radical effects more widely in society.

Turning now to the topic of gender: schooling helps to perpetuate differences in the musical practices and tastes of boys and girls. Teachers, curriculum planners, and pupils in countries as far apart as Britain, Japan, Spain, the United States, Canada, and Hong Kong overwhelmingly associate active engagement in popular music, such as playing electric guitars and drums, with boys and masculinity, whereas classical music practices such as singing in the choir and playing the flute are linked with girls and femininity (Green 1997; O'Neill 1997; Koizumi 2002; Riguero 2000; Koza 1992; Hanley 1998; Ho 2001). Perceptions of gender differences are perhaps most subtle in the realm of composition. For example, in research in England (Green 1997, Legg Forthcoming 2012), paralleled in Canada (Hanley 1998), many teachers declare that girls possess little ability for composition, tend to compose by "merely" following rules or doing what they are told, and lack imagination and creative spark. Girls themselves declare a lack of confidence and a reliance on teacher direction, and even those who enjoy and value composition often decry their own achievements. These assumptions and self-concepts go hand in hand with the association of girls with classical music as a conformist and conservative cultural sphere. Contrastingly, even though teachers quite explicitly see boys as uninterested, disruptive, and more concerned with peer-group opinion than with teachers' assessments, they nonetheless describe them as "naturally" more adept, spontaneous, and creative, while boys themselves display confidence in their creative compositional abilities. These proclivities are linked to boys' associations with popular music, especially its improvisational qualities, its technology, and its greater potential for symbolizing nonconformity—despite, or perhaps even because of, the presence of some "accepted" (or canonized) popular music in the school.

Not only are different musical instruments, practices, and styles associated with girls and boys, but they are also linked to girls' and boys' self-perceptions in terms of musical ability, and to the expectations of teachers. Through labeling and self-fulfilling prophecies, such perceptions and expectations can have a considerable effect on long-term music-educational success (Green 1997). The symbolization of gender through music education thus represents a way in which patterns of musical involvement between the sexes, including educational success and failure in music, are constructed and perpetuated. Again, new teaching strategies may have an effect on this reproductive cycle. In schools where girls and boys are given equal opportunities to play instruments that have traditionally been associated with masculinity, such as electric guitars and drum kits, there are signs that girls take these up with an enthusiasm that is quite equal to that of boys (see Green 2008). However, again it is too early to gauge whether such changes will put down deep roots, or whether old gender-reproductive processes will grow over them. Furthermore, changes in girls' musical involvement towards playing a greater range of instruments associated with masculinity and popular musics do not alter the fact that boys are still not opting in large numbers to take up instruments traditionally associated with femininity and classical music, such as flutes and violins.

While the processes of reproduction through Western classical music tend to reinforce social class and gender differences, the new emphasis upon indigenous classical and traditional musics in the curricula of some countries is explicitly intended to reinforce ethnicities. Such processes occur in Western countries such as Ireland and Wales, and non-Western countries such as Thailand and Hong Kong (McCarthy 1997; Maryprasith 1999; Ho 1999). For example, in Thailand, musical globalization resulted in a two-pronged response during the 1990s: on the one hand, the increased production and purchase of Westernized forms of Thai popular music by the local music industry and consumers; on the other hand, a growing concern by the government, educators, and pressure groups that traditional Thai music was breathing its last breath. The 1997 economic crisis in Thailand then caused a retreat in the production of indigenous popular music, and an increased concentration on British and American popular music by the record industry. At the same time, greater emphasis was placed on traditional Thai music both in schools and the wider society, corresponding with the government's "Amazing Thailand" tourist campaign (Maryprasith 1999). A rather different process of musical nationalization through education has been occurring in Hong Kong. There, formal music education in schools and higher education has operated under the legacy of British imperialism to a large extent. Until recently, courses have been based entirely on Western classical music in a mold derived from British music education. With the end of British sovereignty and the establishment of Hong Kong as an autonomous region of the People's Republic of China in 1997, traditional Chinese music began to enter formal music education (Ho 1999). However, young Thai and Hong Kong Chinese students, like students everywhere, generally prefer Western or Westernized, indigenous, mother-tongue popular music, rather than the classical or traditional music of their national heritage (Maryprasith 1999; Ho 1999).

Distinct from moves to reinforce ethnicity by the inclusion of indigenous music in the curriculum, there have at the same time been increasing moves toward multiculturalism in music education. Claims are often made that "world music" has the capacity to break down ethnic barriers, particularly in multiracial schools. However, such claims are rarely examined, and when they are, a less optimistic perspective can emerge (Green [1999] 2002). During research in an inner-city London primary school, Alden (1998) came across a significant degree of reluctance on the part of Hindi-speaking Asian children to reveal their private musical tastes. In discussion with the whole, mixed-ethnicity class, all the pupils gave the impression that they listened entirely to mainstream chart music. But when Alden interviewed the same pupils in small, single-ethnicity groups, he was presented with a very different picture by the Asian children: "although they were familiar with 'pop' music and sometimes listened to *Top of the Pops* they were all very clear that Hindi film music was the substance of their experience at home and they stated that this was their preferred music" (p. 84). He then conducted another whole-class session in which pupils devised a music curriculum for their school. They included only mainstream popular music and its associated instruments, along with some classroom percussion with which they were already familiar. During discussion afterwards, the Asian pupils were silent. "I pointed out that pupils in the school listened to a much wider range of music than those which had been suggested, and asked if this range should be included. Even with such a clear lead, there was no voice strong enough to say 'yes'" (p. 88). Later, he asked the pupils separately why they had not spoken up, and they said it was because of peer pressure (p. 85). Even in a school such as this, with a written antiracist policy, the multi-cultural curriculum remained unconnected to the musical experiences of many of the children, who appeared to be ashamed of and secretive about their musical tastes. Ethnicity here occurred as a problematic part of musical identity arising from commercial pressures outside, and peer-group pressures inside the school. In such ways, multiculturalism in music education can operate more as an unwitting affirmation rather than a breaking down of ethnic power and status differentials. In newer approaches, particularly those affording pupils the autonomy to choose their own music, there are so far few signs that their choices necessarily resist the pressures of commercial media (e.g. Green 2008, 45–46); however again, this will be an area for researchers to investigate in the future.

Looked at from the perspectives adopted in this chapter, music education appears to have long been affirming pre-existing ideologies of musical value, and their corresponding skills and knowledge, thereby reproducing social group differentiation on the basis of, for example, class, gender, and ethnicity. Even radical challenges, such as the explosion in curriculum content and the turnaround in teachers' attitudes described above, seem to be inveigled. It may be that teaching and learning strategies which give students more autonomy will make significant inroads into social reproductive processes, but more research will be needed to ascertain to what extent this is so. Also, although as individuals it is possible for teachers to step outside of the reproductive effects of the wider social systems to which we all belong, and although many do so in their music classrooms, lecture theaters, and studios every day, overall these social systems are beyond the control of any individual. It is only by taking a critical stance and attempting together to move beyond some of the assumptions and procedures that go to make up our parts in those systems that we can ever come to a deeper understanding of them, and thereby make significant steps toward improving them. The expansion of the music curriculum to include a more global purview and a wider range of teaching and learning strategies has itself grown out of just such a critical perspective, shared across countries, classes, genders, and ethnicities; and, despite the reproductive processes that this expansion involves, it represents a historically necessary recognition of the music, musical tastes, and musical practices of a greater span of humanity than was hitherto represented in education. One task facing music educators, not only in schools but also across the board to higher education, is to ensure that the expansion of teaching and learning strategies which is currently occurring does not happen, on the one hand, at the expense of losing older valued approaches, and does not on the other hand fall into the ruts of the old tracks in terms of restricting musical opportunities to a minority of children.

FURTHER READING

Bourdieu, Pierre, and Jean Claude Passeron. 1999. *Reproduction in education, society and culture.* Translated by R. Nice. Beverly Hills, CA: Sage. [First published as *La réproduction.* 1977.]

Green, Lucy. 1988. *Music on deaf ears: Musical meaning, ideology and education.* New York: Manchester University Press. [2nd ed. Bury St Edmunds, U.K.: Arima Publishing, 2008.]

Green, Lucy. 1997. *Music, gender, education.* New York: Cambridge University Press.

Green, Lucy. 2001. *How popular musicians learn: A way ahead for music education.* New York: Ashgate Press.

Green, Lucy. 2008. *Music, informal learning and the school: A new classroom pedagogy..* New York: Ashgate Press.

Halsey, A. H., Hugh Lauder, Philip Brown, and Amy Stuart Wells. 1997. *Education: Culture, economy, society.* 2nd ed. New York: Oxford University Press.

Hanley, Betty, and Janet Montgomery. 2002. Contemporary curriculum practices and their theoretical bases. Pp. 113–143 in *The new handbook of research on music teaching and learning.* Edited by Richard Colwell and Carol P. Richardson. New York: Oxford University Press.

Lebler, Don. 2007. Student-as-master? Reflections on a learning innovation in popular music pedagogy. *International Journal of Music Education* 25(3): 205–221.

Legg, Robert (Forthcoming 2012) "One equal music": an exploration of gender perceptions and the fair assessment by beginning music teachers of musical compositions. *Music Education Research* 12(2).

Small, Christopher. 1980. *Music—Society—Education.* London: John Calder.

Tagg, Philip. 1998. The Göteborg connection: Lessons in the history and politics of popular music education and research. *Popular Music* 17(2): 219–242.

Vulliamy, Graham. 1977a. Music and the mass culture debate. Pp. 179–200 in *Whose music: A sociology of musical languages.* Edited by John Shepherd, Paul Virden, Trevor Wishart, and Graham Vulliamy. London: Latimer New Dimensions.

Vulliamy, Graham. 1977b. Music as a case study in the "new sociology of education." Pp. 201–32 in *Whose music: A sociology of musical languages.* Edited by John Shepherd, Paul Virden, Trevor Wishart, and Graham Vulliamy. London: Latimer New Dimensions.

CHAPTER 19

MUSIC TECHNOLOGY, OR TECHNOLOGIES OF MUSIC?

BENNETT HOGG

In his introduction to the first edition of the present book Richard Middleton notes "There is no chapter on technology . . . because its importance is taken for granted" (Middleton 2003, 13). In writing this chapter on music and technology I will not challenge this statement which is, effectively, a truism. Instead I would like to look behind it, as it were, to see what elements of a cultural study of music and technology might be obscured or concealed behind the ubiquity of musical technologies. The task of writing about music and technology is problematic not because there is so much to say but rather because of an underlying incompatibility between categories: music, understood as a culturally and historically contingent series of human actions; and Technology (with a capital "T") as essentially an abstraction. Abstractions, in the worst case scenario, give rise to essentialisms that can be politically deployed to underwrite a multitude of misrepresentations, prejudices, and vested interests. Technology, as such, is essentially an abstraction, and as such stands as an obstacle in trying to arrive at any form of culturally contingent understanding.

Rainer Rochlitz, for example, in an otherwise rich and nuanced book on Walter Benjamin (Rochlitz 1996), rehearses the notion of capital-T Technology in ways that foreclose alternative readings. Benjamin wrote, more or less simultaneously with his "Work of Art in the Age of Mechanical Reproduction," a shorter piece called "The Storyteller" (Benjamin [1936] 1973a and b). There is ample evidence in Benjamin's letters to indicate that he saw the two essays as related (Rochlitz 1996, 187–188), but Rochlitz reads the two essays diachronically, suggesting that "The Storyteller" represents a change of heart on Benjamin's part away from the emancipatory potential of Technology in "The Work of Art" towards a more pessimistic position; the fact that the essays deal with completely *different* technologies—cinema and photography in the "Work of Art," printing in "The Storyteller"—is not given serious attention. This reifies Technology and refuses the specificity of the different technologies that led Benjamin to celebrate cinema and photography as potentially democratizing practices, but to mourn the passing of storytelling (understood, with its intimate links to lived lives, as a demotic, oral form) under the impact of the printed word and the pre-digested nature of "information" conveyed through newsprint. If anything, these two essays ought to be read together in order to better understand how *different* technologies interact with culture, rather than as evidence that "The Storyteller" represents Benjamin's position that, as Rochlitz puts it, "[t]he masses and technology no longer have any promising potential" (Rochlitz 1996, 188). Rochlitz's book is excellent, but his insistence on the general term "technology" to discuss radically different phenomena emblematizes a tendency to think in terms of Technology rather than technologies.

The ubiquity of technologies doubtless contributes to the abstraction of Technology, which *as* an abstraction acquires a certain conceptual autonomy; it is ironic that from this historically and socio-culturally determined position the idea of technological determinism can take hold. For determinists technology drives cultural change, following an inexorable logic of rationalization and progress. Such an analysis, where technological causes lead to cultural effects, tends now to be considered unrepresentatively reductive and so, starting from this anti-determinist position, I want to shift the terms of the discussion somewhat, resisting the notion that talking about Technology is productive at all. I take my lead in this from Hård and Jamison whose jointly edited work (Hård and Jamison 1998) insists on the locally and historically specific nature of the meanings that particular technologies accrue to themselves. My first task in writing about music and technology must therefore be to actively refuse to define technology. As Nietzsche put it in *The Genealogy of Morals* (1998, 60), "[o]nly that which has no history can be defined"; definition reduces (or at least establishes exclusionary, unrepresentative limits) and unifies (where culturally speaking there is diversity and difference). "No history" was, of course, a dream of one of the constituent strands of modernism, but projects such as Boulez's *Structures 1a* would become cul de sacs in their respective composers' outputs and, ironically given the idealism with which they seemed to resist history at the moment of their creation, are now more or less experienced only through history books. In refusing to define technology I aim to avoid the cul de sacs of definition to foreground the socio-historical and particular contingencies of individual technologies; refusing to define, then, is also to pluralise. Avoiding the abstract in the interests of the concrete facilitates a contingent understanding of how *some* musical practices interrelate with *some* of their technologies, an approach which seems congruent with an avowedly culturalist position that seeks to evade essentialisation and the general.

Sound recording, one of the key technological developments of the modern period, has a history that long precedes its actual invention. Lisa Gitelman, for example, argues that a reliable historiographical understanding of sound recording needs to take account of Pitman shorthand, itself known as phonography, which arrived some forty or fifty years prior to the phonograph and which, like Edison's invention, was seen as primarily a technology for the office (Gitelman 1999, 62–70). She underlines its utilitarian functions by noting how Edison's phonograph was classified as a "measuring instrument" by the U.S. Patent Office (pp. 98, 171), concretizing the device's technological affinities with technologies that measured environmental or physiological variables—wind speed or heart rate—and recorded the data on a rotating surface, such as those developed by Etienne-Jules Marey (see Rabinbach 1992). For Friedrich Kittler phonography represents an ephochal shift in Western epistemology, and, despite the (arguably) postmodern tonality of his methodology, his claims for its effects on culture resonate with a very modernist hyperbole; nevertheless, such epochal shifts are not understood as rising *ex nihilo* but are constituted as historical moments at which already existing philosophical, technical, and imaginary antecedents converge (Kittler 1990, 21–29).

Though it is true that until the invention of the phonograph musical sound was entirely dependent upon the living, physical presence of musicking humans,[1] and that phonography's erasure of this dependency effected a profound change in the ontology of music, it is interesting how quickly Western culture assimilated the new technology. A culture for which embodied music making was the *only* possible site of the musical imagination might not have so easily assimilated the disembodied sounds of recorded music. Though prior to phonography disembodied music was heard as supernatural, Romantic ideological formations concerning the ineffability of music, music as the least corporeal of the arts, as outpourings of pure spirit, as well as its associations with the other worldly (Orpheus in Hades, music in religious practices the world over), all contributed to providing a cultural ground in which disembodied music could take root and flourish. Adorno, for example, shifted from an argument that recording technology, whatever its potentials, was in large part merely supplementary to live performance ("the reduced transmission, adapted to domestic needs, of pre-existing works" (Adorno [1927] 2002, 272); "a music . . . that was already in existence before the phonograph record and is not significantly altered by it" [Adorno [1934] 2002, 278]) to the view that recording technology, in constellation with capitalism and the culture industry, forces tangible, material changes (for the worse, in Adorno's estimation) on musical culture: a regression of listening due in great measure to the fetish-character of music greatly intensified by the music industry and its attendant technologies (Adorno [1938] 2002). No uncritical technophile, then, Adorno was nevertheless able in his final years to celebrate the invention of the LP record for returning opera to its rightful place as a musical rather than a theatrical form: "[the LP] allows for the *optimal* presentation of music, enabling it to recapture some of the force and intensity that had been worn threadbare in the opera houses. Objectification, that is, a concentration on music as the *true object* of opera, may be linked to a perception that is comparable to reading, to the immersion in a text" (Adorno [1969] 2002, 284–285, emphasis added). For Adorno, opera stagings that are archaic, kitsch, or gratuitously oblique draw attention from the music and move the art form towards obsolescence; in a sense, opera is over-embodied, or at least its embodiment is overdetermined. In making (disembodied) music on LPs the "true object of opera," Adorno plays on the theme of intangibility and the ineffable that had directed much of the cultural reception of music as Art-with-a-capital-A from the late eighteenth century onwards— and particularly in cultures whose philosophical traditions had been formed or informed by German Romanticism. Acknowledging his own former ambivalence to the significance of sound recording (p. 283), he is able to recuperate it precisely at the moment when, within the philosophico-political frames within which he constrains himself to think, it returns music to itself, as it were.

This might be a good moment to reflect upon the specific factors that intertwine with technological developments such that, as I have suggested, any avowedly culturalist position that also seeks to maintain the monolith Technology is severely compromised. Sound recording, for the later Adorno, can return a textuality to music that had been obscured in physical spectacle, yet, only a few years earlier, Pierre Schaeffer, in what was one of the earliest appropriations of sound recording for creative rather than reproductive ends, explicitly opens up music to the embodied and the material through *la musique concrète*. Eschewing formalism and abstract musical materials, *musique concrète* set itself the challenge of making a music structured phenomenologically, without recourse to the dominant abstractions of pitch and duration that Adorno understood as "the true object of opera." Developing the creative and philosophical implications of Schaeffer's investigations, Trevor Wishart sees in sound recording a tool with which to undermine precisely those claims that Western music had made to itself, namely that pitch and duration locate the "true object" (to recontextualize Adorno's phrase) of music. For Wishart, pitch and duration became dominant paradigms in Western music through their being recorded in staff notation. Dating back to the medieval period, Western music notation developed primarily to record "the notes," imposing, in Wishart's analysis, an ontological bias on music that sidelines the corporeal and the oral-aural in favor of the abstract and formalistic. For Wishart, it is no coincidence that such a disciplining of music's materiality goes hand-in-hand with a system developed by a "scribal elite," in service to the royal courts of Europe and the Church. He sees sound recording as "the central watershed in changing our view of what constitutes music" (Wishart 1985, 4), enabling a move "beyond the pitch-duration paradigm," challenging the grounds on which music had been constructed as autonomous, and implying an understanding of the ontology of music more specifically aural/oral in nature (pp. 7–27). Two very divergent readings of recorded sound, then, Adorno's returning music to writing, Wishart's liberating it from writing, remain viable today in the ideologies of progressive Western art music, emphasizing the contingencies at play in the meanings that develop between musics and their technologies.

So far I have focused on phonography (sound recording) and in doing so have reproduced a dominant cultural perspective that "music technology" is electronic. Typing the search terms "music" and "technology" into Google returns sites overwhelmingly devoted to electronic, usually digital, machinery, suggesting (though a social scientist might question my methodology by asking how reliable and sensitive a seismographic of our cultural conditions Google really is) a culturally dominant imaginary in which music technologies are electronic. The particular visibility of this perspective tends to sideline other technological relations, as well as grounding the idea that there is some *thing* that is Technology. For example, phonography has frequently been figured as having a particularly privileged relationship to memory (Draaisma 2000, 24–27). In *Civilization and Its Discontents*, for example, Freud writes of the gramophone record as a prosthesis of our "innate faculty of recall, of . . . memory" (Freud 2004 [1930], 35), and when Joyce's Leopold Bloom fantasizes about "a gramophone in every grave" (Joyce [1922] 1980, 115) he is but one of many for whom phonography emblematizes memory and memorialization. The mnemic aspects of phonography are obvious, as they are with photography. Yet, as Gitelman suggests in her elaborating of connections between Edison's invention and Pitman's phonetic transcription system, and as the etymology of "phonograph" (sound or voice writer) makes plain, the uniquely phonographic storage of memory is grounded on the earlier mnemic technology of writing. As if to articulate this connection, in the year after the phonograph's invention de Moncel relates the physical traces left on the phonograph cylinder to writing (du Moncel 1879, 251–255), and Adorno, writing in 1934, is still fascinated by the phonograph record's "delicately scribbled, utterly illegible writing" (Adorno [1934] 2002, 277, 279). Caution, though, is needed here, because writing is only one model for mnemic technology. As Kittler has argued, phonography's claim to represent a fundamental shift in the circulation of information rests on its inscribing a continuous phys-ical trace rather than an alphabetized code. It took some time for the full implications of this to be felt in musical culture,[2] but as a technology phonography—this, let us say, *non-notational* mode of recording—opens up alternative ways in which a technology may be understood as mnemic. The mnemic, then, is a theme that I will now deploy to move away from electronic technologies and capital-T Technology at large in order to briefly explore some of the alternative ways in which music and technologies interrelate.

Rhyme, in poetry and in oral cultures, has been figured as a mnemic tech-nology, insofar as a rhyme scheme places constraints on what a particular word in a particular place in the poem's structure can be (Ong 1982). Harmonic rhythm—perhaps most acutely in improvised tonal musics such as jazz or Cuban son, though it is also clearly at play in any playing from memory or by ear—is a similar technology, structuring and limiting what can happen next. This remains, though, like writing, a technology that is structured according to what we might call a code, even if that code for an expert jazz musician is so internalized as to feel like an intuition. If not all mnemic technologies store information as code (even though codes such as the rules of tonal harmony, or linguistic grammar, may strongly inform such technologies), I suggest that musical instruments are also mnemic technolo-gies, but ones that depend upon a subtly different model of memory that incorporates human embodiment.

Contemporary moves in cognitive science and consciousness studies have brought into doubt the reliability of the Cartesian model of consciousness, what Daniel C. Dennett has called the "Cartesian theatre" (Dennett 1991). Consciousness (in which memory is, of course, deeply implicated) is increasingly conceptualized in ecosystemic terms (Gibson 1986); as John T. Sanders puts it (Sanders 1996, para. 36), memories are "not only in [human] heads but in their worlds." Sanders cites (para. 31) a number of (now quite long-established) positions that seriously challenge the idea that memory happens exclusively in the brain, or that it is structured like a filing system under the control of an omniscient "I." Francesco J. Varela has also argued for an understanding of consciousness as something we do, not something we have (Varela et al. 1993). Rather than inhabiting the body like a non-material tenant in a material house, consciousness is inseparable from embodiment, from situatedness in an environment, or from social relations. A violin, in terms of such an understanding of consciousness, is embodied (a prosthesis of the body), environmental (part of not-me), and social (a cultural artifact and also the means by which I can socially interact with other musicking humans). It becomes a mnemic technology when, for example, I cannot remember a tune unless I have the instrument in my hands, or when I find myself playing a tune in a folk session that I *don't remember knowing* but can nevertheless play; that tactile encounter with the instrument is what actualizes kinesthetic memory of the tune that would otherwise remain unretrieved, effectively unknown. Though not generally classified as a mnemic technology, in part because that role is so conspicuously monopolized by writing and phonography, an ecologically informed approach to memory and consciousness, understood as enactive phenomena, uncovers the violin's value as a mnemic technology.

From "The letter kills but the spirit gives life" (II Corinthians 3:6) to Mallarmé's unfinished *Livre*, writing has, since ancient times, held associations with death (Weiss 2002, 29–66; Ong 1982, 80–81). As a technology that in effect underwrites phonography, it combines with the phonograph's superficial—if more vivid—spookiness (where the voices of the dead can be heard again, or where ghostly voices emerge from "dead" machinery), to produce "for the fifty years straddling 1900 . . . the machine of choice for repopulating the world by reanimating the dead" (Kahn 1994, 70; see also Sconce 2000, Potts and Scheer 2006). But there is an alternative prehistory to recording that evades writing, in which musical instruments enter into uncanny constellations with murder, guilt, and dead voices. Musical instruments have mythologically been sites of memories that will not be repressed, memories that are not inscribed in codified form but which possess these instruments. Syrinx, the beautiful water nymph desired by Pan who transforms herself into a reed and is then made into a flute, is one of the earlier manifestations of this. In the Scottish ballad "The Twa Sisters," also sometimes known as "Binnorie," a murdered girl's voice returns through a musical instrument to condemn her murderer. Different versions of the ballad have her hair being found long after her murder by a traveling musician, who then twines it into strings for a fiddle or a harp, or else, finding one of her bones, carves it into a flute. Whatever the instrument, the end result is the same: the voice of the dead girl returns when the living musician plays the instrument, and justice is done. The same narrative underlies the Germanic myths the Brothers Grimm drew on for their folk tale "Der singende Knochen" (The Singing Bone), upon which Mahler based his "Das Klagende Lied." What I find resonant in these tales is the way that playing an instrument is not simply a means to engage in an interplay of codified musical sounds (playing the notes), but shares poetic resonances with activating a recording device. In these stories instruments become technologies that return the dead, not on their own, but through their encounter with a living embodied consciousness—completing a circuit, as it were—that actualizes a memory. In fact, *every* time we play an instrument we are in dialogue not just with our individual learning but with a whole culture, or an interrelated series of cultural subsets. The violin, again, emblematizes this interplay; I cannot recall how many times I have been asked what the difference is between a violin and a fiddle, two "different" instruments that share the same technological body, as it were, differentiated only by the histories of their use and the musical cultures in which they participate—and many, mine included, participate in more than one. Ultimately, technologies are susceptible to being, we might say, *ensouled* (see Sconce 2000). Mr Weasley's Ford Anglia in the second Harry Potter book, or Herby the VW Beetle in the 1968 Disney film *The Love Bug*, are comic versions of this tendency, but the general notion that apparently inanimate objects may become animated, and may display all the signs of having an active consciousness, is something resonant in our culture. Musical instruments, as technologies of music, are, I suggest, not only not exempt from this but constitute privileged sites at which embodiment, ensoulment, disembodiment, and memory can be seen to be played out.

The soldier's violin in Stravinsky's *L'histoire du soldat* stands metaphorically, but also quite literally, for his soul. It is his soul he sells to the Devil, not just a cheap fiddle, and the allegory is noted by many commentators on the piece. This seems, albeit somewhat tangentially, related to the mythological instruments noted above. Those particular technologies are places where souls, where lost voices, where wronged ghosts can go to find articulation. But the soldier's tale raises another specific cultural concern where technologies of music are concerned, and that is the issue of mediation and the extent to which notions of authenticity may be problematized by this. Tim Armstrong has differentiated between extensory (the telescope) and compensatory (a wooden leg) prosthetics (Armstrong 1998, 77–105), and most musical instruments can be readily seen as extensory prostheses. However, in the case of *L'histoire du soldat* the violin's prosthetic function may be compensatory, covering a lack rather than extending a capability, and this lack marks an anxiety about the technological mediation of music at several cultural registers. When, having earlier sold his violin/soul to the Devil, the soldier, towards the end of part 1, gets the violin back, he finds that he is unable to play it. In a story filled with magic, is it that the violin plays only for its master, which, having sold it to the Devil, the soldier no longer is? Did he, then, ever *really* know how to play, or was it a magic violin that only made it look as if he could? Now that he is no longer its rightful owner, is his former skill as a violinist revealed as a sham?

Having deployed the theme of memory to move from electronic recording technologies to the violin, I now want to use the issue of authenticity that I see raised by the soldier's violin understood as a technology to move back to electronic technologies. Many electronic devices such as autotune, compression, samplers, and more recently the laptop as musical instrument, bring with them an anxiety that the musician isn't *really* "doing it," or at least couldn't do it unaided. Since the advent of electronics, the technological mediation of sound has been considered, by many, to be a problem, not only intervening in the process of communication with an audience (a naive understanding of communication, it has to be said; see Peters 1999, 1–31) but also opening possibilities for deceit ("faking it"). Anxieties about singers miming in concert, and the illegibility of the connection between a laptop performer and the resultant sounds, are but two factors that inhabit a complex constellation of problematizations of the idea of electronic mediation in music.

But what constitutes electronic mediation is not itself monolithic, any more than technologies are. Gilbert and Pearson note how contingent technologies are *qua* technologies, citing how the folk revival audience had no difficulty accepting electronic mediation when Bob Dylan sang and played his acoustic guitar into a microphone and loudspeakers, but rebelled when he picked up an electric guitar: this "technology" intruded into what had been seen as unproblematically "authentic" folk music and rendered it "inauthentic" (Gilbert and Pearson 1999). Dylan "going electric" fetishizes the technology but the real issue was not, of course, the fact of mediation but the way in which the electric guitar was understood to be part of another cultural formation against whose perceived commercialism and superficiality the folk revival had effectively constructed itself. This example quite neatly shows the contingency and ambiguity of technologies *qua* technologies; loudspeaker and microphone—as well as gramophone records—had been assimilated by the folk revival audience, rendering them invisible as technologies in a way that the electric guitar had yet to become. It is not a case of technological mediation being "bad" in any absolute sense, so much as specific technologies being deployed as markers of particular cultural positions. As I have argued throughout, any attempt to understand music in cultural terms that reduces musical technologies to the abstraction Technology inevitably forecloses the possible directions such understandings might move in. In contrast to this, localizing musics and their technologies in relation to cultural and historical specificities not only makes the investigations—whether hermeneutic or creative—more mobile and flexible but also encourages the emergence of a "thicker"—in Clifford Geertz's terms—understanding of music's cultural situatedness.

NOTES

1 "Musicking" is the term coined by Christopher Small to argue for music as social human action rather than as an object; verb rather than noun (Small 1998).
2 Though there were attempts to deploy sound recordings in musical composition earlier in the twentieth century, the first serious and productive engagement with sound recording as a creative tool on its own terms, rather than as a surrogate for a more conventional instrument within an already established musical practice, is generally considered to be Schaeffer's *musique concrète* of the late 1940s—a view which, however, may be historically over-simple (see Kahn and Whitehead 1994; Kahn 1999; Chadabe 1997, 21–31; LaBelle 2007, 7–11, 24–28).

FURTHER READING

Armstrong, Tim. 1998. *Modernism, technology, and the body.* Cambridge, U.K.: Cambridge University Press.

Birdsall, Caroline, and Anthony Enns. 2008. *Sonic mediations: Body, sound, technology.* Newcastle upon Tyne: Cambridge Scholars Press.

Emmerson, Simon. 2007. *Living electronic music.* Aldershot, U.K.: Ashgate.

Gilbert, Jeremy, and Ewan Pearson. 1999. *Discographies: Dance music, culture, and the politics of sound.* London: Routledge.

Hård, Mikael, and Andrew Jamison. 1998. *The intellectual appropriation of technology: Discourses on modernity, 1900-1939.* Cambridge, MA, and London: MIT Press.

Hegarty, Paul. 2008. *Noise / music: A history.* New York and London: Continuum.

Hugill, Andrew. 2008. *The digital musician.* New York: Routledge.

Théberge, Paul. 1997. *Any sound you can imagine: Making music / consuming technology.* Hanover, NH, and London: University Press of New England.

CHAPTER 20

MUSIC AND MATERIAL CULTURE

WILL STRAW

In his 1993 book *La passion musicale*, Antoine Hennion noted a key difference between the analysis of music and that of other cultural forms. Those studying literature or art history, he suggested, struggle against the self-evident solidity of their objects. The literary scholar or art historian is up against the seemingly irrefutable concreteness of a book or painting, and so confronts prejudices which assert the self-sufficiency of the artistic object unto itself. In the face of this concreteness, skill and perseverance are required to expose the mediations (the social structures and processes) that made such an object possible, and to convince others that they are of more than secondary interest. For the analyst confronting music, in contrast, "critical discourse finds itself thrown off balance." Music, Hennion writes, "far from concealing the mass of its interpreters and instruments behind the object that they make visible, is all too happy to reveal them; they are the only visible guarantees of its existence" (Hennion 1993, 13; my translation).

Music arrives in our lives propped up by multiple forms of material culture: instruments, scores, recordings, media technologies, concert halls, bodies, electronic gadgets, and so on. Music itself remains an elusive entity; the very idea of the musical work, as Lydia Goehr reminds us, is an obscure, controversial one (Goehr 1992, 2). The question of music's materiality comes accompanied by a set of contradictions or paradoxes. Long considered one of the most ethereal and abstract of cultural forms, music is arguably the one most embedded in the material infrastructures of our daily lives. In Georgina Born's words, music is "perhaps the paradigmatic multiply-mediated, immaterial and material, fluid quasi-object, in which subjects and objects collide and intermingle" (Born 2005, 7).

THING THEORY

Since the end of the 1990s, something called "thing theory" has rippled across the academic humanities (Brown 2001). "Thing theory" is a self-consciously sloganistic label for a variety of recent developments in cultural analysis which have focused on the status and meaning of objects. Modest versions of "thing theory" have reflected on the role played by objects within such cultural forms as the novel or fine art painting (e.g., Watson 1999). In works of literature, for example, "things" (such as items of clothing or furniture) function in a variety of ways: they may serve as the pretext for descriptions which slow down narrative action, enhance a novel's impression of realism or provide an objectifying balance to a work's pull towards psychological interiority. Bill Brown, a key spokesperson for "thing theory" within literary studies, asks scholars to pursue the question of how literature "renders a life of things" (Brown 1999, 3).

More ambitious and totalizing efforts to develop a thing-centered cultural analysis have taken shape within those forms of cultural study located closer to the social sciences. These are marked by models which work to eliminate or reduce fundamental distinctions between things and human beings. A key argument in this work is that objects and humans possess roughly equal degrees of agency and methodological importance. In actor-network theory, for example, or in the media theory of Friedrich Kittler, human agents interact with objects as part of assemblages in which both should be seen as "thing-like," as nodes or connective materials within network operations (e.g., Glennie and Thrift 2002, 152–154; Kittler 1985).

This concern with things, objects, and assemblages may be understood as part of a broader "material turn" in the study of culture (Hicks and Beaudry 2010). The "material turn" draws ideas and inspiration from many sources, some of which (such as "material culture studies") had been longstanding subfields within such fields as anthropology or museum studies. Some of the earliest glimpses of a broader "material turn" came in the mid-1980s, with the publication of influential, cross-disciplinary books such as the anthology *The Social Life of Things: Commodities in Cultural Perspective* (Appadurai 1986) and Susan Stewart's *On Longing: Narratives of the Miniature, the Gigantic, the Souvenir, the Collection* (Stewart 1984). In academic fields hitherto preoccupied with the character of texts or the politics of representation, these interventions invited scholars to think about the material forms in which culture was embedded. Important ideas in these books, such as Igor Kopytoff's notion of a "social biography" of commodities, would be taken up frequently in cultural scholarship over the next quarter-century (Kopytoff 1986).

In the study of music, it is fair to say that this "material turn" has been no more influential than many of the other turns that have left the humanities and social sciences spinning over the last two decades. A turn to the "material" stands alongside "affective", "spatial", "cognitive", "pictorial," and "computational" turns in a long list of diagnosed shifts whose very number betrays the failure of any single one to bring about a definitive refocusing of cultural analysis. What is special about the "material turn," perhaps, is that it allows us to explore a range of questions with particular pertinence to the analysis of music. Some of these have to do with the "thing" status of music itself—with whether music itself might be considered material or immaterial, object-like or ethereal. Others are concerned with the range of material forms (the objects and technologies) through which music is performed, received, collected and rendered mobile. Put differently, one set of approaches moves "backwards" from music, to consider the material substances of which music might be constituted. Another moves "forward" from music, to examine the material supports which enable music to assume its social and cultural existence.

MATERIALITIES OF MUSIC

Arguments over the extent to which music is a material form have wound their way through the long history of philosophical aesthetics, and must be passed over quickly here. Many of these arguments assert the immateriality of music, then go on to speculate as to the particular substances of which it is thought to be made. In her study of British Romantic ideas concerning poetry and music, Phyllis Weliver traces the shifting meanings of the word "air," from its designation of a particular kind of musical work through considerations of the ethereal substances through which music travels and of which it is made. "Air," she shows, suggested both the weightlessness or immateriality of music and its dependence upon a material-chemical substance (the air that is breathed) whose composition, scientists thought, could be isolated and examined (Weliver 2005, 33). Here, as in so many other cases, assertions about music's lack of ontological thickness are counterbalanced by scientific or pseudo-scientific claims about a vital substance (air, in this case, ether or electro-magnetic fields in others) which provide music with its material basis and means of dissemination.

The most popular recent versions of such arguments center on the concept of "matter," as a primordial substance conceived in physical or natural terms. A strikingly assertive (and newly influential) argument for this kind of materialism is provided in Jane Bennett's book *Vibrating Matter* (2009), whose pertinence to the study of music should be evident from its title (even if music receives little attention within the book). Bennett's renewed vitalism asks us to examine the ways in which both human and nonhuman forms participate in a vibrating matter that dissolves the distinctions between them. We may find more restricted versions of this position in Jacques Attali's account of music as "the audible waveband of the vibrations and signs that make up society" (Attali 1985, 4) or in theorizations of "soundscape" in which the vibration of matter is taken to ensure a continuity between musical and nonmusical, cultural and noncultural forms of sound (e.g., Wrightson 2000). Vibrating matter is the condition to which certain forms of music (rock, most frequently) have been reduced, in descriptions that seek to account for the transformative impact of such musical forms on human bodies. Bruce Baugh's argument that "rock is concerned with the matter of music" (Baugh 1993, 23) is echoed in references by journalists to such phenomena as the "bone-dissolving vibration" felt at rock concerts (Orenstein 2000). Similarly, Larry Grossberg, in an influential analysis of rock music, saw its political effectivity residing in the ways in which "the body vibrates with the sounds and rhythms, and that vibration can be articulated with other practices and events to produce complex effects" (Grossberg 1984, 238). Makagon's study of high-powered car stereo systems as "mobile heterotopias . . . that challenge spatial and temporal constraints of daily life" refers specifically to the physical, sensuous character of loud music as it acts upon material forms like the automobile to produce an experience of vibration (Makagon 2006, 224).

In a variety of musical practices over the past century, the materiality of music has been transferred from musical form itself to the objects with which music is made or performed. In his book *Cracked Media: The Sound of Malfunction*, Caleb Kelly describes the practice of the New York-based artist Christian Marclay: "Throughout the 1980s and 1990s, Christian Marclay wreaked havoc on vinyl records, abusing them and subsequently redefining them as art objects. He has scratched, sanded, cut, drilled, snapped, melted, smashed, thrown, and walked on these fragile and once fetishized objects" (Kelly 2009, 150). Whether Marclay's treatment of vinyl records produces something that we might call music (as distinct from conceptual or performance art) is not clear. Nevertheless, Caleb's book describes Marclay's art-making amidst discussion of a variety of other practices in which the materials of music are destroyed, hacked, distorted or allowed to decay in the name of musical creation. If the theorists of vibrating matter ask of music that it recede into a more primordial set of physical processes, a variety of avant-gardist strategies treat the material foundations of music (or other cultural forms) as resistant forces to be struggled against. As Carol Armstrong has suggested, summarizing one of the key tenets of artistic modernism, "the material dimension of the object is . . . at least potentially a site of resistance and recalcitrance, of the irreducibly particular, and of the subversively strange and pleasurable" (Armstrong 1996, 28).

Music's Material Extensions: Mobility

Ideas about the essential "matter" of music are more far-reaching and less common in musical scholarship than studies of the more small-scale interactions of music with material forms. This section discusses a variety of ways in which music's relationship to different kinds of material culture— to different classes and assemblages of "things"— might be conceptualized.

The study of music has seen few examples of the sorts of analysis recently fashionable within literary studies and long practiced within art history: those concerned with the representation of objects. Historians and connoisseurs of popular music have pointed to the important song cycles devoted to such things as cars or trains, but there are few other examples of any note. A "thing-theory" of music bumps up against the longstanding prejudice against lyric analysis in music studies. It must contend, as well, with the fact that such material phenomena as cars or trains (or Heartbreak Hotels) quickly become symbols of more abstract states, like freedom or loss, in which their materiality appears to dissolve. The title of the second Talking Heads album, *More Songs About Buildings and Food*, gained much of its irony from the fact that popular music has rarely been about either.

It is more common to look for the material culture of music outside of the musical text, in those technologies and forms that we might call the "material extensions" of music. Very schematically, these material extensions are marked by two predominant tendencies, each with its corresponding body of scholarly treatments. One, the focus of greatest collective interest, consists of all those material forms through which music becomes mobile— through which it is dispersed, scattered across mobile devices, spaces and practices of listening, and so on. The other, less remarked upon, involves those material forms in which music is aggregated, its individual instances brought together in places of storage or collection. Each of these tendencies corresponds to a widespread perception of contemporary musical culture: on the one hand, that music is to be found everywhere, in virtually all interstices of social and cultural life; and, on the other hand, that music is available in greater and greater abundance, gathered up or stockpiled in ever more comprehensive and easily accessible inventories.

The idea that music moves, perhaps more easily than other cultural forms, has multiple foundations. It may be based in ideas concerning music's ethereality and weightlessness as expressive substance, or grounded in beliefs about music's universality relative to those cultural forms (like literature) whose movement is more obviously constrained by linguistic difference. More and more, claims about music's greater mobility invoke the material forms in which music is embedded—the recording formats, playback devices, and other technologies within and through which music moves. These form the outer surfaces of musical expression, the encasements within which music is carried and through which it comes to be attached to other structures and material forms.

In their manifesto-like call for a "circulatory" approach to culture, Gaonkar and Povinelli ask the following questions, which we might see as effective parameters for the analysis of music's mobility: "Why is it that some forms move or are moved along? What limits are imposed on cultural forms as the condition of their circulation across various types of social space? What are the materialities of form that emerge from, and trace, these movements . . .?" (Gaonkar and Povinelli 2003, 387) If music seems to be a more circulatory cultural form than others, this is in part because the "uses" of music in daily life are increasingly about the ongoing repurposing of music, its integration within ever more varied activities and situations. In their circulation, bits of music come to stick to other material configurations in ways that invite study. Music sticks to contexts of sociability, such as places of night-time congregation. It sticks to other media, through such phenomena as telephone ringtones or computer game soundtracks. Most importantly, perhaps, music is bound to other, human and nonhuman forms of mobility, in phenomena ranging from soundwalks through car-based iPod-docking modules. Portable listening devices, from the Walkman onwards, have inspired a wide range of studies of the mobile experiences of music.

It is common, in considering the effect of portable music devices, to concentrate on transformations of the subjective experience of their users as they move through space. Polemics over the extent and character of this transformation include David Beer's wilfully "gentle" disagreement with Michael Bull over the effect of portable MP3 players on the mobile subject's experience of cities (Beer 2007; Bull 2000). Against Bull's claims about the mobile listener's retreat into a privatized space, in which private soundtracks serve to "manage" the experience of urban time and space, Beer offers a more nuanced account of such soundtracks as perpetually interacting with elements of the surrounding sonic and physical environment. As should be clear, this dispute rejoins broader debates over the character of present-day participation in public life.

What is striking in this polemic is the subject-centered character of the analysis and the shared conviction that the key effects of portable music-listening devices have to do with levels of personal engagement with sonic environments. With a reversal of perspective, however, we might begin to see mobile human subjects as desubjectified agents engaged in the transportation of music through urban space. Indeed, from a perspective that seeks to map the mobility of music rather than of human beings, bodies adorned with MP3 players form part of material systems that include bus loudspeakers, shop music systems, taxi radios, and other material forms through which music of widely varying levels of loudness is made to occupy public space. If one roving MP3 listener is the locus of a subjective experience of urban sensuality, several thousand such listeners represent an infrastructure (however uncoordinated) for the movement of cultural materials.

Music's Material Extensions: Aggregation

The other tendency in the material life of music is towards what we might call its aggregation: its gathering up and accumulation in physical and virtual sites, from compilation discs through hard drives, file sharing clouds and junk stores selling old vinyl. This aggregation also includes the ordering of music within spaces of storage whose materiality is less obvious: charts, canons and the playlists of websites or radio stations. These latter examples show the difficulty of pinpointing the moment at which a cultural form becomes material. A music singles chart is material in relationship to an inchoate, immaterial phenomenon like popularity, of which it stands as a physical embodiment. At the same time, a chart is an immaterial simulacrum of a variety of material processes involving the exchange of money and commodities. Similarly, canons and playlists are both the material instantiation of multiple judgments and idealized, immaterial means of bringing order to the chaotic abundance of material cultural commodities.

In his deliberately reductionist enumeration of the functions of media, Friedrich Kittler invites us to ask, of any medium, what role it plays in the storage, processing and transmission of information (Griffin 1996, 710.) We may ask these questions of the various recording formats which, for a century and more, have served to store and transmit musical expression. As key elements in the material culture of music, formats—like the 78 rpm record, vinyl album, and compact disc—were marked by distinctive sizes, storage capacities, and characteristic relationships between musical and nonmusical information. In the examples that follow, we will pay particular attention to the aggregative features of these formats, to what Kittler would call their capacity for storage.

In his history of the Columbia Records label, Gary Marmorstein suggests that the introduction of the Long Playing record in the late 1940s facilitated an international traffic in popular music and its performers (Marmorstein 2007, 231). By bringing ten to twelve songs by a single artist together in the LP form, the album allowed performer identities to assume coherence across a significant body of vocal performances. The LP made it possible to overcome the estrangement of foreign performers and foreign languages in ways that the two-song 78 rpm record did not. Each of the performances on a Long Playing record nourished and illuminated the others, acclimatizing listeners both to the particularities of an individual voice and to the broader characteristics of a national musical style. Albums by Edith Piaf or Juliette Greco, introduced into the United States, were of sufficient length that the novelty of the French song tradition for Americans was diminished over the experience of 30–40 minutes of listening. At the same time, Marmorstein writes, the LP, unlike the 78 rpm or 45 rpm single, provided the space for elaborate textual commentary, through which artists might be endowed with a context and through which the broader coherence of an album might be constructed.

In this respect, the LP album, as a material form, carried with it a distinctive protocol of listening, one in which a sense of performer personality and generic coherence were elaborated across multiple tracks. The relationship between these tracks, and between the album and its paratexts (the liner notes and images), was in part a pedagogical one, whose effect was that of teaching listeners the skills and dispositions required for their satisfaction. The characteristics of the LP record just described resided in its capacity for aggregation, for collecting together multiple instances of music in ways that transformed the intelligibility of any one.

A very different case of aggregation may be found in the MP3-filled CDs which, for a few years, have lingered on the margins of the music business. In the mid-2000s, Madacy, a Canadian company devoted to the anthologizing of cheaply acquired cultural materials, began marketing CD packages containing two hundred or so MP3s organized by genre. (Examples of these packages include such titles as *Best of the Classics* and the *Workout Music Collection*.) Intended for sale over the internet and in Wal-Mart stores, these "Instant MP3 Packages" were directed at the new, middle-aged owners of iPods and other MP3 players, who were blocked by ethical considerations or technological ignorance from downloading MP3 files over the Internet.

We may contrast these packages with the pirated MP3 discs which, at roughly the same time, had come to dominate the street markets for music in Mexico City. I have written of such packages elsewhere, noting how they had replaced pirated versions of individual albums in a context of heightened, illegal competition (Straw 2009). In Canada, one might buy two hundred "tracks" of classical music performed by no-name orchestras and remastered from unidentified recordings of the 1950 or 1960s. In Mexico City, one could purchase the whole of The Smiths' back catalogue on one or two discs. In the difference between these two sorts of packages, we see two very different practices of musical aggregation. MP3 discs in Mexico City represented the furthest reaches of an illegal practice threatened by official, imminent moves against street commerce and by the eventual disappearance of the CD itself as a material form. Madacy's "Instant MP3 packages" were designed precisely to protect consumers from the slightest contact with practices (downloading or CD-burning) tainted with illegality.

At the same time, the MP3 discs of Mexico City street markets accomplished the transmission through time of an authoritative musical canon dominated by the global North and West. These discs reasserted the centrality of that canon and, in the very abundance contained in any one set, enshrined the career as a meaningful unit of understanding. In contrast, the MP3 discs sold by Madacy, under conditions of pristine legality, were full of budget recordings (such as live performances from the 1960s by rock-and-roll stars of the 1950s) long associated with exploitative music industry practices and fly-by-night labels. As such, they served to dismantle notions of the official release or the definitive version. As has occurred in every shift of recording format in the last half-century, this repertory of dubious provenance and low canonical status has been handed down to a new set of entrepreneurs, to be circulated in contemporary material forms.

In the difference between these two examples, we may glimpse some of the complexities of the material culture of music. The illegal compilations of the Mexico City street market further consolidate a critical and commercial canon by expanding its availability, while marginal musical detritus long associated with practices of exploitation and deception enters the homes of Canadian consumers fearful of any association with music in its illicit forms. At the same time, each class of MP3-filled CD discussed here is engaged in a double mobility: its own movement as a material, commodity form, from places of commerce to contexts of listening, and the transmission, through this material form, of a legacy of musical expression.

Conclusions

If there has been a material turn in music studies, it has, for the most part, gone unnamed. The disciplines studying music are many, and the sites in which it is studied even more so. The sense of a disciplinary center that might uniformly "turn" is more difficult to imagine in the case of music than in relation to other cultural forms. At the same time, the study of music's material forms—its "thingness"—has escaped the polemical claims and accusations that have marked the material turn in other fields.

Elsewhere in the humanities, and most notably in literary studies, a turn to materiality has been enshrined either as a triumphant return to the certainties of a pre-poststructuralist age or as a purifying gesture through which the lingering idealisms of that age have been eradicated. At the same time, this turn has been condemned as a reactionary flight from theory, or as a retreat from the messiness of the human and corporeal into the comforting solidity of the thing.

If the concern with materiality has seemed less controversial in the study of music, this is perhaps because, as Antoine Hennion suggested, the material manifestations of music are everywhere to be noticed (1993, 13). It is through its material extensions that music is encountered in cultural life, and through the specialized study of such extensions that so much of the scholarship on music has developed. In music, as Georgina Born noted, "subjects and objects collide and intermingle" (Born 2005, 7). The endless variety of this process of collision and intermingling makes music distinct and ensures its continued fascination to those who study it.

NOTE

Thank you to Caylin Smith for valuable research assistance.

FURTHER READING

Bodker, Henrik. 2004. The changing materiality of music. *Papers from the Centre for Internet Research.* Aarhus, Denmark: University of Aarhus (http://cfi.au.dk/fileadmin/www.cfi.au.dk/publikationer/cfis_skriftserie/008_boedker.pdf).

Born, Georgina. 2005. On musical mediation: Ontology, technology and creativity. *Twentieth-Century Music* 2(1): 7–36.

Brown, Lee B. 2000. Phonography, repetition and spontaneity. *Philosophy and Literature* 24: 111–124.

Chanan, Michael. 1994. *Musica practica.* London: Verso.

Keightley, Keir. 2004. Long play: Adult-oriented popular music and the temporal logics of the post-war sound recording industry in the U.S.A. *Media, Culture and Society* 26: 375–391.

Kelly, Caleb. 2009. *Cracked media: The sound of malfunction.* Cambridge, MA: MIT Press.

Leonard, Marion. 2007. Constructing histories through material culture: popular music, museums and collecting. *Popular Music History* 2: 147–167.

Leppert, Richard. 1993. *The sight of sound: Music, representation and the history of the body.* Berkeley, CA: The University of California Press.

McCracken, Grant. 1988. *Culture and consumption.* Bloomington and Indianapolis: Indiana University Press.

Miège, Bernard. 1979. The cultural commodity. *Media, Culture and Society* 1: 297–311.

Sterne, Jonathan. 2003. *The audible past: Cultural origins of sound reproduction.* Durham, NC: Duke University Press.

Straw, Will. 2000. Exhausted commodities: The material culture of music. *Canadian Journal of Communication* 25: 175–185.

Thompson, Stacy. 2004. Crass commodities. *Popular Music and Society* 27: 307–322.

PART 4

WHOSE?
Social Forces and Musical Belongings

CHAPTER 21

MUSIC AND SOCIAL CATEGORIES

JOHN SHEPHERD

The starting point of this chapter is the question, to what extent do musical structures and practices reflect, model, or resonate with the identities, experiences, or structural positions of social classes, and gendered and ethnic groups? This issue is a vast one, encompassing an impressive and imposing literature going back almost forty years and raising some major questions in social and cultural theory. It is an issue to which I contributed during the 1970s and 1980s. My intent in this chapter is to explain why I think this issue and its exploration were important to the development of the cultural study of music during this time; why the work that resulted was superseded by other, more sophisticated work; and why the legacy of some of the thinking that occurred during the 1970s and 1980s might remain pertinent to an emergent paradigm for the cultural study of music. This chapter is thus tinged with an element of intellectual autobiography.

It is also written largely, but not exclusively, from the point of view of popular music studies. This is because the issues discussed here found a striking focus during the 1970s and 1980s in work in this discipline, even though it can be argued that they are important to the cultural study of all music. Popular music studies were, however, influenced by wider developments, including some outside the study of music as a whole. Some of these developments are discussed in this chapter. Also, developments important to the issues discussed in this chapter occurred independently of popular music studies in disciplines such as ethnomusicology (e.g., Blacking 1973; C. Keil 1979). As the 1990s dawned, the importance of ethnomusicology to these issues increased considerably (e.g., Slobin 1993).

MUSIC AND PARADIGMS

When I studied music during the late 1960s and early 1970s, I did so in what was then a very conventional way. I studied the history of Western art music, and with only marginal reference to social and cultural forces. The emphasis was overwhelmingly on "the music itself," a music that was judged to be autonomous. The assumption was that, although Western art music was created at particular points in history, it was essentially beyond the influence of social and cultural forces. It was assumed to embody within itself universal, "otherworldly" values and truths immune to the impact of everyday life.

This same period witnessed considerable cultural and social turmoil. In the United States, this was evident in the Civil Rights movement and opposition to the war in Vietnam. Developments in the United Kingdom were less dramatic, but there was nonetheless considerable opposition to established social, cultural, and moral values, with an emphasis on a cultural rebirth emanating from younger generations. Common to all this "anti-establishment" activity was the role of popular culture, and particularly popular music. Much popular music of the time was for younger generations imbued with and expressive of a broadly based and broadly felt sense of cultural and political opposition and renewal. It had to do with the realities of everyday life, and was self-evidently and palpably "social."

For many studying music in institutions of higher education at the time, it was not difficult to perceive a disjunction between music as understood academically, and music as experienced as a part of everyday life. There existed few if any alternatives to the way that music was studied. By contrast, the role of popular music in the cultural politics of everyday life was unmistakable and compelling. To those of us naive enough to suggest that popular music and its politics were a legitimate object for study, the reply was swift and final. Popular music was inferior to "classical" music, and should not therefore be included in the curriculum. Its inferiority was marked and guaranteed by its clear social "content," which served to compromise its tonal values. "Classical" music was superior precisely because it was immune to such undesirable social forces. The cultural, musical, and, indeed, academic battle lines of the late 1960s and early 1970s were drawn very clearly.

This book on the cultural study of music comes from a very different moment. While it would be misleading to say that the old "high cultural" attitudes are no longer evident in university music departments, there had undoubtedly been significant changes even at the time the first edition appeared, changes whose impact has continued to ramify. This has been due to several factors: the contributions made to the study of music by a wide range of disciplines outside music, such as sociology, anthropology, and communication; the increasing and sustained influence of ethnomusicology, a discipline for which existing and interacting with the people whose music is being studied have been a central and defining methodology; and major changes within the historically more conservative disciplines of academic music.

The suggestion has been made that these disciplines have interacted with an intimacy that makes possible a new paradigm for the cultural study of music. This paradigm will certainly be in contrast to the one dominant during the quarter century following the end of World War II. It is of significance that this earlier paradigm became susceptible to challenge in part because of the advent of the term and concept of *paradigm*. The concept's widespread currency derived from Thomas S. Kuhn's influential book *The Structure of Scientific Revolutions* (1962). Kuhn argued that scientific knowledge did not progress steadily toward "the truth," with erroneous knowledge being discarded and replaced by new, more accurate knowledge. He suggested that, when one scientific paradigm, or body of premises, axioms, and theories, could no longer answer the questions it had generated, a crisis would occur in the scientific community supporting and advocating the paradigm. The crisis would be followed by a revolution in which the old paradigm would be replaced by a new one capable of answering the previously unanswerable questions. This new paradigm would be based on a different set of premises, axioms, and theories, and would, quite literally, see the world differently. A classic example of one such paradigm shift is that instigated by Einstein's theories of relativity early in the twentieth century. Scientists who accepted his theories at an early stage did so not because of any empirical "proof," which had to wait some years, but because of the elegance and effectiveness of their explanations. Kuhn concluded that scientists shifted paradigm allegiance not for scientific reasons but for reasons that were primarily aesthetic.

While Kuhn did not say that scientific knowledge was a social construct, he opened the door for this controversial argument to be made in later years. The argument that *reality* is a social construct was, however, made in 1966 in Peter L. Berger and Thomas Luckmann's *The Social Construction of Reality*. According to Berger and Luckmann, reality was not something given that we receive and perceive neutrally, but something that is constructed by people acting together. These two books provided the intellectual basis for arguing that the way in which music was studied after the end of World War II was not something natural, given, self-evident, or unquestionable, but something that had been constructed socially for political and cultural reasons. What followed from this realization was that something that was made by people could be changed by people. The stage was set for a major paradigm shift in the academic study of music. Fundamental to this paradigm shift was the foundational premise that all music, including "classical" music, was a social construct, and thus something that had to be understood both socially and culturally.

Social categories played an important role in the early days of this paradigm shift. If music was a social construct, it followed that connections should exist between social groups and their music. This chapter traces the lines of this development, the problems to which such work gave rise, and the more sophisticated work that followed it. However, the chapter remains cognizant of something recognized by Kuhn: namely, that with paradigm shifts there are losses as well as gains. More specifically, Kuhn observed, with a paradigm shift questions that were previously important become much less important and sometimes get lost to view. A theme underlying this chapter is that, if a new paradigm for the cultural study of music is now in view, then, in the spirit of the continual problematization of objects and methods of study, there should be a sensitivity to questions that appear to have receded from view.

MUSIC AND SOCIAL CATEGORIES

The idea that connections exist between social groups and the characteristics of their music began to emerge in the 1970s. In 1970, Andrew Chester drew a distinction between extensional and intensional forms of musical expression:

> [Western classical music] is the apodigm of the *extensional* form of musical construction. Theme and variations, counterpoint, tonality . . . are all devices that build diachronically and synchronically outward from basic musical atoms. The complex is created by combination of the simple, which remains discrete and unchanged in the complex unity. Thus a basic premise of classical music is rigorous adherence to standard timbres.

By contrast:

> Rock . . . follows . . . the path of *intensional* development . . . the basic musical units (played/sung notes) are not combined through space and time as simple elements into complex structures. The simple entity is that constituted by the parameters of melody, harmony and beat, while the complex is built up by modulation of the basic notes, and by inflection of the basic beat.
>
> (Chester [1970] 1990, 315)

Chester saw important connections between musical characteristics and social groups. While "the internal coordinates of a musical form are not mechanically determined by its social base," he said, "to each social group correspond certain acceptable genres" (pp. 318–319).

This idea that the characteristics of a musical form could give life to the social reality of a culture gained increasing currency during the 1970s and 1980s. In 1977, I argued that the characteristics of functional tonality as the "language" of classical music embodied and gave expression to the temporal and spatial senses underlying and making possible industrial capitalism as a social form. In 1978, Paul Willis argued that early rock 'n' roll and progressive rock articulated the social realities of biker boy subculture and hippy counterculture, respectively. In 1982, I attempted to set out an encompassing model for the social analysis of classical music and many forms of African-American and African-American-influenced popular music important during the twentieth century. The idea behind this model was that of a "harmonic-rhythmic framework," comprised of three chords (the tonic, dominant, and subdominant) and simple duple and triple meters, which was common to both classical and popular musics. This basic framework, with its centralized and "controlling" keynote, was a code for, and articulation of, the encompassing social structures of industrial capitalism. Those with power and influence could manipulate this framework extensionally—hence the complex architectonic harmonic structures of classical music. Those with little power or influence tended to live within this social-musical environment—taking it for granted—and to develop musical complexity intensionally, through individualized sounds or timbres, and through the bending of pitches and rhythms in ways that would be unacceptable within classical music (hence Chester's reference to "modulation"—actually an incorrect use of the term—and "inflection" in his description of intensional modes of musical development). The model thus incorporated the sociological categories of class, ethnicity, and, to a degree, age. In 1987, I extended this kind of analysis to gender, arguing that different voice types or timbres in popular music gave expression to different kinds of gender identities. It is symptomatic that all this work reflected the clearly drawn battle lines of the 1960s and 1970s.

Illuminating though this work seemed, it brought with it problems. Despite Chester's observation that "musical practice has a relative autonomy" ([1970] 1990, 319), the impression lingered that music was a secondary symptom of social and cultural forces. Music, in other words, seemed to be produced by the "social base." Second, this work operated *only* at the level of social groups. Little attention was paid to the social and cultural identities of individuals. Such identities could exist only because of group membership. Third, the fit between music and social and cultural realities was too tight and convenient. It was not difficult to demonstrate that the practice of music was more complex than theoretical models would allow. This problem was identified by Will Straw (1991) when he drew a distinction between musical communities and musical scenes. A musical community, observed Straw, "may be imagined as a particular population group whose composition is relatively stable . . . and whose involvement in music takes the form of an ongoing exploration of a particular musical idiom said to be rooted organically in that community." By contrast, a musical scene ("the most appropriate term for designating centres of musical activity today") is "that cultural space within which a range of musical practices co-exist, interacting with each other within a variety of processes of differentiation and according to widely varying trajectories of change and cross-fertilization." The break with the work of the 1970s and 1980s is clear in Straw's assertion that cultural theorists like himself encountering such studies for the first time "after an apprenticeship in the hermeneutics of suspicion may be struck by the prominence within them of notions of cultural totality or claims concerning an expressive unity of musical practices" (1991, 369–373).

At one level, Straw's observations signaled real changes in musical and cultural life as captured in concepts such as "globalization" and "postmodernism." The battle lines of the 1960s and 1970s had been replaced by an understanding that the musical world is more complicated than the work emanating from those politics and battles could reveal. Since then, cultural commodities including music had to a degree been drained of ideological or organically rooted meaning as a consequence of their increasing number and variety, and the speed and efficiency with which they were transmitted across the surface of the globe. One consequence was that musical practices no longer occurred just within the delimited geocultural spaces within which particular communities lived. Communities in part and musical communities in particular were created as a consequence of the transmission of music. The notion of place and its role in identity construction thus had to be reconceptualized, a process evidenced in the work of George Lipsitz (1994), Martin Stokes (1994), and Andrew Leyshon, David Matliss, and George Revill (1998). At another level, however, Straw's observations are more profound, signaling the distinct possibility that musical life has always been characterized by complex patterns of cross-fertilization and cultural hybridity, and that notions of organic rootedness and "authenticity" are largely mythical. It has only been the more modest rate of such changes during the course of history that has allowed for the *appearance* of tight fits between music and society.

It is perhaps not without coincidence that, in the same year that Straw was making his observations, Sara Cohen was also calling for a change in approaches to the cultural study of music. In an observation symptomatic of a move away from theory, she argued that "what is particularly lacking in the literature . . . is ethnographic data and micro-sociological detail" (1991, 6). Such detail has been provided not only by Cohen but by Ruth Finnegan (1989), Deena Weinstein (1991), and Susan Crafts, Daniel Cavicchi, and

Charles Keil (1993). It has also been provided by a generation of ethnomusicologists interested in world popular music (e.g., Manuel 1988; Waterman 1990; Stokes 1992; Guilbault et al. 1993; Slobin 1993; Erlmann 1996; Langlois 1996).

The 1990s seemed to evidence a watershed in the cultural study of music. A concern with particular social categories (class, gender, ethnicity, age, subculture, counterculture, and so on) was replaced with a more embracing and pervasive concern with identity. This concern with identity subsumed established social categories in markedly complex ways, and at the same time has required and been evidenced by an attention to the specific details of lived cultural–musical realities to a degree not on the whole characteristic of earlier work. The move to ethnography, together with a partial shift in focus from "traditional" to "popular" music in ethnomusicology, can be seen as a defining moment in the emergence of the new paradigm for the cultural study of music. As Georgina Born and David Hesmondhalgh observed, "a common problematic across musicology, ethnomusicology and popular music studies in recent years has been the theorization of music and identity and, by implication, difference" (2000, 2).

Music and Meaning

In the early pages of *Studying Popular Music* (1990), Richard Middleton refers to Gramsci's distinction between "situations" and "conjunctures." In Middleton's words, "situation" refers to "the deepest, the organic structures of a social formation; movement there is fundamental and relatively permanent, the result of crisis"; "conjuncture" refers to "more immediate, ephemeral characteristics, linked to the organic structures but changing at once more rapidly and less significantly, as the forces in conflict within a situation struggle to work out their contradictions" (1990, 12). A question that might be asked of an emergent new paradigm for the cultural study of music is the extent to which the growing, necessary, and legitimate concern with the details of lived cultural–musical realities has nonetheless allowed the situational to recede in relative importance in musical analysis. It is symptomatic, perhaps, that, according to Born and Hesmondhalgh, "much recent work has attempted to move beyond the neo-Gramscian concepts of hegemony and resistance" (2000, 5). They also report that the postcolonial theory so central to many recent developments in the cultural study of music "has been criticized" for treating issues of power "almost entirely in terms of textuality and epistemology" and sidelining "material conditions and the possibility of political practices oriented towards changing material conditions" in a manner that "has been the cause of some bitter Marxist polemics against the field" (p. 6).

A second and related question has to do with musical meaning. The paradigm shift that began in the 1970s had as much to do with the question of musical meaning as it did with the foundational premise of music's social and cultural constitution. Susan McClary (1991), in a book that played a seminal role in the development of critical thinking on questions of gender in music, identified the importance of this issue. "I was drawn to music," she said, "because it is the most compelling cultural form I know. I wanted evidence that the overwhelming responses I experience . . . are not just my own, but rather are shared." However, McClary soon discovered that "musicology fastidiously declares issues of musical signification off-limits to those engaged in legitimate scholarship" (1991, 4). In instigating the beginnings of a paradigm shift, the work of the 1970s and 1980s began to throw light on this question precisely by way of the premise that music was constituted socially and culturally. If music were constituted in this way, then it followed that its characteristics—its harmonies, melodies, rhythms, and sound qualities or timbres—embodied and gave expression to meanings that were pervasively social and cultural.

The work of the 1970s and 1980s spoke as much to the situational as it did to the conjunctural. If one question that might be asked of the new paradigm is the extent to which the situational has receded in relative importance in musical analysis, an allied question might be that of the extent to which questions of signification in music have likewise been allowed to recede. A concentration on the details of lived cultural–musical realities quite correctly involves a heavy reliance on the verbal accounts of those involved in musical practices. This concentration has nonetheless been consistent with the placing of considerable emphasis on the role of connotation in musical significance: the feelings and images capable of descriptive encapsulation that are customarily associated with such musical characteristics as, for example, the feelings of apprehension created by the use of high tremolo violins in film music, or in the images of the ocean—visual, rhythmic, sonic, and even, perhaps, olfactory—evoked by Debussy's *La Mer*. This is an emphasis that seems to have detracted from a concern with the way in which the structural elements of music—harmonic, melodic, rhythmic, and timbral—can speak directly to the structures of social, cultural, and individual realities, and thus to the identities and structural positions of social classes and gendered and ethnic groups. This shift in emphasis is consistent with the Foucauldian "linguistic turn" that has been so influential in a wide range of disciplines in the humanities and social sciences. Although Foucault himself stressed the way in which discourses are embedded in the material practices and apparatuses of institutions (see for example, Foucault 1970, 1972, 1978, 1979), this turn nonetheless draws on a long line of French-language linguistic and cultural theory that has tended to eschew the material, whether the material bases of lived realities or those of various signifying practices such as music (in the case of music, its sounds). It is perhaps not without relevance that Born and Hesmondhalgh have recently quite baldly claimed that "connotation is undoubtedly the dominant mode of musical signification" (2000, 56).

If there is a new paradigm for the cultural study of music, then, it may be important to ensure that the situational and the structural, in both life and music, do not get obscured from view. Any reassertion of the situational and structural will have to take on board the important insights resulting from more recent research on the ways in which music is involved and implicated in the construction of cultural identities. A hint as to how such analysis might work can be drawn from the opening pages of Middleton's book. One moment of situational change identified by Middleton "begins sometime after the Second World War—most strikingly with the advent of rock 'n' roll" (1990, 14). The role of Elvis Presley in this upheaval has been debated. As Greil Marcus observes, "it is often said that if Elvis had not come along to set off the changes in American music and American life that followed his triumph, someone very much like him would have done the job as well." However, concludes Marcus, "there is no reason to think this is true, either in strictly musical terms, or in any broader cultural sense" ([1976] 1982, 166). Because of his particular biography and musical talents, it can be argued that Presley was able to identify intuitively many of the cultural contradictions evident in the United States at the time—between black and white communities, rural and urban life, men and women, working and middle classes, young and old, the South and the North—and give them musical expression. This expression was not simply reflective but also evidenced the relative autonomy of which Chester speaks. As Marcus notes, "Elvis inherited these tensions, but more than that, gave them his own shape" (p. 166). Middleton echoes these sentiments in saying that "Elvis's importance . . . lies not so much in the mix of elements (blues/country/Tin Pan Alley) which he helped to bring into rock 'n' roll, but in what he did with it. He transformed them into particular patterns" (1990, 21). Presley gave a specifically musical shape to a situational moment in a manner that was structural as well as connotative, and powerfully corporeal. The question is whether this would have been possible through any other medium than music, and whether an understanding of this moment could be achieved without a heightened awareness of the social categories through which situational contradictions are generated and find expression.

FURTHER READING

Born, Georgina, and David Hesmondhalgh, eds. 2000. *Western music and its others.* Berkeley: University of California Press.

Bradby, Barbara. 1990. Do-talk and don't talk: The division of the subject in girl-group music. Pp. 341–368 in *On record: Rock, pop and the written word.* Edited by Simon Frith and Andrew Goodwin. New York: Pantheon.

Frith, Simon, and Angela McRobbie. [1978] 1990. Rock and sexuality. Pp. 371–389 in *On record: Rock, pop and the written word.* Edited by Simon Frith and Andrew Goodwin. New York: Pantheon.

Koskoff, Ellen, ed. 1987. *Women and music in cross-cultural perspective.* Urbana: University of Illinois Press.

Maróthy, János. 1974. *Music and the bourgeois, music and the proletarian.* Budapest: Akademiai Kiado.

McClary, Susan. 1991. *Feminine endings.* Minneapolis: University of Minnesota Press.

Middleton, Richard. 1990. "Roll over Beethoven"? Sites and soundings on the music-historical map. Pp. 3–33 in *Studying popular music.* Milton Keynes, U.K.: Open University Press.

Peña, Manuel. 1985. *The Texas-Mexican conjunto: History of a working-class music.* Austin: University of Texas Press.

Radano, Ronald, and Philip Bohlman, eds. 2000. *Music and the racial imagination.* Chicago: University of Chicago Press.

Shepherd, John. 1991. *Music as social text.* Cambridge, U.K.: Polity.

Stokes, Martin, ed. 1994. *Ethnicity, identity and music: The musical construction of place.* Oxford: Berg.

Taylor, Jenny, and Dave Laing. 1979. Disco-pleasure-discourse: On "Rock and sexuality.'" *Screen Education* 31: 43–48.

CHAPTER 22

MUSIC AND MEDIATION
Toward a New Sociology of Music

ANTOINE HENNION

After a century of studies, there is no agreement on what it means to construct a sociology of music. From the beginning this "of" has been a place of tension, not of smooth coordination. If music has easily attracted social readings, there has been strong resistance to a systematic sociology of music whose aim would be to explain musical values or content through reference to sociological factors. The most vehement prosecutor of such alleged reductionism was undoubtedly Adorno (e.g., 1976)—even though he himself became the worst reductionist when it came to popular culture (Adorno [1941] 2002); for him, only musics that are not really art deserve sociological treatment (it is difficult to know if this is more disrespectful of popular music or sociology!). By contrast, the opposite program—a positive explanation of the ways in which music is produced, diffused, and listened to— has been attacked on the grounds that, given its refusal to address "music itself," it cannot acknowledge music's specificity.

In this opposition between two programs, a part of the question is specific to the case of music, but another is common to the social interpretation of any art. To a large extent, the sociology of art has defined itself through opposition to aesthetics. The aim was both to criticize any claim of autonomy for works of art and aesthetic judgment, and to return the experience of aesthetic pleasure—often regarded as immediate and subjective—to its social and historical determinations. The two types of causality mobilized above have often been described in social studies of art in terms of a distinction between studying either "the art object sociologically" or "the art object as a social process" (Zolberg 1990, chapters 3 and 4). One approach displays the mediators of art, the other how art mediates society. The latter takes art as an empirical given reality, and provides explanations of its social conditions; it can be respectful vis-à-vis the "artistic nature of art": the task of sociology is to give an account of the social conditions of its production, diffusion, and reception. The former shows art as a social artifact, or construction, of a group—an "art world"; as such, it is more invasive (it looks for the social nature of art, as Blacking (1973) would put it, not for wider social factors), and sees the claim of art to be autonomous as problematic.

These two directions, one clearly empiricist and more devoted to specific case studies, the other more theoretical, are themselves divided into different trends. Across the board, though, sociology has set itself against a purely internal and hagiographic aesthetic commentary on artworks, "filling out" an art world formerly including only a very few *chefs-d'œuvre* and geniuses. Mainstream productions and copies, conventions and material constraints, professions and academies, performance venues and markets, on the artistic side of the scene; and, on the social side, codes and rites of consumption, gender and ethnicity, and, in the specific case of music, modes of circulation in a "glocal" world: these are what have been pushed to the front of the scene. These mediations range from systems or devices of the most physical and local nature, to institutional arrangements and collective frames of appreciation such as the discourse of critics, right up to the very existence of an independent domain called art. In pursuing this program, scholars have given up global, abstract systems of interpretation, and produced instead a practical theory of mediation, conceived as the reciprocal, local, heterogeneous relations between art and public through precise devices, places, institutions, objects, and human abilities, constructing identities, bodies, and subjectivities.

A Sociology of Aesthetic Pleasure?

Nevertheless, the relationship of sociology and art remained problematic. For most of the classical forms of sociology, for critical theory (Bourdieu 1984), and for interactionist (Becker 1982) or constructivist (DeNora 1995) currents, the sociological analysis of art has always been less interested in creation, genius, or the works "in themselves" than in what makes these categories appear as such. For Bourdieu, who took the critical intention furthest, it means unmasking the magical role of "creation." In this view, culture is a façade disguising social mechanisms of differentiation, artistic objects being "only" means to naturalize the social nature of tastes; aesthetic judgments are but denegations of this work of naturalization that can be made only if unknown as such. This critique of taste and of its social reproduction has led to many empirical surveys of musical consumption (e.g., DiMaggio 1987; Lamont and Fournier 1992; Peterson and Kern 1996). A radical lack of concern for the works themselves characterizes most of these studies. Sociology refuses subjectivism, the cult of genius, and the self-glorifying discourse of artists, preferring to demonstrate the constraints through which artists and amateurs are unknowingly determined, the conventions through which they recognize and create their world, and the formats used to mold the social construction of masterpieces.

In these conditions, any report on artistic experience in terms of beauty, sensation, emotion, or aesthetic feeling is automatically regarded as a manifestation of actors' illusions about their own beliefs (Bourdieu 1990), or the conventional products of a collective activity. The works do nothing, and the processes involved in their appreciation lose their specificity or specialness (a view deplored by Frith (1996) in his plea for the importance of the evaluation of popular cultures); works and tastes—meaningless in and of themselves—are returned to the *arbitrariness* (a key word in any analysis in terms of belief) of a collective election based on a social, nonartistic principle. The argument is a powerful one, and should not be overlooked if we want to avoid the celebration of autonomous art simply being taken literally again. But one also has to measure the limits of such a view, particularly in view of the dominant position it has had in the sociology of art. It is becoming essential to reconsider sociology's lack of interest in works of art and the aesthetic experience as, echoing cultural studies (Hall and Jefferson 1976; Grossberg et al. 1992; Frow 1995), music sociologists have done (DeNora 2000; Hennion [1993] 2007, 2004; A. Bennett 2000; Gell 1998): what do we do with art or music, and what does it produce, emotionally and collectively? Otherwise, there is a danger of reinforcing the great divide between expressive comments and analytical writings: between literary, subjective, "hot" accounts of musical experience on one side, as provided for example by cultural, gender, or queer studies (but often with insufficient rigor—the "what allows you to say so?" syndrome); and explicative, objective, "cold" sociological analyses on the other side, with a higher requirement for evidence—but keeping too far from what art or music are about to be acknowledged by the "groups concerned" (Dewey 1927).

Understanding the work of art as a mediation, in keeping with the lesson of critical sociology, means reviewing the work in all the details of the gestures, bodies, habits, materials, spaces, languages, and institutions that it inhabits. Without accumulated mediations—styles, grammar, systems of taste, programs, concert halls, schools, entrepreneurs, and so on—no beautiful work of art appears. At the same time, however—and against the usual agenda of critical sociology—we must recognize the moment of the work in its specific and irreversible dimension; this means seeing it as a transformation, a productive work, and allowing oneself to take into account the (highly diversified) ways in which actors describe and experience aesthetic pleasure (Hennion 2007; DeNora 2011).

For various reasons, this was for many years not the case within social studies of music. The sterile opposition between theoretical and empirical programs was not clearly superseded. In the case of literature or the visual arts, the sociological approach was prepared by lengthy debate over the merits of internal and external explanations. Even if the terms of this debate proved to be unsatisfactory in the end, the debate has at least occurred; in the case of music, the fight has not taken place. Music has always puzzled the critical discourse of the social sciences: here there is an art obviously collective but technical and difficult to grasp, and with no visible object to contest. As music had *a priori* no explicit "content," the opposition between internal and external approaches was difficult to mobilize. To what could one refer an opposition between a formalist and a realist interpretation of musical works? The positivistic character of much traditional musicology, with little theoretical self-questioning, has often been criticized, while a purely grammatical analysis of musical language produced its own closed sphere. With little relationship to either, a history of music could then describe all the concrete forms through which music had been created, performed, and listened to. The social status of musicians, the technical and economic development of musical instruments, changes in concerts and musical life: studies of all these elements have accumulated, producing rich insights and results, but without any possibility of relating them to musical works, languages, or "contents" in other than very intuitive or metaphorical terms. Instead of giving birth to fruitful controversies and passionate polemics, music has allowed different disciplines to grow, and to ignore one another.

In the case of the visual arts, the materiality of the works, even and especially if challenged by the artists, has allowed a debate to take place about the social production and reception of art. Music is in the reverse situation: its object is elusive; social interpretations just take it as the expression of a social group (ethnic trance, rock concert), aesthetic studies as a nonverbal language of immediacy. Music has nothing but mediations to show: instruments, musicians, scores, stages, records. The works are not "already there," faced with differences in taste also "already there," overdetermined by the social. They always have to be played again or, to say it better, performed anew (Schechner 2002; Butler 2005).

THE LESSON OF MUSIC

But what was a handicap for the older, formerly dominant critical approach can become an asset if the aim is to envisage a positive conception of mediation (Hennion [1993] 2007). Patrons, sponsors, markets, academies: from the first undertakings of the social history of art, mediations have always had a crucial role in social analyses (e.g., Baxandall 1972; Haskell 1976). Their critical dimension has been used against aestheticism to recall that works and tastes are constructed and socially determined. But music enables us to go beyond the description of technical and economic intermediaries as mere transformers of the musical relationship into commodities, and to do a positive analysis of all the human and material intermediaries of the "performance" and "consumption" of art, from gestures and bodies to stages and media. Mediations are neither mere carriers of the work nor substitutes that dissolve its reality; they are the art itself, as is particularly obvious in the case of music: when the performer places a score on his music stand, he plays that music, to be sure, but music is just as much the very fact of playing; mediations in music have a pragmatic status—they are the art that they reveal, and cannot be distinguished from the appreciation they generate. Mediations can therefore serve as a base for a positive analysis of tastes, and not for the deconstruction of these tastes.

Various authors have foregrounded the specificity of music's construction, on the basis of either ethnomethodologist or reflexivist claims to take into consideration the way people themselves construct a reality that they call music (Frith 1981; Bergeron and Bohlman 1992), or to account for the fact that we find in music a very particular way of putting a social reality into a form and a practice, and need to cope with the enigma of this art, which is both very immediate, subjective, and emotive, and also highly symbolic, so powerfully able to mobilize groups and carry social identities. To make a sociological analysis of taste does not mean to acknowledge the existence of some general underlying social mechanisms responsible for the presumably stable and necessary relationship between self-enclosed works and pre-existing tastes. Rather, taste, pleasure, and meaning are contingent, conjunctural, and hence transient; and they result from specific yet varying combinations of particular intermediaries, considered not as the neutral channels through which predetermined social relations operate, but as productive entities that have effectivities of their own.

One could expect that musical practices, publics, and amateurs would be privileged objects of study for sociologists of music. This is the case with changes in concert life and the development of new musical tastes (Weber 1975, 1992; Morrow 1989; Johnson 1995). The invention of a tradition and the social production of the past have been traced for several repertories, ranging from Beethoven (DeNora 1995) to country music (Peterson 1997).

From a more political point of view, Fulcher (1987) has discussed French "Grand Opera" not as a mere petit-bourgeois form of divertissement, as usual, but as a vehicle for the risky political production of the newly restored monarchy's national-popular legitimacy. And after Benjamin's much-debated essay (1973), modern media and the socio-economic transformation of music and listening that they entail have been widely discussed, for example, in relation to the production of a new "*aurality*" through early music recordings (Maisonneuve 2009), to jazz (Berliner 1994), and to rock and popular culture (Laing 1985; Hennion 1989; Frith and Goodwin 1990). More generally, popular music and rock have been sites for rich critical rethinking within cultural, gender, and ethnic studies (Willis 1978; Hebdige 1979; Whiteley et al. 2004; A. Bennett, 2005): what appears to be a blasphemy for occidental music is inescapable for popular music, which is studied as a mixture of rites, of linguistic and social structures, of technical media and marketing strategies, of instruments and musical objects, and of politics and bodies. Often implicitly, social analysis refers to the power of music to establish and actualize the identity of a group, an ethnicity, and a generation, and points to the ambivalence of its political function: music both helps a social entity to access reality, and prevents it from expressing itself through more political means (Brake 1980; Frith 1981; Yonnet 1985; Middleton 1990; Wicke 1990). And after all, Max Weber ([1921] 1958) had done something similar in his much earlier essay—tentative and speculative but full of deep insights—establishing new relations among musical language, technique, and notation, and the social division of labor among audiences, musicians, and composers.

The theme of mediation as an empirical means for identifying the progressive appearance of a work and its reception is very rich; it is the means (for the sociologist) to reopen the work-taste duality, a duality that represents a closure of the analysis, with works on one side left to aestheticians and musicologists, who attribute the power of music to the music itself, and, facing them, a sociological denunciation, the reduction of music to a rite. In the next three sections I briefly exemplify such a "mediation perspective" from some of my own studies.

"BACH TODAY"

Bach was not a "modern composer," author of a "Complete Works," catalogued in the *Bach-Werke-Verzeichnis*, before musicology, the record industry, and the modern amateur. One can trace through the nineteenth century the long transformation of what was "music," and how it produced our taste for Bach as a musician, giving him the strange ability of being both the object and the means of our love for music (Fauquet and Hennion

2000). Bach is neither the solitary individual born in 1685 to whom history would ascribe an oeuvre, nor an artificial construct of our modern taste. We listen to him today by way of three hundred years of collective labor, and of the most modern mechanisms, mechanisms that we created to listen to him but also *because* we were listening to him. Those mechanisms keep on perfecting themselves in the desire for a "return to Bach" (thanks to musicology, organology, computerized recording, the progress made by performers, and the historicization of our appreciation). But in so doing, they invest themselves more and more in this active production of "Bach today," and the more and more modern they become!

How can one analyze Bach's grandeur? To answer such a question, one cannot just study "Bach's reception" musicologically. To speak of reception is already to admit that the oeuvre is constituted. Beauty is also in the eye of the beholder: the formation of a taste cultivated for classical music is not simply an independent development that enables the "reception" of the great composer always to be more worthy of him. But one cannot just sociologically critique the cult of Bach: there was, and continues to be, a simultaneous production of a taste for Bach, of an oeuvre corresponding to this taste and, more generally, of a new mechanism for musical appreciation. The hand is not dealt to two partners (Bach and us) but to three (Bach, us, and "the music"), none of which can be separated from the others: Bach's music continually changes in the process, and reciprocally, all through the nineteenth century, Bach helped a complete redefinition of the love for music to take place.

Bach "becomes music": not only a reference, an ancient Master, the statue of the Commendatore in the shadow of whom the music of the present time is written, but a contemporary composer. But the reverse is also true: classical music "becomes Bach," it is reorganized around his figure (and Beethoven's), resting on their production. Bach is not integrated into an already made musical universe: he produces it, in part, through the invention of a new taste for music. Throughout the century, we witness the formation both of a new way to love music, as a serious, demanding activity—a development that was primarily due to the influence of Beethoven and Bach—and of a new repertoire of masterpieces that respond to this appreciation. Bach's "early adopters" in France (Boëly, Fétis, Chopin, Alkan, Gounod, Franck, Liszt, Saint-Saëns) copied, paraphrased, transcribed—not because they were unfaithful, but because Bach was a means for making music, not a composer of the past. Through the way that each incorporated the insights that they discovered in Bach's work into their own compositions, these composers gradually developed our modern form of musical appreciation. Paradoxically, their interaction with Bach's oeuvre also led to the current stipulation that the past be respected, a stipulation that calls us to reject this nineteenth century that brought Bach to us, so as to return to a more original, more authentic Bach, a Bach who is "better" understood (Hennion and Fauquet 2001).

This account reveals the "musicalization" of our taste for the music: the formation of a specific competence, increasingly well defined and self-sufficient, that makes us appreciate the works according to a regime of connoisseurship—a format that we stop seeing as we come to belong to it most naturally and intimately. This is at the heart of the paradoxes surrounding the baroque revival (Hennion 1997): the appearance of a past to listen to in a particular fashion, by respecting its modes of production, is the incredibly elaborated—and very modern—fruit of a hypertrophy of musical taste, based on musicology and the progress in recording. It is the culmination of a transformation of musical taste, not a passive and anachronistic "return to sources." Nothing is more modern than an historical approach to an old repertoire.

JAZZ, ROCK, RAP, AND THEIR MEDIA

Comparing musics and genres on the basis of the media and modes of performance they use does not mean taking their self-descriptions at face value. It is too easy, for instance, to oppose the freedom of playing together and the pleasure of dancing bodies, identified in jazz or rock, to the way written music gives itself airs, while it is suspected by its opponents to be already dead. Against the supposed rigidity of a corseted classical music—prisoner of scores, orchestral hierarchies, harmonic "laws"—jazz, which is so fond of old records, assumes its sweetest voice to sing praises of improvisation. But, busy adorning the object of her love with these praises, the jazz lover forgets that this splendid transgression of centuries of written music did not come about by going back to the oral sources of a traditional music that cannot be written down on paper, but on the contrary by going forward with the use of new means to overfix music, through a medium that no former genre could lean on: jazz has been written by recordings. Testimonies from all the jazz greats converge: they have trained, they have practiced scales, with one ear stuck at the gramophone and radio. Parker learns how to "chorus" by listening hundreds of times to Hawkins's or Young's solos on an old record player, just as previous generations wore out their eyes on old scores, and he looks for the same thing they did: to read a music he could not hear at its source, but that these recordings allow him to work and rework, to analyze and copy, and to play, note by note, faster and faster (DeVeaux 1997).

As a result, far from obeying the millennial rhythm of traditional musics that (transmitted only through collective repetition) continuously change without changing, never stop moving while thinking themselves eternally the same, jazz covered in fifty years a history classical music took five hundred years to write. Between an old blues and a chorus by Coltrane, both officially improvised, lies a transition from orality to a music that on the contrary is overwritten, even more written than classical pieces. Records have written jazz's library. Its living history is the fruit of mechanical recording.

Another example: the sudden passage from rock to rap, quite similar to the revolution of rock itself in the 1950s, also displays a conflict between different media—stage versus record. Through a face-to-face confrontation between the star and the public, rock constructed its power around a mythic stage in the quest for a lost hand-to-hand clinch between idols and people. This central place given to the stage was destroyed by rap from the very start, giving way to another definition of musical truth: where you live, where you hang out. The denunciation of rock's too-sophisticated techniques, already made by punks, and the bricolage with record decks and boom boxes, exposed rock's "archaic" conception of stage performance on the basis of an unexpected promotion of recording: not as a faithful reproduction medium but as a cheap means for local creation.

By explicitly refusing to refer to a place other than where one lives—the street, the pavement, shared and invaded places, where one talks, fights, discusses—rap at its origin interrupted the very gesture of the great stage performance. It commuted rivalries and fights into an improvisatory sparring match based on a given background music, played on equipment whose quality did not matter as long as the music was loud enough, to be listened to on the spot, by buddies, equals. The truth of music is not in music itself, not in any reconstituted collective, it is in the present performance you can give, here and now. The initial hostility of rappers toward the music business, money, and the mass media is to be interpreted less as political radicalism than as the technical means to stop the move of identities toward the big stage, always in the hands of intermediaries—and of the white man. So defined, rap is not so new: bebop in its time, punk more recently, or neobaroque musicians all began by escaping from the big stage and the media, before being seized back or dying. Rap has already suffered this common fate. But before it became just another musical genre and social style—racking up huge sales for the record industry—rap had produced, besides a blow to rock grandeur, a new and lasting instrumental use of "reproduction" technology.

FIGURES OF AMATEURS

When a sociologist questions somebody nowadays on what he or she likes, the subject apologizes. "My family is very bourgeois, my sister plays the violin . . ." Far from revealing the hidden social reality of tastes thought of by amateurs as personal and subjective, irreducible and absolute, sociology has become one of the main registers in which to speak about them. Music lovers, fully aware that tastes are relative, historical, and the supports of various social rites, display them as arbitrary, socially determined signs. Strange paradox of a highly reflexive field: it is the sociologist who must henceforth "desociologize" the amateur if the former wants her to speak back of her pleasure, of what holds her, of the astonishing techniques and tricks she develops in order to reach, sometimes, her joy.

Far from being the cultural dope at whose expense the sociology of culture built its critical fortune, the amateur (in the broad sense of art lover) is a virtuoso of experimentation, be it aesthetic, technical, social, mental, or corporeal. She is the model of an inventive and reflexive actor, tightly bound to a collective, continuously forced to put into question the determinants of what she likes. She is as self-aware about pieces and products as about the social determinants and mimetic biases of her preferences; about the training of her body and soul as about her ability to like music, the technical devices of appreciation and the necessary conditions of a good feeling, the support of a collective and the vocabulary progressively designed to perform and intensify her pleasure. Studying diverse amateurs, then, provides a better understanding of our attachments (Gomart and Hennion 1999; Hennion 2001).

Such a survey of classical music lovers, through all the means they can use to reach music (instruments, choirs, singing, but also records, concerts, media, and the Internet), displays the various and heteronomous moments, formats, and configurations in the careers of amateurs, their pattern depending less on past determinants than revealing the stages of a problematic relation to an evasive object (Hennion 2007). A systematic comparison between wine amateurs and music lovers puts under scrutiny the variable role of the heterogeneous mediations of taste: techniques of buying and tasting; belonging to clubs or organized groups; use of an idiomatic vocabulary somewhere between technical discourse and emotive self-expression; the role of critiques and guides; modes of evaluation, status games, and so forth. Bodies, spaces, durations, gestures, regular practice, technical devices, objects, guides, apprenticeship: both music as a performing art and wine because of its focus on a corporeal contact with the eye, the nose, and the palate allow us to understand taste not as a recording of fixed properties of an object, not as a stable attribute of a person, and not as a game played between existing identities, but as an accomplishment. It is not about liking music or being a wine taster, but about being touched by this piece or liking this bottle, here, now, with these people: a strange activity, the conditions of which are continuously discussed by amateurs themselves. It relies closely upon moments, places, opportunities: taste is not only an activity, it is an event, oversensitive to the problematic relationship between—as they nicely say—a combination of circumstances.

A POSSIBLE RETURN TO THE WORK?

A last point, about the work "itself"—this silent other side of the coin for the sociology of art. A rewriting of music from the viewpoint of mediation makes artistic creation somewhat less distant, less difficult to think of for sociology. Creation does not need to be "taken away" from the great composers and given back to society or consumers: it is just more distributed. Creation is not only on the side of the creator; on the contrary, the more there is a collective work in defining and thus creating a domain such as music, the more we will end up attributing the origins of the works exclusively to certain creators—the paradox of the "author," which the theoreticians of literature have clearly pointed out (Foucault 1969). This mechanism is profoundly circular: it takes all the collectivity's love to be able to say that everything comes from Rembrandt or Mozart. This is why Elias (1993) is caught in a double bind when he speaks of Mozart as a "socially unrecognized" genius—a paradoxical pleonasm, considering how much this "unrecognition" is a central figure of the social recognition of "genius." Highlighting the work of mediation consists of descending a little from this slightly crazy position of attributing everything to a single creator, and realizing that creation is far more widely distributed, that it takes place in all the interstices between these successive mediations. It is not despite the fact that there is a creator, but so that there can be a creator, that all our collective creative work is required.

This collective redistribution of creation is a counterpoint to the single attribution—the "all to the author"—in the preceding period. There is an optimistic note here: This redistributed creation, always out of line, has no need to be compared to the original work as if to a sort of paralyzing challenge. Creation uses only the elements that it holds to make—with a slight discrepancy—something else: a new creation. It is less a question of understanding everything (a formula whose epistemological terrorism is readily apparent) than of grasping something at work, from which a constantly changing interpretation can be presented.

FURTHER READING

Bennett, H. Stith. 1980. *On becoming a rock musician.* Amherst: University of Massachusetts Press.

Bennett, Tony, Simon Frith, Larry Grossberg, John Shepherd, and Graeme Turner, eds. 1993. *Rock and popular music: Politics, policies, institutions.* London: Routledge.

Bennett, Tony, M. Emmison, and J. Frow. 1999. *Accounting for tastes: Australian everyday cultures.* Cambridge, U.K.: Cambridge University Press.

Chaney, David. 2002. *Cultural change and everyday life.* Basingstoke, U.K.: Palgrave.

Cutler, Chris. 1985. *File under popular: Theoretical and critical writings on music.* London: November Books.

Durant, Alan. 1984. *Conditions of music.* London: Macmillan.

Frith, Simon. 1978. *The sociology of rock.* London: Constable.

Gumplowicz, Philippe. [1987] 2001. *Les travaux d'Orphée: Deux siècles de pratique musicale amateur en France; harmonies, chorales, fanfares.* Paris: Aubier.

Hennion, Antoine, Sophie Maisonneuve, and Émilie Gomart. 2000. *Figures de l'amateur: Forme, objets et pratiques de l'amour de la musique aujourd'hui.* Paris: La Documentation française.

Jacobs, J. M. 1996. *Edge of empire: Postcolonialism and the city.* London, New York: Routledge.

Laborde, Denis. 1997. *De Jean-Sébastien Bach à Glenn Gould: Magie des sons et spectacle de la passion.* Paris: L'Harmattan.

Leppert, Richard, and Susan McClary, eds. 1987. *Music and society: The politics of composition, performance and reception.* Cambridge, U.K.: Cambridge University Press.

Savage, Mike, G. Bagnall, and B. J. Longhurst. 2005. *Globalisation and belonging.* London: Sage.

Scott, Derek. 2000. *Music, culture, and society.* Oxford: Oxford University Press.

Weinstein, D. 2000. *Heavy metal: The music and its culture.* New York: Da Capo Press.

White, Avron Levine, ed. 1987. *Lost in music: Culture, style and the musical event.* London: Routledge and Kegan Paul.

CHAPTER 23

MUSIC AND THE SOCIAL

GEORGINA BORN

November 2010: a telematic music performance is taking place linking the Sonic Lab of the Sonic Arts Research Centre, Queen's University, Belfast, to venues in Graz and Hamburg. Internet connections sustain for an hour or so live transnational interactions between performers in three remote settings—musical interactions that amount to a real-time distributed sociality. The composer has orchestrated interactions such that each group drops periodically in and out of the others' hearing, eruptions of disconnection and absence. The audience in Belfast, where I am sitting, strains to catch the socio-musical and gestural theater between the performers, perceptible live in the room and projected on giant screens. Another arena of sociality is engendered between performers and audiences, one that follows the conventions of silent and immobile audiencehood that for two centuries have governed the concert hall. The technical dimensions of the event are experimental; they depend on a further vector of sociality: a division of labor between technicians, composers, and musicians manifest in the room and in the event's networked infrastructure.

The musical sounds emitted and the constellation of corporeal, social, technological, and discursive mediations in which they are embedded, as well as the venue's architecture, all locate this event generically: it belongs to the genre of computer art music, although part of its experimentation consists in the way that it mixes this heritage with adjacent genres—free improvised music, sound installation and new media art. The genre is, then, reanimated by the event and projected as an evolving entity. Musicians, composers, and many audience members have a tacit understanding of this generic location and share an identification with the genre: an affective relation—whether fascination, burgeoning or passing interest, or sceptical engagement—which has brought them to SARC this evening. This is an affective identification that is at one and the same time musical, cultural, and social; the genre, as an aggregation of the affected, forges a heterogeneous musical public (Warner 2005) or imagined community (Anderson 1983; Born 1993a). And while it is manifest in the event, this imagined community predates and will outlive it. At the same time audience members, performers, and technicians bear the demographic inscriptions of their individual histories such that the socialities of this event are crossed by the social identity formations to which they belong by affiliation or involuntary association. Being an art-music-technology scene of the global North, a palpable if "unmarked" race, class, and gender profile characterizes those who make and listen to the music: white middle-class men predominate. SARC is itself a complex social form. Part of the public University, connected to the departments of Music, Engineering, and Anthropology, as well as internationally to other computer music and media arts centres, its ethos, staffing, and funding are also hybridized through links to industry. Through its population, organization, and technical resources, SARC proffers a set of social-institutional conditions that afford certain kinds of musical practice, while discouraging others.

July 1989: a recording is taking place in a studio in Johannesburg.

> Alton Ngubane and his band are recording a cassette of Inkatha Freedom Party songs . . . Tom, the [white sound] engineer, sets up the mikes, prepares the console for the backing tracks, and programs a drum track. . . . Bongani [the bass player] lugs the amp into the little booth. He starts to plug in. "No", says Tom, holding down the talkback button. Bongani looks up. He plugs in anyway. He starts twisting the amp controls. "No", says Tom. Tom calls Bongani back into the control room. "The bass must go directly into the console. Much cleaner sound", he explains. "Sorry, no half-assed sound is going out of this studio". The band wants the bass amped and miked. Period. [But] "We're dedicated to sound quality in this studio", Tom insists.
>
> (Meintjes 2003, 144)

Cut to February 1992:

> [G]uitarist Nogabisela is warming up in his booth. He has set a stinging sound on the amp alongside him, just the way he likes it. . . . Lee [a white engineer] is trekking in and out of the recording booths, moving microphones. In passing, he cuts Nogabisela's amp settings to zero, dry. Then he returns to the control room to set initial sound levels and

EQs. . . . While Lee is preoccupied, Nogabisela turns his mix back up on his amp.

(p. 106)

Through such ethnographic moments, in which white sound engineers who know little about black styles are setting up to record black musicians, Louise Meintjes captures how recording in South Africa becomes a site of struggles over musical gestures. These are struggles in which black musicians employ tactics to wrest back musical control from the white engineers. Probing the social relations of the studio, Meintjes stresses that "The layering of technological mystification onto the South African social matrix . . . empowers white men in the mbaqanga studio" (p. 104).

In terms of genre, Meintjes shows how such struggles extend to aesthetic judgments in the mediation by white engineers of Zulu styles and sounds for the much-sought world music markets. Infinitesimal shifts in intonation or timbre determine whether a track is deemed to merit international distribution. She shows also how aesthetic imperatives issued by producers serving international markets can tempt musicians to proffer Zulu stereotypes, pandering to essentialist and primitivist imaginaries. The racialized dynamics of the studio thus mediate the sounds that will circulate globally as "authentic Zulu" music. The institutional conditions for these events are provided by the existence in South Africa at the end of Apartheid of a white-controlled recording industry, itself enmeshed in an avalanche of social and political transitions: "studio processes, industrial politics, civic organisation, and state negotiations produce a context within which [these sounds] take on particular characteristics" (ibid., 5). By shifting analysis across scales, Meintjes makes plain how the recording studio is a locus that produces its own irreducible social relations, manifest in the division of labor and the hierarchization of technical skills, while these relations are themelves refracted by the wider social inequalities of race and class of the South African polity, inequalities that intimately mediate musical sound.

In both the ethnographic scenarios described I have drawn attention to the social, and the socio-technical, in music. In both cases the social is not singular but multiple. Music is socially mediated, but this social mediation occurs on a number of distinct and mutually modulating or intersecting planes. Such an analytics can be taken to historical as well as present-day musical assemblages and events. It departs from previous frameworks, which tend to foreshorten music's social mediation, reducing it to one or other plane or to simple determinations between them. The complexity evident in the two scenarios raises the critical question: how should we understand the social in music? In what follows I suggest that music poses generative challenges to social theory, challenges that are symptomatic of an urgent felt need to reconceptualize the very notion of the social. Music, it seems, indicates fertile new lines of enquiry, catalyzing the wider debates. The interdisciplinary perspective opened up by rethinking the social through music is one that abandons older notions of coherent social totalities, as well as the reductive theories of determination or articulation with which these concepts are often associated.

Two writers, Marilyn Strathern and Bruno Latour, have been at the forefront in articulating the "crisis" of the social, and in proffering theoretical alternatives. Strathern develops a comparative stance that enables her to supersede the twin reifications—society or social structure on the one hand, asocial individual on the other—that underpin Durkheimian social theory. As she puts it, in this line of thought

> "society" was reified as an individual thing, set up as an entity in antithesis to entities of a similar conceptual order: society versus economy, the material world, even biology or nature. . . . The theoretical task then becomes one of elucidating "the relationship" between it and other entities.
>
> (Strathern 1990, 5)

Instead she proposes to "retain the concept of sociality to refer to the creating and maintaining of relationships." For Strathern,"Social life consists in a constant movement . . . from one type of sociality to another" (Strathern 1988, 13–14), and she enjoins us to trace how such socialities are constituted by the creation of relations and aggregations, whether by the elimination of difference and resulting unities or by the elaboration of heterogeneity. Latour also rejects the reductive Durkheimian or Marxian "sociology of the social" and advocates instead a "sociology of associations," a nonteleological focus on the action of assembling the social, where this is conceived as multiple. Highlighting the "many . . . contradictory cartographies of the social" (Latour 2005, 34), Latour insists on the contribution of nonhuman as well as human actors in making social connections, mediations that compose an assemblage. Together these writers suggest a new analytical topos of the social that can be taken to music; they pose, without solving, the question of the interrelations between plural socialities.

It is a similar dissatisfaction with reification and reductionism that stoked the questioning in music sociology, ethnomusicology, and popular music studies of Durkheimian and Marxian models that portrayed the link between musical style and social formation in terms of homology or reflection. In sociology the departure from such models is evident in the work of Tia DeNora and Antoine Hennion. Their concern is with the bidirectional nature both of music's mediation and of human and nonhuman agency:

music constituting human subjectivities and socialities, while music is itself constituted in discourse and practice and through its copious socialities and socio-technical relations. As DeNora puts it, "Music is active within social life: just as music's meanings may be constructed in relation to things outside it, so, too, things outside music may be constructed in relation to music"(DeNora 2000, 3). Hennion, for his part, dwells on the intimate mediation between music lover and musical sound in the co-production of taste, where taste is understood as a transformative relation cultivated through heterogeneous practices and techniques (Hennion 2001). There is great merit in these perspectives, which are influenced not only by Latour but by ethnomethodology and symbolic interactionism. At the same time, there is a risk of privileging a singular and micro-social conception of mediation, neglecting other dimensions of the social in music.

Alternative directions are evident in ethnomusicology and popular music studies. Steven Feld proposed to overcome the music–social dualism by analyzing musical cultures as immanently social, "sound structure as socially structured" (Feld 1984). To achieve this he called for ethnographic enquiry into such matters as whether cooperative or competitive social relations emerge in performance, how expressive ideology and performance mark social differences and social inequalities, and whether there is a stratification of musical knowledge. In his research on ethnicity, identity, and music, Martin Stokes suggested in turn that "music does not . . . simply provide a marker in a prestructured social space, but the means by which this space can be transformed" (Stokes 1994, 4). Stokes argued that music can act variably as a medium for both negotiating social identities and enforcing dominant social categories; hence, the musical performance of ethnicity "can never be understood outside the wider power relations in which [it is] embedded" (ibid., 7). These writers attend not only to the socialities of musical practice and how they are freighted ontologically but also, crucially, to how such socialities are entangled in and mediate wider social relations and modalities of power.

Popular music studies have seen further generative developments. Through detailed critique, Richard Middleton undermined simplistic accounts of a homology between social group or subculture and musical style. Drawing on Gramscian theories, he proposed a model of their articulation. While he extended the analysis of social formations beyond a focus solely on class to gender, age, ethnicity, and nationality, and employed extenuating terms (such as relative autonomy), Middleton retained a Marxian insistence on the primacy of class or of overdetermination by "ruling interests" (Middleton 1990, 10) in framing processes of articulation. It was a break with this framing that underlay the next decisive move. In Will Straw's theory of musical scenes, exemplified by alternative rock and electronic dance musics, music is detached from any grounding in a given social ontology. Instead, "scene" captures music's capacity to create "affective alliances" (Straw 1991, 374), engendering musical collectivities that are irreducible to prior forms of social identity. Scene points to the significance and the autonomy of two planes of sociality produced by music: the immediate socialities of musical performance and practice—which Straw portrays through the engrossing corporeal activity of the dance floor—and the diverse musical publics conjured into being by musical tastes and experiences, which he invokes through the "coalitions" created by certain dance musics in the late 1980s between "black teenagers, young girls listening to Top 40 radio, and urban club-goers" (ibid., 384–385). But scene recognizes also the importance of their mutual mediation: how the intimate socialities of performance catalyze music's imagined communities, just as those imagined communities imbue the socialities of performance with collective emotion. Straw makes two further moves. Having established their autonomy, he reconnects these two planes of sociality to wider identity formations—whether class, race, or gender—which may be marked or unmarked by the actors, arguing that the politics of popular music stem from music's capacity to create affective alliances that traverse such pervasive social differences. He then introduces a further plane: the institutions— dance clubs, radio, record stores—"within which musics are disseminated," providing "the conditions of possibility of [those affective] alliances" (ibid., 384). Although incipient, then, Straw's theory of musical scenes recognizes and traces connections between four planes of music's social mediation. The point is that each—performance socialities, imagined communities, social identity formations, institutions—has an autonomy. By opening up each plane to enquiry, as well as their interrelations, they can be analyzed as contingent, as taking a variety of forms—and as the potential conduit for a politics.

It is now possible to advance the core argument of this chapter. It is that music necessitates an expansion of previous conceptions of the social; that if music engenders myriad socialities, it is productive to analyze them in terms of four planes of social mediation. In the first plane, music produces its own diverse socialities in the guise of the intimate microsocialities of musical performance and practice, the social relations enacted in musical ensembles, and the musical division of labor. In the second, music has powers to animate imagined communities, aggregating its listeners into virtual collectivities or publics based on musical and other identifications, collectivities that may be more or less unified or heterogeneous. In the third, music refracts wider social identity formations—formations of class, race or ethnicity, gender or sexuality, nationality or locality. In the fourth, music is entangled in the institutional forms that enable its production, reproduction, and transformation, including nonmarket or market exchange, elite or religious patronage, public or subsidized cultural organizations, or late capitalism's multipolar cultural economy. In short, as demonstrated by scene theory as well as the opening ethnographic vignettes, all four planes of social mediation—which are often disassociated in discussions of music and the social—enter in dynamic ways into the musical assemblage. The first two planes amount to socialities and social imaginaries that are assembled specifically by musical practice and experience. In contrast, the last two planes amount to wider social formations and institutions that condition music, affording certain kinds of musical practice. Such conditions do not amount to an inert "context": they are folded into musical experience; they both permeate and are permeated by music's intimate socialities and imagined communities.

A number of propositions follow. To begin with, the four planes of music's social mediation are irreducible to one another and are articulated in contingent and nonlinear ways through relations of affordance, conditioning, or causality. Strikingly, the first two planes—music's microsocialities and imagined communities—are irreducible to and have a certain autonomy from the last two—music's social conditions. Moreover, all four planes can be the locus of significant and unpredictable transformations. It is the complex potentialities engendered by both the autonomy of and the mutual interference between the four planes that are particularly generative of experimentation, transformation, and emergence in musical assemblages, whether this entails experimentation with the socialities of performance or practice, with the aggregation of the musically affected, with the crystallization via musical affect of novel coalitions of social identities, or with music's institutional forms. That is to say, the irreducibility and the complex interactions between the four planes of music's social mediation—their capacity to synergize and compound—afford spaces of agency and experimentation in the musical assemblage. This is why all four planes have the potential to animate music's aesthetic, ethical, and political operations. At stake is an analytics of the social in music that acknowledges openness and experimentation in the musical assemblage, and thereby the potential for a micropolitics (Deleuze and Guattari 1987, ch. 9). This is a politics "played out at the molecular level in terms of social affinities . . . and varieties of communal belonging" (Patton 2000, 43); music's affordances stem from its capacity to destabilize and re-orchestrate not only affect and desire but criteria of belonging and affiliation, and therefore new collective solidarities.

The concept of assemblage invokes another influential lineage of social thought. For Deleuze an assemblage is a "multiplicity which is made up of heterogeneous terms and which establishes liaisons, relations between them

. . . [where] the assemblage's only unity is that of a co-functioning" (Deleuze and Parnet 1987, 69). Moreover, an assemblage is characterized by "relations of exteriority" such that its component parts may be detached from it and plugged into different assemblages in which their interactions will be different. Each component therefore has a "certain autonomy," while the interactions between them are nonlinear and mutually catalyzing, "only contingently obligatory" (DeLanda 2006, 11, 12). Taken to music, the notion of an assemblage allows not only for music's social mediation but for its multiple simultaneous forms of existence. It suggests that music has no essence but a plural and distributed socio-material being, enabling music to be cognized as a constellation of mediations of heterogeneous kinds: sonic and social, corporeal and technological, visual and discursive, temporal and ontological (Born 1993b, 2005, Forthcoming). Scale and temporality also characterize musical assemblages. In the analytics of music's social mediation developed in this chapter, although scale differentiates the four planes of the social, they defy any linear or nested organization (cf. Delanda 2006, 18–38); instead, the focus is on their cross-scalar interrelations (Strathern 1995), including the potential for disjunctures. And in as much as mediation refers to transformational processes, it ineluctably signals questions of temporality: the relative endurance or stability of certain socialities or aggregations, as against the unstable or fleeting quality of others. In the telematic concert at SARC, these issues were signaled on several planes—concert socialities, musically imagined community, demographics, institution—all of which, while reanimated by the event, predate and outlive it. An analytics of music's social mediation must therefore be attuned to the temporalities immanent in the assemblage, which are differentiated; some mediations will exhibit historical depth and stability—albeit that their "contents" are constantly in formation—achieving a type of "mobile stasis" (Born 1995, 326), while others will be transient.

In this final section, I take the preceding analytics of music and social mediation to three areas of existing work. In each case, the aim is show the anti-reductionist gains of analyzing both the autonomy of distinctive planes of music's social mediation and, thereby, cross-scalar relations between them—including the potential for disjuncture or contradiction. The first area concerns the socialities of musical performance. A number of writers take these intimate socialities as the sole locus for theorizing the social in music. Commonly, they are idealized through a metaphysics of musical co-presence (e.g., Schutz [1951] 1971; Attali 1985, ch. 5; Small 1998, 13). Such accounts contrast with studies that provide a more empirically informed rendering of performance socialities by examining the interaction between the first and third planes of the social: how the socialities of performance are traversed by wider social relations. Examples are Charles Keil's *Urban Blues* (Keil 1970), Ingrid Monson's *Saying Something* (Monson 1996), and Louise Meintjes's *Sound of Africa!* (Meintjes 2003), all of which address how performance socialities refract formations of race and class. Keil's description of the relations enacted between blues singer Bobby Bland, his band, and their audience captures the ways in which social solidarities and collective catharsis are performed moment by moment through voice, gesture, humor, and innuendo, all of them riffing on the "stylistic common denominators" (Keil 1970, 143) linking blues performance and preaching in the lives of black Chicagoans in the 1960s.

A crucial further stage is evident in studies focused on how performance socialities are not only entangled in wider identity formations but have the capacity to catalyze or act on them. Thus, Jocelyne Guilbault stresses the transformative capacities of live soca performance in Trinidad as it produces "public intimacies": social interactions between artists and audience that "reiterate identities," while enabling "new points of connection [to be] developed (for example among artists and audience members of different ethnicities, nationalities and generations, and across musical genres)" (Guilbault 2010, 17). The socialities enacted in performance, she says, can either reinforce or work against social intimacies and social antagonisms. Equally striking is Marina Roseman's account (Roseman 1984) of how the gender relations and cosmologies immanent in the musical performances of the Temiar people of peninsular Malaysia invert the hierarchical gender relations that characterize their everyday social lives. Indeed, historical and anthropological research suggests repeatedly that it is the autonomy of the socialities of musical performance and practice that enables them to promote experimentation, in the sense that they may enact alternatives to or inversions of, and can be in contradiction with, wider hierarchical and stratified social relations. These are performed contradictions that contribute powerfully to the nature of socio-musical experience by offering a compensatory or utopian social space—one that fashions experience differently even as it may fail to overturn wider social relations (although such an outcome is not foreclosed).

A second area enhanced by the analytics proposed in this chapter is that of music and genre; here, insights derive from attending to the interrelations between the second and third planes—musically imagined communities and wider identity formations. Indeed genre is commonly taken to be the primary mechanism for the mutual articulation of social identities and musically imagined communities, communities that are often taken to derive from those same social identities. Already obvious here is how genre theory risks teleology. In his work on corporate genre cultures, Keith Negus emphasizes their contingency, given that "the genre boundaries associated with commercial markets, radio or media formats and wider cultural formations do not coincide in any straightforward way" (Negus 1999, 29). Yet at other times, despite his exemplary concern with "how corporate organization actively intervenes in the production . . . of genres" (ibid., 28), Negus closes down contingency, noting "how genres operate as social categories; how rap cannot be separated from the politics of blackness, nor salsa from Latinness, nor country from whiteness and the enigma of the 'South'" (ibid., 29). In this way he threatens to elide conceptually what must strenuously be held apart: the mutual mediation between musically imagined community, on the one hand, and identity formations, on the other. Here David Brackett's stress in his work on black popular musics on the "paradoxes (and tautologies) of genre" (Brackett 2005, 82) is salutary: "the notion of genre speaks to transitory divisions in the musical field that correspond in discontinuous and complex ways to a temporally defined social space." Brackett indicates how historically labile have been the apparently established links between black musical genres and African-American social formations; yet he cautions against over-arbitrary accounts of genre categories as mere "social constructions" (ibid., 75).

Brackett's studies underline the insights afforded by focusing on both the temporalities and the *attempted* teleologies of genre. That is to say, genre works by projecting temporally, into the cauldron of evolving social identity formations, potential reconfigurations of those formations coded as musical transformations that are proffered as analogous to the social. When the teleology works, music may effect either the reproduction of identity formations, or a redirection or novel coalition of such formations. Brackett illustrates these processes through Isaac Hayes's 1969 hit crossover soul version of Jimmy Webb's 1967 ballad "By the Time I Get to Phoenix," arguing that Hayes's musical gestures reveal "how intersubjective awareness of the audience . . . is in play" (ibid., 86) and results in the attachment of new audiences. Genre can therefore be understood as a process enabling potential convergence or translation between musical figure (and thence musically imagined community) and social identity formations. Genre should be analyzed not as embodying any assured linkage, but as an evolving constellation constituted by the mutual mediation between two self-organizing entities (music, identity formations), *both* reliant on the collective production of memory as well as the anticipation of futures (Born 2005, 20–23); conceiving of genre in this fashion—as a *radically contingent process that is, however, oriented to the production of teleology and thus the erasure of its own contingency*—enables us to understand the way that wider social formations are refracted in music, and that musical genres entangle themselves in evolving social formations. In this light, genre theory can illuminate how music's creation of affective coalitions mediates wider identity formations, but in the anti-teleological terms of affordance, catalysis, and contingency as opposed to determination or singular articulation.

The final area that I want to address through the social analytics of music outlined in this chapter is the fourth plane: music's institutional forms. This can only be indicative, but the goal is again anti-reductionist: to indicate the autonomy and heterogeneity of these forms, as well as the benefits of analyzing interrelations between this and other planes of social mediation. Certainly, there is a continuing salience in distinguishing between two broad spheres of music's institutional forms that evolved over the twentieth century: between those musical activities afforded by capitalist industrialization and internationalization, and those oriented primarily to state subsidized or patronage-endowed institutions—the sphere of art, academic, and nationalist musics (Born 1987). However a primary focus on the inequities and disorders of capitalist music markets can entail a neglect of surprising features of both spheres: the progressive potential of the corporate music industry, as well as the repressive or inequitable tendencies of statist and subsidized music institutions (e.g., Wicke and Shepherd 1993; Baker 2011). On the former: Chris Lawe Davies gives an exemplary analysis of the entry of Australian Aboriginal rock groups into the industry mainstream in the late 1980s and early 1990s, stressing how effective this was in exposing a "massively heterogeneous audience" to a "social narrative of Aboriginality" (Lawe Davies 1993, 262) that is systematically denied in Australia's public culture. At issue is the uncertain capacity for novel engagement across the third and fourth planes: between subaltern group and corporate industry. On the latter: in my study of a globally influential, state-funded Parisian institution, IRCAM, oriented to the future of Western art music (Born 1995), I chart how IRCAM hosted a gendered and racialized (if "unmarked") division of labor while proving unable to revivify its modernist musical idiom—efforts predicated on a kind of aesthetic involution, alongside a repression of "other," nonmodernist musics and musical ontologies.

Analysis of the fourth plane must also entail a focus on experimentation and transformation in music's institutional forms, and thus on their autonomy and heterogeneity. Here I want to effect an important conceptual reorientation. I take my cue from Dipesh Chakrabarty's critique of the totalizing flavor of Marxist theories of global capitalism in which, from a postcolonial standpoint, he develops a distinction between "histories 'posited by capital' and histories that do not belong to capital's 'life process'" (Chakrabarty 2000, 50). His intention is to resist "the idea that the logic of capital sublates differences into itself" (ibid.) by disturbing universalizing and teleological readings of noncapitalist lifeworlds as remnants destined for capitalist incorporation, or, if unincorporated, as residual or insignificant. Martin Stokes takes these ideas to music: drawing on ethnographies of the circum-Mediterranean region, he shows how music and musical labor are variably commodified, arguing against any "teleological, historicist assumption about the [inevitable . . .] 'incursion' of money into musical worlds" (Stokes 2002, 139). Stokes contrasts two successful Turkish popular musicians from the northeastern area of Trabzon: the first with a strong sense of music and musical labor as commodities, keen to see them "circulate freely [and] fluidly, . . . in a system of generalised commodity exchange" (ibid., 143); the second exhibiting "extreme indifference to the cash economy" in favour of an economy of hospitality and honor, communal pleasures, and poetic sentiments. Stokes points out that musical worlds like that of the second musician animate this entire region; they are not destined to disappear, nor are they less modern, less rational, or less well adapted to the exigencies of cosmopolitan existence than the first. Indeed they are common in diasporic and migrant communities. In this way he insists that noncommoditized musics are not pre-capitalist leftovers, nor a secondary sphere of practice, but alternative modernities engaged in a "turbulent dialectic" (ibid., 150) with capital.

The same shift in perspective is compounded by Ana Maria Ochoa and Carolina Botero's account of novel forms of exchange in Colombian popular musics. They uncover a spectrum of practices that unsettle dualistic and economistic models predicated on an opposition between the formal music industry and informal practices of exchange. Instead, Ochoa and Botero trace numerous hybrid forms including economic cross-subsidies between different spheres of musicians' activities and lives; movements between "multiple forms of economic network"; "'alternative economies [that] become economies of subsistence"; an "economy of sacrifice"; and an economy of *rebusque*—of "inventing whatever it is in order to be able to make a living" (Ochoa and Botero 2009, 163–165). The analysis points to initiatives and adaptations that generate multiple forms of exchange enabling music's creation and circulation, forms ranged between the free and the monetized, each entangled in intimate musical socialities and imagined communities as well as wider social relations. It is a portrait not of marginality, necessity or overdetermination, but of embedded and conditioned yet dynamic experimentation and invention: of a certain musical and social autonomy.

If earlier popular music studies took as exceptional or unsustainable such models as punk DIY (Laing 1985) or the independent labels and networks associated with post-punk and electronic dance musics (Hesmondhalgh 1998, 1997), this scholarship goes further. It forges a radical shift in theoretical perspective by prioritizing those ubiquitous but under-recognized worlds of musical practice (Finnegan 1989) that moderate or sublate both music's commodification and statist frameworks. Stokes, Ochoa and Botero impel us to understand the practices they describe not as marginal to or failures of capitalist modernization in music, but as viable, experimental, and pervasive activities and micro-institutional forms. Such an account shifts institutional analysis away from reductive suppositions about the inescapable progress of capitalist relations in music to a nuanced awareness of the spectrum of music's non- or petty-market forms as modes of musical and social organization. (I avoid the term "proto-markets" because of the teleological implication of an eventual goal of "full" commodification: cf. Toynbee 2000, 25–32; Hesmondhalgh 2002, 171.) This approach responds to the condition of many contemporary non-Western and Western musics, dignifying them with substance and significance rather than reducing them to a transitional state destined to be brought under capitalist relations.

Augmenting this approach by tracing dynamic interrelations between institutional form and other planes of social mediation is Aditi Deo's analysis of a congeries of changes to *Khyal*, an improvisatory genre of North Indian classical music, over the twentieth century (Deo 2011). Deo draws out synergistic shifts between the third and second planes—social identity formation and musically imagined community: a transition from hereditary Muslim practitioners to middle- and upper-class Hindus, alongside the classicization of *Khyal*, previously a syncretic practice, as emblematic of a modernizing Hindu cultural nationalism. At the same time she points to tensions between transformations on the fourth and first planes: institutional form and performance sociality. Where formerly *Khyal* relied on feudal patronage and master–disciple transmission of musical knowledge, in the first decades of the twentieth century *Khyal* pedagogy was partly relocated to novel secular institutions, its knowledge abstracted from embodied methods, notated, and standardized. Yet *Khyal* defies a simplistic account of these shifts. On the one hand, training in its aesthetic principles remains bound to master–disciple lineages; subtleties of musical gesture and their social embeddedness work against *Khyal*'s rationalization. On the other hand, institutional processes mediate even those musical and social practices rooted in master–disciple relations. Deo argues that while public discourse reduces *Kyhal*'s socialities to an opposition, practitioners experience them as multiple and juxtaposed. *Khyal* as an assemblage is self-contradictory.

I have proposed that an analytics of four planes of social mediation throws new light on music's socialities, extending the plural and anti-reductionist currents in recent social theory while retaining a concern with scale, time, and power. Scale is addressed through the distinctive nature of and cross-scalar relations between the four planes. Temporality is understood in the sense of transformation given by mediation, and as a variable property of each plane of the social, as well as of their dynamic interactions. Power is conceptualized in the terms of critical social theory, given that "relations of power are constitutive of the social" (Mouffe 2000, 125). Rather than conceive of social relations as organic or oriented to community, the intention must be to address them in all their complexity as constituted also by difference, contradiction, and antagonism. While some writers have addressed the articulation between different planes of music's social mediation, the framework advanced here foregrounds this perspective. In place of reduction it probes the multiplicity and autonomy, as well as the mutual mediation and entanglement, of music's socialities. It suggests finally, as evidenced by the readings of Meintjes and Brackett given in this chapter, that through such an analytics the study of music as sound and as social form are fully reconcilable (cf. Martin 2006; Born 2010a).

FURTHER READING

Born, Georgina. 2005. On musical mediation: Ontology, technology and creativity. *Twentieth-Century Music* 2(1): 7–36.

Born, Georgina. 2010. For a relational musicology. *Journal of the Royal Musical Association*, 135(2): 205–243.

Brackett, David. 2005. Questions of genre in black popular music. *Black Music Research Journal* 25(1/2): 73–92.

Guilbault, Jocelyne. 2010. Music, politics, and pleasure: Live soca in Trinidad. *Small Axe* 14(1): 16–29.

Latour, Bruno. 2005. *Reassembling the social: An introduction to actor-network-theory.* Oxford: Oxford University Press.

Meintjes, Louise. 2003. *Sound of Africa!: Making music Zulu in a South African studio.* Durham, NC: Duke University Press.

Ochoa, Anna Maria, and Carolina Botero. 2009. Notes on practices of musical exchange in Colombia. *Popular Communication* 7(3): 158–168.

Roseman, Marina. 1984. The social structuring of sound: the Temiar of peninsular Malaysia. *Ethnomusicology* 28(3): 411–445.

Stokes, Martin 2002. Marx, money, and musicians. Pp. 139–166 in *Music and Marx: Ideas, practice, politics.* Edited by Regula Burkhardt Qureshi. London: Routledge.

Strathern, Marilyn. 1990. The concept of society is theoretically obsolete. Pp. 60–66 *in Key Debates in Anthropology.* Edited by Tim Ingold. London: Routledge.

Straw, Will 1991. Systems of articulation, logics of change: Communities and scenes in popular music. *Cultural Studies* 5(3): 368–388.

CHAPTER 24

LOCATING THE PEOPLE
Music and the Popular

RICHARD MIDDLETON

Who are "the people"? The Founding Fathers of the United States of America had no doubt about the answer to this question: "We the people . . .," they declared in the new Constitution (1787), with the confidence proper to a new epoch. A few years later, Thomas Paine, defending the French Revolution with equal assurance, insisted that "the Authority of the People [is] the only authority on which Government has a right to exist in any country" (Paine [1791–92] 1969, 131). Such confidence was inspiring but oversimple. The Revolutionary Terror set a cautionary precedent for a host of subsequent attempts to establish popular authority by violence. The founding "we" of the United States was not universal but limited to men of property, excluding not only less-affluent white males but also Native Americans, all women, and (naturally) all slaves. The political moment was in any case part of a broader shift, in which, as Raymond Williams (1983) has shown, the rise of commodity culture led to an emergent and soon predominant usage of the term *popular* to mean "well-liked by many people." By the time that Alexis de Tocqueville was dissecting American society—the 1830s, a period when "Jacksonian democracy" was refocusing U.S. politics on the interests of the "common man"—he was as amazed that "The people reign in the American political world as the Deity does in the universe; everything comes from them, and everything is absorbed in them" (Tocqueville [1835] 1956, 58) as he was depressed by the prospect of leveling down that he saw resulting from the "tyranny of the majority."

From an early-twenty-first-century vantage point, the tiredness of the people idea seems self-evident. The grotesqueness of the concept of the

Nazi *Volk* (from which Jews, gypsies, and homosexuals were excluded: no *Volkswagen* for them) was matched, for cynicism, by that of the "People's Democracies" of the post-World War II Soviet bloc; Brecht's ironic advice to his masters, on the occasion of the failed East Berlin uprising of 1953, that they should perhaps dissolve the people and elect another, was the definitive riposte to "totalitarian populism" (Esslin 1959, 165). Popular Fronts for the Liberation of X (and, usually, the oppression of Y) have lost their allure (as marked by the comic demolition job on the phenomenon in the Monty Python movie *The Life of Brian*). Those of us who lived through the period of Blairite, and perhaps also Thatcherite Britain became wearily accustomed to the routine invocation of "the people" in the service of a multitude of reactionary causes. Anything can be justified by "popularity", and everywhere, it seems, distinctions between "the popular" and its others struggle to survive amid the assumptions of a vulgar relativism.

But the complexities were endemic from the start. The German Romantic W. G. Herder (1968, 323) carefully distinguished the folksinging people (*das Volk*) from the "shrieking mob" (*der Poebel*), and in many ways the "mob", a key (if under-defined) actor in the theater of eighteenth- and nineteenth-century political and cultural discourses, came to govern those of the twentieth: the idea, explored by such diverse writers as George Orwell and T. W. Adorno, that capitalism's best hope for defending class injustice would lie in a program of cultural debasement of the masses is worth taking seriously at the same time that we note the element of condescension implicit in a perspective that fed a history of "moral panics" over "mobs" of ragtimers, jazzers, rock 'n' rollers, punks, and hip-hoppers. The nineteenth century saw a host of new communities imagined into being (Anderson 1991), in Europe and elsewhere, almost always with an appeal to a "national soul" embodied in their folk culture heritage. Small wonder that such a company of Celts, Magyars, Poles, Bohemians, generic Slavs (etc.—not to mention, further toward the margins, gypsies, Jews, "niggers," and orientals) danced and sang its way through the popular musical repertories of the period. Yet it jostled for space both with political and revolutionary songs fixed to class projects (from "La Marseillaise" through songs of the British Chartists, for whom, to quote one of their banners from 1848, "The voice of the People is the voice of God," to socialist anthems like "The Red Flag" and the "Internationale"), and with a huge expansion in market-oriented production, which by 1900 demanded that, in the words of Tin Pan Alley's Charles Harris, "A new song must be sung, played, hummed and drummed into the ears of the public, not in one city alone, but in every city, town and village, before it ever becomes popular" (Hamm 1979, 288). The character of the "people," despite its radical origins and potential, journeys through a landscape which, to use Althusser's phrase, is "structured in dominance," both in general and in the specific forms generated by the historical unfolding of capitalism; and in the maintenance of these hierarchized formations, cultural distinctions play an important role, as Pierre Bourdieu (1984) has taught us. Today, the historical trajectories, in exhausted anticlimax, precipitate inversion, detritus, and perversion, as in (to choose examples almost at random) the "turbo-folk" used as an instrument of ethnic cleansing in the Yugoslav wars of the 1990s; in the embarrassed "Red Flag" performances at Blair-era Labour Party Conferences; and in the unashamed market cynicism of the wave of TV pop talent discovery shows, globally successful in the early twenty-first century, under the celebrity guidance of their ideologist, impresario Simon Cowell.

The people/popular concept, then, is irrevocably "dirty," and in two ways at least. First, it covers a discursive space whose content is mutable and open to struggle; just as, according to Bourdieu (1993a), there is no such thing as an objective "public" but only a shifting social character defined by varying survey methodologies, so, in the words of Stuart Hall (1981, 239), "there is no fixed content to the category of 'popular culture' . . . [and] there is no fixed subject to attach to it—'the people.'" Second (and connected), the politics of the concept are "always already" corrupted (always already, because they are produced in a discourse with no clear origin), and, today, their rescue for progressive uses would require considerable cultural work—not least by intellectuals, so often popular culture voyeurs, but also fellow travelers and even would-be guides, for whom Fanon's injunction (1967, 187) to "work and fight with the same rhythm as the people" represents both an imperative and an impossibility.

The discourse we are uncovering is one specific to modernity. "The people" names a character seen as inhabiting an imagined social space (which is not to say that there is not a real social space in a relation with this). The configuration of this space varies historically and in accordance with ideological assumptions, and hence the character of "the people" is variably delineated too—as a social body, a political actor, a cultural voice—with implications for interpretation of its musical manifestations. The stage on which "the people" moves is commonly structured in alteritous fashion, and a variety of psychic mechanisms come into play: projection, overcompensation, objectification, abjection. Something in the term "people" wants to figure its object as a wayward and subordinate other—a prodigal underside challenging, but also validating by difference, the elite ego of a centered collective self. This figure is both gendered (popular culture is "effeminate": sentimental, passive, intuitive, affective, hysterical [Modleski 1986; Huyssen 1986]) and racialized (the popular is imagined as "barbaric" and/or "exotic"—mapped, most commonly, onto "black"). But peripheral elements can be appropriated by "the center," as they have been, arguably, in much of today's hegemonic popular music culture in the advanced societies. Alternatively they can answer back, as spectacularly evidenced in the long-lived, intricate workings of the "Black Atlantic" (Gilroy 1993); when, for instance, according to Lhamon (1998), an early-nineteenth-century New York cross-racial (miscegenating?) working-class fraction used the blackface mask to construct a subversive alternative to elite culture—a "Plebeian Atlantic"—at the very moment when the Founding Fathers were construing "we the people" as men of property and education. And of course, "the people" can go further, as we have seen, and make their bid for sovereignty: as "the voice of God" (*Vox Populi, Vox Dei*), their authority—cultural, commercial, political—brooks no dissent. The working out of these tensions takes hugely varied forms; but running through and overdetermining this variability is a bifurcating dynamic, what we might call a *structure of exception*: on the one hand, the People constituting itself as an excluding (i.e. would-be sovereign) power, on the other, a "people" as, precisely, the excluded; a "we" and a "they" in whose reciprocal embrace exception functions as the condition of totality. As Gorgio Agamben (1998, 176–177) puts it, "It is as if what we call 'people' were in reality not a unitary subject but a dialectical oscillation between two opposite poles: on the one hand the set of the People as a whole political body, and on the other, the subset of the people as a fragmentary multiplicity of needy and excluded bodies."

The subject/object people, then, is not only fragmented, variable, and unstable—in the language of Freud and Lacan, *split*—but also *contested* across the boundary-forming structures of social subjectivity. As such, its very appearance is dependent on an apparatus—the regime of *representation*—specific to post-Renaissance (Cartesian) modernity (Foucault 1970), and given a new twist by Hegel's dialectics of subject and object, self and other. Earlier, the commoners were simply what was left over, but with the Cartesian revolution they became bound into a system whereby the out-there is a constituent of the problematic of the self: the representation of "reality" reflects, refracts, distorts, and guarantees the subject's presence, and the dynamics of popular and nonpopular interaction become an aspect of the processes of subjectivity. For Enlightenment thinkers, the evident contradiction between alterity (the inescapability of difference) and a politics of inclusivity could in theory be squared through the principle of universalism: all of humankind could potentially perfect itself in Reason. Mozart's *The Magic Flute* (1791) represents a neo-Kantian essay along these lines: Reason triumphs, with the "lower" characters located, musically and socially, firmly in the place appropriate to their cultural stage of development, yet at the same time narratively shadowing the revelatory trajectory followed by their "betters." By 1824, Beethoven's cry in the Ninth Symphony, "O ye millions, I embrace you," has moved on to a neo-Hegelian reach for the Absolute. The shift from Kant's programmatic universalism of taste to Bourdieu's critique of distinction and its socio-economic basis exemplifies a later skepticism. It remains true, however, that it was only with the advent of "modern" thought that this type of discourse became available at all. In the early eighteenth century, Giambattista Vico offered the innovatory means to think all of a society, and even all of humanity, together, through a world-historical image of human development. Tracing the journey from the Enlightenment to twentieth-century modernism reveals metaphors of cultural ladders (progress; upward mobility) joined by, perhaps giving way to, more synchronically structured models (highbrow–middlebrow–lowbrow; the interrelations of modernism, mass, folk, and primitive). At this point the figure of the "cultural field" (variably mapped to corresponding social and politico-economic fields) achieved a dominance eventually theorized by Bourdieu (1993b) among others, and in the Gramscian concept of "hegemony" (Gramsci 1971).

Although the European Union's adoption of Beethoven's Ninth Symphony "freedom tune" as its anthem might suggest that the Enlightenment project is still under way, it also marks its trivialization: the European masses "embraced" as little more than subjects of a free market. Living (arguably) in the climactic crisis of the modernity system, we often, it seems, find it problematic, embarrassing, or even ludicrous merely to name "the people." This grand subject appears to have turned into a simulacrum of subjectivity constituted in the reification of desire in advertising—"one market under God," as Thomas Frank's ironic rewriting of an earlier national-democratic ambition puts it (2002). At best, the people are elsewhere—in unnoticed Third World catastrophes, asylum camps, sweatshops; at worst, the popular is figured in terms of the mystifying populism of meritocratic "opportunity." And yet . . . Is it possible that such pessimism is premature, even self-indulgent? At the time of writing, the "Arab Spring" of 2011 is exploding across the Middle East, and the reports, the chants, the demands of the demonstrators insistently name a self-mobilizing, seemingly authentic revolutionary subject—"the People." For one Egyptian writer, Ahdaf Soueif, reporting from the streets of Cairo, "what was there was The People," and one of their chants, according to another, Alaa Al Aswany, was "The people say, out with the regime" (*The Guardian*, January 27, 2011, 1, 38). Perhaps there is life, still, in the popular.

The foundations of the structure outlined here, in its recognizable modern form, were laid in the twentieth century. In a first phase, dominated musically by the "jazz family," the framework was constituted by the conflicts between liberal/imperial capitalism, fascism, bolshevism and Stalinism. A second phase, dominated by the "rock/pop family," was molded by the Cold War and its aftermath. Throughout, the forces of de- (and re-)

colonization were important too, as were the successive waves of feminist struggle. However mixed and, often, fraught the outcomes, each of these intersecting moments represents an opening, in which, mediated by technological and social changes (most importantly, for music, the evolving mechanisms of mass media and mass culture), new democratic possibilities, new senses of who "we" could be, were at issue. I will focus on the second of the historical phases, as the backdrop against which I can then, in the final section of this chapter, consider the conditions of our situation today. Searching for symptoms of the popular within the musical currents of this period, can we find ways of locating its subject?

Think of John Lennon's "Working Class Hero" (*John Lennon/Plastic Ono Band*, Apple PCS 7124, 1970). This is, evidently, a song about the people conceived in terms of class—or more exactly, about the disjunction of this relationship, that is to say, the culture forced on working-class people as a result of their lack of political consciousness; implicitly, it is also a song about leadership, or perhaps its lack or failure: "a working-class hero is something to be," as Lennon bitterly if ambivalently puts it. The style is terse, stern, and didactic, with lyrics foregrounded, melody plain, and accompaniment limited to simple acoustic guitar, summoning up memories of the equally spartan approach of the early Bob Dylan, down to the relentless ("deathly") guitar riff keeping the singer right on the straight and narrow message, forbidding all semiotic play. But an element of doubt about the references of pronoun shifters ("I," "we," "you," "they") clouds the issue: the flow of identifications is disrupted. Similarly, behind the stern paternal voice we hear a shadow—a would-be lyrical, "feminine" reach beyond the meaningful surface, audible in occasional tremulous cracks in timbre, anxious stretching for high pitches, and little inflections and melismas around the main melody notes; and perhaps also in the disruption of the otherwise insistent minor tonic chord, once toward the end of every verse, by a single appearance of the "yielding" major chord on the subdominant (conventionally coded "feminine" in the Western tonal system, in relation to the "masculine" dominant). Will Lennon *cry*, we ask?

Historically, the song is richly contextualized. On a biographical level, it comes between, on the one hand, the traumatic Beatles breakup and Lennon's primal scream therapy earlier in 1970 with Californian psychotherapist Arthur Janov, when he spent much of his time crying and screaming, and on the other hand, the "silence" of the period 1975–79, when Lennon gave up musical production to be a ("feminized") house-husband. In terms of cultural history, it punctuates the transition from "John Beatle" to "John Lennon," taking this to stand for the shift from the fetishizing, macho heroics of the 1960s star system (false hero worship, in Lennon's eyes) to the more skeptical, ironic, often gender-bending discourses around star presence characteristic of the 1970s. On the level of political economy, it engages the contemporaneous restructuring of class associated with the move away from social democracy toward the Thatcherism to come. "Working Class Hero" is both suspiciously insistent and revealingly fractured, signaling what Lawrence Kramer (1990) calls a hermeneutic window organized around scream/cry on the one hand and silence/death on the other. Lennon's figure of the people here is inscribed in the complex relationships and shifting meanings set up at the intersection of "leadership" and "class," generating a tantalizing image of the popular other, desired but errant, and always receding from grasp.

The Spice Girls' "Wannabe" (*Spice*, Virgin CDV2812, 1996), noisily surrounded by proclamations of "girl power," focused on gender rather than class. The singers issue instructions, give us their demands, tell us "what they really really want"; and the verses, where they do this, are delivered in a sort of rap style, borrowing and inverting the machismo of male hip-hop. Female vocal groups, however, can hardly avoid summoning references to 1960s girl groups, especially those of Motown, with their approach oriented around more traditional themes of "romance"; and, sure enough, the choruses turn to a poppier style, complete with vocal harmonies, a melodic hook, and a stress on togetherness. The bridging of individual empowerment (verses) and collective feeling (choruses) is meant to target and construct girl power's own community (eliding the issue of class, of course). But verse and chorus are also contrasted: rapped call-and-response backed by rock-style minor-pentatonic bass riff in the first, major-key vocal harmonies in the second; it is as if the inclusivity strategy couples popular music's two main ideological categories and their gender associations, "feminine" pop fantasy being grounded by "masculine" rock realism. The claim of contrast is deceptive, however. Verse and chorus flow seamlessly into each other, the rhythm track is continuous, and bits of vocal style from the verse increasingly find their way into the choruses; moreover, the bass/harmonic patterns of the two sections perform closely related gestures. Similarly, the dialogues within the verses are superficial: calls and responses from the different girls are much the same, and come from much the same place on the stereo spectrum. The song is a closed binary—nothing is left over—and the hint of teleology (tonally, the relationship of the two bass patterns—minor pentatonic and major, respectively—recalls that between *passamezzo antico* and *passamezzo moderno* which marked the dawn of "modernity" in the sixteenth and seventeenth centuries) leads nowhere.

Just as girl power offered a fake individual and collective empowerment at the extreme end of Thatcherism (there is no such thing as society, she told us), so "Wannabe" rehearses a simulacrum of difference, a wannabe teleology, a fantasy in which nobody fails and nothing is left out: rock and pop, romance and raunch, black (rap) and white (singalong), past and future are seamlessly stitched together. But the stitching (the suturing, as Lacan would call it) is overdone: it could not last—as became evident, on the level of biography, with the Spice Girls' disintegration, and, on the level of society, with the passage from Thatcherite power-feminism to the pseudo-meritocratic populism that followed, accompanied as this was by a wave of emollient girl and boy bands on the one hand, and an underground subchorus of unorthodox gender poses on the other.

White rappers became commonplace in the 1990s. Most notoriously, the success of working-class white trash Eminem demonstrated the continuing potency of the blackface stance, his records exploiting (by implication) the blackface mask to proclaim white disempowerment. Though often collaborating with black rapper and producer, Dr Dre, Eminem has been most conspicuously successful (as with most rap by this date) with a middle-class white market. His extravagantly brutal, misogynistic, and homophobic narratives work against the background of a cross-race, class-based economic split in the United States (bourgeois affluence; workers impoverished, neglected, or imprisoned), but also draw a traditional *frisson* from the image of violence long associated with black ghetto society: rap's "posses" and "gangstas" reinscribe the discourse of mob and moral panic. Eminem's "My Name Is" (*The Slim Shady LP*, Interscope 490 287-2, 1999) adds further dimensions to the masking operation. The insistent repetitions in the choruses of the statement "My name is . . ." summon memories of the long African-American tradition of naming games and rituals (the street game, the dozens, for instance); they also echo boxer Muhammed Ali's equally insistent question, "What's my name?" to his opponent Sonny Liston, soon after the name change accompanying his conversion to Islam, and Black Muslim refusals of slavery surnames (by Malcolm X, for example). Small wonder that the persona Eminem adopts here, named for us by a distant, other, and highly technologized voice, way back in the mix, is a marker of miscegenation: "Shady."

In a sense, the narrative of the song, telling of Shady/Eminem's brutal, oppressive early life and schooling, and bringing together issues of identity, charisma, and class, works similar territory to that of "Working Class Hero." But the fragmentation of voice is much more overt here. Shady's apparent identity and location shift constantly, and are embedded in complex dialogues with other voices. The play of name, identity, and voice is a work of what black theorists such as Gates (1988) have termed Signifyin(g), a key practice in African-American culture that operates through manipulation of a "changing same" by constant variation of given material, disrupting the signifying chain in the interests of semiotic play. Another element in this intra- and intertextual work is the instrumental backing, shaped—typically for rap—from a sample, here a four-chord riff taken from Labi Siffre's "I Got The," which repeats in varied forms throughout. Again, technology (digital sampling in this case) mediates a shift in the parameters of the popular music community. The process of Signifyin(g) makes fun (play; play as fun; funny, incongruous, or uncanny connections) of sense, of the signification process itself, its orientation around doing rather than meaning pointing toward the sphere of the body. Although "My Name Is" adheres to the typical rap duality of "rhymes" and "beats" (word and act, logos and body), the lyrics are noticeably "musicalized" through the operations of the vocal polyphonies, and the underlying riff, reduced to the basic drum/bass groove, is what fades out the song, inviting but always retreating from bodily response, and, in the context of the racial location of Eminem's performance, implicitly posing the question, what the *body* of the people, its social body, would be like.

These three songs are offered as symptomatic rather than representative examples. Their intricate maneuvers around the registers of race, gender, and class remind us of Hall's point that there is no *essence* of the popular—"the people" can only be defined dialogically. Their points of address from "below," no less (and no more) than their positionings in the power textures of capitalist society, confirm that the discourse of "the popular" is closely tied to the project of modernity. This, as we have seen, guaranteed the subjectivity of the emergent Western self through an apparatus of representations of his others, "masters" and "slaves" warring on, but also maintaining, each other (to draw on Hegel's celebrated dialectical image, produced [1807] in the same moment that the "people," conceived as potential subject, made such a dramatic historical step forward).

It might be argued, though, that the very multivalency of subject-position made available in such songs, their particularity of attachment to racial, gender, or class locations, represents a weakness, an accommodation to the force of market hegemony: an argument all the more plausible from an early-twenty-first-century standpoint when the fit between the liberal pluralist positions characteristic of reductive "identity-politics" and the voracious niche-marketing appetite of Big Capital in its current neo-liberal mode becomes readily apparent (Badiou 2002); difference—of class, race, gender, sexuality—is all too easily appropriated and sold back to its celebrants. And in that case, the mode of analysis practiced above risks falling victim to the same critique. With the end of the Cold War, the emergent neo-liberal hegemony—the "Restoration", as Badiou calls it—found its appropriate musical vehicle in the pseudo-democratic populism of the "reality-based" (i.e. phantasmatic) TV talent show. The unlikely commercial success in 2009 of *Britain's Got Talent* runner-up, Susan Boyle, with its fairy-tale air (she performed "I Dreamed a Dream", from—ironically—a musical based on Victor Hugo's novel of revolutionary sympathies, *Les Misérables*), perfectly mirrored the spectral pantomime of Capital after the twin "deaths" of its epicenter, first time as tragedy, second as (black) farce (Žižek 2009a): at the World Trade Center, 2001, in Wall Street, 2008–9; the "undead" of Capital, staggering grotesquely, robotically, if so far successfully forward in the face of on-rushing catastrophes of ecology, resource depletion, huckster finance and social injustice. The (successful) online campaign to prevent Simon Cowell's 2009 *X-Factor* winner achieving its expected Christmas Number One single spot, through multiple downloads of Rage Against the Machine's 1992 hit "Killing in the Name," marks the limit of resistance at this level of the system: the radical politics of the rap-metal band's record left not a dent in the hegemonic armour, and in any case it was marketed by the same multinational corporation as Cowell's products (Sony). This is not to say that elsewhere, "below" this level, there are not instances of practice figuring the popular in ways possessing genuinely independent, subversive or resistant qualities and impact (for a study of one such strand, see Dale 2011); just that positing a simple alternative—"we" or "they", univocal People or multitudinous popular identities—is plainly inadequate to the demands of this situation.

Number *is* key, however. One or Many—or (after all) Two? It is no coincidence that in much recent writing on "democracy"—that is, on the politics of the popular—what I have called the "structure of exception" is a key trope. Here an almost absent referent of my discussion so far needs to come to the front: the world beyond that of Western popular music and its cultural hinterland—not "world music", a commercial category, but the world as such, or what commonly these days goes under the name of "globalization." The structure of exception has its (Western) roots in, on the one hand, traditions of political philosophy going back, most prominently at least, to the French Revolution (Agamben 2005), on the other hand, in philosophical traditions stemming from Hegelian logic (Žižek 2002). (And the "world" referent of this lineage reveals its historical dimension if we follow Žižek's injunction (2009a, 111–114) to think Hegel and the Haitian revolution together. Haiti was, arguably, the absent referent for Hegel's master-and-slave dialectic.) In both cases, a One (a totality, a sovereignty, a set) is constituted only through the work of boundary-forming exceptions. A One—the People's voice as voice of God, say—is always incipiently a Two (through its formative exclusions); but this "originary two" can itself only be *forced* from the play of infinite multiplicity, that is, it must be *produced* in a specific act or event (Badiou 2007); and this becomes all the clearer in a world that is rapidly "filling up," that is running short of external exceptions:

as exception "rebounds" back inside, so "inside" and "outside" interpenetrate each other as never before, "we" and "they" turning each other inside out in what is truly described as a play of *miscegenation*. If difference is mundane ("infinite alterity is quite simply *what there is*": Badiou 2002, 25), then forcing in any given moment a Deleuzian "event of becoming-people" (Žižek 2009b, 110) is to work towards a conception of fraternity (of a "we") whose "being-together" is not that of a "quasi-military 'I'" but operates through "immanent disparity" or "inseparate articulation," always devolving towards a decisive choice (Badiou 2007, 96–97, 123). The location of the people is to be thought within a structure that is *aporetic* (Spivak 2009); People and people, "we" and "they," are—to adapt Adorno (2002, 244)—"torn halves of an integral freedom, to which, however, they do not add up": a negative dialectic that represents not blockage but the potential always inherent in internal contradiction.

The cultural study of the musical popular, then, is always already immersed in its politics. The best approach to the global dimension will therefore lie not in any (impossible) attempt at a purely cultural survey but in a focus on exemplary fault lines, points of fracture, in the global body politic. Here we might return to the case of the Middle East, mentioned in passing earlier. No fault line vibrates with more pregnant energy than the location that, at the level of geopolitical fracture, constitutes the epicentre of the tensions of this region: Palestine/Israel (even if the great powers persistently struggle to keep it offstage). Two "peoples" contest the same ground. Each stands at a point where the intersecting vectors of nation and diaspora cross. Each, an epitome of exception, in relation both to the other and to wider geocultural formations, twines around and interpenetrates the other, encapsulating the multivalent tensions of home and exile, in a figure that at the same time registers the residues of twentieth-century racisms, totalitarianisms, and imperialisms as well as the absolutely current forcefield structured by the struggle between resource-hungry international capital and dispossessed (that is, in effect, equally stateless) masses. Two recordings cast a brilliant light on this aporia. (I have written on them in more detail elsewhere: see Middleton 2009, 324–325; Middleton 2006, 131–134.)

"Al-Quds," by the Jewish Israeli Gilad Atzmon, featuring Palestinian singer Reem Kelani (*Exile*, Enja TIP-888 844 2, 2003), brings together Jewish tune, Arab melody and lyrics, and hectic post-bop improvising in a lament for (the divided city of) Jerusalem (Al-Quds). The musical transitions and overlays—the fit is uncanny, that is, never quite at home—drawing on the diasporic spirit of both jazz and klezmer, produce an exemplary image of exile as also potential exodus: a departure whose singularity is, because "voided," precisely universalized. "Diva," the 1998 Eurovision Song Contest winner by Jewish transsexual vocalist Dana International (*Diva*, IMP 2048, 1998), presents a multivalent subaltern position (she is of immigrant working-class Yemeni background, the lowest of the Israeli low—except for Arabs—as well as a sexual outlaw) but does so through a certain kind of hyper-technologized, almost cyborgian international pop style and in the context of an instance of precisely that pseudo-democratic cultural process—a sort of "Europe's Got Talent"—which any genuine popular must subvert. Rather than local being universalized, here global is, via the mechanisms of outrageous camp, given a quite singular punch, Dana International's exceptionality undermining Israeli social norms but then, at a higher level, bringing the Jewish exception itself, previously excreted from the body of imperial Europe, right back to Europe's cultural heart.

Žižek (2009b, 4–6) has argued that the Jewish tradition, via the apparently contradictory myths of "cosmopolitanism" and "ghetto," stands for both universality and exception *at the same time*. To a greater or lesser extent, perhaps, this is true of all diasporas, not least the Afro-diasporic traditions that constituted the greatest single influence in the emergence of a world popular music in the twentieth century. Žižek (2009a, 91–94) goes further and suggests that, under the conditions of contemporary capitalism—commodification of the remaining commons, indeed of the very gifts of Being (water and air; memory, thought and subjectivity; human bodies—in fact, the codes of life itself), along with the concentration of power and wealth into fewer and fewer hands, and its corollary, the progressive outsourcing and pauperization of labor at the global level—the tendency is towards a *universalization of exception*; "proletarianization" and "exile" both, from different perspectives, name this state. And, just as Jewish critics of Israel (such as Atzmon and Dana International) become "Jews of the Jews themselves" (Žižek 2009b, 6), so more broadly "we" and "they" produce each other simultaneously, as exclusion is introjected into the social body. This is a condition for any authentic popular today.

In July 2010 a Palestinian inhabitant of Jerusalem was convicted by an Israeli court of "rape by deception," after having consensual sex with an Israeli woman who believed him to be a fellow Jew. The specter of miscegenation is still, it seems, at large. Indeed, as an acute pressure-point in the structure of exception, where the inside-out relations of self and other are inscribed on the body itself—social as well as personal—it can be taken as the very mark of the popular. Whenever the People presents itself as the "voice of God," the miscegenating demiurge will not be far away. The "we" of the people could never attain the purity it wanted. Where, then, is it to be found, how can we locate its voice? Not *there*, is the answer; not where it was, not where it is supposed to be. For Ernst Bloch (2009), the God of Christianity, of a properly atheistic Christianity, could only be one who is absent, who has *absconded*. The voice we must listen for, then, is that of a *populus absconditus*.

FURTHER READING

Adorno, Theodor W. 1991. *The culture industry*. London: Routledge.

Badiou, Alain. 2007. *The century*. Translated by Alberto Toscano. Cambridge: Polity Press.

Bennett, Tony. 1986. The politics of the "popular" and popular culture. Pp. 6–21 in *Popular culture and social relations*. Edited by Tony Bennett, Colin Mercer, and Janet Woollacott. Milton Keynes, U.K.: Open University Press.

Born, Georgina, and David Hesmondhalgh, eds. 2000. *Western music and its others: Difference, representation and appropriation in music*. Berkeley: University of California Press.

Bourdieu, Pierre. 1984. *Distinction: A social critique of the judgement of taste*. Translated by Richard Nice. London: Routledge.

Gilroy, Paul. 1993. *The black Atlantic: Modernity and double consciousness*. London: Verso.

Levine, Lawrence. 1988. *Highbrow/lowbrow: The emergence of cultural hierarchy in America*. New Haven, CT: Yale University Press.

Middleton, Richard. 2006. *Voicing the popular: On the subjects of popular music*. New York: Routledge.

Middleton, Richard. 2009. *Musical belongings: Selected Essays*. Farnham, U.K.: Ashgate.

Mowitt, John. 2002. *Percussion: Drumming, beating, striking*. Durham, NC: Duke University Press.

Stallybrass, Peter, and Allon White. 1986. *The politics and poetics of transgression*. London: Methuen.

Williams, Raymond. 1983. *Keywords: A vocabulary of culture and society*. Rev. ed. London: Fontana.

CHAPTER 25

MUSIC AND THE MARKET
The Economics of Music in the Modern World

DAVE LAING

[W]ho would think seriously of minimising the role of the market? Even in an elementary form, it is the favoured terrain of supply and demand, of that appeal to other people without which there would be no economy in the ordinary sense of the word. . . . The market spells liberation, openness, access to another world. It means coming up for air.

(Fernand Braudel)

This chapter is concerned with the various ways in which the idea of the market can be used to help us understand how music works as a business. It begins with a consideration of markets as actual geographical spaces where goods and services are exchanged, and then discusses some different concepts of what, borrowing from Anderson (1991), I call "imagined markets." Such music markets can involve consumers of musical goods and services, employers of musicians' labor power, and/or businesses that use music. Here, ideas such as market failure, public goods, and intellectual property are introduced. Finally, the chapter briefly deals with new ways in which music is being consumed online and with the limits of the market idea.

THE MARKET AS BASIC PLACE OF EXCHANGE

In his book *The Wheels of Commerce*, the eminent social historian Fernand Braudel reminds us that "exchange is as old as human history" (Braudel 1982, 225). The simplest modes of exchange are those involving no or few intermediaries between producer and consumer, and these are modes where supply and demand for goods or services fluctuate little. Exchange may take a variety of forms including the bartering of goods or services without the intermediation of money, but for some centuries the predominant sites of exchange have been various forms of market. Some musical examples are performances at fairs or street markets ("the elementary form" mentioned by Braudel in the epigraph to this chapter), over many centuries to the present day, in all parts of the world, and the sale there of musical commodities in the form of instruments, cassettes, or CDs.

Popular music has had a presence at markets for centuries. In England in 1595, a writer complained that, at every market, ballad singers were "singing their wares" (Clark 1983, 185), while cassette sellers are found in the markets of most, if not all, African, Asian, and Latin American cities today. In contemporary Africa, Sandaga market in Dakar is a center of legitimate cassette production, and in Kankan (Guinea) cassette stalls are set up near the Grand Marché. Chris Waterman's classic study of jùjú music in Nigeria in the 1980s also discussed the role of markets in the dissemination of recordings (Waterman 1990, 152–153).

As far as music is concerned, the most important role of contemporary street markets is as venues for the sale of pirate discs and tapes. In his study of street markets in Mexico City, John C. Cross points out that such "informal economic activity" is more complex than the standard definition of it as "the pursuit of legal ends with illegal means." Cross says that, while the sale of unauthorized music cassettes "violates a number of laws" (i.e., laws regulating intellectual property) apart from laws concerning selling in the street, "enforcement rarely reaches the retail level . . . [and] . . . vendors selling these articles behave in the same way as those selling legal goods" (Cross 1998, 85). Elsewhere in Latin America, the main street market of Lima has become a target for music industry antipiracy teams. More than two million recordable (CD-R) discs were seized in a raid by over five hundred police officers on three hundred stalls at the El Hueco market in June 2001 (IFPI 2001). Even in Europe, music is sold in street markets from Sarajevo (where the biggest market is a major outlet for pirate CDs) to London, whose large weekend market in Camden Town is famous (or notorious) for the sale of bootleg tapes and CDs of concerts by David Bowie, Bob Dylan, and dozens of other performers.

Diawara (1998) and Bohlman (1988) have stressed the continuing strategic significance of street markets in separate ways. Diawara powerfully evokes and analyzes the antiglobalization role of such markets in West African life: "By producing disorder through pricing, pirating, smuggling and counterfeiting African markets participate in the resistance to multinational control of the national economy and culture" (Diawara 1998, 151). In his description of the "bazaar" in North Africa, Bohlman emphasizes its condition as a space of "cultural simultaneity" where musics of different styles, commodity forms, and technologies interact and overlap. He also points up the historical continuity of such musical melanges: "the cultural simultaneity that obtains . . . is not a recent phenomenon. . . . Marketplaces whether in pre-Islam middle east, mediaeval Europe, or 19th century American Midwest have been a locus for diversity" (Bohlman 1988, 123).

MARKET AS CONCEPT IN CLASSICAL ECONOMICS

In the eighteenth century, Western economic theory elaborated the term *market* into a concept denoting an abstract space where supply and demand meet and find equilibrium through the pricing of commodities or services. When demand exceeds supply, prices rise, and where supply is in excess of demand, prices tend to fall. This theory, in its extreme form, claims that distortion by alien forces such as governments or monopolistic practices compromises the operation of a "free" market in providing equilibrium between supply (the producers) and demand (the consumers). At this point, the "market" becomes an autonomous, almost mystical force—Robert Nelson has written of the "religion of economics" (Nelson 2001)—epitomized in Adam Smith's famous phrase from his *The Wealth of Nations*, "the invisible hand" that leads the merchant "to promote an end that was no part of his intention" (A. Smith [1776] 1910, IV, ii, 9).

In practice, the free market concept developed by Smith and later "neoclassical" economists remained an ideal type rather than a precise description of observable markets. Instead of an equilibrium deriving from the possession by producer and consumer of the same information, disequilibrium and asymmetry beset each specific market. In the case of music markets, disequilibrium is most frequently produced when the greater power of the suppliers (the record companies and retailers) determines the recordings to be made available and the prices to be charged. The monopoly status conferred by copyright ownership plays a role here too. On the demand side, disequilibrium is created when the participants (notably the potential audience) do not act as rational economic beings whose behavior can be reliably influenced by such factors as pricing and publicity.

By the mid twentieth century, the concept of a free market had spilled over from purely economic discourse to become central to much conservative and even social democratic political ideology. It was counterposed to the planned economies of state socialism where the supply of recorded music was controlled by a state monopoly such as Amiga in the German Democratic Republic. Amiga's decision to issue an album was not primarily determined by perceived demand but as "evidence of the official recognition of the artist." Consequently, "[a]s the print run of the record was fixed in advance and second editions rarely appeared, musicians had no (economic) interest in record production, only a chance to gain a reputation" (Maas and Reszel 1998, 269).

If the abstraction of the market in neoclassical orthodoxy remains an ideal type, it nevertheless underlines the fact that in many contemporary economies the face-to-face character of exchange in street markets has generally been supplanted by "imagined markets" where the relationship between producer and consumer is highly mediated. The term *imagined markets* is adapted from Benedict Anderson's description of nation-states as "imagined communities" produced by the action of print media and other forms that connect individuals who can never meet face-to-face (Anderson 1991).

Authors who stress the exceptional character of the culture industries have challenged the idealization and homogenization of the market idea by neoclassical economics. Miège (1989) and Garnham (2000) have commented on the special characteristics of markets for cultural commodities, in particular the unpredictability of consumer demand for such items as songs, books, and films. This unpredictability is a sign that consumer (and often producer) behavior in markets for cultural goods and services frequently deviates from the neoclassical theorists' presentation of these subjects as "homo economicus," concerned only with their own economic welfare. In his important study of large record companies, Negus brings together the motifs of the imagined market and the uncertainty of demand by emphasizing the *construction* of markets and consumers by such companies. He writes that "[m]arkets are not simply out there in the world, forming as members of the public gravitate towards certain recordings and not others. Markets have to be carefully constructed and maintained" (Negus 1999, 32).

Three strategies for the construction of markets where demand can be managed can be identified. First, Miège and Negus (and other authors) emphasize what the latter calls the "portfolio" approach, whereby a large record company will promote a wide range of recordings in the expectation that at least some of them will prove to be successful. According to Miège, in order to reduce the risks of failure, cultural producers such as record companies and film studios bring to the market a "catalog" of a large number of different items in the expectation that profits from the small number of hits will compensate for the losses incurred by unsuccessful titles.

The second strategy is systematically to gather information about consumer preferences and behavior. Here record companies, especially in the United States, are increasingly using the tools and methods of contemporary market research. Negus (1999, 53) describes the Soundata system based on an interview panel of twelve hundred U.S. consumers, and Anand and

Peterson argue that information about the market "is the prime source by which producers in competitive fields make sense of their actions and those of consumers, rivals and suppliers that make up the field" (2000, 271). They point out that while some producers can undertake private research such as public opinion surveys, the provision of a generalized "market information regime" by an independent research firm is generally the most important source of such data. In the music industry, the crucial feature of the regime is of course the chart of weekly or monthly soundcarrier sales or radio airplay.

A third strategy is to influence the various gatekeepers or intermediaries perceived to be influential in consumer decisions. These include broadcasting executives, disc jockeys, and journalists. The methods used have often been controversial and unlawful, as the term *payola* testifies (Segrave 1994; Dannen 1990). Since the early 1990s, a more radical version of such marketing has been targeted at supposed opinion formers or taste makers within the audience itself. This is the use of "street teams" that, according to a record company executive interviewed by Negus, are "going to places where consumers are and hitting them where they live" (Negus 1999, 97).

The only actors with the resources to deploy such strategies consistently in order to limit their exposure to uncertain demand are, of course, large corporations. At the start of the second decade of the twenty-first century, four major companies—EMI, Warner, Sony, and Universal—controlled the global distribution of over 80 percent of (nonpirate) CDs and cassettes. This situation has given rise to numerous claims and complaints that these companies operate a *de facto* cartel that keeps prices high and denies smaller companies the opportunity to compete in the market on equal terms. In the sphere of market regulation, notably in North America and Europe, the oligopolistic tendencies of the record industry have led government agencies to prohibit mergers in the sector, and to outlaw certain marketing practices. Additionally, researchers analyzing the provenance of hit records have argued that the dominance of the major companies inhibits innovation in music markets (Peterson and Berger 1990; Rothenbuhler and Dimmick 1982; Lopes 1992; Christianen 1995).

MUSICAL LABOR MARKETS

In the past, hiring fairs for musicians could be found in specific parts of cities, such as Archer Street in central London. Today the distribution of musical labor is carried out by imagined markets where the "uncertainty" or "unpredictability" that characterizes consumer markets is echoed in the oversupply of musicians and singers for the available work and income opportunities. A study of the British market for classical singers by Towse (1993) found that the market was "distorted" because the supply of labor was far greater than the demand from opera companies, choirs, and so on. According to mainstream economic theory, such a disequilibrium should be corrected by the surplus workers moving to other industries where labor is in short supply. Towse concluded that the singers were motivated more by the aesthetic attraction of music than their economic self-interest.

Discussion of the general market for opera and classical music performances has been dominated by the so-called cost disease first diagnosed in the 1960s by the American economist William Baumol. This "disease" is intended to explain the need for subsidy or sponsorship of arts performances. Baumol asked his readers to

> [c]ompare what has happened to the cost of producing a watch with the cost of a musical performance over the centuries. There has been vast, labour-saving technical progress in watchmaking, which is still continuing. But live violin playing benefits from no labour (or capital)-saving innovations—it is still done the old-fashioned way, *as we want it to be.*
> . . .
> This is another way of saying that cost per attendee or per performance must rise faster than the average price of other things: arts budgets therefore must rise faster than the economy's rate of inflation, which is simply the average increase in the prices of all the economy's outputs.
> (Baumol and Bowen [1966] 1997, 214; my emphasis)

Baumol's theory has become widely accepted among economists of the arts but it is open to some major criticisms. First, it ignores the fact that many sectors of the music business *have* been restructured by "laborsaving technical progress." For example, the introduction of amplification permitted bands to play to larger audiences (and thereby cut the cost per attendee), while innovation in instrument design enabled the size of bands to be reduced as synthesizers and drum machines have replaced performers. Perhaps more crucially, Baumol ignores the role of "technical progress" in recording and broadcasting, two media that have provided many participants in the labor-intensive performance-based sector with additional income.

A second criticism of the Baumol thesis is that it ignores an important source of cost inflation in classical performance: the escalating payments to star conductors and soloists in the contemporary classical music industry. In his analysis of the industry, Norman Lebrecht (1996) shows that a cartel of agents and administrators has increased the fees of star musicians at a rate far greater than any increase in the salaries of orchestral musicians and opera choruses. Lebrecht's data emphasize the degree to which the contemporary classical music market is characterized by a complex mixed economy of public subsidy and oligopolistic commercialism.

MUSIC AND MARKET FAILURE

Economists use the concept of "market failure" to describe situations where suppliers are unable or unwilling to provide certain commodities or services for which there is a demand. Examples of remedies for market failure in the music industry include subsidies for performances through state funding or private sponsorship to remedy the cost disease in order to make tickets affordable, and the production and distribution of low-priced soundcarriers when the previously available copies are priced too highly for some consumers. A graphic example is the success of the Naxos record company, which since its formation in 1987 has become a leading firm in classical music by selling newly made recordings at about one-third of the price charged for new releases by other labels.

Another remedy for market failure is the sale of pirate or unauthorized copies of recordings, notably in developing countries where "legitimate" copies of certain music on CDs or cassettes are unaffordable for most of the population or are simply unavailable because no company holds the rights in a particular country. This situation is graphically portrayed in Waterman's study of jùjú music in Ibadan, Nigeria. Waterman reproduces newspaper reports of the clash between bandleaders and cassette sellers over the propriety of this mode of exchange. While a musician complains that piracy robs musicians of income, a market trader is quoted as saying that the common people cannot afford to buy the vinyl discs made by the bandleaders and their record companies:

> Fuji musician Ayinde Barrister has these [sic] to say: "The record pirates make all the money leaving little for us and nothing for the government. It is ridiculous that in a country of over 80 million people, a successful musician cannot boast that his record would sell over one million."
> Mr. Lanre Lawal . . . cassette seller at Ogunpa says: "music should not be for only the rich men alone, poor people should also enjoy good music. . . . We offer recording services for people who cannot afford to buy records and this, to my mind, is a kind of promotion for the musicians themselves."
> (Waterman 1990, 152–153)

Despite the authoritarian rigidity ascribed to state socialist "unfree" markets, they were as much subject to the condition of market failure as were free markets. In the words of Verdery, "the socialist economy needed the black market to fulfil its shortcomings" (1991, 423) and "audiences and performers experimented in the interstices of official culture" (Silverman 1996, 239). Unofficial performances and cassette recordings constituted a "second market" for popular music throughout the socialist bloc, providing audiences with music excluded from the official repertoire, both locally created and foreign. The extent to which the second market was tolerated by the official institutions varied considerably according to the overall political and economic stresses and policies of each country at any particular time. In the Bulgarian case, the growth of the second market for music was associated with the relaxation of state controls on the "petty form of private enterprise" in rural areas, and farmers benefiting from such enterprise could afford to pay for the "wedding music" of such performers as the clarinettist Ivo Papazov (Rice 1996, 182–184).

PUBLIC GOODS AND COPYRIGHT

A public good is defined by economists as one whose consumption by an individual does not preclude its consumption by others. While a loaf of bread is a private good (if I consume it, you are prevented from doing so), a free-to-air radio or television broadcast has the status of a public good. The public good idea has been applied to cultural production in contrasting ways by Baumol and Garnham.

In a somewhat tortuous justification of state funding for the high arts, the former seeks to define performances of drama, opera, and classical music as public goods insofar as their existence has intrinsic value for society in general in addition to their direct benefit for the small minority that actually attends such performances. He writes that "Government must provide funds only where the market has no way to charge for all the benefits offered by an activity" (Baumol and Bowen 1997, 260). The difficulty with this formulation is that it provides no systematic way to determine these "benefits," which are mostly potential in the sense that they remain available to a larger audience should that audience one day materialize. Garnham emphasizes a different aspect by linking the concept of a "public good" to a discussion of the "free rider." He begins by asserting that, in dealing with "media or information," "the market model of provision has serious problems" (Garnham 2000, 57). The most fundamental of these is the lack of scarcity of cultural products and services (market economics holds that the price of a commodity is determined by its availability: a scarce "out of season" fruit will cost more than a fruit plentifully available). But when a free-to-air broadcast is available to all or a digitized recording can be easily copied or cloned, there is no automatic or internalized pricing mechanism. The "free rider" is the consumer (or competing producer), who thereby can acquire the commodity free of cost. Garnham goes on to list three ways in which the market is adapted to "solve" this problem and to ensure that the producer recovers the cost of production. One (adopted by commercial broadcasters) is through selling audiences to advertisers; another is to erect box-office barriers such as pay-per-view television broadcasts; the third, and the most significant for music economics, is through the granting by governments of a legal right to intellectual property, notably the copyright. This last is in many cases the overdetermining factor in music market structures, introducing "a monopoly and the producers' right to a monopoly rent" (p. 57).

Rental is an idea familiar from markets for housing and other expensive goods such as video recorders or automobiles. Its application to music is less obvious but is based on the legal status of a song or recording as the inalienable property of an individual or company. A useful economist's explanation of the application of "rent" to the music business can be found in Andersen and James (2000). As intellectual property, the song or recording cannot pass wholly into the ownership of another (although the physical object embodying it can), and any subsequent user of the music is liable in law to pay a "rent" in the form of a royalty until the duration of its property status has expired. Currently the expiration date for compositions is seventy years following the death of the author, and for recordings is at least fifty years after a track's first release. A royalty is the customary form of payment in business-to-business markets, such as those linking recording artist and record company or broadcaster and composer. The latter market involves an important intermediary, the authors' collection society. Examples are the Performing Right Society in Britain or the competing groups ASCAP and BMI in the United States.

The "free rider" problem reached crisis point with the advent of the Internet and the most prevalent form of online music exchange, the numerous P2P (peer-to-peer) file-sharing networks whose best-known example is Napster. Within such networks, any music tracks stored on the computer of any participant can be copied by any other participant and held on the latter's computer (see Alderman 2001). The music industry considered such behavior to be both unethical and illegal since no money is paid to copyright owners when such copies are made. In legal terms, the practice of P2P is a version of "private copying," a term invented to describe the use of audiotape cassettes by consumers to make copies of recordings, a practice that became widespread in the 1980s. At that time, a legal remedy was found by legislators in the "blank tape levy," a fee paid by manufacturers of tapes that was used to pay "compensation" to composers and record companies. This solution is not possible in the case of P2P since it involves no tangible copying product apart from the computer itself.

There is, however, another perspective from which to view the practice of P2P—the notion of the "gift economy." This concept was introduced into

Western thought by the anthropologist Marcel Mauss, whose book *The Gift* (1954) was a study of the economics of gift-giving in precapitalist societies. This alternative economy has drawn much interest from philosophers and political scientists in recent years. For some of these, the gift economy is important for its diametrical opposition to the logic of the conventional economy of exchange. In the words of Derrida, "for there to be a gift there must be no reciprocity, return, exchange, countergift or debt" (Derrida 1992, 12). The significance for the music market of this resistance to the logic of exchange among music consumers is not yet clear, especially after the failure of the record companies' attempt to prevent file-sharing by the deployment of digital rights management (DRM) technology. For the present, P2P activity coexists on the Internet with the efforts of the music industry to establish an exchange economy there, notably through the sales of MP3 files from Apple's iTunes online stores. Some experts believe that coexistence is a form of symbiosis: "the gift economy and the commercial sector can only expand through mutual collaboration within cyberspace" (Barbrook 1998). One practical application of this approach is the Creative Commons license, whereby a copyright owner can relinquish some of her rights to enable works to be used creatively by others (see Lessig 2008).

LIMITS OF THE MARKET

This chapter has sought to show the usefulness of the idea of the market in understanding music as a business. But this process has its limits, which are twofold.

First, even in an era whose dominant economic mode is capitalist globalization, many musical activities have no connection, or only a tenuous connection, to markets. These include religious practices, military bands, ceremonial music, work songs, and music for political causes. Bohlman notes of such music making that music "articulates the organisation of society" through its "role in ritual" and through "transforming labour into a communal activity" (1988, 1). Second, there is much evidence to show that there is an important aspect of the music economy that is surplus to, or exterior to, the market relation. For example, considering the supply of music, Toynbee discusses "proto-markets" that "bring together performer and audience in arenas which are not fully commodified. Examples include local rock scenes, dance music networks or jazz performance by players taking time out from regular session work" (Toynbee 2000, 27). And echoing Towse's comments on classical singers, he concludes that, in such contexts, "the level of activity cannot be explained by economic factors alone" since the financial rewards are minimal or nonexistent.

From the aspect of consumption, the previously noted features of unpredictability and irrationality are symptoms of what Jacques Attali has called "the extra-market production of demand" (Attali 1985, 42). They also underlie Toynbee's proposition that "in order for culture to be sold it must be shown to be (partially) external to the economic system" (Toynbee 2000, 3). In other words, market forces can never be autonomous, only "themselves." They are always in flux, vulnerable to the impact of an aesthetico-musical unconscious that overflows the economic and problematizes exchange relations.

FURTHER READING

Baumol, William J., and William G. Bowen. [1966] 1997. On the rationale of public support. Pp. 243–260 in *Baumol's cost disease: The arts and other victims*. Edited by Ruth Towse. Cheltenham, U.K.: Edward Elgar.

Garnham, Nicholas. 2000. *Emancipation, the media and modernity: Arguments about the media and social theory*. New York: Oxford University Press.

Laing, Dave. 1993. The international copyright system. Pp. 25–36 in *Music and copyright*. Edited by Simon Frith. Edinburgh: Edinburgh University Press.

Laing, Dave. 2002. Copyright as a component of the music industry. Pp. 171–194 in *The business of music*. Edited by Michael Talbot. Liverpool: Liverpool University Press.

Lebrecht, Norman. 1996. *When the music stops . . . Managers, maestros and corporate murder of classical music*. London: Simon and Schuster.

Manuel, Peter. 1993. *Cassette culture: Popular music and technology in North India*. Chicago: University of Chicago Press.

Miège, Bernard. 1989. *The capitalization of cultural production*. New York: International General.

Negus, Keith. 1999. *Music genres and corporate cultures*. London: Routledge.

Peterson, Richard, and David Berger. [1975] 1990. Cycles in symbol production: The case of popular music. Pp. 140–159 in *On record: Rock, pop and the written word*. Edited by Simon Frith and Andrew Goodwin. London: Routledge.

Stamm, Brad K. 2000. *Music industry economics: A global demand model for prerecorded music*. New York: Edwin Mellen Press.

Wallis, Roger, and Krister Malm. 1984. *Big sounds from small peoples: The music industry in small countries*. London: Constable.

CHAPTER 26

MUSIC, SOUND, AND RELIGION

JEFFERS ENGELHARDT

I take as my point of departure here a set of commonplace observations: The pervasive, profound relation between the sonic and the sacred is an essential aspect of musical practice, thought, and discourse and an enduring theme in music scholarship. Some of the first musicologies are sonic theologies—the Rig Veda, the Gītassara Sutta, the Psalms of David, the Epistles of Paul, the Surah 96 "al-'Alaq." Long before the disciplining of music scholarship, texts such as these inspired the musicological thinking of figures like Purandara Dasa, Zhuhong, Maimonides, Augustine, and al-Ghazālī as Dharmic and Abrahamic traditions transformed into world religions. Within world religions, the applied musicologies of reform and renewal movements like Sufism, bhakti, the Second Vatican Council, or Hasidism have engaged debates about the propriety of sonic expression and aural experience to clarify doctrine, meet the spiritual and social needs of specific communities, and situate the sacred in relation to a particular soundscape. And through their early modern encounters with non-Europeans, missionaries, mercantilists, colonists, and thinkers like Jean de Léry (Harrison 1973) and Bernard Picart (Hunt et al. 2010) documented a developing sense of a universal relation between music, sound, and religion—a relation intensified through recognition, fascination, violence, ethnocentrism, and civilizational stereotype. In these ways, religion has become such an essential part of music scholarship that to critically rethink its naturalness might seem unnatural.

MUSIC AND RELIGION AS CATEGORIES

This universality and naturalness is emblematic of the emergence of religion as a *sui generis*, secular, Enlightenment category (Asad 1993; Masuzawa 2005; Taylor 2007)—what Derrida famously terms the "globalatinization" (*mondialatinisation*) of religion (2001, 50). Religion becomes the same thing everywhere, something people have that is distinct from other spheres of experience, action, and belief and, like culture, comparable across time and distances. Similarly, the kinds and qualities of sound that are recognized, objectified, and disciplined as music (Bohlman 1999, 25–26) establish music as a delimited, universal category of human expressive, affective, and sensory experience. Given the pervasiveness of these epistemological categories, the coupling of music and religion in music scholarship seems intuitive and natural when we speak of and represent Jewish music, music and Islam, Christian musical repertoires, Buddhist musical traditions, or Vedic music theory, for instance.

In these cases, music is something known that gives voice to, mediates, and is fundamentally shaped by what is known as religion. Here, religion is circumscribed as doctrine, text, ritual, sincere belief, power, and transcendence, and music is the sound, style, and performance that religion legitimates. The secular concept of religion makes Buddhism and Islam, Hinduism and Judaism, Christianity and Sikhism discrete, comparable domains of spiritual experience, ethical and moral action, and human being that subjects inhabit. And when musics are linked to religions, they too become comparable and metaconceptually the same; the -isms of world religions that suggest some kind of coherence, orthodoxy, and equivalence also suggest that the musics of those religions are alike in terms of style and efficacy.

For anyone attuned to the varieties of religious modernity and secularity that take shape through different understandings of personhood, polity, and society, this conventional way of thinking music and religion is unsatisfying, however. What sense to make of the substantial sonic and theological disjunctures between the Christian musics of Pentecostal Romani in Hungary (Lange 2003), House of God sacred steel musicians in the United States (Stone 2010), women in the Church of the Nazarites (*ibandla lamaNazaretha*) in South Africa (Muller 2000), popular Catholic ensembles in Brazil (Reily 2002), Tanzanian *kwayas* (Barz 2003), and Trinidadian Full Gospel musicians (Rommen 2007)? What sense to make of the popular, marketable, public religiosity of musicians like Matisyahu, Arvo Pärt, Aretha Franklin, Mos Def, or Lupe Fiasco? What sense to make of spiritualized, de-ideologized religious musics at *kīrtan* sessions in Moscow, Mexico City, and Melbourne or at the Fes Festival of World Sacred Music (Kapchan 2008)? What sense to make of the folklorization of religious musics through tourist-oriented performance (Hagedorn 2001)? What sense to make of religious performance that precedes and enables belief (Engelhardt 2009) or models "real" trance and spiritual ecstasy (Becker 2004; Jankowsky 2007; Kapchan 2007)? And what sense to make of the renunciation or coercive, violent proscription of music in the name of religion?

Perfect sense, I would say, but only when concepts of music and religion are continually and critically examined and their taken-for-grantedness suspended. As spiritual life, ethical and moral action, theology, and the sonic converge in the secular modern, music makes religion, and vice versa. Engaging this, however, means thinking, listening, and writing in terms of the *sui generis*, secular, Enlightenment categories of religion and music— acts that limit perforce the kinds of knowledge scholars can produce.

SECULAR EPISTEMOLOGIES AND MUSIC SCHOLARSHIP

Ethnomusicologists and historians of music are good at representing and interpreting the musical texts that establish religious repertoires, the ways in which religious musics enable ritual and devotion, the ways in which the religious and the secular interact sonically, the details of doctrine and tradition that shape religious musics, the ideologies and aesthetic values of religious sounds, and the far-reaching effects of religious performance. We are good at this because these kinds of representation and interpretation emerge quite easily from the secular concepts of music and religion that help establish our disciplinary commitments; we are able to stop short of invoking faith and the supernatural. Both ethnography and historiography appeal to Enlightenment reason, the hermeneutics of suspicion, verifiability, critical reflexivity, and the nonabsolute, nontranscendental worldliness of secular knowledge (Said 1983), which is what locates ethnomusicology and historical musicology in the discourses of the social sciences and humanities as opposed to religious discourses. As secular epistemological categories, music and religion are about humanness and humanism (even, and especially, as that assertion might be critiqued in the language of the social sciences and humanities). Perhaps nothing gets at the secular epistemology of music and religion better than John Blacking's rightly famous definition of music— religious musics included—as "humanly organized sound" ([1973] 1995).

Yet the effects and affects of what can be called religious musics may arise precisely because music is not humanly organized sound. Rather, the musicking body and subject may be a sonic medium for divine revelation, spiritual presence, and cosmic union, reframing (or effacing) the role of human agency in the efficacies of religious musics (Friedson 2009, 9). Here we reach an epistemological limit established by secular concepts of music and religion because we verge on matters of faith, the veracity of experience, the possibility of ritual failure as nonparadoxical, and the reality of revelation and presence. When "faith may be the ultimate touchstone" (Becker 2004, 34) for the kinds of questions scholars endeavor to address about music and religion, the answers that come may well be beyond the privileged knowledge of secular reason, and may therefore not count as knowledge at all. Or by speaking in the language of secular reason and stopping short of invoking faith and the supernatural, scholars may considerably limit the kinds of representations and interpretations they are able to produce.

This is the epistemological divide across which the study of religious musics must continually operate and translate. On one side of this divide is the commitment of secular critique to continually reveal the worldliness of religious musics—their contingency on forms of power, their stylistic affinities to nonreligious sounds, their particular historicity, and their mythic origins, for instance. In its strongest terms, secular critique concerns the human creation of God and the place of religious musics therein. From this position, scholarly discourse places implicit scare quotes around its representations and interpretations of religious musics' efficacies and truths: It is the "voice of a deity," not the voice of a deity, "sacred tradition," not sacred tradition, "divine silence," not divine silence, "authentic," not authentic. The knowledge produced in critical secular ethnography and historiography is of the worldliness of religious musics' transcendence.

On the other side of this epistemological divide is the position of the believer, the convert, or the practitioner. This is a kind of knowing that comes about by being present to the truth, mystery, or utility of transcendence in religious musics, and thereby relativizing the commitments of secular critique as anthropocentric. Like the native ethnographer or the performer who deeply identifies with a style or genre, the religious subject for whom music is efficacious and true can produce knowledge of consciousness and experience precisely because of the selfness that makes articulating that efficacy and truth a challenge. In its strongest terms, the knowledge of faith and experience is the provocation of no scare quotes: It is the voice of a deity, sacred tradition, divine silence, authentic. Period. This is the transcendence of religious musics' worldliness.

In reality, scholars continually mediate this epistemological divide in their production of knowledge. Many, myself included, work with the language and paradigms of secular critique while remaining deeply empathetic to the truth claims and lived faith of those who practice and believe in ways different than our own, and mindful of the epistemological limits of our work for those same reasons (Engelhardt 2009, 51–52). This is not unlike the relationship of the ethnographer or historian to the category of culture writ large. Many others are active participants in or become initiated into the religious traditions in which they work (see, for instance, Bergeron 1998, xi;

Butler 2000, 38–40; Hagedorn 2001, 5; Summit 2000). The dynamics here are of a different sort, marked by scholars' self-distancing from communities, practices, and doctrines and empathetic engagement with the language and paradigms of secular critique in order to address broad, plural audiences by drawing on the knowledge of faith and experience. And beyond the North American and European scholarly traditions I have in mind here, this kind of mediation takes shape in numerous other ways.

MEDIATING ORTHODOXIES AND SECULAR NORMS

In this part of the chapter, I note some ways this mediation takes shape in the study of music, sound, and religion as orthodoxies encounter secular norms, and vice versa. At the heart of this mediation is ontological difference—the fact that a sound that might be perceived and thought of as music is decidedly not music in a secular, Enlightenment sense, or that the power of religious performance derives from the metaphysics of sound rather than from its sonic qualities. This is the difference between *qirā'ah* and *mūsīqā*, *fanbai* and *yinyue*, chanting and singing, and this difference is one of the enduring epistemological concerns and ethnographic fascinations of music scholarship. The question of whether ontology is "just another word for culture" (Rollason 2008) is transposed into religious practice, experience, and doctrine, bringing matters of subjectivity, materiality, ideology, and alterity to bear on the provocative question of sounds being sacred *per se*.

In Orthodox Christianity, for instance, the human voice is the privileged sound of worship because of its capacity to pray and its perfection as a creation of God. But many Orthodox Christians would hold that the voice of worship is ontically grounded where the aural and the spiritual converge in a gendered subject disciplined by fasting and prayer. The religious metaphysics of the voice, in this case, are directly linked to the spiritual condition of the body and soul, and may not register in the realm of the aural. More generally, when anxieties and debates arise over the performances of professional musicians in any number of religious traditions, ontological difference is articulated in terms of how sincerity and purity matter in religious practice. Despite the exemplary qualities of their performances, professionals may not be religious subjects who can perform authentically. The concern is that their intentions, bodies, and spirits are not disciplined by and reproductive of the religious ideology of a community and that their presence is predicated on monetary payment.

Ontological difference articulates just as forcefully when the opposite is true—when the power of religious performance is not contingent upon the sincerity and purity of performers as religious subjects. In cases where the performance of religious repertoires and sacred sounds precedes belief or is potentially efficacious in any context, it is the ontological strength of those sounds that unsettles and relativizes the secular norms of modern scholarship, since religion is not something private, but something people might become vulnerable to. Similarly, in contexts of public performance where those who listen have different religious and nonreligious dispositions, listeners' pleasure, affection, or pious engagement might be taken as responses that reproduce religious meanings and subjectivities, when, in fact, they mark an ontological distinction between the religious and the spiritual.

The mediation of ontological difference happens in numerous other ways as well. Within a normative secular modernity, the immediacy of revealed sounds—the Qur'an, the *śruti* texts of the Vedas, the songs of shamanic healers—establishes forms of religious subjectivity and concepts of individual agency that chafe against the figure of the autonomous moral subject of a liberal democratic order, thereby invoking competing discourses of blasphemy and freedom as these sounds circulate within secular publics (Mahmood 2009). Immediacy also matters when hearing and listening to the voice and its sacred utterances, which are forms of touching, require a degree of proximity and presence. In these cases, amplification, broadcasting, and recording are mediations that ontologically transform the voice in ways that undermine religious doctrine and ritual efficacy.

Mediation and immediacy bear on the materiality of sound and religious discourses about its sources. Musical instruments are proscribed in many Christian denominations, for instance, because only the voice is mentioned in the New Testament as being apt for worship—organs, drums, and guitars cannot be baptized. In Jewish practice, the Talmud lays out discrete guidelines regarding the kind of animal horn that can be used to make a shofar and the kinds of repairs that can be made without altering its sacred ontology, ensuring that the mitzvah of hearing the shofar is fulfilled. And in Dharmic traditions, there is a wealth of interpretive tropes attending to the conch shell, its physical qualities, and the auspiciousness and spiritual power of its sound. In each of these cases, material ontologies are the bases of sonic ontologies, which are recognized and reproduced in religious practice.

These understandings of mediation and materiality take shape in relation to religious technologies and media and the forms of mediation and materiality attending to them. This includes traditional forms of notation and circulation and conventional globalized electronic media (Frishkopf 2009; Hirschkind and Larkin 2008; Oosterbaan 2008) as well as *salat* apps for mobile media devices, digitized manuscripts and recordings, remote ritual participation using Skype, other VoIP services and virtual studio technologies, electronic *śruti* boxes, online instruction in religious performance, or emergent broadcasting networks (Lee 1999). Whether old or new, technologies elicit responses from religious subjects and institutions and shape experiences and practices. They may enable fuller realizations of religious doctrine, transform modes of pious listening and techniques of sensory self-fashioning (Greene 1999; Hirschkind 2006; Schulz 2010), intensify discourses of religious power through repetition, standardization, and schizophonia, and require clarification or alteration of understandings of how embodied performance, authorized voices, and specialist practitioners function in the poetics of religion. In each case, mediations and materialities index the historical specificity and worldliness of religious musics and sounds.

Markets are another productive field through which to critically examine the mediation of religion as tradition and ideology. Following the dissolution of the Soviet Union, for instance, the marketplace metaphor was a means of conceptualizing the ways religious discourses and sounds took root and took on new meanings. Throughout Eurasia, sounds from "the West" and sounds from the past presented new possibilities for religious practice and identification in a time of profound social dislocation and religious renewal. Following the marketplace metaphor, these possibilities were to be realized through choice and consumption—hallmarks of the personal freedom enshrined in the secular liberal order that was the goal of many post-Soviet transitions. When ideas about individual autonomy resonate with religious ethics and theology, markets can become fields in which religious forms and spiritual power are authorized or produced through acts of consumption. Record sales can embody consensus about religious truth, and exchange can become part of religious practice, in other words.

Markets are also indices of charisma, divine favor, and spiritual flourishing. Pentecostal preachers I have done fieldwork with in Estonia and Kenya invest significant resources into acquiring high-quality equipment, nurturing contacts with studio owners and music distributors, and producing and promoting cassettes and VCDs of their music. Recordings are media of their religious charisma, and responses to their voices, styles, and messages recognize the spiritual power they mediate. For these preachers and their congregants, the market is a field for evangelism and gauging the spiritual needs of listeners as prospective congregants. Market success becomes a sign of God's presence and blessing in the lives they live.

As indices of charisma, divine favor, and spiritual flourishing, markets may dramatically impact established religious orders and institutions. The voices and practices that circulate in markets create religious networks and communities that obscure conventional boundaries between religious traditions, laypeople and authorities, or between private religion and the supposed secularity of markets. Furthermore, markets may amplify the charisma of star performers and the significance of sacred places, reinvesting singers and shrines, saints and pilgrimages, styles and repertoires with the accord of market recognition (Chen 2005; Kapchan 2007; Qureshi [1986] 1995). This accord emerges from the forms of competition that markets organize (freedom in choice and novelty, freedom in orthodoxy and tradition), which are symbolized in competitive religious performances like Qur'anic recitation competitions.

For scholars of music and religion, markets are essential fields for understanding the dynamics of religion and its social surround. Markets can afford performers, practitioners, and listeners a means of establishing religious meanings in the world as they circulate sacred sounds in public spaces, but their worldliness might also impinge upon the efficacy and purity of those sacred sounds as they are decoupled from sites of religious power. My point is that markets mediate these extremes through their different forms of secularity. Believers make music for and consume music with their co-religionists, but not only, since engagement with religious sound is predicated on forms of exchange and labor rather than on the sincerity or expediency of belief, once again invoking ontological difference. In this way, markets make music and religion valuable and exchangeable across multiple differences, thereby making the conditions for a secular epistemology of music and religion.

My final point about mediating orthodoxies and secular norms in music scholarship concerns the complicated concepts of hybridity and syncretism. Hybridity and syncretism are everywhere in the scholarly discourse of music and religion, perhaps most notably in thinking about Santería, Candomblé, Vodun, and other Afro-Atlantic Orisha worship practices and the globalization of Pentecostal and Catholic Christianities. However, these interpretive tropes rely upon essentialized, secular concepts of religion and music antecedent to the novel forms of practice they inspire. This privileging of religious origins risks reproducing the dynamics of colonial domination, missionization, and global power that scholars have long been committed to critically rethinking (Engelhardt 2006). Hybridity and syncretism are always relative, always for someone, in other words, and the orthodoxies, centers of religious power, and marginal, derivative practices that these concepts naturalize may create more problems than they solve. The banality of hybridity and syncretism in musics and religions shifts scholarly attention to religious performance as a form of consciousness and efficacy that is always integral and historically specific.

CONCLUSION

I have meditated here on the critical urgency of thinking about the secularity of music and religion when we think about music and religion. Far from questioning the essential place of religion in musical thought and discourse or writing off the universal associations of music, sound, and religion, this is meant to clarify what we talk about and know through these concepts. Scholars often turn to debates about reform, fundamentalism, and innovation in religious performance and aural piety, for instance, because these debates clearly bear on how people inhabit the world musically as religious subjects, act ethically and morally through sound, or invoke religion and style out of expediency. On the other side of these debates, however, are embodied experiences of sacred sound and the consciousness of listening, practicing subjects that are incompletely addressed through the bounded, secular categories of music and religion. This is the alterity that, like the concept of culture, establishes the disciplinary and epistemological boundaries within which music scholarship takes place. Short of imagining nonsecular ways of knowing that are not reducible to belief and faith, the critical imperative is to listen for voices across the differences that music, sound, and religion bring into being within secular modernities.

FURTHER READING

Asad, Talal. 1993. *Genealogies of religion: Discipline and reasons of power in Christianity and Islam.* Baltimore: Johns Hopkins University Press.

Asad, Talal. 2003. *Formations of the secular: Christianity, Islam, modernity.* Palo Alto: Stanford University Press.

Bakhle, Janaki. 2008. Music as the sound of the secular. *Comparative Studies in Society and History* 50(1): 256–284.

Becker, Judith. 2004. *Deep listeners: Music, emotion, and trancing.* Bloomington: Indiana University Press.

Bohlman, Philip V., Edith Blumhofer, and Maria Chow, eds. 2006. *Music in American religious experience.* New York: Oxford University Press.

Csordas, Thomas J., ed. 2009. *Transnational transcendence: Essays on religion and globalization.* Berkeley: University of California Press.

Hirschkind, Charles. 2006. *The ethical soundscape: Cassette sermons and Islamic counterpublics.* New York: Columbia University Press.

Mahmood, Saba. 2005. *Politics of piety: The Islamic revival and the feminist subject.* Princeton: Princeton University Press.

Sullivan, Lawrence, ed. 1997. *Enchanting powers: Music in the world's religions.* Cambridge, MA: Harvard University Press.

Taylor, Charles. 2007. *A secular age.* Cambridge, MA: Belknap Press of Harvard University Press.

CHAPTER 27

MUSIC, RACE, AND THE FIELDS OF PUBLIC CULTURE

RONALD RADANO

The question of race abounds in contemporary cultural studies of music. What was merely a faint blip on the screen only a decade or so ago has now become an abiding concern for scholars across the musicologies, offering collectively a sound rejection of facile claims that we have entered a post-racial era. The interest in race has increased, in large part, owing to the successes of African-American studies, whose commitment to the matter of institutional racism and music's role in its resistance has historically informed the intellectual conversation. Analyses of race have also grown influential as a result of the popularity of British cultural studies, which, particularly through the work of Paul Gilroy, has helped to illuminate music's historical affiliations with the modern formation of blackness. Gilroy's foundational work, *The Black Atlantic: Modernity and Double Consciousness* (1993), for example, has done more than perhaps any other single monograph to elevate the significance of race in postcolonial analysis, a position that he puts forward through the primary vehicle of U.S. black music. In the wake of these central influences, matters of the racial have assumed an increasingly conspicuous place in studies of music culture, warranting publication of major edited volumes dedicated or attentive to racial subjects (Born and Hesmondhalgh 2000; Brown 2007; Radano and Bohlman 2000). While much of the most recent scholarship still gives primary emphasis to U.S. and transatlantic black musics, scholars from a variety of disciplines have begun to look beyond the United States in order to explore how race identifies a concern of broad consequence in the formation of global history and culture. Studies range from the effects of race in the shaping of national identities (Garrett 2008; Olaniyan 2004; Seigel 2009) to the making of musical localities (Jones 2001; Meinjtes 2003; Sharma 2010); from the coalescence of the racial and the musical within the institutional apparatuses of the state (Baker 2011; Guilbault 2007; Wade 2000) to the musical constitution of racial subjects (Bohlman 2008; Kun 2005; Miller 2010); and from the politics of musical representation (Agawu 2003; Bloechl 2008; Moreno 2004; Tomlinson 2007) to the position of race in the critical appraisal of European musicology (Cook 2007; Potter 1998; Rehding 2000). One senses overall in the musicologies an increasing openness about matters racial, coaxed, in large part, by the scholastic leadership of critics working outside the discipline.

If race has earned a more visible place in the mainstream of musical thought, however, it has yet to be acknowledged as a principal, structuring force in the history of musical production and reception. Despite the shifts outlined above, the subject of race represents in music studies but one of a multitude of possible topics of research, a subject more or less equivalent to any number of genre studies or analytical approaches. If, moreover, race is now recognized as a legitimate concern in musicological inquiry, it is still commonly regarded as a matter exterior to music as such, an issue primarily for the politically motivated and politically minded—those "radical" critics of noncanonical musics. And yet there is nothing inherently radical about the study of music and race. On the contrary, it seems rightly considered as a point of departure for any musicological enterprise attentive to the broad, difficult matters of music as a constitutive force in the production of modern cultures. Race is critical to the cultural study of music for the simple reason that, since at least the mid-nineteenth century, the musical and the racial have been inextricably linked in the popular imagination, and that linkage, deeply connected as it is to economic interpretations of the racialized body, has carried forward into the present day. For reasons that have everything to do with race, "the racial" remains largely relegated to the study of black and ethnic musics, even as we can so readily see and hear how race is always among us. Despite the ever-widening recognition of race as an ideological formation not limited to the domain of African America, the lion's share of musicological scholarship continues to perpetuate the faulty notion that some musics are more racial than others. How might music scholars and cultural critics seek to broaden comprehension of the complex relations of the racial and musical? How do we demonstrate the critical place of race in music studies? Simply put, why does race matter?

One could imagine countless responses to these rhetorical challenges, from a call for continuing studies of various historical and ethnographic sites to a vast rethinking of the "history of Western music," and, indeed, of the place of European art music across the legacies of empire. (How, for example, might a sensitivity to race drive an interpretation of Beethoven's status in the history of popular meaning and taste?) My concern in this brief chapter, however, focuses on a single issue, namely, race as an idea informing the broad contexts of public culture, representing what is perhaps the primary, ideological structuration determining musical significance in the global metropolitan. At the center of this analysis is the legacy of African-American music, which, through a rather bizarre set of historical circumstances, becomes, by the late nineteenth century, the fundamental "race music" of the U.S., Europe, and beyond. U.S. black music's centrality in the formation of popular style is widely acknowledged, and the copious range of studies attesting to its power across various genres, from jazz to blues to funk to hip-hop, has certified its dominant position in the canons of modern music. But explanations of the nature of that power, together with its role in the formation of public imaginations of racial and national subjectivity, remain few and far between. When critics do seek to examine black music's value, they typically depend upon predictable claims of its inherent artistic superiority and moral authority, or assert that these qualities are attributable to a precolonial or pre-capitalist past. While such notions are most certainly important to the ideological formation of black music, they do not in themselves explain the source of its power. They are symptoms rather than causes.

In order to comprehend the value ascribed to black music, then, we need to step away from literal concerns with music as such and acquire some distance from the prevailing voluntarism that orients black music studies. This, ironically, will allow us to focus more deliberately on U.S. black music's place within the circuits of public culture and its status as a key formation in the modern production of race. I want to suggest that the cultural value of U.S. black music rests fundamentally on its materialization of race in the modern, giving audible form to new categories of racial subjectivity and group identification. More specifically, black music has acquired global status and appeal as a result of its unique articulation of a critical antinomy in U.S. history, one resonant with the double-sided sense of liberation and social rationalization characterizing the modern condition (e.g., Durkheim's functionalism, Weber's "Protestant Ethic"). At the heart of this antinomy is the contradiction between persons and things, between free-willed human sentience and the historical background of slavery that established U.S. black music as a key measure in the constitution of racial categories. A public conception of "black music" appears at the very moment when antebellum, southern whites first began to recognize a certain musicality in what was previously deemed bestial noise, to hear qualities signifying human experience in the lone, true possession of possessed slaves (Radano 2010). Significantly, the musical possessions of slaves remained only partially obtainable by whites even though they could otherwise claim ownership of the bodies of the slaves themselves. For in music, slaves had discovered a generative basis of culture whose life-affirming power stood repeatedly in contradiction to the life-denying assertion that blacks were nothing more than property. Black music, that lone possession of an economic property named "slave," becomes the basis of an other humanity, representing a cultural form constituted within the very socio-economic frames that had denied slaves the status of human.

U.S. black music emerged as a public form out of this contradiction. The perpetuation of the blackness of black music would ironically grant to African Americans a form of cultural ownership whose value linked directly to the collective memory of the music's status as the original possession of U.S. slaves. Black music identified the exception to white, southern claims upon property-as-slaves, a critical challenge that would prove to be a key, orienting force in the performative constitution of African-American culture. Black music arose as an economically based racial form that ultimately revealed a tear in the logic of capital, representing a supra-economic interruption of the processes of commodification. In black music, a worldly, listening public could literally hear a miraculous feat of culture-making, whereby a human property produces out of its own living body the original basis for a distinctive and essential cultural form that exceeded the property rights of a white majority. It is this fundamental excess in blackness, as a sound referencing an essential inaccessibility structurally determined by white supremacy's commitments to race, that would inform the musical values of U.S. and world-metropolitan youth cultures. The profundity and depth of black music's influence is what has encouraged scholars to presume race to be the subject exclusively of African Americanists and to comprehend European art forms as not-racial. Demystifying U.S. black music accordingly enables us not only to contemplate its enduring cultural value, but also to position race studies in the greater field of musicological analysis.

The history of U.S. black music is pivotal to the study of race because it is through black music that the linkage of the racial and the auditory enters into popular perceptions of the modern. U.S. black music's public appearance in the early part of the twentieth century and its domination of the sound and style of metropolitan entertainment thereafter were not due to an inherent value in the music itself, but rather were the result of a new set of social relations and political-economic shifts that inspired popular interest in African-American musical forms and encouraged stylistic development. Making this claim is meant neither to devalue the importance of African-American agency nor to suggest that African-American musical innovation was merely an accommodation to market demands. The black performers who migrated northward from around 1900 brought with them traditions of musical learning based in a long history of southern vernacular performance, and these traditions were absolutely central to African-American culture-making. At the same time, however, it is equally critical to recognize how the innovation of distinctive practices of modern "Negro music," as it was then called, grew as part of the emergence of a new professional class of African-American musician-laborers working within the white-controlled social fields of entertainment. The circulation of this new "Negro music" via the affiliated technologies of transmission and reproduction was what introduced the very idea of modern musical blackness into metropolitan cultures worldwide (Miller 2010; Sotiropoulos 2006). Black popular music's qualities of distinctiveness (what we now call authenticity) were attributed to a unique, racial character—to natural rhythm, to hot blood, to a proclivity to dance and sing, to emotional qualities of sympathy and soul—all, tellingly, attributions of the black body. Such somatic-sensual orientations, grounded in the common sense of nineteenth-century Western racism that imagined black soundworlds as an unobtainable, supra-economic excess, would drive public fascination with the new generative machine of black difference-making. The depth of black music's connectedness to race would perpetuate versions of color-line thinking well beyond the era of conspicuous white supremacy, reinforcing racial commitments even as the reality of race would increasingly be put to question.

Here, then, we may identify the fundamental logic of black music's value arising from the ontological uncertainties of race at the onset of the modern. Value arose as an alchemy of sorts that brought into U.S. society by the late nineteenth century an unprecedented cultural phenomenon, what James Weldon Johnson called "a miracle of production" (Johnson 1925), the creation of a publicly recognized, creative form that had emerged within a broad, social and technological matrix of change, from the beginnings of the vast southern migrations to the technological revolution of mass production that revolutionized and transformed the entertainment fields. What was truly miraculous was how this form arose in the first place. Black music stood as a powerful symbol of African-American humanity, representing the creative genius and spiritual freedom of a class of people once enslaved, whose facility to invent culture remained paradoxically suspect among the general white populace (Herskovits 1941). Such suspicions were, of course, a symptom of the racism that commonly shaped prevailing white opinion. And the enduring commitment to that suspicion meant that whites would rarely give up on their belief in the fundamental difference between black and white. No matter how deeply they might have felt otherwise, most white Americans could not allow themselves to embrace black music as American because such an embrace would bring with it the contamination of whiteness itself. As a result, black music would always remain partially contained within the black body to which it referred, and, as such, always be in possession of a racial essence that helped to formalize twentieth-century conceptions of blackness and whiteness.

The structural impossibility for whites to fully appropriate black music, to claim the newly commodified forms as yet another possession in a "world of goods" (Douglas and Isherwood 1979), locates the seat of its power as a popular, cultural phenomenon, one whose putative essence—a quality constituted within the economy of U.S. race relations—repeated the contradiction of the African American as simultaneously citizen and subject, an American and progeny of a U.S. nation built upon the trafficking of slaves. As this contradiction played out, black music's instability and power would grow; the more that U.S. black music circulated within the cultural networks of twentieth-century entertainment, the greater its attachment to an insider culture of mystified "blackness" would seem. Indeed, the belief in a distinctly racialized African-American temporality, of a counter-modern difference, would develop as something part and parcel of African Americans' status as other. And yet black music's appeal was not simply a manifestation of desire for that which was deemed different. It was rather the consequence of a grand contest on the subject of race in which the modalities of blackness and whiteness were materialized as purchasable sound, to be bought and sold, performed, embodied, and acted out within the constitution of the U.S. nation-state and as part of its position within the global modern.

Such anxious, musically bounded negotiations of modern, racial subjects took place in the particular structural locality of a consumer society that encouraged purchase as a means of social play. Constituting and constituted within what Raymond Williams has called the "magic system" of advertising and consumer society, U.S. black music emerged as part of the revolution in industrialization and mass production that overtook the United States and Europe in the late nineteenth century and positioned the U.S. as a global leader in the making of a consumer empire (Hoganson 2007; Williams 1980). Black music's ambiguous, symbolic status as purchasable property and particularized, racial form captured interracial and international youth attention within the new frames of the popular, paralleling the situation of modern consumers as at once subjugated by market forces and enabled by the liberating activity of purchase that linked spending and citizenship (McGovern 2006; Suisman 2009). It is no coincidence that the appeal of black music ignited at the same moment that "youth" emerged as an identifiable consumer class in the 1910s (Savage 2008). The music's popularity arose as part of a popular system of signs, representing a particular materialization of racial ideology resonant with new comprehensions of subjectivity in the global modern. That black music would be constituted as a form whose special qualities and uniqueness grew from its original attachments to the reified, black body—to a performance under slavery claimed by whites yet always ultimately in the possession and control of African Americans—would establish the frames of reference and meaning for the rise of black music in the twentieth century.

Black music's unique status as a material, commodified form accessible to all listeners and capable of signifying a broad array of personal attachments, magnified its potential for modern citizens to act out and negotiate their positions as racial subjects. In black music, U.S. and European youth, both black and white, could hear a soundworld that spoke powerfully to commonality and manufactured difference; racially hybrid in form, it "sounded like" black and white, at once. For U.S. black music, as an acknowledged public form, betrayed the lie of Negro imitativeness as it revealed the truth of African-American civility and humanity, just as it also, in its very "blackness," gave symbolic form to racial separation. Listening to early recorded popular music from a historical distance, one can now hear the obvious similarities between black and white styles from a time when African Americans were ironically closer to the segregated tradition of African-based slave culture. It was within this new, modern soundworld that a consumer class of interracial, internationalized youth audiences learned variously to perform imaginations of self, as style brought into symbolic form the contradictions of similarity and difference.

A principal figuration in modern conceptions of racial subjectivity was that of freedom—that marker of identification constituted within the circumstance of pan-American slave regimes (Buck-Morss 2000). But what did this popular sense of freedom, so common to the rhetoric of early-twentieth-century U.S. black music, really mean? In general terms, black music signified across racial category a new sense of cultural belonging consistent with consumption's value as a mechanism of communication and social coherence. Yet the qualities and dimensions of black music's "freedom" registered differently on opposite sides of the color line. Among African Americans, black music's prominence within the new field of the popular represented, at least to a certain extent, the possibility of "Jazzing Away Prejudice," as in the 1919 *Chicago Defender* headline (Kenney 1993, 123). Even in those instances, however, black music's value never moved very far from the experience of life under Jim Crow, particularly so in African-American religious settings that carried forth the prominence of the spirituals. For many white Americans, on the other hand, value seemed to depend more on the act of forgetting, or, at best, on a simulated recollection of suffering, cast in the mediating languages of modern consumption—for example, the mawkishly sentimental interpretations of the blues and spirituals in the 1920s. It was, indeed, far easier and more convenient for U.S. white listeners to hear black music as a form without history, without conflict, as a widely circulating commodity form obtainable to anyone who had the money to buy it. And so we observe in black music's liberationist valuation an additional dimension of struggle, a racial contest that traces back to the time of slavery and to black music's public origins as a commodity-within-a-commodity. It was the consequence of supremacist efforts to claim black music that would orient African-American innovation across the twentieth century, inspiring black musicians to develop new forms that simultaneously accommodated and resisted the insatiable wants of modern consumers.

Observing the legacy of race and music from the present, it would seem that the peculiar logic of music under white supremacy has eroded considerably. The most egregious claims of black inferiority and natural musicality have largely disappeared, and the derogatory images of the minstrel past have for the most part receded from the public arena. We can still observe, however, how a subtler form of racialist thinking continues to inform musical perceptions across political and ideological position. In some ways, in fact, things have gotten worse. By the 1950s, as U.S. black music assumed a dominant place on the world stage, claims about the racial specificity of "blackness" intensified even as U.S. black music's global circulation grew. Narratives of the music's essential, racial qualities would, in turn, proliferate in direct proportion to the music's availability as a commodity-form. The depth of this racialization appeared in the very indication of African-American performance as "black music." And while the heightened racialization of African-American forms was instrumental to the advance of black civil-rights solidarity, it had the unintended effect of reinforcing racial thinking about black music, bringing into the present what is, in the end, a version of nineteenth-century racialism. The imaginations of racial essence have, in turn, become increasingly decoupled from African-American musical practices at the same time that they continue to orient determinations of popular style and taste. Today, one can hear the influence of U.S. black music in a diversity of expressions, from the vocal styles of pop (consider, for example, the performances on American Idol or the Eurovision Song Contests) to the rhythmic practices of rock. Frequently, these performance practices carry with them a figurative language of liberation yet without clear attachments to the historical legacies of black music and black people. We might wonder, then, about the state of race today in the broad frames of popular musical culture—about how the invisible forces of race inhabit a grand array of humanly organized sound that appears in the name of truth, liberation, and democracy. As Richard Middleton writes with reference to *The Black Atlantic*, "If, as [Paul] Gilroy argues, the presence of a slave and post-slave Afro-diasporic culture within late-modern bourgeois society is not marginal but significantly constitutive for that society, then the emergent role of black American music becomes important not just for popular music but for our understanding of the musical field in this society considered as a whole" (Middleton 2001, 146). Understanding the qualities and character of these complex racial-musical linkages stands as a primary challenge to the future course of music studies in its multiple forms.

FURTHER READING

Agawu, Kofi. 2003. *Representing African music: Postcolonial notes, queries, positions.* New York: Routledge.

Bloechl, Olivia A. 2008. *Native American song at the frontiers of early modern music.* Cambridge, U.K.: Cambridge University Press.

Bohlman, Philip V. 2008. *Jewish music and modernity.* New York: Oxford University Press.

Cook, Nicholas. 2007. *The Schenker project: Culture, race, and music theory in fin-de-siècle Vienna.* Oxford: Oxford University Press.

Gilroy, Paul. 1993. *The black Atlantic: Modernity and double consciousness.* Cambridge, MA: Harvard University Press.

Jones, Andrew F. 2001. *Yellow music: Media culture and colonial modernity in the Chinese jazz age.* Durham, NC: Duke University Press.

Kun, Josh. 2005. *Audiotopia: Music, race, and America.* Berkeley: University of California Press.

Miller, Karl Hagstrom. 2010. *Segregating sound: Inventing folk and pop music in the age of Jim Crow.* Durham, NC: Duke University Press.

Radano, Ronald. 2003. *Lying up a nation: Race and black music.* Chicago: University of Chicago Press.

Radano, Ronald, and Philip V. Bohlman, eds. 2000. *Music and the racial imagination.* Chicago: University of Chicago Press.

Rehding, Alexander. 2000. The quest for the origins of music in Germany circa 1900. *Journal of the American Musicological Society* 53(2): 345–385.

Wade, Peter. 2000. *Music, race, and nation: Música Tropical in Colombia.* Chicago: University of Chicago Press.

CHAPTER 28

Music, Gender, and Sexuality

FRED EVERETT MAUS

Basic Concepts

The terms *gender* and *sexuality* contribute to analysis of social and psychological phenomena. In recent cultural theory, these terms reflect a concern with distinctions between natural or biological attributes of people, on one hand, and constructed, contingent, cultural, or historical attributes, on the other hand.

Gender refers to the classification of people and human traits as masculine, or feminine, or by related terms. Often, theorists of gender distinguish between gender, as culturally variable, and biological sex, understood as something physical, determined by chromosomes, hormones, morphology, and so on. By convention, the terms *male* and *female*, rather than *masculine* and *feminine*, mark differences of sex. (Biological sex, in this contrast between gender and sex, differs from sex in the sense of *sexuality*, as discussed below: the same word has different meanings.)

The difference between gender and sex is politically important, because gender, created and maintained socially rather than naturally, is subject to analysis in terms of cultural issues such as the distribution of power, and is subject to cultural change. If differences of biological sex are physical, they do not appear open to cultural change. However, boundaries between gender and sex, between the natural and the constructed, are controversial. At one extreme, Judith Butler, in *Gender Trouble* (1990), argues that scientific claims about sex difference should be understood politically, not as matters of objective scientific knowledge.

Sexuality refers to feelings, actions, and attributes involving erotic desires, feelings, and behavior. This vague definition reflects the vagueness of the concept, which, like the concept of gender, is contested. As with gender, recent cultural theory typically regards many aspects of sexuality as variable and constructed. In *The History of Sexuality*, Vol. 1 (1978), Foucault argued persuasively that sexuality comprises a range of practices that change historically; most famously, he argued that the conceptualization of homosexuality in the late nineteenth century marked an ontological shift from sexual acts to sexual identities, from kinds of behavior to kinds of person.

Gender expresses itself in many different aspects of individual and social life. While sexuality may seem more narrowly defined, it has also been understood to express itself both directly, in consciously erotic thoughts, feelings, and actions, and indirectly, through various routes of displacement; the work of Sigmund Freud was crucial in expanding the range of phenomena that could be regarded as expressions of sexuality. The diffuse realization of gender and sexuality gives them extensive reach for understandings of many aspects of life and culture, though analytical applications of gender and sexuality are often controversial.

Beyond *gender* and *sexuality*, a complex interrelated vocabulary has developed. *Feminism* denotes a cluster of political movements. Most simply, one can say that feminism advocates for women. But this definition may require complication, to the extent that it endorses a biologically determinate concept of *woman* or treats woman as a cross-culturally unified group. Feminism includes interpretive discourses as well as political activism. The academic field of *women's studies* takes women as its subject matter; *feminist studies* implies, more strongly, an activist political stance. G*ender studies* implies a constructivist emphasis, and invites study of categories beyond femininity, especially *masculinity*.

In the late twentieth century, activists worked to replace the term *homosexual*, used since the late nineteenth century to denote same-sex eroticism, with other terms, especially *gay* and *lesbian*, terms of self-identification rather than diagnostic terms imposed by an external authority. *Gay* and *lesbian* often denote fixed identities, alongside *heterosexual* or *straight*. None of these identity terms include people sexually attracted to both men and women, *bisexual* people. A coalition of non-heterosexual people, that is, gay, lesbian, and bisexual people may be marked with the term GLB or LGB. With LGBT, the grouping expands to include *transgender*, a term for people who in various ways cross between sexes and/or genders. Thus, a gender-related term is added to a list of terms designating sexualities.

During the 1990s, *queer* gained currency. Originally an insult, the word has been reclaimed for self-identification. One goal in using the term *queer* is to refuse specific identity categories marked by terms such as *straight, gay,* or *lesbian,* indicating the diversity of desire and potentially including anyone of minority sexuality. While some people now describe themselves as queer, others continue to prefer self-description as gay or lesbian. The expanded term LGBTQ reflects this. In U.S. academic settings, the term *queer studies,* despite its origins in an intentionally provocative usage, is standard for an interdisciplinary range of studies focused on minority sexualities.

Scholarly studies of gender and sexuality have been more visible in the United States than elsewhere, reflecting a broader tendency to U.S. domination of feminist and queer politics. Further, within the U.S., gender studies and queer studies have often reflected middle-class white norms. Recent scholarly work has attempted to reduce such parochialism.

Relations between gender and sexuality are debatable. Some theories place sexuality at the center of the account of gender, as in the work of radical feminist Andrea Dworkin ([1987] 2006), who argues that the power relations of heterosexual intercourse are fundamental to gender difference. Others emphasize the importance of distinguishing gender and sexuality, while acknowledging the interactions between the two; Gayle Rubin presents this alternative in her essay "Thinking sex" ([1984] 1993). Recently, many scholars have questioned the usefulness of discussions of gender and sexuality that do not also treat their intersections with race, class, nationality, and other social categories.

CONTRIBUTIONS IN THE 1970S

Gender and sexuality did not become major topics in professional music scholarship until the late 1980s. But during the 1970s, feminist, lesbian-feminist, and gay liberation political movements, vigorous from the late 1960s on, already led to impressive interpretive and practical work on music. This work did not originate in academic music programs, but came from journalism, scholarly fields such as cultural studies, and practical music making.

Through the 1970s, music critic Ellen Willis (2011) wrote brilliantly about topics such as male domination of rock, an alternative tradition of female and sometimes feminist musicians, the ambiguous accomplishments of early "women's music," and the gender politics of punk. In 1978, Simon Frith and Angela McRobbie published a fine theoretical essay, "Rock and Sexuality" (Frith and McRobbie [1978] 2007). They reject the commonplace idea that "there is some sort of 'natural' sexuality which rock expresses," arguing instead that "the most important ideological work done by rock is the *construction* of sexuality" (43). They also argue that analysis of lyrics is inadequate to show how rock constructs sexuality, and that a full account must also discuss musical sound (42). Already in 1978, a Foucauldian emphasis on the construction of sexuality contributes to interpretation of music, along with rejection of the alternative conception of a natural sexuality that is repressed or released through music.

Frith and McRobbie distinguish two kinds of popular music. Both are created and performed by men. *Cock rock* is "loud, rhythmically insistent, built round techniques of arousal and climax," with "shouting and screaming" (44). Cock rock presents images of masculine sexuality, for consumption by men who identify with these images. In contrast, *teenybop* presents romantic images of masculine sexuality, for consumption by girls. In teenybop, boys are "sad, thoughtful, pretty and puppy-like" (45). Rock constructs males as collective and active, females as individual and passive, with regard to both musical production and sexual behavior. Male audiences, on this account, relate to performance by identifying with it, rather than understanding themselves as passive in relation to male musicians. Frith and McRobbie also complicate these oppositions, noting that both male and female listeners may find value in cock rock's emphasis on the physicality of sex and teenybop's complementary emphasis on feelings. The essay touches on many other topics—complex images of gender and sexuality in recent popular music, the importance of dance, the need to understand constructions of sexuality in the context of leisure and consumption, and more. (See Frith [1990] 2007 for his later comments on this essay.)

Richard Dyer's essay "In Defense of Disco" ([1979] 1992) notes that socialists generally disparage disco music because of its commodity character. However, disco contributes to the formation of gay identity, and Dyer suggests that it has subversive political potential. Dyer describes "the three important characteristics of disco." He contrasts its *eroticism* with the phallic qualities of rock: "rock's eroticism is thrusting, grinding," whereas disco "restores eroticism to the whole of the body, and for both sexes, not just confining it to the penis" (153, 154). The *romanticism* of some disco emphasizes emotion, "the intensity of fleeting emotional contacts," melancholy. Thus it proposes alternatives to the world of work and obligation. The *materialism* of disco, its lavish use of musical and technological resources, maintains contact with the actual world, refusing the transcendence offered by much art. Dyer suggests that, taken together, these attributes create experiences that could be the basis for a questioning of hegemonic sexual and economic practices.

In 1970, Pauline Oliveros, a composer of experimental music, published a brief article in *The New York Times* (Oliveros 1984, 47–49). Addressing the question why there have been no great women composers, she replies that women historically "have been taught to despise activity outside of the domestic realm as unfeminine," and have been valued for the obedience and support they offer to men. Oliveros observes that women presently have more opportunities to participate in professional musical life than before, although contemporary composers confront a musical culture that gives disproportionate attention to the past. She notes that preoccupation with "greatness" is harmful to appreciation of new compositional work.

Later texts by Oliveros deepen her explorations of gender and sexuality. In a grant proposal (1984, 132–137), she contrasts "active, purposeful creativity" and "receptive creativity, during which the artist is like a channel through which material flows and seems to shape itself" (132). Composers should balance "the analytical way and the intuitive way" (132). But Oliveros identifies a cultural bias toward the analytical, which draws support from gender associations: "traditionally, men are encouraged in self-determining, purposive activity, while women are encouraged to be receptive and dependent" (135). Gender stereotypes support a one-sided account of creativity that emphasizes masculine qualities. When creativity is misconstrued that way, it seems less available to women.

Oliveros also questions a one-sided account of listening. "Browsing in a psychology text, I came across the idea that music is a phallic phenomenon because it penetrates the body! . . . Come now, Freudians, one can *receive* music but also actively penetrate it, not to mention all the other finer variations" (ibid., 113). Listening can have active and receptive aspects. "Maybe the psychologist assumed that only men (probably dead men) write music. According to a certain social paradigm, it follows then, that maybe only women should listen to it! Or eat it." But the "social paradigm," like the parallel account of creation as active, listening as passive, does not reflect experience. "That paradigm leaves out a large assortment of very fine variations in relationships. How many of you out there think you are in the minority? If everyone came out of the closet the world would change overnight" (113). For Oliveros, oppositions between active and passive are simplistic, whether applied to creativity, listening, gender, or sexuality. Oliveros recommends greater attention to experience, to counter stereotypes.

Some of Oliveros's creative work also addresses interactions between activity and receptivity. Her verbal scores, collected as *Deep Listening Pieces* (1990), often ask participants to shift repeatedly between active and receptive roles. Most simply, *Circle Sound Meditation* (1978) asks participants to lie in a circle and, after relaxing, "listen then sound. Alternate between listening and sounding" (9). In *The Tuning Meditation* (1980), participants alternate between singing a pitch that originates in their imagination and, next, matching the note that someone else is singing. Such practices disrupt, and critique, the fixed roles of performer and audience. The active/passive contrast is fundamental to conventional ideas of gender roles and sexual roles; thus, participants in Oliveros's *Deep Listening Pieces* enact subtle forms of gender and sexuality dissidence. (For much more on Oliveros, see Mockus 2007.)

During the 1970s in the United States, *women's music* developed, shaped by feminist and lesbian politics, composed and performed by women, and primarily directed at female audiences. This remarkable application of feminist thought led soon to new record companies and music festivals (Mosbacher 2004). The political character of women's music accounted for its successes and its image as self-limiting. The music was primarily created by lesbians, for lesbian audiences, and, despite the inclusion of African-American musicians, most performers and audiences were white (Hayes 2010). Practices such as the exclusion of men from concert audiences showed strong separatism.

However, stereotypes of women with acoustic guitars, singing simple protest songs and lesbian love songs, are inaccurate. Women's music was stylistically eclectic and often skillful. An early, famous example, Cris Williamson's "Waterfall" (*The Changer and the Changed*, Wolf Moon Records, [1975] 2005), reflects on personal experience and offers advice, using images of water as models for life. A rainy day, she sings, can show you that life will be all right. "When you open up your life to the living / All things come spilling in on you." Then, you will flow "like a river," and you will need to "spill some over," in "an endless waterfall." The lyrics are persistently metaphorical, yet audiences understood and loved the song. The water that spills over could refer to weeping, perhaps a figure for access to one's emotions. The water's flow in and out, filling and spilling, is a non-phallic sexual image. Other feminist texts of the time also represent women's experiences through images of water. In a 1976 novel, Rita Mae Brown writes, "When Carole groaned, 'Now, Ilse, now,' she felt that she had ridden out a tidal wave" ([1976] 1988, 77). More theoretically, Luce Irigaray (1985b) argues that standard scientific and logical symbols represent solids well, but not fluids; she connects this directly to the psychic centrality of the phallus. Femininity, as fluidity, is unrepresentable or nonexistent.

At first, the keyboard-based music of "Waterfall" is slow, and the key is uncertain. The tonic clarifies; the music accelerates, then accelerates again to a repeating four-chord progression, a chorus-like section with momentum and a catchy melody. The music drops off, in a delicate *ritardando*; the first section repeats, just up to the point where the tonic was established, and then the chorus repeats. Along with the non-phallic lyrics, the music offers an image of gently increasing excitement, reaching a plateau, dropping back and then recovering the plateau; the goal is not an orgasmic crisis but a heightened vivacity. A final fadeout suggests that this pleasure has no inherent conclusion.

In France during the 1970s, outstanding feminist theorists such as Julia Kristeva and Luce Irigaray drew on psychoanalysis and philosophy. One such writer, Catherine Clément, published a book on opera in 1978 (translated into English only in 1988, when musicological feminism began to appear in Anglophone settings). Clément explores the deaths of female operatic characters, arguing that opera presents misogynist content in a seductive form. Clément's book neglects music—it is basically about libretti. But it is an auspicious contribution to the feminist analysis of representations of women.

LATER SCHOLARLY CONTRIBUTIONS

As already mentioned, discussions of music, gender, and sexuality did not play a significant role in professional music scholarship until the late 1980s. As this delay reveals, the music scholarship of the time was insular and socially disengaged; the same qualities account for the controversy around the eventual attempts to bring gender and sexuality into music scholarship. However, from the late 1980s on, research on gender and sexuality in relation to music has been a productive and exciting field, with excellent work from professional music scholars and fruitful interaction between musicology and other fields such as cultural studies. By now there is far too much valuable research to summarize, or to represent in a brief reading list. The rest of this chapter indicates the range of more recent scholarly work by commenting on selected texts. In general I emphasize theoretical contributions, though much fine work has appeared that is primarily empirical. And I emphasize work in which gender and/or sexuality are the central themes, though one welcome shift is that it is common, now, for such issues to be included along with many others in a musicological study.

Two excellent anthologies, edited by Jane Bowers and Judith Tick (1987) and by Ellen Koskoff (1987) respectively, exemplify a women's studies approach to music, using careful research—historical in the first case, ethnographic in the second—to explore musical roles of women in many times and places. Since then, many superb studies of women in music have appeared. A fine essay by Marcia J. Citron, "Gender, Professionalism, and the Musical Canon" (1990), returns to Oliveros's question about the scarcity of historical female composers. The creation of knowledge about women in music has flourished as an important part of music scholarship (see, for example, Tick 1997; Locke and Barr 1997; Kisliuk 1998; Koskoff 2000; Whiteley 2000; Feldman and Gordon 2006; Cusick 2009, and much more. The journal *Women & Music*, from 1997 on, has provided excellent resources on women in music as well as feminist and queer studies).

During the 1970s and 1980s, musicologists such as Joseph Kerman (1985) and Leo Treitler (1989) had urged music scholars to take up *criticism,* understood as an interpretive and evaluative discourse in contrast to the more empirical traditions of musicology. One branch of criticism, exemplified by Anthony Newcomb and others, interprets classical instrumental music through the concept of narrative. Susan McClary's book *Feminine Endings* (1991) offers a sustained example of feminist music criticism, discussing Monteverdi, Bizet, Tchaikovsky, and Beethoven, along with recent female musicians. By including chapters on Laurie Anderson and Madonna, McClary juxtaposes canonic male composers with a performance artist and a popular performer, proposing a critical approach that can cross generic boundaries.

Feminine Endings contrasts two ways of shaping time in music. Some music drives toward goals, creating desire for points of climax and resolution. Other music creates a sense of sustained pleasure. McClary finds, in both, powerful images of sensuality and sexuality, which listeners experience as their own, and she associates the two with gendered conceptions of sexuality—masculine and feminine respectively. Like Frith and McRobbie, McClary argues that music participates in the social construction of gender, in part by creating vivid, gendered musical images of sexual experience. A later essay on Schubert ([1994] 2006) finds, in the nonteleological character of some of his music, a related resistance to goal-driven masculinity.

McClary's advocacy of music that embodies feminine sensuality, or music that resists celebrations of masculinity, is provocative; but for some readers, it is problematic. McClary seems to commend female musicians for producing feminine music, and thereby to deny certain resources to women. Long before, Ellen Willis had questioned the absence of rock in "women's music," noting that "it is no accident that women musicians have been denied access to this powerful musical language" (2011, 143). Frith and McRobbie also noted that girls can find value in the physicality of rock music (2007, 50).

In both opera and instrumental music, McClary identifies local stylistic markers of masculinity or femininity, such as evasive chromatic melodies that represent sly, seductive femininity. This approach resembles the topical analysis of Leonard Ratner (1980), or the musematic analysis of Philip Tagg ([1979] 2000), but focuses on gender and sexuality. In sonata form, McClary identifies a temporal and harmonic patterning of masculine and feminine music that communicates a narrative about the subordination of femininity, thus offering an instrumental analog of Clément's work on misogynist narratives in opera.

Philip Brett (1997) made an impressive and challenging contribution to criticism when he entered the scholarly conversation about Franz Schubert's sexuality and its relation to his music. Maynard Solomon (1989) had argued that Schubert may have been homosexual. Debate followed about the biographical claim and its relation to Schubert's music. Brett's essay notes that, up to his own intervention, self-identified gay scholars have been absent from the debate, an astonishing fact. Brett describes his experiences playing Schubert's music for piano, four hands, with a younger gay male friend; he savors the sexual implications of this duet collaboration, in which the two men are physically and musically close. Brett then offers a detailed description of the slow movement of Schubert's four-hand Sonata in C (D. 812). The analysis identifies a contrast between superficial, conformist musical gestures and moments that suggest suppressed rage; near the end, violent emotions hold sway, briefly but impressively, before conventional closure hides them again. Brett notes that this emotional pattern is familiar to present-day gay men. With caution, Brett suggests that similar feelings may have figured in Schubert's life. Still, Brett leaves no doubt that Schubert's social life, sexuality, and feelings are difficult for us to reconstruct, and should be assumed to be different, in various ways, from those of his present-day admirers.

Brett's essay, a model of circumspect historical thought, also restricts the claim it makes for its authority as music criticism: Brett states firmly that "criticism is radical in musicology because it is personal and has no authority whatsoever" (p. 171). Some readers may be disturbed by this relativism; more importantly, Brett is unnerving, in a productive way, in his insistence that writing about music must be thoroughly open and honest.

Brett, McClary, and others have not only discussed classical music in relation to gender and sexuality, but have also turned their attention to professional discourse about music. They join critics like Kerman in arguing that conventional verbal resources of music scholars fail to address important experiential qualities, and they add that professional norms of objectivity make it difficult to articulate issues of gender and sexuality that are pervasive in musical experience. I make such arguments about music theory in "Masculine Discourse in Music Theory" (1993); in a related essay, Marion Guck (1994) writes of her experiences as a female music theorist drawn to experiential description. Such arguments suggest a far-reaching critique of musicological discourse as a defense mechanism, a way of evading aspects of musical experience.

What would bland discourse about music hide? McClary suggests that it hides the messages of gender ideology that music communicates. Another answer is that it hides the eroticism of musical experience. Suzanne Cusick, in a well-known essay ([1994] 2006), explores relationships between her own lesbian sexuality and her musicality. She identifies both music and sexuality as areas where people give and receive pleasure, with intimacy and in relationships configured by power. In view of this broad parallel (or perhaps identity—Cusick wonders, eventually, whether music simply *is* sex), she compares her preferred sexual and musical experiences.

Power relationships emerge as the crucial variable: Cusick identifies the constructed notion of "woman" as "nonpower," and therefore, a relationship between two women as, perhaps, "a relationship based on non-power," or with "a flow of power in both directions. No one in the relationship has been formed to be the power figure, although all can play at it" (p. 72). Similarly, Cusick states her preference for "musics which *invite* and allow me to participate or not as *I* choose, musics with which I experience a continuous circulation of power even when I let the music be 'on top'" (p. 76). And, as a performer, Cusick values moments when "power circulates freely across porous boundaries; the categories player and played, lover and beloved, dissolve" (p. 78). Like Frith and McRobbie, Cusick sees that musical production and reception could be understood as a relationship in which music, or musicians, exert power over listeners; like Oliveros, she prefers to resist this "social paradigm" by seeking out more complex variations in which power relations may shift or become unclear.

There are alternatives, in theories and practices of sexuality, to Cusick's emphasis on mutuality, nonpower, and flexibility of roles. In general, Alan Sinfield (2004) has questioned the cultural habit of praising equality in sexual relationships. Leo Bersani ([1987] 2010) would identify Cusick's description of sexual experience as a "pastoralizing" account; Bersani counters such thinking with an account of sex as "self-shattering". For Bersani, the experience of self-loss in sexuality accounts for its value. Drawing on Bersani, one can suggest alternative descriptions of musical experience that center on the value of being controlled or overwhelmed by music. I have worked on this approach, in different ways, in essays about Edward T. Cone and Hector Berlioz (2006, 2009).

Clément's neglect of voice and singing has been offset by many subsequent studies. John Shepherd (1987) and Suzanne Cusick (1999), using examples from popular music, explore the construction of gender difference through vocal style. Elizabeth Wood's essay on "Sapphonics" ([1994] 2006) identifies a type of female operatic voice, rich and powerful in its lower register yet clear and strong in the upper register, with an awkward break between. Wood documents the historic affinity of lesbian musicians and opera fans with such voices, beloved for their "acceptance and integration of male and female" (32). Wayne Koestenbaum (1993) writes of the culture of "opera queens," gay men whose love of opera centers on the diva; he offers personal descriptions of specific opera scenes, somewhat as Brett offered a personal account of Schubert's music. In a related emphasis on physicality, there has been a good deal of work recently on questions of music and embodiment. Some of these studies explicitly thematize gender and/or sexuality, while others do not. (For an overview, see Maus 2010.)

In popular music studies, there has been rewarding research on musicians in light of the relations between their gender and/or sexuality, their music, and their careers. In a few cases, scholars can write about popular musicians or musical movements explicitly identified with feminism, such as the riot grrrl movement of the 1990s (Leonard 2007). In other cases, when musicians have not called themselves feminists, scholars have nonetheless found proto-feminist positions in their work. Attention to female musicians has potential for significant revision of histories of popular music. Angela Davis's study of women in blues (1998) counters the traditional emphasis on male blues performers, while finding many links between female blues singers and feminism. Jacqueline Warwick's study of girl groups (2007) counters a conventional historical narrative that moves from early rock 'n' roll to the British invasion, with a gap between. In fact, much of the most popular music during that alleged gap was by girl groups; their neglect by historians reflects difficulty with taking young female performers, often black, and their young female audiences seriously.

There is a surprisingly large literature of feminist commentary on Madonna (for example, hooks 1992, 157–164; Bordo [1994] 2004; Fouz-Hernández and Jarman-Ivens 2004). Musical theater has also drawn brilliant commentary, in part because of gay and lesbian fandom (Miller 1998; Wolf 2002; Rogers 2008). Greater openness about sexuality has also permitted illuminating studies of LGBTQ popular musicians (Echols 1999; Hubbs 2004; Gamson 2005; Randall 2008, and many more).

Important contributions have considered audiences of popular music in light of gender and sexuality. Lisa Rhodes (2005) discusses the culture of groupies, with attention to their love of music and their agency in seeking pleasure. Maria Pini's study of women and rave culture (2001), in an unusual and skillful combination of resources, draws on ethnographic interviews along with feminist theory; she shows that rave offers women new kinds of subjectivity, parallel in some ways to subjectivities articulated in speculative feminist philosophy. Walter Hughes (1994), influenced by Bersani, suggests that gay men, dominated by the beat in the discos of the 1970s, experienced an unmaking of their subjectivities that permitted the creation of new identities. The resulting analysis is quite unlike Dyer's. Tim Lawrence (2004), in a completely different style, has written an extraordinary interview-based history of discos in New York City during the 1970s, a crucial contribution to the history of sexuality in the U.S. Judith Peraino (2005) has offered an ambitiously broad synthesis of historical and contemporary relations between music and queer identity, covering classical music, popular music, and more.

Two excellent online resources direct readers to many additional materials on music, gender, and sexuality. The Committee on the Status of Women of the Society for Music Theory maintains a bibliography of research in these areas. And the website of the LGBTQ Study Group of the American Musicological Society includes a full run of the group's fine newsletter, with reviews, articles, and more.

Significant gaps remain in the professional literature on music, gender, and sexuality. Several recent studies address constructions of masculinity, a welcome development that could be taken much further (Pederson 2000; Meintjes 2004; Jarman-Ivens 2007; Biddle and Gibson 2009). Issues of cross-dressing or complexities of gender presentation arise throughout discussions of music, gender, and sexuality. (Examples include Garber 1991; Muñoz 1999; Braga-Pinto 2002; Rodger 2004; Auslander 2006; Head 2006; Dreyfus 2010; Rodger 2010; but related issues are pervasive in the literature.) However, people who identify as transgender or transsexual have received little interpretation or representation in music scholarship (for exceptions, see Swedenburg 1997; Namaste 2000; Middleton 2006, 91–136; Constansis 2008).

Perhaps the most striking absence has been the relative lack of work on sexuality and music in settings beyond classical music and mainstream Anglophone popular music. E. Patrick Smith (2008) has gathered valuable material about gay black men and the choirs of Southern churches. The brief, descriptive studies in Whiteley and Rycenga (2006) are unusual in their geographical range, with chapters on popular music in Germany, Latin America, Israel, and Russia. Gayatri Gopinath (2005) has written usefully about the heterosexual masculinity of recent Anglo-Asian rock and dance music, in contrast to underground South Asian queer scenes. José Quiroga (2000) and Frances Negrón-Muntaner (2004) offer Latin American perspectives on a number of popular music topics, including bolero, Ricky Martin, Madonna, and *West Side Story*. Susan Thomas (2006) writes about representations of lesbians in recent Cuban popular song. There is need for much more work along these lines.

FURTHER READING

Bernstein, Jane A., ed. 2003. *Women's voices across musical worlds.* Boston, MA: Northeastern University Press.

Blackmer, Corinne E., and Patricia Juliana Smith, eds. 1995. *En travesti: Women, gender subversion, opera.* New York: Columbia University Press.

Brett, Philip, Elizabeth Wood, and Gary C. Thomas, eds. [1994] 2006. *Queering the pitch: The new gay and lesbian musicology,* 2nd ed. New York: Routledge.

Citron, Marcia J. [1993] 2000. *Gender and the musical canon.* Urbana: University of Illinois Press.

Cusick, Suzanne G. 1999. Gender, musicology, and feminism. Pp. 471–498 in *Rethinking music.* Edited by Mark Everist and Nicholas Cook. Oxford: Oxford University Press.

Fuller, Sophie, and Lloyd Whitesell, eds. 2002. *Queer episodes in music and modern identity.* Urbana: University of Illinois Press.

Holsinger, Bruce. 2002. *Music, body, and desire in medieval culture: Hildegard of Bingen to Chaucer.* Stanford: Stanford University Press.

McClary, Susan. 1991. *Feminine endings: Music, gender, and sexuality.* Minneapolis: University of Minnesota Press.

Moisala, Pirkko, and Beverley Diamond, eds. 2000. *Music and gender.* Urbana: University of Illinois Press.

Solie, Ruth A., ed. 1993. *Musicology and difference: Gender and sexuality in music scholarship.* Berkeley: University of California Press.

Stras, Laurie, ed. 2010. *She's so fine: Reflections on whiteness, femininity, adolescence, and class in 1960s music.* Aldershot, U.K.: Ashgate Publishing.

Whiteley, Sheila. 2000. *Women and popular music: Sexuality, identity, and subjectivity.* New York: Routledge.

Whiteley, Sheila, and Jennifer Rycenga, eds. 2006. *Queering the popular pitch.* New York: Routledge.

PART 5

WHO?
Musical Subjectivities

CHAPTER 29

WHAT'S GOING ON
Music, Psychology, and Ecological Theory

ERIC F. CLARKE

> Music recognizes no natural law; therefore, all psychology of music is questionable.
>
> (Theodor Adorno)

Never one to miss a polemical opportunity, Adorno's apparently dismissive assessment provides an appropriately perverse starting point from which to argue a defense of the value of psychology to the cultural study of music. Adorno was strongly influenced by the work of Freud among others—not only in his specifically psychological writing but also in his writing on music. However, the assumption that psychology must be concerned with natural laws that is implicit in Adorno's rejection of the psychology of music is unwarranted, and my aim in this chapter is to argue that psychological principles can help to shed important light on music from a variety of natural and cultural perspectives, and that the very idea of a sharp division between "nature" and "culture" is one that psychology itself questions.

Since most people engage with music because they find it in some way meaningful, rewarding, exciting or moving, psychology—variously defined as the "science of mental life" (James 1890) or the study of behavior (Watson 1919)—should have quite a bit to offer to an understanding of music. But that abstract potential arguably remains frustratingly unfulfilled: while the psychology of music has seen dramatic growth since around 1980, its achievements have until recently largely been concerned with establishing, or verifying, the processes by which people produce or make sense of what have been considered the "fundamentals" of music—pitches, duration sequences, the control of tempo and dynamics, basic tonal structures, the timbre of single sounds or small-scale complexes, and so on. Since around 2000, there has been a more concerted attempt to tackle issues on a larger scale and with more sense of the bigger and more social picture (e.g. DeNora 2000, Clarke, Dibben, and Pitts 2010), but there is still a significantly reductionist impetus within the subject (reflecting the generally cognitive, and increasingly neuroscientific outlook that has predominated), and little sense of an engagement with culture. In this chapter I argue that this need not be the case, and that a fruitful interaction between music and psychology is possible that encapsulates a much more richly cultural view. It depends, however, on adopting a rather different view of perception and cognition from the one that has dominated until now—one that places the issue of musical meaning at the center of the whole endeavor.

Psychology is an extraordinarily hybrid subject. It is part philosophy, part biology, strongly influenced by ethology and sociology, and, since the 1960s, by cybernetics, linguistics, and computer science. A crude institutional indicator of this disciplinary uncertainty is that psychology can be found across a whole range of university faculties including arts and humanities, social science, pure science, biological science, and cognitive and computing sciences, and that research in psychology in Britain is supported by the Arts and Humanities Research Council, the Economic and Social Research Council, the Engineering and Physical Sciences Research Council, and the Brain and Behavioural Sciences Research Council. A popular introduction to the subject (Butler and McManus 1998, 130) concludes in the following terms:

> Today psychology is a far more diverse subject than it was even fifty years ago, as well as a more scientific one. Its complexity means that it may never develop as a science with a single paradigm, but will continue to provide an understanding of mental life from many different perspectives—cognitive and behavioural, psychophysiological, biological, and social. Like any other discipline, it is the site of conflicting theories as well as agreement.

Note the tone of approval with which psychology's increasingly "scientific" character is mentioned, coupled with the admission of its sometimes uncomfortable heterogeneity. In considering the relationship with psychology, music (itself a diverse and heterogeneous subject) confronts a shifting territory, and, if there are shortcomings in achieving a really rich and productive relationship between the two, it is in part a result of the rather narrow range of encounters that have so far been contemplated.

One central feature of psychology that distinguishes it from musicology (and one of the hallmarks of a science) is that it is primarily concerned with the identification and investigation of general principles rather than particular manifestations. At the level of individual pieces of research this may not always be immediately apparent: A psychological paper may seem to be concerned specifically with the ability of infants to recognize their carers' faces, for example; but the emphasis in such research is invariably on discovering *general principles* for face recognition, which can then be discussed in the context of still more general principles of perception or memory. It is seldom the particular perceptual or mnemonic attributes of one specific face that are the focus of interest. By contrast, a considerable amount of work in musicology (whether analytical, critical, historical, or hermeneutic) focuses on a detailed understanding of particular phenomena: a consideration of Russian folk melodies in Stravinsky's *The Rite of Spring* may engage with broader questions of music and national identity, but the emphasis is likely to be primarily on what's happening in the specific piece. This difference of perspective should represent a fruitful complementarity, an opportunity rather than a problem. But all too often the trade-off between broad explanatory power and local specificity leads research in the psychology of music to seem blandly obvious and lacking in critical awareness to musicologists, while psychologists point to the apparently arbitrary particularity of musicological research, its speculative and discursive character, and raise questions about empirical support and "evidence."

The contemporary phase of the psychology of music dates from around 1980, when within the space of about five years a number of important books were published, and new journals established. The sudden rise of the subject came on the back of what has often been called "the cognitive revolution" in psychology (which began some twenty years earlier) and which has continued to play a powerful role in shaping the psychology of music. The characteristic features of this approach are a combination of controlled experimental procedures, an emphasis on modeling of one kind or another (in the form of either "grammars" or computer programs), and a focus on individual human subjects stripped of their cultural context. Internal representations, mental models, and cognitive capacities are the central preoccupation, with human action, and in particular the cultural context of human action and interaction, held at bay so as to throw into relief fundamental psychological functions in their pristine state.

Deutsch's reference volume, entitled *The Psychology of Music*, originally published in 1982 and in a second edition in 1999, provides one opportunity to assess how the subject represented itself across those two decades. Six of the eighteen chapters of the second edition are concerned with pitch perception, with two chapters on rhythm, and single chapters on a variety of topics including timbre, performance, neurology, hierarchical structures, acoustics, and "comparative music perception and cognition." There are no chapters on emotion or meaning in music, the outlook is almost entirely concerned with the Western classical tradition, and any sense of the way in which music is culturally embedded is almost entirely absent. This looks like a bleakly unlikely prospect for any attempt to argue for the relevance of the psychology of music to its cultural study. But combined with the influence of ethnomusicology and the sociology of music, the picture has begun to change significantly, with the *Oxford Handbook of Music Psychology* (Hallam, Cross, and Thaut 2009) presenting a rather different picture of the subject. The cognitive tradition, for all its dominance in contemporary psychology, is not the only way to study mental life and human behavior, and a rather different prospect for the psychology of music comes into view if a different psychological starting point is adopted. I use the remainder of this chapter to focus on listening understood from a perspective that does make an important connection with the cultural study of music.

Consistent with the overall character of the modern psychology of music given above, listening has been tackled in a predominantly structuralist fashion: It has been widely assumed that the primary aim should be to investigate the kinds of abstract tonal, metric, grouping, melodic, and timbral structures that people accumulate as they listen (e.g., as reviewed in Krumhansl 1991), as well as the more dynamic processes to which these structures give rise. As a number of commentators have pointed out (e.g., Cook 1994; Serafine 1988), the assumption that the basic units of "standard music theory" are necessarily the salient features of listening is unjustified—and indeed, as Cook argues, the very fact that the music-theoretic way of listening has to be learned through aural training programs suggests that these may not be important attributes of spontaneous listening. The kind of highly abstracted structural listening that characterizes both standard music theory and the cognitive tradition looks rather like an artifact or a fictional stereotype.

And yet there is a recognition within this cognitive tradition that listening is far more situated. In a spirited defense of empirical research and its relationship with music theory, Robert Gjerdingen (a former editor of the leading psychology of music journal *Music Perception*) observes that "A little reflection . . . leads one to realise that a great deal of music perception is contingent, situational, and subject to biases of culture and experience" (Gjerdingen 1999, 168). Indeed it would be hard to deny that *all* music perception involves "biases of culture and experience." How might a more situated and cultural approach to listening, but one that is still amenable to empirical inquiry, and based in psychological principles, tackle its subject? As Cook (2001, 180–181) puts it:

How can we understand the cultural production of music as prompted but not determined by acoustical or psychoacoustical phenomena, and correlatively how can we see musical meaning as prompted but not determined by verbal or other discourse? How in other words can we avoid the binary either/or that makes music *either* all nature *or* all culture, and that locates musical meaning *either* all in the music itself *or* all in its verbal or other interpretation?

A number of authors have recently argued for the potential of an ecological approach to listening (Clarke 2005; DeNora 2000; Windsor 2000)—an approach in which the relationship between perceiver and environment (natural and cultural) is taken to be fundamental. Central to an ecological view is the idea that perceptual information specifies objects and events in the world, and that perception and action are indissolubly linked. If I hear glass breaking, for instance, I am likely to turn my head to hear and see where the breakage has occurred, and to make sure that I don't tread on the glass: the perceptual information (the sounds of impact followed by a cascade of irregular and dissipating tinkling sounds) specify an event (breaking glass), which I perceive by means of orienting actions (head turning), and which leads to further adaptive actions (changing my pattern of movements to avoid possible injury). The relationship between stimulus and object or event, and between perception and action, come together in an important concept for which the psychologist James Gibson coined the term *affordance*. The affordances of an object are the uses, functions, or values of an object—the opportunities that it offers to a perceiver:

> I have coined this word as a substitute for *values*, a term which carries an old burden of philosophical meaning. I mean simply what things furnish, for good or ill. What they *afford* the observer, after all, depends on their properties. . . . [T]he human observer learns to detect what have been called the values or meanings of things, perceiving their distinctive features, putting them into categories and subcategories, noticing their similarities and differences and even studying them for their own sakes, apart from learning what to do about them.
>
> (Gibson 1966, 285)

A lump of stone of an appropriate size, for instance, may afford being used as a missile or a paperweight, or being carved into a sculpture, but it does not afford being used as clothing or as a dwelling (for a human being). It simply doesn't have the right properties. The affordances of objects are, however, defined relative to the perceiving organism: "I mean by it [affordance] something that refers to both the environment and the animal in a way that no existing term does. It implies the complementarity of the animal and the environment" (Gibson [1979] 1986, 122). To a human being, a wooden chair affords sitting on, while to a termite it affords eating. Equally, the same chair affords use as a weapon to a human being who needs one (an illustration of the way in which an organism's changing needs and circumstances can affect the perception of affordances)—as in the archetypal barroom brawl. The relationship really is dialectical—neither simply a case of organisms imposing their needs on an indifferent environment, nor a fixed environment determining strictly delimited behavioral possibilities.

A concentration on everyday objects might lead to the erroneous conclusion that affordances are a simple matter of physical properties and perceptual capacities. But even the most cursory consideration of more socially charged objects demonstrates the importance of the social component. A wooden crucifix, for example, affords religious contemplation or prayer; it also affords burning, but social factors ensure that this is a more remote affordance—which might be realized only in extreme circumstances or by an individual who had no regard (or even a deliberate disdain) for the conventional religious context that regulates the affordances of the crucifix. Similarly, objects and events may afford clearly social actions (as when an outstretched hand or a smile affords friendly social engagement with another person), those actions being socially determined in infinitely variable and often highly particular ways—as a fist of solidarity, mistaken for a fist of aggression illustrates. The properties of objects are part of the material of a social fabric—and this makes them no less material.

As these examples demonstrate, there is a complex intertwining of attributes that are commonly ascribed to supposedly subjective and objective properties, and to nature and culture. An ecological approach rejects these supposedly hard and fast distinctions, in the dialectical concept of affordance on the one hand, and in the following explicit statement on nature and culture on the other:

> In the study of anthropology and ecology, the "natural" environment is often distinguished from the "cultural" environment. As described here, there is no sharp division between them. Culture evolved out of natural opportunities. The cultural environment, however, is often divided into two parts, "material" culture and "non-material" culture. This is a seriously misleading distinction, for it seems to imply that language, tradition, art, music, law, and religion are immaterial, insubstantial, or intangible, whereas tools, shelters, clothing, vehicles, and books are not. Symbols are taken to be profoundly different from things. But let us be clear about this. There have to be modes of stimulation, or ways of conveying information, for any individual to perceive anything, however abstract. . . . No symbol exists except as it is realized in sound, projected light, mechanical contact, or the like. All knowledge rests on sensitivity.
>
> (Gibson 1966, 26)

It is in these respects that an ecological approach has something important to offer to the cultural study of music. By considering music in terms of its affordances, discussions of musical meaning, which have often been excessively abstract, or diverted into a consideration of emotional responses to music, or caught up in discussions of music's relationship with language, can combine with a consideration of its social uses and functions in a manner that recognizes the plurality of music's social functions without being swept away by total relativism.

To make this approach clearer, I offer three specific examples. The first comes from Tia DeNora's book *Music in Everyday Life* (DeNora 2000), in which she looks at the way in which music is used in step aerobics classes. An aerobics class typically uses a carefully planned sequence of musical materials that takes the participants through a specific pattern of physical activities: warm-up, pre-core, core, cool down, and floor exercises. Considerable care is taken in assembling these sequences of musical materials, since getting the music right can have a dramatic effect on the success of an aerobics class. In this case the music affords different kinds of physical movement with varying degrees of physical exertion, pace, and stamina. To the women in these classes, the primary affordance of the music is a pattern of physical engagement, arising out of a socially defined context (an exercise class), the properties of the music (tempo, texture, dynamic shape), and the women's particular focus (an exercise motivator and regulator).

A second example of music's affordances comes from Windsor's (2000) discussion of acousmatic music. Windsor points out the paradoxical character of acousmatic sounds: they often specify objects and events of the everyday world with considerable power and explicitness, while at the same time concealing their sources through the very fact of their acousmatic presentation—sound in the absence of its visible or tangible sources. Furthermore, acousmatic presentation allows sound to play with a listener's sense of the relationship between everyday reality and the virtual reality of the objects and events specified by the sounds of the piece. Impossible objects, or impossible relationships between objects, can be specified in acousmatic sound, and one of the consequences of this, Windsor argues, is that listeners are driven to try to find an interpretation of what they hear, somewhere on a continuum between the lawfulness of everyday reality and the special context—the virtual reality—that the piece itself creates. Acousmatic music therefore affords (even demands) interpretation, just as it can also afford emotional catharsis, persuasion, structural listening, the accumulation of cultural capital, synchronized working, group solidarity, and dancing. The question is whether, and how, the specific attributes of both the musical materials and the perceiver's capacities and circumstances, which give rise to any particular affordance, can be determined, and it is here that the psychology of perception could make a real contribution to the cultural study of music.

My third example takes up this last point more directly, and also relates to DeNora's study of music in aerobics. As I discuss in more detail elsewhere (Clarke 2001; 2005), a powerful component in the impact and meaning of music is the sense of motion and agency that listeners may experience. A great deal of contemporary dance music makes use of this—not only to afford the dancing for which it is designed but also to explore various kinds of virtual spaces and virtual motions with which the real spaces and movements of actual dancing interact. There are established techniques that dance music producers use to achieve these effects (filtering techniques; blurring, withholding and emphasising beats, etc.) that not only exploit basic perceptual processes (the sense of occlusion, submersion or distance versus directness and proximity that variable band-pass filtering or reverberation can specify; or the "looseness" versus "tightness" specified by different amounts and styles of synchronization) but also engage with the huge repertory of other dance music. Producers and DJs manipulate this complex environment, using the transformation of dancers' perceptual experiences to elicit both virtual actions in the virtual spaces that the sounds specify, and the real actions of dance. This interaction of the virtual and the real is often powerfully evident at the start of dance tracks, where the texture and meter of the music are often deliberately poorly defined, specifying rather loose and "spacey" environments and making dancing difficult, but becomes either gradually or suddenly more clearly articulated. This process of clarification and articulation will often reach a climactic point where the energizing and anchoring beats of the music slot into place (known as "the drop"—and often focused on the introduction of the kick drum), galvanizing clubbers into coordinated dance and transforming or supplanting the preceding "spacey" virtual environment in their heads. The interdependence of perception and action, a cornerstone of the ecological approach, could hardly be more directly manifested.

This chapter has tackled the relationship between music's social meaning and its material, and has argued that the relationship can be understood as much more perceptual than has hitherto been understood. The resistance to doing so has come on the one hand from a suspicion on the part of musicologists and critical theorists that a perceptual approach implies determinacy, and a failure to recognize the social and historical nature of both human subjects and musical materials; and on the other hand from psychologists, who have regarded accounts of music's social meaning as too speculative, subjective, and discourse-based to be amenable to psychological inquiry or explanation. Both of these resistances are unwarranted: perception is not determinate, as its variability in even quite simple and everyday circumstances illustrates—and in aesthetic contexts it is particularly and deliberately so. If this indeterminacy leads to diverse and sometimes unanticipated perceptions of "what's going on" and what it means, this is, as Marvin Gaye fans will readily agree, no reason for us to reject them, or to regard them as somehow rarified or fantastic. Perception is a matter of being tuned to the opportunities that the environment offers, and aesthetic objects offer exceptionally multivalent opportunities. We shouldn't shy away from recognizing that this leads to diverse perceptions; that some of these will reflect the particular preoccupations and perceptual tuning of an individual; and indeed that perceptual information can be properly described only relative to the capacities, sensitivities, and interests of a perceiver. If people use the perceptions of others (critics, commentators, teachers, friends) to guide their own attention such that they end up perceiving in that way too, this is not evidence for the nonperceptual character of the resulting experience; rather, it is an illustration of the much more general and pervasive principle of perceptual learning.

The contribution of ecological theory is thus to ground the elusive relationship between musical material and social meaning by insisting upon the manner in which musical sound specifies a whole range of invariants—from the instruments and human actions that make it, through the musical structures, styles and genres to which it belongs, to the social conditions from which it arises and to which it contributes (cf. Dibben 2001). The problem is not in bringing these elements together, but is rather to trace explicitly how any particular invariant is specified in the stimulus, and to consider music's affordances in a properly listener-specific fashion. The psychological framework sketched in this chapter is one particular way to understand the relationship between musical materials and social meaning—not through the language of codification and representation, but through the perceptual principles of specification and affordance. An advantage of this approach is that the arbitrariness and abstraction of codification are replaced by the realism and materialism of perception, restoring the connection between the aesthetic consciousness of musical listening and the practical consciousness of "everyday" listening.

It also exposes, however, a deep-seated uncertainty within both music theory and the psychology of music about the significance of musical structure. There have been times when both music theory and the psychology of music have claimed that structure is really all there is—or perhaps all there is that's worth talking about—followed by reactions to such a totalizing stance (Cook 1994; Levinson 1997; Dell'Antonio 2004) that have been more skeptical about how much structure, and of what kind, listeners can really pick up; and that indeed have questioned the whole ideology of "structural listening." The point on which I finish, then, is this: the idea that the social meaning of local, small-scale musical materials can be picked up by listeners is perhaps not too controversial. What is more challenging is the question of whether and how these immediate perceptual meanings relate to larger musical form, and in particular whether this relationship should be understood as abstract, discursive and codified, or as another aspect of a unified perceptual process. I have pushed the perceptual view both because it emphasizes the continuity between different types of listening and because it encourages a close consideration of the properties of musical materials relative to different listeners. But questions about the perceptual directness, or cognitive abstraction, of larger-scale musical organization and meaning may in the end come down to a proper empirical investigation of some of the issues that are raised by such an outlook, and which have so far received little attention.

Further Reading

Clarke, Eric F. 2005. *Ways of listening: an ecological approach to the perception of musical meaning*. New York: Oxford University Press.

Clarke, Eric F., Nicola Dibben, and Stephanie E. Pitts. 2010. *Music and mind in everyday life*. Oxford: Oxford University Press.

Cook, Nicholas. 1990. *Music, imagination and culture*. Oxford: Oxford University Press.

DeNora, Tia. 2000. *Music in everyday life*. Cambridge, U.K.: Cambridge University Press.

Leman, Marc. 2007. *Embodied music cognition and mediation technology*. Cambridge, MA: MIT Press.

Musicae Scientiae 2001. Special issue on *Perspectives on musical meaning*. 5(2).

Windsor, W. Luke. 2000. Through and around the acousmatic: the interpretation of electroacoustic sounds. Pp. 7–35 in *Music, electronic media and culture*. Edited by Simon Emmerson. Aldershot, U.K.: Ashgate.

CHAPTER 30

MUSICAL MATERIALS, PERCEPTION, AND LISTENING

NICOLA DIBBEN

On the basis of the history of research into music perception and cognition one could be forgiven for assuming that the cultural character of music has little to do with the perceptual capabilities of individuals. Research into the perception and cognition of music has largely focused on the perception of auditory events such as pitch, grouping, and tonal and rhythmic structures. One of the most influential accounts of music cognition in the last thirty years has been the idea that listeners hear relationships between abstract underlying structures in music, as well as surface relationships, and that a hierarchy of tonal structures is fundamental to the listening experience (e.g., Lerdahl and Jackendoff 1983). The titles of work in this domain, such as Steven Handel's *Listening*, belie an almost exclusive focus on musical sound conceived in terms of "raw" parameters.

Much of this research converges with a particular branch of music theory and analysis: many theoretical concepts such as pitches, chords, harmonies, scales, keys, voice-leading, and rhythmic structures have received empirical verification. However, while some of these theoretical constructs do seem to be heard, others seem to bear little relationship to listeners' experiences. For example, despite much research into the cognitive reality of large-scale structure there is little evidence that the large-scale hierarchical structures posited by cognitive theories play an important role in listeners' aesthetic appreciation of music. Furthermore, while attempting to describe the perceptions of experienced listeners, these models tend to result in a "view from nowhere": the listening subject is deleted in favor of an apparently objective reading of musical structure (Cross 1998).

The conception of material implicit in these approaches is in direct contrast with historically or socially informed approaches within music theory and criticism. For example, semiotic theories conceive of music not in terms of raw parameters and structures but in terms of "topics" or "archetypes"—musical materials that come with a history of use (e.g., Agawu 1991). And other instances of the "new musicology" present interpretations of works in which musical structures are read in terms of social meanings. Thus, there appears to be a sharp divide between conceptions of musical material implicit in studies of music perception, and those implied by some branches of music theory and history.

One interpretation of the absence of empirical research into the perception of musical "material" is that listeners don't really "hear" the structures and meanings identified in music theory and criticism, and that therefore there is no need, or indeed point, to carrying out perceptual studies to show the cognitive reality of these materials. Indeed, the way in which the relationship between music perception and music theory has generally been conceived is that whereas music perception and cognition studies what listeners hear, music theory persuades the listener of what they might or could hear. Taken at face value, this is a problematic distinction. On the one hand, it seems to suggest that the cultural and social meanings identified by theory and criticism are not related in any way to historically situated musical materials heard by an individual, and that, on the other hand, there is a level of musical experience that is unmediated and to which a sociologically informed hermeneutics is subsequently applied. In this chapter I review some empirical evidence that listeners hear musical "material," not just "sound," and consider implications of the cultural construction of listening for understanding the perception of music. I start by presenting an account of musical structure that brings together a more veridical account of listening with a culturally informed conception of musical material.

ASSOCIATIVE STRUCTURE

An alternative to hierarchical models of musical structure is the idea of "associative" structure—relationships between musical events, or musical events and things "outside" the music, which connect with each other rather than subsume each other. Little empirical or theoretical research has been conducted into associative structure. Leonard Meyer (1973) provides a discussion of the associative structure of melody, and more recently Jerrold Levinson (1997) has argued that music is heard on a "moment-to-moment" basis (what he terms *concatenationism*), rather than in terms of large-scale structural relationships between events separated in time. According to Levinson, knowing that large-scale relationships exist may have some effect on the listening experience, but is not necessary to the aesthetic experience of music. In effect, his theory rehabilitates the untrained listener, and attempts a more veridical account of the listening experience. Despite criticism of the idea of concatenationism by some music theorists (critics have argued that large-scale structural relationships do play a part in the listening experience for them), Levinson's approach is important because it is a systematic attempt to clarify what a nonhierarchical experience of musical structure might be like.

The approach that I propose differs from both Meyer's and Levinson's in that it encompasses associative links in two axes, which are somewhat similar to the syntagmatic and paradigmatic axes of Saussurean linguistics. Meyer primarily discusses the syntagmatic axis, analyzing and categorizing the associative links between elements occurring within the same piece of music but displaced in time. It is in this domain that subsequent empirical research has been conducted. The paradigmatic axis (Saussure himself originally called this the "associative axis") is concerned with the relationship between any instance of an element and the other elements belonging to the same category with which it could be substituted. This axis captures the manner in which musical materials refer beyond themselves to other instances (archetypes, prototypes) that may not be present here and now but that give a basis for evaluating those that are. The difference between this theory of associative structure and hierarchical theories of music perception mentioned earlier is that it treats the substance of musical sound as "material" rather than as raw parameters. This alternative conception of musical material can be thought of as operating in two dimensions: first, intraopus, forging relationships within a particular piece, and giving rise to a sense of coherence; and, second, extraopus, by virtue of reference to other specific, or generic, works and styles.

There are a number of clues to the existence of musical "material." One such clue lies within hierarchical perceptual theories themselves. Although *A Generative Theory of Tonal Music* (Lerdahl and Jackendoff 1983) specifies a set of rules that remove successively higher levels of structure, it is not able to do this with the two-membered cadence. The authors argue that "we must regard cadences as signs, or conventional formulas" (1983, 134), and in doing so they render the theory open to historical style analysis. This treatment of the cadence is an example of a more widespread phenomenon identified by music theory and analysis: the idea that musical material does not consist only of the "raw" parameters of pitch, rhythm, contour, and so on, but is socially and historically constituted. Influenced by semiotics, music theory refers to this material as "topics," "schemata," and "archetypes," and proposes that, owing to the compositional and social use of particular materials, their meanings or functions have become stabilized over time. Drawing on the writings of Theodor Adorno, a number of scholars have elaborated on this idea (Green 1988; Paddison 1996). In very broad terms it suggests that musical materials are heard in terms of their historical usage, such that if they have been associated with particular social (or musical) contexts or functions those meanings remain when they are used outside of those locations. The discourse surrounding music (program notes, narratives, lyrics, visual accompaniment, and so on) provides an interpretative context that reinforces those meanings. This idea underlies Philip Tagg's analytical method (Tagg and Clarida 2003). An often-cited example used to illustrate Tagg's method is the television theme song to the American detective series *Kojak* (Tagg 1982), in which, among other motifs and associated meanings, the use of brass signifies predatory behavior (because of the history of the use of brass instruments in hunting calls) and is associated with masculinity (owing to the hunting reference, but also to other musical and film contexts in which this figure accompanies the appearance of the male hero).

In sum, I argue that listeners make associative links between musical elements that are present in any given piece, and at the same time make associations with similar or functionally equivalent elements or gestures in the wider repertoire of music with which they are familiar—a process akin to that of Steven Feld's (1994a) "interpretive moves," in which we can think of "[musical] sound as structures rooted in our listening experience." My approach is based on the premise that musical materials are heard in terms of their historical usage, whether that be their compositional use with regard to fulfilling particular structural functions, or their association with particular social contexts. The advantage of this approach is that it does away with a crude distinction between intramusical and extramusical attributes: sounds always have a compositional function, and are part of a social situation. This is, in essence, an argument for paying more attention to the historical and social nature of musical material, rather than simply treating it as raw materials in the here and now. And in doing so, one finds that these associative links lead beyond what is commonly regarded as the domain of music into a more general system of cultural reference.

HEARING "MATERIAL"

The idea that people hear music in terms of material rather than sound is central to applications of ecological psychology to music (see the chapter by Eric Clarke in this volume). Drawing on ecological psychology, William Gaver (1993) distinguishes between two listening modes, which he equates with two types of sound: "musical listening," in which the listener attends to the acoustic characteristics of sound, and "everyday" listening, in which the listener attends to the sources specified by sounds (such as the way in which a sound informs about the size and material of the object that produces it, and the manner in which it has been produced). Subsequent applications of ecological psychology to music differ from Gaver's approach in two important respects. First, the distinctions between "everyday" and "musical" listening are theorized not as two different types of sound but as two different listening modes. The question then becomes one of when and why listeners hear sounds in one way rather than another. This is addressed through the notion of "affordance" (the way in which the meanings of things are a function of the mutuality of organism and environment) and captures the way in which the meanings specified by sounds are always meanings for someone rather than being properties of an object. Notably, Feld also emphasizes the role of mutualism in the social construction of musical meaning, arguing that "Interpretive moves . . . emerge dialectically from the human social encounter with a sound object or event" (1994a, 86). The second important difference is the extension of source specification to include not only physical sources of sounds but also the cultural and historical meanings of material, and their compositional functions (cf. the work of Eric Clarke, and of Luke Windsor).

Relatively few empirical studies have investigated the perception of music in terms of this notion of musical "material." Robert Francès's book *The Perception of Music* (1988) includes an account of listening studies that show that listeners are sensitive to the cultural and historical meanings of musical material. Carol Krumhansl (1998) has investigated perception of "topics" in classical music, although this is in terms of their occurrence rather than their specific content. And a number of studies, Francès's among them, have shown that listeners are sensitive to the structural functions in music (for example, the way in which diverse musical material may have a closural function in a piece of music). One study that contextualizes its findings in relation to listening as a cultural practice is John Baily's study of Herati Afghans' perceptions of a range of musical and everyday sounds. Baily asked his listeners to describe a selection of musical and everyday sounds, and found that his informants tended to describe sounds in terms of their meanings and values. Baily concluded that "Afghans do not generally perceive sounds as abstract entities, as pure sounds, in the way that Europeans may do" (1996, 173).

Following from this research, I carried out a listening study that investigated the range of meanings sound material has for Western listeners (Dibben 2001). In one task (similar to that used by Baily), participants were presented with 48 short sound examples of musical and nonmusical sounds, and asked to describe the thing they were hearing. The range of responses included reference to acoustic attributes, physical source, genre, compositional function, physical space, proximity of the sound to the listener, performance skill, emotional character, and social context. Overall, listeners described sounds in terms of their physical and cultural sources more frequently than in terms of their acoustic characteristics. This indicates that, for these listeners, listening to music involves more than listening to its acoustic attributes; it involves hearing meanings specified by sounds. This finding serves to highlight the narrowness with which perception is traditionally conceptualized within music perception research. It also shows that listeners are sensitive to the physical and cultural sources and associations of sounds, contrary to constructions of Western music, and of the Western listening aesthetic as one in which listeners pay attention to "pure" sounds. A subsequent study has provided behavioral and electroencephalographic evidence of this, demonstrating that music can prime particular words, and therefore conveys semantic meaning (Koelsch et al. 2004).

In itself, the findings of these studies are no great revelation; intuitively it seems obvious that listeners hear sounds in terms of their meanings and contexts. What are more important are the questions they raise regarding subjectivity, and the apparent tension between subjectivity and the idea of sedimented meaning—the meanings that accrue to musical material as a result of its history of use. Although there was a great deal of agreement between listeners' descriptions of sounds in my listening study (as might be expected given a shared cultural context and listening conditions), there were nonetheless differences between the descriptions of sounds given by different participants. Why is it that some listeners described sounds in terms of one kind of attribute (acoustic characteristics, the physical source of the sound, and so on) rather than another? These differences seem to be due to a number of factors. First, listeners may simply be mistaken about some aspect of the sound, as for example in the case of a six-second recording of vinyl hiss that listeners described variously as the sound of vinyl, the sound of burning, and the sound of bees. In this case, differences between listeners arise from the paucity of the information presented, leading to confusion over the sound source. Second, listeners may simply not be aware of a culturally significant attribute: some listeners described the sound of a stringed instrument accurately as a koto, whereas others, less familiar with this genre, described the sound in terms of its acoustic attributes. Third, listeners privilege certain meanings over others according to their needs and preoccupations and the information available to them. For example, responses to an excerpt from Beethoven's Violin Concerto in D Major, op. 61, included descriptions of the sound source ("violin concerto—Beethoven"), genre ("Classical"), structural function ("development part"), physical space and social context ("church"), reflecting differences of background and training among other factors. And for one informant—a seventeen-year-old student from a relatively disadvantaged background with little if any training in classical music, and participating in my study as a visitor on an outreach program run by the university—the salient aspect of an extract from Beethoven's Violin Concerto in D Major, op. 61, was its class allegiances ("posh"). On the face of it these differences seem to argue against the idea of sedimented meaning and serve to highlight the question of whose meanings these are. The notion of sedimented meaning is problematic to the extent that it is an analytical convenience—an averaging out of interpretations of material arising from an assumed common cultural context. Yet it is still commensurate with a dialectical notion of the relationship between listener and material: In other words, the perceptual characteristics of the stimulus are dependent on the needs of the individual, and the properties of the object (cf. Eric Clarke, this volume)—although stating it in this way already suggests a misleading polarization.

The descriptions of the extracts given above highlight one way in which this dialectical relationship of listener and material works to produce meanings. Just as the Beethoven example mobilized particular meanings to do with social class for the participant in my listening study, so too DeNora has argued that music focuses particular meanings for musicologists and critics:

> Telling what the meaning is, and deftly deflecting dispreferred meanings and readings, is part and parcel of the semiotic skills of daily life. We need to learn to see professional semioticians in a similar vein—as mobilizing particular features of utterances in order to produce meanings.
>
> (DeNora 2000, 38)

Musicological interpretation and criticism have come to be seen as *formative* of the meanings and significance of music rather than as simply "reflecting" truth. The most notorious example of this type of writing, and one that invited most response along these lines, was Susan McClary's feminist analysis of Beethoven's Ninth Symphony in which she interprets the first movement recapitulation as an episode of horrifying violence (McClary 1991, 128). Detractors of McClary's approach argued that such interpretations were fabrication, arbitrarily related to the musical trace. One reason for the heated debate that surrounded this critical reading was its failure to articulate the basis for its interpretive claims, which led to a mistaken assumption as to how and what music means: McClary's analysis provides a way of perceiving the musical work, and in light of this we may also perceive what she perceives, and mistakenly assume that it was there all along (cf. DeNora 2000; Cook 1990). Seen in this way, musicological writings have a specifically instructional role, often for political ends—whether that be to point up constructions of gender and sexuality in the music of Beethoven in a way relevant to a late-twentieth-century reaction against formalism, and concern with sexual equality, in the case of McClary, or, in the case of some of her detractors, a means of protecting the notion of autonomous music. The important point is that music analysis and criticism are concerned with persuasion rather than proof, with providing ways of experiencing music— the ramifications of which are only slowly becoming apparent for psychological approaches to music listening. As others have argued, one function of theoretical accounts is to provide new ways of hearing (or imagining) music—in effect, to produce music.

LISTENING PRACTICES AND MUSICAL CULTURE

The approach to music listening that I have presented here understands musical materials as having a history of use resulting from their socio-historical associations, and is in direct contrast to the view espoused in hierarchical models of perception and cognition. I have argued that hierarchical models of the perception of music are premised upon the idea that listeners' perceptions can be described adequately without taking into account the historical character of musical material, and that in these models the musical work is viewed as a concrete, self-contained unit specified by the notes of the score. By contrast, the theory of associative structure makes possible the interpenetration of immanent analysis with the socio-historical and extramusical context. The history of research in music perception and cognition reflects a prevailing reception ideology of Western art music in which listening has been conceptualized as attentive but passive listening to musical structures. However, to paraphrase Nicholas Cook on the aesthetics of Western art music: To interpret music in terms of an interest in sound and its perceptual experience does not transcend cultural values, it expresses them (1990, 7).

Knowing how to listen, and what to hear, are parts of what constitutes musical culture. Nicholas Cook has argued that "a musical culture is essentially a cognitive entity . . . to define a musical culture means defining the things a people must know in order to understand, perform and create acceptable music in their culture . . . ear training forms the basic means by which the identity of a musical culture is maintained" (Cook 1990, 222).

From this perspective "contemplative" listening, the act of listening afforded to audience members by Western classical concert music, is just one of a number of ways of listening. An ecological perspective argues that whether one pays attention to the acoustic character of sounds, or to their social and physical specifications, is determined by the needs and preoccupations of the moment. However, it is also determined by a set of listening practices into which listeners are enculturated.

As I have argued, the passive and laboratory-based listening context required by most research in music perception is modeled on a prevailing ideology of Western art music as "works" that are subject to attentive, passive listening. However, as any historical or cross-cultural survey shows, there is a coevolution of beliefs about music and listening practices. James Johnson has traced the way in which changing listening practices coincided with new ways of thinking about music's materials and forms in nineteenth-century France (Johnson 1995). And in terms of more recent developments, the impact of recording technology on listening is the most obvious focus of research into changing listening practices: in particular, the experience of music removed from its original social and cultural context (Benjamin [1936] 1973b; Chanan 1995); and the invention of a new kind of listener produced by a historicized musical repertoire (Hennion and Fauquet 2001). However, this should not be taken solely as an argument for the "impact of recording": In a remarkable reversal of the one-way conception of the relationship between listening and recording (an influence running from recording to listening), Jonathan Sterne has shown how ideas about listening, and about music, have shaped the development and use of sound reproduction technology, as evidenced by that most macabre of hearing devices, the "ear phonautograph," which used a real human ear to trace the soundwaves coming into the eardrum onto a glass surface (Sterne 2001).

One way in which research in music perception can contribute to an understanding of music listening is to offer psychological explanations of why we hear what we hear, and of what effect particular listening practices might have in determining this. For example, there is empirical evidence from ecological psychology that under circumstances where people are unable to explore a particular perceptual event they tend to describe it in terms of its perceptual qualities rather than in terms of its properties and identity. James Gibson (1966, [1979] 1986) found that when presented with a haptic (i.e., tactile or kinesthetic) stimulus participants described it in terms of sensations on the hand, whereas a participant allowed to explore it actively tended to report object properties and identity. In the domain of sound, William Gaver found that listeners tended to describe sounds in terms of their acoustic characteristics when the source of the sound was ambiguous (1993). And in a similarity task in which listeners were asked to pair two out of three sounds related either by acoustic similarity or by source similarity, participants tended to group sounds on the basis of acoustic similarity (Dibben 2001). Luke Windsor has argued that music and other aesthetic objects afford interpretation because of the very ability of music to deny the possibility of exploration with the other perceptual senses one would normally employ to make sense of the world (2000). Where the immediate information from the perceptual source (e.g., sound) is insufficient, the listener searches for additional information from the social and cultural environment: by observing the behavior of others, by discussions with others, and by exploring the music through the discourse and other information that surrounds it. Methods within music perception which remove music from its context therefore encourage participants to adopt some aspects of a listening perspective associated with the Western art tradition of autonomous music—the stereotype of listeners with eyes shut, silent and still that came about during the Romantic period. The point is not that we should therefore do away with these techniques because they reproduce a culturally specific mode of reception, but that we should recognize the potential for research in music perception to shed light on how perceptions and interpretations are produced.

What are the implications of this for a culturally informed approach to research in music perception? First, it suggests that sound should be conceptualized not only in terms of "raw" parameters but also in terms of musical "materials" heard in terms of their history and context of use. Second, it suggests that research needs to investigate the relationship between music theory and music perception—not to show if and how the two match up, but to investigate how musical discourse impinges on experience. Third, and perhaps most importantly, it suggests an alternative theorization—of listening as social action (cf. Small 1998). At the crux of this argument is a critique of the Western ideology that the material of music history lies in the creation of forms rather than social action. This is not to reject the existing tools and theories of music perception, but to recognize that they are produced within and, to some extent, reproduce culturally specific reception ideologies. Once this conceptual shift is made, it allows studies of perception to take into account the social and physical mediation of listening, and to ground observations in a more reflexive understanding of how they are obtained. If we are able to do this then we may really be capable of a culturally informed theory of music perception.

FURTHER READING

Clarke, Eric F. 2005. *Ways of listening: An ecological approach to the perception of musical meaning.* New York: Oxford University Press.

Cook, Nicholas. 1990. *Music, imagination and culture.* Oxford: Clarendon Press.

Cross, Ian. 1998. Music analysis and music perception. *Music Analysis* 17(1): 3–20.

DeNora, Tia. 2000. *Music in everyday life.* Cambridge, U.K.: Cambridge University Press.

Du Gay, Paul, Stuart Hall, Linda Janes, Hugh Mackay, and Keith Negus, eds. 1997. *Doing cultural studies: The story of the Sony Walkman.* London: Sage.

Johnson, James H. 1995. *Listening in Paris: A cultural history.* Berkeley: University of California Press.

Small, Christopher. 1998. *Musicking: The meanings of performing and listening.* Hanover, NH: University Press of New England.

Sterne, Jonathan. 2001. A machine to hear for them: On the very possibility of sound's reproduction. *Cultural Studies* 15(2): 259–294.

Windsor, W. Luke. 2000. Through and around the acousmatic: the interpretation of electroacoustic sounds. Pp. 7–35 in *Music, electronic media and culture.* Edited by Simon Emmerson. Aldershot, U.K.: Ashgate.

CHAPTER 31

MUSIC, EXPERIENCE, AND THE ANTHROPOLOGY OF EMOTION

RUTH FINNEGAN

It is surely a truism that music cannot be equated just with its textual realization, nor even just with its composition and performance or the processes through which it is created and circulated, important—and well-studied—as these topics are. It is also a matter of people's subjective experience.

Attempts to capture this aspect of music have always been problematic but are now attracting growing interest. This was already true at the time of the first edition of this volume (2003), if in sparse and scattered form. In the intervening years a plenitude of further publications have been appearing in the increasingly interdisciplinary study of music and emotion (notably captured in Juslin and Sloboda 2010). Even now however the experiential dimensions of music are regarded as somewhat marginal to the central concerns of musicology, and their study commonly overlooked in favor of perhaps more readily researchable topics. This chapter briefly considers some of the background to this and refers to attempts to overcome the conceptual and ideological dichotomies that have for long impeded the exploration of musical experiencing.

EMOTION, MIND, AND BODY

The background largely lies in that familiar and still-powerful theme-with-variations running through Western thought—the value-laden oppositions between mind and body, intellect and emotion, meaning and feeling. Romanticist accounts used these polarities to celebrate the emotional side.

More commonly reason was set on top, its role to control our lower "animal" nature and lead upward into the scientific, emotion-free enlightenment of human language and writing. It was these cognitive elements, furthermore, that were regularly taken as the self-evident focus for scholarly analysis.

These ideas have long influenced our models of culture and, with it, of music. Western classical music—the assumed norm—has often been implicitly assigned to the "rational" side of the equation, connected with written formulations and the intellectual elements of cultivated human society. Scholars privileged music's cognitive and nonbodily features, highlighting composition, written scores, and the rationality of classic music theory: *these* aspects, not the primeval emotions, seemed the appropriate focus for study. Emotions have certainly not always been disregarded in analyses of music; but in conventional Western musicological models they have commonly been envisaged as something to be controlled and refined by reason. In a common twentieth-century view, "music" (read, Western classical music) is "a language of the emotions, through which we directly experience the fundamental urges that move mankind. . . . A dangerous art. . . . But under the guidance of the intellect and the enlightened moral sense, it is surely as safe as anything human can be" (Cooke 1959, 272).

The musicological task, then, was not to dwell on the "fundamental urges" but to provide the intellectual guidance for regulating them and for analyzing music's rational features: feasible for "true" music, in contrast to unwritten forms like jazz, rock, or African drumming that were cast as irredeemably "physical," the "mindless" outflow of primal emotion. Musicology was the purview of the specialist trained expert, dedicated to the analysis of Western art music. Prolific twentieth-century "listeners' guides" offered intellectual expositions of the expressiveness in the musical work (not in the listeners), focusing on the musical text and teaching listeners "how musical elements fit together" (Ratner 1977, 1). Similarly Leonard Meyer's *Emotion and Meaning in Music* did not treat ordinary people's experiences but the "syntax" of musical works and the judgments of "composers, performers, theoreticians and competent critics" (1956, 197).

This cluster of assumptions is increasingly in question. We are nowadays ready to challenge limiting ethnocentric models, among them those attributed to traditional musicology, and in so doing to go beyond prescription, intellectual theory, and written products into people's (varied) practices. Added to this are new approaches to experience and emotion as subjects for serious study in people's everyday actions rather than as matters of speculation, disapproval, or buried mystery, far less as just confined to the sensibilities of elite and self-selected authorities.

Anthropological approaches to the study of emotion have made a significant contribution here. Anthropologists had long noted links between ritual and sentiment, and in the later twentieth century were explicitly tackling the subject of emotion. The anthropologist John Blacking pointed to experiential processes like falling in love, ecstasy, or joy in dancing (1977, 5), and his analyses of music (1973, 1987) brought together body and thought, feeling and practice. Meantime Vic Turner was developing the "anthropology of experience" (Turner and Bruner 1986), and from the 1980s anthropological work on emotion was increasingly taking off (Crapanzano 1994; Heelas 1996; Lutz and White 1986; Lutz and Abu-Lughod 1990; Schwartz et al. 1992; also, more recently, Klima 2008; Lindholm 2007, 266–295; Magowan 2007; Milton 2002; Milton and Svašek 2005; Wulff 2007).

The emphasis was on cultural relativity. This was rooted not only in changing theoretical insights but also—an essential component—in detailed ethnographic studies. Contrary to what had often been assumed, emotions came to be seen not as universal facts of nature but as differently formulated in different times and places. We *learn* how to feel, and how to deploy particular emotions in ways and contexts appropriate to our situation. People also learn the discourses through which their emotions are more, or less, verbalized, for conceptualizations differ too, from the "hydraulic metaphor" underlying many Western views to the Sudanic Dinka concept of forces acting from outside (Lutz and White 1986, 419; Heelas 1996, 182). The study of experience, including musical experience, needs to be cognizant of such cultural specificities.

And it is a matter not just of passive feelings but of the active "management" of feeling. Emotions can be socially arranged and manipulated. Thus flight attendants were trained to shape their feelings to their job (Hochschild 1983). The medieval Christian Church organized sights and sounds to encourage reverence and exaltation just as religious and political movements today deliberately deploy identity-bringing musical performances. Indeed, as Gordon pertinently comments (1990, 168), elites everywhere endeavor to control the material and symbolic resources for emotion production.

Such perspectives have enabled analysts of music to bypass the tendentious mind–body polarity together with the prescriptive—and ethnocentric—model of music associated with it, so as to explore the *diverse* ways people actually experience music in practice. And for *all* participants. In Ola Stockfelt's provocative overstatement, "the listener, and only the listener, is the composer of the music" (1994, 19). Musical experience in other words belongs not just to musical work, composer, or accredited "expert" but also, crucially, to the variegated practitioners and audiences.

It is true that anthropological work has now increasingly diversified, interacting with the surges of interest in emotion across other disciplines and with transdisciplinary feminist, post-structuralist, biological, environmental, and phenomenological approaches (see for example Bendelow and

Williams 1998; Berger 2007; Juslin and Sloboda 2010; Lupton 1998; Milton 2002; Williams 2001). But, behind the diversity of perspectives, the emphasis on cultural/historical specificity remains, something that can and should be explored through in-depth understanding of context and culture. In Helga Kotthoff's succinct summary, "feelings are no longer regarded as something innate and inward, but rather as a culturally interwoven and shaped mode of experience" (2001, 169).

STUDYING MUSICAL EXPERIENCES

A handful of brief examples can give a flavor of the ways studies of musical experience are now attempting to transcend the old dichotomies. Differ as they do, they build on anthropological insights in sharing a preparedness to attempt in-depth ethnographic study, culture-sensitive and nonjudgmental, in pursuit not of universals but of the embodied experiences of participants in music in specific situations.

Take the anthropologist Steven Feld's now-classic study, *Sound and Sentiment* (1990), based on long participant observation among the New Guinean Kaluli. He explores their music as interwoven into all the associations that Kaluli learn to feel between "birds, weeping, poetics, and song." Feld uncovers the complex sonic world in and through which Kaluli live, the ways they describe and experience it, and the interaction among the sorrowful songs of their night-long ceremonies, the tears these stir in their hearers, the rage with which these deeply moved participants retaliate—and are expected to retaliate—against their mythically informed experiences, and the acoustic epistemology that resonates through their lives. The songs, thoughtfully composed and deliberately rehearsed, are oriented to making the listeners sad and nostalgic, organizing feelings of sadness and rage and eventually moving them to tears. They are performed by a dancer whose demeanor and actions create "an image of loneliness and isolation," and what dominates both the aftermath and the remembrances of the event is "the way the songs persuaded the audience to tears" (Feld 1990, 215, 7)

Other traditions differ. The anthropologist Simon Ottenberg describes the freelance Limba musician Sayo in northern Sierra Leone, his vocal-instrumental performances marked by a sense of sadness and misfortune, of a lack of ability to control life or destiny. But the listeners to these sorrowful songs do not show sadness. As members of the chorus—participant listeners—they seem concerned not with the words but with the enjoyment of responding, clapping, and dancing (Ottenberg 1996, 92–93). Their reactions stand in stark contrast to those of the Kaluli—but are no less a real dimension of their musical experiences.

Different again is the musical lamenting in (Caucasian) Georgia, where the women "carry out emotion work" for the community (Kotthoff 2001, 25). Their laments are not the outcome of spontaneous irrational forces but worked-on artistic performances. The singers' management of their feelings structures the emotional occasion and enables the audience to grieve.

> For the lamenters aesthetical grieving means to keep control over their feelings. They cannot let themselves go. For some of the listeners the process is the other way round. They are inflicted with their pain. . . . [The occasion] involves the audience in grieving . . . coming to terms with the loss.
>
> (Kotthoff 2001, 192, 25)

Another example is Daniel Cavicchi's work on music and meaning among Bruce Springsteen fans (it is not just among "other cultures" that musical experience can be studied). Cavicchi uncovers the complex ways fans experience the music: their shared enthusiasms, experiential conventions in "becoming-a-fan" narratives, sense of personal connection with Springsteen. The performances are not to watch passively, but to join. "I'm tired after seeing a Bruce show," says one fan, "I've been on my feet, I've been applauding and I've been yelling and screaming" (Cavicchi 1998, 93). Another describes "the feeling that one has just been to a religious revival. . . . Faith and Hope and Joy!," while for yet another:

> It gets you into it physically, because you're dancing, you're moving around, you're waving your arms, you're clapping your hands. You get into it mentally because you know the lyrics or you're listening to them again, maybe you're getting another meaning out of them, a new meaning or an old meaning, whatever. It's just such an energizing experience, and it's a spiritual experience. So, it gets you, mind, body, and soul.
>
> (Cavicchi 1998, 95)

It is not just "fun" but personal critical appreciation. Rejecting armchair generalizations about illusion or hegemony, Cavicchi explains how fans' experiences interact with their individual lives. "During the commute, at work, at school, . . . most fans are still 'listening' . . . making associations between perceived musical structures, potential messages, and the contexts of their experiences" (p. 126).

The complexity of musical experience—mind, body, movement, environment, sensation—also comes out vividly in Fiona Magowan's study of music and emotion in an aboriginal community in northern Australia (Magowan 2007). She traces the connections between the emotions formulated and experienced in women's crying songs (and their hearing and danced participation) and the modes through which children's musical learning is intimately intertwined with knowledge about sea and land, about individual and clan identity, the role of ancestral beings, and an expanding multisensory experiencing of the world. Learning music and dance is to experience and reproduce environmental rhythms and perceive ancestral presence, enacted in sounding, singing and moving (ibid., 99, 188). This deeply grounded background of shared emotive, sensory, somatic, and cognitive meaning gives the setting for musical display, above all for the senior women's obligation to perform crying songs in public mourning, vehicles for capturing and expressing deeply felt emotion. Such singing depends on a conscious decision "to speak out and share emotions performatively, extending the personal and private realm of grieving to the broader realm of public life" (ibid., 85).

The experiencing of music, in short, emerges not as random but as molded through specific groups, genres, and contexts. So too in the English town of Milton Keynes, people's experiences in the contrasting "worlds" of jazz, folk, or classical music are interwoven with differing practices and conceptualizations of performance, composition, and learning (Finnegan 1989; see also Hennion 1997). In the Balkans, Serbian epic-singing is heard with pride by many Serbs but with terror by some of their Croat neighbors (Petrovic in Baily 1995, 69), while in Ulster listeners experience the emotive sounds of Orange flutes and drums in contrasting ways, bound into long historical-mythic associations. Expectations differ over time as well. An early listener to Chopin playing the piano, for example, formulated the experience through the otherworldly metaphors then current but less likely to come to mind today: "[The music] seems to descend from heaven—so pure, and clear, and spiritual" (Kallberg 1994, 52). Specific genres come to have particular associations at given times or places: for some overtones of nostalgia and loss; for others excitement, dance, or rowdy laughter; for others again gaiety, solemnity, exuberance, reverence, humor, protest, or affront, where, again, it makes no sense to draw an opposition between thought and feeling.

Amidst the inescapable diversities—part of the findings—some points are worth drawing out. It is striking how often rituals are intershot with music, managing fraught situations in human lives and presenting organized public occasions for emotional deployment. Through music, public ceremonies can exploit the encompassing capacity of sound to marshal a sense of *communitas*, where, as Van Leeuwen suggests (1999, 197), "listening is connection, communion." Experience is dynamically co-created too as people dance with each other, beat time, move together, construct and reexperience their recollections later—realizations of human sociality that recall Schutz's "mutual tuning-in relationship" (1951, 92). The collective experiencing of music can divide as well as unite of course. Its military usages have been a common feature through the ages, powerful in stirring not only feelings of identity but hostility and aggression. As Gerd Baumann rightly insists,

> Every experience of collective "communion" . . . forging an experiential "us" . . . can [also] be abused. Whether it is engendered by [raindances in the Nuba mountains], or associated with the rousing rendition of a Nazi hymn . . . it can be exploited, and perhaps even induced, in the interests of powerful elites, sectional interests, or seductive hegemonic ideas.
>
> (Baumann in Baily 1995, 38)

Another recurrent theme in the literature is the consciousness-changing potential of music. The Georgian lamenters created "a non-ordinary experiential and imaginative involvement and a space where the living are seemingly in contact with the dead" (Kotthoff 2001, 173), while among Liverpool rock performers music "creates its own space and time where all kinds of dreams, emotions, and thoughts are possible" (Cohen 1991, 191). Limba musical performances altered everyday time and thought, overshadowing the here and now (which in Sierra Leone could be grim indeed). Instrumentalists and chorus were "happy in a sort of pleasant, timeless musical world" as troubles and conflicts were publicly expressed, an opening for people to "deal with the reality of their feelings under the appearance of happiness" (Ottenberg 1996, 192–193):

> The repetitiveness of the instrumental music and song, the steady rhythm, sometimes the repetitive movements of dancers in a circle, and the minimizing of everyday time allowed not only for a sense of momentary social solidarity but also for a special sort of inner individualism . . . swinging back and forth between full consciousness and daydreaming.

The varying experiences of time and imagination in differing contexts, elusive as these are, are now accepted topics for in-depth research, exploring the complex and subtle intertwining of cultural expectation, specific setting, and individually embodied practice.

The focus now, therefore, is not primarily on endeavoring to chart universal emotions (though some such background is not necessarily denied). "Emotion" on its own may still elude clear bounded definition, but the term has acted as a useful prompt to indicate a broad and variegated facet of human life to which words like *emotion, affect, mood, imagination, expressiveness,* and *passion* direct our attention. One prominent manifestation of this is found in the organized expression of such emotions as grief, joy, anger, or aggression, enacted and intensified in music (and, often dance) in the public rituals that have so often caught anthropologists' particular attention. But it is also a thread running through more low-key but still emotive everyday aspects of life, as people hear, practice, and engage in music. Consider for example the overtones of Wagner's music for some listeners; or the multilayered clusters of associations, partly personal, partly shared, of a childhood carol, a Beatles song, the opening of Beethoven's Fifth symphony. Amusement, happiness, intellectual satisfaction, excitement, disapproval—in specific contexts these too are part of people's musical practice. It is not always self-conscious internalized "feelings"—though in some cultural settings that is indeed one recognized element—but also the *manner*, variably practiced and conceptualized in different contexts, in which people are personally involved in their musical engagements: joyfully, fearfully, inattentively, reflectively, proudly; in a spirit of exaltation or energy or irritation; in sorrowful, celebratory, or nostalgic mood; with boredom (that too!), with tranquility. Whether in deeply intense fashion or more light-touch action, music provides a human resource through which people can enact their lives with inextricably entwined feeling, thought, bodily engagement and imagination. Such aspects have in the past been downplayed by scholars but by now we can surely find something recognizable in detailed studies like those mentioned above, the more so because these accounts are tied into overt and specific practices.

The notable feature of these studies is the way they straddle the once rigidly conceived boundaries between mind and body, cognition and emotion, inner and outer. Musical experience is envisaged as embodied and lived, entangled with culturally diverse epistemologies and practices. The Enlightenment ideology of language and the scholars' preoccupation with cognition and verbalized texts are undermined and enlarged by a growing appreciation of human life as everywhere intershot with imagination, with value, with connotation. In Michelle Rosaldo's memorable formulation, "feeling is forever given shape through thought . . . and thought is laden with emotional meaning" (Rosaldo 1984, 137).

COMMENTARY

The study of music and emotion is still scarcely accepted as central to musicology, and even recent publications present it as a relatively new, if expanding, area. But studies like those sketched above suggest a growing confidence in its validity, and, amidst the welcome multidisciplinary take on the subject from many different perspectives (see especially Juslin and Sloboda 2010), a reinforced inclination to go beyond the limitations of the older mutually exclusive oppositions: body/mind; emotion/meaning; Western/other. Replete with problem and controversy as they remain, such attempts to bridge these apparent divisions deserve serious attention.

Let me end by urging the importance of two particular trends in current studies. The first is the modification of earlier anthropological emphases on cultural pressures. Rich as they were and essential in elucidating cultural diversity, the classic works of the 1980s and 1990s tended to downplay individual agency. The last decade has seen not only something of a rapprochement between the once starkly opposed culturalist and universalist approaches to emotion—each offers a useful complementary perspective— but also, more particularly, a growing focus on individual motivations and experience. The traditional model of "culture" as homogeneous external entity has been supplanted among anthropologists—and others too—by talk of differentiation, multiplicity, and individual agency and, as a consequence, an avoidance of cultural determinist perspectives. Interest in personal, not just collective, experience has also been fired by that aspect of the reflexive turn which encourages analysts to recognize their personal emotive experience, sensitizing them to that in others and illuminating the creative roles of individuals as they interact with, and themselves mold, cultural expectations. This does not imply rejecting the earlier insistence that people's experiences are indeed interwoven with conceptualizations and conventions that are shared (more or less) with others—and not always equitably so. But these are now being elucidated not solely as cultural constraints but also as resources that human agents actively draw on and fashion to their own occasions—"a dialectic," as Harris Berger well puts it, "of culture and agency" (2007, 104).

Thus Tia DeNora's *Music in Everyday Life* presents music as "a material that actors use to elaborate, to fill out and fill in, to themselves and to others, modes of aesthetic agency and, with it, subjective stances and identities . . . a resource for producing and recalling emotional states" (DeNora 2000, 74, 107). Her "Lucy" uses Schubert's Impromptus to "retreat into" and "soothe" herself, actively putting together memories, musical recordings, furniture, current emotional state, timing, and biographical associations (DeNora 2000, 42–43). Ottenberg traces how the individual lives of three blind musicians interpenetrate their musical performances (1996), just as Cavicchi (1998) describes individual fans intertwining their personal histories with how they experience Springsteen's music and build it into the fabric of their lives. The imagery of Chopin listeners, Kaluli myth, classical music ideologies, Yolngu musical ecologies, biographical particularities—all in their different ways offer resources through which people actively construct their experiences.

We are thus now more aware that people participate in music in multifarious individual ways, colored not only by recognized cultural convention but also by their personal histories. Different participants organize their experiences differently, and even in collective musical rituals people may move in and out of the "appropriate" emotions. Here again textual analysis or cultural generalization cannot replace time-consuming ethnographic investigation of the actual experiences of variegated participating individuals in all their dynamics and multiplicities. We must leave space for such personal creativities and the active constructing of experience.

Second, it is worth remarking on the now-fashionable awareness of the bodily dimensions of human action. This is directly pertinent for the study of music. We do not have to accept the old body–mind polarities to recognize that sound resonates in the body, and that the experience of music includes its corporeal engagements. Once again traditional dichotomies are challenged, here those that pitted popular and "other" music, in the past often stereotypically categorized as solely of the body, against the classical Western canon with its assumed intellectual quality. Thus funk has often been pictured as the epitome of "blackness," the antithesis of Western art music, and quintessentially "body music"—yet Anne Danielsen's detailed and down-to-earth study convincingly reveals it as being "as much a condition of mind as of body . . . funk is body *and* soul, a body-soul" (2006, 217). And while classical music conventions may control the body in different ways, there too a somatic element is far from absent. Again and again analysis in depth uncovers the bringing together of cognitive, emotive, and bodily dimensions in people's engagement with music, whether in high art forms or "popular" musics like jazz, heavy metal, or rap. Simon Frith sums it up felicitously when he insists that "*all* music-making is about the mind-in-the-body" (1996, 128).

This embodied musical experiencing is the more compelling in that it is so often multimodal, a feature to which the cross-disciplinary popularity of sensory studies has made us more attentive (Howes 2005; Porcello et al. 2010; Sensory Studies 2011). We are now in a better position to appreciate the experiential implications of Barthes's characterization of music as in part manual and muscular ("as if the body was listening, not the 'soul'" (1986, 261), Blacking's delineation of musical performances as "multimedia events" (1987, 123), or Leppert's depictions of the "visual-performative" aspects of music (1993, xxi). All this brings yet further resonances to music's experiential potential—images of place, artifacts (instruments, dress, programs), visual associations, tactile impressions, bodily rhythms, somatic remembrances, intertextualities across a range of senses. These complex multimodalities deserve a central rather than marginal place in our experience-ful analyses of music.

We should welcome this multiplicity of musical experiencings, interfused overlappingly with thought, embodied affect, multiple senses and personal creativity. But, as my final point, let me urge that they can fully emerge only through studies which not only have the theoretical awareness to open the mind to facets not before fully recognized but also—no quick and easy task—pay sensitive attention to ethnographic specificities with all their complications of multiple groups, roles, outlooks, senses, artifacts, and individuals. Sidestepping earlier ill-founded dichotomies and widening the analysis of music to include such issues can lead to both a more realistic appreciation of music and a richer model of human beings and human culture.

FURTHER READING

Becker, Judith. 2010. Exploring the habitus of listening: anthropological perspectives. Pp. 127–157 in *Handbook of music and emotion: theory, research, applications*. Edited by Patrick N. Juslin and John A. Sloboda. Oxford: Oxford University Press.

Berger, Harris M. 2007. *Stance: Ideas about emotion, style, and meaning for the study of expressive culture.* Middletown, CT: Wesleyan University Press.

Danielsen, Anne. 2006. *Presence and pleasure: The funk grooves of James Brown and Parliament.* Middletown, CT: Wesleyan University Press.

DeNora, Tia. 2000. *Music in everyday life.* Cambridge, U.K.: Cambridge University Press.

Feld, Steven. 1990. *Sound and sentiment: Birds, weeping, poetics, and song in Kaluli expression.* 2nd ed. Philadelphia: University of Pennsylvania Press.

Juslin, Patrick N., and John A. Sloboda, eds. 2010. *Handbook of music and emotion: theory, research, applications.* Oxford: Oxford University Press.

Magowan, Fiona. 2007. *Melodies of mourning: Music & emotion in Northern Australia.* Oxford: James Currey.

Milton, Kay and Maruška Svašek, eds. 2005. *Mixed emotions: anthropological studies of feeling.* Oxford: Berg.

Ottenberg, Simon. 1996. *Seeing with music: The lives of three blind African musicians.* Seattle: University of Washington Press.

Schwartz, T., Geoffrey M. White, and Catherine A. Lutz, eds. 1992. *New directions in psychological anthropology.* Cambridge, U.K.: Cambridge University Press.

Turner, Victor, and Edward Bruner, eds. 1986. *The anthropology of experience.* Urbana: University of Illinois Press.

Wulff, Helena, ed. 2007. *The emotions: A cultural reader.* Oxford: Berg.

CHAPTER 32

TOWARDS A POLITICAL
AESTHETICS OF MUSIC

DAVID HESMONDHALGH

This chapter outlines a political aesthetics of music. The aim is to produce a framework that would allow for the evaluation of musical institutions, processes, and developments, in terms of how music, in its various institutional, technological, and textual forms, might inhibit or promote human flourishing. This aesthetics is "political" in a broader sense of politics than that which is concerned with analyzing, for example, how social movements use music or whether certain musical texts reinforce or resist ideology—though this is not to deny the importance of these matters, and it can include them too.

In modern capitalist societies, music is a mode of communication and culture oriented primarily towards artistic expression and experience. To consider music's ability or otherwise to enhance people's lives requires engaging with the significance of the domain of art and aesthetics in modern society. I mean "art" in a broad sense: the use of skills to produce works of the imagination, to invoke feelings of pleasure, beauty, shock, excitement, and so on. The social value of artistic practices and experiences, like education and culture more broadly, has come under attack in recent years. Politicians and commentators question the value of art (see O'Connor 2006 for a brilliant critique of one such case) and, in the British context in which I write, savage cuts in education, library, and arts funding are under way. This will almost certainly have an enormous effect on musical practice. The U.K. case is not untypical: in many societies, music and other forms of culture and knowledge are increasingly prone to being treated as activities inferior to the accumulation of profit, or the pursuit of personal and corporate advantage. Artistic practices and experiences can, it seems, be defended only on the basis of their contribution to the economy, or to some kind of amelioration of social damage (Miller and Yúdice 2002).

In such circumstances, the artistic practices and experiences afforded by music need defending in other terms—in terms of their ability to promote human flourishing. However, this needs to be a critical defence, which recognizes the ways in which power, history, and subjectivity interlock in the highly complex and unequal societies of today. Massive inequalities persist in the realm of culture, information, and knowledge, just as they do in the economic sphere.

Defending Artistic Experience—and Musical Experience

Where, in such circumstances, might we turn for a critical defence of culture, of artistic experience, and of music? Disappointingly, much serious analysis of culture has offered only occasional and limited resources in this respect. There is no space to back up my point by surveying all the different fields. But a brief look at one especially important set of approaches—those associated with the interdisciplinary project known as cultural studies— might help contextualize my approach here. Cultural studies has been highly influential on the cultural study of music, the subject of this volume.

Cultural studies developed in the 1960s and 1970s, with the explicit aim of contributing to a democratization of culture. It did so partly through critical analysis of how inequality was etched into artistic and cultural expression in modern societies. It also aimed to question the way that humanities scholarship had been approached, and in particular the idea of studying culture as the analysis of the "best which has been thought and said in the world," to quote Matthew Arnold's *Culture and Anarchy* (1869). Cultural studies developed important insights concerning the way in which audiences contributed to meaning, and the importance of class, ethnic, and gender difference in relation to culture. As much a movement across disciplines as a discipline in itself, cultural studies drew on the new social activism of the post-countercultural period, notably feminism and anti-racism, and also on longer traditions of socialism that sought to defend working-class cultural experience. Post-structuralist versions claimed to offer much more developed conceptions of relations between culture, power, and subjectivity than "traditional" or classical Marxism. The influence of the Marxist political theorist Louis Althusser was important in this respect, as was that of the radical psychoanalyst Jacques Lacan, and the historian Michel Foucault. As these authors were translated and imported into Anglophone cultural analysis (and eventually the cultural analysis of music), their work encouraged much greater engagement with the incomplete, uncertain and open nature of human subjectivity.

But this engagement came at a cost. The profound hostility of these writers and their followers to humanism swayed many cultural studies analysts towards a suspicion of categories such as aesthetics, experience, and even emotion ("affect" being the preferred anti-humanist concept). Such ways of thinking—which were by no means peculiar to cultural studies but influenced a range of critical thought in the humanities and social sciences—may have ended up unwittingly strengthening the hand of social groups who might seek to benefit from the erosion of intellectual and artistic autonomy, especially big business and its allies in the state apparatus. (Of course not all cultural studies followed this route. Exceptions include Frith 1996; Negus and Pickering 2004; and the work of Raymond Williams.)

Times change, and different approaches are called for. I believe that we need a much richer account of the role of culture in people's lives, and the relation of culture to people's attempts—always uncertain, constrained and uneven, often failing—to live a good life. This particular focus on experience needs an account of subjectivity that understands people as *emotional* beings, recognizing that culture has a problematic but important relationship to this dimension of our lives. Dynamics of power, history, and inequality, forefronted by the best versions of cultural studies, need integrating with these issues.

We must turn to other traditions if we are to evaluate in a more rounded way the role of artistic experience in modern societies, and specifically music as a form of artistic experience. I have chosen to address only two here, neo-Aristotelianism and pragmatism, since they raise questions of emotion and experience in relation to artistic practice, questions that I find of particular interest. This is necessarily abstract, and abstraction is good because it allows for the identification of underlying principles. But I'll then make the discussion more sociologically concrete by discussing some potential relations of music to human flourishing (or otherwise) in modern societies. As I do so, I'll explore in greater depth what I mean by a *critical defence* of music—one that recognizes that the deeply scarred nature of modern societies is bound to affect music.

Music, Emotion, and Experience

One notable tradition that has been neglected for many years by those who pursue the critical cultural study of music can be designated "Aristotelian." The concept of human flourishing that I have already referred to in passing derives from this. The neo-Aristotelian philosopher Martha Nussbaum (2003) has provided one recent attempt to explain how the experience of art might enhance human life. The context for her account is an analysis of the ethical importance of emotions, against the preference for the application of detached intellect apparent in much philosophy (and reflected in some forms of cultural policy). Nussbaum first argues that emotions have a narrative structure. "The understanding of any single emotion is incomplete," she writes, "unless its narrative history is grasped and studied for the light it sheds on the present response" (p. 236). This suggests a central role for the arts in human self-understanding, because narrative artworks of various kinds (whether musical or visual or literary) "give us information about these emotion-histories that we could not easily get otherwise." (p. 236) So narrative artworks are important for what they show the person who is eager to understand the emotions; also because of the role they play in people's emotional lives.

Importantly, Nussbaum grounds her conception of emotions in a psychoanalytically informed account of subjectivity. Rather than the bizarrely nonfeeling subject to be found in the Lacanian tradition favored by much post-structuralist cultural studies, she draws on object relations analysts such as D. W. Winnicott (1971). For Nussbaum and Winnicott, the potentially valuable role that artistic experience might play in people's lives is suggested by studies of infant experience of stories and of play. Storytelling and narrative play cultivate the child's sense of her own aloneness, her inner world. The capacity to be alone is supported by the way in which such play develops the ability to imagine the good object's presence when the object is not present, and play deepens the inner world. Narrative play can help us understand the pain of others, and to see them in noninstrumental ways. Children can be given a way of understanding their own sometimes frightening and ambivalent psychology, so that they become interested in understanding their subjectivity, rather than fleeing from it. Stories and play can militate against depression and helplessness, by feeding the child's interest "in living in a world in which she is not perfect or omnipotent" (237). They contribute to the struggle of love and gratitude versus ambivalence, and of active concern against the helplessness of loss. These dynamics continue into adult life—this of course is a fundamental insight of psychoanalytically informed thought—and adults too benefit from narrative play.

How might this relate to music as a special case of cultural and aesthetic experience? Rightly, in my view, Nussbaum claims that much music, in most modern societies, is closely connected to emotions, or at least is ideally thought to be so. But music as such doesn't contain representational or narrative structures of the sort that are the typical objects of concrete emotions in life, or in other kinds of aesthetic experience such as films or novels. This makes it less obvious how music itself can be about our lives. Music is of course often linked to stories, in songs, operas, ballads, and so on, and, even when it isn't, is often highly discursively mediated, by the use of titles, instructions on scores, or critical discourse that seeks to interpret what music means. But we still need an account of the way musical sounds address emotion and feeling.

Nussbaum delineates (p. 272) a number of ways in which narrative fiction, such as novels and plays, allow for emotion on the part of the reader/spectator. Emotions can be felt

- towards characters, sharing emotion through identification or reacting against the emotions of a character
- towards the sense of life embodied in the text as a whole, reacting to it sympathetically or critically
- towards one's own possibilities
- in response to coming to understand something about life or about oneself.

Musical artworks can play the same role, says Nussbaum, but with the emotional material embodied in peculiarly musical forms. Music's distinctive language is one of compressed and elliptical reference to our inner lives and our prospects; for Nussbaum, it is close to dreaming in this respect. Our responses to music are crystallizations of general forms of emotion, rather than reactions to characters, as in narrative fiction; so most musical emotions, for Nussbaum, fall into the second and third of the categories listed above. Nussbaum agrees with Schopenhauer that music is "well-suited to express parts of the personality that lie beneath its conscious self-understanding" (p. 269), bypassing habit and intellect. Music "frequently has an affinity with the amorphous, archaic, and extremely powerful emotional materials of childhood' (ibid.). Its semiotic indefiniteness gives it a superior power to engage with our emotions.

Using examples from Mahler, Nussbaum claims that musical works can contain structures in which great pain is crystallized and which construct "an implied listener who experiences that burning pain" (p. 272); or they may "contain forms that embody the acceptance of the incredible remoteness of everything that is good and fine" and construct a listener who experiences desolation. Or a musical work may contain forms that embody the "hope of transcending the pettiness of daily human transactions." Music is somehow able to embody "the idea of our urgent need for and attachment to things outside ourselves that we do not control" (p. 272). This capacity is not natural; it is the product of complex cultural histories, and experience of such emotions depends on familiarity with the conventions that allow them, either through everyday experience of musical idioms or through education. These emotions might be hard to explicate as they happen, and not all works invoke deep emotion—they can just be enjoyable or interesting. But music provides its own version of the ways in which stories and play potentially enhance our lives, by cultivating and enriching our inner world, and by feeding processes of concern, sympathy, and engagement, against helplessness and isolation.

Nussbaum suggests the fruitfulness of an approach that relates the value of art to human well-being, emotion, and experience, and which also addresses the specificity of music as part of that account. Of course, music might fail much of the time to do this. Nussbaum is suggesting what music *can* offer, how it *might* add to our capabilities, our prospects for living different versions of a good life. It may be, however, that her explication is centered too much on a model of a listening self that is contemplative and self-analytical. This suggests that the defence of a wider range of artistic experience might need to look to other sources. One potential starting point is the American educationalist and pragmatist philosopher John Dewey, who, in the helpful gloss of Richard Shusterman, argues that art's special function and value lie "not in any specialized particular end but in satisfying the live creature in a more global way, by serving a variety of ends, and above all by enhancing our immediate experience which invigorates and vitalizes us, thus aiding our achievement of whatever further ends we pursue" (Shusterman 2000, 9). Art is thus at once instrumentally valuable and a satisfying end in itself. Art "keeps alive the power to experience the common world in its fullness," in Dewey's words ([1934] 1980, 138), and provides the means to make our lives more meaningful and tolerable through the introduction of a "satisfying sense of unity" into experience. This emphasis on experience in no way precludes the importance of meaning and reflection, and does not rely on a naive romantic notion of immediacy as the basis of art's power. Dewey confusingly merged artistic and aesthetic experience, but to see the experience of music, stories, and visual art as ordinary, as part of the flow of life, and as continuous with other forms of aesthetic experience (such as finding a person or a landscape deeply attractive) fits well with Raymond Williams's statements about the simultaneous ordinariness and extraordinariness of culture and creativity (for example in Williams 1965). It makes room for forms of artistic expression and entertainment that are less about contemplation, and more about energetic kinesthesis, and (thoughtful) engagement of the body. Shusterman (2000, 184) gives the example of how funk embodies an aesthetic, which he sees as derived from Africa, of "vigorously active and communally impassioned engagement." Shusterman is rather too inclined to dismiss other experiences of music as "dispassionate, judgemental remoteness" in his efforts to defend popular art; and not all dancing experiences are as communal as he suggests. Simon Frith's sociologically informed aesthetic of popular music (1996) may get closer to what goes on in music which is focused more on rhythm than on harmony and melody. A steady tempo and an interestingly patterned beat, observes Frith, enable listeners to respond actively and to experience music "as a bodily as well as a mental matter" (p. 144). This is often as much about order and control as going wild—a pronounced steady beat often underlies dance music. The point though is that a whole range of popular musics offer deeply pleasurable, feelingful, and absorbing experiences—and Frith (who is not a pragmatist in the philosophical sense), Dewey and Shusterman help us to see the value of this combination of mental and bodily experiences through music.

Nussbaum and Dewey/Shusterman come from very different philosophical, intellectual, and political traditions, but their Aristotelian and pragmatist ethics can be mutually complementary. They suggest ways in which artistic experience, including musical experience, might be valued in modern societies. Now, however, I want to elaborate on the suggestion I made earlier, that the kind of defence of such experience I have in mind needs to be a *critical* defence, so that we avoid producing the kind of pious, ethnocentric, and complacent celebrations that now seem to characterize some earlier writing about culture and music, and which post-structuralism and cultural studies did such important work in helping us to demystify.

MUSIC AND HUMAN FLOURISHING: FIVE DIMENSIONS

How might a more critical orientation towards culture, and towards music, balance the claims we might want to make for its emancipatory potential to allow human flourishing? To put this another way, how might we incorporate into our analysis the recognition that the world is severely marred by injustice, inequality, alienation, and oppression, and that music is unlikely to remain unaffected by these broader social dynamics? Perhaps the most durable body of critical work on culture and music in modernity is that of Theodor Adorno. No one applied a historical understanding of power and subjectivity so relentlessly to musical culture as a whole than did Adorno. For Adorno ([1932] 2002, 393), music could contribute to bettering the world only through "the coded language of suffering." From the perspective sketched here, Adorno's work is limited by its excessive austerity, his idealist requirement that art should aspire to extremely demanding levels of autonomy and dialectic, by his failure to recognize adequately the ambivalence in both "high culture" and "popular culture," and, linked to all this, his seeming contempt for everyday cultural experience in modern societies. A significant challenge for critical analysts, then, is to produce a historically informed but *non-Adornian* account of music-related subjectivity (see Hesmondhalgh 2008). This section of the chapter merely sketches such an account, based on Nussbaum, Shusterman, and others. I try to make the discussion more sociological, more concrete, by listing just five ways in which music might enhance well-being or flourishing in modern societies. At the same time I address some aspects of music–society relations which prevent music from fulfilling that potential.

First, music can *heighten people's awareness of continuity and development in life*. It seems powerfully linked to memory, perhaps because it combines different ways of remembering: the cognitive, the emotional, and the bodily-sensory (van Dijck 2006). It allows us to remember things that happened, how we felt, and what it's like to move, dance, and feel to a certain set of sounds, rhythms, textures. This ability for music to get stuck in our minds has surely been enhanced by recording technologies: most of us hear a lot more music now than most of our ancestors, and we are likely to hear some of it repeatedly, often in great bursts of repetition over a few weeks when a recording is initially a hit, when it's played regularly in public spaces. This tends to happen to people more when they're young, and so, for older people, music can be powerfully evocative of loss as well as continuity. Nostalgia is neither good nor bad in itself, as it has the potential to make us aware of things that we might be justified in regretting (Boym 2002). But it can involve a negatively sentimental relationship to our past: for example, older people might project onto their youth the feeling that things were better then, when in fact life involved a mixture of different emotions and processes, and may often have been extremely difficult. Attachment to the familiar records of the past can crowd out the inclination and desire to add new experiences to people's lives, inhibiting development and flourishing. Arguably, the commodification of music has encouraged that negative sentimentality through economics and aesthetics that make it cheaper and easier to invoke musical pasts than to encourage real innovation.

Second, music might *enhance our sense of sociality and community*, because of its great potential for providing shared experiences that are corporeal, emotional, and full of potential meanings for the participants. Parties and festive occasions are, for many people, unthinkable without music. This sense of sociality and community can be pleasurable, moving, and even joyous. Such occasions provide opportunities for the forging of new friendships, and the reaffirmation of old ones. Music plays an especially powerful communal role by encouraging people to move to the same sounds at the same time, but in different ways (wilder and more restrained, skillfully and not so skillfully, ironically or sincerely). Music, then, combines a responsive form of individual self-expression with the collective expression of shared taste, shared attachments. But, as I tried to show in earlier work (Hesmondhalgh 2008), building on the insights of social theorists such as Axel Honneth (2004), dynamics of emotional self-realization through music are closely linked to status battles in contemporary societies marked by competitive individualism; indeed, music, precisely because of its links to the emotions, and therefore to privileged modes of modern personhood involving emotional intelligence and sensitivity, might be a particularly intense site for such struggles.

Third, music can combine *a healthy integration of different aspects of our being, combining reflection and self-awareness with kinetic pleasure*, as Shusterman (2000) suggests. The connecting glue is some kind of emotional awareness. Musicians consciously and subconsciously seek to produce certain moods in those who are hearing or who at some time will hear their music. In moving to music, from almost imperceptibly tapping a foot or a steering wheel while the radio plays at a traffic light, through swaying at a concert, to full-on dancing at a club or party, people are both thinking and feeling. Of course, those thoughts might involve the mind wandering along a chain of associations; and they will feature preoccupations that have nothing to do with the music at all. It often takes us a while at concerts to "attune" ourselves to music, and, in a live music setting, after the initial rush of excitement when a band or orchestra begin playing, we might lose our way for a while. But when certain kinds of music *work*, they put mind and body together. This is one of the reasons why "the primitivist understanding of black music" (Danielsen 2006, 27, 28) is so objectionable. It reduces the complex interplay of thought, reflection, and skillful practice in the varieties of African-American music Danielsen examines to an unmediated expression of some inner essence, and in so doing often reduces people of color to one aspect of themselves: their sexuality. As she shows, the skill of great funk musicians is to conceal the remarkable amount of work that goes into making their music sound as though it flows naturally from the impulse to dance. But the common misreading of such forms of music suggests, again, how difficult it is for even the most remarkable genres and practices to escape the effects of the inequality and racism that so profoundly scar modern societies.

Fourth, as Nussbaum suggests, music can *heighten our understanding of how others might think and feel.* It can do so because music encodes human emotions into sounds that can be transmitted and transported across time and space, and because the understanding of these sounds is not limited by the need to learn verbal languages (which makes it easier to transmit than stories and poems). This has synchronic and diachronic dimensions. Synchronically, it is true of our potential understanding of music that comes from other societies in our own time; diachronically, it's true of music that comes from previous eras. This potentially *sympathetic* (*sym* = with, *pathetic* = related to feeling) quality of music is severely limited however by the deceptively transparent nature of musical communication. All communication, including spoken language, relies on convention. When we hear a foreign language of which we have no knowledge, we are completely reliant for our interpretation of what is happening on the paralinguistic features of speech—tone and volume of voice, and so on. We will always be aware of the "gap" left by not knowing the language. When we hear music from a society that we don't know well, by contrast, we may often be deceived into thinking we understand its resonances and potential meanings better than we really do. Of course, some musical features may "translate"— certain combinations of musical sounds may reliably indicate happiness or sadness whether emanating from Nigeria or Nebraska. But many more subtle indications of mood, emotion, and purpose will be much more elusive. The sympathetic quality of music—its potential heightening of our understanding of how others think and feel—is also limited by the same dangers of projection that I discussed in the previous point: inequality and ideology might mean that musical practices and values are radically mis-understood—either devalued or highly valued for the wrong reasons. This is one reason why education about culture might be life-enhancing. The sensitive teaching of conventions and discourses can help us to get more realistically at what kinds of experiences and emotions are being coded into music.

Fifth, music is *potentially very good at being a practice* in the Aristotelian sense, where practice is used to mean cooperative activities which involve the pursuit of excellence, and which emphasize the "internal" rewards of achieving standards appropriate to those forms of activity, rather than external compensations of money, power, prestige, and status (MacIntyre 1984, Keat 2000). It is an activity deeply loaded with ethical significance for many people. Musicians put enormous amounts of time into practicing so that they can be adept in making the sounds that they are required to make, and this is often for the intrinsic rewards associated with making music, rather than for fame itself. As Mark Banks (2012) has aptly put it, jazz is a particularly acute example of a practice in this sense, because of the "sharply delineated contrast and tension between the durable ethical pull of the internal goods of the practice (the virtues of community participation and engagement and the 'good of a certain kind of life' that jazz provides) against the contingent external goods that musicians and institutions might seek to accumulate in jazz." But this emphasis on intrinsic rewards can lead to self-exploitation in artistic labor markets characterized by massive over-supply of willing workers, and reward systems hugely skewed towards the successful few (Hesmondhalgh and Baker 2011).

Concluding Comments

There are of course many other ways in which music might contribute to human well-being, even if, in doing so, it is subject to constraints. But in this final section, I want merely to address a couple of potential objections to the way of thinking about music that I have advocated in this chapter. First of all, given my emphasis on emotion and experience, is the critical defence of music sketched here an attempt to smuggle back bourgeois individualism into the critical cultural analysis of music? We experience the world as individuals, and it is good to recognize that fact, while understanding that individual experience is always socially determined and mediated. Aristotelianism and pragmatism can be complements to the socialism, feminism, and multiculturalism that guide much progressive thinking. Marx himself had a deeply Aristotelian conception of humanity (Elster 1985).

Second, is this outline of a political aesthetics of music based on human flourishing an abnegation of real politics, given that politics is inevitably about collectivities? It is certainly a counter to the equation of a politics of music with the question, "Can music change the world?" There is nothing wrong with this question, as long as it is not assumed to exhaust our understanding of the politics, or social significance, of music. Nothing can change anything by itself! However much we want to see the world become a better place, surely none of us would want to see music evaluated solely on the basis of the degree to which it contributes to social change. It has other purposes which might be thought of as indirectly political. What I'm suggesting is that the best way to approach this array of potential functions is in terms of the distinctive abilities of music—distinct from other forms of human endeavor, and from other forms of artistic practice and experience—to contribute to human flourishing, and the ways in which social and political dynamics inhibit or promote these capacities.

Further Reading

Frith, Simon. 1998. *Performing rites: On the value of popular music.* Oxford: Oxford University Press.

Gracyk, Theodore. 1996. *Rhythm and noise: An aesthetics of rock.* London and New York: I. B. Tauris.

Hesmondhalgh, David. 2008. Towards a critical understanding of music, emotion and self-identity. *Consumption, Markets and Culture* 11(4): 329–343.

Keat, Russell. 2000. *Cultural goods and the limits of the market.* London and New York: Routledge.

Negus, Keith, and Michael Pickering. 2004. *Creativity, communication and cultural value.* London, Thousand Oaks, CA, and New Delhi: Sage.

Nussbaum, Martha. 2003 *Upheavals of thought: The intelligence of emotions.* Cambridge, U.K.: Cambridge University Press.

Shusterman, Richard. 2000. *Pragmatist aesthetics: Living beauty, rethinking art.* 2nd edn. Lanham, MD: Rowman and Littlefield.

Toynbee, Jason. 2007. *Bob Marley: Herald of a postcolonial world?* Cambridge, U.K.: Polity.

CHAPTER **33**

MUSIC AND THE SUBJECT
Three Takes

JOHN MOWITT

TAKE ONE

In the discourse of Hegelian Marxism the subject is born of struggle. Indeed the subject is read as the philosophical, we might also say theoretical, expression of the form of human being made possible by the economic emergence of the capitalist mode of production and the political consequences of the bourgeois revolutions of the eighteenth century. To this extent the subject is not simply another name for identity or person. It is, to risk a paradox, the objective ground of such iterations of the self. Thus, the despair that progressively gripped this discourse during the course of the last century might be said to be consummately embodied in the circulation, since 1979, of *Self*, a health and fitness magazine addressed to the former readers of *Women's Sports and Fitness*, that is, white, Anglophone, middle-class women of the North. One is sorely tempted by Adorno's "pessimism" when faced with a monthly invitation to consume, in the name of fit self-determination, that which philosophy deemed a precarious spoil of war.

In the August 2010 issue of *Self* there appears an excerpt from Stephanie Dolgoff's *My Formerly Hot Life*. In recounting her discovery of her former hotness Dolgoff writes: "And finally one morning as I rocked out to the Blondie song, 'One Way or Another,' I realized it was the soundtrack of a Swiffer commercial blaring from the TV. This anthem from my high school days was now being used to market cleaning supplies! Even worse, I owned a Swiffer and felt strongly enough about it to have recommended it to friends" (Dolgoff 2010, 36). The excerpt goes on to detail Dolgoff's becoming reconciled with her lost hotness (she decides "current happiness" is satisfactory compensation), but surely what is striking, even painfully familiar, is the place that music plays in this re-*Bildungs* narrative. Paralleling the shift from hot to happy, is a musical shift—and the fact that we are dealing here with a "girl power" tune from the late 1970s is far from insignificant—a shift from anthem to jingle. If one regards the shift from hot to happy as a shift bearing on the lived reality of Dolgoff's subjectivity (and I urge the reader to suppress the easy cynical giggle), then what this excerpt puts in play is a decisive version of the articulation of music and the subject. Stated abstractly Dolgoff's remarks underscore the profound role that music can play in the articulation of time and the subject. Clearly, the theme of lost hotness is tinged with a certain nostalgia. Dolgoff is reflecting upon two moments in time: the past—specifically, given the allusion to high school, her late teens when she experienced herself as an object of desire—and the present when she is struggling to come to terms with a new experience, that of being happy with, presumably, the existential fact that she may no longer be an object of desire. Although the point of the excerpt is to remove the sting of nostalgia, its temporal structure and evaluative tone—the past has been lost—is nostalgic. But more than that, to the extent that they draw attention to desire, Dolgoff's remarks urge us to see that nostalgia is not simply an attitude, a sentiment, but something active in the very lived character of subjectivity, at least as it is construed by the readership of *Self.*

"One Way or Another" fits here because it places Dolgoff in time, it places her, literally situates her both in her teens, and now, albeit differently, in middle age. Precisely to the extent that this is a cliché—who hasn't observed the general point here about "the way we were" and music?—it touches on something that has little if anything to do with Blondie or Dolgoff, something general if not precisely universal. That said, there are details worthy of attention that might otherwise simply disappear in the cliché. I will emphasize two. If, as I have suggested, the shift from hot to happy finds its echo in the shift from anthem to jingle, it is worth thinking a bit about the anthem (versus the jingle) as a temporal marker, as a monument. Perhaps most immediately one thinks of the anthem as an index of national identity. It marks, with a distinctly sacred power, the coming into existence of a particular national project of the sort celebrated at the Olympics or the World Cup. One is obliged to stress the unique temporality of the anthem because it touches on the temporality of transcendence, that is, the marking in time of that which—technically—is timeless. The anthem is a crucifix. Brushed against its philological grain, this marker locates the subject in a space of reactivity, of passivity, in that "anthem" derives from the Greek *antiphonos*, that is, "sung responses." The anthem thus marks the timeless moment, by soliciting in the subject a response, within time, to the vanishing, but ever present, past.

Of course, something slightly different is being said about "My Generation" or "Born to Run" or "One Way or Another" when characterized as "anthems." But only slightly. The frame may be decidedly less nationalistic, but the paradoxical temporality, the reactivity, persists. In this respect, "One Way" may seem entirely unsuitable as an anthem—with its catchy, insistent stress (the lyrics tend not to toggle between verse and refrain) on agency: "One way, or another, I'm gonna getcha, getcha, getcha, getcha. . . ." One imagines Dolgoff and her BFFs singing along, living the song as an expression of their collective decision to make the switch, the conversion from objects to subjects of desire. The contrast with "jingle" would virtually imply this. However, the lyrics—and certainly the urgent stasis of the music—complicate this. First, by producing a disturbing link between becoming a subject of desire, and stalking. As if blazing the groove within which Britney's "Piece of Me" rocks and rolls, "One Way" plays insistently with the affective crossover between fanaticism, the obsessive fan, and the agent of love. Reactivity thus reappears in the very logic of obsession. Second, the thematic arc of the tune, as if tracing the flip into reactivity, moves from find, to get, to lose. Unlike the backbeat one cannot lose, the "you" ("ya") shifts away with an inevitability that has both a psychological ("when I become a subject of desire, I *always* fail," or, "I'm a Loser") and a structural ("desire *is* the missing of its object") dimension. Even if one stresses the paradigmatic resonances of "lose" (go crazy, wild, or get rid of, dump or shake), in the end "One Way" actually does work as an anthem in the strict sense of "sung response," a marker of the subject's impossible (that is, both active and passive) relation to time.

But is this really different from a jingle? Dolgoff's excerpt prompts such a question by the way she sets up her anecdote. Here we touch on the second theme bearing on music and the subject that calls out for attention. She tells us that the question of her lost hotness pressed upon her while she "rocked out" to Blondie's tune, learning that it had become a jingle for a cleaning product. Setting aside the disconcerting image of a woman, home alone, perhaps preparing for work, with her television "blaring" (the whole anecdote depends on the moment of disillusionment, that is, the fact that something first perceived as a music video [??] became a commercial), what juts forward here is Dolgoff's body. "Rocked out" is another way to say physical performance (dance, under such circumstances, maybe too strict a word), and what is crucial here is the way the anthem seizes her at the level of her body. She "lets herself go," and in doing so points directly to the way music articulates not only the subject and time but the psychical and the somatic. Music addresses itself to the seam, the frontier between thought and extension, to, in effect, the space of sound as a lived event. Although this might suggest that a more unequivocal embrace of agency is on offer here— Dolgoff is passionately *doing* whatever it is that she is doing—here too a certain reactivity of the subject repeats.

Dolgoff draws this out when she narrates her discovery that she has been gyrating to a commercial, where the accent falls not primarily on the mistake ("I thought it was one thing, but it's another"), but on the motif of consumption. As if wrestling with this very matter, Dolgoff stresses that she does not simply passively consume Swiffers, but she "markets" them to her friends as well. A body performing to/with music restages this precise scene. When "you got the beat," you have engaged a pattern set for you by someone or something else. Even if the beat is familiar, if it is one chosen by you on your iPod shuffle, responding to it physically, is a response, a re-action. It is an act of surrendering agency, in the name of enjoyment. Or, to re-invoke the excerpt, it is a discovery of happiness lived as a moment of exuberant physicality. While the reference here to the body is surely an important index for hotness—is it still desirable, can it still perform, does it still feel? etc.— it is also a gesture that underscores the vital link between music and the incarnation of the subject. In ways that Western thought has not always respected, music—and this is true whether we are speaking of dance music or not—draws out the crucial way in which the subject is, however restlessly (think here of Descartes's doubts about the reliability of his sense of sight), embodied. It is also, of course, gendered, raced, and classed, but in ways— indeed, one way or another—that massively presuppose the subject's restless embodiment. Not in the sense that anatomy is destiny, but in the sense that destiny, the so-called adventure of the spirit in the flesh, cannot avoid anatomy entirely. Ask the trannie.

Thus Dolgoff—who otherwise seems bent on getting us to hear the verb "to fit" in fitness—underscores for us the necessary, if insufficient, series: subject, time, body, music, desire.

Take Two

What do the Vatican Embassy in Panama City, Panama, Mount Carmel in Waco, Texas and the detention center (GTMO) in Guantanamo Bay, Cuba, have in common? All are sites where a very distinct, brutally distinct, articulation of the relation between music and the subject either has taken or is taking place.

In December of 1989 then President George Bush I authorized a long-planned invasion of Panama. The invasion, dubbed "Operation Just Cause," was launched in order to effect a coup against Mañuel Noriega, a former U.S. ally who had become inconvenient to the Bush regime despite his prior resistance to Left insurgencies in both El Salvador and Nicaragua. Because Navy SEALs, through what was dubbed "Operation Nifty Package," had eliminated Noriega's means of escape (his plane and his boat), he was forced to seek sanctuary in the Apostolic Nunciature, in effect, the embassy of the Vatican in Panama City. Early in January of 1990, less than a month later, Noriega surrendered. He was driven from the embassy by a cunning, even perverse PSYOP campaign: known to loathe "rock 'n' roll," Noriega and the embassy were bombarded day and night by a sound system broadcasting rock music at an earth-shattering volume. It has been widely reported that the tunes in steady rotation were, "Welcome to the Jungle" by Guns 'n' Roses, and the Clash's cover of "I Fought the Law."

A few years later, in February of 1993, the U.S. Bureau of Alcohol, Tobacco, and Firearms (BATF) and the FBI under the authority of then Attorney General Janet Reno laid siege to and ultimately overran the Branch Davidian compound, known to followers as Mount Carmel, outside Waco, Texas. The purpose was to bring to justice the controversial Branch Davidian leader, David Koresh. As in Panama City, a key part of the siege involved a PSYOP campaign involving both sound and light. In effect, a stadium show. On the soundtrack, according to Dick Reavis (author of *The Ashes of Waco*) were, in addition to tape recordings of rabbits being slaughtered, snippets from talk shows and the sounds of dental drills revving, several pieces of music: a selection of Tibetan chants (later the object of a formal protest), Christmas carols from both Andy Williams and Mitch Miller, and Nancy Sinatra's "These Boots Were Made for Walking." As is well known, this campaign failed to drive Koresh from Mount Carmel. Indeed, according to Reavis, some occupants could be seen around the compound "rockin' out" to the government's playlist.

In a later moment, under President Bush II, "detainees" at Guantanamo Bay were subjected to a similar PSYOP campaign. In addition to the time-honored techniques of abuse (including "enhanced interrogation," that is, torture), isolation and humiliation, "detainees" have been forced to listen to extremely loud, recorded music. According to Jon Ronson in *The Men Who Stare at Goats*, "detainees" have been blasted with material from Fleetwood Mac ("Don't Stop"), Kris Kristofferson, Matchbox 20, and the British singer David Gray, notably his song "Babylon." Ronson also reports that "enemy combatants" captured in Iraq and confined in enormous metal shipping containers were routinely "entertained" with relentless, earsplitting recordings of the theme song from *Barney the Purple Dinosaur*, "I Love You," an undisguised melodic replica of the enigmatic classic, "This Ol' Man."

When the Waco episode was covered in the *New York Times*, resident music critic Jon Pareles baptized the music blared into the compound, "siege rock." Although he quoted, with legible incredulity, Robert Lauden (a former hostage negotiator) who insisted, "the idea is not so much to drive them from their lair [*sic*], as it is to reaffirm the communication process" (Pareles 1993, 2), Pareles focused his remarks exclusively on the "failure to communicate" between Koresh and Reno. The problem was that perhaps Reno (famously spoofed by Will Ferrell on *Saturday Night Live*) had the wrong siege rock selection in rotation at Waco. Somewhat facetiously, but only somewhat, Pareles recommended: an alternation between Einstürzende Neubauten and the Archies' "Sugar, Sugar"; and then, in no particular sequence, "Hit the Road Jack" by Ray Charles, "They're Comin' to Take Me Away" by Napoleon XIV, "Losing my Religion," by R.E.M, and "Stairway to Heaven" by Led Zeppelin.

Clearly, Pareles—otherwise a very astute musical commentator—fails to appreciate the full impact of the encounter between musical sound and PSYOPs. If the latter concerns itself, as is stated in Joint Publication 3-13.2 of January 7, 2010, with "support of combat operations, influence of perception, attitudes, objective reasoning and behavior," then lyric content, song titles, or thematic content are really only a very small part of what matters in Guantanamo and elsewhere. After all, the command of English (or German) on the part of "detainees" is doubtless rather limited. What Lauden gets right is that blaring music works to remind its target audience that the communication channel is open, as is said, 24:7. To some degree this is about access, even if in a certain sense frustrated, but it is also surely about deprivation, about distraction, exhaustion, and harassment. As a set of lyrics, "I Fought the Law" is merely a taunt. More profound, more disturbing is the earsplitting character of the amplified sound. While important, the duration and volume of *any* tune presume for their efficacy what Gregory Whitehead memorably said about the human ear: it is a hole in the head. As the official term implies, PSYOP seeks to operate on the psyche, and what the preceding examples illuminate is that this operation can be focused with excruciating and nerve-racking intensity on the ear as the, difficult if not impossible to shut, communication channel through which the body can be at once permeated and turned against the mind. In effect, what Panama, Waco, and Guantanamo all demonstrate is that music is widely perceived to articulate with the subject so as precisely to disarticulate, to disorient, to, when all is said and done, destroy it. While cast in silhouette what emerges here is the intimately profound way in which music is part of the very production of the subject, not simply at the level of its fitness, but at the level of the bearer of experience whether fit or unfit.

Take Three

With the recent publication of Adorno's radio writings, *Current of Music*, most of his work in English produced in exile in the late 1930s is now widely available. An important exception is a memorandum prepared for his colleagues at the Princeton Radio Research Project whose subject line reads: "Plugging, Like and Dislike in Light Popular Music," a typescript of which sits in the Max Horkheimer archive in Frankfurt. As with most of his English memoranda of the period, this one proposes some ideas and models for carrying out a largely empirical analysis of the phenomenon of plugging, that is, repetition, specifically when focused on the work of promotion. The typescript is undated, but it twice refers to the essay Anglophone readers now know as "The Fetish-Character in Music and the Regression of Listening" (Adorno [1938] 2002), where plugging is also discussed, and extended passages of it (re-)appear in Adorno's collaboration with George Simpson, "On Popular Music" ([1941] 2002) where plugging is linked to standardization, placing it somewhere between 1938 and 1942. It thus dates from the period of Adorno's early work on radio.

Three crucial issues recommend the "plugging study" (as it is referred to in the typescript) for consideration here. First, as with his other work on radio, Adorno's memorandum seeks to explore the essential impact of technology on music. In "The Radio Symphony" Adorno resists the notion that radio might be used to democratize taste for "serious" music, arguing that the very medium of the radio contradicted this aim by destroying symphonic music from within. In a nutshell, radio deprived symphonic music of its sonic force, thus urging precisely the wrong sort of listening (culinary or atomized) for the comprehension of a symphony. Although framed in negative terms, this is an argument that refuses the notion that technology simply delivers or conveys sound, thus affecting music, if at all, from the outside. If, as Adorno insists, music is caught up in the subjective act of reception (listening), then the conditions of this reception, conditions that include the very character of the human subject, are *inside*, not outside, music. Plugging is a further manifestation of this dynamic, in that it embodies a means by which to use the very logic of broadcasting to produce and sustain the ambivalence of the listener, an ambivalence that finds expression in the impassioned boredom of the consumer's attachment to musical hits.

Second, the memorandum expressly sets out to model studies of what in his other writings Adorno calls "pseudo-individualization," that is, the process whereby the subject is positioned to misrecognize forms of self-expression in instances of total manipulation. At its most acute, "pseudo-individualization" displaces the subject altogether, or, as it is put in "On Popular Music": "standardization of song hits keeps the customers in line by doing their listening for them" (Adorno [1941] 2002, 445). In the film theory of the 1970s, this was precisely how the basic cinematographic apparatus was understood to produce ideological effects: spectators took imaginary possession of a visual field in reality produced by something or someone who saw for them. In the memorandum Adorno, somewhat uncharacteristically, insists that psychoanalysis must inform any study of the wily process of "pseudo-individualization." What this foregrounds, even as an overstatement, is the way music, once subjected to the technologies and techniques of mass distribution, engages the subject well below the level of conscious taste formation ("I Like It Like That"). It compels us to ask whether there *is* a subject for music.

Doubtless the most immediately pertinent aspect of "the plugging study" (aside from squarely conceding that race has something fundamental to do with the musical status of jazz) is that it states in the form of a blunt thesis what in "The Fetish-Character" and "On Popular Music" is mentioned largely in passing. On page 25 of the typescript Adorno writes: "Thesis: I am inclined to compare the general attitude of the listener masses toward light popular music to that of the prisoner who finally loves the little green spot he can see through the jarred [*sic*] window of his cell, or, if worst comes to the worst, the cell itself" (Adorno n.d., 24–25). In "On Popular Music" the insight is nuanced thus: "A strong-willed political prisoner may resist all sorts of pressure until methods such as not allowing him to sleep for several weeks are introduced. At that point he will readily confess to crimes he did not commit" (Adorno [1941] 2002, 464). Either way, what Adorno is concerned to tease out is the way music—especially though not uniquely popular music—plays a fundamental role, in a present that is still with us, in altering the composition of individuality itself.

Over-dubbed with the use of music in PSYOPs campaigns, what leaps forward in the mix is, on the one hand, the unsettling thought that plugging—the ordinary practice of developing playlist rotations for radio (even those organized by randomization algorithms)—is a low-intensity PSYOPs campaign. What it achieves is a surrender, not to an imperial power *per se* but to a mode of subjectivation not only useful to such power, but one confused with the means, the personal will, by which to stand up to it. On the other hand, the link between plugging and PSYOPs suggests that the logic of consumer society, the very libidinal economy of fetishism—and the point would surprise neither Marx nor Foucault—organizes military strategy, especially when that strategy expressly engages what it takes to be the domain of the psychological, the space of the subject. In this respect, what took place in Panama City, or Waco, is something like what Adorno calls fury, the ambivalent rage that is vented on a prisoner whose treatment exposes one's own status as a prisoner. If Pareles and others can so quickly spin out alternative playlists, perhaps this is because a chain linking music and the subject that subtends fury is linked to them.

The point here is not to succumb to despair or to hole up in the Grand Hotel Abyss, but first to appreciate that a certain account of the articulation of music and the subject obliges one, in the name of the subject's happiness (if not its hotness), to confront the conditions, the possibility of that despair. This keeps the discussion serious, focused, not tangled up in the distractions of identities. Put differently, perhaps happiness is less about recognition, especially nostalgic recognition, than about rigor, about one's capacity to grasp the mechanisms whereby happiness is offered as consolation for what refuses to change. Famously, the ever dour Adorno ends "On Popular Music" by saying (and the allusion to Kafka is plain): "To become transformed into an insect [he is thinking of the jitterbug], man needs that energy which might possibly achieve his transformation into man" (Adorno [1941] 2002, 468), a formulation which points to the ambivalence that, in defining the very structure of the encounter between music and the subject, reminds us that this encounter has an historico-ontological character and that for this reason, if no other, a revolution at which we might all dance remains possible.

FURTHER READING

Adorno, Theodor W. 2006. *Philosophy of the new music.* Translated by Robert Hullot-Kentor. Minneapolis: University of Minnesota Press.

Adorno, Theodor W., and Max Horkheimer. 2002. *Dialectic of enlightenment: Philosophical fragments.* Translated by Edmund Jephcott. Palo Alto, CA: Stanford University Press.

Cusick, Suzanne G. 2008. 'You are in a place that is out of the world . . .': Music in the detention camps of the 'Global War on Terror'. *Journal of the Society of American Music* 2 (1): 1–26.

Deleuze, Gilles, and Félix Guattari. 1987. 1837: Of the refrain. Pp. 310–350 in *A thousand plateaus.* Translated by Brian Massumi. Minneapolis: University of Minnesota Press.

Evans, Aden. 2005. *Sound ideas: Music, machines, and experience.* Minneapolis: University of Minnesota Press.

Kramer, Lawrence. 2010. *Interpreting music.* Berkeley: University of California Press.

McClary, Susan. 2004. *Modal subjectivities: Self fashioning in the Italian madrigal.* Berkeley, CA: University of California Press.

McRobbie, Angela. 1999. *In the culture society: Art, fashion and pop culture.* New York: Routledge.

Middleton, Richard. 2006. *Voicing the popular: On the subjects of popular music.* New York: Routledge.

Mowitt, John. 2002. *Percussion: Drumming, beating, striking.* Durham, NC: Duke University Press.

Savage, Roger. 2010. *Hermeneutics and music criticism.* New York: Routledge.

Sterne, Jonathan. 2003. *The audible past: Cultural origins of sound reproduction.* Durham, NC: Duke University Press.

CHAPTER 34

OF MICE AND DOGS
Music, Gender, and Sexuality at the Long Fin-de-Siècle

IAN BIDDLE

This chapter is an attempt to work through some of the difficulties we have encountered (and continue to encounter) in seeking to analyze the "relationship" (to put it no more ambitiously for the moment) of music to gender and sexuality. At what might be termed the "long fin-de-siècle" (that period which stretches from the last decades of the nineteenth century to the First World War), three profound epistemological revolutions impacted significantly on the possibility of talking about music in this "relationship": (1) the invention of recording technology (1877); (2) Freud's psychoanalytic revolution; (3) the collapse of what Friedrich Kittler has called the "universal translatability" of media, a notion to which I shall return shortly.

We begin, in perverse counter-chronological logic, with Lacan:

> you will see that, far from speaking of the emergence of this gaze as of something that concerns the organ of light, [Sartre] refers to the sound of rustling leaves, suddenly heard while out hunting, to a footstep heard in a corridor.
>
> (Lacan [1964] 1979, 84)

The gothic frisson of this passage from *The Four Fundamental Concepts of Psycho-Analysis* is remarkable for its faithfulness to the epistemological shifts that characterized the long fin-de-siècle. The uncanny reciprocity of looking and listening that so fascinates Lacan in Sartre's *Being and Nothingness* is a curious articulation of the fatal tendency, in discourses about the modern personality since Freud, for the one looking or listening to readily turn into the one looked at or listened to. For Lacan, "sound" (or its figuration) enters when the subject *comes under threat*:

> And when are those sounds heard? At the moment when he has presented himself in the action of looking through a keyhole. A gaze surprises him in the function of a voyeur, disturbs him, overwhelms him and reduces him to a feeling of shame.
>
> (p. 84)

The source of the "threat" (or shame) here is perhaps best explained in terms of what Bruce Fink has termed "the neurotic's 'education'" (Fink 1999, 97). In other words, the "sound of footsteps" the subject imagines s/he has heard can be understood as a symptom flowing from the processes of what might be termed "socialization" (Fink refers to this also as a process of "Oedipalization and de-Oedipalization" [ibid.]). In other words, the inner ear hears what it hears as the result of a certain attachment to a *regimen*, a process of becoming subject to the "law of the father," of taking up one's place *in relation to gender*. Sartre's choice of sound, the "rustling of leaves" or a "footstep in a corridor," to mark the uncanny anxiety of "being beside oneself" draws on the rather ancient conceit that sound is somehow beyond the limits of what we can rationally know: in other words, sound stands here for a kind of short-circuiting of the affective fields of the senses such that "the gaze" (the subject looking through the keyhole) slips sideways to its proxy, sound, that affective field which, perhaps more than any other, seems to seep through every boundary, and pierce the bubble of autonomy that classical philosophy since Descartes has always imputed to the subject.

Sound, then (and, for our purposes here, music in particular), has been made to work in those affective fields that language seems to have failed to capture. This is by no means a recent injunction. Indeed, it is an ancient commonplace to conceive of sound or music as operating from an other-worldly dimension, as "transporting" the listener, or as shifting the register of consciousness. It is made to work as a marking of a passage into another place. And, like so many overdetermined boundaries and passages, music is often seen as bringing a certain epistemological danger (it seduces, under-mines, mollifies, stupefies) and has tended to occasion, therefore, a certain moral anxiety. But boundaries and passages are also the sites of discourse formation and/or dissolution, the border zones where the shape and scope of discourse can be tested and reformulated. In this perilous play at the edge of discourse, boundaries and passages are intensely and frequently con-tested: as many scholars have shown, in this contested zone, a "dangerous crossroads" as George Lipsitz termed it, discourse is anxious (Sedgwick 1985, 1990; Butler 1990; Haraway 1991).

Feminist commentators have amply demonstrated that the terms on which discursive boundaries have been drawn up, contested, and shaped—the epistemological and ideological means by which they are put into play—are *densely gendered* (Irigaray 1985a; Cixous 1980, 1990). This insight is grounded in the observation, made most explicitly by Jacques Derrida in his critique of Lacan's seminar on Poe (Derrida 1987; Lacan [1978] 1988, 191–205), that Western epistemology is characterized by a ubiquitous *phallogocentrism*. A conflation of "*phallo-*" and "*logo*-centrism", the term designates the "old and enormous root" that characterizes our use of language: "the 'description' is a 'participation' when it induces a practice, an ethics, an institution, and therefore a politics that ensure the truth of the tradition" (Derrida 1987: 481n). For Derrida language arrives to us *always already* marked by the deployment of a misogynistic discourse. It is not surprising therefore, if we are to accept Derrida's diagnosis, that the tendency to figure music as a boundary or passage has facilitated its appropriation as a way of doing important cultural work, especially the work of gender.

Kafka's Mice, or, Music and Gender

When music is characterized as a boundary, it is so characterized in order to place it under pressure to do the cultural work that discourses grounded in the kinds of language forms favored by Lacan and Freud cannot undertake for themselves. When it comes to the cultural work of gender and sexuality—both discursive formulations and yet both impish in their refusal of the constraints rational discourse seeks to place on them—music can operate as a way of effecting a particular discursive outcome: she sings like an angel; he marches with conviction; she dances like a woman possessed; he really hammers that piano. In each case, the "description" is densely gendered, sounding out the production of what Derrida would call an "ethico-institutional discourse" in its appeal to deeply embedded assumptions about femininity and masculinity.

The phallogocentrism of the Western rational epistemology marks music out as a particularly volatile yet profoundly effective (and affective) cultural resource in the imagining, policing, and managing of discourses on gender. This is clear in a striking passage from the short story "Josephine the Singer, or the Mouse Folk" by Franz Kafka:

> So there she stands, the delicate creature, shaken by vibrations especially below the breastbone, so that one feels anxious for her, it is as if she has concentrated all her strength on her song, as if from everything in her that

does not directly subserve her singing all strength has been withdrawn, almost all power of life, as if she were laid bare, abandoned, committed merely to the care of good angels, as if while she is so wholly withdrawn and living only in her song a cold breath blowing upon her might kill her.

(Kafka [1922] 1993a, 236–237)

A multitude of discursive effects is activated here: the alignment of physical delicacy with femininity; song as a site for the construction and performance of female gender; the body as the primary site for the construction of the feminine; the proximity of the feminine to sickness and so on. And it is to a sort of degraded "song" (whistling) that Kafka looks for a site at which to lay out in ironic form the complexities of fin-de-siècle gender designations. In Josephine's singing, as Boa (1996) has shown, Kafka is able to articulate the material conditions that sustain the "profession" of the female singer, her closeness to images of prostitution, her manner of *representing* a particular (misogynist) imagination of the feminine as itself a marker of the alienation of feminine labor, its aestheticization (Boa 1996, 179).

Nonetheless, as a "'singer" that merely "whistles," one that is so precariously endangered by this act of whistling and so comprehensively de-eroticised, Josephine serves also to subvert the hysterical misogyny that attends the construction and consumption of the diva in the long fin-de-siècle. The cultural work that Kafka asks musical performance to undertake here is activated in no small measure by the use of music to mark a contested boundary between erotic play and the law. It is music that denies the appropriation of the feminine form as an object of desire and generates a discursive play in the confrontation of the narrator's masculinity—itself ironically performative of a certain masculine "assuredness", "rationality" etc. ("she cannot very well go on limping forever . . .")—with Josephine's femininity. This play is furthermore reliant on music's performative qualities: the "arbitrary" distinction the mice folk draw between Josephine's whistling and the everyday whistling of other mice is reflected in her spatial deployment on a stage, away from the others. What marks her whistling out from the others' equally mundane whistling is an agreement amongst the members of the mouse community that her whistling is *different*. In appealing to a model of musical meaning that relies first and foremost on the active construction of meaning by a community of the music's users, Kafka thereby also draws our attention to the performative dimension of gender. If music's meanings are made, and performed, so, by implication, are the meanings of gender: we learn to subvert the "given" nature or "law" of meaning by witnessing the ironic juxtaposition of music and gender. The proximity here helps undo the phallogocentric work of language.

This structural trope, the proximity of music and gender performativity, is grounded in the working through of a relationship between the various "stuffs" of discourse—between media—that Friedrich Kittler has described as "to a degree arbitrary, a manipulation". In this view, the passing of "messages" (*Botschaften*) from music into literature or literature into music, for example, comes to be viewed, somewhere around 1900, as a process that has to be constantly remade, refashioned at every delicate site of exchange:

> Given Medium A, organized as a denumerable collection of discrete elements $E^a_1 \ldots E^a_n$, its transposition into Medium B will consist in reproducing the internal (syntagmatic and paradigmatic) relations between its elements in the collection $E^b_1 \ldots E^b_m$. Because the number of elements n and m and the rules of association are hardly ever identical, every transposition is to a degree arbitrary, a manipulation. It can appeal to nothing universal and must, therefore, leave gaps.
>
> (Kittler 1990, 265)

If music is often deliberately implicated in debates about gender, then it is inevitably thereby implicated in debates about how discourse transposition (from "gender" in law, biology, or popular psychology to "gender in music") is possible. It is crucial to recognize in Kittler's theory of media a profoundly historicist articulation of the exchange: the nature and scope of discourse exchange is reliant upon the local technologies and cultural resources that are available to the wielders of discourse. The extent of the implication of discourses on gender in literary or operatic forms, for example, is intimately connected to the ways in which the various data of those discourses came to be stored:

> color and sound, light and the voice have become recordable, become part of the general acceleration, "in the sense of the technical maximization of all velocities, in whose time-space modern technology and apparatus can alone be what they are" [Heidegger]. Henceforth, command will conflict with command, medium with medium.
>
> (p. 267)

In this conflicted economy of exchange, the relationship between gender and music at the long fin-de-siècle must be explored, therefore, in the context of developments in the *technology of recording*. If, for example, the singing or spoken voice can be *recorded*, it can thus also be constituted as a *fixed* object of scrutiny; sounds can thereby be transported, moved from one location to another and yet remain sounds, remain within their medium; there is no longer a need for discourse translation in order to achieve a circulation of the "stuff" of sound in culture; the sounds of the voice can thereby become stable carriers of human character, and of sexual and gender pathologies that hitherto resided only in the internal invisible world of the psyche; these externalized sounds become mobile, powerfully characterized markers of healthy communicative norms and pathological deviance; voice now comes under the scrutiny of the rationalizing medical impulse. The operatic voice (especially the "pathological" feminine voice), for example, can thereby be seen as an elaboration of this new knowledge. Lulu/*Lulu* is unthinkable before the phonograph.

KAFKA'S DOGS, OR, MUSIC AND SEXUALITY

Eve Sedgwick (1985, 1990) has famously shown how the phallogocentric tendency is invariably accompanied by its complement, homophobia. The conceptual pairing hetero/homo, which Sedgwick locates in fin-de-siècle medical discourses, is possible only after the term (and type) "homosexual" has entered medical discourse. This is also the point at which the need to "police" sexuality becomes particularly acute since to "medicalize" homosexuality is not only to "recognize" it (thereby constituting it for the first time as a sexual *identity* and thus bringing with it the need to conceive of *rights* and *laws* for that identity) but also to bring it into existence as a sexual *pathology*. This effects homophobia as we know it, the rise of which is dependent upon new conceptions of a medicalized "perverse" or nonnormative sexuality incubated in the already well-formed fin-de-siècle fascination for criminology, pathology, and raciology. One need only look to the densely sexualized reception of Gustav Mahler in order to see how sexual "perversion," gender "deviance," and racial "difference" overlap in the musicocritical discourses at the end of the nineteenth century (Franklin 1991; Knittel 1995).

If, as Foucault (1978) would have us believe, sexuality operates in the manner of a deployment, then it is only in the *act* of its deployment, in a kind of discursive gear shift or discourse transposition, that sexuality can be said to exist at all: in this sense, sexuality, like gender, is the "invention" of the 1900 discourse network, reliant on a location of desire within a logic of exchange that is framed by the immutability of media. This observation is crucial to our understanding of sexuality at the fin-de-siècle. Just as Freud liquidates the "material" phenomenon of the dream in his *The Interpretation of Dreams* (1900) by seeking to differentiate fundamentally "dream stuff" from the language we use to interpret it, so media transpositions "liquidate the Medium from which they proceed" (Kittler 1990, 275). Sex is obliterated in the act of writing; writing is obliterated in the production of sound. Only desire, the emptied out brilliant, fluid, overwhelming structurality of sex, seems to remain. It operates as a ghostly polymorphous carrier of shifting object relations from one medium to another, yet never quite entering the medium, never quite being taken up, always somehow outside.

Hence, the "deployment" that sexuality might be said to constitute will necessarily be activated at those same contested regions we have identified as music's operational territory at the fin-de-siècle, the boundary and the passage. How, then, does this border zone operate for discourses of sexuality? And how can music intervene in this operation? As we have already seen in the medicalization of the interior life of the psyche at the fin-de-siècle, music continued to help shape or articulate debates about *gender* through its appropriation by the wielders of discourse as a territory in which these debates can be rehearsed (a "zone" or site). Its encounter with *sexuality* was, as we might expect, similar but by no means the same. Whereas music was often appropriated as a secondary "site" or proxy for debates about gender, in its encounter with fin-de-siècle sexuality, music was often called upon to undertake a rather different but no less highly contested work: it would often have to conjure up, even as it announced its cultivated artifice, the very "stuff" of desire as an aestheticized material "flow". This powerful yet ultimately banal transposition allows the polymorphous nature of desire to find a crude analogue in the "flux" of sound. In Kafka's short story "Investigations of a Dog" ([1922] 1993b), for example, music is given precisely this affective work:

> the music gradually got the upper hand, literally knocked the breath out of me and swept me far away from those actual little dogs, and quite against my will, while I howled as if some pain were being inflicted upon me, my mind could attend to nothing but this blast of music which seemed to come from all sides, from the heights, from the depths, from everywhere, surrounding the listener, overwhelming him, crushing him, and over his swooning body still blowing fanfares so near that they seemed far away and almost inaudible.
>
> (p. 424)

The omnidirectionality, the overwhelming plurality of this music, its ego-debilitating effects, the source of an unbearable pain: all these figurations of music point to an extraordinarily terrifying bodily encounter with the underside of paternal law. Indeed, as the narrator observes, "those dogs were violating the law" and, like all idealized others, they fail to answer the Lacanian *che vuoi?* ("what do you—the Other—want?") of the young narrator's entreaty:

> But they—incredible! incredible!—they never replied, behaved as if I were not there. Dogs who make no reply to the greeting of other dogs are guilty of an offence against good manners which the humblest dog would never pardon any more than the greatest.
>
> (p. 425)

The law is invoked here in a dialectical formulation: the one side of the law generates its opposite, transgressive Other. What is particularly striking in this passage is the disturbing incursion of the gaze into the narrative:

> could I not see the last and youngest dog, to whom most of those cries were addressed, often stealing a glance at me as if he would have dearly wished to reply, but refrained because it was not allowed? But why should it not be allowed, why should the very thing which our laws unconditionally command not be allowed in this one case?
>
> (p. 425)

Sound—the cries of the other dogs and the debilitating music—both *disturbs* the surreptitious gaze of the youngest dog at the narrator and *frames* its transgressive frisson: sound is both the marker of transgression and a carrier of desire; it is both a *signifier* of moral deviation and its *enabler*. The same sex intimacy that might ensue between the lawful and the lawless is transposed (foreclosed) by the music: whenever the narrator re-enters his legalistic phallogocentric discourse, the world falls silent; whenever sound intervenes (and especially music which is here juxtaposed with occult knowledge or "magic") the narrator misses the transgression, lets it slip past unnoticed.

> Great magicians [*Zauberer*] they might be, but the law was valid for them too . . . and having recognized that, I now noticed something else. They had good grounds for remaining silent, that is, assuming they remained silent from a sense of shame [*Schuldgefühl*]. For how were they conducting themselves? Because of all the music I had not noticed it before, but they had flung away all shame, the wretched creatures were doing the very thing which is both most ridiculous and indecent in our eyes; they were walking on their hind legs. Fie on them! They were uncovering their nakedness, blatantly making a show of their nakedness . . . as if Nature were in error.
>
> (p. 426)

The display of the genitals, which Freud had already by 1905 linked to the interplay of exhibitionism and scopophilia (Freud [1905] 1977, 67), takes on the role here of an ironic, hyperbolic over-Freudian imagery. This ironic play on the Freudian orthodoxy also returns us to the extraordinary uncanny reciprocity of looking and listening that Lacan recognized in Sartre: since music causes the narrator to miss the "shame" (in Freud, "*Scham*") of exhibitionism, it functions here as a way of exploring taboos in a highly charged but safely "transposed" manner; for Lacan too, sound is safely "figured" only when its devastating effects have been silenced. Kittler's view of the 1900 discourse network as locked into media specificity is thus particularly apposite here: Lacan and Sartre's reciprocity of looking and listening, Kafka's dialectic of law and transgression, Freud's interplay of exhibitionism and scopophilia, all these fragile attempts at conjuring forms of equivalence across media are responses to the devastating fixity of media at the long fin-de-siècle.

CONCLUSION: THE HOMOLOGIZING IDEOLOGY

The devastation of this fixity is implicated in every anxious overwrought "homological" coupling that stalks musicological attempts to implicate music in gender performance and to mark it as a proxy for the deployment of sexuality. I will begin this final section by contending that homology, the interpretive strategy whereby the structural proclivities of one cultural form or medium are made to find a structural equivalent in another medium, uncritically reproduces the kinds of cultural patternings that characterize the phallogocentric impulse. Such patternings in musicology characterize an uncritical practice that is still grounded in what might be termed an Oedipal logic (the logic whereby paternal/filial affiliations are privileged and notions of "inheritance" dominate the symbolic field), a practice, therefore, which fundamentally avoids explicit examination of *how* the connectedness of music to gender and sexuality is brought about (taking for granted, that is, the patrilineal affiliational structures that still dominate the field). We might map a typical example of this practice as in Figure 34.1.

In this schema, a male homosexual composer, living and working in Europe, seen through the lens of someone living after the explicit pathol-

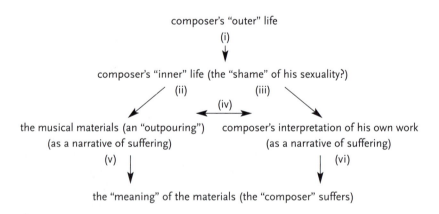

FIGURE 34.1 A typical relay of homological couplings in the Oedipal economy of deviant creativity

ogization of homosexuality, is implicated in a deviant (or subversive, but always *spectacular*) compositional practice because of his sexuality. The composer's outer public life (his succumbing to an external law) is taken into his inner world (what Freud has termed the "superego", the internalized law of the father). The suffering (shame) that the composer thereby feels is transformed by a cathartic creative act into the aestheticization of that suffering, into "suffering" (note the quotation marks here), but safely doubly coded by the composer's public counter-pronouncements on the work's meanings. The task of the musicologist in this sentimentally Oedipal scheme is to consider the "meaning" of the composer's work by considering the evidence of contemporaneous legal and popular discourses on sexuality and thereby constructing a template of how the composer will suffer *for us*. And it is, indeed, for "us" that the composer suffers: the sentimental homological series is based on a view of that "suffering" (i.e., the suffering of the composer as "figured" in the musical work) as a spectacle. We might summarize this process as follows:

1. The composer's "suffering" is a titillating spectacle for the liberal heterosexual critic fascinated by (desirous of) the Other.
2. The status of the "suffering" as spectacle is reliant upon the authority granted to that "suffering" by the same epistemological mechanisms that generate the suffering in the first place.
3. The work's signifying energies are largely focused on displaying that "suffering."

The heterosexist assumptions of this view aside, the Oedipal logic of the homological chain mistakes the epistemological *content* of the Freudian revolution for its radical *consequences*. It is in the *mediality* of Freud's revolution—in his unwillingness to accept the homological coupling of dream content to dream interpretation, for example—that the revolution recognized by Kittler is grounded. In Kafka's ironic over-Freudian narrator-dog, in Lacan and Sartre's fractious discourse of the subject haunted by footsteps in the corridor or the rustling of leaves, in Freud's dream revolution, we encounter a profound and far-reaching realignment of the order of things. This singular "revolution" marks a shift from the romantic hagiography of the male creative personality as coupled to and expressive of the male life force, to the halting and delicate circulation of mentalities. In this new dispensation, music's connectedness to gender formation and the deployment of sexuality is extraordinarily fragile and much more contested than musical scholarship has so far been willing to acknowledge. But that fragility is not the end of the story. It presents us with a challenge to think music (and sound more broadly) as operating in, through and against the newly autonomous affective fields of (very) late Capitalism (what Clough et al. [2007] have termed "affect-itself").

FURTHER READING

Blackmer, Corinne E., and Patricia J. Smith, eds. 1995. *En travesti: Women, gender subversion, opera.* New York: Columbia University Press.

Brett, Philip, Gary Thomas, and Elizabeth Wood, eds. 1994. *Queering the pitch: The new gay and lesbian musicology.* London and New York: Routledge.

Citron, Marcia. 1993. *Gender and the musical canon.* Cambridge, U.K.: Cambridge University Press.

Cook, Susan, Judy S. Tsou, and Susan McClary. 1994. *Cecilia reclaimed: Feminist perspectives on gender and music.* Urbana: University of Illinois Press.

Ericson, Margaret, 1996. *Women and music: A selected annotated bibliography on women and gender issues in music, 1987–1992.* New York: G. K. Hall.

Gill, John, 1995. *Queer noises: Male and female homosexuality in twentieth-century music.* Minneapolis: University of Minnesota Press.

Green, Lucy, 1997. *Music, gender, education.* Cambridge, U.K.: Cambridge University Press.

Groos, Arthur, and Roger Parker, eds. 1988. *Reading opera.* Princeton: Princeton University Press.

McClary, Susan, 1991. *Feminine endings: Music, gender and sexuality.* Minneapolis: University of Minnesota Press.

Nattiez, Jean-Jacques. 1993. *Wagner androgyne.* Princeton: Princeton University Press.

Sedgwick, Eve Kosofsky. 1994. *Tendencies.* London: Routledge.

Solie, Ruth, ed. 1993. *Musicology and difference: Gender and sexuality in music scholarship.* Berkeley and Los Angeles: University of California Press.

CHAPTER 35

Subjectivity Unbound
Music, Language, Culture

LAWRENCE KRAMER

Words and music do not get along; they never have. Even song bends words at will without necessarily worrying about how they are supposed to sound or what they are supposed to mean. And why not? Music is supposed to be beyond words. Talking about what it expresses is an exercise in futility. So we're still told; at some point in cultural history music became ineffable, became *the* ineffable, so that although we can talk *around* it we can't really talk *about* it. Either words will overgeneralize—"compared with music," wrote Nietzsche ([1901] 1969, 428), "all communication by words is shameless; words dilute and brutalize; words depersonalize; words make the uncommon common"—or words will overspecify, channeling the evocativeness of music into narrow referents and concepts. Either way, the lack of a systematic musical semantics will render whatever the words say irresponsibly subjective.

No doubt music, as a product of culture and history, cannot entirely escape either meaning in general or meaning in particular. But for roughly the past two centuries the cultural value of music has depended on the postulate that far more escapes than gets caught. This attitude is not only epistemic but also aesthetic; music is supposed to heed it along with performers and listeners. For Nietzsche, music that fails to cultivate its difference from language betrays "the law of its being" (p. 441). For Adorno, music "suffers" from its similarity to language but "its similarity to language is fulfilled as [music] distances itself from language" (Adorno 1993, 411, 405).

Nietzsche and Adorno clearly, and given their own epistemologies, oddly, believe themselves to be speaking on behalf of the true nature of music. (One of them forgets the will to power, the other negative dialectics, and both of course use words to do it.) But what they are actually talking about is a cultural ritual. Music does not by nature lack, surpass, transcend, or escape involvement with the multitude of things that words address. But a certain cultural ritual, repeated in many forms from everyday uses of music to scholarly accounts of it, *extracts* music symbolically from those worldly meshes.

The custom has an intriguing history and it has too many adherents to ignore. It lends to music of any style or genre what Richard Leppert (2005) has shown to be a utopian impetus that carries considerable appeal in a less than perfect world. But to acknowledge the custom need not be to endorse it or repeat it or, for that matter, to exaggerate its presence in and around music. The purpose of this chapter is to affirm the things that the custom of musical speechlessness ignores or denies. It is to affirm, in so many words, that music is unthinkable—not impossible but unthinkable—without language. This is true not despite but because of two inescapable conditions: that language about music is culture-bound on one hand and subjective on the other. The subjective speech acts that cluster around music are both the effects of its cultural force and the foundation of its cultural study. Neither the speech nor the subjects nor the cultural formations they invoke—this point can't be stressed too much—is "extrinsic" to the music, any music; the three terms are inseparable in both theory and practice.

With that we have reached the end before we have half begun. We navigate music by triangulating culture, subjectivity, and speech, and like the triangle in an orchestra's percussion section the result yields a pure tone only via the resonance of all three sides. But there is still work to be done. What are the implications of this triangle for the cultural study of music? How might those implications change our conception of what music is and does? What happens when we take the ceremony of the ineffable as a symptom, a point of departure, and hear music not as a prohibition on speech but as a provocation to it?

I propose to answer that question by offering five theses, stated as bluntly as possible. Illustrations and further comments will follow.

First, the cultural study of music is necessarily the study of language about music. The link between these terms is the subject who both hears and speaks. The question of how music is heard is inextricable from the question of who hears it, and therefore of who *replies* to it; music is a call. But the question of who hears, who speaks, who replies is never to be answered in the singular. The subject speaks through culture; culture speaks through the subject; both speak because both are linguistic through and through. Language does not attach to them; it permeates them. Every voice is many voices. The cultural study of music is thus, whatever else it may be, a study of the speech genres (Bakhtin), actual and possible, with which historical subjects envelop the practices of making and listening to music.

At the same time, the cultural study of music *is* one of those speech genres. It participates in and validates the passage of music through the mesh of language. Contrary to received wisdom, the subjectivity of language about music is not an obstacle to understanding but the means of understanding. The cultural study of music is both the study of subjectivity and the exercise of it. There is no alternative that does not default on understanding itself. I should add in passing that these questions are inseparable from those of musical performance, which in this context is effectively a speech genre in itself. The topic will be touched on later, albeit too briefly.

Second, the traditional complaint that language about music is merely subjective (unless it is merely technical) misunderstands both language and subjectivity. It ignores something the complainants surely know, that both language and subjectivity are above all cultural agencies, each of which acts through the other. Each addresses music exactly as it addresses everything else, including phenomena such as feeling and sensation which, like music, are commonly regarded as ineffable. Music does cultural work in being spoken of. Subjectivity does cultural work in speaking about music. Discourse about music is revealing about every term in the nexus of music, subjectivity, and culture.

Such discourse discloses credible meanings that act both retrospectively and prospectively. It does so both in its first iterations as performative utterance and in subsequent reflective appropriations that take it (and through it each term that informs it) as an object of interpretation. Music acts culturally by modeling modes of subjectivity toward which its listeners and performers take a determinate position. Subjective language about music is the record of this negotiation, which becomes interpretable just through that language.

Third, revealing discourse about music tends to take a specific form, finding its nucleus in a specific genre of utterance. The discourse depends on framing or seeking a special type of speech act that changes the things it describes, and that does so not as an exceptional but as a normal function of language. I propose to call this type of utterance *constructive description.* Its musical elaboration takes the overlapping forms of metaphors about music and accounts of how music unfolds, most often in narrative modes that I have elsewhere identified as parable and paraphrase—roughly speaking, a story we imagine a piece of music to tell and the story we tell about a piece of music (Kramer 2001, 14–20).

Fourth, the familiar notion of "cultural context" is insufficient to circumscribe the cultural study of music (or anything else). This study is impossible to confine within an empirical framework. It is inescapably hermeneutic and bound up not only with the descriptive powers and limits of language but also with the uncertainties, equivocations, and figurative energies of language. We cannot be satisfied with modest, limited efforts that apologize for what they say in the act of saying it and/or confine themselves to simple affective or descriptive categories and/or demote themselves to the categories of the "personal" or "poetic." Instead we must address music—must, that is, if we want to understand it—with the same rich conceptual and verbal resourcefulness routinely applied to texts and images.

Fifth, the cultural study of music is conditioned, though never merely determined, by the cultural work of culture itself. Culture endows contingent historical forms of agency and practice with universalizing value. It does so openly but often without avowing it explicitly. As Jacques Lacan says of the symbolic order, a concept closely related to "culture" in the sense intended here and derived from Claude Lévi-Strauss's version of cultural anthropology, the fact that the forms thus endowed are not actually universal does not matter. They are universal in principle; their effects mimic those we expect from the universal (Lacan 1988, 29–31). Both music and its cultural study are driven in part by a tension between the recognition and the forgetting of what happens when we endow contingent phenomena with the status of truth, law, or value.

The cultural work of culture fosters that tension through a familiar but almost imperceptible paradox. Pierre Bourdieu calls it "the paradox [that] defines the 'realization' of culture as *becoming natural*. Culture is . . . achieved only by negating itself as such, that is, as artificial and artificially acquired, so as to become second nature, a habitus, a possession turned into being" (Bourdieu 1993, 234). Music, with its almost limitless capacity to adapt to particular circumstances, lends itself to this affirmative self-forgetfulness all too well. Both everyday life and ceremonial occasions fill themselves with music—and "fill" is an understatement in today's world of proliferating media, where music is routinely devalued and rendered virtually unhearable, though not inaudible, by its very ubiquity—whenever they need to realize culture as second nature in immediate, effective form. Music is used to elevate the ordinary and aggrandize the occasional. It may work against our better judgment but it certainly seems to work.

This usage does not need to involve explicit claims of universality; perhaps it does better without them. It comports quite well with enthusiasm for specific, and therefore culturally relative, types of music. It asks us only to assume a certain emphasis or disposition, to find a groove and follow it, to act out a judgment in the form of participation without reserve. The privilege, if it is that, and certainly the problem of music is that music not only participates in the transformation of culture into second nature but is commonly appointed to embody it. Music stages the scene in which cultural self-forgetfulness remembers to affirm itself.

Because culture presents itself semantically and music, apparently, does not, music has the capacity to assume oracular value. It can claim—be granted, be endowed with—an eloquent inarticulateness that seems to touch the ground beyond the relativity of culture. The effect of this usage is to help validate the very culture it seems to transcend. The music regarded as proper to a cultural milieu is invested with an unsurpassed power to strip away its own contextual specificity and thus to render its culture-bound values categorical. Music regarded as culturally external, that is, as bearing the semantic marks of an alien milieu, undergoes a parallel but opposite process that renders it excessively particular, an expression of either a parochial Other that must be surmounted or a revolutionary Other that aims to usurp categorical force (and may be welcome for it). Either way, the instituted ineffability of music provides a relief from the ubiquitous demands of meaning without surrendering the culturally grounded sense of meaningfulness.

This custom supplies most of the language still used conventionally to talk about music—and also *not* to talk about it, which is where the real problem lies. It is one thing to enjoy not filling in music's semantic blanks and quite another to prohibit filling them: to turn a custom into a law. The prohibition is pointless in any case. Semantic energies are irrepressible; the voices of invention refuse to be stilled; the possibility of talking at all includes the possibility of talking back. It makes little sense to label as ineffable something we talk about as incessantly as we talk about music. But until the development, starting around 1990, of "New Musicology" and "Critical Musicology," approaches for which meaningfulness without meaning was not enough, there was a broad consensus that enforced a certain silence about music—a silence where it really counts—by requiring that any meanings ascribed to music be both vague and expendable, as befits their origin in mere subjectivity.

These disciplinary developments were not systematic and they are now generally conceded to have been absorbed into mainstream practice. One way to describe them is to say that both their "method" and their aim was to revalue ways of speaking and writing about music that would formerly have been considered mistaken, nonsensical, impressionistic, or lacking in rigor, the better to reveal the cultural work that music performs, in part, by the art of concealment.

This project brings us to constructive description: in effect a description that makes what it sees—or hears (Kramer 2010, 52–66). The cultural study of music benefits from constructive description by both recognizing it and practicing it, though in many instances these two activities are indistinguishable. Constructive descriptions are statements that "stick" to the objects they address, forming an independent layer of appearance that is nonetheless part of the object's phenomenal presence. Snatches of poetry, lines one gets by heart (Derrida 1991, 223–237), often assume this surplus vividness, so perhaps it is only fitting that constructive description is itself perhaps best evoked—constructively described—in a philosophical poem by Wallace Stevens, "Description without Place" (1940). Constructive description both records and produces "the difference that we make in what we see." It is less a representation than an invention, but like any good invention it reveals something about what it makes happen: "Description is revelation. It is not / The thing described, or false facsimile. // It is an artificial thing that exists, / In its own seeming" (Stevens 1954, 344). Such speech acts may be either fleeting or enduring; the enduring ones become part of the lore surrounding their objects, though one has to be careful (and it is not always possible) to keep them from ossifying into clichés or dead metaphors.

To show how constructive description works, and how it can be put to work for the cultural study of music, I turn to one of Frédéric Chopin's twenty-four Preludes for Piano (no. 20 in C minor), Op. 28 (1839), and to some famous remarks about the Preludes overall by George Sand, writing in part in her capacity as Chopin's companion. The remarks are teasingly equivocal, part memoir, part metaphor. They are candidly evocative and would not traditionally have been regarded as a source of real musical insight, though their way with words about music was not unusual when they were written. But what if they have real cognitive value after all? What happens if we take them as constructive descriptions rather than as mere "figures of speech"? The point would not be to equate what the music expresses with what the words say—a ventriloquist's trick; who would want to do that even if it could be done? The point, rather, is to see why what Sand says of the music has stuck to it and in so doing enabled the music to disclose potential knowledge about both itself and its cultural investments.

Sand's remarks come from her autobiography. She is recalling a stay in Majorca where she and Chopin had gone for Chopin's health, and where he composed four of the Preludes:

> [In Majorca] he composed the most beautiful of those short pages that he modestly entitled Preludes. They are masterpieces. Several present to thought [*présentent à la pensée*] visions of defunct monks and the resonance [*l'audition*] of the funeral chants that beset them [*l'assiégeaient*]; others are melancholy and sweet—they came to him in hours of sun and health, from the noise of children's laughter beneath the window, from the

distant sound of guitars, from the song of birds under the moist leaves, from the sight of small pale roses blooming on the snow.[1]

(Sand 1893, 439)

Sand deploys her imagery, part of a common stock of images in nineteenth-century French poetry before Baudelaire, to emphasize the brevity and disorderly particularity of these "short pages." She is in good company; both Liszt and Schumann had done the same thing, helping to initiate a tradition of hearing the Preludes as fragments, even fragments of fragments. The pieces certainly fit the description. They form an expressive grab-bag despite a rather rigid arrangement on the grid of all the major and minor keys. Most of them sound like musical epigraphs based on a single rhythm; many flit by too quickly to be absorbed or become absorbed in; most break off with an abrupt halt followed by an arbitrary cadence formula. Sand was right to speak of "pages" rather than "works"; these are "pieces" in a strikingly literal sense.

In their resistance to completeness and definition, the Preludes count as among the earliest "avant-garde" compositions. They are not Romantic fragments—works of ideal incompletion, parts that are paradoxically also wholes—but fragments in the sense of something broken off, something subtracted, so that they stand at the limit of being "something" at all. This quality is resonant in Schumann's metaphors once one takes them seriously as acts of constructive description: the Preludes are "sketches, beginnings of Etudes; or, so to speak, ruins, eagle wings, a wild motley" (Higgins 1973, 91). As music *sui generis*, the Preludes are demonstrations of an emergent resistance to stable identity—a continuous, ontologically open "transit of identity" (Kramer 1984, 92–95) that requires historical explanation. At the same time these piecemeal pieces are conduits for the insertion of unstable identity into historical experience. By maintaining their own identity as a mode of tenuousness, an extreme but not unique position in Chopin's output, the Preludes refuse to mirror the identity of the listener. They address the person who plays or hears them with a short-circuit of the Hegelian process whereby the self appropriates its identity from the Other that confronts it.

Sand seems to find this surplus particularity a source of pleasure; her language reflects as much. She is even inspired to invent parallel pleasures, recalling or conjuring up fragrant flowers and gamboling children although there is obviously nothing in the music to mandate them; the monkish funerals are easier to spot—we will come to that. But Sand is not merely engaging in a baseless effusion. The contrast she draws between the gloomy and sunny preludes activates numerous contraries typical of early nineteenth-century aesthetics: the beautiful and the sublime, the natural and the supernatural, the pastoral and the gothic, and secular sentiment and religious awe. These oppositions supply a lucid framework within which anyone so disposed—or anyone puzzled by the strangeness of the music— can find a listening post.

It is suggestive in this respect that Sand's metaphors are anchored in acoustic impressions that Chopin's music is said to recall—not to imitate, exactly, but to make present without actually making audible: the resonance of the chants, the laughter of the children, the remoteness of the guitars. The language already suggests, even before any interpretation of it begins, a world of acoustic meanings in which both the music and the listener are situated. Start to press the description interpretively, and the meanings begin to multiply, in part by what they omit: modernity, the city and its streets, the salon and its chatter. The acoustic world in question is in one respect real; it is the world of the Majorcan countryside where Chopin worked on the Preludes. In another respect that world is idyllic, a fantasy, and even, in its openness to archaic, gothic impressions, phantasmal. But the difference between these alternatives is more tenuous than it may first seem; the spatial distance of the guitars blurs into the temporal distance of the monkish funerals. The music dissolves identities. It makes fluid what seems solid.

What happens, then, if we press even further? What cultural, what historical need does this perception of the music, and the music through this perception of it, seek to satisfy?

As noted earlier, Sand's statement includes elements like the roses in the snow and children's laughter that at first seem unaccountable, and that do not so much come from the object described as lead to it. Their presence is typical for constructive descriptions. It is just these unique elements that hold out the promise of a deeper engagement with the culture and subjectivities hovering somewhere between the music and the description. Probably the most striking instance in Sand's statement consists of those defunct monks. What are they doing there and what can we learn from their presence?

More than one might suppose, if we allow our own constructive agency some latitude. Sand does not identify which of Chopin's "pages" she has in mind. Several are possible, but the C minor Prelude stands out because it is immediately recognizable as a miniature funeral march. If the defunct monks are anywhere, they are probably (also) here.

This music is at once simple and confounding. It is only thirteen measures long and might just as well have been eight; in several post-publication album versions, Chopin transcribed only the first eight: four measures *fortissimo* over resonant octaves reaching to the deepest bass, and four measures *piano* over a bass descending in octaves by step and half-step, starting high but ending low as the music, slow to begin with, drags its feet in a ritenuto. The remainder in one sense adds nothing, but from the perspective suggested by Sand it adds everything. First there is a repetition of the four *piano* measures, but taken down to *pianissimo* until the last measure and half, where a gradual crescendo appears (to what level remains open); then, while the last beat of the last measure introduces the pedal, a final, extra measure containing only a single chord cancels the crescendo and ends the piece.

There are at least three venues here for Sand's defunct monks to haunt: the prelude's genre, the shape of the bass line in its double second half, and the anomalous extra measure at the end. The genre is not simply funereal or ecclesiastical, but gothic. The booming bass octaves of the first half and the echoing and re-echoing of them in the two second halves seem to emanate, by acoustic mimicry, from a resonant vault. Sand's image of the "defunct monks . . . beset" by "funereal chants" points more to ominous gloom than to religious dignity; it registers the music's imaginary space as gothic more in the sense of popular fiction than of architectural form. The popular gothic is built on the ruins of a religious awe lost with the Middle Ages; its haunted spaces mark the decline of naive piety, now an object of nostalgia, to the "thrilling" presence of spectral forms—defunct, yes, but still animate. The prelude registers this decline by its extreme miniaturization, which reduces the sublime to a squib.

This pocket gothic is the scene of an imaginary visit by a detached, alienated modern observer for whom awe has lost its intimidating but also its elevating power and become a mood. The prelude is an ironic realization of the survival of medieval sublimity into the modern age as envisioned by a book that probably influenced both Chopin's musical imagery and Sand's description of it, the Vicomte de Chateaubriand's *The Genius of Christianity* (published 1802): "How readily the poets and novelists of this infidel age . . . introduce dungeons, specters, castles, and Gothic churches into their fictions,—so great is the charm associated with [medieval] religion. . . . The more remote were those times the more magical they appeared" (Chateaubriand [1802] 1856, 384–385). The Prelude measures the historical distance between medieval and modern subjectivity in terms one can call allegorical: the shift from the arresting immediacy of the opening clamor to the proliferating distances of the two or, counting the extra measure, three fading echoes that follow it, again in terms redolent of Chateaubriand: "Past ages, conjured up by these religious sounds, raise their venerable voices from the bottom of the stones. . . . The sanctuary re-echoes like the cavern of the ancient Sibyl; loud-tongued bells swing over your head, while the vaults of death under your feet are strangely silent" (p. 387).

The bass line of the first two echoes concentrates the impression that the observing subject is grounded in an absence of spirit. The absence is actually produced by the music. At first, and with impressive inexorability, the bass descends along an artificial scale composed of all the notes available in the three scalar forms of C minor—all, that is, but one. The descent breaks off just before reaching the threshold of completion, at the point where D, the second scale degree, should be. Before this missing tone is finally recaptured, albeit not in the bass, the music resonates precisely around its absence. The absence is not an abstraction but a gap felt immediately in the disruption of the scale pattern. With this break the music once more shifts into the mode of allegory, hovering around the vacancy in, or of, spirit that defines the exemplary self of its era. That vacancy may seem like a big burden for a small piece to carry, but the disproportion is part of the point. The vacant space of self is all too familiar; it is even popular, a Byronic and heroic flaw; it needs no more than an allusion to bring it into play.

Its presence may help explain the perplexing final echo, the unlucky thirteenth measure. The final chord is one of the arbitrary closing gestures scattered throughout the collection of Preludes, but it is really unnecessary either rhetorically or harmonically. Its true force seems to lie with the crescendo it cancels. The crescendo is another feature that in some sense should not be there. If the *pianissimo* of the repeated second half suggests a recession to the distance, the fading sounds should if anything get softer, and certainly not louder, as the music slows. (Did the cortège take a wrong turn down some catacomb or other?) The fluctuation in sound suggests that the distances embedded in the piece are not spatial but historical. The motion involved concerns memories or fantasies, not bodies. Sand's description of a vision presented to thought, like Chateaubriand's of spectral gothic, is exact in its observation of a mode of perception. But this is a mode that the Prelude does not elicit simply, but comes to elicit progressively. The crescendo marks a decisive turn from the illusion of space to the reality of mind. The final chord, for reasons of its own, then shuts things down beyond appeal.

This ending challenges both perception and performance. The fadeout starting with the *pianissimo* serves in part as a reflection on the strange time scale of the piece. It marks and heightens the contrast between long pace and short duration: the music asks us to imagine an event that happens slowly, with gravitas, while the depiction of the event takes up only about a minute and a half. The listener who complies might be described as hearing the past in the process of assuming its pastness, acquiring the distance without which it could not be perceived. The temporal form of that distance is the brevity of compression, which stands as a musical parallel to the spatial form of the ruin, the only form in which the past can be preserved.

But the listener might also be a performer, as for a long time virtually any piano student would be at some time. In that case—and this brings us back to the point made in passing earlier, that musical performance may act as a speech genre—the question of the past would be posed in a different medium. As a performer I might ask how I can touch the keys softly enough to capture the immense distance introduced by the extra segment and the extra measure. And, whether playing or listening, I might also ask what impression the sound leaves or should leave as it becomes, though it wavers, more impalpable. Is its solemnity archaic, ecclesiastical, ceremonial, supernatural or—the list is not complete—parodistic?

And here, running counter to conventional wisdom and some scholarly protocols (both of which might crop up by now, or have already), we should take note of some things that do not matter. There are quite a few of them. It does not matter if Chopin did not imagine any defunct monks in the C minor Prelude and it does not matter if he thought about nothing else and let that slip in an unguarded moment to Sand. It does not matter if "we," in another epoch, cannot locate the monks' spirits in the "vaults of death" or if we find their trail faintly ridiculous and so prefer not to follow it. What matters is that Sand, in her own epoch, could respond to this music, or to music like it, with the imagery of dead—that is, long ago dead—monks and could do so with a certain assurance that she would be understood as making sense, not spouting nonsense. That historical reality draws both musical and cultural formations together within a framework that they disclose and that potentially discloses something about them, or, more exactly, discloses something about their semantic potentiality.

The potential mode is of the essence here. Sand's constructive description does not form a boundary; it is not authoritative or pre-emptive. On the contrary, it establishes the potentiality of other descriptions, other frameworks, that neither Sand nor Chopin might have recognized but that the music of the one and the language of the other not only do not exclude but positively invite.

For example, consider the stony thirteenth measure one last time. I have described it, via Sand, as spectral, but is it also a reflection on the spectrality of what precedes it, a *mise-en-abîme* that places the whole Prelude at a historical distance from itself? Or is this extra finish a false signifier of closure meant to halt the infinite repeatability of the B section of the funeral march implied by its double statement and reviving dynamic level? Is the extra measure a way of curtailing the universal metastasis of the funereal?

Whatever the answers—my guess is that they are all "Yes"—the description involved in posing the questions brings us back to a key point. That description, any constructive description, necessarily goes beyond the "facts" before it and any available code for deciphering them. One might derive the idea of ecclesiastical space in the C minor Prelude from the sound of the solemn march over resonant octaves, but the derivation would not extend from there to the impression of archaic time—the music sounds neither archaic nor chant-like—and even less to the monks, let alone defunct monks. (Are they the ones being entombed or are they doing the entombing?) For that image we need precisely the alienated modern subject whose condition this listening registers. The subject must proffer the constructive description and see what follows from it. If the music evokes the medieval scene, it does so precisely because it is addressed to a modern ear for whom the medieval is still, if freshly, the lost scene of cultural unity and infinite mystery. That again is why the Prelude is so graphically minimized—it is one of the shortest in the set; we hear it as through the wrong end of an acoustic telescope.

Some of these impressions are so ingrained in the score and so supported by the surviving remnants of nineteenth-century culture that the music may be heard from a Sand-like listening post even by listeners who have no inkling of her description. By addressing the piece interpretively from the perspective she provides, we engage in acts of explication and recovery; we situate these acts of listening in a culturally as well as acoustically resonant space. To do that, we need only put to work the five theses proposed earlier. As always with reading the texts of "reception," what we want to know is not just what was said but rather what was being done in the saying. The saying without the doing is inert. It is not even historical. But put them together, energize them with the finding and making of constructive descriptions, and the result is the cultural study of music.

FURTHER READING

Adorno, Theodor. 2002. *Essays on music: Selected, with introduction, commentary, and notes by Richard Leppert.* New translations by Susan Gillespie. Berkeley: University of California Press.

Brown, Marshall. 2010. *The tooth that nibbles at the soul: Essays on music and poetry.* Seattle: University of Washington Press.

Chapin, Keith, and Lawrence Kramer, eds. 2009. *Musical meaning and human values.* New York: Fordham University Press.

Klein, Michael. 2005. *Intertextuality in Western art music.* Bloomington: Indiana University Press.

Kramer, Lawrence. 1990. *Music as cultural practice, 1800-1900.* Berkeley: University of California Press.

Kramer, Lawrence. 1995. *Classical music and postmodern knowledge.* Berkeley: University of California Press.

Kramer, Lawrence. 2001. Chopin at the funeral: Episodes in the history of modern death. *Journal of the American Musicological Society* 54: 97–126.

Leppert, Richard. 1993. *The sight of sound: Music, representation, and the history of the body.* Berkeley: University of California Press.

McClary, Susan. 2000. *Conventional wisdom: The content of musical form.* Berkeley: University of California Press.

Middleton, Richard. 2006. *Voicing the popular: On the subjects of popular music.* New York: Routledge.

Scott, Derek. 2003. *From the erotic to the demonic: On critical musicology.* Oxford: Oxford University Press.

Williams, Alastair. 2001. *Constructing musicology.* Aldershot, U.K.: Ashgate.

REFERENCES

Abbate, Carolyn. 2004. Music—drastic or gnostic? *Critical Inquiry* 30: 505–536.

Adler, Guido. 1885. Umfang, Methode und Ziel der Musikwissenschaft. *Vierteljahrsschrift für Musikwissenschaft* 1: 5–20.

Adler, M. 1985. Stardom and talent. *American Economic Review* 75(1): 208–212.

Adorno, Theodor W. [1927] 2002. The curves of the needle. Pp. 271–276 in *Essays on Music*. Edited by Richard Leppert. Translated by Susan H. Gillespie. Berkeley: University of California Press.

—— [1932] 2002. On the social situation of music. Pp. 391–436 in *Essays on Music*. Edited by Richard Leppert. Translated Susan H. Gillespie. Berkeley: University of California Press.

—— [1934] 2002. The form of the phonograph record. Pp. 277–282 in *Essays on Music*. Edited by Richard Leppert. Translated by Susan H. Gillespie. Berkeley: University of California Press.

—— [1938] 2002. On the fetish-character of music and the regression of listening. Pp. 288–317 in *Essays on Music*. Edited by Richard Leppert. Translated by Susan H. Gillespie. Berkeley: University of California Press.

—— [1941] 2002 (with George Simpson). On popular music. Pp. 437–469 in *Essays on Music*. Edited by Richard Leppert. Translated by Susan H. Gillespie. Berkeley: University of California Press.

—— [1969] 2002. Opera and the long-playing record. Pp. 283–287 in *Essays on Music*. Edited by Richard Leppert. Translated by Susan H. Gillespie. Berkeley: University of California Press.

—— 1973. *Philosophy of modern music*. Translated by Anne G. Mitchell and Wesley V. Bloomster. London: Sheed and Ward.

—— [1973] 2003. *The jargon of authenticity*. Translated by Knut Tarnowski and Frederic Will. New York: Routledge.

—— 1976. *Introduction to the sociology of music*. New York: Seabury Press.

—— 1984. *Aesthetic theory*. Edited by Gretel Adorno and Rolf Tiedemann. Translated by C. Lenhardt. New York: Routledge and Kegan Paul.

—— 1993. Music, language, and composition. Translated by Susan Gillespie. *The Musical Quarterly* 77(3): 401–414.

—— 2002. *Essays on music*. Selected and introduced by Richard Leppert. Berkeley: University of California Press.

—— n.d. Plugging, like and dislike in the field of light popular music. Max Horkheimer Archive, Frankfurt, Box XIII, Folder 18, 1–39.

Agamben, Giorgio. 1998. *Homo sacer: Sovereign power and bare life*. Translated by Daniel Heller-Roazen. Stanford: Stanford University Press.

Agamben, Giorgio. 2005. *State of exception.* Translated by Kevin Attell. Chicago: University of Chicago Press.

Agawu, V. Kofi. 1991. *Playing with signs: A semiotic interpretation of classic music.* Princeton: Princeton University Press.

—— 2003. *Representing African music: Postcolonial notes, queries, positions.* New York: Routledge.

Alden, Andrew. 1998. What does it all mean? The national curriculum for music in a multi-cultural society. M.A. thesis. London University Institute of Education.

Alderman, John. 2001. *Sonic boom: Napster, P2P and the battle for the future of music.* London: Fourth Estate.

Allanbrook, Wye Jamison, ed. 1998. *The late eighteenth century.* Vol. 5 of *Strunk's source readings in music history,* rev. ed. Edited by Leo Treitler. New York: Norton.

Alpert, Michael. 1994. Liner notes to *Brave old world: Beyond the pale.* Rounder Records CD 3135.

Anand, N., and Richard A. Peterson. 2000. When market information constitutes fields: Sensemaking of markets in the commercial music industry. *Organization Science* 11(3): 270–284.

Andersen, Birgitte, and Vanus James. 2000. *Copyrights and competition: Towards policy implications for music business development.* Manchester: ESRC Centre for Research on Innovation and Competition.

Anderson, Benedict. [1983; 1991] 2006. *Imagined communities: Reflections on the origins and spread of nationalism.* New York: Verso.

Aparicio, Frances R. 1998. *Listening to salsa: Gender, Latin popular music, and Puerto Rican cultures.* Hanover, NH: University Press of New England.

Appadurai, Arjun. 1990. Disjuncture and difference in the global economy. Pp. 1–24 in *Global culture: Nationalism, globalization and modernity.* Edited by Mike Featherstone. London: Sage.

—— 1992. Disjuncture and difference in the global cultural economy. *Public Culture* 2(2): 1–24.

—— 1996. *Modernity at large: Cultural dimensions of globalization.* Minneapolis: University of Minnesota Press.

——, ed. 1986. *The social life of things: Commodities in cultural perspective.* Cambridge, U.K.: Cambridge University Press.

Aracena, Beth K. 1999. Singing salvation: Jesuit musics in colonial Chile, 1600–1767. Ph.D. thesis, University of Chicago.

Armstrong, Carol. 1996. Contribution to "Visual culture questionnaire." *October* 77: 25–70.

Armstrong, Tim. 1998. *Modernism, technology, and the body.* Cambridge, U.K.: Cambridge University Press.

Arnold, John H. 2000. *History: A very short introduction.* New York: Oxford University Press.

Arnold, Matthew. [1869] 1963. *Culture and anarchy.* Edited by J. Dover Wilson. Cambridge, U.K.: Cambridge University Press.

Arthur, W. Brian. 2009. *The nature of technology: What it is and how it evolves.* London and New York: Penguin.

Asad, Talal. 1993. *Genealogies of religion: Discipline and reasons of power in Christianity and Islam.* Baltimore: The Johns Hopkins University Press.

Ashby, Arved. 2010. *Absolute music, mechanical reproduction.* Berkeley: University of California Press.

Aston, Elaine, and George Savona. 1991. *Theatre as sign-system: A semiotics of text and performance.* London: Routledge.

Attali, Jacques. 1985. *Noise: The political economy of music.* Translated by Brian Massumi. Minneapolis: University of Minnesota Press.

Augustine, St. 1991. *Confessions.* Translated by Henry Chadwick. Oxford: Oxford University Press.

Auslander, Philip. 2006. *Performing glam rock: Gender and theatricality in popular music.* Ann Arbor: University of Michigan Press.

Austin, J. L. 1962. *How to do things with words.* Edited by J. O. Urmston. Oxford: Clarendon Press.

Averill, Gage. 1997. *A day for the hunter, a day for the prey: Popular music and power in Haiti.* Chicago: University of Chicago Press.

Back, Les. 1996. X amount of Sat Siri Akal! Apache Indian, Reggae music, and the cultural intermezzo. *New Formations* 27: 128–147.

Badiou, Alain. 2002. *Ethics: An essay on the understanding of evil.* Translated by Peter Hallward. London: Verso.

—— 2007. *The century.* Translated by Alberto Toscano. Cambridge, U.K.: Polity Press.

Baily, John. 1976. Recent changes in the dutar of Herat. *Asian Music* 8(1): 26–64.

—— 1984. *Amir: The life of an Afghan refugee musician in Pakistan.* Documentary film. Boston: Documentary Education Resources.

——, ed. 1995. *Working with Blacking: The Belfast years.* [Special issue] *The World of Music* 37(2).

—— 1996. Using tests of sound perception in fieldwork. *Yearbook for Traditional Music* 28: 147–173.

—— 2004. Music censorship in Afghanistan before and after the Taliban. Pp. 19–28 in *Shoot the singer: music censorship today.* Edited by M. Korpe. New York: Palgrave Macmillan.

Baker, Geoffrey. 2011. *Buena Vista in the club: Rap, reggaetón, and revolution in Havana.* Durham, NC: Duke University Press.

Bakhtin, Mikhail M. 1981. *The dialogic imagination. Four essays.* Edited by Michael Holquist. Translated by Caryl Emerson and Michael Holquist. Austin: University of Texas Press.

Balter, Michael. 2004. Seeking the key to music. *Science* 306: 1120–1122.

Banks, M. 2007. *The politics of cultural work.* Basingstoke, U.K.: Palgrave.

—— 2012. Macintyre, Bourdieu and the practice of jazz. *Popular Music* 29.

Baraka, Amiri. 1967. *Black music.* New York: William Morrow.

Barbrook, Richard. 1998. The hi-tech gift economy. http://firstmonday.dk/issues/issue3_12/barbrook/index.html (accessed August 6, 2002).

Barfield, Thomas, ed. 1997. *The dictionary of anthropology.* Oxford: Blackwell.

Barnes, Ken. 1988. Top 40 radio: A fragment of the imagination. Pp. 8–50 in *Facing the music.* Edited by Simon Frith. New York: Pantheon.

Barthes, Roland. 1977. The death of the author. Pp. 142–148 in *Image/Music/Text.* London: Fontana.

—— 1986. *The responsibility of forms: Critical essays on music, art, and representation.* Translated by Richard Howard. Oxford: Blackwell.

Barz, Gregory F. 2003. *Performing religion: Negotiating past and present in Kwaya music of Tanzania.* New York: Rodopi.

Barz, Gregory F., and Timothy J. Cooley. [1997] 2008. *Shadows in the field: New perspectives for fieldwork in ethnomusicology.* New York: Oxford University Press.

Baugh, Bruce. 1993. Prolegomena to any aesthetics of rock music. *Journal of Aesthetics and Arts Criticism* 51(1): 23–29

Baumol, William J., and Hilda Baumol. [1985] 1997. On the cost disease and its true policy implications for the arts. Pp. 213–224 in *Baumol's cost disease: The arts and other victims.* Edited by Ruth Towse. Cheltenham, U.K.: Edward Elgar.

Baumol, William J., and William G. Bowen. [1966] 1997. On the rationale of public support. Pp. 243–260 in *Baumol's cost disease: The arts and other victims.* Edited by Ruth Towse. Cheltenham, U.K.: Edward Elgar.

Baxandall, Michael. 1972. *Painting and experience in fifteenth century Italy: A primer in the social history of pictorial style.* Oxford: Oxford University Press.

Becker, Howard S. 1982. *Art worlds.* Berkeley: University of California Press.

Becker, Judith. 2004. *Deep listeners: Music, emotion, and trancing.* Bloomington: Indiana University Press.

—— 2010. Exploring the habitus of listening: anthropological perspectives. Pp. 127–157 in *Handbook of music and emotion: Theory, research, applications.* Edited by Patrick N. Juslin and John A. Sloboda. Oxford: Oxford University Press.

Beckwith, John. 1982. Kolinski: An appreciation and list of works. Pp. xvii–xxiv in *Cross-cultural perspectives on music (Essays in memory of Mieczyslaw Kolinski from his students, colleagues, and friends).* Edited by Robert Falck and Timothy Rice. Toronto: University of Toronto Press.

Beer, David. 2007. Tune out: Music, soundscapes and the urban mise-en-scène. *Information, Communication and Society* 10: 846–866.

Bendelow, Gillian, and Simon J. Williams, eds. 1998. *Emotions in social life: Critical themes and contemporary issues.* London: Routledge.

Benjamin, Walter. [1936] 1973a. The storyteller. Pp. 83–109 in *Illuminations.* Edited by Hannah Arendt. Translated by Harry Zohn. London: Fontana Books.

Benjamin, Walter. [1936] 1973b. The work of art in the age of mechanical reproduction. Pp. 217–251 in *Illuminations.* Edited by Hannah Arendt. Translated by Harry Zohn. London: Fontana Books.

Bennett, Andy. 2000. *Popular music and youth culture: Music, identity and place.* Basingstoke: Macmillan.

Bennett, Andy. 2005. *Culture and everyday life*. London: Sage.

Bennett, Jane. 2009. *Vibrant matter: A political ecology of things*. Durham, NC: Duke University Press.

Berger, Harris M. 2007. *Stance: Ideas about emotion, style, and meaning for the study of expressive culture*. Middletown, CT: Wesleyan University Press.

Berger, Peter L., and Thomas Luckmann. 1966. *The social construction of reality*. London: Allen Lane.

Bergeron, Katherine. 1998. *Decadent enchantments: The revival of Gregorian chant at Solesmes*. Berkeley: University of California Press.

Bergeron, Katherine, and Philip V. Bohlman, eds. 1992. *Disciplining music: Musicology and its canons*. Chicago: University of Chicago Press.

Berliner, Paul F. 1994. *Thinking in jazz: The infinite art of improvisation*. Chicago: The University of Chicago Press.

Bernstein, Charles, ed. 1998. *Close listening: Poetry and the performed word*. New York: Oxford University Press.

Bernstein, Jay M. 1992. *The fate of art: Aesthetic alienation from Kant to Derrida and Adorno*. Cambridge, U.K.: Polity Press.

Bersani, Leo. [1987] 2010. Is the rectum a grave? Pp. 3–30 in *Is the rectum a grave?: And other essays*. Chicago: University of Chicago Press.

Besseler, Heinrich. 1931. *Die Musik des Mittelalters und der Renaissance*. Potsdam, Germany: Akademische Verlagsgesellschaft Athenaion.

Bhabha, Homi. 1994. *The location of culture*. New York: Routledge.

Bhaskar, R. 1998. *The possibility of naturalism: A philosophical critique of the contemporary human sciences*. London: Routledge.

Biddle, Ian, and Kirsten Gibson, eds. 2009. *Masculinity and western musical practice*. Aldershot, U.K.: Ashgate Publishing.

Birley, Margaret, Heidrun Eicher, and Arnold Myers. 2000. *Voices for the silenced: Guidelines for interpreting musical instruments in museum collections*. Electronic publication (this update, January 17, 2000). http://www.music.ed. ac.uk/euchmi/cimcim/iwte.html.

Björk. 2001. *Björk*. London: Little-i.

Blacking, John. 1973. *How musical is man?* Seattle: University of Washington Press.

——, ed. 1977. *The anthropology of the body*. New York: Academic Press.

—— 1987. *"A commonsense view of all music": Reflections on Percy Grainger's contribution to ethnomusicology and music education*. Cambridge, U.K.: Cambridge University Press.

—— 1995. *Music, culture, and experience: Selected papers of John Blacking*. Chicago: University of Chicago Press.

Blanning, Tim. 2008. *The triumph of music: Composers, musicians and their audiences, 1700 to the present*. London: Penguin.

Bloch, Ernst. 2009. *Atheism in Christianity*. Translated by J. T. Swan. London: Verso.

Bloechl, Olivia A. 2008. *Native American song at the frontiers of early modern music*. Cambridge, U.K.: Cambridge University Press.

Bloomfield, Terry. 1993. Resisting songs: Negative dialectics in pop. *Popular Music* 12(1): 13–31.

Blum, Stephen. 1991. European musical terminology and the music of Africa. Pp. 3–36 in *Comparative musicology and anthropology of music: Essays in the history of ethnomusicology*. Edited by Bruno Nettl and Philip V. Bohlman. Chicago: University of Chicago Press.

Boa, Elizabeth. 1996. *Kafka: Gender, class, and race in the letters and fictions*. Oxford: Clarendon Press.

Bogin, Barry. 1999. *Patterns of human growth*. Edited by C. G. N. Mascie-Taylor and M. A. Little. 2nd ed. Cambridge Studies in Biological Anthropology. Cambridge, U.K.: Cambridge University Press.

Bohlman, Philip V. 1988. *The study of folk music in the modern world*. Bloomington: Indiana University Press.

—— 1993. Musicology as a political act. *Journal of Musicology* 11: 411–436.

—— 1999 Ontologies of music. Pp. 17–34 in *Rethinking music*. Edited by Nicholas Cook and Mark Everist. Oxford: Oxford University Press.

—— 2000. The remembrance of things past: Music, race, and the end of history in modern Europe. Pp. 644–676 in *Music and the racial imagination*. Edited by Ronald Radano and Philip V. Bohlman. Chicago: University of Chicago Press.

—— 2002. Landscape-region-nation-reich: German folk song in the nexus of national identity. Pp.

104–127 in *Music and German national identity*. Edited by Celia Applegate and Pamela M. Potter. Chicago: University of Chicago Press.

—— 2004. *The music of European nationalism: Cultural identity and modern history*. Santa Barbara, CA: ABC-CLIO.

—— 2007. The politics of power, pleasure, and prayer in the Eurovision Song Contest. *Musicologia/Musicology* 7: 39–67.

—— 2008. *Jewish music and modernity*. New York: Oxford University Press.

—— 2009. Music before the nation, music after nationalism. *Musicology Australia* 31: 79–100.

—— 2011. *Focus: Music, nationalism, and the making of the New Europe*. New York: Routledge.

Bohlman, Philip V. and Nada Petković, eds. 2011. *Balkan epic: Song, history, modernity*. Lanham, MD: Scarecrow Press.

Bohlman, Philip V. and Martin Stokes. 2010. Foreword. Pp. vii–viii in *Music and displacement: Diasporas, mobilities, and dislocations in Europe and beyond*. Edited by Erik Levi and Florian Scheding. Lanham, MD: Scarecrow Press.

Bonds, Mark Evan. 1997. Idealism and the aesthetic of instrumental music at the turn of the nineteenth century. *Journal of the American Musicological Society*, 50(2–3): 387–420.

Bordo, Susan. [1994] 2004. "Material girl": The effacements of postmodern culture. Pp. 245–276 in *Unbearable weight: Feminism, western culture, and the body*. Berkeley: University of California Press.

Boretz, Benjamin. 1992. Experiences with no names. *Perspectives of New Music* 30: 272–283.

Born, Georgina. 1987. On modern music culture: On shock, pop and synthesis. *New Formations* 2: 51–78.

—— 1993a. Afterword: Music policy, aesthetic and social difference. Pp. 266–293 in *Rock and popular music: Politics, policies, institutions*. Edited by S. Frith, T. Bennett, L. Grossberg, J. Shepherd, and G. Turner. London: Routledge.

—— 1993b. Understanding music as culture: Contributions from popular music studies to a social semiotics of music. Pp. 211–228 in *Tendenze e metodi nella ricerca musicologica*. Edited by R. Pozzi. Florence: Olschki.

—— 1995. *Rationalizing culture: IRCAM, Boulez, and the institutionalization of the musical avant-garde*. Berkeley: University of California Press.

—— 2005. On musical mediation: Ontology, technology and creativity. *Twentieth-Century Music* 2(1): 7–36.

—— 2010a. For a relational musicology: Music and interdisciplinarity, beyond the practice turn. *Journal of the Royal Musical Association* 135: 205–243.

—— 2010b. On Tardean relations: temporality and ethnography. Pp. 232–249 in *The social after Gabriel Tarde: Debates and assessments*. Edited by Mattei Candea. London: Routledge.

—— Forthcoming. Music: Ontology, agency, and creativity. In *Material agencies*. Edited by Liana Chua and Mark Elliot. Oxford: Berg.

Born, Georgina, and David Hesmondhalgh, eds. 2000. *Western music and its others: Difference, representation, and appropriation in music*. Berkeley: University of California Press.

Bourdieu, Pierre. 1973. Cultural reproduction and social reproduction. Pp. 71–112 in *Knowledge, education and cultural change*. Edited by Richard K. Brown. London: Tavistock.

—— 1977. *Outline of a theory of practice*. Cambridge U.K.: Cambridge University Press.

—— 1984. *Distinction: A social critique of the judgment of taste*. Cambridge, MA: Harvard University Press.

—— 1990. *In other words: Essays towards a reflexive sociology*. Cambridge, U.K.: Polity.

—— 1993a. Public opinion does not exist. Pp. 149–157 in *Sociology in question*. Translated by Richard Nice. London: Sage.

—— 1993b. *The field of cultural production: Essays on art and literature*. Edited by R. Johnson. Cambridge, U.K.: Polity Press.

Bourdieu, Pierre, and Jean Claude Passeron. [1977] 1999. *Reproduction in education, society and culture*. Translated by Richard Nice. Beverly Hills, CA: Sage.

Bowers, Jane, and Judith Tick, eds. 1987. *Women making music: The western art tradition, 1150–1950*. Urbana: University of Illinois Press.

Boyd, Robert, and Peter J. Richerson. 2009. Culture and the evolution of human cooperation. *Philosophical Transactions of the Royal Society B: Biological Sciences* 364, 1533: 3281–3288.

—— 2010. Transmission coupling mechanisms: Cultural group selection. *Philosophical Transactions of the Royal Society B: Biological Sciences* 365, 1559: 3787–3795.

Boym, Svetlana. 2002. *The future of nostalgia.* New York: Basic Books.

Brackett, David. 1994. The practice and politics of crossover in American popular music, 1963–65. *Musical Quarterly* 78(4): 774–797.

—— 1995. *Interpreting popular music.* Cambridge, U.K.: Cambridge University Press.

—— 2002. (In search of) musical meaning: Genres, categories, and crossover. Pp. 65–83 in *Popular music studies.* Edited by David Hesmondhalgh and Keith Negus. London: Arnold.

—— 2005. Questions of genre in black popular music. *Black Music Research Journal* 25(1/2): 73–92.

Braga-Pinto, César. 2002. Supermen and Chiquita Bacana's daughters: Transgendered voices in Brazilian popular music. Pp. 187–207 in *Lusosex: Gender and sexuality in the Portuguese-speaking world.* Edited by Susan Canty Quinlan and Fernando Arenas. Minneapolis: University of Minnesota Press.

Brake, Mike. 1980. *The sociology of youth cultures and youth subcultures.* New York: Routledge and Kegan Paul.

Braudel, Fernand. 1982. *The wheels of commerce.* London: Collins.

Braziel, Jana Evans, and Anita Mannur. 2003. Introduction. Pp. 1–22 in *Theorizing diaspora: A reader.* Edited by J. Braziel and A. Mannur. Malden, MA, and Oxford: Blackwell.

Breedveld, Keon. 1996. Le loisir et le travail en période post-fordiste: changements idéologiques et sociaux. *Loisir et société* 19(1): 67–90.

Brett, Philip. 1997. Piano four-hands: Schubert and the performance of gay male desire. *19th Century Music* 21(2): 149–176.

Brett, Philip, Elizabeth Wood, and Gary C. Thomas, eds. [1994] 2006. *Queering the pitch: The new gay and lesbian musicology.* New York: Routledge.

Brothers, Thomas. 2006. *Louis Armstrong's New Orleans.* New York: Norton.

Broughton, Simon, Mark Ellingham, David Muddyman, and Richard Trillo. 1994. *The rough guide to world music.* London: Penguin.

Broughton, Simon, Mark Ellingham, and Richard Trillo, eds. 1999–2000. *World music: The rough guide.* 2nd ed. Vol. 1, *Africa, Europe and the Middle East.* Vol. 2, *Latin and North America, Caribbean, India, Asia and Pacific.* London: The Rough Guides.

Brown, Bill. 1999. The secret life of things (Virginia Woolf and the matter of modernism). *Modernism/Modernity* 6(2): 1–28.

—— 2001. Thing theory. *Critical Inquiry* 28 (1): 1–22.

Brown, Julie, ed. 2007. *Western music and race.* Cambridge, U.K.: Cambridge University Press.

Brown, Rita Mae. [1976] 1988. *In her day.* New York: Bantam Books.

Brubaker, Rogers. 2005. The "diaspora" diaspora. *Ethnic and Racial Studies* 28: 1–19.

Buck-Morss, Susan. 2000. Hegel and Haiti. *Critical Inquiry* 26 (Summer): 821–865.

Bull, Michael. 2000. *Sounding out the city: Personal stereos and the management of everyday life.* Oxford: Berg.

—— 2007. *Sound moves: iPod culture and urban experience.* New York: Routledge.

Bürger, Peter. 1984. *Theory of the avant-garde,* 2nd ed. Translated by Michael Shaw. Minneapolis: University of Minnesota Press.

Burke, Peter. 1987. *The historical anthropology of early modern Italy: Essays on perception and communication.* Cambridge, U.K.: Cambridge University Press.

Burnett, Robert. 1996. *The global jukebox: The international music industry.* London: Routledge.

Burnham, Scott. 1995. *Beethoven hero.* Princeton: Princeton University Press.

—— 2001. How music matters: Poetic context revisited. Pp. 193–216 in *Rethinking music.* Edited by Nicholas Cook and Mark Everist. Oxford: Oxford University Press.

Butler, Gillian, and Freda McManus. 1998. *Psychology: A very short introduction.* Oxford: Oxford University Press.

Butler, Judith. 1988. Performative acts and gender constitution: An essay in phenomenology and feminist theory. *Theatre Journal* 40: 519–531.

—— 1990. *Gender trouble: Feminism and the subversion of identity.* New York: Routledge.

——. 2005. *Giving an account of oneself.* New York: Fordham University Press.

Butler, Melvin L. 2000. Musical style and experience in a Brooklyn Pentecostal church: An "insider's" perspective. *Current Musicology* 70: 33–60.

—— 2010. Ethnomusicology and the African diaspora. Pp. 213–233 in *The African diaspora and the disciplines.* Edited by T. Olaniyan and J. H. Sweet. Bloomington and Indianapolis: Indiana University Press.

Campbell, Patricia Shehan. 1991. *Lessons from the world: A cross-cultural guide to music teaching and learning.* New York: Schirmer Books.

Caplan, Patricia. 1989. *The cultural construction of sexuality.* New York: Routledge.

Carr, Edward H. 1961. *What is history?* New York: St. Martin's Press.

Cavicchi, Daniel. 1998. *Tramps like us: Music and meaning among Springsteen fans.* New York: Oxford University Press.

Chadabe, Joel. 1997. *Electric sound: The past and promise of electronic music.* Upper Saddle River, NJ: Prentice-Hall Inc.

Chakrabarty, Dipesh. 2000. *Provincializing Europe: Postcolonial thought and historical difference.* Princeton: Princeton University Press.

Chanan, Michael. 1995. *Repeated takes: A short history of recording and its effects on music.* London: Verso.

Charry, Eric. Forthcoming (2012). Music in a twenty-first century globalizing Africa. In *Hip hop Africa and other new African music in a globalized world.* Edited by Eric Charry. Bloomington and Indianapolis: Indiana University Press.

Chateaubriand, François René. [1802] 1856. *The genius of Christianity; or, the spirit and beauty of the Christian religion.* Translated by Charles I. White. Baltimore: John Murphy.

Chen, Pi-yen. 2005. Buddhist chant, devotional song, and commercial popular music: From ritual to rock mantra. *Ethnomusicology* 49(2): 266–286.

Chernoff, John Miller. 1997. "Hearing" in West African idioms. *The World of Music* 39(2): 19–25.

Chester, Andrew. [1970] 1990. Second thoughts on a rock aesthetic: The band. Pp. 301–319 in *On record: Rock, pop, and the written word.* Edited by Simon Frith and Andrew Goodwin. New York: Pantheon.

Chisholm, S. L., J. K. Caird, and J. Lockhart. 2008. The effects of practice with MP3 players on driving performance. *Accident Analysis and Prevention* 40: 704–713.

Christianen, Michael. 1995. Cycles in symbol production? A new model to explain concentration, diversity and innovation in the music industry. *Popular Music* 14(1): 55–93.

Christiansen, Anna Sofie. 2001. Mechanical music in Weimar Germany: "Absolute music" as performance paradigm. Paper presented at Second Biennial International Conference on 20th-century music, Goldsmiths College, London.

Chua, Daniel K. L. 1999. *Absolute music and the construction of meaning.* Cambridge, U.K.: Cambridge University Press.

Citron, Marcia J. 1990. Gender, professionalism, and the musical canon. *The Journal of Musicology* 8(1): 102–117.

Cixous, Hélène. 1980. Sorties. Pp. 90–98 in *New French feminisms.* Edited by Elaine Marks and Isabelle de Courtivron. New York: Schocken.

—— 1990. *Reading with Clarice Lispector.* Edited by Verena Andermatt Conley. Minneapolis: University of Minnesota Press.

Clark, Peter. 1983. *The English alehouse: A social history, 1200–1830.* New York: Longman.

Clarke, David. 1996a. Language games: Is music like language? *The Musical Times* 137(1835): 5–10.

—— 1996b. Speaking for itself: How does music become autonomous? *The Musical Times* 137(1836): 14–18.

Clarke, Eric F. 2001. Meaning and the specification of motion in music. *Musicae Scientiae* 5: 213–234.

—— 2005. *Ways of listening: an ecological approach to the perception of musical meaning.* New York: Oxford University Press.

Clarke, Eric F., Nicola Dibben, and Stephanie E. Pitts. 2010. *Music and mind in everyday life.* Oxford: Oxford University Press.

Classen, Constance, ed. 2005. *The book of touch.* Oxford and New York: Berg.

Clausen, Bernd, Ursula Hemetek, Eva Sæther, and the European Music Council, eds. 2009. *Music in motion: Diversity and dialogue in Europe.* Bielefeld, Germany: Transcript Verlag.

Clayton, Martin R. L. 2000. *Time in Indian music: Rhythm, metre and form in North Indian rāg performance.* Oxford: Clarendon Press.

Clayton, Martin, Rebecca Sager, and Udo Will. 2005. In time with the music: The concept of entrainment and its significance for ethnomusicology. *ESEM Counterpoint* 1: 1–45.

Clément, Catherine. 1988. *Opera, or, the undoing of women.* Translated by Betsy Wing. Minneapolis: University of Minnesota Press. First published in French in 1979.

Clifford, James. 1988. *The predicament of culture: Twentieth-century ethnography, literature, and art.* Cambridge, MA: Harvard University Press.

—— 1992. Travelling cultures. Pp. 96–116 in *Cultural studies.* Edited by Lawrence Grossberg, Cary Nelson, and Paula A. Treichler. New York: Routledge.

—— 1994. Further inflections: Toward ethnographies of the future. *Cultural Anthropology* 9(3): 302–338.

Clifford, James, and George E. Marcus, eds. 1986. *Writing culture: The poetics and politics of ethnography.* Berkeley: University of California Press.

Clough, Patricia Ticineto, Greg Goldberg, Rachel Schiff, Aaron Weeks, and Craig Willse. 2007. Notes towards a theory of affect-itself. *Ephemera* 7(1): 60–77.

Cohen, Robin. 1998. Series editors' statement for the series Global diasporas. [No page number.] In Nicholas Van Hear. *New diasporas: The mass exodus, Dispersal and regrouping of migrant communities.* Seattle: University of Washington Press.

Cohen, Sara. 1991. *Rock culture in Liverpool: Popular music in the making.* Oxford: Clarendon Press.

Collins, John. 1992. *West African pop roots.* Philadelphia: Temple University Press.

Collins, Tim. 2010. 'Tis like they never left: Locating "home" in the music of Sliabh Aughty's diaspora. *Journal of the Society for American Music* 4(4): 491–508.

Comaroff, Jean, and John Comaroff. 1992. *Ethnography and the historical imagination.* Boulder, CO: Westview Press.

Committee on the Status of Women, Society for Music Theory. *Bibliography of sources related to women's studies, gender studies, feminism, and music.* https://ccrma.stanford.edu/~leigh/csw/csw/CSWBib2.html.

Conard, Nicholas J., Maria Malina, et al. 2009. New flutes document the earliest musical tradition in Southwestern Germany. *Nature* 460, 7256: 737–740.

Constansis, Alexandros N. 2008. The changing female-to-male (FTM) voice. *Radical Musicology* 3. http://www.radical-musicology.org.uk/2008/Constansis.htm.

Cook, Nicholas. 1990. *Music, imagination and culture.* Oxford: Clarendon Press.

—— 1994. Perception: A perspective from music theory. Pp. 64–95 in *Musical perceptions.* Edited by Rita Aiello and John A. Sloboda. Oxford: Oxford University Press.

—— 2001. On qualifying relativism. *Musicae Scientiae, Discussion Forum* 2: 167–189.

—— 2007. *The Schenker project: Culture, race, and music theory in fin-de-siècle Vienna.* Oxford: Oxford University Press.

Cook, Nicholas, and Mark Everist, eds. 1999. *Rethinking music.* Oxford: Oxford University Press.

Cooke, Deryck. 1959. *The language of music.* Oxford: Oxford University Press.

Cooke, Peter. 1999. Was Sempeke just being kind? Listening to instrumental music in Africa south of the Sahara. *The World of Music* 41(1): 73–83.

Cottrell, Stephen. 2010. An interview with Ben Mandelson. *Ethnomusicology Forum* 19(1): 57–68.

Coupland, Justine, Nikolas Coupland, et al. 1992. "How are you?": Negotiating phatic communion. *Language in Society* 21(2): 207–230.

Crafts, Susan D., Daniel Cavicchi, and Charles Keil. 1993. *My music.* Hanover, NH: Wesleyan University Press.

Crapanzano, Vincent. 1994. Réflexions sur une anthropologie des émotions. *Terrain: carnets du patrimoine ethnologique* 22: 109–117.

Crofton, Ian, and Donald Fraser, eds. 1985. *A dictionary of musical quotations.* New York: Schirmer.

Cross, Ian. 1998. Music analysis and music perception. *Music Analysis* 17(1): 3–20.

—— 1999. Is music the most important thing we ever did? Music, development and evolution. Pp. 10–39 in *Music, mind and science.* Edited by Suk Won Yi. Seoul: Seoul National University Press.

—— 2003. Music and evolution: Causes and consequences. *Contemporary Music Review* 22(3): 79–89.

—— 2005. Music and meaning, ambiguity and evolution. Pp. 27–43 in *Musical Communication.* Edited by D. Miell, R. MacDonald, et al. Oxford: Oxford University Press.

—— 2007. Music and cognitive evolution. Pp. 649–667 in *Handbook of evolutionary psychology.* Edited by Robin I. M. Dunbar and Louise Barrett. Oxford: Oxford University Press.

—— 2009. The evolutionary nature of musical meaning. *Musicae Scientiae.* Special Issue: Music and Evolution: 147–167.

Cross, Ian, and Ghofur Eliot Woodruff. 2009. Music as a communicative medium. Pp. 113–144 in *The Prehistory of Language*. Edited by Rudie Botha and Chris Knight. Oxford: Oxford University Press.

Cross, John C. 1998. *Informal politics: Street vendors and the state in Mexico City*. Stanford: Stanford University Press.

Currid, Brian. 2006. *A national acoustics: Music and mass publicity in Weimar and Nazi Germany*. Minneapolis: University of Minnesota Press.

Currid, Elizabeth. 2007. *The Warhol economy: How fashion, art, and music drive New York City*. Princeton: Princeton University Press.

Currie, James. 2009. Music after all. *Journal of the American Musicological Society* 62: 145–203.

Cusick, Suzanne G. [1994] 2006. On a lesbian relationship with music: A serious effort not to think straight. Pp. 67–83 in *Queering the pitch: The new gay and lesbian musicology*. Edited by Philip Brett, Elizabeth Wood, and Gary C. Thomas. New York: Routledge.

—— 1999. On musical performances of gender and sex. Pp. 25–48 in *Audible traces: Gender, identity, and music*. Edited by Elaine Barkin and Lydia Hamessley. Zürich: Carciofoli.

—— 2008. Fifth column: Musicology, torture, repair. *Radical Musicology* 3. http://www.radical-musicology.org.uk: 24 pars.

—— 2009. *Francesca Caccini at the Medici court: Music and the circulation of power*. Chicago: University of Chicago Press.

Cutietta, Robert. 1991. Popular music: An ongoing challenge. *Music Educators Journal* 77(8): 26–29.

Dahlhaus, Carl. 1989a. *The idea of absolute music*. Translated by Roger Lustig. Chicago: University of Chicago Press.

—— 1989b. The metaphysic of instrumental music. Pp. 88–96 in *Nineteenth-century music*. Translated by J. Bradford Robinson. Berkeley: University of California Press.

Dale, Pete. 2011. Anyone can do it: Punk and the politics of empowerment. Ph.D. thesis, Newcastle University.

Danielsen, Anne. 2006. *Presence and pleasure: The funk grooves of James Brown and Parliament*. Middletown, CT: Wesleyan University Press.

Dannen, Fredric. 1990. *Hit men: Power brokers and fast money inside the music industry*. New York: Times Books.

Darwin, Charles. [1871] 2004. *The descent of man and selection in relation to sex*. 2nd ed. 2 vols. London: Penguin Books.

Davies, Martin L. 1989. History as narcissism. *Journal of European Studies* 19: 265–291.

Davis, Angela Y. 1998. *Blues legacies and black feminism: Gertrude "Ma" Rainey, Bessie Smith, and Billie Holiday*. New York: Pantheon Books.

Dawe, Kevin. 2001. People, objects, meaning: Recent work on the study and collection of musical instruments. *The Galpin Society Journal* 54: 219–232.

—— 2007. *Music and musicians in Crete: Performance and ethnography in a Mediterranean island society*. Lanham, MD: Scarecrow Press.

—— 2010. *The new guitarscape in critical theory, cultural practice and musical performance*. Farnham, Surrey, and Burlington, VT: Ashgate.

de Certeau, Michel. 1988. Ethno-graphy: Speech, or the space of the other: Jean de Léry. Pp. 209–243 in *The writing of history*. Translated by Tom Conley. New York: Columbia University Press.

DeLanda, Manuel. 2006. *A new philosophy of society: Assemblage theory and social complexity*. London: Continuum.

de Léry, Jean. 1578. *Histoire d'un voyage faict en la terre du Brésil*. La Rochelle, France: Antoine Chuppin.

Deleuze, Gilles, and Félix Guattari. 1987. *A thousand plateaus: Capitalism and schizophrenia*. Minneapolis: University of Minnesota Press.

Deleuze, Gilles, and Claire Parnet. 1987. *Dialogues*. Translated by Hugh Tomlinson and Barbara Habberjam. London: Athlone.

Dell'Antonio, Andrew, ed. 2004. *Beyond structural listening? Postmodern models of hearing*. Berkeley: University of California Press.

Dennett, Daniel C. 1991. *Consciousness explained*. Boston: Little, Brown, and Co.

DeNora, Tia. 1995, *Beethoven and the construction of genius: Musical politics in Vienna, 1792–1803*. Berkeley: University of California Press.

—— 1999. Music as a technology of the self. *Poetics* 26: 1–26.

—— 2000. *Music in everyday life*. Cambridge, U.K.: Cambridge University Press.

—— 2011. *Music-in-action: Essays in sonic ecology*. Aldershot, U.K.: Ashgate.

Deo, Aditi. 2011. Alternative windows into tradition: Non-hereditary practices in Hindustani khyal music. Ph.D. thesis, Indiana University.

Derrida, Jacques. 1978. *Writing and difference*. Translated by Alan Bass. Chicago: University of Chicago Press.

—— [1975] 1987. Le facteur de la vérité. Pp. 411–496 in *The post card: From Socrates to Freud and beyond*. Translated by Alan Bass. Chicago: University of Chicago Press.

—— 1991. "Che cos'è l'poesia?" Pp. 221–237 in *The Derrida reader: Between the blinds*. Edited by Peggy Kamuf. New York: Columbia University Press.

—— 1992. *Given time 1: Counterfeit money*. Translated by Peggy Kamuf. Chicago: University of Chicago Press.

—— 2001. *Acts of religion*. New York: Routledge.

Desan, S. 1989. Crowds, community and ritual in the work of E. P. Thompson and Natalie Davis. Pp. 47–71 in *The new cultural history*. Edited by Lynn A. Hunt. Berkeley: University of California Press.

Deutsch, Diana, ed. [1982] 1999. *The psychology of music*. 2nd ed. New York: Academic Press.

DeVale, Susan C. 1989. Power and meaning in musical instruments. Pp. 94–110 in *Music and the Experience of God*. Edited by M. Collins, D. Power, and M. Burnim. Edinburgh: T. and T. Clark Publishers.

—— 1990. Organizing organology. Pp. 1–34 in *Issues in organology*. Edited by Sue Carole DeVale. *Selected Reports in Ethnomusicology* 8.

DeVeaux, Scott. 1997. *The birth of bebop: A social and musical history*. Berkeley: University of California Press.

Dewey, John. 1927. *The public and its problems*. New York: Holt.

—— [1934] 1980. *Art as experience*. New York: Perigree.

Diamond, Beverley, M. Sam Cronk, and Franziska von Rosen. 1995. *Visions of sound: Musical instruments of first nations communities in Northeastern America*. Chicago: University of Chicago Press.

Diawara, Manthia. 1998. *In search of Africa*. Cambridge, MA: Harvard University Press.

Dibango, Manu (with Danielle Rouard). 1994. *Three kilos of coffee: An autobiography*. Chicago: Chicago University Press.

Dibben, Nicola. 2001. What do we hear when we hear music? Musical material and the perception of meaning. *Musicae Scientiae* 5(2): 161–194.

Diehl, Keila. 2002. *Echoes from Dharamsala: Music in the life of a Tibetan refugee community*. Berkeley and Los Angeles: University of California Press.

Dietrich, Gregory. 2004. Dancing the diaspora: Indian Desi music in Chicago. Pp. 103–116 in *Identity and the arts in diaspora communities*. Edited by T. Turino and J. Lea. Warren, MI: Harmonie Park Press.

DiMaggio, Paul. 1987. Classification in art. *American Sociological Review* 52: 440–455.

Dolgoff, Stephanie. 2010. Formerly hot, finally content. *Self* (August): 36–39.

Doubleday, Veronica. 2008. Sounds of power: An overview of musical instruments and gender. *Ethnomusicology Forum* 17(1): 3–39.

Douglas, Mary, and Baron Isherwood. 1979. *The world of goods*. New York: Basic.

Dournon, Geneviève. 1981 *Guide for the collection of traditional musical instruments*. Paris: UNESCO Press.

Draaisma, Douwe. 2000. *Metaphors of memory: A history of ideas about the mind*. Translated by Paul Vincent. Cambridge, U.K.: Cambridge University Press.

Dreyfus, Laurence. 2010. *Wagner and the erotic impulse*. Cambridge, MA: Harvard University Press.

du Moncel, Théodore Achille Louis. 1879. *The telephone, the microphone and the phonograph*. New York: Harper.

Durkheim, Emile. 1912. *Les formes élémentaires de la vie religieuse: Le système totémique en Australie*. Paris: Presses universitaires de France.

Dworkin, Andrea. [1987] 2006. *Intercourse*. New York: Basic Books.

Dyer, Richard. [1979] 1992. In defense of disco. Pp. 149–158 in *Only entertainment*. London: Routledge.

Eagleton, Terry. 1983. *Literary theory: An introduction*. Minneapolis: University of Minnesota Press.

—— 2000. *The idea of culture*. Oxford: Blackwell.

Echols, Alice. 1999. *Scars of sweet paradise: The life and times of Janis Joplin*. New York: Metropolitan Books.

Eco, Umberto. 1976. *A theory of semiotics.* Bloomington: Indiana University Press.

Edge, John T. 2010. The tortilla takes a road trip to Korea. *New York Times,* July 28, 2010.

Eggebrecht, Hans Heinrich. 1991. *Musik im Abendland: Prozesse und Stationen vom Mittelalter bis zur Gegenwart.* Munich: Piper.

Ehrlich, Cyril. 1985. *The music profession in Britain since the eighteenth century.* Oxford: Clarendon Press.

—— 1990. *The piano: A history.* rev. ed. Oxford: Clarendon Press.

Elias, Norbert. 1993. *Mozart: Portrait of a genius.* Cambridge, U.K.: Polity.

Eliot, T. S. 1963. *Collected poems 1909–1962.* New York: Harcourt, Brace, and World.

Ellison, Ralph. 1964. *Shadow and act.* New York: Random House.

Elster, Jon. 1985. *Making sense of Marx.* Cambridge, U.K.: Cambridge University Press.

Elton, Geoffrey R. 1967. *The practice of history.* London: Methuen.

Engelhardt, Jeffers. 2006. Inculturation: Genealogies, meanings, and musical dynamics. *Yale Institute of Sacred Music Colloquium: Music, Worship, Arts* 3: 1–6.

—— 2009. Right singing in Estonian Orthodox Christianity: A study of music, theology, and religious ideology. *Ethnomusicology* 53(1): 32–57.

Erlmann, Veit. 1996. *Nightsong: Performance, power and practice in South Africa.* Chicago: University of Chicago Press.

——. 1999. *Music, modernity and the global imagination: South Africa and the West.* New York: Oxford University Press.

Esslin, Martin. 1959. *Brecht, a choice of evils: A critical study of the man, his work and his opinions.* London: Heinemann.

Ethnomusicology. 1992. Vol. 36(3). Special issue on *Music and the Public Interest.*

Evans, Richard J. 1997. *In defence of history.* London: Granta Books.

Evans, Graeme. 2009. Creative cities, creative spaces, and urban policy. *Urban Studies* 46: 1003–1040.

Eze, Emmanuel Chukwudi. 1997. *Race and the enlightenment: A reader.* Oxford: Blackwell.

Fabbri, Franco. 1982. A theory of musical genres: Two applications. Pp. 52–81 in *Popular music perspectives: Papers from the first international conference on popular music research, Amsterdam, June 1981.* Edited by David Horn and Philip Tagg. Göteborg: IASPM.

Fanon, Franz. 1967. *The wretched of the earth.* Translated by C. Farrington. Harmondsworth, U.K.: Penguin.

Faulks, Sebastian. 2011. *Faulks on fiction.* London: BBC Books.

Faultline. 1999. *Closer colder* [CD]. Leaf: bay 12cd.

Fauquet, Joël-Marie, and Antoine Hennion. 2000. *La grandeur de Bach: L'amour de la musique en France au XIXe siècle.* Paris: Fayard.

Feld, Steven. 1981. "Flow like a waterfall": The metaphors of Kaluli musical theory. *Yearbook for Traditional Music* 13: 22–47.

—— 1983. Sound as a symbolic system: The Kaluli drum. *Bikmaus* 4(3): 78–89.

—— 1984. Sound structure as social structure. *Ethnomusicology* 28(3): 383–409.

—— [1982] 1990. *Sound and sentiment: Birds, weeping, poetics and song in Kaluli experience.* 2nd ed. Philadelphia: University of Pennsylvania Press.

—— 1994a. Communication, music, and speech about music. Pp. 77–95 in *Music grooves: Essays and dialogues.* Edited by Charles Keil and Steven Feld. Chicago: University of Chicago Press.

—— 1994b. From schizophonia to schismogenesis: On the discourses and commodification practices of "world music" and "world beat." Pp. 257–289 in *Music grooves.* Edited by Charles Keil and Steven Feld. Chicago: University of Chicago Press.

—— 2000. The poetics and politics of Pygmy pop. Pp. 254–279 in *Western music and its others.* Edited by Georgina Born and David Hesmondhalgh. Berkeley: University of California Press.

Feldman, Martha, and Bonnie Gordon, eds. 2006. *The courtesan's arts: Cross-cultural perspectives.* Oxford: Oxford University Press.

Ferguson, Niall. 2011. *Civilisation: The West and the rest.* London: Allen Lane.

Fineberg, Joshua. 2006. *Classical music, why bother? Hearing the world of contemporary culture through a composer's ears.* New York: Routledge.

Fink, Bruce. 1999. *A clinical introduction to Lacanian psychoanalysis: theory and technique.* Cambridge, MA: Harvard University Press.

Finnegan, Ruth. 1989. *The hidden musicians: Music-making in an English town.* Cambridge, U.K.: Cambridge University Press [republished, Wesleyan University Press, 2007].

Fisher, Erik, Annelie Kirsten, and Sarah Bosack. 2006. *Musikinstrumentenbau im interkulturellen Diskurs.* Stuttgart: Franz Steiner Verlag.

Floyd, Samuel A., Jr. 1991. Ring shout! Literary studies, historical studies, and black music inquiry. *Black Music Research Journal* 11(2): 265–288.

—— 1995. *The power of black music: Interpreting its history from Africa to the United States.* New York: Oxford University Press.

Foley, Robert, and Clive Gamble. 2009. The ecology of social transitions in human evolution. *Philosophical Transactions of the Royal Society B: Biological Sciences* 364, 1533: 3267–3279.

Ford, Charles. 1991. *Così: Sexual politics in Mozart's operas.* Manchester: Manchester University Press.

Forkel, Johann Nicolaus. 1967. *Allgemeine Geschichte der Musik* (Leipzig, 1788). Facsimile ed. Edited by Othmar Wessely. Graz, Austria: Akademische Druck und Verlagsanstalt.

Forty, Adrian. 1986. *Objects of desire: Design and society since 1750.* London and New York: Thames and Hudson.

Foucault, Michel. 1969. Qu'est-ce qu'un auteur? *Bulletin de la Société Française de Philosophie* 69(3): 73–104.

—— 1970. *The order of things: An archaeology of the human sciences.* London: Tavistock.

—— 1972. *The archaeology of knowledge.* Translated by Alan Sheridan. New York: Pantheon.

—— 1978. *The history of sexuality.* Vol. 1. Translated by Robert Hurley. New York: Pantheon.

—— 1979. *Discipline and punish: The birth of the prison.* Translated by Alan Sheridan. New York: Random House.

Fouz-Hernández, Santiago, and Freya Jarman-Ivens, eds. 2004. *Madonna's drowned worlds: New approaches to her cultural transformations, 1983–2003.* Aldershot, U.K.: Ashgate.

Francès, Robert. 1988. *The perception of music.* Translated by W. Jay Dowling. Hillsdale, NJ: Erlbaum.

Frank, Thomas. 2002. *One market under God: Extreme capitalism, market populism and the end of economic democracy.* London: Vintage.

Franklin, Peter. 1991. *Mahler: Symphony No. 3.* Cambridge Music Handbooks. Cambridge, U.K.: Cambridge University Press.

Freud, Sigmund. [1900] 1955. *The interpretation of dreams.* Vols. 4 and 5 of the *Standard edition of the complete psychological writings of Sigmund Freud.* London: Hogarth Press / Institute of Psycho-Analysis. [*Trumdeutung. Gesammelte Schriften,* vols. 2 and 3. Leipzig, Vienna, and Zürich: Internationaler Psychoanalytischer Verlag, 1930]

—— [1905] 1977. *On sexuality: Three essays on sexuality and other works.* Vol. 7 of *The Penguin Freud library.* New York: Penguin Books. [*Drei Abhandlungen zur Sexualtheorie. Gesammelte Schriften,* vol. 5. Leipzig, Vienna, and Zürich: Internationaler Psychoanalytischer Verlag, 1924: 1–119]

—— [1930] 2004. *Civilization and its discontents.* Translated by David McLintock. London: Penguin Books.

Friedson, Steven M. 2009. *Remains of ritual: Northern gods in a Southern land.* Chicago: University of Chicago Press.

Frishkopf, Michael. 2009. Mediated Qur'anic recitation and the contestation of Islam in contemporary Egypt. Pp. 75–114 in *Music and the play of power in the Middle East, North Africa, and central Asia.* Edited by Laudan Nooshin. Burlington, VT: Ashgate.

Frith, C. D. 2008. Social cognition. *Philosophical Transactions of the Royal Society B-Biological Sciences* 363, 1499: 2033–2039.

Frith, Simon. 1978. *The sociology of rock.* London: Constable.

—— 1981. *Sound effects: Youth, leisure and the politics of rock 'n' roll.* London: Constable.

—— [1990] 2007. Afterthoughts. Pp. 59–64 in Frith, *Taking popular music seriously.* Aldershot, U.K.: Ashgate.

—— 1998. *Performing rites: On the value of popular music.* Cambridge, MA: Harvard University Press.

—— 2000. The discourse of world music. Pp. 305–322 in *Western music and its others.* Edited by Georgina Born and David Hesmondhalgh. Berkeley: University of California Press.

Frith, Simon, and Angela McRobbie. [1978] 2007. Rock and sexuality. Pp. 41–57 in Frith, *Taking popular music seriously.* Aldershot, U.K.: Ashgate.

Frith, Simon, and Andrew Goodwin, eds. 1990. *On record: Rock, pop, and the written word.* New York: Pantheon Books.

Fritz, Thomas, Sebastian Jentschke, et al. 2009. Universal recognition of three basic emotions in music. *Current Biology* 19(7): 573–576.

Frow, John. 1995. *Cultural studies and cultural values.* Oxford: Clarendon Press.

Fukuyama, Francis. 1992. *The end of history and the last man.* New York: Free Press.

Fulcher, Jane F. 1987. *The nation's image: French grand opera as politics and politicized art.* New York: Cambridge University Press.

Fuss, Diana, ed. 1991. *Inside out: Lesbian theories, gay theories.* New York: Routledge.

Gamson, Joshua. 2005. *The fabulous Sylvester: The legend, the music, the seventies in San Francisco.* New York: Henry Holt.

Gaonkar, Dilip Parameshwar, and Elizabeth A. Povinelli. 2003. Technologies of public forms: Circulation, transfiguration, recognition. *Public Culture* 15: 385–397.

Garber, Marjorie. 1991. The transvestite continuum: Liberace-Valentino-Elvis. Pp. 353–374 in *Vested interests: Cross-dressing and cultural anxiety.* New York: Routledge.

Garnham, Nicholas. 2000. *Emancipation, the media and modernity: Arguments about the media and social theory.* Oxford: Oxford University Press.

Garrett, Charles Hiroshi. 2008. *Struggling to define a nation: American music and the twentieth century.* Berkeley: University of California Press.

Gates, Henry Louis III. 1986. *"Race," writing, and difference.* Chicago: University of Chicago Press.

—— 1988. *The signifying monkey: A theory of African-American literary criticism.* New York: Oxford University Press.

Gauntlett, D. 2007. *Creative explorations: New approaches to identities and audiences.* London: Routledge.

Gaver, William. W. 1993. What in the world do we hear? An ecological approach to auditory event perception. *Ecological Psychology* 5(1): 1–29.

Geertz, Clifford. [1972] 1973. Deep play: Notes on the Balinese cockfight. Pp. 412–453 in *The interpretation of cultures.* New York: Basic Books.

—— 1973. Thick description: Toward an interpretive theory of culture. Pp. 3–30 in *The interpretation of cultures.* New York: Basic Books.

—— [1974] 1977. "From the native's point of view": On the nature of anthropological understanding. Pp. 480–492 in *Symbolic anthropology: A reader.* Edited by Janet L. Dolgin, David S. Kemnitzer, and David Murray Schneider. New York: Columbia University Press.

—— [1980] 1983. *Local knowledge: Further essays in interpretive anthropology.* New York: Basic Books.

—— 1988. *Works and lives.* Stanford: Stanford University Press.

Gell, Alfred. 1998. *Art and agency: An anthropological theory.* Oxford and New York: Oxford University Press.

—— 2006. *The art of anthropology: Essays and diagrams.* Edited by Eric Hirsch. New York and London: Berg.

George, Nelson. 1985. *Where did our love go? The rise and fall of the Motown sound.* London: Omnibus Press.

Gibson, James J. 1966. *The senses considered as perceptual systems.* Boston: Houghton Mifflin.

—— [1979] 1986. *The ecological approach to visual perception.* Hillsdale, NJ: Erlbaum.

Gilbert, Jeremy, and Ewan Pearson. 1999. *Discographies: dance music, culture, and the politics of sound.* London: Routledge.

Gilroy, Paul. 1993. *The black Atlantic: Modernity and double consciousness.* Cambridge, MA: Harvard University Press.

Ginzburg, Carlo. 1980. *The cheese and the worms: The cosmos of a sixteenth-century miller.* Translated by John and Anne Tedeschi. Baltimore: Johns Hopkins University Press.

—— 1985. *The night battles: Witchcraft and agrarian cults in the sixteenth and seventeenth centuries.* Translated by John and Anne Tedeschi. New York: Penguin.

Gitelman, Lisa. 1999. *Scripts, grooves, and writing machines: Representing technology in the Edison era.* Stanford: Stanford University Press.

Gjerdingen, Robert. 1999. An experimental music theory? Pp. 161–170 in *Rethinking music.* Edited by Nicholas Cook and Mark Everist. Oxford: Oxford University Press.

Glasser, Irene. 1995. *My music is my flag: Puerto Rican musicians and their New York communities, 1917–1940.* Berkeley and Los Angeles: University of California Press.

Glennie, Paul, and Nigel Thrift. 2002. The spaces of clock times. Pp. 151–174 in *The social in question: New bearings in history and the social sciences.* Edited by Patrick Joyce. London and New York: Routledge.

Godlovitch, Stan. 1998. *Musical performance: A philosophical study.* London: Routledge.

Goehr, Lydia. 1992. *The imaginary museum of musical works: An essay in the philosophy of music.* Oxford: Clarendon Press.

—— 1993. "Music has no meaning to speak of": On the politics of musical interpretation. Pp. 177–190 in *The interpretation of music: Philosophical essays.* Edited by Michael Krausz. Oxford: Clarendon Press.

—— 2000. "On the problems of dating" or "looking backward and forward with Strohm." Pp. 231–246 in *The musical work: Reality or invention?* Edited by Michael Talbot. Liverpool: Liverpool University Press.

Gomart, Emilie, and Antoine Hennion. 1999. A sociology of attachment: Music lovers, drug addicts. Pp. 220–247 in *Actor network theory and after.* Edited by John Law and John Hassard. Oxford: Blackwell.

Gonzalves, Theodore. 2010. *The day the dancers stayed: Performing in the Filipino/American diaspora.* Philadelphia: Temple University Press.

Goodman, Elaine. 2000. Analysing the ensemble in music rehearsal and performance: The nature and effects of interaction in cello–piano duos. Ph.D. thesis, Royal Holloway (University of London).

Gopinath, Gayatri. 2005. Communities of sound: Queering South Asian popular music in the diaspora. Pp. 29–62 in *Impossible desires: Queer diasporas and South Asian public cultures.* Durham, NC: Duke University Press.

Gordon, Steven. 1990. Social structural effects on emotions. Pp. 145–179 in *Research agendas in the sociology of emotions.* Edited by Theodore Kemper. Albany: State University of New York Press.

Gramsci, Antonio. 1971. *Selections from the prison notebooks.* Edited and translated by Quintin Hoare and Geoffrey Nowell-Smith. London: Lawrence and Wishart.

Green, Lucy. 1988. *Music on deaf ears: Musical meaning, ideology and education.* New York: Manchester University Press. [Second edition: Bury St Edmunds, U.K.: Arima Publishing, 2008.]

—— 1997. *Music, gender, education.* New York: Cambridge University Press.

—— 1999. Ideology. Pp. 5–17 in *Key terms for popular music and culture.* Edited by Bruce Horner and Thomas Swiss. New York: Basil Blackwell.

—— 2001. *How popular musicians learn: A way ahead for music education.* New York: Ashgate.

—— [1999] 2002. Research in the sociology of music education: Some fundamental concepts. In *Teaching music in secondary schools: A reader.* Edited by Gary Spruce. New York: RoutledgeFalmer.

—— 2002. From the Western classics to the world: Secondary teachers' changing perceptions, 1982 and 1998. *British Journal of Music Education* 19(1): 5–30.

—— 2005. Musical meaning and social reproduction: A case for retrieving autonomy. *Educational philosophy and theory,* 37(1): 77–92.

—— 2008. *Music, informal learning and the school: A new classroom pedagogy.* New York: Ashgate.

Green, Richard E., Johannes Krause, et al. 2010. A draft sequence of the Neandertal genome. *Science* 328, 5979: 710–722.

Greenblatt, Stephen. 1991. *Marvelous possessions: The wonders of the new world.* Chicago: University of Chicago Press.

Greene, Paul D. 1999. Sound engineering in a Tamil village: Playing audio cassettes as devotional performance. *Ethnomusicology* 43(3): 459–489.

Greene, Paul D., and Thomas Porcello, eds. 2005. *Wired for sound: Engineering technologies in sonic cultures.* Middletown, CT: Wesleyan University Press.

Griffin, Matthew. 1996. Literary studies +/– literature: Friedrich A. Kittler's media histories. *New Literary History* 27: 709–716.

Griffiths, Paul. 1978. *Modern music: A concise history from Debussy to Boulez.* London: Thames and Hudson.

Grimley, Daniel. 2006. *Grieg: Music, landscape, and Norwegian identity.* Woodbridge, U.K.: Boydell and Brewer.

Gross, Joan, David McMurray, and Ted Swedenburg. 1997. Arab noise and Ramadan nights: Rai, Rap, and Franco-Maghrebi identity. *Diaspora* 3(1): 3–39.

Grossberg, Lawrence. 1984. Another boring day in paradise: Rock and roll and the empowerment of everyday life. *Popular Music* 4: 225–258.

Grossberg, Larry, et al., eds. 1992. *Cultural studies.* London: Routledge.

Guck, Marion A. 1994. A woman's (theoretical) work. *Perspectives of New Music* 16(2): 28–43.

Guilbault, Jocelyne. 1997. Interpreting world music: A challenge in theory and practice. *Popular Music* 16(1): 31–44.

—— 2005. Audible entanglements: Nation and diasporas in Trinidad's calypso music scene. *Small Axe* 9(1): 40–63.

—— 2007. *Governing sound: The cultural politics of Trinidad's carnival musics.* Chicago: University of Chicago Press.

—— 2010. Music, politics, and pleasure: Live soca in Trinidad. *Small Axe* 14 (1): 16–29.

Guilbault, Jocelyne, with Gage Averill, Édouard Benoit, and Gregory Rabess. 1993. *Zouk: World music in the West Indies.* Chicago: University of Chicago Press.

Guridy, Frank Andre. 2010. *Forging diaspora: Afro-Cubans and African Americans in a world of empire and Jim Crow.* Chapel Hill: University of North Carolina Press.

Hadley, Peter. 2007. The didjeridu dispersion: The transmission and transformation of a hollow log. Ph.D. dissertation, Wesleyan University.

Hagedorn, Katherine J. 2001. *Divine utterances: The performance of Afro-Cuban Santeria.* Washington, DC: Smithsonian Institution.

Hall, Stuart. 1980. Cultural studies: Two paradigms. *Media, Culture and Society* 2: 57–72.

—— 1981. Notes on deconstructing "the popular". Pp. 227–240 in *People's history and socialist theory.* Edited by Raphael Samuel. London: Routledge.

—— 1991. The local and the global: Globalization and ethnicity. Pp. 19–40 in *Culture, globalization and the world system.* Edited by Anthony King. London: Macmillan.

—— 2000. Conclusion: The multi-cultural question. Pp. 209–241 in *Un/Settled multiculturalisms: Diasporas, entanglements, "transruptions."* Edited by Barnor Hesse. London and New York: Zed Books.

Hall, Stuart, and Tony Jefferson, eds. 1976. *Resistance through rituals: Youth subcultures in post-war Britain.* London: Routledge.

Hallam, Susan. 2001. *The power of music.* London: The Performing Right Society.

Hallam, Susan, Ian Cross, and Michael Thaut, eds. 2009. *The Oxford handbook of music psychology.* New York: Oxford University Press.

Hamm, Charles. 1979. *Yesterdays: Popular song in America.* New York: Norton.

Handel, Stephen. 1989. *Listening: An introduction to the perception of auditory events.* Cambridge, MA: MIT Press.

Hanley, Betty. 1998. Gender in secondary music education in British Columbia. *British Journal of Music Education* 15: 51–69.

Hanslick, Eduard. [1885] 1974. *The beautiful in music: A contribution to the revisal of musical aesthetics.* 7th ed. Translated by Gustav Cohen. New York: Da Capo Press.

Haraway, Donna. 1991. *Simians, cyborgs, and women: The reinvention of nature.* London: Free Association.

Hård, Mikael, and Andrew Jamison. 1998. *The intellectual appropriation of technology: Discourses on modernity, 1900–1939.* Cambridge, MA, and London: MIT Press.

Harker, Dave. 1997. The wonderful world of IFPI: Music industry rhetoric, the critics and the classical Marxist critique. *Popular Music* 16(1): 45–80.

Harrison, Frank. 1973. *Time, place and music: An anthology of ethnomusicological observation c. 1550 to c. 1800.* Amsterdam: Frits Knuf.

Harvey, David. 1990. *The condition of postmodernity: An enquiry into the origins of cultural change.* Cambridge, MA: Blackwell.

—— 2003. *Paris: Capital of modernity.* New York: Routledge.

Haskell, Francis. 1976. *Rediscoveries in art: Some aspects of taste, fashion and collecting in England and France.* Oxford: Phaidon Press.

Haskell, Francis, and Nicholas Penny. 1981. *Taste and the antique: The lure of classical sculpture 1500–1900.* New Haven, CT: Yale University Press.

Hayes, Eileen M. 2010. *Songs in black and lavender: Race, sexual politics, and women's music.* Urbana: University of Illinois Press.

Head, Matthew. 2006. Beethoven heroine: A female allegory of music and authorship in *Egmont*: *19th Century Music* 30(2): 97–132.

Hebdige, Dick. 1979. *Subculture: The meaning of style*. London: Methuen.
Heelas, Paul. 1996. Emotion talk across cultures. Pp. 171–199 in *The emotions: Social, cultural and biological dimensions*. Edited by Rom Harré and W. Gerrod Parrott. London: Sage.
Hegel, Georg Wilhelm Friedrich. [1807] 1910. *The phenomenology of mind*. Translated by J. B. Baillie. London: Allen and Unwin.
—— [1822–28] 1975. *Lectures on the philosophy of world history*. Translated by H. B. Nisbet. Cambridge, U.K.: Cambridge University Press.
Heller, J. R. 1990. *Coleridge, Lamb, Hazlitt, and the reader of drama*. Columbia: University of Missouri Press.
Hennion, Antoine. 1989. An intermediary between production and consumption: The producer of popular music. *Science, Technology and Human Values* 14(4): 400–424.
—— 1997. Baroque and rock: Music, mediators and musical taste. *Poetics* 24: 415–435.
—— 2001. Music lovers. Taste as performance. *Theory, Culture, Society* 18(5): 1–22.
—— 2004. Pragmatics of taste. Pp. 131–144 in *The Blackwell companion to the sociology of culture*. Edited by Mark Jacobs and Nancy Hanrahan. Oxford and Malden, MA: Blackwell.
—— [1993] 2007. *La passion musicale: Une sociologie de la médiation*. Paris: Métailié.
—— 2007. Those things that hold us together. *Cultural Sociology* 1(1): 97–114.
Hennion, Antoine, and Joël-Marie Fauquet. 2001. Authority as performance. The love of Bach in nineteenth-century France. *Poetics* 29: 75–88.
Hennion, Antoine, Sophie Maisonneuve, and Emilie Gomart. 2000. *Figures de l'amateur: Formes, objets et pratiques de l'amour de la musique aujourd'hui*. Paris: La Documentation Française.
Henrotte, Gayle. 1985. Music as language: A semiotic paradigm? Pp. 163–170 in *Semiotics 1984*. Edited by John Deely. Lanham, MD: University Press of America.
Herder, Johann Gottfried. 1778–79. *Stimmen der Völker in Liedern* and *Volkslieder*. 2 vols. Leipzig, Germany: Weygandsche Buchhandlung.
—— 1968. *Sämtliche Werke*, vol. 25. Edited by Bernhard Suphan. Hildesheim, Germany: G. Olms.
Herndon, Marcia, and Norma Mcleod. 1979. *Music as culture*. Norwood, PA: Norwood Editions.
Herskovits, Melville. [1941] 1990. *The myth of the Negro past*. Boston, MA: Beacon Press.
Hesmondhalgh, David. 1997. Post-punk's attempt to democratise the music industry: the success and failure of Rough Trade. *Popular Music* 16 (3):255–274.
—— 1998. The British dance music industry: a case study of independent cultural production. *British Journal of Sociology* 49 (2):234–251.
—— 2000. International times: Fusions, exoticism and anti-racism in electronic dance music. Pp. 280–304 in *Western music and its others*. Edited by Georgina Born and David Hesmondhalgh. Berkeley: University of California Press.
—— 2002. *The cultural industries*. London: Sage.
—— 2008. Towards a critical understanding of music, emotion and self-identity. *Consumption, Markets and Culture* 11(4): 329–343.
Hesmondhalgh, David, and Sarah Baker. 2011. *Creative labour: Media work in three cultural industries*. Abingdon, U.K.: Routledge.
Hesse, Barnor. 2000. Introduction. Pp. 1–30. In *Un/Settled multiculturalisms: Diasporas, entanglements, "transruptions"*. Edited by Barnor Hesse. London and New York: Zed Books.
Hicks, Dan, and Mary C. Beaudry. 2010. Introduction. Material culture studies: A reactionary view. Pp. 1–21 in *The Oxford handbook of material culture studies*. Edited by Dan Hicks and Mary C. Beaudry. Oxford: Oxford University Press.
Higgins, Thomas. 1973. *Chopin: Preludes Op. 28: An authoritative score*. New York: W. W. Norton.
Hirschkind, Charles. 2006. *The ethical soundscape: Cassette sermons and Islamic counterpublics*. New York: Columbia University Press.
Hirschkind, Charles, and Brian Larkin. 2008. Introduction: Media and the political forms of religion. *Social Text* 26(3): 1–9.
Ho, Wai-chung. 1999. The sociopolitical transformation and Hong Kong secondary music education: Politicization, culturalization, and marketization. *Bulletin of the Council for Research in Music Education* 140: 41–56.
—— 2001. Musical learning: Differences between boys and girls in Hong Kong Chinese co-educational secondary schools. *British Journal of Music Education* 18(1): 41–54.
Hochschild, Arlie. 1983. *The managed hear: The commercialization of human feeling*. Berkeley: University of California Press.

Hoffmann, E. T. A. [1810] 1989. Review of Beethoven's fifth symphony. Pp. 234–251 in *E. T. A. Hoffmann's musical writings: Kreisleriana, the poet and the composer, music criticism*. Edited by David Charlton. Translated by Martyn Clarke. Cambridge, U.K.: Cambridge University Press.

Hoganson, Kristin L. 2007. *Consumers' imperium: The global production of American domesticity, 1865–1920*. Chapel Hill: University of North Carolina Press.

Honneth, Axel. 2004. Organized self-realization: some paradoxes of individualization. *European Journal of Social Theory* 7(4): 463–478.

hooks, bell. 1992. *Black looks: Race and representation*. Boston: South End Press.

Horn, David. 2000. Some thoughts on the work in popular music. Pp. 14–34 in *The musical work: Reality or invention?* Edited by Michael Talbot. Liverpool: Liverpool University Press.

Hornbostel, Erich Moritz von. [1905] 1975. The problems of comparative musicology. Translated by Richard Campbell. Pp. 247–270 in *Hornbostel opera omnia*, vol. 1. Edited by Klaus P. Wachsmann, Dieter Christensen, and Hans-Peter Reinecke. The Hague: Martinus Nijhoff.

—— 1928. African Negro music. *Africa* 1(1): 30–62.

Hornbostel, Erich Moritz von, and Curt Sachs. [1914] 1961. A classification of musical instruments. *Galpin Society Journal* 14: 3–29.

Hornby, Nick. [1995] 2000. *High fidelity*. London: Penguin Books.

Howes, David, ed. 2005. *Empire of the senses: The sensual culture reader*. Oxford and New York: Berg.

Hubbs, Nadine. 2004. *The queer composition of America's sound: Gay modernists, American music, and national identity*. Berkeley: University of California Press.

Hughes, Walter. 1994. In the empire of the beat: Discipline and disco. Pp. 147–157 in *Microphone fiends: Youth music, youth culture*. Edited by Andrew Ross and Tricia Rose. New York: Routledge.

Hunt, Lynn A., ed. 1989. *The new cultural history*. Berkeley: University of California Press.

Hunt, Lynn, Margaret C. Jacob, and Wijnand Mijnhardt. 2010. *The book that changed Europe: Picart and Bernard's religious ceremonies of the world*. Cambridge, MA: Belknap Press of Harvard University Press.

Hutton, Thomas. 2010. *The new economy of the inner city*. New York: Routledge.

Huyssen, Andreas. 1986. *After the great divide: Modernism, mass culture, postmodernism*. Bloomington: Indiana University Press.

IFPI. 2001. Peru raids net 2m CD-Rs. *IFPI network* 8 (October): 3.

Irigaray, Luce. 1985a. *Speculum of the other woman*. Translated by Gillian C. Gill. Ithaca: Cornell University Press.

—— 1985b. The "mechanics" of fluids. Pp. 106–118 in *This sex which is not one*. Translated by Catherine Porter with Carolyn Burke. Ithaca: Cornell University Press. First published in French in 1977.

Ivy, Marilyn. 1995. *Discourses of the vanishing: Modernity, phantasm, Japan*. Chicago: University of Chicago Press.

James, William. 1890. *The principles of psychology*. New York: Holt.

Jameson, Fredric. 1988. The politics of theory: Ideological positions in the post-modernist debate. Pp. 372–383 in *Modern criticism and theory: A reader*. Edited by David Lodge. New York: Longman.

Jankowsky, Richard C. 2007. Music, spirit possession and the in-between: Ethnomusicological inquiry and the challenge of trance. *Ethnomusicology Forum* 16(2): 185–208.

Jarman-Ivens, Freya, ed. 2007. *Oh boy!: Masculinities and popular music*. New York: Routledge.

Jarvis, Simon. 1998. *Adorno: A critical introduction*. Cambridge, U.K.: Polity Press.

Jenkins, Henry. 2006. *Convergence culture: Where old and new media collide*. New York: New York UniversityPress.

Jenkins, Jean L., and Paul Roving Olsen. 1976. *Music and musical instruments in the world of Islam*. London: Horniman Museum: World of Islam Festival Publishing Company Ltd.

Jenkins, Keith. 1995. *On "What is history?": From Carr and Elton to Rorty and White*. New York: Routledge.

Jessop, Bob. 2005. Critical realism and the strategic-relational approach. *New Formations* 56: 40–53.

Johnson, James H. 1995. *Listening in Paris: A cultural history*. Berkeley: University of California Press.

Johnson, James Weldon, ed. 1925. *The book of American Negro spirituals*. New York: Viking.

Johnson, Julian. 2002. *Who needs classical music? Cultural choice and musical value.* Oxford and New York: Oxford University Press.

Jones, Andrew F. 2001. *Yellow music: Media culture and colonial modernity in the Chinese jazz age.* Durham, NC: Duke University Press.

Jones, Arthur Morris. 1959. *Studies in African music.* 2 vols. Oxford: Oxford University Press.

Jones, Mari Riess, and Marilyn Boltz. 1989. Dynamic attending and responses to time. *Psychological Review* 96(3): 459–491.

Joyce, James. [1922] 1980. *Ulysses.* Harmondsworth, U.K.: Penguin Modern Classics.

Jung, C. G. 1977. *Symbols of transformation* . Collected works of C. G. Jung, volume 5. 2nd edition. Princeton: Princeton University Press.

Juslin, Patrick N., and John A. Sloboda, eds. 2010. *Handbook of music and emotion: Theory, research, applications.* Oxford: Oxford University Press.

Kafka, Franz. [1922] 1993a. Josephine, the singer or the mouse folk. Pp. 233–250 in *Franz Kafka: Selected stories.* Translated by Willa and Edwin Muir. Edited by Gabriel Josipovici. London: David Campbell. ['Josephine, die Sängerin oder Das Volk der Mäuse.' *Franz Kafka: Erzählungen. Franz Kafka: Gesammelte Werke.* Frankfurt am Main: Fischer Verlag, 1998: 200–218.]

—— [1922] 1993b. Investigations of a dog. Pp. 420–459 in *Franz Kafka: Selected stories.* Translated by Willa and Edwin Muir. Edited by Gabriel Josipovici. London: David Campbell. ['Forschungen eines Hundes.' *Franz Kafka: Beschreibung eines Kampfes: Novellen, Skizzen, Aphorismen aus dem Nachlass. Franz Kafka: Gesammelte Werke.* Frankfurt am Main: Fischer Verlag, 1998: 180–215.]

Kahn, Douglas. 1994. Death in light of the phonograph. Pp. 69–103 in *Wireless imagination: Sound, radio, and the avant-garde.* Edited by Douglas Kahn and Gregory Whitehead. Cambridge, MA: MIT Press.

—— 1999. *Noise water meat: A history of sound in the arts.* Cambridge, MA, and London: MIT Press.

Kahn, Douglas, and Gregory Whitehead, eds. 1994. *Wireless imagination: Sound, radio, and the avant-garde.* Cambridge, MA: The MIT Press.

Kallberg, Jeffrey. 1994. Small fairy voices: Sex, history and meaning in Chopin. In *Chopin studies. vol. 2.* Edited by John Rink and Jim Samson. Cambridge, U.K.: Cambridge University Press.

Kant, Immanuel. [1790] 1952. *The critique of judgement.* Translated by James Creed Meredith. Oxford: Clarendon Press.

—— [1790] 2000. *Critique of judgment.* Translated by John Henry Bernard. New York: Prometheus.

Kapchan, Deborah. 2007. *Traveling spirit masters: Moroccan Gnawa trance and music in the global marketplace.* Middletown, CT: Wesleyan University Press.

—— 2008. The promise of sonic translation: Performing the festive sacred in Morocco. *American Anthropologist* 110(4): 467–483.

Kartomi, Margaret. 1990. *Concepts and classifications of musical instruments.* Chicago: University of Chicago Press.

Kaye, Nick. 1994. *Postmodernism and performance.* London: Macmillan.

Kearns, Katherine. 1997. *Psychoanalysis, historiography, and feminist theory: The search for critical method.* Cambridge, U.K.: Cambridge University Press.

Keat, Russell. 2000. *Cultural goods and the limits of the market.* London and New York: Routledge.

Keightley, Keir. 2001. Reconsidering rock. Pp. 109–142 in *The Cambridge companion to pop and rock.* Edited by Simon Frith, Will Straw, and John Street. Cambridge, U.K.: Cambridge University Press.

Keil, Charles. 1970. *Urban blues.* Chicago: University of Chicago Press.

——. 1979. *Tiv song.* Chicago: University of Chicago Press.

Kelly, Caleb. 2009. *Cracked media: The sound of malfunction.* Cambridge, MA: MIT. Press.

Kenney, William Howland. 1993. *Chicago jazz: A cultural history, 1904–1930.* New York: Oxford University Press.

Kerman, Joseph. 1985. *Musicology.* London: Fontana.

Kershaw, Baz. 1992. *The politics of performance: Radical theatre as cultural intervention.* London: Routledge.

Kisliuk, Michelle. 1997. (Un)doing fieldwork: Sharing songs, sharing lives. Pp. 23–44 in *Shadows in the field: New perspectives for fieldwork in ethnomusicology.* Edited by Gregory F. Barz and Timothy J. Cooley. New York: Oxford University Press.

——— 1998. *Seize the dance! BaAka musical life and the ethnography of performance.* New York: Oxford University Press.

Kittler, Friedrich. 1985. *Discourse networks 1800/1900.* Translated by Michael Metteer with Chris Cullens. Foreword by David E. Wellbery. Stanford: Stanford University Press.

——— 1990. *Gramophone, film, typewriter.* Translated with introduction by Geoffrey Winthrop-Young and Michael Wutz. Stanford: Stanford University Press.

Klima, Alan. 2008. Thai love Thai: Financing emotion in post-crash Thailand. Pp. 121–136 in *The anthropology of globalization: A reader.* Edited by Jonathan Xavier Inda and Renato Rosaldo. Oxford: Blackwell.

Knittel, K. M. 1995. "Ein hypomoderner Dirigent": Mahler and anti-Semitism in *fin-de-siècle* Vienna. *19th-Century Music* 18 (3): 257–276.

Koelsch, Stefan, Elizabeth Kasper, Daniela Sammler, Katrin Schulze, Thomas Gunter, and Angela D. Friederici. 2004. Music, language and meaning: brain signatures of semantic processing. *Nature Neuroscience* 7(3): 302–307.

Koestenbaum, Wayne. 1993. *The queen's throat: Opera, homosexuality, and the mystery of desire.* New York: Poseidon Press.

Koestler, Arthur. 1975. *The act of creation.* 2nd ed. London: Picador.

Koizumi, Kyoko. 2002. Popular music, gender and high school pupils in Japan: Personal music in school and leisure sites. *Popular Music* 21(1): 107–125.

Kopytoff, Igor. 1986. The cultural biography of things: commoditization as process. Pp. 64–91 in *The social life of things: Commodities in cultural perspective.* Edited by Arjun Appadurai. Cambridge, U.K.: Cambridge University Press.

Korsyn, Kevin. 1999. Beyond privileged contexts: Intertextuality, influence, and dialogue. Pp. 55–72 in *Rethinking music.* Edited by Nicholas Cook and Mark Everist. Oxford: Oxford University Press.

Koskoff, Ellen, ed. 1987. *Women and music in cross-cultural perspective.* Westport: Greenwood Press.

——— 2000. *Music in Lubavicher life.* Urbana: University of Illinois Press.

Kotthoff, Helga. 2001. Aesthetic dimensions of Georgian grief rituals: On the artful display of emotions in lamentation. Pp. 167–194 in *Verbal art across cultures: The aesthetics and proto-aesthetics of communication.* Edited by Hubert Knoblauch and Helga Kotthoff. Tübingen, Germany: Narr.

Koza, Julia Eklund. 1992. Picture this: Sex equity in textbook illustrations. *Music Educators' Journal* 78(7): 28–33.

Kramer, Lawrence. 1984. *Music and poetry: The nineteenth century and after.* Berkeley: University of California Press.

——— 1990. *Music as cultural practice, 1800–1900.* Berkeley: University of California Press.

——— 1993. Music criticism and the postmodern turn: In contrary motion with Gary Tomlinson. *Current Musicology* 53: 25–35.

——— 1995. *Classical music and postmodern knowledge.* Berkeley: University of California Press.

——— 2001. *Musical meaning: Toward a critical history.* Berkeley: University of California Press.

——— 2007. *Why classical music still matters.* Berkeley: University of California Press.

——— 2010. *Interpreting music.* Berkeley: University of California Press.

Krims, Adam. 2000. *Rap music and the poetics of identity.* Cambridge, U.K.: Cambridge University Press.

——— 2001. Marxism, urban geography, and classical recordings: An alternative to cultural studies. *Music Analysis* 20(3): 347–363.

——— 2007. *Music and urban geography.* New York: Routledge.

——— 2010. Music theory, historically-informed performance, and the significance of cities. *Zeitschrift der Gesellschaft für Musiktheorie* 7(3). http://www.gmth.de/zeitschrift.aspx.

Kristeva, Julia. 1987. Narcissus: The new insanity. Pp. 103–121 in *Tales of love.* Translated by Leon S. Roudiez. New York: Columbia University Press.

Krumhansl, Carol L. 1990. *Cognitive foundations of musical pitch.* New York: Oxford University Press.

——— 1991. Music psychology: Tonal structures in perception and memory. *Annual Review of Psychology* 42: 277–303.

——— 1998. Topic in music: An empirical study of memorability, openness, and emotion in Mozart's string quintet in C major and Beethoven's string quartet in A minor. *Music Perception* 16(1): 119–134.

Krumhansl, Carol L. 2000. Music and affect: Empirical and theoretical contributions from experimental psychology. Pp. 88–99 in *Musicology and sister disciplines past, present, future*. Edited by David Greer. Oxford: Oxford University Press.

Kuhn, Thomas S. 1962. *The structure of scientific revolutions*. Chicago: University of Chicago Press.

Kun, Josh. 2005. *Audiotopia: Music, race, and America*. Berkeley: University of California Press.

Kuper, Adam. 1999. *Culture: The anthropologists' account*. Cambridge, MA: Harvard University Press.

LaBelle, Brandon. 2007. *Background noise: Perspectives on sound art*. New York and London: Continuum.

Lacan, Jacques. [1953] 1977. The function and field of speech and language in psychoanalysis. Translated by Alan Sheridan. Pp. 30–113 in *Écrits: A selection*. London: Tavistock.

—— [1964] 1979. *The four fundamental concepts of psycho-analysis*. Translated by Alan Sheridan. New York: Penguin.

—— [1987] 1988. *The seminar of Jacques Lacan. Book II: The ego in Freud's theory and in the technique of psychoanalysis, 1954 –1955*. Translated by Sylvia Tomaselli. Edited by Jacques-Alain Miller. New York: W. W. Norton.

Laing, Dave. 1985. *One chord wonders: Power and meaning in punk rock*. Milton Keynes, U.K.: Open University Press.

—— 1986. The music industry and the "cultural imperialism" thesis. *Media, Culture and Society* 8: 331–341.

Lakoff, George, and Mark Johnson. 1980. *Metaphors we live by*. Chicago: University of Chicago Press.

Lamont, Michèle, and Marcel Fournier, eds. 1992. *Cultivating differences: Symbolic boundaries and the making of inequality*. Chicago: University of Chicago Press.

Lange, Barbara Rose. 2003. *Holy brotherhood: Romani music in a Hungarian Pentecostal church*. New York: Oxford University Press.

Langlois, Tony. 1996. The local and global in North African popular music. *Popular Music* 15(3): 259–273.

Lassiter, Luke. 2000. *The Chicago guide to collaborative ethnography*. Chicago: University of Chicago Press.

Latour, Bruno. 2005. *Reassembling the social: an introduction to actor-network theory*. Oxford: Oxford University Press.

Lawe Davies, Chris. 1993. Aboriginal rock music: Space and place. Pp. 249–265 in *Rock and popular music: Politics, policies, institutions*. Edited by S. Frith, T. Bennett, L. Grossberg, J. Shepherd, and G. Turner. London: Routledge.

Lawrence, Tim. 2004. *Love saves the day: A history of American dance music culture, 1970–1979*. Durham, NC: Duke University Press.

Lebler, Don. 2007. Student-as-master? Reflections on a learning innovation in popular music pedagogy. *International Journal of Music Education* 25(3): 205–221.

Lebrecht, Norman. 1996. *When the music stops: Managers, maestros and corporate murder of classical music*. London: Simon and Schuster.

Lee, Tong Soon. 1999. Technology and the production of Islamic space: The call to prayer in Singapore. *Ethnomusicology* 43(1): 86–100.

Legg, Robert. Forthcoming (2012). "One equal music": An exploration of gender perceptions and the fair assessment by beginning music teachers of musical compositions. *Music Education Research* 12(2).

Le Huray, Peter, and James Day, eds. 1981. *Music aesthetics in the eighteenth and early-nineteenth centuries*. Cambridge, U.K.: Cambridge University Press.

Leman, Marc. 1995. *Music and schema theory: Cognitive foundations of systematic musicology*. New York: Springer.

Leonard, Marion. 2007. *Gender in the music industry*. Aldershot, U.K.: Ashgate.

Leppert, Richard. 1993. *The sight of sound: Music, representation, and the history of the body*. Berkeley: University of California Press.

—— 2005. Music "pushed to the edge of existence" (Adorno, listening, and the question of hope). *Cultural Critique* 60: 92–133.

Leppert, Richard, and Susan McClary. 1987. *Music and society: The politics of composition, performance and reception*. Cambridge, U.K.: Cambridge University Press.

Lerdahl, Fred, and Ray Jackendoff. 1983. *A generative theory of tonal music.* Cambridge, MA: MIT Press.

Leslie, A. M. 1987. Pretence and representation: The origins of "Theory of mind." *Psychological review* 94(4): 412–426.

Lessig, Lawrence. 2008. *Remix: Making art and commerce thrive in the hybrid economy.* New York and London: Penguin.

Levi, E., and F. Scheding, eds. 2010. *Music and displacement: Diasporas, mobilities, and dislocations in Europe and beyond.* Lanham, MD: Scarecrow Press.

Levin, Theodore, and Valentina Suzukei. 2006. *Where rivers and mountains sing.* Bloomington: Indiana University Press.

Levine, Lawrence W. 1988. *Highbrow/lowbrow: The emergence of cultural hierarchy in America.* Cambridge, MA: Harvard University Press.

Levinson, Jerrold. 1997. *Music in the moment.* Ithaca: Cornell University Press.

Ley, David. 2003. Artists, aestheticisation, and the field of gentrification. *Urban Studies* 40(12): 2527–2544.

Leyshon, Andrew, David Matliss, and George Revill, eds. 1998. *The place of music.* New York: Guilford.

LGBTQ Study Group, American Musicological Society. Includes issues of the group's newsletter. http://www.ams-lgbtq.org/.

Lhamon, W. T. 1998. *Raising Cain: Blackface performance from Jim Crow to hip-hop.* Cambridge, MA: Harvard University Press.

Ligota, Christopher R. 1982. "This story is not true": Fact and fiction in antiquity. *Journal of the Warburg and Courtauld Institutes* 45: 1–13.

Lindholm, Charles. 2007. *Culture and identity: The history, theory, and practice of psychological anthropology.* Revised ed. Oxford: Oneworld Publications.

Lipsitz, George. 1994. *Dangerous crossroads: Popular music, postmodernism, and the poetics of place.* London: Verso.

Liu, David, Henry M. Wellman, et al. 2008. Theory of mind development in Chinese children: A meta-analysis of false-belief understanding across cultures and languages. *Developmental Psychology* 44(2): 523–531.

Locke, Ralph P., and Cyrilla Barr, eds. 1997. *Cultivating music in America: Women patrons and activists since 1860.* Berkeley: University of California Press.

Lomax, Alan. 1968. *Folk song style and culture.* Washington, DC: American Association for the Advancement of Science.

Lomax, Alan, and Norman Berkowitz. 1972. The evolutionary taxonomy of culture. *Science* 177: 228–239.

Longinovic, Tomislav. 2000. Music wars: Blood and song at the end of Yugoslavia. Pp. 622–643 in *Music and the racial imagination.* Edited by Ronald Radano and Philip V. Bohlman. Chicago: University of Chicago Press.

Lopes, Paul D. 1992. Innovation and diversity in the popular music industry 1969 to 1990. *American Sociological Review.* 57(1): 56–71.

Lott, Eric. 1993. *Love and theft: Blackface minstrelsy and the American working class.* New York: Oxford University Press.

Lundberg, Dan. 2003. Assyria—A land in cyberspace. Pp.289–308 in *Music, media, multiculture: Changing musicscapes.* Edited by Dan Lundberg, Krister Malm, and Owe Ronstrom. Stockholm: Svenskt Visarkiv.

Lupton, Deborah. 1998. *The emotional self.* London: Sage.

Lutz, Catherine, and Geoffrey M. White. 1986. The anthropology of emotions. *Annual Review of Anthropology* 15: 405–436.

Lutz, Catherine, and Lila Abu-Lughod, eds. 1990. *Language and the politics of emotion.* Cambridge, U.K.: Cambridge University Press.

Lyotard, Jean-François. 1991. *The inhuman: Reflections on time.* Translated by Geoffrey Bennington and Rachel Bowlby. Oxford: Basil Blackwell.

Lysloff, René T. A. and Leslie C. Gay, Jr., eds. 2003. *Music and technoculture.* Middletown, CT: Wesleyan University Press / University Press of New England.

Maas, Georg, and Hartmult Reszel. 1998. Whatever happened to? . . . The decline and renaissance of rock in the former GDR. *Popular Music* 17(3): 267–278.

MacDonald, Ian. 1995. *Revolution in the head: The Beatles' records and the sixties.* London: Pimlico.

MacIntyre, Alasdair. 1984. *After virtue: A study in moral theory.* London: Duckworth.

Magowan, Fiona. 2007. *Melodies of mourning: Music and emotion in Northern Australia*. Oxford: James Currey.

Mahmood, Saba. 2009. Religious reason and secular affect: An incommensurable divide? Pp. 64–100 in *Is critique secular? Blasphemy, injury, and free speech*. Berkeley: University of California Press.

Maisonneuve, Sophie. 2009. *L'invention du disque, 1877–1949*. Paris: EAC.

Makagon, Daniel. 2006. Sonic earthquakes. *Communication and Critical/Cultural Studies* 3: 223–239.

Manuel, Peter. 1988. *Popular musics of the non-Western world: An introductory survey*. New York: Oxford University Press.

—— 2000. The construction of a diasporic tradition: Indo-Caribbean "Local classical music." *Ethnomusicology* 44(1): 97–119.

Marcus, George E., and Michael M. J. Fisher. 1986. *Anthropology as cultural critique: An experimental moment in the human sciences*. Chicago: University of Chicago Press.

Marcus, Greil. [1976] 1982. *Mystery train: Images of America in rock 'n' roll music*. New York: Dutton.

Marcus, Scott. 2007. *Music in Egypt: Experiencing music, expressing culture*. Globalisation series. New York: Oxford University Press.

Marett, Allan. 2005. *Songs, dreamings, and ghosts: The Wangga of North Australia*. Hanover, CT: Wesleyan University Press.

Marmorstein, Gary. 2007. *The label: The story of Columbia Records*. New York: Thunder's Mouth Press.

Martin, Peter. 1995. *Sounds and society: Themes in the sociology of music*. Manchester: Manchester University Press.

—— 2006. *Music and the sociological gaze: art worlds and cultural production*. Manchester: Manchester University Press.

Maryprasith, Primrose. 1999. The effects of globalisation and localisation on the status of music in Thailand. Ph.D. thesis, London University Institute of Education.

Masuzawa, Tomoko. 2005. *The invention of world religions: Or, how European universalism was preserved in the language of pluralism*. Chicago: University of Chicago Press.

Maus, Fred Everett. 1993. Masculine discourse in music theory. *Perspectives of New Music* 31(2): 264–293.

—— 2006. The disciplined subject of musical analysis. Pp. 13–43 in *Beyond structural listening? Postmodern modes of hearing*. Edited by Andrew Dell'Antonio. Berkeley: University of California Press.

—— 2009. Virile music by Hector Berlioz. Pp. 113–133 in *Masculinity and Western musical practice*. Edited by Ian Biddle and Kirsten Gibson. Farnham, U.K.: Ashgate.

—— 2010. Somaesthetics of music. *Action, criticism, and theory for music education* 9(1): 9–25.

Mauss, Marcel. 1954. *The gift: Forms and functions of exchange in archaic societies*. Glencoe, IL: Free Press.

McAlister, Elizabeth. (2011). Listening for geographies: Music as sonic compass. In *Geographies of the Haitian diaspora*. Edited by Regine O. Jackson. New York: Routledge.

McAllester, David. 1989. Videotaped lecture at Brown University, April 10, 1989, for the Seminar in the History of Ethnomusicological Thought.

—— 2006. Reminiscences of the early days. *Ethnomusicology* 50: 200.

McCarthy, Maree. 1997. Irish music education and Irish identity: A concept revisited. *Oideas* 45: 5–22. Dublin: Department of Education and Science.

McClary, Susan. 1991. *Feminine endings: Music, gender, and sexuality*. Minneapolis: University of Minnesota Press.

—— [1994] 2006. Constructions of subjectivity in Schubert's music. Pp. 205–233 in *Queering the pitch: The new gay and lesbian musicology*. Edited by Philip Brett, Elizabeth Wood, and Gary C. Thomas. New York: Routledge.

McClary, Susan, and Robert Walser. 1990. Start making sense! Musicology wrestles with rock. Pp. 277–292 in *On record: Rock, pop and the written word*. Edited by Simon Frith and Andrew Goodwin. London: Routledge.

McGovern, Charles F. 2006. *Sold American: Consumption and citizenship, 1890–1945*. Chapel Hill: University of North Carolina Press.

McGraw, Ted. 2010. The McNulty family. *Journal of the Society for American Music* 4(4): 451–474.

McGuigan, Jim. 1992. *Cultural populism*. London: Routledge.

McLeod, Norma. 1974. Ethnomusicological research and anthropology. *Annual Review of Anthropology* 3: 99–115.

Meintjes, Louise. 2003. *Sound of Africa! Making music Zulu in a South African studio.* Durham, NC: Duke University Press.

—— 2004. Shoot the sergeant, shatter the mountain: The production of masculinity in Zulu ngomba song and dance in post-apartheid South Africa. *Ethnomusicology Forum* 13(2): 173–201.

Melrose, Susan. 1994. *A semiotics of the dramatic text.* London: Macmillan.

Mendonça, Maria. 2002. Javanese gamelan in Britain: Communitas, affinity and other stories. Ph.D. dissertation, Wesleyan University.

Merriam, Alan P. 1964. *The anthropology of music.* Evanston, IL: Northwestern University Press.

—— 1969. The ethnographic experience: Drum-making among the Bala (Basongye). *Ethnomusicology* 13: 74–100.

Metzler, Fritz. 1938. Dur, Moll und "Kirchentöne" als musikalischer Rassenausdruck. Pp. 1–27 in *Zur Tonalität des deutschen Volksliedes.* Edited by Guido Waldmann. Wolfenbüttel, Germany: Kallmeyer.

Meyer, Leonard B. 1956. *Emotion and meaning in music.* Chicago: University of Chicago Press.

—— 1973. *Explaining music: Essays and explorations.* Berkeley: University of California Press.

Middleton, Richard. 1990. *Studying popular music.* Milton Keynes, U.K.: Open University Press.

—— 2000. Work-in-(g) practice: Configuration of the popular music inter-text. Pp. 59–87 in *The musical work: Reality or invention?* Edited by Michael Talbot. Liverpool: Liverpool University Press.

—— 2001. Popular music in the West. Pp. 128–166 in *The new Grove dictionary of music and musicians,* Volume 20. Edited by Stanley Sadie. London: Macmillan.

—— 2003. Music studies and the idea of culture. Pp 1–15 in *The cultural study of music: A critical introduction.* Edited by Martin Clayton, Trevor Herbert, and Richard Middleton. New York and London: Routledge.

—— 2006. *Voicing the popular: On the subjects of popular music.* New York: Routledge.

—— 2009. *Musical belongings: Selected essays.* Farnham, U.K.: Ashgate.

Miège, Bernard. 1989. *The capitalization of cultural production.* New York: International General.

Miller, Daniel, ed. 2005. *Materiality.* Durham, NC: Duke University Press.

Miller, D. A. 1998. *Place for us: Essay on the Broadway musical.* Cambridge, MA: Harvard University Press.

Miller, Karl Hagstrom. 2010. *Segregating sound: Inventing folk and pop music in the age of Jim Crow.* Durham, NC: Duke University Press.

Miller, Toby, and George Yúdice. 2002. *Cultural policy.* London, Thousand Oaks, CA, and New Delhi: Sage.

Milton, Kay. 2002. *Loving nature: Towards an ecology of emotion.* London: Routledge.

Milton, Kay, and Maruška Svašek, eds. 2005. *Mixed emotions: anthropological studies of feeling.* Oxford: Berg.

Mingus, Charles. 1995. *Beneath the underdog.* Edinburgh: Payback Press.

Mitchell, Tony. 1996. *Popular music and local identity.* London: Wesleyan University Press.

—— 2009. Sonic psychogeography: A poetics of place in popular music in Aotearoa/New Zealand. *Perfect Beat* 10(2): 145–175.

Mithen, Steven. 2005. *The singing Neanderthals: The origins of music, language, mind and body.* London: Weidenfeld and Nicolson.

Mockus, Martha. 2007. *Sounding out: Pauline Oliveros and lesbian musicality.* New York: Routledge.

Modleski, Tania. 1986. Femininity as mas(s)querade: A feminist approach to mass culture. Pp. 37–52 in *High theory, low culture: Analysing popular television and film.* Edited by Colin McCabe. Manchester: Manchester University Press.

Monson, Ingrid. 1996. *Saying something: Jazz improvisation and interaction.* Chicago: University of Chicago Press.

Montagu, Jeremy, and John Burton. 1971. A proposed new classification system for musical instruments. *Ethnomusicology* 15(1): 49–70.

Montaigne, Michel Eyquem de. [1580] 1952. *Essais.* Paris: Editions Garnier Frères.

Moore, Allan. 1993. *Rock: The primary text.* Milton Keynes, U.K.: Open University Press.

Moreno, Jairo. 2004. Bauzá—Gillespie—Latin/jazz: difference, modernity, and the Black Caribbean. *South Atlantic Quarterly* 103(1) (Winter): 81–99.

Morley, David, and Kuan-Hsing Chen, eds. 1996. *Stuart Hall: Critical dialogues in cultural studies.* London: Routledge.

Morrow, Mary Sue. 1989. *Concert life in Haydn's Vienna: Aspects of a developing musical and social institution.* Stuyvesant, NY: Pendragon Press.

Mosbacher, Dee, director. 2004. *Radical harmonies.* DVD. San José, CA: Wolfe Video.

Mouffe, Chantal. 2000. Hegemony and new political subjects: toward a new concept of democracy. Pp. 295–309 in *Readings in Contemporary Political Sociology.* Edited by Kate Nash. Oxford: Blackwell.

Mugglestone, Erica. 1981. Guido Adler's "The scope, method and aim of musicology" (1885): An English translation with an historico-analytical commentary. *Yearbook for Traditional Music* 13: 1–21.

Muir, Edward, and Guido Ruggiero, eds. 1991. *Microhistory and the lost peoples of Europe.* Translated by Eren Branch. Baltimore: Johns Hopkins University Press.

Mulhern, Francis. 2000. *Culture/metaculture.* New York: Routledge.

—— 2009. The idea of culture. *New Left Review* 55 (January–February): 32–45.

Muller, Carol Ann. 2000. *Rituals of fertility and the sacrifice of desire: Nazarite women's performance in South Africa.* Chicago: University of Chicago Press.

Muñoz, José Esteban. 1999. "The white to be angry": Vaginal Creme Davis's terrorist drag. Pp. 93–115 in *Disidentifications: Queers of color and the performance of politics.* Minneapolis: University of Minnesota Press.

Namaste, Viviane K. 2000. "A gang of trannies": Gendered discourse and punk culture. Pp. 73–92 in *Invisible lives: The erasure of transsexual and transgendered people.* Chicago: University of Chicago Press.

Negrón-Muntaner, Frances. 2004. *Boricua pop: Puerto Ricans and the Latinization of American culture.* New York: New York University Press.

Negus, Keith. 1992. *Producing pop: Culture and conflict in the popular music industry.* London: Edward Arnold.

—— 1999. *Music genres and corporate cultures.* London: Routledge.

Negus, Keith, and Michael Pickering. 2004. *Creativity, Communication and Cultural Value.* London: Sage.

Nelson, Richard. 2001. *Economics as religion.* Philadelphia: Pennsylvania State Press.

Nettl, Bruno. [1973] 1992. Comparison and comparative method in ethnomusicology. *Yearbook for Inter-American Musical Research* 9: 148–161.

—— 1987. *The Radif of Persian music: Studies of structure and cultural significance.* Champaign, IL: Elephant & Cat.

—— 2005. *The study of ethnomusicology: Thirty-one issues and concepts.* 2nd ed. Urbana and Chicago: University of Illinois Press.

Nettl, Bruno, Ruth M. Stone, James Porter, and Timothy Rice, eds. 1998–2002. *The Garland encyclopedia of world music.* 10 vols. New York: Garland.

Neuenfeldt, Karl, ed. 1997. *The Didjeridu: From Arnhem Land to Internet.* Sydney: John Libbey / Perfect Beat.

——, ed. 1998. Old instruments in new contexts. Special Edition of *The World of Music* 40(2).

Newcomb, Anthony. 1980. *The madrigal at Ferrara, 1579–1597.* Princeton: Princeton University Press.

Newlin, Dika. 1980. *Schoenberg remembered: Diaries and recollections (1938–76).* New York: Pendragon Press.

Nietzsche, Friedrich. [1887] 1998. *On the genealogy of morals.* Translated by Douglas Smith. Oxford: Oxford University Press.

—— [1901] 1969. *The will to power.* Edited by Walter A. Kaufmann. Translated by Walter A. Kaufmann and R. J. Hollingdale. New York: Random House.

North, Adrian C. and David J. Hargreaves. 2008. *The social and applied psychology of music.* Oxford: Oxford University Press.

Nussbaum, Martha. 2003. *Upheavals of thought: The intelligence of emotions.* Cambridge, U.K.: Cambridge University Press.

Nye, Sean. 2009. Love parade, please not again: A Berlin cultural history. *ECHO* 9(1) (accessed January 3, 2011).

Ochoa, Anna Maria, and Carolina Botero. 2009. Notes on practices of musical exchange in Colombia. *Popular Communication* 7 (3):158–168.

O'Connor, Justin. 2006. Art, popular culture and cultural policy: variations on a theme of John Carey. *Critical Quarterly* 48(4): 49–104.

Olaniyan, Tejumola. 2004. *Arrest the music! Fela and his rebel art and politics.* Bloomington: Indiana University Press.

Olaniyan, T., and J. H. Sweet, eds. 2010. *The African diaspora and the disciplines.* Bloomington and Indianapolis: Indiana University Press.

Olatunji, Babatunde. 2005. *The beat of my drum: An autobiography.* Philadelphia: Temple University Press.

Oliveros, Pauline. 1984. *Software for people: Collected writings 1963–80.* Baltimore: Smith Publications.

—— 1990. *Deep listening pieces.* Kingston, NY: Deep Listening Publications.

Olsen, Dale. 1986. Note on "corpophone." *Newsletter of the Society for Ethnomusicology* 20(4): 5.

O'Neill, Susan. 1997. Gender and music. Pp. 46–63 in *The social psychology of music.* Edited by David J. Hargreaves and Adrian C. North. New York: Oxford University Press.

Ong, Walter J. 1982. *Orality and literacy: The technologizing of the word.* New York and London: Methuen.

Oosterbaan, Martijn. 2008. Spiritual attunement: Pentecostal radio in the soundscape of a favela in Rio de Janeiro. *Social Text* 26(3): 123–145.

Orenstein, J. B. 2000. Mosh-pit mania. *Salon,* June 13. http://www.salon.com/entertainment/music/feature/2000/06/13/moshpit (accessed January 15, 2011).

Ottenberg, Simon. 1996. *Seeing with music: The lives of three blind African musicians.* Seattle: University of Washington Press.

Ovid. 1986. *Metamorphoses.* Translated by A. D. Melville. Oxford: Oxford University Press.

Pacheco, Christina Diego. 2009. Beyond church and court: City musicians and music in Renaissance Valladolid. *Early Music* 37(3): 367–378.

Pacini Hernandez, Deborah. 2010. *Oye como va: Hybridity and identity in Latino popular music.* Philadelphia: Temple University Press.

Paddison, Max. 1996. *Adorno, modernism and mass culture. Essays on critical theory and music.* London: Kahn and Averill.

Pagden, Anthony. 1993. *European encounters with the New World: From Renaissance to Romanticism.* New Haven, CT: Yale University Press.

Paine, Thomas. [1791–92] 1969. *Rights of man.* Edited by Henry Collins. Harmondsworth, U.K.: Penguin.

Palan, Ronan, ed. 1996. *Global political economy: Contemporary theories.* London and New York: Routledge.

Pareles, John. 1993. It's got a beat and you can surrender to it. *The New York Times,* The Week in Review, section 4: (March 28), 2.

Parry, Hubert. 1896. *The evolution of the art of music.* New York: D. Appleton.

Patton, Paul. 2000. *Deleuze and the political: Thinking the political.* London and New York: Routledge.

Pederson, Sanna. 2000. Beethoven and masculinity. Pp. 313–331 in *Beethoven and his world.* Edited by Scott G. Burnham and Michael P. Steinberg. Princeton: Princeton University Press.

Penley, Constance, and Andrew Ross. 1991. *Technoculture.* Minneapolis: University of Minnesota Press.

Peraino, Judith A, 2005. *Listening to the sirens: Musical technologies of queer identity from Homer to Hedwig.* Berkeley: University of California Press.

Perrault, Charles. 1991/1697. Parallels between the ancients and the moderns. Treating astronomy, geography, navigation, war, philosophy, music, medicine, etc. Translated by Robert Martin. *Turkish Music Quarterly* 4(1): 10–11.

Peters, John Durham. 1999. *Speaking into the air: A history of the idea of communication.* Chicago and London: University of Chicago Press.

Peterson, Marina. 2010. *Sound, space, and the city: Civic performance in downtown Los Angeles.* Philadelphia: University of Pennsylvania Press.

Peterson, Richard A. 1997. *Creating country-music: Fabricating authenticity.* Berkeley: University of California Press.

Peterson, Richard A., and David Berger. [1975] 1990. Cycles in symbol production: The case of popular music. Pp. 140–159 in *On record: Rock, pop and the written word.* Edited by Simon Frith and Andrew Goodwin. London: Routledge.

Peterson, Richard A., and Roger M. Kern. 1996. Changing highbrow taste: From snob to omnivore. *American Sociological Review* 61: 900–1007.

Philip, Robert. 1992. *Early recordings and musical style: Changing tastes in instrumental performance, 1900–1950.* Cambridge, U.K.: Cambridge University Press.

Pini, Maria. 2001. *Club cultures and female subjectivity: The move from home to house.* New York: Palgrave.

Pinker, Steven. 1994. *The language instinct.* London: Allen Lane.

Pinker, Steven, and Ray Jackendoff. 2005. The faculty of language: What's special about it? *Cognition* 95(2): 201–236.

Porcello, Thomas, Louise Meintjes, Ana Maria Ochoa, and David W. Samuels. 2010. The reorganization of the sensory world. *Annual Review of Anthropology* 39: 51–66.

Potter, John. 1998. *Vocal authority: Singing style and ideology.* Cambridge, U.K.: Cambridge University Press.

Potter, Pamela M. 1998. *Most German of the arts: Musicology and society from the Weimar Republic to the end of Hitler's Reich.* New Haven, CT: Yale University Press.

Potts, John, and Edward Scheer. 2006. *Technologies of magic: A cultural study of ghosts, machines and the uncanny.* Sydney: Power Publications.

Pritchard, Matthew. 2007. Review of *The cultural study of music: A critical introduction.* Edited by Martin Clayton, Trevor Herbert, and Richard Middleton (New York: Routledge, 2003). *Musica Scientiae* XI(1): 145–151.

Quiroga, José. 2000. *Tropics of desire: Interventions from queer Latino America.* New York: New York University Press.

Qureshi, Regula Burckhardt. 1987. Musical sound and contextual input: A performance model for musical analysis. *Ethnomusicology* 31(1): 56–86.

—— [1986] 1995. *Sufi music of India and Pakistan: Sound, context, and meaning in Qawwali.* Chicago: University of Chicago Press.

—— 1997. The Indian sarangi: Sound of affect, site of contest. *Yearbook for Traditional Music* 29: 1–38.

——, ed. 2002. *Music and Marx: Ideas, practice, politics.* New York: Routledge.

Rabinbach, Anson. 1992. *The human motor: Energy, fatigue, and the origins of modernity.* Berkeley: University of California Press.

Radano, Ronald. 2003. *Lying up a nation: Race and black music.* Chicago: University of Chicago Press.

—— 2010. On ownership and value. *Black Music Research Journal* 30(2) (Fall): 363–369.

Radano, Ronald, and Philip V. Bohlman, eds. 2000. *Music and the racial imagination.* Chicago: University of Chicago Press.

Ramnarine, Tina. 2007. *Beautiful cosmos: Performance and belonging in the Caribbean diaspora.* London: Pluto Press.

Ramsey, Guthrie P., Jr. 2003. *Race music: Black cultures from bebop to hip-hop.* Berkeley: University of California Press.

Randall, Annie J. 2008. *Dusty!: Queen of the postmods.* Oxford: Oxford University Press.

Ratner, Leonard G. 1977. *Music: The listener's art.* New York: McGraw-Hill.

—— 1980. *Classic music: expression, form, and style.* New York: Schirmer Books.

Raynor, Henry. 1972. *A social history of music.* New York: Taplinger.

Regev, Motti. 1997. Rock aesthetics and musics of the world. *Theory, Culture and Society* 14(3): 125–142.

Rehding, Alexander. 2000. The quest for the origins of music in Germany circa 1900. *Journal of the American Musicological Society* 53(2): 345–385.

Reich, David, Richard E. Green, et al. 2010. Genetic history of an archaic Hominin group from Denisova Cave in Siberia. *Nature* 468, 7327: 1053–1060.

Reily, Suzel. 2002. *Voices of the magi: Enchanted journeys in Southeast Brazil.* Chicago: University of Chicago Press.

Reyes Schramm, Adelaida. 1986. Tradition in the guise of innovation: Music among a refugee population. *Yearbook for Traditional Music* 18: 91–102.

Reynolds, Simon. 1998. Rave culture: Living dream or living death? Pp. 84–93 in *The club cultures reader.* Edited by Steve Redhead. Oxford: Blackwell.

Rhodes, Lisa. 2005. *Electric ladyland: Women and rock culture.* Philadelphia: University of Pennsylvania Press.

Rice, Timothy. 1994. *May it fill your soul: Experiencing Bulgarian music.* Chicago: University of Chicago Press.

—— 1996. The dialectic of economics and aesthetics in Bulgarian music. Pp. 176–199 in *Retuning culture. Musical changes in central and eastern Europe.* Edited by Mark Slobin. Durham, NC. Duke University Press.

Rich, Adrienne. 1986. Compulsory heterosexuality and lesbian existence. Pp. 23–75 in *Blood, bread and poetry: Selected prose 1979–1985.* New York: Norton.

Riguero, Patricia Digon. 2000. An analysis of gender in a Spanish music text book. *Music Education Research* 2(1): 57–73.

Roberts, Jennifer L. 2007. Copley's cargo: Boy with a squirrel and the dilemma of transit. *American Art* 21(7): 21–41.

Robins, Kevin, and David Morley. 1996. Almanci, Yabanci. *Cultural Studies* 10(2): 248–254.

Rochlitz, Rainer. 1996. *The disenchantment of art: The philosophy of Walter Benjamin.* Translated by Jane Marie Todd. New York and London: The Guilford Press.

Rodger, Gillian M. 2004. Drag, camp, and gender subversion in the music and videos of Annie Lennox. *Popular Music* 23(1): 17–29.

—— 2010. *Champagne Charlie and Pretty Jemima: Variety theater in the nineteenth century.* Urbana: University of Illinois Press.

Rogers, Bradley. 2008. The interpellations of interpolation: or, the disintegrating female musical body. *Camera Obscura* 23(1): 89–111.

Rollason, William. 2008. Ontology—just another word for culture? *Anthropology Today* 24(3): 28–29.

Rommen, Timothy. 2007. *Mek some noise: Gospel music and the ethics of style in Trinidad.* Berkeley: University of California Press.

Rosaldo, Michelle Z. 1984. Toward an anthropology of self and feeling. Pp. 137–157 in *Culture theory: Essays on mind, self and emotion.* Edited by Richard A. Shweder and Robert A. LeVine. Cambridge, U.K.: Cambridge University Press.

Rose, Tricia. 1994. *Black noise: Rap music and black culture in contemporary America.* Hanover, NH: University Press of New England.

Roseman, Marina. 1984. The social structuring of sound: the Temiar of peninsular Malaysia. *Ethnomusicology* 28 (3):411–445.

Rosen, Charles. 1994a. *The frontiers of meaning: Three informal lectures on music.* New York: Hill and Wang.

—— 1994b. Music à la mode. *New York Review of Books*, June 23, 55–62.

Rosenwald, Lawrence. 1993. Theory, text-setting, and performance. *Journal of Musicology* 11: 52–65.

Rosselli, John. 1984. *The opera industry in Italy from Cimarosa to Verdi: The role of the impresario.* Cambridge, U.K.: Cambridge University Press.

—— 1991. *Music and musicians in nineteenth-century Italy.* Portland, OR: Amadeus Press.

Rothenbuhler, Eric W., and John Dimmick. 1982. Popular music: Concentration and diversity in the industry, 1974–1980. *Journal of Communication* 32(1): 143–149.

Rothstein, William. 1995. Analysis and the act of performance. Pp. 217–240 in *The practice of performance: Studies in musical interpretation.* Edited by John Rink. Cambridge, U.K.: Cambridge University Press.

Rubin, Gayle. [1984] 1993. Thinking sex: Notes for a radical theory of the politics of sexuality. Pp. 3–44 in *The lesbian and gay studies reader*, edited by Henry Abelove, Michèle Aina Barale, and David M. Halperin. New York: Routledge.

Rumph, Stephen. 1995. A kingdom not of this world: The political context of E. T. A. Hoffmann's Beethoven criticism. *19th Century Music* 19(1): 50–67.

Sahlins, Marshall. 1985. *Islands of history.* Chicago: University of Chicago Press.

Said, Edward W. 1983. *The world, the text, and the critic.* Cambridge. MA: Harvard University Press.

—— 1992. *Musical elaborations.* London: Vintage.

Sand, George. 1893. *Oeuvres complètes de George Sand*, vol. 4: *Histoire de ma vie.* Edited by Calmann Levy. Paris: Levy.

Sanders, John T. 1996. An ecological approach to cognitive science. *The Electronic Journal of Analytical Philosophy* 4. http://ejap.louisiana.edu/EJAP/1996.spring/sanders.1996.spring.html.

Sarrazin, Thilo. 2010. *Deutschland schafft sich ab: Wie wir unser Land aufs Spiel setzen.* Munich: Deutsche Verlags-Anstalt.

Sassen, Saskia. 1991. *The global city: New York, London, Tokyo.* Princeton: Princeton University Press.
—— 1998. *Globalization and its discontents: Essays on the new mobility of people and money.* New York: New Press.
Savage, Jon. 2008. *Teenage: The prehistory of youth culture, 1875–1945.* New York: Penguin.
Sayer, Derek. 1987. *The violence of abstraction.* Oxford: Blackwell.
Schechner, Richard. 1998. *Performance theory.* Rev. ed. New York: Routledge.
—— 2002. *Performance studies.* London: Routledge.
—— 2004. Performance studies: The broad spectrum approach. Pp. 7–9 in *The performance studies reader.* Edited by Henry Bial. London and New York: Routledge.
Scherzinger, Martin. 2004. In memory of a receding dialectic: The political relevance of autonomy and formalism in modernist musical aesthetics. Pp. 68–100 in *The pleasure of modernist music: Listening, meaning, intention, ideology.* Edited by Arved Ashby. Rochester, NY: University of Rochester Press.
Schott, Rüdiger. 1968. Das Geschichtsbewusstsein schriftloser Völker. *Archiv für Begriffsgeschichte* 12: 166–205.
Schulz, Dorothea. 2010. "Channeling" the powers of God's word: Audio-recordings as scriptures in Mali. *Postscripts: The Journal of Sacred Texts and Contemporary Worlds* 4(2): 135–156.
Schutz, Alfred. 1951. Making music together: A study in social relationship. *Social Research* 18: 76–97 [republished, pp. 159–178 in *Collected papers.* The Hague: Nijhoff].
Schwartz, Theodore, Geoffrey White, and Catherine A. Lutz, eds. 1992. *New directions in psychological anthropology.* Cambridge, U.K.: Cambridge University Press.
Schwarz, David. 1997. Oi: Music, politics and violence. Pp. 100–132 in *Listening subjects: Music, psychoanalysis, culture.* Durham, NC: Duke University Press.
Sconce, Jeffrey. 2000. *Haunted media: Electronic presence from telegraphy to television.* Durham, NC, and London: Duke University Press.
Scott, Alan. 2000. *The cultural economy of cities.* London: Sage.
Scott, Derek B. 1994. The sexual politics of Victorian music aesthetics. *Journal of the Royal Musical Association* 119(1): 91–114.
Sedgwick, Eve Kosofsky. 1985. *Between men: English literature and male homosocial desire.* New York: Columbia University Press.
—— 1990. *Epistemology of the closet.* New York: Penguin Books.
Seeger, Anthony. 1987. *Why suya sing.* Cambridge, U.K.: Cambridge University Press.
Seeger, Charles. 1977. *Studies in musicology 1935–1975.* Berkeley: University of California Press.
Segrave, Kerry. 1994. *Payola in the music industry: A history 1880–1991.* London: McFarland.
Seigel, Micol. 2009. *Uneven encounters: Making race and nation in Brazil and the United States.* Durham, NC: Duke University Press.
Sensory Studies. 2011. http://www.sensorystudies.org/ (accessed January 17, 2011).
Serafine, Mary Louise. 1988. *Music as cognition: The development of thought in sound.* New York: Columbia University Press.
Sharma, Nitasha Tamar. 2010. *Hip hop desis: South Asian Americans, blackness, and a global race consciousness.* Durham, NC: Duke University Press.
Sharma, Sanjay, John Hutnyk, and Ashwani Sharma. 1996. *Dis-orienting rhythms: The politics of the new Asian dance music.* London: Zed Books.
Shelemay, Kay Kaufman. 1998. *Let jasmine rain down: Song and remembrance among Syrian Jews.* Chicago: University of Chicago Press.
Shepherd, John. 1977. The musical coding of ideologies. Pp. 69–124 in *Whose music? A sociology of musical languages.* Edited by John Shepherd, Phil Virden, Graham Vulliamy, and Trevor Wishart. London: Latimer New Dimensions.
—— 1982. A theoretical model for the sociomusicological analysis of popular musics. *Popular Music* 2: 145–177.
—— 1987. Music and male hegemony. Pp. 151–172 in *Music and society: The politics of composition, performance and reception.* Edited by Richard Leppert and Susan McClary. New York: Cambridge University Press.
—— 1991. *Music as social text.* Cambridge, U.K.: Polity.
Shilling, Chris. 2005. *The body in culture, technology, and society.* London: Sage Publications.
Shiloah, Amnon. 1995. *Music in the world of Islam: A socio-cultural study.* London: Scholar Press.

Shusterman, Richard. 2000. *Pragmatist aesthetics: Living beauty, rethinking art.* 2nd ed. Lanham, MD: Rowman and Littlefield.

Silverman, Carol. 1996. Music and marginality: Roma (Gypsies) of Bulgaria and Macedonia. Pp. 231–253 in *Retuning culture: Musical changes in central and eastern Europe.* Edited by Mark Slobin. Durham, NC: Duke University Press.

Sinfield, Alan. 2004. *On sexuality and power.* New York: Columbia University Press.

Slobin, Mark. 1982. *Tenement songs: The popular music of the Jewish immigrants.* Urbana: University of Illinois Press.

—— 1989. *Chosen voices: The story of the American cantorate.* Urbana: University of Illinois Press.

—— 1993. *Subcultural sounds: Micromusics of the West.* Hanover, NH: University Press of New England.

—— 1994. Music in diaspora: The view from Euro-America. *Diaspora* 3(3): 243–252.

—— 2001. *Fiddler on the move: Exploring the klezmer world.* New York: Oxford University Press.

—— 2008. *Global soundtracks: Worlds of film music.* Middletown, CT: Wesleyan University Press.

Sloboda, John A., and Susan O'Neill. 2001. Emotions in everyday listening to music. Pp. 413–429 in *Music and emotion: Theory and research.* Edited by Patrick N. Juslin and John A. Sloboda. Oxford: Oxford University Press.

Small, Christopher. 1987. Performance as ritual: Sketch for an enquiry into the true nature of a symphony concert. Pp. 6–32 in *Lost in music: Culture, style and the musical event.* Edited by Avron Levine White. London: Routledge and Kegan Paul.

—— 1998. *Musicking: The meanings of performing and listening.* Hanover, NH: University Press of New England.

Smith, Adam. [1776] 1910. *An enquiry into the nature and causes of the wealth of nations.* London: Everyman.

Smith, Chris. 1998. Miles Davis and the semiotics of improvised performance. Pp. 261–289 in *In the course of performance: Studies in the world of musical improvisation.* Edited by Bruno Nettl with Melinda Russell. Chicago: University of Chicago Press.

Smith, E. Patrick. 2008. Church sissies: gayness and the black church. Pp. 182–255 in *Sweet tea: Black gay men of the South.* Chapel Hill: University of North Carolina Press.

Solie, Ruth, ed. 1993. *Musicology and difference: Gender and sexuality in music scholarship.* Berkeley: University of California Press.

Solomon, Maynard. 1989. Franz Schubert and the peacocks of Benvenuto Cellini. *19th Century Music* 12(3): 193–206.

Sontag, Susan. 1966. *Against interpretation and other essays.* New York: Farrar, Straus and Giroux.

Sotiropoulos, Karen. 2006. *Staging race: Black performers in turn of the century America.* Cambridge, MA: Harvard University Press.

Spencer, Herbert. 1858. *Essays, scientific, political and speculative.* Vol. 1. London: Williams and Norgate.

Sperber, D. 1999. Culture, cognition and evolution. Pp. cxi–cxxxii in *MIT encyclopedia of cognitive sciences.* Edited by Robert A. Wilson and Frank C. Keil. Cambridge, MA: MIT Press.

Spivak, Gayatri Chakravorty, with Ellen Rooney. 1989. In a word [Interview]. *Differences* 1(2): 124–156.

—— 2009. They the people: Problems of alter-globalization. *Radical Philosophy* 157. http://www.radicalphilosophy.com/arrticle/they-the-people

Stanyek, Jason. 2004. Transmissions of an interculture: Pan-African jazz and intercultural improvisation. Pp. 87–130 in *The other side of nowhere: Jazz, improvisation, and communities in dialogue.* Edited by Daniel Fischlin and Ajay Heble. Middletown, CT: Wesleyan University Press.

Steiner, George. 2001. *Grammars of creation.* London: Faber.

Sterne, Jonathan. 1997. Sounds like the mall of America: Programmed music and the architectonics of commercial space. *Ethnomusicology* 41(1): 22–50.

—— 2001. A machine to hear for them: On the very possibility of sound's reproduction. *Cultural Studies* 15(2): 259–294.

Stevens, Catherine, and Tim Byron. 2009. Universals in music processing. Pp. 14–23 in *Oxford handbook of music psychology.* Edited by Susan Hallam, Ian Cross, and Michael Thaut. Oxford: Oxford University Press.

Stevens, Wallace. [1945] 1954. *The collected poems.* New York: Alfred A. Knopf.

Stewart, Susan. 1984. *On longing: Narratives of the miniature, the gigantic, the souvenir, the collection.* Baltimore and London: The Johns Hopkins University Press.

Stockfelt, Ola. 1994. Cars, buildings and soundscapes. Pp. 19–38 in *Sound-scapes: Essays on vroom and moo.* Edited by Helmi Järviluoma. Tampere, Finland: Department of Folk Tradition University of Tampere and Institute of Rhythm Music Seinäjoki.

Stokes, Martin. 1992. *The Arabesk debate: Music and musicians in modern Turkey.* Oxford: Clarendon Press.

——, ed. [1994] 1997. *Ethnicity, identity and music: The musical construction of place.* Oxford: Berg.

—— 2001. Ethnomusicology IV/2, Contemporary theoretical issues. Pp. 386–395 in *The new Grove dictionary of music* vol. 8. Rev. ed. Edited by Stanley Sadie. London: Macmillan.

—— 2002. Marx, money, and musicians. Pp. 139–166 in *Music and Marx: Ideas, practice, politics.* Edited by Regula Burckhardt Qureshi. London: Routledge.

Stone, Robert. 2010. *Sacred steel: Inside an African American steel guitar tradition.* Urbana: University of Illinois Press.

Strathern, Marilyn. 1988. *The gender of the gift: problems with women and problems with society in Melanesia.* Berkeley: University of California Press.

—— 1990. The concept of society is theoretically obsolete. Pp. 60–66 in *Key debates in anthropology.* Edited by Tim Ingold. London: Routledge.

—— 1995. *The relation: issues in complexity and scale.* Cambridge. U.K.: Prickly Pear Press.

Stratton, Jon. 1982. Reconciling contradictions: The role of artist and repertoire in the British record industry. *Popular Music and Society* 8(2): 90–100.

Straw, Will. 1991. Systems of articulation, logics of change: Communities and scenes in popular music. *Cultural Studies* 5(3): 368–388.

—— 2009. The music CD and its ends. *Design and Culture* 1(1): 79–92.

Strohm, Reihhard. 2000. Looking back at ourselves: The problem with the musical work-concept. Pp. 128–152 in *The musical work: Reality or invention?* Edited by Michael Talbot. Liverpool: Liverpool University Press.

Stumpf, Carl. 1911. *Die anfänge der Musik.* Leipzig, Germany: Barth.

Subotnik, Rose Rosengard. 1976. Adorno's diagnosis of Beethoven's late style. *Journal of the American Musicological Society* 29: 242–275.

—— 1991. The challenge of contemporary music. Pp. 265–293 in *Developing variations: Style and ideology in Western music.* Minneapolis: University of Minnesota Press.

Suisman, David. 2009. *Selling sounds: The commercial revolution in American music.* Cambridge, MA: Harvard University Press.

Summit, Jeffrey A. 2000. *The Lord's song in a strange land: Music and identity in contemporary Jewish worship.* New York: Oxford University Press.

Sunardi, Christine. 2010. Making sense and senses of locale through perceptions of music and dance in Malang, East Java. *Asian Music* 41(1): 89–126.

Swanwick, Keith. 1968. *Popular music and the teacher.* Oxford: Pergamon Press.

Swedenburg, Ted. 1997. Saida Sultan/Danna International: Transgender pop and the polysemiotics of sex, nation, and ethnicity on the Israeli–Egyptian border. *Musical Quarterly* 81(1): 81–108.

Sweeney, Philip. 1991. *Virgin directory of world music.* London: Virgin.

—— 1992. The world made flesh: In the beginning. *The Independent,* Thursday July 9. http://www.independent.co.uk/arts-entertainment/rock—world-music-the-world-made-flesh-in-the-beginning—five-years-ago-in-a-london-pub-the-phrase-world-music-was-coined-by-a-cabal-of-music-industry-types-philip-sweeney-describes-how-the-term-entered-the-language-and-how-the-sounds-have-changed–1532098.html.

Tagg, Philip. [1979] 2000. *Kojak – 50 seconds of TV music.* Larchmont, NY: Mass Media Music Scholars' Press.

—— 1982. Analysing popular music: Music theory, method and practice. *Popular Music* 2: 37–69.

—— 1998. The Göteborg connection: Lessons in the history and politics of popular music education and research. *Popular Music* 17(2): 219–242.

Tagg, Philip, and Bob Clarida. 2003. *Ten little title tunes: Towards a musicology of the mass media.* New York: Mass Media Music Scholar's Press.

Taiwo, Olufemi. n.d. Exorcising Hegel's ghost: Africa's challenge to philosophy. http://web.africa.ufl.edu/asq/v1/4/2.htm (accessed August 6, 2002).

Talbot, Michael, ed. 2000. *The musical work: Reality or invention?* Liverpool: Liverpool University Press.

Taruskin, Richard. 1995. *Text and act: Essays on music and performance.* New York: Oxford University Press.

—— 1997. *Defining Russia musically: Historical and hermeneutical essays.* Princeton: Princeton University Press.

—— 2008. *On Russian music.* Berkeley: University of California Press.

Taylor, Charles. 1994. *Multiculturalism: Examining the politics of recognition.* Edited by Amy Gutman. Princeton: Princeton University Press.

—— 2007. *A secular age.* Cambridge, MA: Belknap Press of Harvard University Press.

Taylor, Timothy. 1997. *Global pop: World music, world markets.* London: Routledge.

—— 2002. *Strange sounds: Music, technology and culture.* New York: Routledge.

Tchaikovsky, P. [1878] 1970. Letter: Florence, 17 February, 1878. Pp. 57–60 in *Creativity: Selected readings.* Edited by Philip E. Vernon. Harmondsworth, U.K.: Penguin Books.

Théberge, Paul. 1998. *Any sound you can imagine: Making music/consuming technology.* Hanover, NH, and London: University Press of New England.

Thomas, Nicholas. 1991 *Entangled objects: Exchange, material culture, and colonialism in the Pacific.* Cambridge, MA: Harvard University Press.

Thomas, Susan. 2006. Did nobody pass the girls the guitar? Queer appropriations in Cuban popular song. *Journal of Popular Music Studies* 18(2): 124–143.

Thompson, Edward P. [1963] 1968. *The making of the English working class.* London: Pelican.

Tick, Judith. 1997. *Ruth Crawford Seeger: A composer's search for American music.* Oxford: Oxford University Press.

Titon, Jeff Todd. 1988. *Powerhouse for God.* Austin: University of Texas Press.

—— 1995a. Bi-musicality as metaphor. *Journal of American Folklore* 108: 287–297.

—— 1995b. Text. *Journal of American Folklore* 108: 432–448.

—— 1997. Knowing fieldwork. Pp. 87–100 in *Shadows in the field: New perspectives for fieldwork in ethnomusicology.* Edited by Gregory F. Barz and Timothy J. Cooley. New York: Oxford University Press.

Titon, Jeff Todd, and Mark Slobin. 1996. The music-culture as a world of music. Pp. 1–16 in *Worlds of music.* Edited by Jeff Todd Titon. New York: Schirmer Books.

Titon, Jeff Todd, Elwood Cornett, and John Wallhausser. 1997 and 2003. *Songs of the old regular Baptists.* Vols. 1 (1997) and 2 (2003). Washington, DC: Smithsonian Folkways CD 40106.

Tocqueville, Alexis de. [1835] 1956. *Democracy in America.* Edited and abridged by Richard D. Heffner. New York: Mentor Books.

Tololyan, Khachig. 1991. The nation-state and its others: In lieu of a preface. *Diaspora* 1(1): 3–7.

Tomasello, Michael, M. Carpenter, et al. 2005. Understanding and sharing intentions: The origins of cultural cognition. *Behavioral and Brain Sciences* 28(5): 675–691.

Tomlinson, Gary. 1993. Musical pasts and postmodern musicologies: A response to Lawrence Kramer. *Current Musicology* 53: 18–24.

—— 1999. *Metaphysical song: An essay on opera.* Princeton: Princeton University Press.

—— 2007. *The singing of the New World: Indigenous voice in the era of European contact.* Cambridge, U.K.: Cambridge University Press.

Tomlinson, John. 1991. *Cultural imperialism.* London: Pinter.

Toop, David. 1994. Sleevenotes to [Various artists], *Artificial Intelligence II.* Warp, LP23.

Touma, Habib Hassan. 2003. *The music of the Arabs.* London: Amadeus Press.

Towse, Ruth. 1993. *Singers in the marketplace: The economics of the singing profession.* Oxford: Clarendon Press.

——, ed. 1997. *Baumol's cost disease: The arts and other victims.* Cheltenham, U.K.: Edward Elgar.

Toynbee, Jason. 2000. *Making popular music: Musicians, creativity, institutions.* London: Arnold.

—— 2002. Mainstreaming: Hegemony, market and the aesthetics of the centre in popular music. Pp. 149–163 in *Popular music studies.* Edited by David Hesmondhalgh and Keith Negus. London: Arnold.

—— 2007. *Bob Marley: Herald of a postcolonial world?* Cambridge, U.K.: Polity.

Tracey, Hugh. 1954. The state of folk music in Bantu Africa. *African Music* 1(1): 8–11.

Treitler, Leo. 1989. *Music and the historical imagination.* Cambridge, MA: Harvard University Press.

Trumpener, Katie. 1996. Imperial marches and mouse singers: Nationalist mythology in central European modernity. Pp. 67–90 in *Text and nation: Cross-disciplinary essays on cultural and national identities.* Edited by Laura García-Moreno and Peter C. Pfeiffer. Rochester, NY: Camden House.

Tsing, Anna. 2002. Conclusion: The global situation. Pp. 453–482 in *The anthropology of globalization: A reader.* Edited by Jonathan Inda and Renato Rosaldo. Oxford: Blackwell.

Tsuda, Takeyuki, ed. 2009. *Diasporic homecomings: Ethnic return migration in comparative perspective.* Palo Alto, CA: Stanford University Press.

Turino, Thomas. 1999. Signs of imagination, identity, and experience: A Peircian semiotic theory for music. *Ethnomusicology* 43(2): 221–255.

—— 2008. *Music as social life: The politics of participation.* Chicago and London: The University of Chicago Press.

Turner, Victor, and Edward Bruner, eds. 1986. *The anthropology of experience.* Urbana: University of Illinois Press.

Tylor, Edward Burnett. 1871. *Primitive culture.* London: John Murray.

UNFPA. 2007. Urbanization: A majority in cities. http://www.unfpa.org/pds/urbanization.htm (accessed December 22, 2010).

Van Dijck, José. 2006. Record and hold: popular music between personal and collective memory. *Critical Studies in Media Communication* 23(5): 357–374.

Van Glahn, Denise. 1996. A sense of place: Charles Ives and Putnam's Camp, Redding, Connecticut. *American Music* 14(3): 276–312.

Van Hear, Nicholas. 1998. *New diasporas: The mass exodus, dispersal and regrouping of migrant communities.* Seattle: University of Washington Press, 1998.

Van Heur, Bas. 2010. *Creative networks and the city: Towards a cultural political economy of aesthetic production.* Bielefeld, Germany: Transcript Verlag.

Van Leeuwen, Theo. 1999. *Speech, music, sound.* Basingstoke, U.K.: Macmillan.

Varela, Francesco J., Evan Thompson, and Eleanor Rosch. 1993. *The embodied mind: Cognitive science and human experience.* Cambridge, MA, and London: MIT Press.

Venturi, Robert, Denise Scott Brown, and Steven Izenour. 1977. *Learning from Las Vegas: The forgotten symbolism of architecture.* Rev. ed. Cambridge, MA: MIT Press.

Verdery, Katherine. 1991. Theorising socialism: A prologue to the transition. *American Ethnologist* 18(3): 419–439.

Vergo, Peter, ed. 1991. *The new museology.* London: Reaktion Books.

Vico, Gianbattista. 1968. *The new science of Gianbattista Vico.* Translated by Thomas Guddard Bergin and Max Harold Fisch. Ithaca: Cornell University Press.

Virolle, Marie. 1995. *La Chanson Rai: De l'Algerie profonde à la scene internationale.* Paris: Karthala.

Volk, Therese. 1998. *Music, education, and multiculturalism: Foundations and principles.* New York: Oxford University Press.

Vulliamy, Graham. 1977a. Music and the mass culture debate. Pp. 179–200 in *Whose music: A sociology of musical languages.* Edited by John Shepherd, Paul Virden, Trevor Wishart, and Graham Vulliamy. London: Latimer New Dimensions.

—— 1977b. Music as a case study in the "new sociology of education." Pp. 201–232 in *Whose music: A sociology of musical languages.* Edited by John Shepherd, Paul Virden, Trevor Wishart, and Graham Vulliamy. London: Latimer New Dimensions.

Wachsmann, Klaus P. 1971. Universal perspectives in music. *Ethnomusicology* 15(3): 381–384.

Wade, Peter. 2000. *Music, race, and nation: Música Tropical in Colombia.* Chicago: University of Chicago Press.

Waksman, Steve. 1999 *Instruments of desire: The electric guitar and the shaping of musical experience.* Cambridge, MA: Harvard University Press.

Wallin, Nils, Bjorn Merker, and Steven Brown, eds. 2000. *The origins of music.* Cambridge, MA: MIT Press.

Wallis, Roger, and Krister Malm. 1984. Big sounds from small peoples. World music in the 1990s. *Public Culture* 8(3): 467–488.

Walser, Robert. 1993. *Running with the devil: Power, gender and madness in heavy metal music.* Hanover, NH: University Press of New England.

Walton, Kendall. 2007. Aesthetics—what? why? and wherefore? *Journal of Aesthetics and Art Criticism* 65(2): 147–161.

Warner, Michael. 2005. *Publics and counterpublics.* New York: Zone.

Warwick, Jacqueline. 2007. *Girl groups, girl culture: Popular music and identity in the 1960s.* New York: Routledge.

Waterman, Christopher. 1990. *Jùjú: A social history and ethnography of an African popular music.* Chicago: Chicago University Press.

—— 1991. The uneven development of Africanist ethnomusicology: Three issues and a critique. Pp. 169–183 in *Comparative musicology and anthropology of music.* Edited by Bruno Nettl and Philip V. Bohlman. Chicago: University of Chicago Press.

Watson, Janelle. 1999. *Literature and material culture from Balzac to Proust: The collection and consumption of curiosities.* Cambridge: Cambridge University Press.

Watson, John B. 1919. *Psychology from the standpoint of a behaviorist.* 2nd ed. Philadelphia: J. B. Lippincott.

Weber, Max. [1921] 1958. *The rational and social foundations of music.* Carbondale: Southern Illinois University Press.

Weber, William. 1975. *Music and the middle class: The social structure of concert life in London, Paris and Vienna between 1830 and 1848.* London: Croom Helm.

—— 1992. *The rise of the musical classics in eighteenth-century England: A study in canon, ritual and ideology.* Oxford: Clarendon Press.

Weinstein. Deena. 1991. *Heavy metal: A cultural sociology.* New York: Lexington.

Weiss, Allen S. 2002. *Breathless: Sound recording, disembodiment, and the transformation of lyrical nostalgia.* Middletown, CT: Wesleyan University Press.

Weliver, Phyllis. 2005. *The figure of music in nineteenth century British poetry.* Aldershot, U.K., and Burlington, VT: Ashgate.

Wenner, Jann. 1972. *Lennon remembers: The Rolling Stone interviews.* Harmondsworth, U.K.: Penguin.

White, Hayden V. 1973. *Metahistory: The historical imagination in nineteenth-century Europe.* Baltimore: Johns Hopkins University Press.

Whiteley, Sheila. 2000. *Women and popular music: Sexuality, identity, and subjectivity.* New York: Routledge.

Whiteley, Sheila, Andy Bennett, and Stan Hawkins, eds. 2004. *Music, space and place: Popular music and cultural identity.* Aldershot, U.K.: Ashgate.

Whiteley, Sheila, and Jennifer Rycenga, eds. 2006. *Queering the popular pitch.* New York: Routledge.

Wicke, Peter. 1990. *Rock music: Culture, aesthetics, and sociology.* Cambridge, U.K.: Cambridge University Press.

Wicke, Peter, and John Shepherd. 1993. "The Cabaret is Dead": Rock culture as state enterprise—The political organization of rock in East Germany. Pp. 25–36 in *Rock and popular music: Politics, policies, institutions.* Edited by S. Frith, T. Bennett, L. Grossberg, J. Shepherd, and G. Turner. London: Routledge.

Williams, Raymond. 1961. *Culture and society 1780–1950.* Harmondsworth, U.K.: Penguin.

—— 1965. *The long revolution.* Harmondsworth, U.K.: Penguin.

—— 1980. *Problems in materialism and culture: Selected essays.* New York: Verso.

—— 1981. *Culture.* London: Fontana.

—— 1983. *Keywords: A vocabulary of culture and society.* Rev. ed. London: Fontana.

Williams, Simon. 2001. *Emotion and social theory. Corporeal reflections on the (ir)rational.* London: Sage.

Willis, Ellen. 2011. *Out of the vinyl deeps: Ellen Willis on rock music.* Edited by Nona Willis Arnowitz. Minneapolis: University of Minnesota Press.

Willis, Paul E. 1978. *Profane culture.* London: Routledge and Kegan Paul.

—— 1990. *Common culture: Symbolic work at play in the everyday cultures of the young.* Milton Keynes, U.K.: Open University Press.

Wilson, Olly. 1974. The significance of the relationship between Afro-American music and west African music. *The Black Perspective in Music* 2 (Spring). 3–22.

Windsor, W. Luke. 2000. Through and around the acousmatic: The interpretation of electroacoustic sounds. Pp. 7–35 in *Music, electronic media and culture.* Edited by Simon Emmerson. Aldershot, U.K.: Ashgate.

Winnicott, Donald. 1971. *Playing and reality.* London: Tavistock.

Wishart, Trevor. 1985. *On sonic art.* York: Imagineering Press.

Wolf, Stacy. 2002. *A problem like Maria: Gender and sexuality in the American musical.* Ann Arbor: University of Michigan Press.

Women & Music: A Journal of Gender and Culture. International Alliance for Women in Music, 1997–2007. Lincoln: University of Nebraska Press, 2008–.

Wood, Elizabeth. [1994] 2006. "Sapphonics." Pp. 27–66 in *Queering the pitch: The new gay and lesbian musicology*. Edited by Philip Brett, Elizabeth Wood, and Gary C. Thomas. New York: Routledge.

Woodward, Ian. 2007. *Understanding material culture*. London: Sage.

Wrightson, Kendall. 2000. An introduction to acoustic ecology. *Soundscape: The Journal of Acoustic Ecology* 1(1):10–13.

Wulff, Helena, ed. 2007. *The emotions: A cultural reader*. Oxford: Berg.

Wynne, Derek, and Justin O'Connor. 1998. Consumption and the postmodern city. *Urban Studies* 35(5–6): 841–864.

Yonnet, Paul. 1985. *Jeux, modes et masses: La société française et le moderne, 1945–1985*. Paris: Gallimard.

Zaslaw, Neal. 1989. *Mozart's symphonies: Context, performance practice, reception*. Oxford: Clarendon Press.

Zbikowski, Lawrence M. 2002. *Conceptualising music: Cognitive structure, theory, and analysis*. New York: Oxford University Press.

Zemp, Hugo. 1978. 'Are'are classification of musical types and instruments. *Ethnomusicology* 22(1): 37–68.

Zheng, Su. 2010. *Claiming diaspora: Music, transnationalism, and cultural politics in Asian/Chinese America*. New York: Oxford University Press.

Žižek, Slavoj. 2002. *For they know not what they do: Enjoyment as a political factor*. 2nd ed. London: Verso.

—— 2009a. *First as tragedy, then as farce*. London: Verso.

—— 2009b. *In defence of lost causes*. London: Verso.

Zolberg, Vera L. 1990. *Constructing a sociology of the arts*. Cambridge, U.K.: Cambridge University Press.

Zukin, Sharon. 1982. *Loft living: Culture and capital in urban change*. Baltimore: Johns Hopkins University Press.

INDEX